EE FILE COPY
PLEASE DO NOT REMOVE

D1327938

Family Business

The International Library of Critical Writings in Business History

Series Editor: Geoffrey Jones
Professor of Business History,
University of Reading

Family Business

Edited by

Mary B. Rose

Department of Economics
The Management School
Lancaster University, UK

THE INTERNATIONAL LIBRARY OF CRITICAL WRITINGS IN BUSINESS HISTORY

An Elgar Reference Collection
Aldershot, UK • Brookfield, US

© Mary B. Rose 1995. For copyright of individual articles please refer to the Acknowledgements.

All rights reserved. No part of this publication may be reproduced, stored in a retrieval system, or transmitted in any form or by any means, electronic, mechanical, photocopying, recording, or otherwise without the prior permission of the publisher.

Published by
Edward Elgar Publishing Limited
Gower House
Croft Road
Aldershot
Hants GU11 3HR
UK

Edward Elgar Publishing Company
Old Post Road
Brookfield
Vermont 05036
US

British Library Cataloguing in Publication Data
Family Business. – (International Library
of Critical Writings in Business History;
Vol. 13)
  I. Rose, Mary B. II. Series
  338.7

Library of Congress Cataloguing in Publication Data
Family business / edited by Mary B. Rose.
      p. cm. — (International library of critical writings in
business history ; 13)
   Includes bibliographical references and index.
   1. Family corporations. 2. Family-owned business enterprises.
I. Rose, Mary B. II. Series
HD62.25.F335 1995
658'.045—dc20
                                                              95–11877
                                                                CIP

ISBN 1 85898 049 6

Printed in Great Britain by Galliard (Printers) Ltd, Great Yarmouth

Contents

Acknowledgements

The editor and publishers wish to thank the following who have kindly given permission for the use of copyright material.

American Economic Association for article: Robert A. Pollak (1985), 'A Transaction Cost Approach to Families and Households', *Journal of Economic Literature*, **XXIII**, June, 581–608.

British Journal of Sociology and Routledge for articles: Michael Lisle-Williams (1984), 'Beyond the Market: the Survival of Family Capitalism in the English Merchant Banks', *British Journal of Sociology*, **XXXV** (2), June, 241–71; Siu-lun Wong (1985), 'The Chinese Family Firm: A Model', *British Journal of Sociology*, **XXXVI** (1), March, 58–72.

Business History Conference for article: Wayne Broehl (1989), 'The Family Business', *Business and Economic History*, **18**, Second series, 1–10.

Cambridge University Press for article: David S. Landes (1949), 'French Entrepreneurship and Industrial Growth in the Nineteenth Century', *Journal of Economic History*, **IX** (1), 45–61.

Frank Cass & Co. Ltd for articles: Roy Church (1986), 'Family Firms and Managerial Capitalism: The Case of the International Motor Industry', *Business History*, **XXVIII** (2), April, 165–80; Roy Church (1993), 'The Family Firm in Industrial Capitalism: International Perspectives on Hypotheses and History', *Business History*, **35** (4), October, 17–43; Philip Scranton (1993), 'Build a Firm, Start Another: The Bromleys and Family Firm Entrepreneurship in the Philadelphia Region', *Business History*, **35** (4), October, 115–51; Keetie E. Sluyterman and Hélène J.M. Winkelman (1993), 'The Dutch Family Firm confronted with Chandler's Dynamics of Industrial Capitalism, 1890–1940', *Business History*, **35** (4), October, 152–83.

Harvard Business School for articles: Johannes Hirschmeier (1970), 'The Japanese Spirit of Enterprise, 1867–1970', *Business History Review*, **XLIV** (1), Spring, 13–38; Hidemasa Morikawa (1970), 'The Organizational Structure of Mitsubishi and Mitsui Zaibatsu, 1868–1922: A Comparative Study', *Business History Review*, **XLIV** (1), Spring, 62–83; Wellington K.K. Chan (1982), 'The Organizational Structure of the Traditional Chinese Firm and its Modern Reform', *Business History Review*, **LVI** (2), Summer, 218–35.

Indian Economic and Social History Review for article: Thomas A. Timberg (1973), 'Three Types of the Marwari Firm', *Indian Economic and Social History Review*, **X** (1), March, 1–36.

JAI Press Inc. for article: W. Mark Fruin (1980), 'The Family as a Firm and the Firm as a Family in Japan: The Case of Kikkoman Shōyu Company Limited', *Journal of Family History*, **5** (4), Winter, 432–49.

Jossey-Bass Publishers Inc. for article: Peter Dobkin Hall (1988), 'A Historical Overview of Family Firms in the United States', *Family Business Review*, **1** (1), Spring, 51–68.

Jürgen Kocka for his own excerpt: (1981), 'The Entrepreneur, the Family and Capitalism: Some Examples from the Early Phase of Industrialisation in Germany', in the German Society for Business History (eds), *German Yearbook on Business History 1981*, 53–82.

Population Council for article: Yoram Ben-Porath (1980), 'The F-Connection: Families, Friends, and Firms and the Organization of Exchange', *Population and Development Review*, **6** (1), March, 1–30.

Routledge for excerpt: Edward Goodman (1989), 'Introduction: The Political Economy of the Small Firm in Italy', in Edward Goodman and Julia Bamford with Peter Saynor (eds), *Small Firms and Industrial Districts in Italy*, 1–30.

Singapore University Press (PTE) Ltd for article: J.W. Cushman (1986), 'The Khaw Group: Chinese Business in Early Twentieth-century Penang', *Journal of Southeast Asian Studies*, **XVII** (1), March, 58–79.

University of Chicago Press for articles: E. Wayne Nafziger (1969), 'The Effect of the Nigerian Extended Family on Entrepreneurial Activity', *Economic Development and Cultural Change*, **18** (1), Part 1, October, 25–33; Hanna Papanek (1972), 'Pakistan's Big Businessmen: Muslim Separatism, Entrepreneurship, and Partial Modernization', *Economic Development and Cultural Change*, **21** (1), October, 1–32; Nathaniel H. Leff (1978), 'Industrial Organization and Entrepreneurship in the Developing Countries: The Economic Groups', *Economic Development and Cultural Change*, **26** (4), July, 661–75: Philip Scranton (1986), 'Learning Manufacture: Education and Shop-Floor Schooling in the Family Firm', *Technology and Culture*, **27** (1), January, 40–62.

University of Tokyo Press for excerpts: Shoji Ito (1984), 'Ownership and Management of Indian Zaibatsu', in Akio Okochi and Shigeaki Yasuoka (eds), *Family Business in the Era of Industrial Growth: Its Ownership and Management*, 147–66; Peter L. Payne (1984), 'Family Business in Britain: An Historical and Analytical Survey', in Akio Okochi and Shigeaki Yasuoka (eds), *Family Business in the Era of Industrial Growth: Its Ownership and Management*, 171–206; Maurice Lévy-Leboyer (1984), 'The Large Family Firm in the French Manufacturing Industry', in Akio Okochi and Shigeaki Yasuoka (eds), *Family Business in the Era of Industrial Growth: Its Ownership and Management*, 209–33; Alfred D. Chandler, Jr. (1986), 'Managers, Families and Financiers', in Kesaji Kobayashi and Hidemasa Morikawa (eds), *Development of Managerial Enterprise*, 35–63.

Every effort has been made to trace all the copyright holders but if any have been inadvertently overlooked the publishers will be pleased to make the necessary arrangement at the first opportunity.

In addition the publishers wish to thank the Library of the London School of Economics and Political Science, the Photographic Unit of the University of London Library, and the Marshall Library, Cambridge University, for their assistance in obtaining these articles.

Introduction

Family businesses, which have been instrumental in the industrialization of most countries, remain an important dimension of modern economies world wide. Yet analyses of international differences in Western micro- and macroeconomic performance, since the late nineteenth century, have usually been focused upon the rise and capabilities of the American-style business corporation. In this context, whilst family business has not been without its champions, these firms were often dismissed as inferior alternatives to managerial capitalism and the source of economic decline. As a result they have received, until comparatively recently, less attention than they deserve. This collection of essays, which spans more than forty years of scholarship on family business, is not confined to the discussion of Western firms. Instead contributions cover their role, capabilities and performance on four continents and includes the work of leading institutional and development economists and sociologists, as well as business and economic historians.

In the British industrial revolution of the eighteenth century 'the power of heredity and the vitality of the family as an economic group [was quite remarkable]' (Payne, 1984, reprinted in this volume as Chapter 4). The popularity of family oriented enterprise in eighteenth and nineteenth century Britain, was a product of a complex array of legal, economic, and cultural forces. With the spectre of bankruptcy ever present, a combination of the common law partnership and unlimited liability meant that many businessmen preferred to be associated with their family connections than with outsiders. Since business activity was heavily localized, the canvas of action was usually the local business community. As a result, the boundaries of the family firm with respect to finance, managers and labour were most often the community. This was less a reflection of conservatism than a strategy to ameliorate the worst effects of uncertainty.

It was, however, the rapid entry and exit of many small firms in commerce and manufacturing that proved an important source of change in the eighteenth century British economy. It was not that failure outweighed success, but that a turnover of firms was both a symptom and a cause of expansion (Hoppit, 1987: pp. 63 and 75). Since the eighteenth century the proliferation of small family businesses has been critical to the initiation of industrialization elsewhere. In the early phases of industrialization family firms have proved the principal agents of change, their rapid turnover providing the dynamism which fuelled the growth process (Habakkuk, 1955: p. 155).

The Family Firm Debate: Conservatism and Decline or an Alternative Strategy?

Few would doubt that rapid family firm formation was a major source of dynamism during the early stages of modern industrialization in many countries. However, family-owned business outlived both the Industrial Revolution and the Second Industrial Revolution to remain the predominant form of business organization up to the present (Jones and Rose, 1993). Family firms account for between 75 per cent and 99 per cent of all companies in the EU, and 65 per cent of GDP and employment in Europe. While the huge majority of family businesses are very small-scale, many are not. In the United States one-third of 'Fortune 500' companies are currently family controlled (*Financial Times*, 30 March 1993). The list of leading US and European corporations which are family-owned in the 1990s includes Michelin, the world's biggest tyre manufacturer, Mars, the confectionary manufacturer, and C & A, the department chain store. Half of the largest 20 Swedish multinational manufacturing firms belong to Sweden's biggest industrial group which has been owned and managed by several generations of the Wallenberg family (see *Financial Times*, 3 May 1994, for an analysis of their holdings). Jardine Matheson, the diversified Far Eastern trading company and business conglomerate, has been controlled by the Keswick family since its foundation in the mid-nineteenth century. On a smaller scale, the international success achieved by northern Italian family firms, producing textiles and knitwear for fashion-oriented markets, has become a symbol for the potential of small-scale manufacturing, supported by an international commercial network, in the late twentieth century (Toyne *et al.*, 1984: pp. 150–51).

Beyond Europe and the United States the family firm has been, and continues to be, the norm. Family businesses – the vast majority of which are small – have been the basis of the dynamic overseas Chinese capitalism which has transformed the economies of much of Southeast and East Asia over the last three decades (Redding, 1990: pp. 143–82). The huge *chaebol* conglomerates, which have led South Korean industrialization in the contemporary era, are family businesses (Amsden, 1989; Hattori, 1984: pp. 121–42). The Marwari, Parsee and other ethnic or caste groups which have dominated private sector business in modern India operate, without exception, family businesses. The largest of these family houses, such as the Tatas and Birlas, have survived several generations (Timberg, 1978; Bagchi, 1972; Ray, 1979). Family ownership also has remained universal among the diversified business groups which developed in the Arabian peninsular since the early 1970s (Field, 1984). In this respect, Japan provides a major exception in the non-Western world. Between the late nineteenth century and 1945 the *zaibatsu* – powerful diversified commercial, industrial and service enterprises – were family-owned and, for a time, family-managed. However, there was a strong trend towards the separation of ownership and control and the professionalization of management, even before Japan's defeat in the Second World War led to the dissolution of the family-owned *zaibatsu* – although not of the tradition of co-ordination through interfirm networks which they had helped to establish (Fruin, 1992). Yet, if dominant enterprises are the most visible in modern Japan, 99% of businesses are small or medium sized family firms (Fruin 1980, reprinted in this volume as Chapter 12).

In view of the extraordinary persistence and dynamism of family businesses, it is curious that business historians have sometimes regarded them as forces for conservatism and backwardness. The explanation might be found in the experience of the United States where, from the nineteenth century, large business corporations emerged whose ownership was separated from control. Large firms, where family control endured well into the twentieth century, such as DuPonts in chemicals, Fords in automobiles and Cargills, the multinational commodity trading company, have been seen as exceptional (Broehl 1989, reprinted in this volume as Chapter 7; Broehl 1992; Church 1986, reprinted in this volume as Chapter 5; Church 1993, reprinted in this volume as Chapter 8).

Against this national experience it is understandable that American historians were amongst the most prominent sceptics of the efficiency of family firms outside the United States. The coincidence of the advent of managerial capitalism with the emergence of the United States as the world's largest industrial economy, displaying the highest levels of labour productivity, was also significant. It meant that the starting point and bench mark for best practice, after 1880, for many economic and business historians, and not just Americans, became the United States.

In the four decades after the late 1940s, the potentially damaging consequences of family capitalism have found wide currency in the literature. Landes (1949) for example, (reprinted in this volume as Chapter 1), developed a powerful explanatory model of the lacklustre performance of the French economy in the nineteenth century, which was based around the intrinsic conservatism of family-oriented business. In extending his analysis to Britain, he concluded that by the late nineteenth century the once dynamic family firms of the industrial revolution had become moribund (Landes, 1965: pp. 563–4). Echoed in Wiener's cultural interpretation of British economic decline, the implication was that business success encouraged gentrification and consequent neglect of or withdrawal from business (Wiener, 1981). Business historians have, however, demonstrated the fundamental shortcomings in the so-called 'third generation thesis or Buddenbrooks syndrome' as an explanation of economic decline. They have defended the performance of individual late nineteenth century firms, citing well known examples of continuity, advanced organizational structure and technological dynamism in long-lived family firms (Hannah, 1982: p. 3; Barker and Lévy-Leboyer, 1982: pp. 12–13). From a macroeconomic perspective however, the 'case against' a third generation explanation of British industrial decline is even more convincing. In the first place there is no evidence that the rate of gentrification rose in the late nineteenth century (Coleman, 1973). In addition, Payne (1984, reprinted in this volume as Chapter 4) has shown that only a minority of firms survived more than one generation, let alone three. Instead he concluded that it was the tendency, in the late nineteenth century and interwar period, of one time family owned firms to form horizontal holding companies, with inadequate managerial structures that accounted for relatively poor British business performance.

More recently, Chandler (1986, reprinted in this volume as Chapter 2) explored the retardative influences of family business, a thesis which he later developed in *Scale and Scope* (1990). The persistence of personal capitalism lies at the core of this impressive analysis of the reasons for Britain's relative economic decline from the late nineteenth century, as compared with the United States and Germany. British entrepreneurs, he argued, viewed their firms as family estates to be preserved for future generations. This desire to maintain control, combined with a preference for short term income rather than long term growth, Chandler believed, distinguished British entrepreneurs from their principal competitors. It meant that they failed to make the required three-pronged investment in production, distribution and management which was necessary to exploit fully economies of scale and scope in the industries of the Second Industrial Revolution (Chandler, 1990: pp. 286 and 390).

This theme was picked up and developed by Lazonick. Whilst recognizing the central contribution of 'proprietary capitalism' to the international competitive advantage of Britain's nineteenth century staple industries, he believed that within it lay the seeds of decay. In the changing world of the twentieth century, when the organizational basis of competitive advantage was increasingly managerial capitalism, the very ethos of proprietary capitalism, in all its dimensions, proved resistant to change (Lazonick, 1992: pp. 25–7; 45–9).

For their insights into the role of technological innovation in the economic growth process and the understanding of economies of scale and scope in business corporations the respective contributions of Landes and Chandler to business history have been considerable. Similarly, Lazonick's insights into the relationship between history and business organization are of vital importance to the understanding of international shifts in competitive advantage. Yet for the study of family business, within and outside America, the implications of concentration on the strengths of the professionally managed, technologically advanced, capital intensive business corporation in manufacturing industry, has been considerable.

Within the United States, for example, it meant that before Scranton's compelling analysis of flexible specialization in Philadelphia, the city's 'proprietary capitalists' were dismissed as backward (Scranton, 1983; Scranton, 1989; Jeremy, 1981: pp. 51–2). Elsewhere, as an alternative basis for capitalism, the late nineteenth and twentieth century family business was for some time viewed as at best, a conservative anachronism of a bygone age, at worst, a major contributor to economic decline. Moreover, with attention heavily focused on manufacturing, where America's competitive advantage resided, there was a comparative neglect of those sectors, such as trade and financial services, where it did not. Yet it is precisely in those sectors, internationally, where family business has proved most resilient and successful (Chapman, 1985: pp. 230–51).

The distinctive behaviour of American industrial firms, not least the apparently rapid demise of personal capitalism in the United States, in the nineteenth century, has been explained in a number of ways. Considerations include the rapid growth of the domestic market, differences in resource allocation and in attitudes within the family firm (Chandler 1977; Rosenberg, 1972: p. 48; Habakkuk, 1962: pp. 11–16; Temin, 1966: pp. 277–95; Saul, 1970: p. 4). However, concentration on the organizational and technological characteristics of business and its prowess, has sometimes left the developmental, political, legal and cultural peculiarities of the United States obscure. The United States was the only country of recent settlement to industrialize in the nineteenth century and it would have been extraordinary had experience mirrored that elsewhere. Indeed it has been suggested that the vertical integration so characteristic of American business was initially a sign of backwardness rather than modernity (Stigler, 1951: p. 190). Similarly there is ample evidence that family business strategy in a new country was shaped by different cultural influences and expectations from those in the 'old world' (Broehl, 1989, reprinted in this volume as Chapter 7). Equally, it seems that from the Civil War onwards, a combination of economic and political forces worked against family business in the United States (Hall, 1988, reprinted in this volume as Chapter 6).

In 1954 Gerschenkron (reprinted in this volume as Chapter 3) pointed to the pitfalls of assuming that cultural deviations from an American norm would necessarily impede economic performance elsewhere. Given the distinctiveness of American experience it is especially unfortunate that this timely warning went largely unheeded. It meant that comparative analysis of business strategy and performance *within* culturally similar regions, such as Europe or the Far East, where family capitalism has proved a successful alternative to the

US-style corporation, was long delayed. As a result analysis has sometimes concentrated more on how family business measured up to the business corporation than on the understanding of its variety and capabilities. In addition, whereas Chandler explains Britain's economic decline in terms of the persistence of personal capitalism, the irony of superior German business performance remains. There, the transition to integrated, diversified industrial enterprises, at least until the 1930s, did not see family business replaced by managerial capitalism (Pohl, 1982: p. 108).

The assumption that micro-, still less macroeconomic, performance can be explained primarily in terms of organizational structure or of the ownership characteristics of firms has not proved particularly robust. In an internationally comparative study of the motor industry Church (1986, reprinted in this volume as Chapter 5) found the evidence, relating to the impact of family control on behaviour and performance, inconclusive. Returns on equity were, for example, the same irrespective of ownership, whilst in the UK large owner-controlled firms achieved higher rates of profit than managerial firms. Equally it cannot be concluded that looser forms of organizational structure were always inferior to US-style business corporations. Whereas the horizontal holding company structure, adopted in inter-war Britain, has been linked to poor business performance (Payne, 1984, reprinted in this volume as Chapter 4), it cannot be universally condemned. In Japan in the same period, for example, the vertical holding company facilitated the growth of the highly successful Zaibatsu (Morikawa, 1992). Nor is Church convinced (1993, reprinted in this volume as Chapter 8) by Chandler's contention that the owners of family firms necessarily display a preference for short term income rather than long term growth. He found the evidence on dividend to profit ratios slightly ambiguous, but maintained that high and stable dividends need not be a sign of income maximization. In any event recent cries of short-termism have more often been directed at multidivisional firms than family owned businesses. In both Britain and the United States since 1960, heavy reliance on equity finance and fears of hostile takeover have meant that managers have been more concerned with the bottom line of their balance sheets, in six months time, than with long term perspectives. This tendency towards short-termism has been further reinforced by internal accounting procedures and managerial incentive schemes of the multidivisional firms. With managerial bonuses tied to the annual performance of independent profit centres, it is not surprising that the importance of long term commitments has not always been appreciated (Dore, 1985: pp. 17–19). Despite the well known problems of leadership succession large family firms, by contrast, have a reputation for adopting a longer term perspective often linked to a strong corporate culture (Ketsde Vries, 1992).

Family and Firm: Theory, Concepts and Culture

The comparison of the behaviour of family business with the business corporation has not, therefore, proved entirely fruitful. Internationally comparative evidence suggests that whilst family businesses may adopt strategies and structures which are different from those in publicly owned business corporations, these are by no means always inferior alternatives. Whilst it would be dangerous and misleading to discount or minimize the impact of economic influences on business behaviour, they should not be viewed in a cultural vacuum.

The notion that international diversity in the structure and strategies of firms may be a reflection of socio-cultural considerations has already been raised. It is clearly unhelpful to draw general conclusions concerning *best practice* between culturally different regions. Nevertheless, in establishing why family business has proved more resilient and successful in some regions and sectors than others and why, despite some common characteristics, its form and capabilities may vary it is necessary to look beyond purely economic variables. The analysis of such issues as attitudes to the family, to inheritance, and to the community are critical to any understanding of family firm reactions to risk, uncertainty and other economic stimuli in different societies. Equally they inform any discussion of the international differences in the strategy and structure of family business.

In the early stages of industrialization a hazardous economic environment, combined usually with imperfect formal institutions, goes a long way towards explaining the predominance of family firms. Thus, whether discussion is of eighteenth century Britain or twentieth century developing countries, the owners of mainly small scale firms have seen the family as the ideal interface between the market and the firm (Ben-Porath, 1980, reprinted in this volume as Chapter 9; Nafziger, 1969, reprinted in this volume as Chapter 11). The family, widely defined to include that extended kinship group of cousins, in-laws and connections in the local business community, especially from within religious groupings, therefore represented more than just a reservoir of skill, labour and finance. It was a network of trust, the use of which reduced the transaction costs and the dangers and uncertainties of business activity. Thus, although the family might represent an internal market for managerial labour, a source of funds for establishment and expansion and of market information, the boundaries of the family business have usually lain within a rather wider group with a shared culture and values. (Casson, 1982: pp. 302–7; Casson, 1991: pp. 169-70; Casson, 1993: pp. 30–54; Pollak, 1985, reprinted in this volume as Chapter 10).

Established businesses normally choose to reinforce their position and reduce uncertainty by diversification. For the family business operating within, for example, a localized business community, such insurance strategies often involved externalization rather than internalization. Not only was this facilitated by a common culture, but such strategies reinforced the founding family's security within a community. In labour markets too, family business owners have sometimes tried through paternalist strategies, to create or mould community culture in an effort to reduce conflict and uncertainty. This is not to say that competition is not intense in developing communities. Rather it is to suggest that where the external environment is potentially volatile, the desire to reduce the danger of failure will inform the policies of family businesses. Since family and family firm strategy are inseparable, decisions will, in turn, be shaped by cultural norms, value and legal systems. Inevitably, therefore, the characteristics of family businesses may vary internationally or even intranationally.

There are two striking differences if, for example, offshore Chinese and Japanese family values and practices are compared. In the first place the Japanese are alone amongst Far Eastern industrializers in the practice of primogeniture. In addition, whereas in China, and indeed the West, the family is defined in genealogical or biological terms, in Japan the distinction between kin and non-kin in the household is unimportant. Rather, the family is defined as those contributing to the economic welfare of the group or *ie*, irrespective of lineage. Moreover, in Japan collective values override the interests of the individual whether applied at the level of the family, the firm or the nation (Fruin, 1980, reprinted in this volume as Chapter 12). In the Chinese family or kia, not only is kin and lineage of overriding importance, but Overseas Chinese communities display a far higher degree of individualism than is to be found in Japanese society. Moreover, their status as foreign migrants undoubtedly influenced attitudes and behaviour. These differing perspectives have been reflected in differences in both the ownership and control of firms and in general business behaviour (see Parts IV and V).

Cultural influences on the Indian family are different again and have again contributed to distinctive behaviour by the owners of family businesses. Central to Hindu thinking is a collective responsibility to create continuity in the family through the male line (Smith, 1993: p. 49). This tendency, combined with a social system which led to the dominance of Indian business by a few caste groups, such as the Marwaris, has helped to shape Indian family firms in important ways. It has contributed to longevity in family businesses, with the extended Hindu family having collective responsibility for succession. Equally, from the eighteenth century onwards it has led to the consistent reinforcement of traditional networks among families which shared both religion and caste. Three types of Marwari firm had emerged before 1914 – the great multi-branch firm, the brokers and banians and those speculating in futures. Whilst they belonged to different epochs, they all shared a common family and hence commercial culture. They were all, in their different ways, dependent upon extended family and community for personnel. Moreover many firms displayed extraordinary longevity, even where initial wealth had been gained speculatively, either in the opium trade or in commodity markets before the First World War (Timberg, 1973, reprinted in this volume as Chapter 13).

Training and Organization of Work

If the cultural characteristics of societies contribute to the structure and capabilities of family business, they are inseparable from attitudes to training and the organization of work. Moreover, it is clear that an important explanation of competitive advantage in differentiated or speciality products lies in the distinctive features of particular communities. It has derived in large degree from that combination of indigenous skill, proprietary capitalism and shared culture which has sustained systems of flexible production from the eighteenth to the twentieth century. In the Birmingham metal trades in the eighteenth century, the speciality textile producers of Philadelphia in the nineteenth century and the Northern Italian clothing and footwear producers of the late twentieth century, networks of specialist producers have successfully served rapidly changing markets (Berg, 1993; Scranton, 1983; Goodman, 1989, reprinted in this volume as Chapter 15).

In nineteenth century America the vertically integrated, bulk sheeting corporations of Northern Massachusetts employed a mainly unskilled female labour force, and served the homogeneous frontier markets. In Philadelphia in 1860 by contrast 'there existed a complex of specialized and flexible manufacturing enterprises of all sizes, employing labor of recognized skill in the production of wools, cottons, blends, hosiery, carpets, silks and trimmings' (Scranton, 1983: 10). The symbiotic relationship between the immigrant owners of factories and workshops and the skilled, largely foreign born craft workers helped to give the Philadelphia textile industry its distinctive character. The immigrant hand loom weavers were the linchpin of Philadelphia's flexible manufacturing system. It was their skill which facilitated rapid pattern changes in response to demand fluctuations in differentiated markets. It is, however, the relationship between community and business which is of interest here. The values and attitudes of foreign handloom weavers, often living in close-knit, ethnically distinctive neighbourhoods, reinforced existing Philadelphian traditions. These both influenced the product strategies of the City's manufacturers and had profound effects on business culture.

The origins of the competitive advantage of Philadephia producers in speciality markets can be traced to the cultural characteristics and technical competence of the city's skilled communities. Nevertheless it was also critical that there was some coincidence of values between proprietors and skilled workers. This was achieved in part, by the ease with which workers could become proprietors. In addition the tendency for successors in family firms to serve a shopfloor apprenticeship was also important. It gave them the technical competence necessary to earn the respect of the skilled workforce and an understanding of craft culture which was crucial to harmonious labour relations (Scranton, 1986, reprinted in this volume as Chapter 14).

Similar cultural considerations help to explain why flexible specialization has proved so successful in late twentieth century Italy. After an abhortive experiment with US-style corporate enterprise between 1945 and 1970, Italy emerged as the fastest growing European economy in the 1980s. Success, especially in the clothing trades, has been based upon small, specialized family firms using skilled local labour. The shift, which was government inspired, was precipitated by rising levels of unemployment, and was designed to build upon the high degree of localism, both political and financial in Italian society and was facilitated by computerization which made specialization feasible. The shared values of family and community and co-operation on both education and innovation, has created a highly successful business system, capable of penetrating both domestic and European high income clothing markets. It is, therefore, both a reflection and a projection of Italian socio-cultural characteristics (Goodman, 1989, reprinted in this volume as Chapter 15).

Diversification

Contrary to Chandler's suggestion that personal capitalism constrains growth and dynamism, established businesses, irrespective of ownership, diversify, not least to reduce uncertainty. This may involve internalization, but it need not. It has been demonstrated that in different environments, especially where a shared culture leads to low transaction costs, various forms of externalization may extend the boundaries of the firm considerably. Ties of control may well be looser than in US-style business corporations. Yet the differing strategies and structures of family businesses are more a reflection of their capabilities in particular economic and socio-cultural circumstances than of their shortcomings.

In characterizing nineteenth century French business as conservative and small scale, Landes (reprinted in this volume as Chapter 1), consigned to a footnote numerous large scale enterprises, including many family businesses. There were in nineteenth century France, a number of old, large scale family businesses in merchant banking, textiles and iron. More interestingly French firms proved both successful and dynamic in the Second

Industrial Revolution. Family firms such as Saint-Gobain, Renault, Schneider and Citröen all emerged as dominant large scale firms. In common with family firms elsewhere in Europe, the Far East and in America prior to the Sherman Acts, a combination of holding companies, trusts and preference shares meant that family control was not diluted until quite late in the twentieth century. Yet cultural influences do distinguish French and indeed German family firms from, for example, their British neighbours. Attitudes to education in Britain have been significantly different from those on the Continent. In France, for example, the prestige of business families was enhanced by education, whilst advanced technological and vocational education had especially high status. Thus, family directors were often as highly educated as their salaried managers, a characteristic which enhanced performance of these family firms in technologically advanced industries (Lévy-Leboyer, 1984, reprinted in this volume as Chapter 16).

If French family firms displayed a greater potential for growth and dynamism than either Landes or Chandler would have predicted, the same must also be true of the Netherlands. Twentieth century Dutch family businesses have been able to grasp the opportunities of scale and scope and have been competitively successful in both fine chemicals and electricals. Dutch family firms share characteristics with both Britain and Germany and are thus best viewed in a northern European context. In an environment where, until the 1930s at least, personal capitalism was common and where, from that decade, co-operative agreements were supported by governments, diversification through the establishment of separate companies proved just as successful as internalization (Sluyterman and Winkelman, 1993, reprinted in this volume as Chapter 20).

It has been demonstrated that in nineteenth century Philadelphia, the emergence of flexible specialization was inseparable from the culture of the city's immigrant craft workers. This reservoir of skill was also instrumental in the survival of those few family firms which grew. The plentiful supply of skilled labour allowed the Bromleys, the large carpet manufacturers, to diversify from the 1860s onwards. They moved, first into lace, then into household furnishing and finally into silk and were able to maintain a high degree of competitiveness until the 1930s. Then expansion to the South, by separating them from their skill base proved disastrous (Scranton, 1993, reprinted in this volume as Chapter 19).

Elsewhere evidence of the growth, diversification and flexibility of family business is plentiful, whilst the wide range of strategies reflect striking differences in both the economic base and in the culture of families. Differences in the role of government, the sectoral base and market opportunities undoubtedly help to distinguish the behaviour of family firms owned by offshore Chinese from, for example, the Japanese *zaibatsu*. Nevertheless distinctive attitudes to family and inheritance have also been significant. In the *zaibatsu* such as Mitsui or Mitsubishi diversification from commerce into manufacturing, mining, insurance shipping and ship building, saw a divorce of ownership from control, although mechanisms of control did vary between firms. In Japan collective, as opposed to individualistic, values have permeated all aspects of family and business. It has been shown that biological ties were of less significance than the welfare of the household. In the context of the *zaibatsu* the acceptance of well educated, 'adopted' sons as managers, meant that despite strong ties of family ownership, managerial control in these vertically integrated holding companies increased significantly in the 1930s (Fruin, 1980, reprinted in this volume as Chapter 12; Morikawa, 1970, reprinted in this volume as Chapter 17; Hirschmeier, 1970, reprinted in this volume as Chapter 25).

The businesses owned by the overseas Chinese in Taiwan, Hong Kong, Singapore and more generally in East Asia on the other hand have displayed very different characteristics. Family firms have generally been small scale and comparatively shortlived. In the early twentieth century considerable diversification both geographically and in terms of range of goods was achieved by Hong Kong merchants and in retailing without any loss of family control or tradition (Chan, 1982, reprinted in this volume as Chapter 18). Equally diversification of industrial activity in the late twentieth century has not involved the combination of family ownership and informal transorganizational control which characterized the *zaibatsu*. Rather it has involved the development of complex external networks within which traditional family control, broadly paternalistic management and flexibility have been retained and where the scope of activity in such industries as textiles, clothing, electronics and precision equipment has been considerable (Redding, 1990: pp. 41–78).

The explanation of this distinctive Chinese capitalism can be found in part in the cultural influences on the family which were so different from those in Japan. Amongst the Chinese although the head of the family firm holds the business in trust for future generations, the emphasis is on individual advancement rather than collective welfare. The strong link between social status and business success discourages retirement or the recruitment of outsiders, limiting the scale and sometimes the longevity of individual firms.

Co-operative Behaviour and Groups

It has been demonstrated that the rapid entry and exit of family firms helped to fuel industrialization. Yet in most societies the opportunity for co-operative activity by the owners of family businesses has been considerable. Since the eighteenth century there has been a tendency, in the face of uncertainty, for inter- and intra-family co-operation by successful family businesses. Thus in the hazardous environment of Britain in the eighteenth century, survival and success was as much dependent upon the position of a firm within a community as upon innovation. Continued access to credit during financial crises, for example, was underpinned by a family's position within networks of trust, based upon shared values and pooled information. These especially favoured those few families who, through that combination of reputation and goodwill which is only born of long establishment, were best able to survive in times of adversity (Rose, 1994).

Co-operative activity of one form or another, between established commercial and industrial families, will be found wherever concentrations of wealth have emerged in the hands of a business elite. Bound by common ties of religion, intermarriage and experience, such groups enjoy the high levels of trust and low transaction costs, which are the product of a common culture (Casson, 1991: pp. 3 and 169). The relationship between the cultural characteristics of elites and collective action means that the precise form of group activity will vary internationally and even within societies.

In nineteenth century Germany, for example (Kocka, 1981, reprinted in this volume as Chapter 22), business owners were anything but isolated individualists, deriving support and security from a network of family connections. Indeed, intermarriage between industrial families formed the basis of cartel-type arrangements which united the fortunes and business strategies of interconnected families. Such co-operative activity found support from governments and later from the banks. Similarly it was the informal and subtle collusion within the City of London, underpinned by a shared experience of education and club membership, and with the tacit approval of the Bank of England, which perpetuated British merchant banking dynasties until the 1960s (Lisle-Williams, 1984, reprinted in this volume as Chapter 23). Even under normal conditions this close knit group of banking aristocrats favoured co-operation rather than competition. When panics, like the Baring Crisis of 1890 or the world financial turmoil of 1931 and 1932, threatened the very fabric of the City's prosperity, the merchant bankers closed ranks.

In nineteenth century Britain, and indeed in twentieth century East Asia, businesses were sometimes founded which were dependent upon established firms. This meant that networks could develop which helped to create market stability and reduce transaction costs (Nenadic, 1990: p. 192; Redding, 1990: pp. 149–690). The development of financial services and public utilities in Manchester in the 1820s were, for example, the result of coordinated action by the commercial elite wishing to reduce the uncertainty of their business environment. There, a 'charmed circle' of mainly Unitarian mercantile families remained dominant socially, economically and politically, at least until 1850 (Pearson, 1991: pp. 379–414). In nineteenth century America, on the other hand, the wealth and cohesion of the Boston Associates allowed them to respond collectively to increasing threats to their prosperity and standing as merchants. The result was an all-embracing, regional industrialization, based upon interlocking business corporations, producing a standardized product and supported by a range of ancillary services (Dalzell, 1987). Externalization and collusion, therefore, have been, and remain, a common family business response to risk whether firms are large or small.

The formation of interlocking economic groups, where capital and management transcend a single family, are a familiar feature of twentieth century business activity in Latin America, Asia and Africa (Leff, 1978, reprinted in this volume as Chapter 21). Based upon interpersonal ties of trust and loyalty, economic groups facilitate diversification in response to uncertainty or market failure. As such they represent an important and often highly successful alternative to internalization of activity within a single, tightly controlled, firm. Sometimes, as in the case of the Chinese Khaw group, family groupings were comparatively shortlived. Operating in Penang before the First World War, the Khaw group was a response to British commercial infiltration of the Thai peninsular and received the support of the Thai government. The power of the Khaw family, and its ability to combine mining, smelting, shipping, financial and insurance interests, through a network of interlocking companies, was therefore dependent upon a combination of commercial strength and local political power. When changed circumstances, following the First World War, eroded the family's political strength, and with it its government support, the group began to disintegrate (Cushman, 1986, reprinted in this volume as Chapter 24). More generally in the Far East, however, economic groups have proved more resilient, though in common with the Khaw case, their effectiveness and success has often been in part dependent upon government support.

During the early twentieth century and the interwar period inter-family financial cooperation led to the dramatic expansion of the *zaibatsu* into vertically integrated groupings (Hirschmeier, 1970, reprinted in this volume as Chapter 25). Although these were swept away after the Second World War, family groups have persisted elsewhere in the Far East and have dominated industrial activity in Hong Kong, India, Pakistan and Korea in the late twentieth century (Wong, 1985, reprinted in this volume as Chapter 26; Ito, 1984, reprinted in this volume as Chapter 27; Papanek, 1972, reprinted in this volume as Chapter 28; Hattori, 1984). In Hong Kong, for example 54% of stockmarket capitalization is controlled by ten family groups, seven of them Chinese (Redding, 1990: pp. 151–2). It has already been suggested that contrasting national and local economic, socio-cultural, political and legal characteristics in different countries have meant that the strategies of family businesses may vary internationally. Such diversity is reflected in both the origins and the organization of economic groups.

It has been shown, for example, that the Japanese Zaibatsu reflected the collective culture which extended from family to business to nation and received handsome subsidies from the government (Hirschmeier, Chapter 25). In late twentieth century Hong Kong, by contrast, the informally allied business groups held together by interlocking directorships have emerged without government intervention. The development of family controlled economic groups within an individualistic and hence competitive culture at first seems an anomaly. However it can partly be explained by the status of the Overseas Chinese as migrants, who have been prepared to pursue a form of cooperative competition on the basis of their own cultural cohesion as a minority group. In addition, partible inheritance and the desire to compensate for subdivision of profits within extended families have contributed to the development of these groupings (Wong, 1985, reprinted in this volume as Chapter 26).

In India and Pakistan too, the combination of partible inheritance and the pre-eminence of the biological family help to explain the existence of economic groups where ownership and control is united. Yet again differing cultural and indeed political influences lead to some distinguishing characteristics. In India, in contrast to Hong Kong, private business has long been dominated by specific castes and ethnic groups, whilst several large firms have displayed considerable longevity. Underpinned by a shared Hindu culture the owners of these firms have behaved as an elite group, maintaining their existing position. In the relatively new Pakistan, on the other hand, the co-operation within economic groups has usually, though not exclusively, been connected with membership of the Muslim League and was supported by the emergent government (Ito, 1984, reprinted in this volume as Chapter 27; Papanek, 1972, reprinted in this volume as Chapter 28).

Conclusions

The family business is far too important in both Western and Far Eastern economic life to be discounted as either an outmoded anomaly or a source of economic decline. The essays in this volume reflect the development of the debate surrounding its characteristics and capabilities. It has become clear that while family firms do inevitably display some common features their strategies vary internationally.

Much more research is needed to establish whether family business is more successful in some sectors and indeed societies than others. The evidence in this volume suggests that family business has been especially successful in those sectors where competitive advantage is dependent on skill and flexibility, rather than on the cost advantages of mass production. This has been especially true in clothing and textile industries. In addition since family businesses tend to pursue long term goals they may enjoy competitive advantage in more technologically advanced sectors, such as pharmaceuticals, where investment in human capital is critical. Equally, family dominance has persisted in the service sector. This suggests that it may prove resilient in those sectors where the development was dependent upon contacts and socialization, especially in an East Asian environment which has proved so hospitable for family enterprise. Far more research is needed to establish the precise relationship between the cultural characteristics of different societies and business behaviour, yet they clearly add an important dimension to the understanding of diversity in the structure capabilities and performance of family businesses world wide.

References

Amsden, Alice H. (1989), *Asia's Next Giant*, New York and Oxford: Oxford University Press.

Bagchi, A.H. (1972), *Private Investment in India 1900–39*, Cambridge: Cambridge University Press.

Barker, T.C. and Lévy-Leboyer, M. (1982), 'An Inquiry into the Buddenbrook Effect in Europe', in Hannah (ed.), *From Family Firm to Professional Management*, Budapest: Akadémiai Kiadó.

Berg, M. (1993), 'Small Producer Capitalism in Eighteenth Century England', *Business History*, **35**, 17–39.

Broehl, Wayne G. (1992), *Cargill. Trading the World's Grain* Hanover NH: University Press of New England.

Casson, M.C. (1982), *The Entrepreneur*, London: Mark Robertson.

Casson, M.C. (1991), *The Economics of Business Culture: Game Theory, Transaction Costs and Economic Performance*, Oxford: Oxford University Press.

Casson, M.C. (1993), 'Entrepreneurship and Business Culture', in J. Brown and M.B. Rose (eds), *Entrepreneurship, Networks and Modern Business*, Manchester: Manchester University Press.

Chandler, A.D. Jr, (1990), *Scale and Scope*, Cambridge, Mass: Harvard University Press.

Chapman, S.D. (1985), 'British Based Investment Groups before 1914', *Economic History Review*, **38**, 230–51.

Church, Roy (1986), 'Family Firms and Managerial Capitalism: The Case of the International Motor Industry', *Business History* **28** (2), April, 165–80.

Church, Roy (1993), 'The Family Firm in Industrial Capitalism: International Perspectives on Hypotheses and History', *Business History*, **35** (4), 17–43.

Coleman, D.C. (1973), 'Gentlemen and Players', *Economic History Review*, **26**, 92–116.

Dalzell, R. (1987), *Enterprising Elite: The Boston Associates and the World they Made*, Cambridge, Mass: Harvard University Press.

Dore, R.P. (1985), 'Financial and the Long Term View', *Policy Studies*, **6** (1) 10–29.

Field, Michael L. (1984), *The Merchants*, London: John Murray.

Fruin, W. Mark, (1992), *The Japanese Enterprise System*, Oxford: Oxford University Press.

Habakkuk, H.J. (1955), 'The Historical Experience on the Basic Conditions of Economic Progress', in L.H. Dupriez (ed.), *Economic Progress*, Louvain: Louvain University Press.

Habakkuk, H.J. (1962), *British and American Technology*, Cambridge: Cambridge University Press.

Hannah, L. (1982), 'Introduction', in L. Hannah (ed.), *From Family Firm to Professional Management: Structure and Performance of Business Enterprise*, Budapest: Akadémiai Kiadó.

Hattori, T. (1984), 'The Relationship between Zaibatsu and Family Structure: the Korean case', in A. Okochi and S. Yasuoka (eds), *Family Business in the Era of Industrial Growth*, Tokyo: University of Tokyo Press.

Hirschmeier, Johannes (1970), 'The Japanese Spirit of Enterprise, 1867–1970', *Business History Review*, **44** (1), 13–38.

Hoppit, J. (1987), *Risk and Failure in English Business, 1700–1800*, Cambridge: Cambridge University Press.

Jeremy, David J. (1981), *Transatlantic Industrial Revolution: The Diffusion of Textile Technology between Britain and America*, Oxford: Basil Blackwell.

Jones, G. and Rose, Mary B. (1993), 'Family Capitalism', *Business History*, **35**, 1–16.

Ketsde Vries, M.F.R. (1992), 'The Family Firm: An Owners Manual', *Insead Working Paper Series*, No 92/03/0B.

Landes, David S. (1965), 'Technological Change and Development in Western Europe, 1750–1914', in M. Postan and H.J. Habakkuk (eds), *Cambridge Economic History of Europe*, Vol 6, Cambridge: Cambridge University Press, 563–4.

Lazonick, W. (1991), *Business Organisation and the Myth of the Market Economy*, Cambridge: Cambridge University Press.

Morikawa, H. (1992), *Zaibatsu: The Rise and Fall of the Family Enterprise Group*, Tokyo: University of Tokyo Press.

Nenadic, S. (1990), 'The Life Cycle of Firms in Late Nineteenth Century Britain' in P. Jobert and M. Moss (eds), *The Birth and Death of Companies: An Historical Perspective*, Carnforth: Parthenon, 181–196.

Pearson, Robin (1991), 'Collective Diversification: Manchester Cotton Merchants and the Insurance Business in the Early Nineteenth Century', *Business History Review*, **65**, 379–414.

Pohl, H. (1982), 'On the History of Organisation and Management in Large German Enterprises since the Nineteenth Century', *German Yearbook on Business History*, Berlin: Springer, 99–122.

Ray, Rajat (1979), *Industrialisation in India*, New Delhi: Oxford University Press.

Redding, S. Gordon (1990), *The Spirit of Chinese Capitalism*, Berlin: de Gruyter.

Rose, Mary B. (1986), *The Gregs of Quarry Bank Mill: the Rise and Decline of a Family Firm, 1750–1914*, Cambridge: Cambridge University Press.

Rose, Mary B. (1994), 'The Family Firm in British Business, 1780–1914', in Maurice Kirby and Mary B. Rose (eds), *Business Enterprise in Modern Britain from the Eighteenth to the Twentieth Centuries*, London: Routledge.

Rosenberg, N. (1972), *Technology and American Economic Growth*, New York: Harper and Row.

Saul, S.B. (1970), *Technological Change: the United States and Britain in the Nineteenth Century*, London: Methuen.

Scranton, P. (1983), *Proprietary Capitalism: The Textile Manufacture of Philadelphia, 1800–1885*, Cambridge: Cambridge University Press.

Scranton, P. (1989), *Figured Tapestry: Production, Markets and Power in Philadelphia Textiles, 1885–1941*, Cambridge: Cambridge University Press.

Smith, S.(1993),'Fortune and Failure: The Survival of Family Firms in Eighteenth Century India', *Business History*, **35** (4), 44–65.

Stigler, G.J. (1951), 'The Division of Labour is Limited by the Extent of the Market', *The Journal of Political Economy*, **LIX.**

Temin, P. (1966), 'Labor Scarcity and the Problem of American Industrial Efficiency in the 1850s', *Journal of Economic History*, **26**, 277–95.

Timberg, Thomas A. (1978), *The Marwaris: From Traders to Industrialists*, Bombay: Asia Publishing House.

Toyne, B. *et al.* (eds.) (1984), *The Global Textile Industry*, London: Routledge.

Wiener, M. (1981), *English Culture and Economic Decline*, Cambridge: Cambridge University Press.

Part I
The Family Firm Debate:
Conservatism and Decline or an
Alternative Strategy?

[1]

French Entrepreneurship and Industrial Growth in the Nineteenth Century

I

THE study of French enterprise and entrepreneurship is rewarding for two major reasons. In the first place, anything that
will help explain the present weakness of French industry and commerce throws light in turn on one of the most important political
phenomena of the last 150 years: the fall of France from hegemony
under Napoleon to the position she holds today. Secondly, the history of French business and businessmen is significant precisely
because of France's relatively minor place in the economic world.
If we are to weigh the validity of the recent emphasis of theorists
on the role of the entrepreneur qua se in the over-all process of economic change—on the contribution of the personal element to the
impersonal operation of the system—we must consider not only the
more "modern" nations but those less industrialized as well. It will
not suffice to study the progress of American or German business
and deduce therefrom impressive theories on the importance of the
businessman. The converse must also be examined: To what extent
are certain attitudes and values inimical to the development of
enterprise? Or concretely in the case of France to what extent have
the character and mentality of the French financier, industrialist, or
merchant been responsible for the relatively retarded status of the
country's economy?

Unfortunately, owing to certain inhibiting factors, some of them
the temporary reflection of postwar instability and impoverishment,
others the semipermanent result of outdated academic traditions
and an unfavorable social milieu, French scholars have not only
neglected the subject almost entirely but are unlikely to give it much
attention for a long time to come.[2] This, of course, makes the problem of research that much more difficult—the historian must in

---

[1] It would take me far beyond the scope of this article to analyze in detail the economic
position of France in the world today. There is a whole literature on the subject. A convenient survey is offered by A. Martel, ed., *Grandeur et déclin de la France à l'époque contemporaine* (Paris: Société d'Organisation et de Gestion, [1946]).

[2] There have been few attempts to treat the history of enterprise as such, and these primarily along the lines of an introduction to an elementary course in business administration.
Works like J.-P. Palewski's *Le Rôle du chef d'entreprise* (Paris: Presses Universitaires, 1924),
of which his *Histoire des chefs d'entreprise* (Paris: Gallimard, 1928) is simply a popular
summary, and Germain Martin's and P. Simon's *Le Chef d'entreprise: évolution de son rôle
au XX* siècle* (Paris: Flammarion, 1946) fall into this class.

effect start from scratch. But at the same time it renders all the more urgent, in so far as scholarly needs may be termed "urgent," a provisional synthesis that will introduce the question and furnish a solid foundation for future specialized effort. This article does not quite pretend to be such a synthesis. It is meant more as a suggestive outline, directed especially at other students of entrepreneurship in the hope of arousing, first, interest and, second, criticism.

For the study of French entrepreneurship, the years from about 1815 to 1870 are undoubtedly the most important.[3] This was the period of France's industrial revolution, the critical era of change and growth that in large measure fixed the economic structure of the country. It is precisely during this time of decision, therefore, that the influence of the individual may be expected to have been paramount. Furthermore, from a purely practical standpoint, the researcher is best off in the nineteenth century. The student of entrepreneurship obviously needs private archives, family records, and the papers of various firms. Such materials are almost nonexistent for the prerevolutionary period, and after 1789 their inaccessibility varies directly with their contemporaneity. In a country where every businessman fears the fisc and every bourgeois worships privacy, it would be utter presumption to ask for documents of recent date. Even those of a century ago are rarely opened to outsiders, as the rebuffs of many a French scholar will testify.

II

What, then, was the French entrepreneur of the industrial revolution like Here a word of caution is in order. As one writer put it: France is diversity.[4] It is astonishing to note the geological, climatic, ethnographic, cultural, and other variety found in an area smaller than the state of Texas. In one sense, therefore, there is no such thing as *the* French businessman. On the other hand, the development of a single, conscious nation with its implications for economic, social, and spiritual unity has inevitably shaped the individual more or less to the common mold. In spite of nuances and exceptions, there are definitely certain characteristics of entrepreneurship during this period generalized enough to constitute a type.

[3] For the purpose of this article, the entrepreneur is not only the "innovator" as such but the adapter and manager as well. In other words, the entrepreneur is the businessman who makes the decisions.

[4] L. Febvre, "Que la France se nomme diversité," *Annales: économies, sociétés, civilisations*, I (1946). 271–74.

French Entrepreneurship 47

To begin with, the average French entrepreneur was a small businessman acting for himself or at most on behalf of a handful of partners. This was especially true in 1815. To take the two most important industries, in textiles he was still at that time the "undertaker," the little capitalist who furnished the raw material to scattered spinners and weavers and then collected the finished goods for market, and in metallurgy he was the isolated *maître de forges,* with his furnace built along some country stream in the neighborhood of iron deposits and forests. Transportation in those days was provided by a multitude of *maîtres de poste,* haulers, boatmen, and, especially for local shipments, peasants exploiting their livestock in the quiet season. Foreign trade was in the hands of small commission and shipping firms, some of them with perhaps one or two coasting vessels, others with as many as half a dozen ocean-going sailers, while retail trade continued in the small, cluttered shops of the eighteenth century. Finally, such credit as was available came from private lenders or from small local banks, many of them built on profits made in commerce and industry and most of them restricting their clientele to an intimate circle of trusted friends and relatives. The corporation, to all intents and purposes, did not exist.

Naturally, the years that followed changed this picture in many important respects. Certain districts, notably Alsace, the Nord, and Normandy, saw the rise of impressively large cotton factories. If the woolen industry, owing to slower mechanical progress, cannot show developments of comparable magnitude, companies like Paturle-Seydoux at Câteau-Cambrésis and Holden at Reims nevertheless represented important concentrations of capital and labor. In the manufacture of iron and steel, where a more important outlay of capital was required, the Schneider plant at Le Creusot and the De Wendel mills at Hayange and Stiring were only the best known of the larger units. During these years, the railroad, which necessitated an unprecedented accumulation of private capital, completely transformed land transport. Foreign trade was similarly affected, though to a lesser degree, by the steamship. It was during this period also that retail commerce made its first significant departure from the tradition of centuries with the introduction of fixed prices and the creation under the Second Empire of the first successful department stores and branch outlets. As for finance, it required the boom psychology of the 1850's and 1860's to launch the first corporative investment and deposit banks.

David S. Landes

Nevertheless, a survey of French business in 1870 quite clearly shows that these new concentrations of economic strength were still the exception. In land transport the change was complete; the very nature of the new technique imposed regional monopolies and large corporations. But in the other primary economic sectors, the small entrepreneur remained the norm, even in those areas where the factory system had come to prevail.[5]

In the second place, the French businessman was a fundamentally conservative man, with a firm distaste for the new and unknown. Security was his first concern, and it was generally felt that the quickest road to success was the slow but sure one. The main thing was to watch the sous; the francs would take care of themselves. Thus enterprise was generally characterized on the one hand by a high rate of book amortization—also intended incidentally to conceal the size of profits—and on the other by slow turnover of equipment. The average French producer was reluctant to buy machines to begin with; when he bought them, he wanted them to last. How much this emphasis on caution and thrift was due to the influence of the peasant mentality it is hard to say. Suffice it to point out that even today the visitor to France is struck by the passion for conservation of the most trivial objects, even *la ficelle* of Maupassant.

A third major characteristic of the French entrepreneur was his independence: the typical firm was pretty much self-sufficient. Since the cost of expansion usually came out of company revenues and, if necessary, the pockets of the owner or his relatives and friends, the goal of enterprise was the highest possible *rate* of profit. Naturally, all were not equally successful in this endeavor, but the fact remains that most French industrial growth in this period was financed precisely in this manner. To choose merely one striking example among many, the unusually prolific and prosperous Motte textile interests of Roubaix, who were said to purchase or build a new mill every time a Motte was born, never found it necessary to request outside credit or funds of any sort.[6]

---

[5] It would be easy to substantiate this with the official statistics, especially since the figures are weighted in favor of the small units. But French statistics have always been notoriously unreliable: no businessman worth his salt would think of telling the truth. For this reason, any attempt to "quantify" French economic and social history soon reduces itself to arithmetical guesswork, certain fields like price history excepted.

[6] *Motte-Bossut: un homme, une famille, une firme, 1843–1943* (Tourcoing: Privately printed, 1944), *passim*. See below, p. 53, for the De Wendel family.

French Entrepreneurship 49

It is fairly obvious, however, that cautious management, obsolescent plants, and high profits are not a combination designed to flourish in a world of cutthroat competition. As stated above, the French entrepreneur prized security above all, and a secure market meant one well protected from foreign inroads. For all but the last few years of this period, therefore, French industry and commerce were protected by a series of impassable duties and prohibitions, which for most businessmen came to represent as much a permanent element of the environment as the ground on which their factories stood.

Nevertheless, the elimination of foreign competition was not in itself sufficient to guarantee the prosperity of any and all producers. This was, after all, a period of technological change, and certain firms inevitably fell behind in capacity and efficiency. Theoretically, the competion between these marginal units and the more progressive firms should have been enough in itself to eliminate the laggards and hasten modernization. In many cases it did have this effect. Yet the fact remains that backward forms of production and distribution remained widespread in France for a surprisingly long period side by side with far more efficient techniques. In part, of course, this was due to the cost of transportation, which made it difficult, especially in the heavy industries, to compete far from the base of operations. But there are far too many cases where this explanation will not suffice, and there it would seem that the usual mechanism of competition was not operative. It is not easy to find concrete examples owing to the inaccessibility of records of business costs and prices, but the data available in the many government tariff inquiries and similar sources would seem to show quite definitely that the more efficient French producer was not inclined to push his advantage. In most cases he preferred a healthy amount of what Joseph Schumpeter has called "entrepreneurial profit" to the elimination of rivals and a consequent rapid expansion of capacity.[7] The latter involved much more effort to begin with, and might well have necessitated appeals to outside credit.

---

[7] Perhaps the best example is that of the Anzin coal mines which, though quite capable of undercutting the other basins on the Paris market, found it much more profitable to live and let live. Indeed, at the tariff inquiry of 1832 we have the amusing spectacle of Anzin arguing against a decrease in the duty so that its competitors should not suffer.—*Enquête sur les houilles* (Paris, 1832), p. 472 f.

David S. Landes

Furthermore, this dependence on high tariffs was only one aspect of a general reliance on the aid and protection of the government. Under the old regime the French manufacturer had been more a functionary than an independent entrepreneur; industry had been in large measure a sort of hothouse growth, nurtured by and derived from the central administration. The Napoleonic period, if anything, strengthened these characteristics.[8] It is not surprising, therefore, that the businessman came to look on the government as a sort of father in whose arms he could always find shelter and consolation. This fundamentally infantile attitude, which must be distinguished from the predatory outlook not uncommon in the United States, was carried in this period to remarkable lengths and characterized businessmen from one end of the scale to the other. There is essentially no difference between the request of a wheelchair maker of Belleville that the state purchase twelve of his devices for donation to various hospitals and the petition in 1848 of three of France's biggest iron firms, Schneider, Boigues, and Bougueret-Martenot, that the government take over the defaulting Paris-Lyons Railroad and make good on four million dollars owed for delivery of rails.[9]

To be sure, there were important exceptions to this widespread conservatism and timidity. Contrary to popular assumption, France has had her share of pioneers, and indeed the French rather pride themselves on their imagination and ingenuity. The powerful innovating influence of the Saint-Simoniens comes perhaps first to mind. These disciples of a utopian reformer, many of them trained engineers, combined keen business instincts with the vision of a new economic world, and their role in the French industrial revolution, especially in the fields of transport and banking, cannot be overestimated. Or take retail trade, where Boucicaut established the world's first successful department store, the Bon Marché, Potin produced the first packaged foods for sale through branch outlets, and Révillon revolutionized the French and, on occasion, the world fur business.[10]

---

[8] Cf. the recent work of O. Viennet, *Napoléon et l'industrie française* (Paris: Plon, 1947).

[9] Letter of M. Dupont to Minister of Interior, March 18, 1848, *Archives nationales* F 12 2224; Letter of MM. Schneider, Boigues, and Bougueret-Martenot to the Président du Conseil, July 1848, *Archives nationales* F 12 2223.

[10] There is an excellent history of the Révillon firm by Marcel Sexé, *Histoire d'une famille et d'une industrie pendant deux siècles, 1723–1923* (Paris: Plon, 1923). It is several cuts above the usual anniversary publication.

Nevertheless, the influence of these and other innovators was considerably dampened by certain characteristics of French enterprise. In this connection, one factor is worthy of special consideration: the difficulty for the *novus homo* of obtaining funds. Under the old regime, the shortage of business capital in France had been just about chronic. Such money as was available went by preference to the various government *charges* or into landed property.[11] During the nineteenth century the situation was apparently much improved. Superficially, at least, the demand for capital was satisfied by reinvestment of profits and the loans of relatives and friends. But this condition was obviously not calculated to facilitate the advent of those newcomers whose only assets were their talent and imagination. Moreover, these difficulties were accentuated by the relatively limited role of the corporation in the French industrial revolution. The unprecedented potentialities of this new business form lay not only in its ability to concentrate thousands of anonymous petty fortunes, the aspect most often emphasized, but in its use as a vehicle for the penniless innovator. In France, however, this use was sharply circumscribed for various reasons, not least among them the red tape and legal difficulties involved and the keen distaste of the saving public for aleatory business investments.[12] It is easy to show that even in those fields where the *société anonyme* predominated, the new form of organization served more to consolidate the position of established financial interests than to open the way for new men. The railroads are an excellent example.

This shortage of risk capital serves to explain in turn, at least in part, why France has so often failed to appreciate its own inventors. From Lebon's discovery of gas lighting at the turn of the eighteenth century, through Girard's spinning machine, Sauvage's screw propellor, and Verguin's accomplishments in artificial dyes, to Tellier's refrigerator and beyond, the list of innovations which originated in France only to find their quickest and greatest development abroad is quite impressive.

---

[11] See, on this point, the brief comparative survey of J. Koulischer, "La grande industrie aux XVII° et XVIII° siècles: France, Allemagne, Russie," *Annales d'histoire économique et sociale*, III (1931), 11–46.

[12] It was not until 1867 that the formation of a firm with completely limited liability and transferable ownership was permitted by the mere act of registration. On the complications and obstacles imposed by the previous regime, see C. Coquelin, "Des Sociétés commerciales en France et en Angleterre," *Revue des Deux-Mondes* (N.S.), XIII, iii (1843), 397–437.

52   *David S. Landes*

Finally, even in those cases where newcomers succeeded in imposing themselves, they usually did so only at the expense of important
concessions to the *status quo*. It is no coincidence that so many of
the self-made pioneers should appear in the field of retail trade where
the scattered shops already in existence were in no position to resist,
or that among the Saint-Simoniens, the Péreire brothers, who insisted
on carrying the fight to the vested interests, were eventually broken,
while an entrepreneur like Talabot, who withdrew from competition with Schneider and the other big ironmasters when warned of
the possible consequences, died with his fortune intact.[13] France has
been prolific of talent and genius, but she also has had an effective
way of putting innovators in their place.[14]

III

It is not within the scope of a short article to discuss and evaluate
the many factors that undoubtedly concurred to make the French
businessman of the industrial revolution what he was. Nevertheless,
certain of these seem more important than others, particularly the
structure of French society and the traditions on which it rested.

In discussing the typical firm of this period, one important feature,
its family character, was deliberately omitted in order to differentiate clearly between the economic and social aspects of the problem.
With rare exceptions, French enterprise was organized on a family
basis and the entrepreneur conceived of his business, whatever its
nature, not as a mechanism for the production or distribution of
goods nor a means to indefinite wealth and power but as a sort of
fief that maintained and enhanced the position of the family, just as
the produce of the manor and the men-at-arms it could muster were
the *material* basis of medieval status. If the family was inclined to
remain in business, there was always room for future generations.
Thus some firms, like the Japy hardware and watchmaking company, had careful rules regulating the right of each partner to introduce a son or son-in-law into the organization. And if, as was only
too often the case, the family was looking forward to "higher"
things, a good business was always a steppingstone to a career in the

---

[13] The best picture of the Péreire-Rothschild conflict is still to be found in J. Plenge,
Gründung und Geschichte des Crédit Mobilier (Tübingen: H. Laupp, 1903). On Talabot,
see A. Ernouf, *Paulin Talabot: sa vie et son oeuvre, 1799–1885* (Paris, 1886). The incident
discussed is to be found on p. 190.

[14] Cf. A. Mayer, *La Crise de la structure de la société française* (New York: Offprint from
the *French Review*, 1942).

government service, possibly even to ennoblement or marriage into the aristocracy. In either case, the *affaire* was never an end in itself, but the means to an end. The obsession of the entrepreneur with the enterprise as such, which Sombart finds so common in America and Germany, to all intents and purposes did not exist in France.[15]

This fact in turn helps to explain some of the other characteristics of French enterprise already discussed. A family firm is first and foremost a private affair, which accounts in large measure for the self-imposed goal of financial self-sufficiency and the slow adoption of the corporative form. In this respect, the extravagant lengths to which the French businessman has carried what is known as *le secret de l'affaire* are worthy of note. When in 1908 the De Wendel interests felt compelled for the first time in their history to call in outside capital, they preferred to pay 4.5 per cent to German investors rather than borrow at 4 per cent on the French market and publish statutes and statements as required by law.[16] It is truly astonishing to follow the evolution of some of these industrial fiefs, which start as simple private firms, take in generation after generation of children and in-laws, and remain through changes in name and legal status, through wars and depressions, in the control of what one writer has called the *dynasties bourgeoises*.[17]

Furthermore, a family firm is necessarily a cautious firm. It is easy to speculate with the money of others; it is sometimes even easy to gamble with one's own funds. But it is somewhat harder to take chances when every question must be approved by a keenly critical circle of relatives primarily interested in the conservation of the patrimony. And in France at least as much attention has always been given to the preservation as to the creation of wealth.[18]

This characteristic also explains in part the paradox of entrepreneurial dependence on government aid and the undeclared war

---

[15] W. Sombart, *Quintessence of Capitalism* (London: T. F. Unwin, Ltd., 1915), 172–75.

[16] H. Grandet, *Monographie d'un établissement métallurgique sis à la fois en France et en Allemagne* (Chartres: E. Garnier, 1909), p. 119. Like most of the few French business historians who have had access to private archives, Grandet is a member of the family concerned.

[17] Cf. E. Beau de Loménie, *Les Responsabilités des dynasties bourgeoises* (2 vols.; Paris: Denoël, 1947–48).

[18] See in this regard the fascinating works of P. Leroy-Beaulieu, *L'Art de placer et gérer sa fortune* (Paris: C. Delagrave, 1906), and J. Bainville, *Comment placer sa fortune* (Paris: Nouvelle Librairie Nationale, 1919), which provide an exceptional insight into the psychology of the French investor.

54   *David S. Landes*

between business and the state which is so often shocking to the
foreign observer. If the administration has always been the tutor of
French commerce and industry, it has also been the bureaucratic
overseer and prying fisc, half meddler, half thief. Moreover, in France
the government has come to be a relatively transitory phenomenon.
Rulers come and go, republics rise and fall, but the family goes on.
No wonder that taxes are and always have been evaded with a clear
conscience. As the founder of the Boussardel clan put it: "More
willingness, spirit of sacrifice, and fortitude is expended in our homes
in the interest of the family than in our country for the service of the
nation." [19]

Although the fundamental business unit was the family, these
families were in turn parts of the larger whole, and their outlook
was inevitably colored by the prevailing mores, traditions, and attitudes of French society. In every society there exists a hierarchy of
status based in part on function, in part on customary values.[20] This
hierachy is in effect a scale of social approval and consideration and
is unquestionably a primary factor in channeling the aspirations
and activities of the group. Moreover, this scale is especially susceptible to "cultural lag" and represents an essentially conservative force.

In the French social structure the businessman had always held
an inferior place. Three major forces conduced to this result. In the
first place, he was detested from the start by the nobility, which
rightly saw in him a subversive element. The aristrocracy, its military
and administrative functions slowly but surely ossifying in a new
world of gunpowder and mercenaries, centralization and bureaucracy, turned at bay on its bourgeois adversaries and wreaked revenge
with the strongest weapon it had left, prestige. Unable to compete
with the driving spirit of these ambitious newcomers, unable to
defeat them on their chosen ground of business with their chosen
weapon, money, the nobility deliberately turned its back and tilted
its nose. Against the practical, materialistic values of the businessman
it set the consciously impractical, unmaterialistic values of the gentleman. Against the restless ambition of the parvenu, it placed the

[19] P. Hériat, *La Famille Boussardel* (Paris: Gallimard, 1946). The story, while fictional,
is based on actual fact and presents a remarkable picture of the rise of a *dynastie bourgeoise*.
[20] There is no need to analyze in detail the concept of social status. A useful introduction
is to be found in T. Parsons, "The Analytical Approach to the Theory of Social Stratification," *American Journal of Sociology*, XLV (1940), 841–62.

French Entrepreneurship 55

prestige of birth; against the mercurial efficacy of money, the solid stability of land; against the virtues of diligence and austerity, the dignity of leisure and the splendor of pomp and circumstance.[21]

If anything, the revolutions of 1789 and 1830 strengthened this attitude. Those few nobles who under the old regime had been active as ironmasters, glass manufacturers, and so on, or had followed the Colbertist tradition of encouragement of and investment in industry, were now for the most part impoverished. To be sure, many of the new generation, especially those whose titles were of recent vintage, were to lend their names and prestige to entrepreneurial efforts and place their capital in railroads, insurance, and other corporative enterprises. But the aristocracy as a group had hardened its heart. The early years of the July Monarchy saw a marked reaction against the new way and the consecration of the myth of noble superiority, social, spiritual, and even physical. One has only to read the flood of scornful literature that followed the Revolution of 1830 to feel the bitterness approaching revulsion on the part of the dispossessed toward anything smacking of bourgeois business and money.[22]

That the entrepreneur was considerably influenced by the prestige of this "superior" group is obvious from his continued efforts to rise into its ranks, either directly or through marriage. For the same reasons, the businessman was rare who did not acquire sooner or later a landed estate, considered the safest of investments and an important criterion of social status. Obviously, most of these new gentry were simply absentee landlords. In some districts like Bordeaux the practice was just about unanimous, and there shippers and merchants were at least as well known for their vineyards and vintages as for their commercial activities.[23] It is impossible to say with any precision how much of the national wealth was diverted from business enterprise on this account, but most writers are agreed that, whether made as a form of conspicuous consumption or for more serious reasons, such investments by businessmen and nonbusinessmen were a significant obstacle to industrialization.

---

[21] Cf. the succinct article, "Gentleman, Theory of the," in the *Encyclopedia of the Social Sciences*.

[22] See, for example, the "dime novels" of Baron de Lamothe-Langon, especially *La Femme du banquier* (2 vols.; Paris, 1832).

[23] Cf. the list of viticulturers given by E. Féret, *Supplément à la statistique générale de la Gironde (partie vinicole)* (Bordeaux, 1880).

The hostility of the aristocracy would not have been enough in itself, however, had it not been for the acceptance of this concept by the nonbusiness elements of the *bourgeoisie*. This heterogeneous group, which is more easily defined negatively than positively since it includes almost everyone not falling into the small category of nobility or the large mass of the people, had developed in the course of centuries of slow ascension a scale of status heavily weighted with the prejudices of an aristocratic society. Of the multitude of professional groups that composed the *bourgeoisie*, the businessmen were generally relegated to the bottom of the ladder, other things being equal. In the last analysis, this social inferiority was what made possible the system of *charges* under the old regime, which by conferring on the *nouveaux riches* the prestige, security, and sometimes ennoblement of public office further depreciated the entrepreneurial classes and intensified their efforts to rise up and out of their "sordid" occupations.

These prejudices by no means died with the Revolution. Instead, the older *bourgeoisie*, dominated by civil servants and the liberal professions, tended to stress their prestige in the face of rising capitalist elements. In this they were, generally speaking, quite successful, and the invidious distinction between the two groups has continued right up to the present, though with considerably less force since the economic and monetary disasters due to World War I. Considerations of status, moreover, were strengthened by such factors as the security of official or professional positions and the character of the French educational system, a primary force for social conservatism. For these reasons, the best talents in France almost invariably turned to the traditional honorific careers such as law, medicine, or government. This was true even of the children of businessmen. To be sure, the important entrepreneurs were succeeded by their own offspring, but here the importance of conserving the family heritage was a vital consideration, and, besides, great wealth has always excused many a fault. The average businessman was not so fortunate. Apparently, this "curse of *fonctionnarisme*" and the rush toward the liberal professions created in turn a certain pernicious instability on the lower entrepreneurial levels. One observer, struck by the age of the Flavigny wool firm of Elbeuf, was moved to write: "This inheritance of ownership in industry is something very rarely found in France; the designation 'and son', so common in England, is almost

French Entrepreneurship 57

unknown in France. Is it the fault of our legislation or of our fickle character?" [24]

The forces of aristocratic snobbery and bourgeois aspiration were significantly assisted by a third, the pressure of literary and artistic opinion. The war between bourgeois and intellectual in France is of long standing, and the progress of the industrial revolution, which coincided with the surge of romanticism, only embittered the quarrel. For the bourgeois, especially the businessman, the intellectuals were suspect if only for their nonconformity. For the intellectual, the genus *épicier,* which included any and all moneymakers, was the essence of crass, hypocritical Philistinism. And if in this fight the Philistine held the purse strings, the pen and brush proved at least as effective. The novels of Balzac, the comedies of Scrive and Augier, and the caricatures of Daumier perpetuated the tradition of Molière and Lesage and fixed as never before the unflattering picture. MM. Jourdain, Turcaret, Poirier, and Robert Macaire are all members of the same family.

The effect of these forces was a general atmosphere that can best be termed anticapitalistic. The medieval concept of production for use and not for profit, of a static as opposed to a dynamic society, never lost its validity. The vitality of the guild idea in France right up to the present day bears witness to this. This current of thought was by no means an insignificant feature of the economic environment and was directly reflected, to choose only one example, in the hostility often encountered by French business at the hands of officials and in the national and local legislatures. The most spectacular cases were perhaps the attacks in the Chamber on private railroad corporations during the 1830's and 1840's and Napoleon III's temporary prohibition on new stock issue in 1856, but these were less discouraging in the long run than the persistent, silent opposition of an unfriendly bureaucracy. Furthermore, it is in the light of this spirit of antagonism toward the new world of industry and commerce that the historian must assess such important phenomena as the traditional French emphasis on quality as against quantity, the preference for handwork over machine work, the keen distaste

---

24 J. Turgan, *Les grandes usines: études industrielles en France et à l'étranger* (Paris: Vol. I, Librairie Nouvelle, 1860; Vols. II-X, Michel Lévy, 1862–74), V, 71. The reference to legislation is to the French Code Civil, which, in imposing a relatively equal division of estates, necessitated the liquidation of business property whenever the heirs could not come to an agreement on continued operation.

58   *David S. Landes*

for anything smacking of speculation or easy money, the frequent
praise of agriculture and the land as opposed to business and the
city, and so on.

Nor was the entrepreneurial community itself immune to this pervasive sentiment. It is surprising how many of the attacks on the
new capitalism came from businessmen, who if generally opposed
more from interest than principle, nevertheless made use of and
reinforced the traditional conservative arguments. Even the more
progressive entrepreneurs, those naturally most favorable to the
economic revolution, were affected. The student of French industry,
impressed by the social-security systems, technical schools, housing
projects, canteens, churches, and other philanthropies characteristic
of almost every firm of any size, cannot help feeling that the
businessman was often leaning over backward to appease public
opinion.[25] Moreover, how else explain the fact that the majority of
the more important manufacturers and merchants personally undertook, even sought, the responsibility of what were frequently minor
administrative functions at the expense of business duties? Not for
the political influence—entrepreneurs have never lacked for instruments to this end. Nor for the negligible prestige of the mayoralty
of a provincial village. The desire to show that the businessman was
more than a moneygrubbing egoist, that he too could be civic
minded, was undoubtedly a factor.

The discussion of the anticapitalist stream of sentiment brings us
to the important question of religion as a factor in entrepreneurship.
Long before Weber observers had noted that the more advanced
industrial and commercial populations of Europe were predominantly Protestant. The rough congruence of capitalism and Reform
seemed to indicate a mutual compatibility and reciprocal stimulation of the Calvinist ethic and those qualities which go to make a
good businessman.

The proponents of this thesis have found much in French history to support their contention. From the seventeenth century on,
the role of Protestant bankers, merchants, and industrialists has been
utterly, almost astonishingly, out of proportion to their place in the
total population. In the period we are studying, the leading financial

---

[25] This is not to exclude the genuine paternal sentiment that at times inspired these
efforts, nor, on the other hand, their usually indispensable role as a supplement to miserably
inadequate wages.

French Entrepreneurship 59

houses of France, the so-called Haute Banque, were for the most part Calvinist; so were many, if not most, of the leading shipping and commission houses, especially in Le Havre, Bordeaux, and Montpellier-Sète; and in industry, the remarkable prosperity of the cotton manufacturers of Mulhouse was only the most striking example of Protestant accomplishment.

Obviously this was more than coincidence. Whether, however, the very nature and ethic of the Calvinist faith shaped its adherents for business success, as Weber maintained, is something else again. It is quite clear that in the beginning the Reform found recruits among all classes and that, if, owing in part to requirements of moral discipline and the literacy imposed by individual Bible reading, Protestant members of the working class tended to rise in the social scale, the new ethic nevertheless proved just as favorable to the constitution of a prosperous and zealous peasantry as to the creation of capitalists.

French scholars have been inclined instead to emphasize the minority character of the French Calvinists, with all that such a position implies in the way of effort, determination, and cohesion. As members of a group that had long been openly or tacitly persecuted, the dissenters of the nineteenth century were in a sense the products of a *passé de sélection sociale*.[26] Moreover, from a purely practical standpoint, the Protestants were long more or less excluded from precisely those honorific professional and official careers that attracted the best of their Catholic compatriots. In a way, the capable and ambitious Protestant was almost forced into business.

But, and here Weber's stress on the Calvinist ethic is relevant, the success of Protestant entrepreneurship was not simply a negative phenomenon, a success sought and accepted for want of anything better. It was unquestionably bound up with the very nature and origin of the new faith, with that very quality expressed in the name, "Protestantism." The essential thing is not that the French Calvinists were diligent, thrifty, honest, and so on (they certainly had no monopoly of these virtues) but that they were revolutionaries, not only against Rome, but against the whole medieval-Catholic tradition. For them it was no disgrace to do business; rather it was a disgrace to be idle. Where the Catholic entrepreneur felt keenly the

---

[26] For this interpretation, see the excellent, if somewhat chauvinistic, lectures of E. Léonard at the Institut d'Etudes Politiques published in *La Société française contemporaine; études religieuses études politiques* (Paris: Les Cours de Droit, 1947-48), fasc. II.

slights of an aristocratic social hierarchy, the dissenter, fortified by the consciousness of his election, was impervious to the sharpest shafts of genteel scorn. His concepts of social value and levels of aspiration were almost diametrically opposed to those of the Catholic majority. There is all the difference in the world between a family like the Seillière, perhaps the most important Catholic representatives of the Haute Banque, who, once ennobled under the First Empire, never again married with commoners, and the competing Protestant houses, the Mallet, Hottinguer, Odier, Vernes, Mirabeau, Neuflize, and others, who never dispersed their fortunes in glorious but unremunerative alliances and intermarried with one another until their lines have become almost inextricable.

On the other hand, the matter is not so simple as all that. Certain Catholic circles, notably the textile manufacturers of the Nord and of Lyons, have shown precisely the same tendencies: the intense, almost exclusive, concentration on the pursuit of gain, the pride in business activities and the firm, scorn of the idle no matter how highborn and how highly placed, and intermarriage with other business families. And these groups, especially the spinners and weavers of Lille, Roubaix, and Tourcoing, are among the pillars of the Roman church in France.[27]

Furthermore, there is good reason to believe that the Reform, while favorable to sustained and self-respecting entrepreneurial effort, nevertheless tended as time went on to dull the spirit of innovation. The puritan virtues, which suited ideally the steady, unspectacular enterprise of the seventeenth and eighteenth centuries, were not so well adapted to the daring and imagination required by the fast pace of modern business. When to this is added the vested nature of much French Calvinist enterprise (by 1848 most of the Protestant entrepreneurial dynasties were already firmly established and more concerned with maintaining their position than in taking chances), it is not surprising that the actual pioneers of the French industrial revolution were for the most part non-Protestant. At the same time, it should be noted that these same qualities of sane, steady, and concentrated effort were perhaps those best adapted to the economic structure of the country; the Protestant businessman was in one sense simply a bigger and better edition of the average

---

[27] Cf. *Les grandes familles de Lille, Armentières et environs* (Lille: La Croix du Nord, 1937) and *Les grandes familles de Roubaix, Tourcoing et environs* (Lille: La Croix du Nord, 1936–37).

enterpriser already described. Many of the radicals have come and gone. The *haute société Protestante* is as powerful as ever.

IV

It is obviously impossible in a short paper to cover every factor directly or indirectly conditioning French entrepreneurship. For this reason I have not specifically discussed such less fundamental considerations as the political, fiscal, or legal environments. Nor have I attempted to weigh the importance of the business mind as one of the major forces shaping France's over-all economic development Even if it is true that the average French enterpriser has lacked drive, initiative, and imagination—and the evidence indicates that he has—the question still remains of to what extent this failing is attributable to the entrepreneur qua se and to what extent it reflects severe, external handicaps with which he has been unable to cope. Which is the greater factor in the stagnation of a given French steel firm: the timidity of the directors or the cost of coal? It is a nice point, and one that can only too rarely be decided with any precision.

This much may be said: Questions of ultimate causality aside, ideas once formed are as powerful as the strongest material forces, the two types of phenomena continuously interact; and the influence of French entrepreneurial psychology on her general economic structure has been and is extremely important. It is so important that many observers of the present day, from the impatiently chauvinistic American tourist to the leading figures of French commerce and industry, are inclined to give it first priority on the list of France's economic problems. As Lucien Febvre put it: "We shall buy machines, fine machines, when we have acquired from top to bottom a mechanical mentality. We shall organize production effectively when we have freed ourselves of a certain Louis-Philippic petty-bourgeois psychology. Think first. Act afterwards. Then, yes, France, regenerated, will be able to resume a role of leadership in the world. Then, yes, the mortgage will be lifted, the heavy mortgage placed on our country by its cult of old ideas, its serene but stubborn museum-piece traditionalism." [28]

Harvard University   DAVID S. LANDES

---

[28] L. Febvre, in Introduction to C. Morazé, *La France bourgeoise, XVIII*-*XX* siècles* (Paris: A. Colin, 1946), p. ix.

[2]

Managers, Families, and Financiers

Alfred D. Chandler, Jr.
Harvard University

One of the most significant economic phenomena of modern times has been the transformation of business enterprises from small, personally managed partnerships to giant corporations administered through extensive hierarchies of lower, middle, and top managers. This bureaucratization of business came later than that in the military and in government; but when it came, it came much more quickly. As late as the mid-nineteenth century no business enterprise was administered through a managerial hierarchy comparable to that depicted in Figure 1. Within a century such managerial enterprises had come to dominate the major sectors of all industrial, urban, technologically advanced economies.

The sudden appearance and rapid growth of the new bureaucracies reflected fundamental changes in the technology of production and distribution and in the size, nature, and location of markets. Because these new hierarchies were created to manage new and rapidly changing technologies whose output went to growing and ever-changing markets, the middle and top managers in these hierarchies acquired new specialized, product-specific skills. These skills could only be acquired through continuing experience in managing the new processes of production and distribution. The more complex the technology and the more extensive the market, the more critical were such skills to the profitability and continuing growth of the enterprise. Very few families, even extended kinship groups, were numerous enough or experienced enough to manage personally the new high-volume production for national and international markets. The founding families had to rely on nonfamily managers if they were to retain a profitable share of these markets.

35

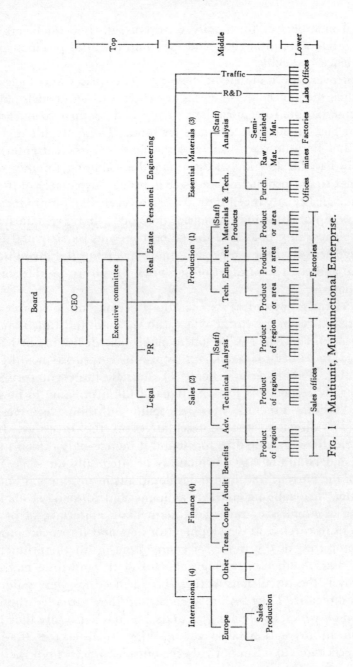

Fig. 1 Multiunit, Multifunctional Enterprise.

And if members of the family were not full-time managers, they were rarely able to acquire and maintain essential product-specific knowledge and skills.

Moreover, the founders of these new enterprises and their families often did not have the necessary capital to build such national and international organizations. They had to turn to outside investors and financial institutions for funds. These outside investors, who thus became part-owners of the new hierarchical enterprises, usually had far less knowledge than the founding families of the complexities of production and distribution, particularly in the new technologically advanced industries. However, like family members who were not full-time managers, they or their representatives sat on the governing boards of the enterprises and participated in top management decisions, especially those involving the investment of capital and the recruitment of personnel for future production and distribution.

As a firm grew and as its operations became more complex, the representatives of the stockholders who were not full-time managers had less and less to say in top management decisions, at least as long as the full-time managers kept the enterprise healthy and profitable. The governing board of the new large enterprise that was legally responsible for the affairs of the firm came to be made up of "inside" directors, who were senior full-time executives, and "outside" directors, the representatives of the investors. In all countries these outside directors found it increasingly difficult to get a full understanding at their monthly or often only quarterly meetings of the current and future developments in production and distribution, of changing markets at home and abroad, of changing sources of supplies of raw and intermediate materials, of progress made in research and development of new and improved products and processes, of the moves of competitors in all these functional areas, and of other operating concerns of the full-time managers. Moreover, the discussions at these board meetings were guided by inside directors. They set the agenda, and they provided the information on which the board was to decide and act. Only they could implement any action taken at a meeting. In time, too, the inside managers came to select not only the outside directors but their own successors. By then the firm had become what I have termed a managerial enterprise.

To understand this transformation of the relationship between ownership and management requires an understanding of why managerial hierarchies appeared at the time that they did and in the industries that they did, and why they grew in the way that they did. For it was only the appearance of such hierarchies that brought a separation between ownership and management. However, the timing, location, and processes of growth of these hierarchies and the resulting relationships between managers and representatives of the owners, that is, between inside and outside directors, did vary with time and place. Such historical variations in "the development of managerial enterprise in different countries" (Morikawa Hidemasa's definition of one major theme of this conference) reveal much about "the causes and inevitability of the development of the managerial enterprise" (his definition of its other basic theme). Let me begin, then, by reviewing in a highly condensed form what I have been writing about the coming of managerial enterprises and then consider variations in the evolution of such enterprises in three leading Western economies—those of Britain, Germany, and the United States.

I. The Growth of Modern Hierarchical Business Enterprise

As is now well known, the first managerial hierarchies appeared during the 1850s and 1860s to coordinate the movements of trains and the flow of goods over the new railroad networks and of messages over the new telegraph system.[1] They then quickly came into use to manage the new mass retailing establishments—the department stores, mail-order houses, and chains or multiple shops—whose existence the railroad and the telegraph made possible. Such administrative hierarchies grew to a still greater size in industrial enterprises that, again on the basis of modern transportation and communication, integrated new processes of mass production and mass distribution within a single business enterprise.

One way to review the emergence of managerial enterprises is, then, to focus on the evolution of the largest and most complex of managerial hierarchies, those of integrated industrial enterprises. These integrated enterprises had much in common. They appeared at almost exactly the same moment in history in the United States and Europe; they clustered in much the same types of industries; and finally, they grew in much the same manner. In nearly all cases they became large first by integrating forward, that is, investing in marketing and distribution facilities and personnel; next by moving backward into purchasing and often into the control of raw and semifinished materials; finally, though much less often, by investing in research and development. In this way they created the multifunctional organization that is depicted in Figure 1. They soon became multinational by investing abroad, first in marketing and then in production. Finally, they continued to expand their activities by investing in product lines related to their existing businesses, thus creating the organization depicted in Figure 2.

Tables 1–5 show where—that is, in what industries—the large and increasingly managerial enterprise appeared. Table 1 indicates the location by country and by industry of all industrial corporations in the world that in 1973 employed more than 20,000 workers. (The industries are those defined as two-digit industrial groups by the U.S. Census Standard Industrial Classification [S.I.C.].) In 1973, 263 (65%) of the 401 companies were clustered in food, chemicals, oil, machinery, and primary metals. Just under 30% were in three-digit categories of other two-digit groups—subcategories that had the same industrial characteristics as those in which the 65% clustered, such as cigarettes in tobacco; tires in rubber; newsprint in paper; plate glass in stone, glass, and clay; cans and razor blades in fabricated metals; and mass-produced cameras in instruments. Only 21 companies (5.2%) were in remaining two-digit categories—apparel, lumber, furniture, leather, publishing and printing, instruments, and miscellaneous.

A second point that Table 1 reveals is the predominance of American firms among the world's largest industrial corporations. Of the total of 401 companies employing more than 20,000 people, more than half (212, or 52.6%) were American. The United Kingdom followed with 50 (12.5%), Germany with 29 (7.3%), Japan

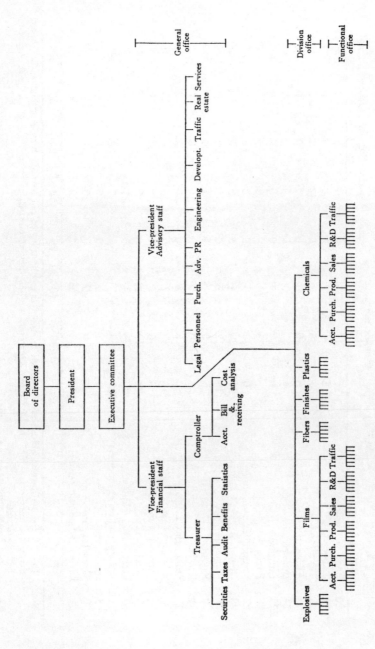

FIG. 2 The Multidivisional Structure.

TABLE 1   The Distribution of Manufacturing Firms with more than 20,000 Employees, by Industry and Nationality, 1973.

S.I.C.		U.S.	Outside the U.S.	U.K.	Germany	Japan	France	Others	Total
20	Food	22	17	13	0	1	1	2	39
21	Tobacco	3	4	3	1	0	0	0	7
22	Textiles	7	6	3	0	2	1	0	13
23	Apparel	6	0	0	0	0	0	0	6
24	Lumber	4	2	0	0	0	0	2	6
25	Furniture	0	0	0	0	0	0	0	0
26	Paper	7	3	3	0	0	0	0	10
27	Printing & publishing	0	0	0	0	0	0	0	0
28	Chemical	24	28	4	5	3	6	10	52
29	Petroleum	14	12	2	0	0	2	8	26
30	Rubber	5	5	1	1	1	1	1	10
31	Leather	2	0	0	0	0	0	0	2
32	Stone, clay & glass	7	8	3	0	0	3	2	15
33	Primary metal	13	35	2	9	5	4	15	48
34	Fabricated metal	8	6	5	1	0	0	0	14
35	Machinery	22	12	2	3	2	0	5	34
36	Electrical machinery	20	25	4	5	7	2	7	45
37	Transportation equipment	22	23	3	3	7	4	6	45
38	Instruments	4	1	0	0	0	0	0	5
39	Miscellaneous	2	0	0	0	0	0	0	2
	Diversified/conglomerate	19	3	2	1	0	0	0	22
	Total	211	190	50	29	28	24	59	401

Note: In 1970 the 100 largest industrials accounted for more than one-third of net manufacturing output in the United States and more than 45% in the United Kingdom. In 1930 they accounted for about 25% of total net output in both countries.

Source: *Fortune*, May 1974 and August 1974.

with 28, and France with 24. Only in chemicals, metals, and electrical machinery were there as many as four or five more firms outside the United States than there were within it.

Table 2 shows that throughout the twentieth century large industrial corporations clustered in the United States in the same industries in which they were concentrated in 1973. The pattern depicted in Tables 3, 4, and 5 is much the same for Britain, Germany, and also Japan. Other data document what is indicated here, that the American firms were larger, as well as more numerous, than those in other countries. For example, in 1948 only 50 to 55 of the British firms had assets comparable to those of the top 200 in the United States. In 1930 the number was about the same. For Germany and

TABLE 2   The Distribution of the 200 Largest Manufacturing Firms in the United States, by Industry.

	S.I.C.	1917	1930	1948	1973
20	Food	30	32	26	22
21	Tobacco	6	5	5	3
22	Textiles	5	3	6	3
23	Apparel	3	0	0	0
24	Lumber	3	4	1	4
25	Furniture	0	1	1	0
26	Paper	5	7	6	9
27	Printing & publishing	2	3	2	1
28	Chemical	20	18	24	27
29	Petroleum	22	26	24	22
30	Rubber	5	5	5	5
31	Leather	4	2	2	0
32	Stone, clay & glass	5	9	5	7
33	Primary metal	29	25	24	19
34	Fabricated metal	8	10	7	5
35	Machinery	20	22	24	17
36	Electrical machinery	5	5	8	13
37	Transportation equipment	26	21	26	19
38	Instruments	1	2	3	4
39	Miscellaneous	1	1	1	1
	Diversified/conglomerate	0	0	0	19
	Total	200	200	200	200

Note: Industries are ranked by assets.

TABLE 3   The Distribution of the 200 Largest Manufacturing Firms in the
United Kingdom, by Industry.

	S.I.C.	1919	1930	1948	1973
20	Food	63	64	52	33
21	Tobacco	3	4	8	4
22	Textiles	26	24	18	10
23	Apparel	1	3	3	0
24	Lumber	0	0	0	2
25	Furniture	0	0	0	0
26	Paper	4	5	6	7
27	Printing & publishing	5	10	7	7
28	Chemical	11	9	15	21
29	Petroleum	3	3	3	8
30	Rubber	3	3	2	6
31	Leather	0	0	0	3
32	Stone, clay & glass	2	6	5	16
33	Primary metal	35	18	28	14
34	Fabricated metal	2	7	8	7
35	Machinery	8	7	7	26
36	Electrical machinery	11	18	13	14
37	Transportation equipment	20	14	22	16
38	Instruments	0	1	4	3
39	Miscellaneous	3	4	3	1
	Diversified/conglomerate	0	0	0	2
	Total	200	200	204	200

Note: Industries are ranked by sales for 1973 and by market value of quoted capital
for the other years.

Japan it was smaller. Well before World War II the United States
had many more and much larger managerial hierarchies than did
other nations—underlining the fact that managerial capitalism first
emerged in that nation.

These tables also suggest (though only barely) basic differences
within the broad pattern of evolution. For example, in the United
States large enterprises were to be found throughout the twentieth
century in the production of both consumer and industrial goods.
Britain had proportionately more large firms in consumer goods
than the United States, while the largest industrials in Germany and
Japan concentrated much more on producer's goods. Even as late
as 1973 (as Table 1 shows) 13 of the United Kingdom's 50 firms

TABLE 4   The Distribution of the 200 Largest Manufacturing Firms in Germany, by Industry.

	S.I.C.	1913	1928	1953	1973
20	Food	23	28	23	24
21	Tobacco	1	0	0	6
22	Textiles	13	15	19	4
23	Apparel	0	0	0	0
24	Lumber	1	1	2	0
25	Furniture	0	0	0	0
26	Paper	1	2	3	2
27	Printing & publishing	0	1	0	6
28	Chemical	26	27	32	30
29	Petroleum	5	5	3	8
30	Rubber	1	1	3	3
31	Leather	2	3	2	1
32	Stone, clay & glass	10	9	9	15
33	Primary metal	49	47	45	19
34	Fabricated metal	8	7	8	14
35	Machinery	21	19	19	29
36	Electrical machinery	18	16	13	21
37	Transportation equipment	19	16	14	14
38	Instruments	1	2	4	2
39	Miscellaneous	1	1	1	1
	Diversified/conglomerate	0	0	0	1
	Total	200	200	200	200

Note: Industries are ranked by sales for 1973 and by assets for the other years.

employing more than 20,000 people were in the production and distribution of food and tobacco products, whereas France and Japan had only one each and Germany none. Before World War II Germany had many more firms in chemicals and heavy machinery than did Britain, while Japan, the late industrializer, still had a greater number of textile firms in its top 200 than did the other nations. As Japan's economy grew, the number of chemical and machinery enterprises on that list increased substantially.

Why did these large integrated hierarchial enterprises appear in some industries but rarely in others? And why did they appear at almost the same historical moment in the United States and Europe? Why did these industrial enterprises in advanced economics grow in the same manner, first integrating forward into volume

TABLE 5   The Distribution of the 200 Largest Manufacturing Firms in Japan by Industry.

	S.I.C.	1918	1930	1954	1973
20	Food	31	30	26	18
21	Tobacco	1	1	0	0
22	Textiles	54	62	23	11
23	Apparel	2	2	1	0
24	Lumber	3	1	0	1
25	Furniture	0	0	0	0
26	Paper	12	6	12	10
27	Printing	1	1	0	2
28	Chemical	23	22	38	34
29	Petroleum	6	5	11	13
30	Rubber	0	1	1	5
31	Leather	4	1	0	0
32	Stone, clay & glass	16	14	8	14
33	Primary metal	21	22	28	27
34	Fabricated metal	4	3	6	5
35	Machinery	4	4	10	16
36	Electrical machinery	7	12	15	18
37	Transportation equipment	9	11	18	20
38	Instruments	1	1	3	5
39	Miscellaneous	1	1	0	1
	Diversified/conglomerate	0	0	0	0
	Total	200	200	200	200

Note: Industries are ranked by assets.

distribution, then taking on other functions, then becoming multi-national and finally multiproduct?

Because these enterprises initially grew larger by integrating mass production with volume distribution, answers to these critical questions require a careful look at both these processes. Mass production is an attribute of specific technologies. In some industries the primary way to increase output was adding more workers and machines. In others it was improving and rearranging the inputs; improving the machinery, furnaces, stills, and other equipment; re-orienting the process of production within the plant; placing the several intermediate processes of production required for a finished product within a single works; or increasing the application of energy (particularly fossil fuel energy). The first set of industries remained labor intensive; the second set became capital intensive. In this second set of industries the technology of production permitted much larger economies of scale than were possible in the first. That is, it permitted much greater reduction in cost per unit of output as volume increased. So in these capital-intensive industries with large-batch or continuous-process technologies, large works operating at minimum efficient scale (the scale of operation that brought the lowest unit costs) had a much greater cost advantage over small works than was true with labor-intensive technologies. Conversely, cost per unit rose much more rapidly when production fell below minimum efficient scale (say, 80% to 90% of rated capacity) than was true in labor-intensive industries.

What is of basic importance for an understanding of the coming of the modern managerial industrial enterprise is that the cost advantage of a large plant cannot be fully realized unless a constant flow of materials through the plant or factory is maintained to assure effective capacity utilization. The decisive figure in determining costs and profits is, then, not rated capacity but throughput —that is, the amount of output processed during a single day or other unit of time. The throughput needed to maintain minimum efficient scale requires careful coordination not only of flow through the processes of production but also of the flow of inputs from the suppliers and the flow of outputs to the distributors and final consumers. Such coordination cannot happen automatically. It demands the constant attention of a managerial team or hierarchy. Thus scale is only a technological characteristic. The economies of scale measured by throughput are organizational. They depend on knowledge, skills, and teamwork—on the human organization essential to exploit the potential of technological processes.

In the S.I.C. classifications in Tables 1–5 where the large firms clustered, the economies of scale as measured by throughput provided substantial cost advantages—advantages that could only be exploited if the founders of an enterprise recruited an effective managerial team. On the other hand, in those classifications where few large firms appeared, that is, in the older, technologically simple, labor-intensive industries, such as apparel, textiles, leather, lumber, and publishing and printing, neither technological nor organizational innovation substantially increased minimum efficient scale. In these industries large plants did not offer significant cost advantages over small ones. In these industries the opportunities for cost reduction through material coordination of high volume throughput by managerial teams remained limited.

The differentials in potential scale economies of different production technologies not only indicate why the large hierarchical firms appeared in some industries and not in others, that is, why they appeared *where* they did. They also explain why these firms appeared *when* they did, that is, why they appeared so suddenly in the last decades of the nineteenth century. Only with the completion of the modern transportation and communication networks—those of the railroad, telegraph, steamship, and cable—could materials flow into a factory or processing plant and the finished goods move out at a rate of speed and volume required to achieve substantial economies of throughput. Transportation that depended on the power of animals, wind, and currents was too slow, too irregular, and too uncertain to maintain a level of throughput necessary to achieve modern economies of scale.

However, such scale and throughput economies do not in themselves explain why the new technologies made possible by the new transportation and communication systems caused the new mass producers to grow in the way they did, that is, why they became large and managerial by integrating forward into mass distribution. Coordination between producers and distributors might have been achieved through contractual agreement with intermediaries—both buyers and sellers. Such an explanation requires a more precise understanding of the process of volume distribution, particularly of why the wholesaler, retailer, and other commercial intermediaries lost their cost advantage vis-à-vis the volume producer.

The intermediaries' cost advantage lay in exploiting both the economies of scale and what has been termed "the economies of scope." Because they handled the products of many manufacturers, they achieved a greater volume and lower unit cost than any one manufacturer in the marketing and distribution of a *single* line of products. Moreover, they increased this advantage by the broader scope of their operation, that is, by handling a number of *related* product lines through a single set of facilities. This was true of the new volume wholesalers in apparel, dry goods, groceries, hardware, and the like and even more true of the new mass retailers—the department store, the mail order house, and the chain or multiple shop enterprise.

The commercial intermediaries lost their cost advantage when manufacturers' output reached a comparable scale. As one economist has pointed out, "The intermediary will have a cost advantage over [his] customers and suppliers only as long as the volume of transactions in which he engages comes closer to that [minimum efficient] scale than do the transactions volumes of his customers or suppliers."[2] This rarely happened in retailing, except in heavily concentrated urban markets, but it often occurred in wholesaling. In addition, the advantage of scope was sharply reduced when marketing and distribution required specialized, costly facilities and skills that could not be used to handle other product lines. By investing in such product-specific personnel and facilities, the intermediary not only lost the advantage of scope but also became dependent on what was usually a small number of producers to provide those supplies.

All these new volume-producing enterprises created their own sales organizations to advertise and market their products nationally and often internationally. From the start they preferred to rely on a sales force of their own to advertise and market their goods rather than to depend on the salesmen of wholesalers and other intermediaries, who sold the products of many manufacturers, including those of their competitors. Of more importance, mass distribution of these products—many of them quite new—often required extensive investment in specialized, product-specific facilities and personnel. Because the existing wholesalers and mass retailers made their profits from handling related products of many manufacturers, they had little incentive to make large investments in facilities and personnel that could only be useful for a handful of specialized products processed by a handful of producers on which they would become dependent for supplies essential to make that investment pay.

For these reasons, then, the large industrial firm that integrated mass production and mass distribution appeared in industries with two characteristics. The first and most essential was a technology of production in which the realization of potential scale economies and the maintenance of quality control demanded close and constant coordination and supervision of materials flows by trained managerial teams. The second was volume marketing and distribution of products, which required investment in specialized, product-specific human and physical capital.

Where this was *not* the case, that is, in industries where technology did *not* have a potentially high minimum efficient scale, where coordination was *not* technically complex, and where mass distribution did *not* require specialized skills and facilities, there was little incentive for the manufacturer to integrate forward into distribution. In such industries as publishing and printing, lumber, furniture, leather, apparel and textiles, and specialized instruments and machines, the large integrated firm had few competitive advantages. In these industries the small, single-function firm continued to prosper and to compete vigorously.

But where this was the case, that is, in those industries that had the two critical characteristics, the most important entrepreneurial act of the founders of an enterprise was the creation of an administrative organization. That is, it was first the recruiting of a team to supervise the process of production, then the building of a national and very often international sales network, and finally the setting up of a corporate office of middle and top managers to integrate and coordinate the two. Only then did the enterprise become multinational. Investment in production abroad followed, almost never preceded, the building of an overseas marketing network. So, too, in the technologically advanced industries, investment in research and development followed the creation of a marketing network. In such a firm this linkage between trained sales engineers, production engineers, product designers, and the research laboratory became a major impetus to continuing innovation in the industries in which it operated. The result of such growth was an enterprise whose organization is depicted in Figure 1. The continuing growth of the firm rested on the ability of its managers to transfer resources in marketing, research and development, and production (usually those that were not fully utilized) into new and more profitable related product lines, a move that carried the organization shown in Figure 1 to that illustrated in Figure 2. If the first step—that of integrating production and distribution—was not taken, the rest did not follow. The firm remained a small, personally managed producing enterprise buying its materials and selling its products through intermediaries.

II. National Comparisons

This review of the coming of the large industrial enterprise in the West emphasizes that personal and family management had little difficulty maintaining itself in labor-intensive, fragmented industries, but that in the capital-intensive, concentrated industries the recruitment of managerial hierarchies was essential for an enterprise to enter and then to maintain and expand market share. The review also suggests that differences in the processes of production and distribution demand different product-specific facilities and skills. Enterprises in industries using less complex processes of production and needing less extensive investment in distribution required smaller hierarchies than did those in industries using complex technologies of production and needing highly product-specific distribution networks. By the same token, the capital requirements were smaller in the former than in the latter industries. Therefore, this explanatory theory suggests that members of the founder's family were able to have a continuing say in top-management decision making, as either inside or outside directors, in less technological, less capital-using industries, and that representatives of banks, other financial institutions, and large investors had more influence as outside directors in the more complex and more capital-using industries.

The historical evolution of the relationship between managers and owners in Britain, Germany, and the United States appears to support these hypotheses. In Britain, where the large firms concentrated more in light consumer industries, requiring relatively small hierarchies and relatively little capital, particularly branded, packaged products, the family continued to play a larger role for a longer period of time than in the other two countries. In Germany, where the large firms clustered in the more capital-using metals, industrial machinery and chemical industries, hierarchies were much larger and banks played a more important role in the funding of the new enterprises. Therefore their representatives shared top-management decisions with members of the founding family and senior full-time salaried managers. In the United States the large firms clustered in those industries mass-producing branded, packaged products, light machinery, metals, and chemicals—industries that had the greatest potential for scale economies—for the world's largest and fastest-growing market. Their founders had to recruit even larger hierarchies than did their British and German counterparts. At the same time the cost advantages of scale provided funds for continued growth, so that American entrepreneurs had far less need of external financial aid than did those in Germany. As a result the senior full-time managers came, as inside directors, to dominate top-level decision making more quickly than they did in either Britain or Germany.

III. Britain: The Persistence of the Family Enterprise

The family firm persisted in Britain longer than elsewhere primarily because British entrepreneurs were reluctant to make a substantial investment in new and other untried processes of production; to invest heavily in marketing, distribution, and research personnel and facilities; and above all, to turn the administration of at least part of the enterprise over to nonfamily, salaried managers. Thus, although Britain was the world's first industrial nation, by the second decade of the twentieth century its largest industrial firms were producers of branded, packaged consumer products. During the interwar years five of the seven largest firms in terms of the market value of their securities were Imperial Tobacco, Distillers' Corporation (Scotch whisky), Lever Brothers (soap), Guinness (ale), and Anglo-Iranian Oil (kerosene and gasoline). As was pointed out earlier, in 1973 Britain had 13 food companies employing more than 20,000 employees, while Germany and Japan had only one each.

As late as 1948 all but a small number of the largest firms were operated through two types of organizational structures that had all but disappeared among the top 200 American companies. Either they were personally, usually family, managed enterprises whose stockholders made the coordinating, monitoring, and allocating decisions, or they were federations of such family firms legally unified under the control of a holding company with almost no central administrative staff or organization. The large British firms had integrated high-volume production with high-volume distribution, but it was usually the founder, and then members of his family with one or two close associates, who administered the production, sales, and operating departments. These firms rarely competed vigorously with one another, relying instead on contractual agreements to determine price and production schedules and to allocate markets. However, because British common law forbade combinations in restraint of trade, such agreements could not be legally enforced in courts of law. Therefore competitors formed a holding company, with the constituent companies exchanging shares of their stock for that of the new holding company. Its central office was then able to legally enforce the decisions as to price and production determined by the heads of the constituent companies.

In these federations each firm continued to operate much as it had before the merger.[3] It continued to handle its own production and its own distribution. This was true of Imperial Tobacco, Lever Brothers, and Distillers and in very large mergers in the textile industries, such as the Calico Printers' Association, the Bleachers' Association, and British Cotton and Wool Dyers. It was also true of much smaller mergers (in terms of the number of firms involved) between industry leaders, such as British Cocoa and Chocolate (a merger of Cadbury and Fry), Associated Biscuit Manufacturers (a merger of Peak Frean and Huntley & Palmer), and Cross & Blackwell (a merger of three jam and confectionery companies), and comparable mergers in the brewing industry. In such mergers family firms were able to continue to compete with one another in a gentlemanly manner for two or three generations. Of these federations only Lever Brothers began to create a corporate office with an extensive managerial staff before World War II.

There were exceptions. In the few industries where British entrepreneurs did make the investment in production and distribution and did recruit the essential managerial hierarchies, they were able to compete at home and abroad in the new global oligopolies. They did so in oil, rubber, plate and flat glass, rayon, explosives, and synthetic alkalies. In each industry, the first firm to make the investment and recruit the managers quickly dominated the industry at home and became the British representative in the global oligopoly abroad. In glass, rayon, and synthetic alkalies (Pilkington, Courtaulds, and Brunner, Mond) the members of the founding family continued to be recruited into the firm. As full-time managers these family members continued to dominate the board. In rubber (Dunlop) the family was removed after a financial crisis and the firm was reorganized in 1921–22. The restructured firm became one of the earliest of British managerial enterprises, along with Anglo-Iranian Oil and Nobel Explosives. In the oil company (later British Petroleum) there never was a founding family. Two years after its first refinery went into operation in 1912, the British government took 51% of the company's voting shares. The founders of Nobel Explosives, the inventor Alfred Nobel and large investors, such as Charles Tennant, were deeply involved in other business activities and so relied from the start on salaried managers to administer their enterprise.

In other basic new industries, however, British entrepreneurs failed to make the essential investment in production, sales, and purchasing and failed to recruit the necessary managerial hierarchies. In these industries they lost not only the global market but the British home market as well. Such entrepreneurial failure was particularly devastating in the production and distribution of light mass-produced machinery, more specialized heavy machinery, and industrial chemicals. American firms quickly overpowered British competitors in the production and distribution of light mass-produced machines, including sewing, office, and agricultural machinery; household appliances; and until the 1920s automobiles. The Germans and Americans quickly took over the electrical machinery industry, the producers of light and of the energy so critical to increased productivity in manufacturing and increased efficiency in urban transportation. In 1912, for example, two-thirds of the electrical manufacturing output within Britain was produced by three companies, the subsidiaries of the American General Electric and Westinghouse and of the German Siemens.[4] The dye story is even more dramatic.[5] An Englishman, William H. Perkin, invented the first synthetic dyes. Dyes were made of coal tar, of which Britain had an inexhaustible supply. The huge British textile industry was the largest market in the world for dyes. And in 1870 the chemists who would head the industrial laboratories of the great German dye firms were all working in Britain. Yet within a very brief period German enterprises completely dominated the new industry. By 1913, of the 160,000 tons of dyes produced the Germans made 140,000 tons and their Swiss neighbors another 10,000, while British producers made only 4,000, most of which were of low quality.

The British entrepreneurs were not held back in these industries because of the lack of funds. London was the largest and most sophisticated money market in the world. Americans and Germans had no difficulty raising money in Britain for British and European plants and distribution facilities, nor did the successful British companies like Anglo-Iranian Oil and Dunlop. Nor was labor a handicap, since nearly all the workers in the American and German factories in Britain were British. The British failure resulted from the inability or unwillingness of British entrepreneurs to make the necessary investment and to recruit the management organization necessary to exploit the cost advantage of large-scale production in these industries. The price paid for the persistence of the family enterprise was that Britain's entrepreneurs and the British economy as a whole failed to harvest many of the fruits of the second industrial revolution, which was made possible by the advent of modern transportation and communication.

IV. Germany: The Importance of the Banks

Before World War II German entrepreneurs were never as effective as their British and American counterparts in branded, packaged products or as effective as the Americans in mass-produced light machinery. One reason may have been that in both broad sets of industries foreign firms were the first in Germany to build plants with scale economies and to set up national sales forces. Thus, the German subsidiaries of Lever, Nestlé, Quaker Oats, and Corn

Products came to dominate the market in their industries, as did the subsidiaries of Singer Sewing Machine, International Harvester, National Cash Register, American Radiator, Ford, and Otis Elevator in theirs. Nevertheless, the success of the Stollwerck family in creating a much larger cocoa and chocolate multinational empire than any British or American competitors suggests that where the German entrepreneurs were the first movers in branded, packaged products, they could perform effectively.

German entrepreneurs, like British ones, did create at least one major company to represent their nation in the global oligopolies in oil (European Petroleum Union, founded in 1905 under the aegis of the Deutsche Bank), in rubber (Continental), in rayon (Vereinigte Glanzastoff Fabriken), and in explosives and synthetic alkalies (members of the Nobel and Solvay alliances).[6] It was, however, in metals, both ferrous and nonferrous, and even more in complex industrial machinery and chemicals that the Germans excelled. In the last two, the managerial hierarchies were needed to exploit the economies of scope even more than those of scale. (The economies of scope in manufacturing can be defined as those resulting from making several end products from the same set of materials and intermediate processes.) Some management teams in production were even greater in size than those in American firms. In the 1880s and 1890s these enterprises also built extended networks of branch offices throughout the world to market products, most of which were technologically new, to demonstrate their use, to install them when necessary, to provide continuing after-sales service, and to give customers the financial credit they often needed to make such purchases. Once abroad, these enterprises built and acquired branch factories. Finally, they invested far more heavily than any British and most American enterprises in research and development.

The founders of these new industrial giants relied much more heavily on banks to fund their operations than did their counterparts in either Britain or the United States. Their production processes and product development required much more initial capital than did the production of branded, packaged products or mass-produced light machinery. Moreover, in Germany in the 1870s and 1880s there were no capital markets of the size and sophistication of those of London and New York. As a result, the entrepreneurs turned to the German all-purpose "great" banks that had come into being to finance the railroad networks of Germany and eastern Europe. These banks not only marketed the securities of the new corporations but, as was not true of British or American financial institutions, held their shares on their own account and normally voted the proxies of the investors to whom they sold the securities. They also appear to have had more direct supervision over the internal finances of their clients than British or American banks ever had. At the turn of the century representatives of these banks had joined those of founding families and occasionally wealthy investors on supervisory boards of most large German industrial enterprises. (Germany with its two-tiered board was the only country to make a legal distinction between the inside directors who made up the *Vorstand*, or managing board, and the outside directors who made up the *Aufsichtsrat*, or supervisory board.)

Nevertheless, after the initial investment was made in production and distribution at home and abroad, the companies that prospered —and most of them did—came to rely primarily on retained earnings to finance continued growth. So the bankers' influence waned. By the turn of the century banks and bankers had little to say on the strategic decisions in the chemical industry. By World War I their influence had also lessened in metals and machinery. Leading historians of German industry—Gerald Feldman, Hans Pohl, Wilfred Feldenkirchen, and Norbert Horn—all agree with Jürgen Kocka that Rudolph Helferding's famous "theory of the dominance of banks over industry was basically outdated when it was formulated," that is, in 1910.[7] However, the losses in both world wars meant that the industrialists had to continue to rely on banks for financing far more than they did in other Western countries.

If the influence of banks declined, that of founders and their families continued. But whereas in Britain many families continued to manage their firms personally, in Germany they stood at the head of extensive, well-organized managerial hierarchies. The Siemenses, Thyssens, Krupps, Haniels, Klöckners, and, later, Quandts and Flicks continued to have a major say in the affairs of their concerns. Nevertheless, even before the turn of the century salaried general directors, such as Emil Kirdof and Wilhelm Beukenberg in steel, Paul Reusch in machinery, and Carl Duisberg, Karl Bosch, and Heinrich von Brunk in chemicals, ruled their enterprises even more completely than the Siemenses and Krupps did theirs. As time passed the strength of the managers increased and that of the families lessened. In Feldman's words, "The tension between the continued effort at personal rule by the owner and the progress of bureaucratized management was being decided painfully but fatefully in favor of the latter."[8] Yet as late as the 1930s and indeed in the years after World War II, representatives of families, like those of banks, had a far greater influence on the boards of large industrial firms in Germany than they did in the United States.

V. The United States: The Dominance of the Managers

In the United States, where large enterprises came more quickly and in greater numbers and appeared in a wider range of industries, banks played a much less important role in the initial financing than they did in Germany, and families remained less influential in top management than they were in Britain. In other words, managerial enterprises appeared more quickly and in a purer form in America than they did in Europe. These differences reflect not only the much larger and much faster growing domestic market that provided many more opportunities to exploit economies of scale. They can also be traced to the massive turn-of-the-century merger movement in that country. The financing of mergers and, much more important, the financing of the rationalization of production and distribution that followed the mergers for the first time brought representatives of financial institutions on to the boards of American industrials. In many, that same rationalization also lessened family control by bringing a reorganization of management in which nonfamily managers replaced owners of constituent companies in the administration of large sectors of an industry.

In the United States, the initial financing of the large new industrial enterprises (as differentiated from financing of the rationalization after mergers) was personal rather than institutional. The funds came from local investors who had made their money in railroads, banking, and land. Soon, too, the most successful of the new industrialists—the Rockefellers, the Armours, the Bordens, the Dukes of American Tobacco, the Clarks of Singer Sewing Machine, the Havemayers of American Sugar, and a little later the du Ponts —provided capital for new ventures in other industries. They were joined by traction magnates like the Wideners, Whitneys, Elkinses, and Bradys. The continuing high rate of return resulting from the exploitation of the new technologies meant that the leaders had little need to go to the New York or Chicago money markets. Growth was financed by retained earnings.

Investment bankers and brokers first became deeply involved in American industry when they helped finance consolidations during the mergers of the 1890s, which reached a crescendo between 1898 and 1901. First these financiers helped facilitate the funding of the mergers. Because this usually involved little more than exchanging the stock of a new holding company for that of the many small personally managed firms coming into the merger, the cash involved was minimal. However, these bankers and brokers were then committed to raising the funds needed to centralize the administration and then to rationalizing the production and distribution facilities of the new consolidated enterprise so that it might take more effective advantage of the economies of scale and scope. In production the management of the plants of the constituent companies was centralized under a single production department. Some factories were disbanded, others combined, and new ones built to assure continuous operation at close to minimum efficient scale. The different sales forces were consolidated into a single unit with a multitude of regional offices. Purchasing was also centralized, and corporate research laboratories were set up. In this way mergers led to the creation of extensive managerial hierarchies in industries in which up to that time enterprises had been personally managed. At the same time the stock issued by a new consolidated enterprise to finance the resulting rationalization was widely marketed, and the number of stockholders was greatly enlarged.

As I have indicated, such rationalization, recruitment of managers, and an increased scattering of ownership did not occur in

Britain. There a merger remained a federation of family firms whose activities continued to be personally managed in the same way as they had been before the merger. Since there was no rationalization to be financed, much of the stockholding of the enterprise usually remained in the hands of the owners of the constituent companies. In Germany, where cartels were legal and industry-wide agreements could be enforced in courts of law, far fewer industry-wide mergers occurred than in the United States and Britain.

In the United States bankers' influence in top-level decision making that resulted from mergers remained short-lived. Once the managers in the newly created hierarchies had learned their trade and once continued growth was funded through retained earnings, the influence of these outside directors on top-level decisions waned even more quickly than that of bankers on German supervisory boards. Moreover, unlike their German counterparts, American financial institutions rarely held the securities of the companies they helped finance or voted the proxies of the investors who purchased those securities. In the United States proxies were voted by the inside directors, by managers, not bankers. Also, the staffs of American banking and brokerage houses were much smaller than those of the German "great" banks. In Germany the bankers on company boards could rely on these staffs for information about a company and the industry in which it operated. In the United States they had to rely almost entirely on the inside directors for such information. As a result in American firms these banking representatives soon became little more than financial advisers to the inside directors.

In American companies that did not come into being through merger, or in industry-wide mergers that were engineered by one or two enterprises, bankers rarely became directors. And in such companies personal management had all but disappeared by the 1930s. The dismal performance of the Ford Motor Company, one of the rare examples of an entrepreneur and his son operating a large firm with a small, lean management staff in the British manner, suggests the weakness of such control. Ford's share of the market dropped from 55% in 1921 to 16% in 1937, while the share of General Motors, with its massive managerial hierarchy, rose from

11.5% to 45% in the same period. Between 1927 and 1937 Ford's losses were well over $100 million.[9] In the same decade General Motors' profits after taxes were $2 billion.

By the 1920s industrial families still involved in the enterprises they or their forebears had founded were far fewer than they were in Germany or in Britain. By the 1920s there were no Rockefellers in oil, no Carnegies in steel, no Armours in meatpacking, no Dukes in tobacco, no Procters or Gambles in soap, no Otises in elevators, no Babcocks or Wilcoxes in industrial machinery, no Worthingtons in pumps, no Havemayers in sugar, no Westinghouses in electrical equipment, and no Pullmans in transportation equipment. Where du Ponts, Swifts, McCormicks, Deeres, Wrigleys, and Heinzes still influenced their enterprises, they did so as full-time inside directors sharing the decisions and responsibilities with the other inside directors, who stood at the head of extended managerial hierarchies. By the 1930s very few of their competitors had representatives of the founding families or major investors as inside directors. By then, in probably a majority of the 200 largest industrial enterprises outside directors were selected by the full-time inside directors, who together rarely held as much as 5% of the stock outstanding. By the approach of World War II the separation between ownership and management had become clearly defined in the dominant firms of the leading American industries.

VI. Conclusion: The Inevitability of Managerial Enterprise

One point this paper stresses is that managerial enterprise was not inevitable. Indeed, before the mid-nineteenth century it was unnecessary. In nearly all industries the technical skills required by the processes of production and distribution were simple enough and the capital need was small enough to be met by one or two entrepreneurs, their families, and a small number of investors. (Such industries continued to flourish throughout the twentieth century.) Then in the 1870s and 1880s the completion of the new transportation and communication systems, and the coming of the new source of energy, electricity, created in some, but certainly not all, industries a potential for cost savings through economies of scale and scope. These savings could only be fully exploited by building large plants, by recruiting management teams to coordinate flows through the processes of production, and in most cases by making an extensive investment in marketing and distribution facilities. In such industries those entrepreneurs who failed to recruit the essential management teams and to make investment quickly lost out to those who did, as the British experience so dramatically attests. Where these entrepreneurs did both and where they were able to personally raise initial funding, they and their families managed their enterprises. They continued to do so, however, only if the members of their families were trained in the necessary product-specific functional and administrative skills and remained full-time managers of the enterprises. If the family members did not receive such training and did not make a career of the family business but instead became part-time outside directors, the family influence rapidly waned.

Where the founders required institutional financing or where mergers brought reorganization and rationalization of the plants and facilities of the constituent firms, representatives of financial institutions came on the boards of these industrial combinations. But because they had little knowledge of the firms' product-specific processes of production and distribution, they probably had less influence on top-level decision making than did the outside directors representing family and other large investors.

As long as an enterprise remained solvent and as long as it was able to finance growth largely through retained earnings (as was indeed the general rule in the three economies studied, at least up to World War II), the full-time managers on the governing board dominated top-level decision making. They did so because they knew the business better than any outsider. They had developed the critical functional and administrative skills essential if their firm was to continue to compete in national and international markets. Even if a firm encountered financial difficulties that made it necessary for outside directors to remove inside ones, their replacements needed to have comparable training and experience if the enterprise was to maintain market share on which profits were based. Such an enterprise could not be effectively managed by untrained, inexperienced part-time outside directors. In industries where complex product-specific technical and managerial skills were essential to maintain market share in national and international markets, managerial enterprise became inevitable.

NOTES

1. The following paragraphs closely follow what I have written in "The Emergence of Managerial Capitalism," *Business History Review*, Vol. 59, Winter 1984. Because they present my views on the beginning of modern, multiunit industrial enterprise as concisely as I can define them, some paragraphs are taken verbatim from that article.
2. Scott J. Moss, *An Economic Theory of Business Strategy*, Oxford, 1981, pp. 110–11.
3. These brief statements on British firms are based on archival materials, journal articles, and company histories, including works by such distinguished writers as Charles Wilson on Unilever, Theodore Barker on Pilkington, Donald Coleman on Courtaulds, Ronald Ferrier on British Petroleum, and William Reader on Nobel Explosives and Brunner, Mond. The story will be told in detail in my forthcoming *Global Enterprise*.
4. I. C. R. Byatt, *The British Electrical Industry, 1875–1914: The Economic Returns of a New Technology*, Oxford, 1979, p. 150.
5. John J. Beer, *The Emergence of the German Dye Industry*, Urbana, Ill., 1959, chaps. 5–6, 8–9.
6. As in the case of the statements on the British firms, these are based on published histories, journal articles, and archival information and will be presented in detail in my forthcoming study.
7. Jürgen Kocka, "Entrepreneurs and Managers in German Industrialization," in Peter Mathias and M. M. Postan, eds., *The Cambridge Economic History of Europe*, Vol. VII, Cambridge, 1978, p. 570; Gerald D. Feldman, *Iron and Steel in the German Inflation, 1916–1923*, Princeton, N.J., 1977, pp. 19–20; Norbert Horn, "Company Law and the Organization of Large Enterprises 1860–1920—Germany, Great Britain, France and U.S. in Comparative Perspective," in Norbert Horn and Jürgen Kocka, eds., *Law and the Formation of the Big Enterprise in the 19th and 20th Centuries*, Göttingen, 1979, pp. 183–84; Hans Pohl, "On the History of Organization and Management in Large Enterprises Since the Nineteenth Century," *German Yearbook on Business History 1982*, Berlin, 1982, p. 111; Wilfred Felden-

kirchen, "The Banks and the Steel Industry in the Ruhr," *German Yearbook on Business History 1981*, Berlin, 1981, pp. 34–51.

8. Feldman, *op. cit.*, p. 25.
9. Alfred D. Chandler, Jr., *Giant Enterprise: Ford, General Motors and the Automobile Industry*, New York, 1963, pp. 3–7.

[3]

SOCIAL ATTITUDES, ENTREPRENEURSHIP, AND ECONOMIC DEVELOPMENT

The following paper was presented to the Round Table on Economic Progress, held by the International Economic Association in Santa Margherita Ligure in the late summer of 1953. Its subject had been assigned to me by Professor Leon Dupriez of Louvain University who was in charge of program arrangements. As is frequently the case with assigned topics carrying a firm deadline, all that could be done was to provide some starting point for discussion. As I reread my paper, I feel that the desire to provoke an exchange of opinions on the subject probably has led - or misled - me in spots into overstating whatever case I may have. Since the Explorations are essentially designed to serve as a forum for discussion, I have not considered it necessary to change the character of the paper. Except for some abridgments and minor alterations, it remains essentially in the form in which it was originally submitted. But it may be in order to assure the reader that a certain definiteness in the tone of the paper has not been intended to obscure its preliminary and tentative nature. I should like to thank Professor Dupriez for his permission to reproduce the paper here well in advance of its publication by the Association in the volume containing the papers and the proceedings of the Conference.

"Social attitudes" is not a very precise term. It must be treated with restraint. Otherwise it will quickly expand to embrace the whole ambit of governmental economic policies, - a topic very properly assigned to a special session of this Conference. We shall deal here essentially with the significance for a country's economic development of popular evaluations of entrepreneurs and entrepreneurial activities; that is to say, of the general climate of opinion within which entrepreneurial action takes place. Even when so restricted, the problem remains vast, and a great deal of patient mono-graphic research is necessary before any firm conclusions can be reached. The following impressionistic remarks, therefore, purport to do no more than to present briefly some general lines of thought that have been pursued so far, to issue some warnings against too ready an acceptance of certain abstract models, and to illustrate these warnings by reference to some segments of European economic history of the 19th century. With regard to the latter, the emphasis is on earlier stages of industrialization rather than on conditions in mature economies. Except for a brief allusion, the question as to what extent European historical experience can be used for elucidating the current problems of underdeveloped countries must likewise remain outside the scope of this paper.

Research on the problem under discussion is still in its infancy. However, the Harvard Research Center in Entrepreneurial History under the able leadership of Professor Arthur Cole has devoted, during the past five years, much time and thought to an "entrepreneurial approach to economic history," and it has paid a good deal of attention to the question of social attitudes towards entrepreneurship. Entrepreneurial research in the United States has received its intellectual stimulus primarily from two sources. It has been, of course, greatly influenced by Schumpeter's theory of economic development, which assigns to the innovating entrepreneur a focal role in the process of economic change. In fact, Professor Schumpeter remained in intimate association with the Research Center at Harvard until his death in 1950, and the wealth of Schumpeterian hypotheses - and intuitions - quite naturally predetermined many of the paths of research to be followed. At a very early stage, however, as the problem of the entrepreneurial position within the community impressed itself upon those working in the field, the need was felt for a more rigorous and comprehensive sociological framework. Such a framework has been developed over a wide range of recent writings in the field of social psychology, anthropology, and sociology and has found perhaps its most powerful systematic expression in the theoretical structure which over the past two decades has been erected by Professor Talcott Parsons and the scholars assembled around him.

Even if the writer felt qualified to do so, there still would be neither need nor possibility to enter within the scope of these pages into a discussion of the Parsonian System. But a few words on some specific concepts to the extent that they have affected entrepreneurial research - and only to that extent - may be in order.(1) The interest in this respect centers upon the so-called theory of roles. The individual members of the community are seen as performing specific social roles, and it is the role which "for most purposes [is] the conceptual unit of the social system."(2) "The primary ingredient of the role is role expectation(3) which denotes what role the individuals expect each other to perform. Compliance with role expectation is enforced through positive and negative sanctions (rewards and retributions). The role expectancies and sanction patterns are institutionalized into generalized value systems of the community. In a well integrated society these values are "internalized in personality systems," i.e., they are accepted and adopted by the individuals. As a result, the value system becomes the crucial determinant of action.(4)

One cannot suppress some wonderment as to why these particular concepts should have proven attractive to those interested in explaining the process of economic change. It does seem that these concepts essentially pertain to a static system. Of course, the system is still in evolution. Professor Parsons' writings and those of his collaborators are shot through with multifarious warnings. It is said explicitly that the work has not proceeded far beyond the "categorical" stage on the road to the formulation of the general "laws" of the system.(5) One is warned that the "empirical significance of selective or value standards as determinants of concrete action may be considered problematical and should not be prejudged,"(6) that there are dangers in imputing "too much rigidity to behavior" and to over-estimating its "uniformity within a given society."(7) Most importantly, it is emphasized that very often it is in the failure to maintain social integration at the achieved level that lie "many of the most important seeds of social change."(8) The impression is that the static character of the system is well recognized. Still it is claimed that "in principle, propositions about the factors making for maintenance of the system are at the same time propositions about those making for change."(9) Thus social dynamics is said to be included within the framework; and it is essentially in the conflicts between value systems, that is, in an analysis of what Florence Kluckhohn called dominant, variant, and deviant (i.e., prescribed, permissive, and proscribed) values(10) that the processes of change will be sought. This, however, is still a promise. For the time being it seems fair to say that it is the social state rather than social change to which main attention is addressed.(11)

Nevertheless, it is both the static and the nascent dynamic elements in the system that have excited the interest of entrepreneurial research. This is clearly in evidence in the pioneering symposium volume Change and Entrepreneur which was published by the Research Center.(12) Thus in this volume Arthur Cole attaches explicit significance to the degree of social approval which the entrepreneur's striving for economic gain will receive in a given economic milieu, and he refers to various social systems from India to France where entrepreneurial activities labor under various degrees of disapproval.(13) In his stimulating contribution Leland Jenks(14) concerns himself in more detail with role factors, that is with prescriptions concerning appropriate behavior of individuals who occupy a set of special positions. And in dealing with the specific behavior of men like the elder Morgan or Cyrus McCormick he stresses that whatever the importance of accidental factors in the make-up of individuals their actions cannot be adequately understood unless they are placed within the context of the cultural patterns of their society.(15) But Jenks moves a step beyond and places particular stress on the dichotomy of personal and social roles and the possibility of discrepancy between them. It is the existence of such discrepancies, he says, that is indicative of the fact that significant social change is in the making.(16) One would expect, therefore, the concept of entrepreneurial deviance to emerge as the primary device for understanding entrepreneurial behavior and the entrepreneur's role as an innovator. But we are quickly led back to the fold. It is again the "social roles" and the sanctioning acts by which the expected behavior is enforced that assume a central position in the explanatory mechanism. And all we are left with is the fact that in the case of entrepreneurs social roles are peculiarly "indistinct" and "flexible" which, we are told, is in tujn the result, among other things, of the fact that the entrepreneurial position "entails the function and opportunity for introducing novelty into the economic structure."(17)

Finally, mention must be made of the essay by Thomas C. Cochran in the same volume.(18) Cochran's essay which is enclosed within the same conceptual framework, is of particular interest from our point of view because of his specific re-definition of deviant behavior. He speaks of sanctions designed to "encourage deviant behavior."(19) Thus, the concept of deviancy is divorced from the discrepancy between social and personal roles, and deviant behavior becomes fully consonant with social role expectations. Obviously, deviance means something else to Cochran than it does to, say, Florence Kluckhohn, who identifies it with socially proscribed behavior.(20) In Cochran's mind deviance is simply associated with innovation, and is seen as an integral part of the dominant value system.

Where does all this lead? Are we witnessing here a new theory of social change in statu nascendi? How can an economic historian use the analytical tools, with which he is being so generously supplied, in his attempts to elucidate empirical processes of economic change, and in particular, to understand entrepreneurial behavior? Surely, only very tentative answers can be given to these questions.

A dynamic theory? It seems that it allows of economic change in a two-fold fashion. On the one hand, a well-integrated society in which economic innovating has become a generally accepted mode of behavior fits the system to a nicety. Since the process of innovation gives rise to what Schumpeter called "creative destruction,"(21) the process of change, one may suspect, will still involve dissident personal values of the victims of economic change, but these may be either neglected or else the community assumed to be integrated to a point where even the loser in the process has so thoroughly "internalized" the social standard of value that

"Mit dem Ceschick in hoher Einigkeit,
Celassen hingestuetzt àuf Grazien und Musen,

> Empfaengt er das Geschoss, das ihn bedraeut,
> Mit freundlich dargebotnem Busen
> Vom sanften Bogen der Notwendigkeit."

Be that as it may, it is this type of "built-in" dynamism that apparently was in Professor Cochran's mind. On the other hand, there is the original, non-denaturalized concept of deviant behavior on the part of the entrepreneur. This concept is intimated, but all too soon abandoned by Professor Jenks in his discussion of discrepancies between personal and social roles.(22)

Both concepts are, of course, meaningful per se. But it may be noted in passing that in Cochran's society the Schumpeterian concept of innovation loses a good deal of its interest. Innovation is regarded by Schumpeter as a "distinct economic function" inter alia because of the environment's resistance to innovators and innovating processes.(23) Once the resistance of the environment is lowered, "personality and will power must count for less."(24) In other words, specific entrepreneurial research offers less opportunity for understanding the processes of social change in such a society. At any rate, Professor Cochran's society has little resemblance to economies which stand at the threshold of industrialization and are heavily burdened with traditional resistances to economic development.

In a sense, deviance which spurns the established value patterns may indeed be regarded as a dynamic force making for economic change. But it is at this point that our theories, both general and entrepreneurial, leave us in the lurch. For while it may make sense in certain historical situations to take a dominant system of social values for granted, it is much less satisfactory to accept the deviant behavior as given. If we deal with an agricultural community based on century-long traditions, we may be willing to accept those traditions as given without caring much about the "whys" and the "where-fores." But if suddenly deviant values make their entry upon the economic scene, the urge for further explanation is irresistible. We must needs ask whence the change in value orientations: what has caused the sudden outburst. There is nothing within the theoretical framework that provides the elements of such an explanation beyond perhaps some implicit and inchoate ideas about the tolerable degree of tension between the deviant and the generally accepted behavior. In general, the concept of deviance is taken up gingerly and dropped abruptly, and the accent shifts back to the dominant value system as the determinant of action and to the social sanctioning of entrepreneurial behavior. Thus, the questions with which we are left focus on the problem of social approval.

How important is social approval for emergence of entrepreneurial activities? In particular, what is its importance at the crucial stages of economic development when a country's economy becomes engaged in a sudden spurt of economic development? Should lack of social approval be regarded as a serious retarding factor? Does it affect in a significant manner the contents of entrepreneurial activities and make for adaptations in entrepreneurial attitudes which can be said to influence speed and character of a country's economic development? These questions cannot be answered, of course, except on the basis of extensive empirical research. In default of such research, the following remarks must be taken as highly tentative impressions from scattered, but perhaps relevant, historical material.

The theoretical formula is persuasively simple: social approval of entrepreneurial activity significantly affects its volume and quality. At times, it even appears as though social approval were regarded as a prerequisite for successful entrepreneurship. But doubts are bound to arise the moment historical material is approached. One might recall the dramatic pages in Augustin Thierry's Tiers État which deal with the fermiers généraux. Hated and despised, their very existence a slap in the face of all the prevailing standards of goodness and decency, perpetually accused and at times subject to monstrous persecutions, they nevertheless progressed and prospered economically and socially, their entrepreneurial vigor remaining unshaken.(25) Toujours maudits et toujours nécessaires, cursed and indispensable, they continued their activity, indulging their greed and maturing their frauds. Why did not social disapproval erase the shame of that office from the face of France? Perhaps because a system of social sanctions is often too weak unless reinforced by the sanctions of the State, and the latter may or may not reflect the dominant value system. Or, perhaps, because the system of social values was not to be taken too seriously; perhaps because behind the articulately expressed but ineffectual value system lay another, an actually operational system. Possibly so, but we must take care. We have set out to examine the determinants of social action. If we begin to deduce social values from the presence of certain action, we have closed a vicious circle and at the same time have foreclosed the road to a reasoned explanation.

Let us take a brief glance at Russian conditions in the second half of the 19th century. After the emancipation of serfs in the early sixties of that century, former serfs and sons of former serfs are known to have engaged on an unprecedented scale in various entrepreneurial activities, including, it might be added, the magnificent venture of constructing and operating the merchant fleet on the Volga River. Again, there is little doubt that their activities were at variance with the dominant system of values, which remained determined by the traditional agrarian pattern. The Good Life which God intended for man to lead implied tilling the land, which belonged to God, and receiving the divine blessing of its fruit. The Good Life certainly did not mean craving for riches, did not mean laying up treasures on earth where moth and rust doth corrupt. In innumerable adages, fairy-tales, and songs the wisdom of the folklore insisted upon the unrighteous origin of wealth. And still, the activities went on unchecked, great fortunes were amassed, and great entrepreneurial innovations were successfully launched.

There is no doubt that throughout most of the 19th century a grave oppro-brium attached to entrepreneurial activities in Russia. The nobility and the gentry (dvoryanstvo) had nothing but contempt for any entrepreneurial activity except its own. And despite some notable exceptions, it failed to make a sig-nificant contribution to modern industrial development. Divorced from the peasantry, the entrepreneurs remained despised by the intelligentsia. The latter's aversion to mercantile pursuits was, if anything, even stronger than that of the peasantry, even though the roots of that aversion doubtless lay in the value system of the peasantry. In a sense, the Populism of the intelligent-sia was a conscious attempt to espouse the standards of values of the "people." Hence came the intelligentsia's aversion to the bourgeoisie, the acquisitive class. Throughout long decades of the 19th century, there was only one among the great figures in Russian intellectual life who did not quite share this negative attitude, - Belinsky, who, at least at one point, refused to believe that a country that had no bourgeoisie could conceivably prosper. And still it was Belinsky who at the very same time used his most fiery vocabulary to decry the merchant, the "base, despicable, vulgar creature who serves Plutus and Plutus alone."(26)

But what of the value system of the entrepreneurial group itself? Were they deviants? They certainly were that as far as their behavior was concerned. But since we are precluded from inferring values from action, we must still ask whether or not they were deviants in the sense that their own standard of values was different from the dominant one. And this appears highly dubious. It took a long time before something like an independent standard of values of the Russian businessman developed. They knew full well that by accepted standards their life was a sinful one, and they tried seriously to make amends by donations to the Church, - "the graft payments to God" as those donations were cynically and probably unjustly called by Vladimir Solov'ev. It is much more sensible and in accordance with such evidence as we have from letters and memoirs to speak of a profound malaise resulting from the discrepancy not between two value systems but between the dominant value system and a social action that was at variance with it. It is out of this conflict that emerged the figure of the "repentant merchant" (which followed that of the "repentant nobleman" of the pre-Emancipation times), a figure so impressively depicted in Chekhov's Cherry Orchard. And the fictitious figure of Lopakhin appears multiplied in the reality of the early 20th century in the shape of merchants and industrialists who supplied generous funds to revolutionary organizations, including the Bolshevik party, of whom Savva Morosov, the leading textile industrialist, was an outstanding but far from solitary example.

No one can deny that some changes in this situation took place in the last decades of the 19th century. An independent value system of the entrepreneurial group began indeed to evolve. One need only compare the uneasy despotism of the merchant types in Ostrovsky's plays with the much more civilized and self-reliant figures of Gor'ki's Foma Gordeev. And a somewhat parallel change is clearly in evidence in the attitudes of the intelligentsia, as it broke away from the traditional Populism and turned with the same radical fervor to the tenets of Marxism. Paradoxical as it is, it was Marxism in Russia which for large strata of intelligentsia, of which revolutionary groups of course constituted but a small minority, brought about around the turn of the century some reconciliation with the bourgeoisie and replaced in their minds the picture of a despicable mercenary by that of a builder and innovator. But one cannot fail to be impressed by the lateness and incompleteness of this development.

What shall one conclude from all that? That social attitudes towards entrepreneurs, that value systems whether dominant or deviant, are unimportant, that they do not influence the development at all? This almost surely would be a wrong inference. First of all, it could be argued that the existence of wide-spread social attitudes in Russia which were so patently unfavorable to entrepreneurship, greatly reduced the number of potential entrepreneurs and thereby reduced the rate of economic development in the country.(27) There is little doubt that there is some plausibility to such an argument. Even in the 20th century, Russian university students showed a good deal of contempt for work associated with practical pursuits and particularly with business activity. When they went to Western Universities, they quickly developed attitudes of scorn for their student colleagues whose attitudes they regarded as glaringly materialistic. "Career" remained a shameful word in the vocabulary of a Russian university student. This attitude presumably retarded in some measure the industrialization of the country. Yet it did not prevent the brilliant period of rapid industrialization in the 1890's when the annual rate of industrial growth was in the vicinity of nine per cent.

It seems more reasonable to suggest that the effect upon economic development of the lingering preindustrial value systems, of aversion to entrepreneurs and to new forms of economic activity in general, was somewhat different. It is likely in some measure to have contributed in Russia - and elsewhere in the history of European industrializations - to the specific compression of industrialization processes into periods of rapid growth. Precisely because some value systems do not change readily, because economic development must break through the barriers of routine, prejudice, and stagnation, among which adverse attitudes towards entrepreneurship are but one important element, industrialization does not take place until the gains which industrialization promises have become, with the passage of time, overwhelmingly large, and the prerequisites are created for a typical spurtlike upsurge. An adverse social attitude towards entrepreneurs may thus indeed delay the beginning of rapid industrialization. But viewed over a somewhat longer run, more important than the mere fact of delay appears the fact that the character of the industrialization process is affected by those attitudes. At the same time, it would be clearly untenable to try to explain these spurts of rapid industrialization in backward countries, simply in terms of a lag in social attitudes. Technological progress, growing advantages of what Nurkse has called "balanced growth," and sudden institutional changes - all these combine to achieve the effect.

Before some general conclusions are drawn, let us shift the scene and follow for a few moments some other empirical work which has been influenced by the general theoretical structure that has been discussed in the preceding. The reference is to France and to attempts to explain the problem of the relatively low rate of economic development in that country. It is essentially the work of Professors David S. Landes and John E. Sawyer that is of interest here.(28)

The similarity between these two writers denotes the common origins in their theoretical thinking. The thesis is simple: it is the character of entrepreneurial behavior in France which has been a very important, perhaps the main retarding factor in France's economic development and that behavior has been largely shaped by the prevailing value system in the country. It is in these terms that must be seen and explained the French entrepreneur's alleged aversion to risk and credit engagements, his conservative spirit, his dislike of sharp competitive practices, his interest in high profits rather than large sales, the family character of the French enterprises and their small-scale size, to name only the few more important points. In addition, the social status of the businessman is said to be low and hence comes the desire of the best talent in France to turn to the "traditional honorific careers."(29) It is essentially the stress on the strength of the ancien régime survivals in the cultural pattern of modern France which Professor Sawyer has added to the picture.

It is perhaps somewhat unfair to seek the source of these views exclusively in general theoretical concepts. In part it is the tertium comparationis chosen by the two authors that appears to have influenced their thinking. Throughout, the comparison is with the United States. Obviously such a comparison is quite adequate if all the writers wished to convey were the indubitable differences that exist between the American and the French economies. But if what they were after was an explanation of the peculiar "weakness of French industry and commerce," the comparison with the United States is hardly a very helpful one, and the proper comparison ought to have been with countries of similar geographic size, position, and historical background, which nevertheless showed a higher rate of economic growth. Germany was the natural choice, and at least an explanation for shunning the obvious ought to have been provided.

Once the comparison is with Germany, most of the factors mentioned by Professor Landes find their counterpart in the German economy. The strength of pre-industrial social values was, if anything, greater in Germany than in France. The family firm remained strong, and the lower entrepreneurial echelons, whose numbers bulked large, behaved in a way which was hardly different from that in France. The pronouncement made at the turn of the century that modern economic development had transformed the top structure of the German economy while everything beneath it still remained medieval was, of course, a deliberate exaggeration. But there was some meaning to that exaggeration, and it was that no more for Germany than it would have been for France.(30)

Of course, the picture presented is one-sided in any case. In order to maintain his thesis, Landes has to relegate vast and most significant fields of French entrepreneurial endeavor, such as railroads, mines, iron and steel industry, automobile production, banks and department stores to qualifying footnotes and dependent clauses. On the other hand, a comparison with Germany would have brought out that in the 19th century French entrepreneurial vigor in some fields was doubtless in excess of that in Germany. The question of exact priority for the introduction of department stores is perhaps still a matter of - a rather useless - dispute,(31) but that the French supplied a whole series of momentous entrepreneurial innovations to the field is beyond doubt; so is the fact that at least till the end of the century Germany still lagged in this respect behind her neighbor in the West. It was a great French entrepreneur, Felix Potin, whom the alleged French value standards did not prevent from coining the famous altogether "American" phrase "Des affaires avant tout, le bénéfice viendra ensuite," and who successfully carried through his great innovations in retailing long before such ideas began to take hold in Germany.(32) At any rate, when Landes is struck by the far-reaching degree of specialization in French food-retailing which rightly seems so downright un-American to him, he should also have expressed his astonishment about the presence of the same phenomenon in Germany. Somerset Maughan justly claimed that to know one foreign country one must also know at least one other foreign country and added that "Arnold Bennett has never ceased to believe in a peculiar distinction of the French to breakfast off coffee and rolls."(33) This seems very sound advice for the field of comparative economic history.

It is true, of course, that the German rate of industrial growth in the second half of the 19th century exceeded that of France. Some of the factors which must in large measure have accounted for the difference in the speed of growth are obvious. The lack of a coal basis comparable to the Ruhr at a time when coal exercised all or nearly all of the locational pull in iron and steel making, surely is one such factor. The prevalence of the family farm with its unfavorable effects upon the flow of labor to industry is another. It may or may not be true that when everything is said and done, and a distribution of emphasis among the individual factors concerned is attempted, some differences in entrepreneurial behavior between France and Germany may be found very much worthy of mention in this respect. But to assume that such differences, if any, need necessarily be explained in terms of roles, role expectations and value orientations is surely unwarranted. Clearly, variations in entrepreneurial behavior may have nothing to do with the dominant value system and the degree of social approval. They can be, and no doubt are, the result of varying income levels, living conditions, degree of endowment with natural resources, and so on.

And in a sense, the same applies even to comparisons with the United States. There can be no doubt that differences in "dominant value systems" can be easily discerned between France and the country whose economy has remained largely, though by no means completely, free from the influences of pre-capitalist traditions. Ernest Renan once adverted to those differences in forceful sentences:

"Nous sommes une race des gentilshommes; notre idéal a été créé par des gentilshommes, non comme celui de l'Amérique, par d'honnêtes bourgeois, de sérieux hommes d'affaires. Les personnes qui poursuivent si avidement l'idéal américain oublient que cette race n'a pas notre passé brillant, qu'elle n'a pas fait une découverte de science pure, ni créé un chef-d'oeuvre, qu'elle n'a jamais eu de noblesse, que le négoce et la fortune l'occupent tout entière."

"Les meilleurs choses (par exemple, les fonctions du prêtre, du magistrat, du savant, de l'artiste et de l'homme de lettres sérieux) sont l'inverse de l'esprit industriel et commercial, le premier devoir de ceux qui s'y adonnent étant de ne pas chercher à s'enrichir, et de ne jamais considérer la valeur vénale de ce qu'ils font."(34)

These sweeping statements cannot lay claim to absolute accuracy and one should beware of easy generalizations.(35) But this is not the point. What is important to note here is that even in this classical case of differences in "value systems" between the United States and France, there is an obvious need for a good deal of careful and undogmatic research before one can begin to form some idea as to just how much significance can be reasonably imputed to those differences as against the host of other incomparabilities between the two countries.

Perhaps some conclusion can be drawn from the foregoing discussion. A rigid conceptual framework is no doubt useful in formulating questions, but at all times it evokes the peril that those questions will be mistaken for the answers. There is a deep-seated yearning in social sciences for the discovery of one general approach, one general law valid for all times and all climes. But these attitudes must be outgrown. They overestimate both the degree of simplicity of economic reality and the quality of scientific tools. As the economic historian organizes and interprets his material, all he can hope for is the discovery of limited patterns of uniformity which may possess some explanatory value for some places and periods but may be utterly inapplicable to others. And this is fully true of the sets of concepts which have been discussed in the foregoing. It seems reasonably clear that the chances for their usefulness are greatest when applied either to stagnant primitive communites in which no development takes place at all or to well-integrated advanced societies with well built-in dynamic elements. Paradoxical as it may sound, the analysis hitched to a general standard of values is best adapted to the case of, say, Navaho Indians on the one hand and to that of the present American society on the other. Hence perhaps also the strong affiliation that exists between anthropology and modern sociology; and hence perhaps also the strong - though illusory - feeling, so frequently expressed, that plus ça change, plus c'est la même chose,(36) - illusory because it overlooks the fact that the conceptual schemata may have held much less well for the intervening stages of the development. At any rate, serious doubts are permissible whether the theory of roles in its present form and everything that it implies can be of much use for understanding processes in the economies within which a rapid change in economic systems is in the making; more concretely, within the economies which experience the specific initial upsurge in the rate of growth of industrial output.

But the reservations must go farther. The preceding discussion may have seemed at times to have skirted perilously the old question of "precedence": does capitalism "create" the capitalist spirit or does the capitalist spirit "create" capitalism. Nothing could be more unfortunate than if work in economic history should once more be dragged down into the depth of metaphysical or at least hopelessly abstract arguments. The question cannot be: are social values important or unimportant? It must read first of all: what is the degree of persistence in value systems, what is their propensity to change in response to what factors? In dealing in particular with periods of economic transformation which in themselves imply a considerable degree of diversity in values within a given community one should least of all try to evoke the impression of a unified and general normative system. If something like "coefficients of changeability" - however crude such a measure must be - are attached to various value systems, one cannot fail to discover that the range of such coefficients must be wide indeed. Some values do not seem to change at all over long periods of time. The attitudes of peasantry who cling to the land even under unfavorable economic circumstances and even when at length forced into urban occupations still keep looking back over their shoulders, ready to return to the land at the earliest possible time - are surely determined by values whose change is exceedingly slow. It is perfectly reasonable to attribute to the existence of such values the well-known difficulties experienced by young industrial countries in building up a reliable permanent labor force in industry. On the other hand, the same hardly could be said of entrepreneurial values. The volatile group of entrepreneurs composed of men who by definition are "ganz besonders traditions - und beziehungslos... und dem System der überindividuellen Werte...ganz besonders fremd"(37) may not be oriented in their actions by any discernible set of values: there may be, as was pointed out above, a far-reaching divorce between their actions and the general value system to which they may still adhere. And, finally, even if a discernible set of special values can be attributed to the entrepreneur, these values are likely to be so recent in origin, so liable to further change, that it would seem highly unsatisfactory to take these values as a basis for interpreting economic action and economic change.

Precisely because in historical reality we are confronted with important cases where entrepreneurs did not appear as disciplined actors performing their pre-assigned roles in well-structured sociological plays but entered the historical stage in response to the challenge of great changes in the economic and social environment, it becomes imperative in dealing with the problem of entrepreneurial values to examine their relationship to the environment in the broadest sense of the term. The Russian entrepreneurs of the 1860's and the subsequent decades, and the French entrepreneurs of the 1850's have no doubt wrought great economic changes, but it is the emancipation of the peasantry in the one case and the establishment of the Second Empire with its liberalizing policies in the other that would seem to explain those changes much more readily and simply than any reference to the value systems.

Family Business

But to say all those things should not imply at all that the conceptual framework used should be banned altogether from the area of entrepreneurial research in economic history. Economic historians must at all times try to combine the use of analytical tools provided by economic theory with those supplied by the other social sciences. The late Professor Heckscher once even defined economic history as characterized by an interest "in the interplay of economic and other influences on the actual course of events."(38) But too enthusiastic an acceptance of abstract sociological models may tend to discredit the value of interdisciplinary approaches to economic history and the "theory of roles" may be a case in point. What is suggested here, therefore, is that a serious effort should be made to try and establish through empirical research the spatial and temporal limitations within which the use of such an approach is reasonable and defensible. The discovery of these limits will in itself push the research work into discovery of other sets of propositions and hypotheses which may be more promising in treating situations and historical sequences which differ widely from those for which the conceptual framework actually was designed. And it is then that one may begin to hope for a synthesis, that is, for plausible distribution of emphasis among a variety of factors yielded from pursuit of a variety of approaches.

The crying need for further research should effectively excuse the lack of any substantive conclusions to this paper. But perhaps one or two remarks to convey some general impressions may be in order. It would seem that adverse social attitudes towards entrepreneurs and entrepreneurships do not emerge as a major retarding force upon the economic development of European countries in the 19th century. This seems also true of Russian industrialization prior to World War I, although it is in that country that one might have expected hostility to entrepreneurs to be of more consequence than in the more advanced countries. In general, one cannot help being impressed by the rapidity with which the numbers of native entrepreneurs multiplied in Russia of the 19th century, and also by the speed with which the character of their behavior became more and more consonant with Western practices.

The temptation is great, of course, to argue from the Russian experience to the present conditions in underdeveloped countries and to arrive - on that score - at somewhat more optimistic prognostications than those currently in use. But it may be hazardous to succumb to such a temptation. Russia until the First World War had benefited greatly from the presence of foreign entrepreneurs. It is true that some degree of animosity against foreign entrepreneurs and technicians was in clear evidence. But such animosity remained within moderate limits and, if anything, served as a stimulus to native entrepreneurial talent. It may well be that conditions in some of the underdeveloped countries are less favorable in this respect.

Moreover, adverse social attitudes to entrepreneurship in Russia stemmed largely from "pre-industrial" value orientations, and those anti-capitalist attitudes which usually arise with the spread of the industrial economy did not seem to affect entrepreneurial activities in any marked degree. Quite on the contrary, as mentioned before, the effects of pre-revolutionary Marxism on attitudes towards entrepreneurs was presumably positive. It is quite possible that in underdeveloped countries of our days the strength of pre-industrial values and the resulting lack of sympathy with entrepreneurs is greater than was the case in Imperial Russia. And, on the other hand, it is perhaps more likely that those values will more readily coalesce with modern anti-capitalist sentiments and persuasions and that, unlike Russia before 1914, such a combination may find effective expression in acts and policies of the governments concerned. While Count Witte's state of the 1890's stood aloof from popular attitudes, this is much less likely to be true of backward countries in the second half of the 20th century. Perhaps the generalization may be ventured that adverse social attitudes towards entrepreneurs do not significantly affect the processes of industrialization unless they are allowed to become crystallized in governmental action. But discussion of the latter would transcend the scope of this paper.

Alexander Gerschenkron

Harvard University

oOo

FOOTNOTES

(1) The following references (unless otherwise stated) are taken from the symposium Toward a General Theory of Action, edited by Talcott Parsons and Edward A. Shils, Cambridge 1952, particulary from the funda- mental Part 2, Values, Motives, and Systems of Action, which comes from the pens of the two editors. This volume, it may be added, provides a most convenient point of entry for an economist who wishes to trespass upon the domain of modern sociology.

(2) Op. cit., p. 190.

(3) Ibid.

(4) Professor Parsons may be quite unwilling to accept the last sentence of this paragraph as a correct reproduction of his views. Elsewhere (The Social System, 1951), he explicitly rejects the "dominant factor theories which were so popular a generation ago" (p.493). Yet, time and again, it is said that "value orientations are used as "major point of reference" (op. cit., p.484); that "the primary emphasis of this volume has been on the integration of social systems at the level of patterns of value orientations as institution- alized in role expectations" (op. cit., p.350); and so forth. It would seem that from a methodological point of view the substantive outcome is the same, and value orientations when so used do in fact assume the role of the "dominant factor." The difference may lie in the greater awareness of the limitations of the approach, but its locus then is without rather than within the system.

(5) Op. cit., pp. 50 et seq.

(6) Op. cit., p. 63.

(7) Op. cit., p. 225.

(8) Op. cit., p. 179.

(9) Op. cit., p. 231.

(10) Op. cit., p. 415.

(11) Perhaps a word on the system as a whole may go unsuppressed. The system is presented as a social equilibrium system thus evoking com- parisons with the general equilibrium concept in economics. But time and again it appears that the concept of equilibrium is extended so far as to

become coterminous with that of organized society, so that what is actually discussed is not so much a set of equilibrium conditions as a set of minimum conditions of social existence, which would mean that most important and most variegated social processes might take place without any change in the basic variables that enter into the system.

(12) Harvard University Press, Cambridge 1949. A good deal of water has gone down the Charles River since the publication of this volume. In quoting the views expressed by the contributors more than four years ago there is, of course, no intention to suggest that those views are necessarily still adhered to in exactly the same form by the writers concerned. In fact, this would be most unlikely in a new and vigorously expanding field. But the volume in question is the only reasonably full statement of problems in entrepreneurial research that is available, and it is used here for this reason. A new venture of the same kind incorporating the thought and the research experience of the intervening years would seem extremely desirable.

(13) Op. cit., pp. 87–88.

(14) "Role Structure of Entrepreneurial Personality."

(15) Op. cit., pp. 131–132.

(16) Op. cit., p. 138.

(17) Op. cit., p. 14.

(18) "Role and Sanction in American Entrepreneurial History."

(19) Op. cit., p. 160.

(20) Cf., Parsons and Shils, op. cit., p. 415.

(21) Cf. in this connection the interesting treatment by Dr. Redlich of what he calls the "daimonic" entrepreneur, e.g. in Fritz Redlich, History of American Business Leaders, (Ann Arbor 1940) Vol. I, pp. 2-6, and "The Business Leader as a Daimonic Figure," American Journal of Economics and Sociology, Vol. XII, Nos. 2 and 3 (January-April, 1953)

(22) It may be mentioned that Professor Parsons is well aware of the two types of processes of change. He speaks of "processes within the system" and "processes of change of the system" and objects to a confusion of the two in the common term "dynamics." The Social System, p. 481.

(23) Cf., J. A. Schumpeter, Capitalism, Socialism, and Democracy, New York 1942, p. 132. Also: Business Cycles, New York and London 1939, Vol. I, p. 100.

(24) J. A. Schumpeter, Capitalism... ibid.

(25) Augustin Thierry, Essai sur l'histoire de la formation et des progrès du tiers état, Paris 1856, Vol. I, pp. 108-110.

(26) Cf., V. G. Belinsky, Pis'ma (Letters), St. Petersburg, 1914, Vol. III, p. 329.

(27) This point was frequently and effectively made by Dr. Hugh Aitken in the writer's seminar.

(28) Cf., David S. Landes, "French Entrepreneurship and Industrial Growth in the Nineteenth Century," The Journal of Economic History, Vol. IX:1 (May, 1949), pp. 45-61; and "French Business and the Businessmen in Social and Cultural Analysis," in Modern France, Edward Mead Earle, ed., Princeton 1951, pp. 334-353, John E. Sawyer, "Strains in the Social Structure of Modern France," op. cit., pp. 293-312; and "The Entrepreneur and the Social Order, France and the United States," in Men in Business, William Miller, ed., Harvard University Press, 1952.

(29) Cf., Landes, Journal of Economic History, loc. cit., p. 56.

(30) Landes is probably right in saying that the reliability of quantitative information on the subject is not very high. But this should not mean that one is justified in ignoring the existing statistics altogether. In comparing the results of the German Census of 1907 with those of the French Census of 1906, it is interesting to see that in Germany 90 per cent of all establishments in industry (including mining) were within the class employing 0 to 5 persons, while the corresponding figure for France was 88.6 per cent. Both in Germany and in France 1.3 per cent of all establishments in industry were in the category of firms employing more than 50 persons. The data on the corresponding classification of establishments in trade, insurance, and banking are very similar: the lowest 0-5 employees' category comprised 93.3 per cent of all such firms in Germany and 94.6 per cent in France. Cf. Statistik des Deutschen Reichs, Vol. 220/221, pp. 46* and 48* and Statistique Générale de la France, Annuaire Statistique, Vol. 29/1909, p. 188. These figures certainly would not countenance the view that the small boutique was in any way more peculiar to France than to Germany. In addition, it is possible that a certain bias inherent in the French figures tends to inflate somewhat the numbers of enterprises in the lowest category.

It is quite true that comparisons of the share of the total labor force engaged in firms of different size-groups do show that the proportion of the labor force which was engaged in the small-scale enterprises (0-5 persons) was not insignificantly smaller in Germany than in France. (For the purpose of such a comparison, it may be added, it has been necessary to adjust the German census data for the numbers of owners, plant managers, and helping family members; if no such adjustments are made, the differences would appear very minor indeed.) But to some extent, though not exclusively, this is the result of differences in the economic top structures in the two countries rather than of differences pertaining to their industrial and commercial structures in their entireties.

(31) Cf., Ralph M. Hower, History of Macy's of New York, 1858-1919, Harvard University Press 1943, pp. 411 et seq.

(32) G. d'Avenal, Le méchanisme de la vie moderne, Paris, 1902, pp. 174 et seq.

(33) Somerset Maugham, A Writer's Notebook, New York 1949, p. 153.

(34) Ernest Renan, "Philosophie de l'histoire contemporaine: la monarchie constitutionelle en France," Revue des Deux Mondes, November 1, 1869, Vol. 84, Seconde Periode, p. 93.

(35) Modern research, for instance, has assembled considerable evidence to show that even the American merchants in mid 19th century frontier regions held merchandizing in low esteem and tried to escape from it as soon as possible into more honorific careers. Cf., e.g., Lewis E. Atherton, The Pioneer Merchant in Mid-America, The University of Missouri Studies, Vol. XIV: 2 (April 1, 1939), pp. 30-31.

(36) Thomas Cochran, loc. cit., p. 174.

(37) J. A. Schumpeter, Theorie der wirtschaftlichen Entwicklung, Munich and Leipsic, 1926, p. 134.

(38) Eli F. Heckscher, "David Davidson," International Economic Papers, No. 2, London-New York, 1952, p. 126. Cf., also Heckscher's Historieuppfattning, materialistic och annan, Stockholm 1944, pp. 30-31; and W. K. Hancock's emphasis on the basic "impurity" of economic history, Economic History at · Oxford, Oxford 1946, p. 5.

[4]

Family Business in Britain:
An Historical and Analytical Survey

Peter L. Payne
University of Aberdeen

I. The Tenacity of the Family Firm in Britain

Family firms have been an integral part of British business for centuries, and their preeminence in the nation's economic institutions undoubtedly reached its peak during the classic period of the Industrial Revolution. Even during the latter half of the nineteenth century, by which time a legal structure existed which made fundamental changes in the structure of the individual enterprise possible, few firms adopted the corporate form. In contrast with the expectations of those responsible for the early Company Acts, there developed the private company (legally unrecognized until 1907) and this, it is safe to say, was initially all but indistinguishable from the family partnerships or unlimited joint-stock companies which had preceded it, the object of private registration being to obtain limited liability while retaining both the original management and the privacy of the past. Thus, until the 1880s entrepreneurs operated within organizations which show little alteration from those of their pioneering forebears. Certainly there was little movement toward the differentiation of management from ownership; toward the elongation of organizational hierarchies; toward, in effect, the emergence of the corporate economy.[1]

Following his examination of the relevant Parliamentary Papers and the files of the *Economist*, Sir John Clapham outlined those branches of British industry and commerce that were still dominated by family business in 1886–87:

All, or nearly all, the wool firms; outside Oldham, nearly all the cotton firms; and the same in linen, silk, jute, lace and hosiery. Most of the smaller, and some of the largest, engineering firms, and nearly all the cutlery and pottery firms. Brewing was a family affair. So, with certain outstanding exceptions, were the Birmingham trades and the great, perhaps the major, part of the shipbuilding industry. In housebuilding and the associated trades there were very few limited companies; few in the clothing trades; few in the food trades. . . . Merchants of all kinds had rarely 'limited' their existing firms, and the flotation of a brand new mercantile company was not easy. Add the many scores of thousands of retail business, 'unlimited' almost to a shop.[2]

Clapham's observations have largely been confirmed by more recent studies; even in the ever increasing number of partnerships being transformed into joint-stock limited liability companies by registration under the Act of 1856, the direction, management and even ownership was virtually identical with those of the former firms. In the vast majority of cases, the adoption of corporate status initially did nothing to disrupt the familial nature of British business organization.[3] Only in the public utilities, particularly the provision of gas, light and water, and in transport (railways and, to a lesser extent, shipping) was family control either eroded or given little opportunity to develop. Of the major manufacturing sectors of the economy, perhaps only cotton witnessed a diminution of family dominance and even this appears to have been confined to certain geographical localities such as Oldham.[4]

Not until the great boom of the early 1870s can there be discerned any significant relaxation of the grip of the partnership. Companies involved in coal mining and iron making led the way. A need for fixed capital beyond the accumulated wealth of the founders and their successors, many of whom wished to withdraw from active participation in the firms that had been instrumental in creating their fortunes, coupled with a desire to reduce their financial responsibilities when the inevitable reaction to the boom set in, brought about the formation of a host of limited companies in coal and iron, shipbuilding and engineering, chemicals and textiles. With a number of important exceptions, most of these companies were "conversions"; that is, cases in which the original members of family partnerships sold their firms, as going concerns, to limited companies, and in payment received an overwhelming proportion of the ordinary share capital. Thus, as Cottrell has emphasized, "although the number of public companies grew, this development did not lead to 'outside' shareholders gaining control of the assets. The equity, which carried voting rights, remained in the hands of the vendors whereas extra funds were raised at the time of conversions, or subsequently, by the issues of either preference shares or debentures. . . By issuing such non-voting securities to 'outside' investors, the management group of a converted company [invariably the members of the original proprietorial family] . . . could continue to control it in an unfettered way and thus were in the same position as the shareholders of a private limited company."[5]

Even the very large mergers that took place in branches of the textile industry and in brewing, iron and steel, cement, wallpaper and tobacco at the close of the nineteenth century often failed greatly to weaken the hold of the founding families, so high a proportion of the issued share capital was retained by the vendors.[6] If to these important companies be added the enormous number of private companies being created at the turn of the century, in which there continued the *complete* marriage of ownership and control characteristic of earlier epochs,[7] the remarkable tenacity of the family firm in Britain's economy is revealed.

Superficially, little change took place in the inter-war period. As the work of Professor Hannah has shown, although there was a perceptible increase in the separation of ownership and control in the largest companies in the decades following the end of the First World War, this had "not progressed far enough to displace founding or family directors from company boards; 110 of the 200 largest firms in 1919, or 55 per cent, had family board members, as did 140, or 70 per cent, in 1930 and 119, or 59.5 per cent, in 1948."[8] Although it should be emphasized that the mere persistence of family names on the board does not *necessarily* mean that they exercised a dominant role in direction and management, there is little doubt that in several sectors, particularly in brewing, shipbuilding and food, founding families retained much power.[9] And if this was so in the case of the *largest* firms, how much more is it true of what the late Professor P.

TABLE 1   Owner-managership and Controlling Interests in Small Firms.

(a)   Number of partners or shareholders having a controlling interest

	1	2	3–5	6–10	11 and over	All
	Percentage of small firms					
Manufacturing	39.4	46.3	13.0	0.8	0.5	100.0
Non-manufacturing	42.0	46.6	10.0	0.5	1.0	100.0

(b)   Number of working partners or shareholders

	1	2	3–5	6–10	11 and over	All
	Percentage of small firms					
Manufacturing	20.8	45.9	29.9	2.2	1.2	100.0
Non-manufacturing	25.2	44.8	27.4	1.3	1.3	100.0

Source: *Bolton Report*, pp. 6–7, based on Bolton Committee Postal Questionnaire Survey, Research Report No. 17.

Sargant Florence called the medium and smaller large companies.[10] And below these were the thousands of small public companies and tens of thousands of companies which by 1938 had virtually superceded the sole proprietorship and the small partnership in manufacturing activity.[11]

Despite the profound changes in the British economy since the end of the Second World War, the family business continues to play an important role, though its relative significance is certainly diminishing.[12] A number of recent studies have shed considerable light on the *small* firm and it is apparent that many concerns so categorized are as much family businesses as their historical predecessors.[13] In their internal structures and control mechanisms they are almost identical to the archetypal firms of the Industrial Revolution. Those small firms[14] who responded to the Bolton Inquiry in 1969–70 were "almost exclusively under their proprietors' control and a large proportion of them were family businesses of one sort or another":

> Over 85 per cent of respondent [firms] are controlled and almost certainly owned by one or two people; this was true for both manufacturing and non-manufacturing. A further 13 per cent (in manu-

Family Business in Britain 175

TABLE 2   Family Ownership of Small Firms (By Percentages).

Ownership Type	Manu-facturing	Con-struction	Wholesale	Motor Trade	Retail
First generation family	18⎫38	11⎫44	46⎫69	35⎫49	49⎫68
Second or greater generation family	20⎭	33⎭	23⎭	14⎭	19⎭
Non-family and family/ non-family shared	62	56	31	51	32
Total	100	100	100	100	100
Number of Firms	126	36	113	109	128

Source: Merrett Cyriax Associates, *Dynamics of Small Firms*, Research Report for the Bolton Committee, No. 12, p. 11.

facturing) are controlled by three, four or five people. Generally speaking the larger the firm the more dispersed the ownership. As a result, although in manufacturing only about a fifth of firms are wholly owned by one person, in the retail trades proprietorship predominates . . . . The majority [of small firms] are managed by those having a controlling interest, usually the founder or members of his family. In 81 per cent of small firms in manufacturing the 'boss' was the founder of the business or a member of the founder's family and over a third of all small manufacturing businesses and over two thirds in the distributive trades are wholly owned by first, second or third generations of the same family [See Tables 1 and 2].[15]

But it is not these saplings in the forest, as the economist Alfred Marshall might have described them, that are our principal concern on this occasion;[16] our attention has been explicitly directed to the larger organizational units. In this category, although family businesses have survived they are now powerful in very few sectors of economic activity. In 1951 Florence indicated that perhaps a third of Britain's very large companies (those with issued capitals of £3 million and more) were still owner-controlled and thus capable, to varying degrees, of being designated family business. But within little more than a decade several of these giant concerns ceased to qualify as such. Among them were Associated Electrical Industries, the Bristol Aeroplane Company, J. & J. Colman Ltd. and Bovril. Furthermore, the trend against familial ownership evident in the largest firms is equally apparent in Florence's next size

TABLE 3   Percentage Distribution of Family and Non-family Companies by Degree of Diversification.

Category	1950		1960		1970	
	No. of Companies		No. of Companies		No. of Companies	
	F	Non-F	F	Non-F	F	Non-F
	(Percent)		(Percent)		(Percent)	
Single Product	36	31	24	15	7	6
Dominant Product	44	36	41	33	40	31
Related Product	18	31	33	45	50	56
Unrelated Product	2	2	2	7	3	7
Total	100	100	100	100	100	100
Sample Size	50	42	42	54	30*	70

Notes: * See Table 3a.
Source: Channon, *Strategy and Structure*, p. 76.

TABLE 3a   The Companies Exhibiting "Significant Elements of Family Control" Included the Following:

	Structure		
Single Product Companies[1] :			
International Distillers and Vintners	F/HC	(M)	Wines and spirits, manufacture and distribution.
Watney Mann	F		Brewing, public houses, hotels, entertainment.
Dominant Product Companies :			
Pilkington Brothers*	M.D.	(M)	Glass
Ford Motor	M.D.	(M)	Automobiles
Swan Hunter*	M.D.		Shipbuilding
I.B.M.	M.D.	(M)	Computers
Related Product :			
Food			
Associated British Foods	M.D.		
Brooke Bond Liebig	M.G.	(M)	
Cadbury/Schweppes*	M.D.	(M)	
J. Lyons*	M.D.		
Mars	M.D.	(F)	
Rank Hovis McDougall*	M.D.	(M)	
Spillers	M.D.		
Materials and Glass			
Marley Tile*	F	(M)	
Engineering			
John Brown	H.C.		

Family Business in Britain   177

Electrical and Electronic Engineering		
Plessey*	M.D.	(M)
Phillips (U.K.)	M.D.	(F)(M)
Thorn Electric*	M.D.	(M)
Textiles and Clothing		
Coats Patons*	H.C.	(M)
Paper and Packaging		
Dickinson Robinson*	M.D.	(M)
Thomson Organization*	M.D.	(M)
Unrelated Product:		
Reckitt & Coleman	M.D.	(M)

Key: F=Functional
        M.D.=Multidivisional
        H.C.=Holding Company
        (M)=Multinational
        (F)=Subsidiary company controlled by a non-British parent company.
         * =Classified as owner-controlled by Nyman and Silberston in 1976 because
             of shareholdings of "directors and their families" or by the Chairman or
             Managing Director being either the founder, his family or descendants.
Notes: 1 Shortly after Derek F. Channon compiled his list, I.D.V. was acquired by
            Watney Mann, which in turn was acquired by Grand Metropolitan Hotels,
            itself "owner-controlled."
Sources: Derek F. Channon, *The Strategy and Structure of British Enterprise*, pp. 52–63,
            supplemented by a personal communication to the author, 18 November,
            1982.
            S. Nyman and A. Silberston, "The Ownership and Control of Industry,"
            Oxford Economic Papers, N. S. Vol. XXX (1978), pp. 74–101, supplemented
            by additional data referred to on p. 84, note 2.

category—the "medium large" concerns with capitals between £1 million and £3 million. Only among companies smaller still was control by the owner still characteristic of the majority of enterprises.[17]

Yet Channon, in perhaps the most penetrating of recent inquiries into the structure of British enterprise, was still able to discern a substantial number of "family" companies within his sample population of the largest British manufacturing firms in 1969/70. Finding, as others have done both before and after his analysis, that "the pattern of share ownership was not in reality an entirely meaningful measure of family control," he deemed it necessary to adopt a more rigorous definition:

> A company was . . . termed family controlled if a family member
> was the chief executive officer, if there had been at least two gener-
> ations of family control, and if a minimum of 5 per cent of the vot-
> ing stock was still held by the family or trust interests associated
> with it.[18]

Using these criteria, Channon found that no less than fifty out of 92
companies in his sample had been controlled by families in 1950
and that even by 1970 thirty of the 100 companies "still contained
significant elements of family control" (See Table 3). And, in a study
completed six years after Channon's investigation, Steve Nyman
and Aubrey Silberston identified 126 companies among the largest
250 enterprises in the United Kingdom as being "owner controlled,"
of which 77 (or, say, 30 per cent of the total) exhibited significant
elements of family control either by virtue of the shareholdings of
the "directors and their families" (62) or because the company
chairman or managing director was a relation of the firm's founder
or his family (15).[19] In such firms, men bearing the family name
continued to occupy directoral seats and to wield considerable
power however diluted their personal ownership of the company had
become.[20] Furthermore, among the ranks of the unquoted private
companies in 1970 were to be found a number of very large businesses in which entrepreneurial power remained almost totally with
the owner-managers: with the Ferrantis in electrical engineering,
the McAlpines in construction, the Moores (Littlewoods) and the
Sainsburys in retailing, the Lithgows in shipbuilding, the Brintons
in carpets, the Clarks in footwear and the Vesteys in the meat trade.[21]
But are these *large* firms which display, in varying degrees, elements of family control the last of their kind? Are they the survivors
of a once numerous and powerful species doomed, if not to extinction,
to play an ever decreasing role in the British economy? I suspect so.
My reason is this. The large-scale business organization which now
dominate so many sectors of the economy operate within an environment fundamentally different from that which existed even as
recently as 1945.[22] The degree of industrial concentration is remarkably high in Britain: the large firms are very large.[23] Furthermore, since it would appear that large, medium and small firms
grow on average by the same proportionate amount (Gibrat's Law),

the concentration of output in the larger firms will doubtless increase.[24] But in this growth process those firms which retain significant elements of family control and management will be at a disadvantage compared with their more "corporate" counterparts, for family firms are increasingly unlikely to be able to grow at the same rate as the latter unless they increase diversification, permit "outside" capital to come into the firm and relax "leadership by inheritance." Hence, only by divesting themselves of those very characteristics which distinguish "family firms" from giant "public" firms will the former be able to successfully compete in the growth race.[25] The conclusion must be that if a family firm chooses to remain of this category, its relative importance within its own industrial or commercial sector must decline; if it chooses to grow, it has little option but to cease to be a "family" firm.[26] Either way, the family firm in the British economy seems destined to be relegated or confined to the medium or even small size range.[27]

Despite their declining relative significance in the British economy as a whole—not least because of the spread of the multinational company and the nationalization of the coal industry (1947) and much of the iron and steel (1967) and shipbuilding (1977) industries—it is apparent that a number of "family firms" are still to be found among the largest individual enterprises in certain fields of activity. How have these firms managed to survive and grow when it is arguable that, generally speaking, the familial character of firms seems to be inversely correlated with the size of the unit (measured by total assets or by sales)? Is it possible to be more specific in outlining the process of change from the family firm to the large-scale corporate concern? Is this transformation to be explained in terms of efforts to overcome the managerial constraints to the growth of the firm? Has the persistence of the family firm been prejudicial to the nation's economic growth? It is to questions such as this that we must turn, but first it is imperative to survey the timing of the separation of ownership from control in British business and the nature of the different control systems exhibited by firms of different size.

II. The Management Structure and Changing Nature of the British Family Firm

The *small* firms to which we have already alluded—be they those which characterized business organizations in the period of early industrialization or those which still form the majority of British firms—rarely possessed a formal management structure. To employ the words of the Bolton Committee: "small firms [were and] are simply run by their owners" (p. 6). In the family firm there was for decades rarely any need to evolve a sophisticated bureaucratic hierarchy. If growth in size necessitated some degree of functional specialization, members of the founding family or a junior unrelated partner —perhaps originally a trusted foreman—would be assigned the responsibility.[28] Not until changing technology dictated an increase in size beyond their combined resources, was it necessary to devise a new structure for the firm. Meanwhile, as Marshall wrote: "The master's eye is everywhere; there is no shirking by his foreman, no divided responsibility, no sending half understood messages backwards and forwards from one department to another."[29]

Indeed, the maintenance and exercise of personal control was regarded as so vital that the growth of the family enterprise cannot but have been inhibited. In the shipbuilding industry, for example, Professor Slaven has shown that although the growing scale of operations in the Clyde yards involved the creation of a hierarchical organization in which "operating or tactical decisions required to implement policy were clearly delegated to departmental heads and then increasingly subdivided and delegated downward in a functional ladder through supervisors, foremen, under-foremen etc. to the shop floor," at these "lower levels the guidelines controlling action . . . were so detailed and precise that decision taking and action fused together to create the impression that the decision was almost automatic and unthinking." The small, management board at the top really exercised control and this meant that severe limits were imposed on the size of the enterprise. The words of Thomas Bell, managing director of John Brown & Co. at Clydebank, to the Board of Trade Committee on Shipping and Shipbuilding in 1916, quoted by Professor Slaven, certainly have a more general applicability. "Personally I may say I am very much against developing individual works too much. It is impossible to manage them if you do. It is the personal factor and I do not care how splendid the works are; the personal factor cannot spread itself out too much."[30]

It is this " 'mechanistic [management] system,' in which authority is concentrated at the top of the organization, work is functionally specialized and organized in sub-units, and interaction between members of the concern is vertical, between superior and subordinate,"[31] that is so often found in the family firm. And it is the adoption of this system that permitted the marriage of ownership and control to prevail for so long in the British economy: whether in the industrial sector, merchandising or in the service industries such as banking and insurance.

Even the establishment of giant firms produced by the multi-firm mergers in the period 1885–1905 failed in perhaps the majority of cases to produce any fundamental internal organizational changes:

> The fact that the majority of them were single-product companies, involving little integration and even less diversification, and that they were inspired by defensive motives rather than by a desire for great efficiency meant that centralized management was still possible, if not appropriate. Thus those who came out on top during the course of the internecine wars of vendor-directors of the new combinations could continue to conduct the affairs of the merged companies as if all that had happened was that what had hitherto been their own particular firms had grown larger by the multiplication of units. . . .[32]

Thus, in iron and steel and in brewing, for example, the descendants and relations of the founders continued to dominate their companies. Many of the multi-unit enterprises emerging at the turn of the century adopted a loose holding company form and remained essentially federations of family firms.[33] Some families—those whose firms constituted a minor part of an amalgamation—undoubtedly experienced a certain diminution of power, it is true, but others—those whose share of the newly created equity capital essentially gave them ultimate control of their giant firms—enhanced their positions within their industries. Members of the Coats family, for example, dominated the board of J. & P. Coats, and hence the entire thread market.

But Coats, perhaps the most efficient of all the nineteenth-century

combinations, clearly evolved a highly efficient bureaucratic structure. Apparently, the board concentrated on central direction; the
creation of statistical departments made possible the interchange
of fully comprehensive information for the formulation of policy;
departments for buying, selling, and other basic functions were
established; the lines of communications between branches and the
central office made explicit, and detailed accounting procedures
instituted.[34] All this meant that in time professional managers were
recruited: accountants, lawyers and technicians (engineers and
chemists, particularly) were increasingly placed in positions of
authority. The genesis of the process whereby ownership and control
became divorced can be perceived even in the very large family
firm. A similar example is provided by Professor Hannah:

> Before World War I . . . the names of board members, the addresses
> of offices, and other information listed for the United Alkali Com-
> pany imply that the firm was still owned by the family that founded
> it, was not administered by salaried managers, put out a single
> product, and was organized as a holding company. . . . More
> detailed research indicates, however, that the number of professional
> managers in the higher echelons was increasing and suggests that the
> company was developing a more diversified range of products, was
> vertically integrated, was organized according to functional depart-
> ments, and was centrally administered.[35]

Three conclusions are inescapable. The first is that inferences based
simply upon knowledge of the names of the board members of the
larger family firms are potentially misleading if it be assumed that the
continued unification of ownership and control meant little or no
structural change. Second, only further case studies will provide the
information necessary for a proper appreciation of the organizational changes that the growth of the firm demanded. And third,
it would appear that if family firms were to grow, they had to evolve
internal management systems that were similar to those of their
corporate counterparts. If they did not do so, their growth was
stunted, limited to a level lower than might otherwise have been
possible and economically desirable.

Following his analysis of large British companies in 1936–51, Florence concluded that "it looks as though control by personal or family

TABLE 4 Distribution of Family and Non-family Companies and Number with Multidivisional Structures.

Category	1950 No. (M.D.No.)		1960 No. (M.D.No.)		1970 No. (M.D.No.)	
	F	Non-F	F	Non-F	F	Non-F
Single product	18(0)	13(2)	10(0)	8(3)	2(0)	4(1)
Dominant product	22(2)	15(2)	17(2)	18(6)	12(8)	22(17)
Unrelated and related product	10(3)	14(4)	15(8)	28(13)	16(13)	44(34)
Total	50(5)	42(8)	42(10)	54(22)	30(21)	70(52)

Source: Channon, *Strategy and Structure*, p. 76.

ownership [is] not possible beyond a certain size of company."[36] If this observation proves to be correct, then the explanation for the diminishing importance of the family firm becomes clearer. With the growth of giant firms in twentieth century Britain—recently investigated by Dr. S. J. Prias and Professor Hannah[37]—the relative significance of those firms which retain elements of family control has inevitably declined. The evolution of their organizational structures has been slower than their corporate counterparts (see Table 4); their reluctance to go to the market for capital and their inability to raise the funds necessary for expansion from alternative sources (by profit retention, or by familial connections and contacts or by bank loans) has retarded growth. Only in certain, increasingly limited, sectors of activity can they retain some vestige of their previous predominance. Furthermore, I believe it would be accurate to say that even those large family firms that have survived are not really comparable with those of even a few decades ago. They may exhibit, as Channon has phrased it, "significant elements of family control,"[38] but among *large firms*, the family firm characteristic of the nineteenth century—even of the inter-war period—no longer exists. Family firms are essentially confined to the medium or small size categories, many of them having consciously decided not to expand.

Family firms, proud of their individualism, wary of outsiders both at board and senior management levels, and anxious to restrict their growth to the level made possible by the retention of profits, were reluctant to follow the lead of their corporate counterparts who, by

the adoption of the multidivisional form, were slowly pushing back
the barriers of the managerial diseconomies of scale. This issue has
been well surveyed by Professor Hannah in his study *The Rise of the
Corporate Economy*. Obsessed by a belief that potential mergers and a
larger scale of operations would lead to a loss of personal dominance
and control, many family-owned firms chose to spurn the opportunities implicit in enhanced size. Perhaps the best documented case
is that of Kenricks, the Midland hardware firm whose records have
been analyzed by Professor Roy Church.[39] Advised in 1937 by their
management consultants, Peat, Marwick, Mitchell & Co., to seek
a merger with their rivals and thoroughly to overhaul and strengthen
the company's management and administration, the recommendations were rejected because to have implemented them would have
"change[d] entirely the character of the business as one controlled
and managed by the principal owners, which had been its constitution from the beginning."[40]

Even without the goad of a management consultant's report, there
must have been many family firms who were forced to acknowledge
the deficiencies of their own organizations but who chose not to
embark on structural change because it was so repugnant to the
boards whose families had for generations owned and controlled the
business and who viewed "with disfavour the [idea] of appointing
from outside the family a stranger [to] an important position of
control."[41] How else can the slower diversification of family-controlled companies and their obvious reluctance to adopt the multidivisional structure, even in the recent past,[42] be explained?

Frequently, some traumatic experience (such as the death or
retirement of a family leader or the dying out of a branch of a dominant family because of a failure to produce male heirs) was required
to induce structural reorganization,[43] though even here it would
appear that unless some widening of the firm's product range by diversification had already taken place(or was necessary for continued
survival) it was likely that fundamental change would be resisted.[44]
And not the least reason for this refusal to change and to cling on to
their own little businesses was "the feudal idea of handing it on to
their family."[45] In such cases can be perceived manifestations of
Chandler's original dictum that strategy dictates structure, and fur-

ther illustrations of the fact that the more family concerns grow, the more they are forced to divest themselves of the characteristics of the true family firm, in which "the whole of the capital . . . is privately held, practically all the important and administrative posts are filled by members of the family, and in which there are no employees in positions of real authority."[46]

With this caveat in mind, a number of large "family businesses" continue to survive in Britain today. They are to be found in the food and drink industries, glass, electrical and electronics components, publishing and printing, construction, carpets, shipping, retailing and other service industries. But, where the details are known, the majority of them increasingly resemble their corporate counterparts. Pilkingtons, until only recently Britain's largest private company in which authority was highly concentrated within a small family caucus, was forced to go to the market to raise the funds necessary for expansion and diversification in 1970 and become a public company. Much of the stock remained in family hands and members of the Pilkington family continued to play a highly important role in the firm, but the adoption of a multidivisional structure in 1969 and the increasing introduction of non-family directors from the mid-1960's, "seem likely to result in an eventual loss of family control."[47]

At Guiness, the brewers, the company may be family-owned and controlled at board level, but there is apparently little family intervention in management. For well over fifty years the running of the business has been left largely to carefully chosen outsiders. Indeed, "the last member of the Guiness family who was managing director of the company . . . retired in 1902." The internal structure retains a holding company form and the pursuit of the maximum profit does not appear to be a major policy objective.[48] Nor does it at Brintons carpets, John Laings, the second largest construction company in Britain, or Ferrantis, the electronics firm, if the utterances of the chairmen of these companies are anything to go by.[49]

Although some of the major family businesses have grown rapidly in size in recent years (e.g. Marks and Spencer,[50] Marley Tiles), others have chosen to eschew the maximum rate of growth rather than go to the stock market or to open their board rooms to outsiders. Sebastian de Ferranti would "sooner become smaller than raise public money," and at Wates and at McAlpines, the building and construction firms, there is evidence that expansion has been restricted until family partners were available to supervise new contracts or take on new responsibilities.[51]

Such examples could be multiplied, though really hard information is difficult to obtain. They would merely illustrate, I suspect, some of the generalizations made earlier in this paper and would tend to confirm explanations of a continuing relative decline of family power in British industry and commerce. Even in merchant banking, a series of mergers in the early 1960's has lessened the family sovereignty once so apparent in this sector.[52] "Financial conglomerates" have emerged offering a wide range of financial services and this has necessitated structural changes, sometimes the adoption of the multidivisional form. More surprisingly perhaps, this was the organizational form favored by the new thrusting property, retailing and hotel companies which were founded only in the late 1950's and mid-1960's by men such as Charles Clore, Max Joseph, John Collier, Isaac Wolfson and Jim Slater, men who were masters at seeking the potential of a deal rather than becoming concerned with day to day operations and who therefore found a variant of the multidivisional system ideal for their purposes.[53] Thus, even in the service industries, where numerous large firms—particularly those involved with the property market—are still led by their original founding entrepreneurs (so recent is their creation), the family business is declining in relative importance and it is difficult to foresee any reversal of this powerful trend.

III. The Family Firm and Economic Development

1. The Charge against the Family Firm

Perhaps the neatest summary of the role of the family firm in a nation's economic development is that provided by Kindleberger, published nearly two decades ago in his *Economic Growth in France and Britain, 1851–1950*. Drawing on the pioneering work of David Landes, John Sawyer and Jesse Pitts, the French family firm, Kindleberger comments:

is said to have sinned against economic efficiency, and hence against growth, by limiting expansion—failing both to extend into new markets when finance was available from internal funds and to seek outside funds when these were required for expansion. Mergers were shunned so as not to get involved with 'others.' Public sale of stock was avoided. When expansion was possible through inside funds, it frequently took the form of purchase of discrete units of limited size, with their markets, to provide an outlet for the energies of other scions of the family; or there would be vertical integration but without the cost accounting that might enable effective control of the various units. Recruiting was undertaken from within the family, except for faithful retainers who assisted the firm against the revolutionary working force.[54]

This general thesis was not without its critics. Alexander Gerschenkron was perhaps the most penetrating, and one cannot but agree with him that to accept its validity one is forced "to overlook vast and significant fields of French entrepreneurial endeavour, such as railroads, mines, iron and steel industry, automobile production, banks and department stores."[55] Taking a comparative view, Habakkuk argued that the family firm in Britain was in fact not only compatible with rapid economic progress but its main agent.[56] The importance of this argument warrants further investigation over a longer time span.

The foremost difficulty encountered in such an examination is that of accurate generalization. Is the typical family firm in textiles during the Industrial Revolution, for example, to be found among those founded by M'Connel and Kennedy, Robert Peel, Jedidiah Strutt, Benjamin Gott and John Marshall, all of whom were thrusting, highly successful and innovative, or among the Needhams of Litton, the Austins of Wotton-under-Edge, John Cartwright of Retford or William Lupton of Leeds, all of whose concerns suffered from serious entrepreneurial failings coupled with gross management?[57] Later, in the mid-nineteenth century, very different conclusions might be drawn concerning the role of the family firm in, for example, the iron industry if these findings were to be based on a collection of firms that included Joshua Walker & Co., John Darwin, Lloyd, Foster & Co. and the Crawshays of Cyfarthfa, all of whose businesses were either wound up or suffered significant decline,[58] or based upon such infinitely more successful firms as those owned and controlled by the Guests of Dowlais, J. P. Budd of Ynyscedwyn, the Dixons of Calder and Govan and the Wrights of Butterley.[59] It is unnecessary to labor this point. It does, however, illustrate the dangers involved in "arguing by example" and raises the crucial question of whether an enterprise whose existence is essentially confined to the tenure of the founding proprietor is in any real sense a *family* firm.

2. The Family Firm and the British Economy since 1870: The Third Generation Argument

Nevertheless, there can be little doubt that the family firm was the vehicle whereby the Industrial Revolution was accomplished. To that extent Habakkuk's belief that the British family firm has been an important engine of economic progress is incontrovertible. The issue that deserves further discussion and, for its resolution, much more intensive research[60] is whether the persistence of the family firm had some causal connection with the apparent loss of economic vitality and retardation in economic growth during the closing decades of the nineteenth century.[61] The verdict of David Landes will be familiar:

> In many [family] firms, the grandfather who started the business and built it by unremitting application and by thrift bordering on miserliness had long since died; the father who took over a solid enterprise and, starting with larger ambitions, raised it to undreamed-of heights, had passed on the reins; now it was the turn of the third generation, the children of affluence, tired of the tedium of trade and flushed with the bucolic aspirations of the country gentlemen. . . Many of them retired and forced the conversion of their firms into joint-stock companies. Others stayed on and went through the motions of entrepreneurship between the long weekends; they worked at play and played at work. . . . Nor were corporate enterprises significantly better. For one thing, family considerations often determined the selection of managing personnel.[62]

In discussing this resounding passage elsewhere,[63] I was concerned to draw attention to what I believed were the weaknesses of Landes' condemnation of British entrepreneurship. My argument on that occasion need not be repeated, but one fundamental issue raised by Landes is highly germane to the subject of this conference. It is whether the typical British family firm did, in fact, exhibit the cycle depicted by Landes: an energetic, aggressive and dedicated founder, followed by a son who expanded the thriving business he had inherited and who in turn was succeeded by the founder's grandchildren, the "children of affluence," who let the business decline. It is highly improbable.

The fact *seems* to be that very few family firms survived long enough to permit a member of the third generation to wreck such havoc upon a hitherto successful enterprise. True, there are examples; the best known being the Marshalls of Leeds, a firm which had been the world's leading concern in flax-spinning in the opening decades of the nineteenth century but which, by the 1880s, had passed into receivership, after the founder's sons had neglected the business and their own sons in turn despised it.[64] Other cases undoubtedly exist—one such was the business established by Benjamin Gott[65]—but firms conforming to the Landes model are suspiciously hard to find. Furthermore, there are notable exceptions to what has been called the "Buddenbrook syndrome." The Pilkington family in glass, the Yarrows in shipbuilding, the Stewarts in steel, the Coats in textiles, are examples of families who continued successfully to play a major role in their firms beyond the third generation.[66]

But these too are almost certainly exceptional. Much more numerous and representative are, I suspect, firms in which the founders' *sons*, not grandsons, choose not to follow in their father's footsteps. Witness a Hawick minister castigating the local tweed-makers in 1909:

> We [have] had many men chiefly in the founders of our business-men not afraid of very hard work, keeping pleasure in its place, sticking fast to their posts. In the *second generation*, however, we have often seen a different spirit; sometimes contempt for trades, an aping of the fine gentleman, an aspiring to be what they were not . . . love of ease, self indulgence and lack of grit and backbone. They must work in the spirit of their fathers . . . study the technique of their business, bend their energies and talents in one direction.[67]

Such examples are legion, as are cases in which the very founders of highly successful firms display waning entrepreneurial energies as soon as sufficient wealth has been amassed to permit them to participate in local or national politics, to assume largely ceremonial public duties, to purchase and enjoy a country estate, and to indulge in manifold sporting activities: the turf, hunting, shooting and fishing, and yachting were all pursuits of the gentleman.[68]

3. Age and Ownership Statistics

However inconclusive, discussion of the third-generation argument does emphasize the desirability of discovering just how many firms remained under the control of the same family for three generations and what proportion of the total number of firms in any industrial, commercial or service sector they constituted. Indeed, just how many firms—even in the early nineteenth century—would qualify as "family companies" under Channon's definition if it were to be applied to periods earlier than that (1950–1970) with which he was concerned?

The partnership in the early period of British industrialization was an infinitely adaptable organizational form. Partnerships appear to have been created, supplemented, remodelled and frequently terminated when conditions called for change. Partnership agreements rarely lasted their full term, which was in any case, frequently only about seven years in duration. Thus, a partnership created in 1825 to establish an iron foundry called, say, Smith, Campbell & Co., with John Smith as the senior partner, might within a decade or so (and after several intermediate transformations) be owned and controlled by the nephew of the original junior partner, Bruce Campbell, and his cousin Forbes McRae, in company with two new men who had earlier been trusted employees in the casting shop and the cash room. Furthermore, by 1845 the business could well have integrated backwards and come to own two blast furnaces. The reason for providing this hypothetical example is to ask whether Campbell, McRae & Co., iron masters, is the same firm as Smith, Campbell & Co., foundrymen? Or has the changing nature of the firm's principal activities and the different composition of the firm's ownership and management created an entirely new enterprise? Problems such as this are often encountered in British business history and bedevil quantitative analysis.

Family Business in Britain   *191*

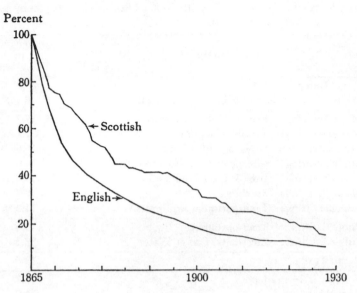

FIG. 1   Percentage Survival of English and Scottish Companies Incorporated between 1956 and 1865.
Source: Payne, *The Early Scottish Limited Companies*, p. 38.

The fact is that we do not possess an age pyramid for nineteenth
century firms. All that we know is that the mortality rate of firms
was remarkably high[69] and one cannot help suspecting that only
a very small proportion of firms created and continued by deed of
partnership survived more than thirty years, a period insufficiently
long to sustain more than two generations of a founding family. But
what of the incorporated company: the company registered with
limited liability under the Joint Stock Act of 1856? Could it be that
the benefits bestowed by such legislation, particularly the advantage
that an incorporated company need not be wound up following the
death of a partner, resulted in a more lengthy life span and thus
facilitated the establishment and continuance of family dynasties?
An analysis of the early Scottish joint-stock companies points to a
positive answer to this question.[70] Although the *average* length of life
of the first three thousand companies registered under the Act of 1856
was only sixteen years, the use of the mean conceals a wide distribution. Despite the high infant mortality of Scottish companies, about

TABLE 5   Average Length of Life of Dissolved Scottish Companies by Selected
Industrial Classification.

Brief description	Average length of life in years
Coal Mining	20.9
Overseas Companies in Mining & Quarrying	6.4
Manufacturing: Food, Drink & Tobacco	17.2
Manufacturing: Textiles, Clothing & Footwear	21.1
Manufacturing: Paper & Allied Products	16.6
Manufacturing: Chemicals & Allied Products	10.0
Manufacturing: Iron & Steel Products	14.8
Manufacturing: Machinery	12.7
Manufacturing: Transportation Equipment	11.9
Public Utilities: Transportation	13.4
Public Utilities: Electricity, Gas & Water	36.1
Retail Trade	13.6
Finance & Insurance	17.7
Real Estate	24.9
Agricultural, Forestry & Fishing	13.6
All Dissolved Companies	16.4

Source: Payne, *The Early Scottish Limited Companies*, p. 101.

25 per cent of those formed between 1856 and 1865 were still in existence on the eve of the First World War and about 12.5 per cent
on the eve of the Second World War. For London-registered companies the figures are approximately 13 per cent and 8 per cent,
respectively[71] (see Fig. 1). Although a disproportionate number of
the long lived companies were public utility companies, a number
of important firms in manufacturing and the service industries did
enjoy a relatively long life (see Table 5) and it is almost certain that
among them were a few family firms. What the information contained in the company files at West Register House, Edinburgh,
did not reveal was just how many could accurately be so described.
I would *guess* that of those companies surviving forty years or more,
family firms constituted less than one per cent of the total. It is to be
hoped that the data being collected by the Company Archives
Survey being conducted by the Business Archives Council in London
may provide more information on this subject.

TABLE 6   Number of Generations in which Founding or Investing Families
Hold Top Offices in Steel Firms.

Number of generations of family control	Number of cases	Percentage of cases
No family managing and owning	14	18
One generation	9	11
Two generations	38	47
Three generations	12	15
Four or more generations	7	9
Total	80	100

Source: Erickson, *British Industrialists*, p. 53.

Meanwhile, we still have Professor Charlotte Erickson's very interesting data on the steel industry. In her pioneering study in the
1950s (i.e. before the nationalization of the industry) she found that
it was possible to trace the duration of family control in eighty
firms. "The founding families were still represented at Butterley,
John Summers, Stewart and Lloyds, United Steel, Dorman Long,
and Partridge, Jones." She also discovered that "frequently the
family which [continued] into the third and fourth generation is
not that of the founder of founders of the firms but a family of later
investors" and that a number of "what might be called 'bureaucratic
dynasties' [had] been established in a number of public companies
in the industry. The father, having worked his way up within the
firm, was able to ease his son's career within the same firm . . . .
Thus the establishment of a family dynasty in the steel industry was
not always the result of founding or investing in the firm. Two
generations of the same family, whose role was primarily managerial
rather than proprietary, have controlled some companies and, in
part, account for the continued presence of 'family careers' in the
industry." Table 6 shows that in thirty-eight of Professor Erickson's
cases, a founding or investing family lost or gave up control after
two generations. "The mean duration of family influence was 66.4
±40 years."[72]

It will be appreciated that Professor Erickson was concerned with
an industry notorious for its family control.[73] It would therefore be
unwise and illegitimate to extend her findings to other sectors of the
British economy.[74] Nevertheless, Erickson's work does suggest the
question that if family influence in steel lasted but two generations,

TABLE 7   Average Ages (in years) of Small Firms in 1963.

	Oldest Quartile	Median	Youngest Quartile
Manufacturing	51	22	10
Construction	93	69	44
Wholesale Trades	66	29	10
Motor Trades	35	19	9
Retail Trades	47	19	7

Source: Merrett Cyriax Associates, *Dynamics of Small Firms*, Research Report for the Bolton Committee, No. 12, p. 12; amended by the Bolton Committee, whose figures are cited (*Report*, p. 7).

how much shorter must have been the domination of the family in large public companies in other spheres of activity? At the other end of the age spectrum, the period of family ownership and control, which was probably relatively short during early industrialization, *may* have lengthened during the course of the twentieth century. It is conceivable that the adoption of corporate status coupled with a rate of growth slow enough to permit continued management by members of the founding family, has enhanced the prospects for survival of individual small family firms. Certainly, the information collected for the Bolton Committee indicates this possibility. The admittedly fragile data are given in Tables 2 and 7. These show that half of those small firms that are wholly owned by one family are in the hands of the second or third generation. In manufacturing industries, half of small firms in 1963 were over 22 years old; in non-manufacturing the median ages ranged from 69 years in construction to 19 in motor trades. The authors of the Bolton Report do note, however, that "the age of a company may be misleading in this context since it may change hands after its foundation."[75]

Certainly, the average ages given in Table 7 could well have been appreciably lower had the firms founded between 1963 and 1970 been included and those that had ceased to operate during these seven years been omitted. What is disappointing is that we have no similar statistics for an earlier period with which to compare these figures. However, we do have a detailed study by Jonathan Boswell, again of *small* firms, which is somewhat more detailed than that of the research associates reporting to the Bolton Committee. Boswell's "Companies House Study"[76] found, *inter alia*, that (i)

TABLE 8   The Performance of Independent Firms: Medians by Age of Firm, 1967 and 1968 (Figures in Percentages).

Measures of performance	Year	Firms Founded				
		Pre-1870	1870–99	1900–18	1914–44	Post-1945
Asset Growth	1967	1.7	2.4	3.9	4.3	8.4
	1968	0.8	1.2	3.7	5.9	15.3
Sales Growth	1968	3.1	10.1	3.5	7.3	8.0
Gross Profitability	1967	13.2	18.4	15.4	20.1	21.8
	1968	11.8	17.2	15.9	19.8	25.5
Net Profitability	1967	7.4	9.5	7.9	15.7	15.2
	1968	6.9	8.7	10.8	13.1	15.5

Source: Boswell, *Small Firms*, p. 245.

founder-run firms were above average in nearly every measure of performance; (ii) the firms run by late inheritors (i.e. third and subsequent generations) performed worst; (iii) in terms of age, the younger firms appeared to perform better in every way (see Table 8).

Taken in conjunction with the earlier discussion, these scattered data suggest that the founders of firms, whether they are partnerships, private joint-stock companies or public companies, are perhaps generally more thrusting and efficient than their successors in managing their businesses. This is not a startling conclusion but it may be vital in evaluating the role of family firms in promoting economic growth, for if it proves to be valid for all time periods, then it indicates that what is of the greatest significance for the promotion of growth is not so much the *form* of company structure as the ability of the founder,[77] the quality of the management, the number of firms coming into existence in any time period and the nature of their activities. Since nearly all founders of firms inevitably start on a relatively small scale, what is important for economic growth is that a legal and financial environment favorable for the *birth* of firms be encouraged. This is because small firms—which almost by definition are *initially* family firms—"provide the means of entry into business for new entrepreneurial talent and the seedbed from which new large companies will grow to challenge and stimulate the established leaders of industry."[78]

IV. Conclusions

Any conclusions that may be drawn from this brief, exploratory survey must be regarded as highly tentative. Greater confidence can only come with the collection and analysis of more data, but even this will fail to clarify the role of the family firm in the development of the British economy unless the "family firm" is carefully defined. If nothing else emerges from this study it will at least be apparent that the family firm today is, except in the small size range, a very different creature from the family firm in the decades preceding the First World War.

Nevertheless, I would agree with Professor Habakkuk that the family firm in Britain has been, and has the potential to continue to be (albeit on a somewhat lesser scale), an engine of economic growth, but paradoxically this is largely because the overwhelming majority of individual family firms in Britain did not and do not enjoy a particularly great longevity. Their importance was and is to serve as a vehicle for the exercise of entrepreneurial energies of the founder and frequently his sons. After this there would on balance appear to have been a marked diminution of drive and business ability. Now this does not seem to have had any markedly deleterious effect in the nineteenth century since very few firms passed into the hands of the third and subsequent generations. Only with the coming of the joint-stock company with limited liability did the life span of firms tend to increase sufficiently to make this possible on an appreciable scale, but since this change in the legal form of the company coincided with the steady advance of professional management recruited from outside the existing firm, its harmful effect was minimized.

It is true that in several branches of activity—steel, coal, pottery, carpets, boots and shoes, cocoa, brewing, sugar and certain types of engineering—"leadership by inheritance" has been discerned,[79] but even here it was by no means as prevalent and stultifying as once was believed.[80] I would argue that if there was any causal connection between the family firm and a loss of economic vitality, it occurred not in the closing decades of the nineteenth century but in the inter-war years when a number of holding companies were still sufficiently familial in nature, being essentially federations of family firms, to be reluctant to adopt a centralized structure and to create a managerial staff that would have permitted them more easily to overcome the diseconomies of size.[81] Indeed, even after 1945 those companies which contained significant elements of family control have been less willing to diversify and more reluctant to adopt a multidivisional organization structure.[82] Put very crudely, the *large* public company which retains elements of family control may retard economic growth; whereas, on balance, the *small* family business positively promotes economic growth.

Lastly, bearing in mind the exceptions to the idea that family management constituted a brake on economic development, it is necessary to emphasize the strong possibility, put forward by Hannah, that in Britain "there is as much variation, if not more, within the two groups of firms—those still controlled by family and those run by salaried managers—as there is between them."[83]

NOTES

1. These issues have been discussed by the author elsewhere. See Payne, *British Entrepreneurship in the Nineteenth Century* (London: Macmillan, 1974), pp. 17–23, and "Industrial Entrepreneurship and Management—Britain, c. 1760–1770," in P. Mathias and M. M. Postan (eds.), *The Cambridge Economic History of Europe*, Vol. VII, *The Industrial Economies: Capital, Labour and Enterprise* (Cambridge: Cambridge University Press, 1978), Part I, pp. 191–93.

2. Sir John Clapham, *An Economic History of Modern Britain* (Cambridge: Cambridge University Press, 1951), Vol. III, p. 203.

3. Clapham, *op. cit.*, Vol. II, pp. 138–40; J.B. Jeffreys, *Business Organization in Great Britain, 1856–1914* (Ph. D. Thesis, University of London, 1938, published in its original form by Arno Press, New York, 1977), pp. 116, 118, 403; P. L. Payne, *The Early Scottish Limited Companies, 1856–1895* (Edinburgh: Scottish Academic Press, 1980), p. 56; P. L. Cottrell, *Industrial Finance, 1830–1914* (London: Methuen, 1980), pp. 104–5.

4. Jeffreys, *op. cit.*, p. 117; D. A. Farnie, *The English Cotton Industry and the World Market, 1815–1896* (Oxford: Clarendon Press, 1979), pp. 244–76.

198   *P. L. Payne*

5. Cottrell, *op. cit.*, p. 164.
6. P. L. Payne, "The Emergence of the Large-Scale Company in Great Britain," *Economic History Review*, 2nd series, XX (1967), Section 2; H. W. Macrosty, "Business Aspects of British Trusts," *Economic Journal*, XII (1902), p. 354; Jeffreys, *op. cit.*, p. 451.
7. It was reported by the Registrar of Joint Stock Companies in 1895, that of the 1,328 companies limited by shares registered in London during the first six months of 1890, "415 [were] more or less of a private character." These were listed and analyzed. It is apparent that of the "private or family companies" (which, incidentally included Bradbury, Wilkinson's, William Hollins, Abram Lyle, Lever Brothers and Reeves & Sons), the bulk of the shares in over a third of them was held by three shareholders or less and well over 80 per cent of the companies had fewer than 15 members. *Report of the Departmental Committee of the Board of Trade on the Company Acts*, C. 7779 (1895), pp. 54–63. Ten years later, in 1906, the Company Law Amendment Committee found that "a *large and increasing proportion* of the companies [formed] under the [Companies] Acts are classed . . . as private companies [in which] the number of members generally does not exceed twenty, and very commonly is not above seven." Of the "well-known concerns . . . carried on as private companies" were listed Harland & Wolff, Huntley & Palmers, Crosse & Blackwell and J. & J. Colman. In the early years of the twentieth century well over 80 per cent of all companies registered were private. *Report of the Company Law Amendment Committee*, Cd. 3052 (1906), pp. 2–3, 17. Emphasis supplied.
8. Leslie Hannah, "Visible and Invisible Hands in Great Britain," in A. D. Chandler and H. Daems (eds.), *Managerial Hierarchies* (Cambridge, Mass: Harvard University Press, 1980), p. 53.
9. Ibid., p. 55. For shipbuilding, see A. Slaven, "Growth and Stagnation in British/Scottish Shipbuilding, 1913–1977," in Jan Kuuse and A. Slaven (eds.), *Scottish and Scandinavian Shipbuilding Seminar: Development Problems in Historical Perspective* (Glasgow, 1980), pp. 19–20.
10. P. Sargant Florence, *Ownership, Control and Success of Large Companies* (London: Sweet & Maxwell, 1961).
11. A. B. Levy, *Private Corporations and Their Control*, 2 vols. (London, 1950), I, pp. 224–29, gives the number of British public companies in 1938 as 14,355 (paid-up capital £4,097m); the private companies numbered 135,221 (paid-up capital £1,894m).

12. Just how much it was diminishing depends partly on the importance attached to the respective *roles* of the large and small firm in the economy.

13. Perhaps the most important recent British inquiry has been that conducted by the Bolton Committee. Its own Report and the associated research reports constitute a remarkably rich quarry of detailed information on the small firm in Britain. See the *Report of the Committee of Inquiry on Small Firms* [*The Bolton Report*]. Cmd. 4811 (London: HMSO, 1971). No less than eighteen research reports were published simultaneously. See also Johnathan Boswell, *The Rise and Decline of Small Firms* (London: Allen & Unwin, 1973). A number of interesting case studies are provided by Philip Clarke, *Small Businesses: How They Survive and Succeed* (Newton Abbot: David & Charles, 1972).

14. The definition of small firms adopted by the Bolton Inquiry is carefully set down in Chapter 1 of the Report, p. 3. For "manufacturing" the statistical definition was that the small firm possessed 200 employees or less and for "retailing," a turnover of £50,000 per annum or less. These definitions covered 94 per cent and 96 per cent of all firms in the respective industries.

15. *Bolton Report*, p. 6.

16. See the recent very interesting article by R. Lloyd-Jones and A. A. Le Roux, "Marshall and the Birth and Death of Firms: The Growth and Size Distribution of Firms in the Early Nineteenth-Century Cotton Industry," *Business History*, XXIV (1982), pp. 141–55.

17. P. S. Florence, *Ownership, Control and Success*, pp. 71–73, Appendix B, pp. 222–65. Although it is legitimate to argue with Florence's definitions and his tests of concentrated ownership, the case he makes is convincing. Only for those companies which were wholly or mainly owned by other (mainly overseas) companies, themselves manager-controlled (such as the British Match Corporation and F.W. Woolworth) would one seriously dispute his figures. See the discussion by M. M. Postan, *An Economic History of Western Europe, 1945–1964* (London: Methuen, 1967), p. 252.

18. Derek F. Channon, *The Strategy and Structure of British Enterprise* (London: Macmillan, 1971), p. 161; cf. P. S. Florence, *op. cit.*, pp. 70–73, 136, and Hannah, *op. cit.*, p. 53.

19. Channon, *op. cit.*, p. 75. Emphasis supplied; Steve Nyman and A. Silberston, "The Ownership and Control of Industry," *Oxford Economic Papers*, N. S., Vol. XXX (1978), pp. 84–5.

20. William Mennell, *Takeover: The Growth of Monopoly in Britain, 1951–1961* (London, 1962), pp. 173ff.

21. A. J. Merrett & M. E. Lehr, *The Private Company Today* (London: Gower Press, 1971), pp. 15, 67–71. Since 1970, a number of these large private companies have gone public. Sainsburys did so in 1973, although in 1981, 45 per cent of the ordinary shares were still owned or controlled by the directors and their families; Ferrantis is now also a public company, a large proportion of its voting stock being held by the National Enterprise Board; the shipbuilding activities of Lithgows was taken into public ownership under the Aircraft and Shipbuilding Act of 1977.

22. Leslie Hannah, *The Rise of the Corporate Economy* (London: Methuen, 1976); S. J. Prais, *The Evolution of Giant Firms in Britain* (Cambridge: C. U. P., 1976).

23. See, for example, Prais, *op. cit.*, p. 5.

24. See the prediction made by G. D. Newbould & A. S. Jackson, *The Receding Ideal* (Liverpool: Guthstead, 1972). On Gibrat's Law, see P. E. Hart, *Studies in Profit, Business Saving and Investment in the United Kingdom, 1920–1962* (London: Allen & Unwin, 1965), pp. 150–51; L. Hannah & J. A. Kay, *Concentration in Modern Industry* (London: Macmillan, 1977), pp. 98–101; S. J. Prais, *op. cit.*, pp. 27–8; Payne, *The Early Scottish Limited Companies*, pp. 102–4.

25. Some issues raised in this paragraph are further considered below, pp. 184–87.

26. It is interesting to note that in one of the most important recent studies of company law, the author observes that for business concerns the "normal rule is to expand or die." Tom Hadden, *Company Law and Capitalism* (London: Weidenfeld & Nicolson, 1972), p. 98.

27. Channon, *op. cit.*, p. 77, indicates that "as the product-market scope of a company increases [i.e. as a company chooses to grow by diversification], it becomes more difficult for a family to maintain managerial control by the family." Professor Channon's most recent work, *The Service Industries: Strategy, Structure and Financial Performance* (London: Macmillan, 1977) and his continuing researches lerd support to this view. Derek F. Channon in a personal communication to the author, November, 1982.

28. See S. Pollard, *The Genesis of Modern Management* (London: Arnold, 1965), pp. 150–51; S. D. Chapman, "The Peels in the English Cotton Industry," *Business History*, XI (July 1969); J. C. Logan, "The Dumbarton Glass Works Company: A Study in Entrepreneurship," *Business History*, XIV (January 1972), pp. 71–81.

29. Quoted by H. J. Habakkuk, "Industrial Organization since the Industrial Revolution," *The Fifteenth Fawley Foundation Lecture* in the University of Southampton, 1968, p. 8.

30. A. Slaven, "Management and Shipbuilding, 1890–1938: Structure and Strategy in the Shipbuilding Firm on the Clyde," in A. Slaven and D. H. Aldcroft (eds.), *Business, Banking and Urban History* (Edinburgh: Donald, 1982), pp. 43–5.

31. *Ibid.*, p. 44. Professor Slaven refers the reader to the paper by T. Burns and G. Stalker, "Mechanistic and Organistic Systems of Management," in *Management of Innovation* (1961), pp. 110–25.

32. Payne, in Mathias and Postan, *op. cit.*, p. 206.

33. Hannah, *op. cit.*, pp. 53, 55; and see the same author's *The Rise of the Corporate Economy*, pp. 96–99. See also Payne, "The Emergence of the Large-Scale Company," pp. 528–29, 533–35.

34. Payne, "The Emergence of the Large-Scale Company," p. 530.

35. Hannah, "Visible and Invisible Hands," p. 52.

36. Florence, *Ownership Control and Success*, p. 192.

37. S. J. Prais, *The Evolution of Giant Firms in Britain* and L. Hannah, *The Rise of the Corporate Economy.*

38. Channon, *op. cit.*, p. 75.

39. R. A. Church, *Kenricks in Hardware. A Family Business. 1791–1966* (Newton Abbot: David & Charles, 1969).

40. *Ibid.*, p. 217, see also p. 213.

41. The words used in the Report by Peat, Marwick, Mitchell & Co. on Kenricks, 1937, quoted Church, *op. cit.*, p. 212.

42. Channon, *op. cit.*, pp. 75–76. Channon's detailed investigation covered the period 1950–1970.

43. *Ibid.*, p. 141; for case studies, see P. L. Payne, *Rubber and Railways in the Nineteenth Century* (Liverpool: Liverpool University Press, 1961), pp. 48–52, and see Stanley Chapman, "Strategy and Structure at Boots the Chemists," in L. Hannah (ed.), *Management Strategy and Business Development* (London: Macmillan, 1976), pp. 95–107.

44. Channon, *op. cit.*, p. 77.

45. P. S. Florence, "Problems of Rationalization" in a discussion reported in the *Economic Journal*, Vol. XL (1930), p. 365, quoted by Hannah, *The Rise of the Corporate Economy*, p. 148.

46. Once again, the words of the Report by Peat, Marwick, Mitchell & Co. on Kenricks, have been adopted. Church, *op. cit.*, p. 211.

47. Channon, *op. cit.*, p. 123; T. C. Barker, *The Glassmakers. Pilkington: the Rise of an International Company, 1826–1976* (London: Weidenfeld and Nicolson, 1977), pp. 406–25. See also T. C. Barker, "A Family

Firm becomes a Public Company: Changes at Pilkington Brothers Limited in the Interwar Years," in L. Hannah (ed.), *Management Strategy and Business Development* (London: Macmillan, 1976), pp. 85–94, and P. L. Cook, *Effects of Mergers* (London: Allen & Unwin, 1958), pp. 242–43.

48. Channon, *op. cit.*, pp. 96–7; Graham Turner, *Business in Britain* (London: Eyre & Spottiswood, 1969), pp. 222, 226–27.

49. Turner, *op. cit.*, pp. 231, 339–41. Professor Edith Penrose has made the point that "family firms" tend to be "content with a comfortable profit." E. T. Penrose, *The Theory of the Growth of the Firm* (Oxford: Blackwell, 1959), p. 34.

50. For Marks & Spencer, see Goronwy Rees, *St. Michael. A History of Marks & Spencer* (London: Weidenfeld & Nicolson, 1969), particularly, pp. 70–78, and Stephen Aris, *The Jews in Business* (London: Johnathan Cape, 1970), pp. 137–54. Until the death of Lord Marks in 1964, only a few of Marks & Spencer's hundreds of thousands of shareholders had the right to vote at the company's meetings: all the voting shares were held by members of the founding family and the Prudential Assurance Co.

51. Turner, *op. cit.*, p. 230.

52. In 1970 even Rothschilds became a private limited company, some years after bringing in much outside talent to the previous private partnership. See Aris, *op. cit.*, pp. 60–63.

53. For these service industries, see D. F. Channon, "Corporate Evolution in the Service Industries," in L. Hannah (ed.), *op. cit.*, pp. 213–34. For a more detailed study of those whose rapid rise was essentially based on the exploitation of rising property values and/or the real as opposed to the balance sheet values of properties owned by businesses engaged in brewing, hotels or retailing, see Oliver Marriott, *The Property Boom* (London: Hamish Hamilton, 1967).

54. Charles P. Kindleberger, *Economic Growth in France and Britain, 1851–1950* (London: Oxford University Press, 1964), p. 115.

55. A. Gerschenkron, "Social Attitudes, Entrepreneurship and Economic Development," *Explorations in Entrepreneurial History*, VI (October 1953), p. 10.

56. H. J. Habakkuk, "The Historical Experience on the Basic Conditions of Economic Progress," in L. H. Dupriez (ed.), *Economic Progress* (Louvain: Institut de Recherches Economiques et Sociales, 1955), p. 159.

57. Payne, *British Entrepreneurship*, pp. 33–34, where references may be found.

58. *Ibid.*, pp. 37–38.

59. For the Guests and J. P. Budd, see T. Boyns, Dennis Thomas and Colin Baber, "The Iron, Steel and Tinplate Industries, 1750–1914," in A. H. John and G. Williams (eds.), *Industrial Glamorgan* (Cardiff, 1980), pp. 112–17; for the Dixons, see I. F. Gibson, "The Economic History of the Scottish Iron and Steel Industry, 1830–1880" (University of London, thesis for the degree of Ph. D., 1955), pp. 117 ff, 168–85; for the Wrights, see R. H. Mottram & C. Coote, *Through Five Generations: The History of the Butterley Company* (London: Faber, 1950), pp. 77–84.

60. It is hoped and expected that two extensive inquiries currently being conducted by the Business History Unit at London University under the direction of Professor Leslie Hannah and the Scottish Business History Project under the direction of Professor A. Slaven at Glasgow University, will produce data sufficient to permit more confident generalizations about the family firm.

61. Kindleberger, *op. cit.*, p. 114.

62. David Landes, "Technological Change and Development in Western Europe, 1750–1914," In H. J. Habakkuk and M. Postan (eds.) *Cambridge Economic History of Europe*, Vol. VI; *The Industrial Revolution and After* (Cambridge: C.U.P., 1965), pp. 563–64.

63. Payne, "Industrial Entrepreneurship," pp. 202–5.

64. W. G. Rimmer, *Marshalls of Leeds, Flax Spinners, 1788–1886* (Cambridge: C.U.P., 1960).

65. H. Heaton, "Benjamin Gott and the Industrial Revolution in Yorkshire," *Economic History Review*, III (1931–2), pp. 15–16.

66. For the Pilkingtons, see T. C. Barker, *op. cit.*, and the Stewarts, *Stewarts and Lloyds Limited, 1903–1953* (Privately printed for Stewarts and Lloyds, n.d. [c. 1954]), p. 7. Information on the Yarrow and Coats families were collected by the author during his tenure of the Colquhoun Lectureship in Business History at the University of Glasgow, 1959–69.

67. C. Gulvin, *The Tweedmakers: A History of the Scottish Fancy Woollen Industry, 1600–1914* (Newton Abbot: David & Charles, 1973), p. 150. Alfred Marshall also criticized the founder's "*sons who had been brought up to think life easy.*" A. Marshall, *Industry and Trade* (London: Macmillan, 1923), pp. 91–92. Emphasis supplied.

68. M. J. Weiner, *English Culture and the Decline of the Industrial Spirit,*
     1850–1980 (Cambridge: C.U.P., 1981) represents a recent examina-
     tion of this phenomenon; see also D. C. Coleman, "Gentlemen and
     Players," *Economic History Review*, 2nd series, XXVI (1973), pp.
     95–96.

69. Research into this subject is currently being conducted by M. S.
     Moss and J. R. Hume who are indexing and analyzing the Scottish
     sequestration (bankruptcy) processes for the period 1839 to 1913.
     I am indebted to them for permitting me to read their unpublished
     paper "Business Failure in Scotland, 1839–1913." The Merrett Cy-
     riax Report for the Bolton Committee found that the proportion of
     small firms existing in 1963 that had gone into liquidation, ceased
     to trade or been taken over by 1970 was very high, ranging from 19
     per cent in the motor trade to 32.5 per cent in wholesaling. Of the
     firms in "manufacturing and construction," 23.1 per cent ceased to
     exist. *Loc. cit.*, p. 18.

70. P. L. Payne, *The Early Scottish Limited Companies, 1856–1895.*

71. H. A. Shannon, "The First Five Thousand Companies and their
     Duration," *Economic History*, II (1931).

72. Charlotte Erickson, *British Industrialists: Steel and Hosiery, 1850–1950*
     (Cambridge: C.U.P., 1959), pp. 52–53.

73. See, for example, Duncan Burn, *The Economic History of Steel Making,*
     1867–1939 (Cambridge: C.U.P., 1940), pp. 296–305; J. H. Burnham
     and G. O. Hoskins, *Iron and Steel in Britain* (London: Allen & Unwin,
     1943), p. 248; J. E. Vaizey, *The History of British Steel* (London:
     Weidenfeld & Nicolson, 1974), p. 10.

74. In carpets, where until nearly the end of the nineteenth century most
     firms were owned and controlled either by one person or more often
     by a partnership, of 31 firms founded in Kidderminster and Stour-
     port, no less than 12 survived less than 11 years and an other ten had
     closed down within fifteen years; five still existed in 1970 but at least
     two of them had lost their original independence. See J. N. Bartlett,
     Carpeting The Millions: The Growth of Britain's Carpet Industry (Edin-
     burgh: John Donald, 1978), pp. 111, 157–58.

75. *Bolton Report*, p. 7.

76. Boswell's "Companies House Study" constitutes Appendix 4 of his
     study, *The Rise and Decline of Small Firms*, pp. 232–53; see also *Bolton*
     Report, p. 17.

77. It is, I believe, worth emphasizing that when Charles Wilson, in his
     defense of British entrepreneurship in late Victorian Britain, drew

attention to the vigor and ingenuity of "the Levers, the Boots, the Harrods, the Whiteleys and Lewises," he was referring to individual founders of what were to become famous firms irrespective of the precise legal nature of such firms. Charles Wilson, "Economy and Society in Late Victorian Britain," *Economic History Review*, 2nd series, XVIII (1965–66), p. 189. The Merrett Cyriax Report for the Bolton Committee found that "Management ability, as evidenced by new markets and products, is the main factor differentiating the fast and slow growers [among small firms], while the founder managed firms showed outstanding growth despite the total absence of formal qualifications and in many cases no direct prior experiences of the industry concerned." Merrett Cyriax Associates, *The Dynamics of Small Firms* (1971), p. 4.

78. Bolton Report, p. 84. Examples of small firms which have "started from nothing and grown to substantial size, even since World War II," are Kenwood, Letraset, Nu-Swift Industries and Racal Electronics. *Ibid.*, pp. 30–31.

79. P. S. Florence, *The Logic of British and American Industry*, pp. 295, 303–4, 320.

80. The only way in which it is possible even to begin to discover just how much influence "a member of the family" had on company policy is to examine the records of the company in question (cf. Nyman & Silberston, *op. cit.*, p. 78). The majority of the shares of Colvilles Ltd., for example, were held by trustees of the Colville family, yet from 1916 control was firmly in the hands of professional managers, and it was made plain that members of the third generation of the Colville family could not expect even to be considered for positions of responsibility within the firm until they had thoroughly learned the trade. See P. L. Payne, *Colvilles and the Scottish Steel Industry* (Oxford: Clarendon Press, 1979), p. 356 and *passim*. To speak, as Florence does (and his argument is cited approvingly by Kindleberger, *op. cit.*, p. 124) of the existence of "leadership by inheritance" in a number of major sectors is apt to be misleading. Were *all* the major units within such sectors similarly affected? Or was it only a small proportion? And, even so, did "amateur" family members on the board really have much influence, or were their views politely received and ignored by the salaried managers on the board? Furthermore, there is a growing body of evidence that in recent years possession of the family name may have eased the way to the boardroom but was insufficient in itself to secure election. The name has to be supported

by professional expertise (see, for example, Mennell, *Takeover*, pp. 137–40; T. C. Barker, "A Family Firm," p. 91; Aris, *The Jews*, pp. 62, 140–1). We need to know more about such matters but my guess would be that the importance of "leadership by inheritance" is declining and from the 1930's was perhaps never as significant as the mere presence of family names on the board would imply.

As for Florence's point (*Logic*, p. 304) that large share holdings in family businesses by distant members of the family—whose interests are often fiercely protected by trustees—are likely to result in a dividend policy prejudicial to the accumulation of reserves and the reinvestment of profits, the evidence is inconclusive. Sir John Craig, the managing director of Colvilles, begrudged paying a penny to the ordinary shareholders, overwhelmingly Colville trustees, during his tenure of office (Payne, *Colvilles*, p. 317), and William Lyons, chairman and managing director of SS Cars Ltd., later Jaguar Cars Ltd., made sure that the profit available for distribution remained low: "I never let them get above £300,000 a year. I thought that was quite enough . . . ." (*Sunday Times*, 29 August, 1982). It is arguable that managing directors in family firms (whether they were salaried managers or members of the family) are in a stronger position to resist appeals for generous dividends than the chairman of public companies.

81. The point made by Hannah, "Visible and Invisible Hands," p. 56.
82. Channon, *op. cit.*, pp. 75–76.
83. Hannah, "Visible and Invisible Hands," p. 55. For the similar findings of an American survey, see R. G. Donnelley, "The Family Business," *Harvard Business Review*, Vol. 42, No. 4 (July–August 1964), pp. 93–105.

[5]

FAMILY FIRMS AND MANAGERIAL CAPITALISM: THE CASE OF THE INTERNATIONAL MOTOR INDUSTRY

By ROY CHURCH

'Family firm' is an expression which is commonly employed yet rarely defined. It is a label which has been applied to various kinds of owner-managed firms ranging from personal enterprises, in which owner control is dominant and where the owner is also chief executive, to entrepreneurial organisations: typically, owner-controlled firms which are staffed by managers and where the owners are essentially *rentiers,* lacking either time or inclination to manage. Three characteristics determine the points of focus for discussions of the family firm, although they are not necessarily related: family generations, family ownership, and family management.[1] In the motor industry, which had barely emerged by the beginning of the twentieth century, yet the economics of which required sizeable production units, even in Europe by the early 1920s, there is little scope for discussion of the significance of inheritance in relation to business and managerial development. Among the major mass producers of motor cars with which we shall be concerned, survival of family ownership and management for a period longer than a single generation was exceptional; for this reason family ownership and management will be regarded merely as a special case of owner management, in which the effective locus of control can be identified with a group of proprietorial interests.

Much of the discussion of ownership and control, principally among economists and sociologists, has been bedevilled by disagreement on the criteria for classifying corporate control. For while majority shareholding confers ownership it is not clear how small a percentage of total votes held by an individual or a clearly defined group has been necessary in order to secure minority control, although this might fall short of actual effective control. A recent review of the literature on ownership and control concluded that only a case by case approach could reveal a perpetuation of control by an individual, group, or family which did not possess substantial share ownership.[2] The classification employed in this article, therefore, depends upon behavioural, as much as upon financial, criteria, for the simple dichotomy of owner-control or control by professional manager is both deceptively inadequate and unsatisfactory for the purpose of establishing both the form and the degree to which family influence has persisted among the world's producers of motor cars, and to assess the effects it has had upon performance.

The separation of ownership from control was accompanied by the development of forms of owner-managed firms which may be categorised as follows: those in which owner-managers worked with minimal

hierarchies, equivalent to the 'personal enterprises' defined by Sargant
Florence; those characterised by extensive hierarchies, defined by Sargant
Florence as entrepreneurial enterprises; and enterprises which were
managerially supervised, in which external directors continued to own a
controlling share of the stock and participated regularly in board and
committee meetings. This represents another variant of owner-management,
differing in the degree to which a contrast was to be found with the manager-
managed firms, in which managers exercised control over the selection of
board members – in accordance with the definitions adopted by Berle and
Means.[3] Managerial enterprises were typically large with diversified stock
ownership, in which full-time salaried managers took decisions at all levels
while the owners, possessing neither the time nor commitment to exercise
authority, concerned themselves more with dividends than with the
operation of their company.[4] As effective competition in national and
international markets required an increasing size of enterprise and greater
financial resources the traditional form of owner-managed enterprise was
gradually transformed, although the overall pattern, in which owner-
managers continued to play a role, persisted. Hitherto, in societies where
business relations depended upon trust and reciprocity and where
information and personal communications were critical to success in
business conducted before the era of large-scale joint-stock enterprise,[5] the
combination of ownership and management within a single institution over
several generations had so often enabled the family firm to provide a
continuous supply of managerial competence and capital. After the
industrial revolution the social, economic, and cultural environment of
Europe, but especially of the United States, provided a climate which
became less congenial to the family firm of the traditional type. By the First
World War the large firm possessing extensive managerial hierarchies was
becoming commonplace in the US, whereas in Europe personal and
entrepreneurial enterprises, owner-managed firms with minimal hierarchies,
were to retain their dominance at least until the second half of the twentieth
century.[6]

   The significance of the transformation from personal and entrepreneurial to managerial organisations depends, of course, upon perceived
discrepancies between the goals and behaviour of owner-managers and
those of the 'professional' managers. In a major comparative study of
British and American firms published in 1953[7] Sargant Florence listed the
defects commonly associated with business leadership in companies where
ownership and managerial control were either in the hands of an
entrepreneur who had grown with his own business or in which the
hereditary, dynastic, or aristocratic type of entrepreneur was in command
(the archetypal family firm). Sargant Florence reckoned that such business
leaders typically soon became resistant to large-scale innovation, that they
were averse to co-operation with other companies, and characteristically
that both types showed caution with respect to reinvestment. Furthermore,
the dynastic leader could be assumed to possess a lower profit maximising
drive than any other category of business leader. Later, Carter and

FAMILY FIRMS AND MANAGERIAL CAPITALISM 167

Williams stressed in particular the retarding effect upon growth of the fear within family firms of losing control through the infusion of external finance.[8] From the historian's standpoint, Kindleberger exhibited agnosticism regarding the restraining influence of family firms upon French industrial performance.[9] Having underlined the systematisation and professionalisation of capital management allied to the specialisation of other economic functions as distinguishing features of managerial capitalism, Alfred D. Chandler, Jr. has since stressed the inhibiting influences of personal and entrepreneurial enterprise which was slower to be replaced by managerial enterprise in the UK by some 50 years.[10]

Hannah has been specific in citing the history of the British motor industry between the wars as an example of the role of major owner-managed firms: 'It is difficult to resist the conclusion that in many companies the family vested interest inhibited change which could have been desirable'.[11] In the German context, Tilly remarked that entrepreneurial enterprise remained characteristic of large-scale industry, which 'may have been a severe hindrance to the development of concentrated and multi-divisional enterprise on the American model',[12] while Kocka minimises the difference in motivation between German owner-entrepreneurs and their salaried counterparts; he regards independent owner-managers as having been more concerned with non-economic matters, such as family consideration. For this reason he detects a more intense 'striving for expansion' among those unencumbered by ownership.[13] The overview of European industrial development by Landes implies a similar relationship between ownership and managerial policies.[14] By contrast, Laux, whose research concentrated upon the French motor industry before 1914, rejected the hypothesis that family firms seriously retarded progress in the business sector.[15] Most recently as a general proposition Payne contrasted the positive contribution to economic growth of *small* family business with that of the large public company retaining elements of family control which, based on a review of the British experience since 1918, he concluded, 'may retard economic growth'.[16]

Most of the observations we have referred to are thus consistent with the notion that by comparison with managerial enterprises, the ceiling on performance of family and owner-managed firms, particularly in the corporate sector, has been inferior. In examining the significance of owner-management in the mass production motor car industry we shall identify the chronology of and reasons for its decline, and consider the history and performance of the European and American survivors which, to a greater or lesser degree, retained some of the characteristics of owner-management -- even of the family firm -- until the second half of the twentieth century.

1

Resembling the pioneering phase of motor production in Europe, family firms were among the first to enter upon the manufacture of luxury motor cars for an upper class clientele. A recent history of the automotive revolution in Detroit describes how, in search of profits to stem their increasingly precarious social and political power, the old families of the Midwest had plunged headlong into the new industry, providing initial finance and a tradition of business enterprise. In 1905 old family companies produced more than half the national vehicle output, a share which by 1910 had fallen to only three per cent, the family firms having sold out to the manufacturers of cars based on interchangeable parts, a consequence of the introduction of mass production methods. At this point many of the old families chose to dispose of their investments in vehicle production completely, rather than change their image and incur greater risks by making lower priced cars, but more importantly, preferring to withdraw from the trade completely rather than lose control of their family firms.[17] Henceforth, successful automobile manufacture demanded mass production and distribution; that, in turn, meant bringing in technical experts, professional managers and additional capital – all of which undermined the traditional prerogatives of the old family stockholders. Even among the early established pioneering firms financial dependence upon financiers doomed the founding engineer-entrepreneurs to progressively diminishing control.[18]

Thus, even before the First World War the American automobile industry had passed beyond the phase when relatively small family firms and owner-managements were characteristic. By the late 1920s even the newcomer owner-managed firms founded by the first generation automotive entrepreneurs proved incapable of challenging the 'big three', two of whom were widely regarded as typical of the new managerial organisations, General Motors and the Chrysler Corporation. The Chrysler Corporation was formed in 1924 from the bankrupt Maxwell Motor Car Co. whose history began in 1903. Owned by a succession of financial institutions, the Chrysler Corporation was none the less managed by Walter Chrysler from its foundation in 1908 until his retirement in 1935. Under his command Chrysler acquired the Dodge Motor Co. in 1927 and established a position among the 'big three' shortly after.[19]

Formed in 1908, the General Motors Corporation is often regarded as the corporate apotheosis of bureaucratic enterprise which, socially neutral and anonymous, came to epitomise the antithesis of the typical family, owner-managed firm. Yet, from the Du Pont reorganisation of GM after 1920 until the US government required GM's owners, the Du Pont Co., to relinquish ownership in the late 1950s, the affairs of GM were closely supervised by the Du Pont family. The Du Pont Co. was in turn controlled by the Christiana Securities Co. which was owned by the Du Pont family, some of whom were active members of the important supervisory committees of the board, the compensation and finance committees. This was the mechanism by which the transformation of GM, although administered through relatively extensive managerial hierarchies, was achieved.[20] Such a pattern in which external directors continued to possess a controlling share in the company, regularly participated in board and committee meetings, and exercised managerial supervision was the GM

FAMILY FIRMS AND MANAGERIAL CAPITALISM 169

model which, though a special case in the precise structure and organisational detail of the form it took, none the less became more common as the size and financial demands of automobile enterprise rendered family succession increasingly problematical.

Ford carried, and carries still, the banner of family enterprise. That company's chequered history between and since the two world wars may be regarded as a direct consequence of the inhibiting influence of family ownership-control and management,[21] although by contrast General Motors' successful reorganisation and performance owed much to the influence and involvement of the Du Pont family.[22] After the withdrawal of Du Pont from General Motors in the late 1950s, Ford demonstrated the ability of a family firm to reach very large size, to be managed successfully, and to survive continuing competition from its most powerful American rival. Ford continued as an owner-managed firm with extensive managerial hierarchies, in which a third-generation Ford inherited control and leadership in the classic mould of family business. It was he who secured a transfusion of bureaucratic expertise from General Motors, thereby harnessing managerial skills as an instrument of radical modernisation of the Ford Motor Co., lifting it for a period after the Second World War from third to second place among the world's largest motor manufacturers.[23]

In Europe, despite the early advantage through the initial design and construction of cars, the existence of a less favourable middle-income market potential combined with a much slower advance of production methods and commercial development provided a more congenial financial environment for the engineer entrepreneurs, which tax and tariff protection perpetuated until after the Second World War. The willingness of some existing family firms to venture risk capital in markets unreceptive to mass-produced vehicles also favoured dominance in the industry by owner-managers. Both in France and Britain the early years of the industry saw company promotions of the kind which characterised the American experience, and in all three countries the newly created firms which succeeded in this industry began with a modest investment, usually obtained by the founders from their savings, from family, friends, or individual investors.[24] Of those European firms which survived the difficulties produced by the First World War and the highly competitive period which followed, all were owner-managed firms and most were managed by founder-owners.

The Renault Co. originated in the imaginative skills of Louis Renault and the commercial flair of his brother, Marcel, sons of a successful clothing manufacturer. Initial financial backing from the family, followed by early success, enabled Louis Renault to assume sole ownership by 1908. Reinvested profits and personal financial backing perpetuated absolute control and the exercise of managerial authority until his death in 1944.[25] In the case of Peugeot the substantial family resources in metal working provided the initial capital for the car-making venture undertaken by Les Fils de Peugeot Freres, although it was to be Armand Peugeot's separately formed enterprise specialising in car production which was to set the pace until financial difficulties began to threaten its future. When the head of Les Fils de Peugeot Freres died in 1907 the two firms merged, Armand consolidating family dominance. Subsequent expansion of Automobiles et Cycles Peugeot occurred on the basis of family resources, supplemented by banking finance, but the family remained in control and continued to manage the company after Armand's death in 1915.[26]

In Germany the family sewing machine and bicycle factory of Opel provided the basis for car manufacture which began shortly after 1900;[27] management by the Opel brothers continued so long as the family was in control. This came to an end in 1929 when General Motors secured ownership in the public issue of that year. The British firms which pioneered large-scale manufacture during the inter-war years were the Austin Motor Co. and Morris Motors. External finance from personal backers, to Herbert Austin from a steel manufacturer, to W.R. Morris from an aristocrat, provided the initial foundations for the major British firms, although by 1914 Austin owned more than 50 per cent of the public company and W.R. Morris was sole owner of his firm, which did not offer shares to the public until 1936; even then the founder retained three-quarters of the ordinary stock.[28] There are resemblances between the financial origins of Morris Motors and Fabbrica Italiana d'Automobili Torino (FIAT), which when formed as a joint-stock company in 1899 was financed by two aristocrats, although the commercial affairs were in the hands of the company secretary, Giovanni Agnelli. Six years later Agnelli formed the R.I.B. ballbearing machine concern, which before long became a holding company possessing a controlling interest in Fiat. Managerial control remained in Agnelli's hands and later Fiat came under the direction of the third-generation Agnelli family.[29] Finally, Citroen, the shortest-lived of the major European companies with owner-manager characteristics, was established in 1914 by André Citroen, whose first business venture was transformed from gear cutting to munitions manufacture during the First World War. Citroen reconverted the plant for car production and, although loan capital was necessary to sustain the firm in the short run, commercial success earned profits sufficient to enable him to repay debts by 1924 and to reorganise the company in which henceforth he held 60 per cent of the stock as the self-styled 'administrateur unique'.[30]

II

When the First World War ended, trends in innovation, output, growth, product development and price competition were similar in kind in Europe to those which had occurred in the United States before the war, and it was the introduction of American-style assembly line plants and the competition from American-owned subsidiaries which brought about increasing industrial concentration in the 1920s and 1930s. In Britain, France, and Germany the largest three producers accounted for more than 70 per cent of national car production by the mid-1930s, while in Italy Fiat alone exceeded that figure.[31] Industrial concentration deriving from the introduction of volume car production and price competition forced firms to invest heavily in plant and machinery in order to survive. This was the phase corresponding to that which had occurred in the United States before the First World War, during which the European managers faced an intensifying challenge to independence and survival.

Success and survival of the owner-managed companies before 1945 was due principally to commercial policies and, critically, the ability to withstand fluctuations in trade which in the downswings forced out firms lacking the strongest financial foundation. Thus, it was in order to survive a financial crisis that Opel accepted an overture from General Motors which, having obtained a majority shareholding in the public issue of 1928, appointed I.J. Reuter, general manager of the Olds division of General Motors, as Opel's managing director.[32] As for Citroen, financial difficulties had been a feature of the company's history since the beginning, and in the 1920s a French banking syndicate had reorganised the firm's finances, temporarily removing from André Citroen the sole managerial control and placing it in the hands of a Board of directors elected by preference and ordinary shareholders.[33] By the 1930s André Citroen had regained control from the Banque Lazard, only to founder in the aftermath of the Great Depression. In 1934 Michelin, a major creditor and a long-established soundly financed family firm, took over 66 per cent of the Citroen stock from the liquidator.[34]

Sir Herbert Austin was compelled to relinquish absolute control of his company as a result of the financial crisis of 1920–21, when considerable limitation of his personal executive power and the establishment of a Board committee of management was the price he had to pay to his creditors, notably the Midland Bank.[35] Attempts first to forge links with Ford and in 1924 to sell equity to General Motors were frustrated, in the latter instance in part by his co-directors who opposed an American solution to Austin's lingering financial difficulties. None the less, until his death in 1941 the founder retained his majority common stock shareholding. The dispersal of ownership of the Nuffield organisation began in 1936, although when merger with Austin occurred in 1952 Lord Nuffield was still the major, if not the majority, shareholder. It is interesting to note that just as Austin had been opposed, for similar reasons, by co-directors in 1924, Lord Nuffield also encountered opposition from his board in 1952. Retirement and the survival of the company he had founded were the reasons why he agreed to the merger to form BMC, to strengthen resistance against American competition.[36]

It was an extraordinary coincidence that neither of the two British leaders could perpetuate their companies in a second generation. Lord Nuffield's marriage was childless, while Lord Austin's son, groomed for succession, was killed on the western front in 1915. In Europe, only at Peugeot, where all six sons of Jules, Robert and Pierre followed their fathers on to the boards of the various Peugeot companies, were second- and third-generation family involved in management and control.[37] Agnelli directed Fiat until his death in 1945 when Vittorio Valetta, an experienced Fiat manager then aged 62, presided over an interregnum. Valetta died in 1966, whereupon two of Agnelli's grandsons, Giovanni and Umberto, resumed managerial dominance for the family.[38] Louis Renault's son was too young to be given responsibility before the company was nationalised in 1944, but a nephew by marriage, François Lehideux, who joined SAUR in 1931, had acted as an important aide to Renault during the 1930s.[39]

While the owner-managers of the motor industry until the Second World War were professional in the sense that they participated in top-level decision-making on a more or less full-time basis, they lacked the professional training which has been suggested as one possible criterion for identifying professionalism in management. Detailed information on this matter is difficult to discover and does not permit unequivocal generalisations. It is clear, however, that only in two instances did the founder acquire a formal professional training of any kind; Austin and Citroen were both qualified engineers. Armand and Robert Peugeot probably received training in the family firm as did the Opel brothers, although Carl Opel was dispatched to England to learn the skills of bicycle manufacture. Louis Renault has been described as a natural mechanic who learned by experience as a designer in an engineering works before launching his own enterprise; Henry Ford I and W.R. Morris were mechanics of sorts, both finding difficulty in reading a blueprint. Giovanni Agnelli's education was at military academy, followed by a career in the army. He was a self-taught mechanic who, on leaving the army, transformed his hobby, tinkering with cycles and engines, into a business venture, culminating in the formation of Fiat.[40] Three of the founding entrepreneurs, Henry Ford I, W.R. Morris and Herbert Austin, experienced early business failure.

The histories of Austin, Fiat, Ford and Morris reveal that while senior professional managers were appointed (at Austin by the company's creditors), the owner-managers themselves retained ultimate power, although somewhat less in Austin's case. They also suggest that, except in the case of Fiat, senior executives from outside the family were able to affect the company's history by exercising independent initiative only in the context of organisational anarchy. Non-family influence was present, despite company policy, and did not represent responsible delegation of managerial power. At Renault, family management underpinned family ownership, and in the 1930s the ageing Louis Renault extended managerial responsibility to a nephew by marriage.[41] Nationalisation ended family participation at Renault in 1945 and within only a few years after the Second World War ended, owner-managed motor producers in Europe had almost completely disappeared, the exceptions being Peugeot and, after an interlude between 1945 and 1966, Fiat, which together remained almost as archetypes of the traditional family firm.

We have excluded the Japanese experience from our review until now because the concept of the family firm translates uneasily into the Japanese business system in which, for the purpose of establishing an indigenous automobile industry, government intervention precipitated trust formation of the 'Japanese Incorporated' type.[42] When this strategy failed, the initiative in the establishment of an indigenous motor industry was seized in the 1930s by two of the younger Zaibatsu, Nissan and Toyoda. The former was a new Zaibatsu in which the leading figure, Yoshisuke Aikawa, found it necessary to finance a merger of his castings and components plant with the Dat car-making firm by forming a public company. The other major firm was Toyota which, while launching the car manufacturing enterprise simultaneously with Nissan, retained its character as an old established local Zaibatsu for which diversification from textiles to textile machinery, financing growth from internal resources, had proved a successful strategy.[43] No fewer than 11 members of the Toyoda family were active directors, vice-presidents, and presidents of the various companies owned by the family between 1920 and the 1970s, although family ownership of the Toyota Motor Co. ended with the financial crisis of 1949. Control passed to the banks, notably the Bank of Japan, and was followed by reorganisation, the establishment of an additional separate motor sales company, and the appointment as President of one of Toyota's sales managers, formerly with G.M.(Japan). At the same time, however, Kiichiro Toyoda, the founder, continued as President of the manufacturing organisation, although he and his board of directors resigned in the course of a labour dispute resulting from a reduction in the workforce in 1950. His successors were Taizo Ishida, hitherto for many years President of the Toyoda Automatic Loom Works, and Fukio Nakagawa of the Teikoku Bank, who it was intended should make way for Kiichiro Toyoda's reinstatement after the repercussions of the labour troubles of 1950 had disappeared. He died, however, in 1952 and cousin Eiji Toyoda succeeded as President.[44] In the mid-1970s both President and Vice-President of Toyota were Toyodas, while Tatsuro Toyoda was director of Toyota Motor Sales Co. Thus, despite the ownership of less than five per cent of share capital the family continues to influence major policy decisions in the management of Japan's largest and most profitable motor company, although these have been much affected, too, by the intervention of the Ministry of International Trade and Industry.[45]

We have charted the chronology of the decline of the family firm and owner-managers in the motor industry, and have identified financial factors as having been critical in their demise. This was the case in the history of the industry in the United States; while Citroen's bankruptcy, Opel's merger with G.M., and Austin's retreat from absolute control are each explained in these terms, too. A combination of the logic of American competition and the absence of heirs eventually brought Austin and Morris together to form B.M.C., the forerunners of British Leyland which, comparable with Renault's transformation to state enterprise, was a political decision. Those business leaders who succeeded in retaining ownership and control until the Second World War pursued conservative financial policies and tended to avoid the capital market.

With the exception of General Motors the growth of large firms in the motor industry before the 1950s occurred as a result of internal expansion rather than by merger, a process which proved favourable to the survival of family influence   although in none of these was family control and influence appreciably greater than that of the Du Ponts in the affairs of General Motors.[46] Since the Second World War financial difficulties, problems of succession and state intervention have hastened the transition between the old family partnership and the managerial bureaucratic enterprise. Chandler attributes Pierre Du Pont's success in transforming General Motors into a modern corporation in part to 'training, lineage, and personality'. These gave him managerial skills, commitment to making a career in the family firm and access to a pool of capital and favourable credit rating.[47]

III

Did the owner-management structure of firms, and in particular family-controlled influence, significantly affect behaviour and performance? For clues to what we might expect we may refer to the findings of economists based on research into the recent history of business organisation. Monsen and Downs have suggested that owner-controlled firms have been less averse to taking risky decisions than organisations described as managerial enterprises.[48] If we regard product policy as the test of risk aversion no clear picture emerges. During the decade prior to the Second World War the American manufacturers combined independent innovation with considerable price competition, whereas both in Britain and France, where owner-controlled enterprises were dominant, manufacturers competed by product differentiation and duplication of models, a policy designed to minimise risk.[49] Yet in all three countries in the 1930s imaginative model design and aggressive marketing saw the resounding, albeit temporary, success of Chrysler in the US, of Rootes and Standard in the UK, and of Citroen, followed by the Fiat-backed Simca, in France. Irrespective of control type, the large motor companies lost ground to the smaller risk-embracing firms reinvigorated by new management.[50] Other recent empirical studies of the relationship between ownership, control, and performance in large corporations, mainly in the period since 1950, suggest caution before concluding that the weakness in management identifiable in the owner-managers of the twentieth century were peculiar to owner-managed firms in general and to family firms in particular.

Reviewing numerous studies of the performance of large owner-manager controlled firms in the US, Kania and McKean concluded that returns on equity indicated both types of firms to have performed equally well and poorly in regard to profit realisation; that there was little support for the hypothesis that managers and owner-managers were motivated towards different goals, and that both sought to maximise owner welfare.[51] Other research on large UK enterprises suggested that owner-controlled firms tend to secure higher rates of profit on average than management-controlled firms and exhibit higher growth rates; although on a different sample another researcher found the difference between mean values of

FAMILY FIRMS AND MANAGERIAL CAPITALISM 175

profits and growth rates for owner and managerially controlled firms were not statistically significant.[52] More recently, a study of large French firms by Jacquemin and de Ghellink found that profitability is not directly influenced by the type and control of the firm; however, the positive effect of the firm's size is significantly higher in the case of familial control as compared with non-familial control.[53] Family firms, it is suggested, seemed to be able to limit the internal bureaucratic inefficiencies linked with large size and to safeguard more profitable capital use. Non-family firms, however, achieved higher profitability as size increased. Their conclusion was that only a combination of size and divergent goals causes deviations from profit maximisation; when ownership and management were combined large size has a systematically better impact upon profitability than when separate.

Taken together, these most recent studies offer little support to the views commonly held by the economists and historians quoted earlier concerning the characteristics of behaviour and performance of family and owner-managed firms. And in so far as motivation and policy of such firms have been found to be similar, in some respects more positive compared with managerial organisations, the justification for attributing to the family and owner-managed firms the inhibiting influences absent in others is considerably diminished. In the United States and in Europe in the period before the 1960s when protected markets differed with respect to geography, taxation, income levels and distribution, and socio-cultural characteristics, factors other than family control or management are seen to have exercised greater influences on the performance of firms. Our review of the rise of the owner-managers before 1939 underlines the inventive and innovative contribution from both new and old established family firms. An informed American assessment of the state of three major European motor manufacturers in 1927, Citroen, Morris and Opel, included favourable remarks upon their productive equipment and commercial practices,[54] and A.P. Sloan made it clear at the time of the merger that in Opel, General Motors was acquiring very much more than a dying European duck.[55]

Historians have condemned W.R. Morris for refusing to merge with Austin in 1924, citing this as a case where the personal preference of the owner-manager seriously inhibited the development of the British motor industry. Such an argument depends upon the counterfactual assumption regarding the effectiveness of Morris's managerial skills, for he would have been chief executive in such a merger.[56] The Nuffield organisation was more profitable than its major British rivals, but at the same time between 1929 and 1939 the production of cars as a percentage of the Big Six fell from 51 per cent to 27 per cent. Overy makes the point that the firm encountered managerial problems in the early 1930s and after 1945, but that they are explicable in terms of a rate of growth which was too fast rather than a failure to grow at all, hardly the qualification to manage the reorganisation which the merger mooted in 1924 would have required. Austin, by contrast, had been prepared to merge with Morris, or with Ford or General Motors, yet it was his professional manager-directors appointed by Austin's creditors in 1921 who, anxious to maintain independence, resisted the proposal and rejected G.M.'s bid in 1924. For, while in terms of voting concentration the Austin Motor Co. was a personal enterprise, in fact Sir Herbert was a prisoner of his debenture holders and of the Bank. While we may not be able to explain the motives of his colleagues, Austin's attitude is clearly inexplicable without reference to the death of his only son and heir in 1915, which thus removed one of the principal driving forces typically regarded as fundamental to the aims and *raison d'être* of family enterprise. Lord Nuffield, on the other hand, also lacked an heir, yet refused to merge with Austin until after the latter's death and his own imminent retirement. Thereafter, the merger proved to be an alliance only in financial terms, while the failure to integrate and rationalise the two constituent organisations occurred even though the owner-managers and their families had long relinquished ownership, control and managerial participation.[57]

Henry Ford's attitude to his son was bizarre, denying Edsel Ford, by all accounts a worthy successor, participation in top-level decision-making. The ageing and eccentric Henry Ford hung on until Edsel's death, whereupon illness and family pressure precipitated Henry II's assumption of power, by which time the company's fortunes had slumped.[58] At Fiat a long hiatus occurred between the founder Agnelli's leadership and his grandsons' resumption of family power, when Jan Agnelli became the leading figure in the family-owned firm; but in the interim the chairman was internally recruited from Fiat's managers.[59] There has been little detailed evidence on training for succession in these firms before the Second World War, although the impression is of minimal preparation, based on experience within the family firm. Yet Ford, Peugeot, and Fiat survived the 1930s with second- or third-generation connections by ownership and management continuing to influence the course of industrial change in competition with the managerial firms and the corporate personalities which guided their fortunes. Thus, while owner-managed firms could be seriously affected one way or another by idiosyncratic decision, since that time owner-managing families have shown imagination either by widening the sources of management recruitment or by ensuring adequate preparation of family heirs for involvement in top-level decision-making. In each of the post-war generation of the Agnelli, Ford, Peugeot and Toyota families are to be found graduates, mostly from Harvard, in engineering or business.

Since the late 1950s Ford has struggled to retain just less than a quarter of the US market, compared with an average of 45 per cent held by G.M. In Europe Ford led G.M. in production and profitability, and both of the American subsidiaries showed superior profit records over the indigenous volume car manufacturers. Among all European car-makers Peugeot was the leading producer in the 1970s, followed by Fiat; and with the exception of Volkswagen, Peugeot, followed by Fiat, was the most profitable.[60] In 1979 approximately 40 per cent of the vehicles produced by the world's largest ten motor manufacturers came from firms in which entrepreneurial families played a major managerial role.[61] Family enterprise, bureau-cratised as in the case of Ford, or of the traditional variety as at Peugeot and Fiat, demonstrates the continuing ability of the family influence to thrive, though more successfully, hitherto, in the more traditional European markets for motor cars where, until the 1950s, the scale of financial commitments required for effective national and international competition rendered the retreat, though not defeat, of family dominance inevitable. Finally, unlike the dynasties of Europe which are protected by majority shareholdings, or that of the US where a significant minority control has buttressed the Ford family's managerial authority, the continuing influence of the Toyoda dynasty depends, it seems, entirely upon non-financial considerations. Such variation between countries and firms suggests that in the motor industry there has been no simple automatic correlation between type of control, managerial style and performance. Increasingly the survival of owner-managed firms came to depend upon large-scale capital investment, organisation and professional management skills and training suited to a large modern co-operation; these were the principal considerations which in the motor industry led to the retreat of families from control as well as from management.

The persistence of a business elite, whether originating in founder families or within the corporate structure long after an economic justification has disappeared, is of intrinsic interest and testifies to the resilience, despite some discontinuities, of those remaining entrepreneurial families, three of which possess business histories pre-dating the motor car by several generations. However, the convergence of structure and behavioural characteristics of the family manager and owner-managed firm, varying in the extent of hierarchical control, points to its lack of analytical and explanatory significance. Our evidence from the international motor industry suggests that even in very large firms it would be unwarranted to infer either strengths or weaknesses in performance from the mere fact of family ownership or management.

University of East Anglia, Norwich

NOTES

A shorter version of this article was presented as a paper to the Eighth International Economic History Congress, Budapest, 1982; Section B9, 'From Family Firm to Professional Management: Structure and Performance of Business Enterprise'. I am grateful for the comments of those who participated in the discussion or who offered observations on an earlier draft.

1. See the discussion in Theo Nicholas, *Ownership Control and Ideology* (1969), pp.19-21; Robert J. Larner, *Management Control and the Large Corporation* (New York, 1970), pp.63-6; C.S. Beed, 'The Separation of Ownership from Control', *Journal of Economic Studies*, Vol.1 (1966), pp.29-46; Philip H. Burch Jr., *The Managerial Revolution Reassessed* (Lexington, MA, 1972), pp.5-19; P. Sargant Florence, *The Logic of British and American Industry* (1953), Ch.V.

2. S. Nyman and A. Silberston, 'The Ownership and Control of Industry', *Oxford Economic Papers,* N.S. Vol.30 (1978), pp.74–8. See also M. Useem, 'Corporations and the Corporate Elite', *Annual Review of Sociology,* Vol.6 (1980), pp.41–69; A. Francis, 'Families, Firms and Finance Capital: The Development of U.K. Industrial Firms with Particular Reference to their Ownership and Control', *Sociology,* Vol.14 (1980), pp.1–26; M. Zeitlin, 'Corporate Ownership and Control: The Large Corporation and the Capitalist Class', *American Journal of Sociology,* Vol.79 (1974), pp.1073–115.

3. A.A. Berle and G.C. Means, *The Modern Corporation and Private Property* (New York, 1937), pp.84–90.

4. Alfred D. Chandler, *The Visible Hand. The Managerial Revolution in American Business* (London, 1979), pp.8–10.

5. N.H. Leff, 'Industrial Organisation and Entrepreneurship in the Developing Countries: The Economic Group', *Economic Development and Cultural Change,* Vol.26 (1978), pp.331–52; J. Kocka, 'Family and Bureaucracy in German Industrial Management, 1815–1914', *Business History Review,* Vol.45 (1971), pp.133–56.

6. Alfred D. Chandler Jr., 'The Development of Modern Management Structure in the U.S. and U.K.', in Leslie Hannah (ed.), *Management Strategy and Business Development* (London, 1976), p.28; A. Jacquemin and E. de Ghellinck, 'Familial Control, Size and Performance in the Largest French Firms', *European Economic Review,* Vol.13 (1980).

7. Sargant Florence, op. cit., pp.295, 303–4, 320.

8. C.F. Carter and B.R. Williams, *Investment in Innovation* (London, 1958), p.40.

9. Charles P. Kindleberger, *Economic Growth in France and Britain, 1850–1950* (Cambridge, MA, 1964), pp.124–7.

10. Alfred D. Chandler Jr., 'The Growth of the Transnational Industrial Firm in the U.S. and the U.K.; A Comparative Analysis', *Economic History Review,* Vol.33 (1980), pp.402–6.

11. Hannah, *Management Strategy and Business Development,* pp.12, 195–6.

12. Richard Tilly, 'The Growth of Large Scale Enterprise in Germany since the mid 19th Century', in H.D. Daems and H. Van der Wee (eds.), *The Rise of Managerial Capitalism* (Louvain, 1974), p.156.

13. Jurgen Kocka, 'Entrepreneurs and Managers in German Industrialisation', *The Cambridge Economic History of Europe,* Vol.VII, Part I (Cambridge, 1978), pp.580–81.

14. David S. Landes, *The Unbound Prometheus. Technological Change and Industrial Development in Western Europe from 1750 to the Present* (Cambridge, 1969), pp.527–8.

15. James M. Laux, *In First Gear. The French Automobile Industry to 1914* (Liverpool, 1976), p.200.

16. However, Payne admitted that this might be a weak hypothesis, referring to Hannah's speculation that variability of performance between firms of contrasting structure might undermine such a conclusion. Peter L. Payne, 'Family Business in Britain: An Historical and Analytical Survey', in Akio Okochi and Shigeaki Yasuoka (eds.), *Family Business in the Era of Industrial Growth* (Tokyo, 1984), p.197; Leslie Hannah, 'Visible and Invisible Hands in Great Britain', in A.D. Chandler and H. Daems (eds.), *Managerial Hierarchies* (Cambridge, MA, 1980), p.55.

17. For an overall analysis of the rise of the American industry, see R.D. Kennedy, *The Automobile Industry* (New York, 1941), Chs.3 and 4; John B. Rae, *The American Automobile* (Chicago, 1969), Chs.1–4. An analysis focusing upon the social aspects of business enterprise is to be found in Donald F. Davis, 'The Social Determinants of Success in the American Industry before 1929', an unpublished paper presented at the Colloque International on 'L'incidence de l'environment exterieur sur l'industrie automobile mondiale', Breau sans Nappe, 1981.

18. Donald F. Davis, loc. cit.

19. Rae, op. cit., pp.100–1.

20. Alfred D. Chandler Jr. and Stephen Salsbury, *Pierre S. Du Pont and the Making of the Modern Corporation* (New York, 1971), pp.564–6, 572, 580–87.

21. Allan Nevins and Frank Ernest Hill, *Ford, Decline and Rebirth 1933–62* (New York, 1963), Chs.I–XII; Harold Livesay, 'Entrepreneurial Persistence through the Bureaucratic Age', *Business History Review,* Vol.LI (1977), pp.431–44.

22. Chandler and Salsbury, *Pierre S. Du Pont,* p.598.

FAMILY FIRMS AND MANAGERIAL CAPITALISM   179

23. Kennedy, op. cit., pp.18-36; Harold Livesay, op. cit., pp.431-43.
24. Donald F. Davis, loc. cit., S.B. Saul, 'The Motor Industry in Britain to 1914', *Business History*, Vol.V (1962), p.31; Laux, op. cit., pp.200-1.
25. P. Fridenson, *Histoire des Usines Renault;* Vol. 1.(Paris, 1972), pp.60, 124.
26. R. Sedillot, *Peugeot: de la crinoline à la 404* (Paris, 1960), pp.58-78.
27. H. Hauser, *Opel. Eindeutches Tor zur Welt* (Frankfurt, 1937), pp.99, 104, 110, 119.
28. Roy Church, *Herbert Austin. The British Motor Industry to 1941* (London, 1979), pp.175-6; P.W.S. Andrews and Elizabeth Brunner, *The Life of Lord Nuffield* (Oxford, 1955), p.66-7, 89-90, 209-11, 214.
29. Franco Arnatori, 'Entrepreneurial Typology in the History of Industrial Italy 1880-1960: A Review Article', *Business History Review,* Vol.LIV (1980), No.3, pp.372-4; Arnolda Mondadori (ed.), *Fiat, A Fifty Year Record* (Turin, 1951), pp.37, 75.
30. H.H. Kelly, 'Development of the Citroen Company', *U.S. Commerce Reports,* 18 July 1927, p.136.
31. George Maxcy and Aubrey Silbertson, *The Motor Industry* (London, 1959), pp.115-21; Fridenson, op. cit., p.181; Hauser, op. cit., p.186; Gerald Bloomfield, *The World Automotive Industry* (North Pomfret, VT), p.299.
32. Alfred P. Sloan Jr., *My Life with General Motors* (Garden City, NY, 1967), p.351.
33. *U.S. Commerce Report,* 18 July 1927.
34. John Sheahan, 'Government Competition and the Performance of the French Automobile Industry', *Journal of Industrial Economics,* Vol.8 (1959-60), p.450.
35. Church, *Herbert Austin,* pp.64-5.
36. R.J. Overy, *William Morris, Viscount Nuffield* (London, 1976), p.98; Graham Turner, *The Leyland Papers* (London, 1971), pp.95-9.
37. Sedillot, op. cit., p.130.
38. Bloomfield, op. cit., p.300.
39. Fridenson, op. cit., pp.124, 283.
40. Valerio Castronovo, *Giovanni Agnelli* (Turin, 1971), Chs.1 and 2.
41. Fridenson, op. cit., p.283.
42. Masaru Udagawa and Seishi Nakamura, 'Japanese Business and Government in the Inter-war Period', *Government and Business* (Tokyo, 1980), pp.93-6.
43. Shotaro Kamiya, *My Life with Toyota* (Tokyo, 1976), pp.31-41, 49-55, 100-1.
44. Ibid.
45. I am grateful to Professor Koichi Shimokawa for this information. See also Masaru Udagawa, 'Historical Development of the Japanese Automobile Industry 1917-1971: Business and Government', presented to the Colloque International, 'Incidence de l'environment exterieur sur l'industrie automobile mondiale', Breau sans Nappe, 1981.
46. Chandler and Salsbury, *Pierre S. Du Pont,* pp.593-7.
47. Ibid., pp.599-600.
48. K.J. Monsen and A. Downs, 'The Behaviour of the Large Managerial Firm', *Journal of Political Economy,* Vol.73 (1965), pp.231-4.
49. Maxcy and Silbertson, op. cit., pp.140-41; Sheahan, loc.cit., pp.202-3.
50. Roy Church and Michael Miller, 'The Big Three: Competition, Management and Marketing in the British Motor Industry 1922-1939' in Barry Supple (ed.), *Essays in British Business History* (Cambridge, 1977), pp.108-83.
51. John J. Kania and John R. McKean, 'Ownership, Control and the Contemporary Corporation: A General Behaviour Analysis', *Kyklos,* Vol.29 (1976), pp.272-87.
52. H.K. Radice, 'Control Type, Profitability and Growth in Large Firms: An Empirical Study', *Economic Journal,* Vol.81 (1971), pp.547-62; P. Holl, 'Effect of Control Type on the Performance of the Firm in the UK', *Journal of Industrial Economics,* Vol.23, No.4 (1974-5), pp.257-71.
53. Alexis Jacquemin and Elizabeth de Ghellink, 'Familial Control, Size and Performance in the Largest French Firms', *European Economic Review,* Vol.13 (1980), p.35.
54. Carl Hicks and G. D. Babcock, 'The Automobile Situation in the World and Europe in 1927', a typescript report to the President of the Dodge Motor Corporation, Detroit Public Library, 1927; H.H. Kelly, 'Automotive Products; Distribution of American

Automotive Products in Europe', *United States Bureau of Foreign and Domestic Commerce* (1928).

55. Sloan, op. cit., pp.349–50.
56. Church, op. cit., pp.103, 142; Overy, op. cit., p.124.
57. K. Cowling, *Mergers and Economic Performance* (Cambridge, 1980), Ch. 6, 'Engineering'.
58. Allan Nevins and Frank Ernest Hill, *Ford, Decline and Rebirth 1933 1962* (New York, 1962), pp.228, 248 51.
59. In 1980 the Agnelli family owned 80 per cent of the capital. I am grateful to Signor G. Sapelli for this information.
60. For comparisons see the relevant tables in Krish Bhasker, *The Future of the World Motor Industry* (London, 1980), pp.93, 105, 162, 165, 220, 230.
61. Jean Pierre Bardan, Jean Jacques Chanaron, Patrick Fridenson, James M. Laux, *The Automobile Revolution. The Impact of an Industry* (Chapel Hill, 1982), Table 9.5.

[6]

A Historical Overview of Family Firms in the United States

Peter Dobkin Hall

How do dynastic families adopt to social and economic forces restricting attempts to transmit family wealth from one generation to the next?

Writing in the 1850s, the physician and novelist Oliver Wendell Holmes summed up the problems faced by Americans who hoped to pass their firms and fortunes intact to their children and grandchildren: "It is in the nature of large fortunes to diminish rapidly, when subdivided and distributed. A million is the unit of wealth, now and here in America. It splits into four handsome properties; each of these into four good inheritances; these, again, into scanty competences for four ancient maidens,— with whom it is best that the family should die out, unless it can begin again as its great-grandfather did. Now a million is a kind of golden cheese, which represents in a compendious form the summer's growth of a fat meadow of craft or commerce; and as this kind of meadow rarely bears more than one crop, it is pretty certain that sons and grandsons will not get another golden cheese out of it, whether they milk the same cows or turn in new ones. In other words, the millioncracy, considered in a large way, is not at all an affair of persons and families, but a perpetual fact of money with a variable human element" (Holmes, 1961 [1860], pp. 15-16).

Holmes knew what he was talking about, for he was heir to two venerable family dynasties. His mother's family, the Wendells of Portsmouth, New Hampshire, had reaped the "fat meadow of craft and commerce" of the eighteenth-century West Indies trade. His father's family belonged to New England Brahmin caste of clergymen and scholars.

Combining these two dynastic strands in a secular and industrial age, Holmes practiced medicine, taught at Harvard, and wrote for his own amusement. As a healer, he ministered to the bodies and minds of Boston's elite, who were struggling to run, pass on, and inherit family firms and fortunes. He distilled their experiences and distinctive outlook into popular poems, novels, and essays that, in a significant sense, gave voice to the critical problems faced by nineteenth-century Boston merchant families. Though pre-eminently concerned with Boston, which Holmes dubbed the "hub of the solar system" in one of his essays, Holmes's conception of the predicament faced by family dynasties in a democratic and capitalist society held true for the United States as a whole.

This paper will give a historically informed, multidisciplinary account of the obstacles to dynastic success in the United States and discuss some of the special means that families have used to surmount them. The following topics will be considered: the impact of the law of inheritance on family property, including its role in dividing and consolidating family interests; the impact of economic and technological processes on ties between families and firms; ideological and political obstacles to dynastic formation; the resolution of the conflict between dynasty and dominant democratic and meritocratic values; and the significance of the family firm and the dynastic process in American social and economic life. Although this paper deals with the past, the purpose is not historical. Rather, it is to provide a cultural framework that helps us to understand some of the problems that family business managers, advisers, consultants, and therapists face today.

The Law of Inheritance

When Alexis de Tocqueville visited the United States in the late 1820s, he wanted not only to observe how world's first modern democracy worked but also to discover how it had become a democracy in the first place. As a French aristocrat, he was exquisitely sensitive to dynastic issues, which for centuries had shaped the political and social life of Europe but which appeared to be entirely absent from the New World. Not only were Americans able to do without a titular aristocracy, they also lacked the sentimental and legal ties that bound European families of all classes to land, crafts, and occupations.

Tocqueville could easily understand how the patchwork character of early settlement, the heterogeneity of the colonists, and the privations of life on the frontier had prevented the establishment of feudalism and its apparatus of family succession. More puzzling was the failure of dynasty to establish itself—even in an informal way, based on wealth or political alliances—once the colonies had advanced beyond the stage of pioneering.

Tocqueville came to view the law of inheritance as the most important single factor shaping American life and character (1945 [1835], I, pp. 50–51): "When the legislator has once regulated the law of inheritance, he may rest from his labor. . . . When framed in a particular manner, this law unites, draws together, and vests property and power in a few hands; it causes an aristocracy, so to speak, to spring out of the ground. If formed on opposite principles, its action is still more rapid; it divides, distributes, and disperses both property and power. Alarmed by the rapidity of its progress, those who despair of arresting its motion endeavor at least to obstruct it by difficulties and impediments; they vainly seek to counteract its effect by contrary efforts; but it shatters and reduces to powder every obstacle, until we can no longer see anything but a moving and impalpable cloud of dust, which signals the coming of democracy." The division of estates broke up family holdings, transforming land from patrimony to commodity and family from corporate group to collections of autonomous individuals. Individualism and the ability to buy and sell property freely created the basis for the democratic state and a capitalist economy.

Americans were curiously ambivalent about the inheritance of property. As responsible citizens, virtually all Americans agreed that accumulation of vast fortunes was inimical to democracy, and for that reason they supported the passage of laws favoring the division of estates. However, as individuals, they continuously sought ways of passing their farms, firms, and fortunes on to the next generation intact. They devised a variety of adaptive strategies to counteract the erosion of family resources by the system of partible inheritance (Farber, 1972; Hall, 1982).

In the eighteenth century, kin-marriage was a basic means of preserving land, labor, skill, and capital from the inheritance system. Kin-marriage circumvented the partition of estates with elegant simplicity. Visualize a three-generation family: generation one consists of two grandparents, generation two of their four children, and generation three of their eight grandchildren. In the normal process of estate partition, generation one's estate would be divided eight ways by the time it was distributed to generation three. However, if the grandchildren were encouraged to marry one another rather than nonfamily members, their one-eighth shares in their grandparental estates would be recombined. The number of divisions of the grandparent's estate would be reduced by half from eight to four.

Another method, sibling exchange, worked even more efficiently. It involved encouraging siblings in one family to marry siblings in another family. Imagine two business partners, each with four children. If each child married outside his or her family, the estates of the partners would be divided eight ways on their deaths. But, if the eight children of the partners married one another, the number of divisions would be reduced to four, and assuming that each couple produced two children, it would only increase to eight in the next generation. Sibling exchange had the particular virtue of both consolidating existing wealth and combining resources that had hitherto been separate.

Cousin-marriage, sibling exchange, the marriage of widows to their husband's brother, and delaying or preventing marriage were among the estate-preserving strategies in common use throughout the colonies by the early 1700s (Farber, 1972; Hall, 1982). The strategy used depended on the needs of the group using it. Farmers and artisans, whose primary interest was preserving land, labor, and skill, encouraged alliances between related male lines: Sons tended to marry the daughters of the father's brothers. Merchants, whose primary interest was increasing capital and extending commercial contacts, favored marriages linking previously unrelated males, such as sibling exchanges between the children of partners, and encouraged sons to marry the daughters of their mother's sisters, which tied the unrelated maternal uncle into the family. Having a widow marry her late husband's brother kept her dower right (one-third share) of his estate as well as the shares of his children within control of the paternal line. Preventing marriage, especially of daughters, assured that their share in their parents' estates would be distributed among their male siblings. This practice had much to do with the large number of unmarried women among elite New England families in the nineteenth century.

Dynasty and Democracy

The use of marriage for dynastic purposes was ultimately limited in its effectiveness. Kin-marriage slowed, but did not stop, the partible division of estates. As holdings became smaller, more effective means of keeping estates intact had to be devised. In any event, children in the post-Revolutionary era were less willing to allow their parents to dictate their marital choices. Under these circumstances, farmers and artisans increasingly left the "family place" or the craft to their younger sons as a trade-off for caring for parents in their old age (Waters, 1978). In more affluent families, older children were provided with educations, with apprenticeships in other crafts, or with farms in other places. Poorer families simply sent them off to seek their fortunes, a practice that had much to do with the growth of the free labor force in the first decades of the nineteenth century.

While farmers and artisans had little to lose by sending their children out to seek their fortunes, those who already possessed fortunes could not afford to take such risks. Each child remained a potential legatee. And, even if a child was disinherited, he or she could challenge a parental will with a fair hope of success. For purely instrumental reasons, elite families had an interest in reining in their children. Beyond this, the social styles of the Enlightenment and the Romantic period promoted the sentimentalization of relations between parents and children. This sentimentalization produced emotional bonds that made it difficult for parents to allow their children to go their own way, and it sapped the desire of children to do so. Finally, because wealthy Americans modeled themselves on their aristocratic European counterparts, they began to view themselves as family founders, as dynasts. The 1780 declaration of Massachusetts *nouveau riche* John Adams typified this sensibility (Smith, 1962, pp. 468–469): "I must study war, that my sons may have liberty to study mathematics and philosophy. My sons ought to study mathematics and philosophy, geography, natural history and naval architecture, navigation, commerce, and agriculture, in order to give their children a right to study painting, poetry, music, architecture, statuary, tapestry, and porcelain."

The urban merchants of the New Republic, rather than leaving their children to fate, turned to formal legal mechanisms to preserve their estates and to keep their children in dynastic orbits. Their wealth enabled them to be more sophisticated about the law and its uses. They rediscovered English law and introduced to America doctrines and practices that their forebears had left behind in the Old World or that had failed to develop when first brought here. One of the most important of these involved equity jurisprudence (Scott, 1939). In equity jurisprudence, it was possible for one person to hold legal title to a piece of property, while another was entitled to receive the benefits of it. This division of ownership and use was the basis for *trusts*. Trusts made it possible to keep capital intact for generations in the legal possession of a trustee; the earnings of that capital could be partibly divided among descendants, the holders of equitable title. Trusts, which could be set up between living persons, under wills, or as perpetual charitable endowments, opened new vistas for the founders of trading and industrial fortunes.

The Massachusetts merchants of the post-Revolutionary era spearheaded the legal innovations that would eventually be adopted everywhere, laying the foundation for dynasties of national significance (Hall, 1973; Marcus, 1983). The changes wrought by these men in the law of inheritance were not, notwithstanding John Adams's assertion, intended to create a European-style aristocracy. They appear to have understood that, in the American setting, the survival of family dynasties depended on continuing commercial, industrial, and financial eminence. This is evident in some of their key contributions to the law of trusts, particularly the introduction of the rule against perpetuities and the prudent man rule.

The rule against perpetuities had its roots in Tudor England. The rising middle class of the sixteenth century had feared that the use of trusts by the aristocracy and the monasteries would ultimately make it impossible to buy or sell property, thus strangling commerce. The English courts began to hand down decisions limiting the length of time that a trust could run before its principal ultimately "vested" in an individual. The basic rule, as handed down in 1682 in the Duke of Norfolk's

Case, stated that the limitation on the duration of a trust was "a life or lives in being" at the time the trust took effect, plus twenty-one years, plus nine months (Newhall, 1942). This seemed to strike a reasonable balance between the desire of families to keep capital intact for two generations and the public good of freely circulating property. By the nineteenth century, however, elites on both sides of the Atlantic had become more dynastically minded. The phrase *life or lives in being,* which comprised the most flexible element in the formula, came to be stretched to the point of absurdity: One will specifying the group to be all the lineal descendants of Queen Victoria living at the time the will was made was upheld by the British courts. This version of the rule was accepted in Massachusetts.

Although the rule against perpetuities strengthened trusts, it still conceded the ultimate necessity of freeing family property from testamentary restrictions. To this extent, it acknowledged the mandates of a triumphant capitalism as well as the extent to which all dynasties both sprang from and returned to the world of market relations.

The prudent man rule, which was enunciated by the Massachusetts courts in 1830, dealt with the investment of trust capital. Much as they wished their capital to be safe, the Massachusetts merchants also wanted it to be available for investment in the region's economic growth. When a group of beneficiaries sued a trustee for investing in the shares of manufacturing corporations, which the beneficiaries regarded as unsafe securities, the court, after reviewing all the possible ways in which money could be invested, declared that there was no perfectly safe investment vehicle. All that could be required of a trustee was that he be guided by the practice of "men of prudence" in managing their own affairs "in regard to the permanent disposition of their funds" (*Pickering's Reports,* 1830, p. 461). This decision had a twofold effect. First, it protected trustees from legal action by beneficiaries, thereby enabling them to pursue their dynastic purposes more effectively. Second, it made trust capital available for investment in the industrial economy. This enabled Massachusetts to lead the nation in industrial growth and to its role as an early center of investment banking.

A third feature of the Massachusetts trust doctrine was the development of charitable endowments. While such endowments dated from Puritan times, their establishment became tied in the early nineteenth century to the mercantile effort to conserve and consolidate family capital. Charitable endowments, whether held by organizations like Harvard College or free-standing like the Lowell Institute, served not only the long-term goal of preventing the division of estates but also the short-term goal of providing for the needs of children and grandchildren. The creation of charitable endowments was the most complex of the dynastic strategies used by Massachusetts families.

The basic business organization used by these families was the partnership firm, in which all members were related by blood or marriage. Before the Revolution, sons generally entered their father's firms and daughters married partners, reducing the erosion of operating capital caused by death and subsequent divisions of estates. Business practice began to change after independence. Freed from the restrictions of British mercantilism, merchants who once traded only with the West Indies and England now expanded to India, China, and Latin America. Such large-scale trade was risky. It was also expensive, often requiring nonfamily capital. For these reasons, firms not only had to begin to admit unrelated partners, who brought their capital with them, but competence became more important than blood.

Responding to these changes in economic life, the merchants began to encourage vocational diversity. Those with an aptitude for business became businessmen; those without such an aptitude were encouraged to enter the law, medicine, or some other respectable occupation. Endowment trusts played a key role in this process. Endowing colleges and professional schools made alternatives to business careers more attractive by raising the status of the professions and by creating positions of influence for family members (Hall, 1973; Story, 1981). Endowments themselves constituted important pools of investment capital that were not only managed by family members of governing boards but also used in underwriting family businesses (White, 1955; Hall, 1973). Family involvement in the governance of endowed charitable corporations, usually via business members, perpetuated intergenerational control and authority and created arenas in which the competence of relatives and in-laws could be assessed.

In devising special means to overcome the centrifugal and individuating dynamic of the inheritance system, the Brahmins never forgot that they were, first and foremost, a business class whose pre-eminence depended on active participation in the new nation's exponentially growing economy. The portrayals of aristocratic disdain for commerce so favored by fictioneers mask the long traditions of managerial and entrepreneurial leadership maintained by some patrician families (Kolko, 1967). The genius of the institutional system devised by the Bostonians and adopted by other urban patriarchates lies in its capacity to sort family members for fitness, recruit and maritally coopt talented outsiders, and constantly produce "golden cheeses" by farming ever new "fat meadows of craft or commerce."

All Americans in the eighteenth and early nineteenth centuries struggled to keep farms, firms, and fortunes intact against the divisive force of the law of inheritance. Not only were some groups more successful than others, but the relative degrees of success profoundly shaped the emerging hierarchy of wealth, power, and influence (Hall, 1982).

Farmers fared worst. Although they were the most numerous group in the population, they became steadily more impoverished and powerless. Land holdings were often successfully preserved through such strategies as kin-marriage and leaving family farms to the youngest son. But, the price of success was enormous. Providing the other sons with apprenticeships and farms in new settlements cost money, which could be earned only by shifting away from self-sufficiency toward commercial agriculture and participation in markets over which the farmers had little control. The outmigration of all but the youngest sons meant that farm families lost invaluable human capital. The most ambitious went West or gravitated to the cities. What remained was the pathetic spectacle of ingrownness, isolation, and poverty so accurately depicted in novels like Wharton's *Ethan Frome* (1911).

The effectiveness of the adaptive strategies that artisan families used is more difficult to assess, because rapidly changing technology and the changing character of the markets played so important a role in shaping relations between family and productive enterprise. In highly skilled and highly capitalized occupations like printing, ties between family and craft were unusually long-lasting. For example, the Green family of Boston remained closely identified with the printing trade for more than five generations (Thomas, 1970). To maintain such enduring ties between family and craft required considerable geographical mobility, since colonial cities could not support an unlimited number of printers. To remain printers, the Greens sent sons to establish shops in Connecticut, Nova Scotia, Maryland, and Virginia.

Other artisans chose to stay where they were, even if it meant altering their occupations. Such highly skilled artisans as silversmiths and cabinetmakers developed a specialized and cooperative division of labor. The woodworkers often became upholsterers, coachmakers, or japanners—all interdependent crafts. In a similar fashion, silversmiths became jewelers, engravers, or clock and instrument makers (Jobe and Kaye, 1984). A few craftsmen became entrepreneurs, moving out of production into financing and marketing the work of others.

Of the major occupational groups in early America, only the merchants succeeded in using the major adaptive strategies—occupational diversification and kin-marriage—to long-term advantage. But, their success in maintaining continuities of family, firm, and fortune depended on their ability to create unified institutional infrastructures that both collectivized their human and financial capital and served as a mechanism for coopting talented new blood. This was not possible everywhere. In cities like Boston, where institutional development was relatively integrated, elite families not only displayed remarkable continuity but remained economic leaders into the twentieth century. However, in New York and Philadelphia, many of the families that were prominent in the late eighteenth century were either swept away or left the great commercial and industrial achievements of the nineteenth century to more ambitious strivers (Baltzell, 1979).

The great industrial fortunes created in the decades after the Civil War were the substance of the final development of dynastic machinery in the United States. These fortunes presented their founders with unique problems, not only because of their enormous size but also because their creation coincided with the appearance of mass poverty and unemployment. For this reason, the final development in the legal machinery of dynastic formation was the charitable foundation, which combined features intended to maintain family control of wealth with socially concerned philanthropy. The emergence of foundations was also tied to the changing structure of family firms, which, as they increased their scale of operations and capital requirements, came to be incorporated enterprises. In this setting, ostensibly charitable foundations served as holding companies that removed control of the firm from the testamentary process, permitting division of income while at the same time perpetuating and formally collectivizing family control. In the late 1930s, with sharp increases in federal income and inheritance taxes, foundations also became a major means of tax avoidance (Hall, 1986).

For many wealthy families, philanthropy itself became an important occupational alternative involving both altruistic and self-interested components. The Rockefeller "family office" in Room 5600 at Rockefeller Plaza served as the nerve center for managing the family's assets, coordinating its public relations, and overseeing its numerous charitable interests (Collier and Horowitz, 1976). As family holdings diversified and as family members scattered occupationally and geographically, it also played a central role in sustaining the family identity and mission (Marcus, 1983).

We should not make too much of the ability of some families—the Rockefellers, the Du Ponts, the Cabots, and others—to resist the divisive dynamic of the inheritance system, because even for the largest and most enduring family fortunes, each new generation presents the challenge of successful transmission. For example, it is by no means clear that the Rockefeller family will continue to exist in any dynastic sense a century from now. Collier and Horowitz (1976, p. 624) point out the problems posed when the number of heirs to a fortune increases from six siblings to twenty-two cousins: "Instead of *the* family, there will be five families—those of each of the male heirs of the Brothers. Long after the Brothers have died, their grandchildren—the fifth generation—will finally inherit the vestige of Senior's fortune, the '34 Trusts, which terminate by law when they reach maturity. The aging Cousins will no doubt worry over the impact this sudden wealth will have on their children and what it will portend for the Rockefellers and their concept of service. But by that time the sense in which this has been the most royal of America's families will have passed, and the question will be largely academic." As Tocqueville wrote a century and a half ago in the passage quoted earlier, the law of inheritance in the end "shatters and reduces to powder every obstacle" placed in its path.

From Firm to Fortune

The perpetuation of a fortune and the perpetuation of a family's ties to a particular business constitute distinct but overlapping issues. Because those who seek guidance from consultants and therapists are often closely tied to the enterprises from which they derived their wealth, it is tempting to focus exclusively on the ties between family and firm. However, doing this arbitrarily excludes those who have successfully diversified their interests beyond a particular enterprise but for whom family economic interests remain centrally important. What makes an activity a family enterprise is the degree of family involvement in the sources of family wealth, however diverse those sources may be.

Diversification, like partible inheritance, is tied to the fundamental dynamics of American economic life. As the inheritance system detached families from the land, it also detached artisans from their crafts. Profits rather than perfection became the artisan's goal, and earning profits— even survival itself—demanded continuous technological and organizational innovation. In this rapidly changing and intensely competitive environment, maintaining close ties to a single productive activity and retaining wealth became virtually incompatible. As the nineteenth-century industrial system grew more complex, success even in a single area—for example, steel—required the control of coal, ores, railroads, and construction companies, as survival increasingly hinged on strategic control of raw materials, market access, and markets themselves. To be sure, many small firms found niches for themselves, either by producing specialty products or by establishing client relationships with larger enterprises. But, over the longer term survival inevitably required the dissolution of ties between family and firm or, under special circumstances, the development of interrelated and interdependent clusters of enterprises, such as those created by the Du Ponts.

The changing scale of market activity also worked against family firms. Until the early nineteenth century, most markets were local, and most enterprises were familial. Economic activity was noncompetitive, and consumer choices were governed not by rational choice but by kinship and loyalty (Jobe and Kaye, 1984). The growth of translocal markets was accompanied by the growing use of money, which provided a standard for making rational economic choices. As market relations grew more impersonal, they also became more competitive, because successful

firms depended increasingly on mechanical efficiency, the quality of decision making, and the rational division of labor.

Under these circumstances, the factors that had made family firms
so vital a part of the colonial social and economic pattern became in
many instances obstacles to their survival. As capital markets grew and
as family firms began to compete with publicly held corporations, depending solely on the family for financing became a disadvantage. Resistance
to employing nonrelatives and reluctance to promote newcomers to positions of responsibility deprived family firms of the talents and skills of
these individuals, many of whom became commercial rivals. Unless family firms were fortunate enough to find a niche through control of
resources and industrial processes, as did the anthracite coal operators
and iron makers of northeastern Pennsylvania (Folsom, 1981), they found
it increasingly difficult to succeed in the emerging national economy of
the nineteenth century.

In the aggregate, such factors could affect the destinies of towns
and cities as they struggled for market dominance in the heady antebellum economy. Nineteenth-century Boston, despite its reputation for Old
Family exclusiveness, was remarkable for its ability to attract and provide
places for the talented. As lesser cities came within its intellectual range,
it drained off their wealth and talent, their promising authors, rising
lawyers, large capitalists, and prettiest girls (Holmes, 1957 [1859]).

Where Boston succeeded, other cities failed. Middletown was the
largest city in Connecticut in 1800, but its economic life was closely
controlled by a small group of traditionally minded families. As early as
1806, a letter in the *Middlesex Gazette* (1806) complained of the unwillingness of "older and wealthier citizens" to "induce young men of property, industry, and enterprise to become inhabitants." Instead of attracting
them, the writer noted, "they have actually been driven from the place."
By 1860, Middletown had fallen from first in population to seventh, and,
in spite of its strategic location on the Connecticut River, the industrial
and commercial growth that had enriched the state's other cities largely
passed it by.

Dynasty and the Polity

The third force that has persistently worked against family firms
is political. In a certain sense, this is the most important force, since it is
the political process that shapes the legal and tax environments so central
to the survival of family firms. Political opposition to dynasticism is
embedded in the earliest legal codes, and it has arisen episodically as a
component of electoral appeals.

Partible inheritance was not introduced to the British colonies of
North America in order to prevent the intergenerational transmission of

farms and firms. On the contrary, its original purpose was to assure patriarchal and patrilineal continuities of authority and property. But, as extraordinary population growth severed the ties between families, land, and traditional occupations, it began to serve a contrary purpose.

In this setting, some families proved more adept than others at operating in the emerging market system, and the countryside witnessed the emergence of a class of landed entrepreneurs (Sweeney, 1984). In the towns and cities, the merchants benefited both from the rise of colonial markets and from the integration of these markets into an international mercantilist system. By the mideighteenth century, significant differences in economic and political interests had begun to divide American society. It was at this point that antidynastic political sentiments began to be voiced.

The revolutionary legislatures abolished entail, the English law that in some colonies had perpetually tied lands and families. Many legislatures also repealed the entire body of English common law and with it the statute of uses (the juridical basis of trusts) and the statute of charitable uses (the basis for endowment). As the propertied worked to form for-profit and not-for-profit corporations, they were opposed at every step of the way by their political enemies, who understood the dynastic implications and the larger political consequences of incorporation, private charity, and testamentary trusts (Hall, 1982).

Thomas Jefferson was the most eloquent spokesman for the populist, antidynastic "Virginia Doctrine." He opposed industrial and commercial development, describing market dependency as "a canker which soon eats to the heart of [a republic's] laws and constitution" (Koch, 1965, p. 393). More important, he believed that every generation should be free to work out its own destinies unencumbered by the past. "The earth belongs to the living," Jefferson declared, "the dead have neither power nor rights over it" (Koch, 1965, pp. 329-330). This position was the kernel of the Virginia Doctrine and the basis for antidynastic legislation and court decisions throughout the United States (Miller, 1961).

The Virginia Doctrine distorted the institutional and economic life of the early republic. In spite of its large population, the Jeffersonian South had few business corporations or cultural institutions. In contrast, Federalist New England possessed two thirds of the business corporations and most of the colleges in the United States (Davis, 1917). These institutional differences were paralleled by advances in economic development, which were in turn closely tied to the use of testamentary and endowment trusts, the fundamental legal mechanisms of dynastic formation.

In the 1820s, Jacksonianism represented the final crystallization of antidynastic politics. This development was especially evident in states like New York, which enacted laws limiting the proportion of estates that could be left to charity, made the size of institutional endowments subject to the will of the legislature, and established governmental over-sight of charitable organizations (Scott, 1951). Although the federal courts eased some of these strictures, antiaristocratic doctrines remained strong. As late as the 1880s, New York courts enforced the Jacksonian statutes against the trustees of Samuel J. Tilden, who had left the bulk of his fortune to establish the New York Public Library. Only a national outcry spearheaded by reformers concerned about the need for private wealth to serve the public good led to a change in the state's laws (Ames, 1913).

Antidynasticism was not the exclusive property of populist politicians. Social Darwinism influenced some founders of the great post–Civil War industrial fortunes to question the wisdom of passing on huge accumulations of wealth. Andrew Carnegie was the most outspoken of these. Proclaiming that he who dies rich dies disgraced, he became the greatest philanthropist of his generation. He advocated a progressive income tax and confiscatory inheritance laws (Carnegie, 1889). Carnegie was echoed by Boston legal scholar John Chipman Gray. In criticizing the legitimation of spendthrift trusts, Gray (1895, p. vi) denounced mechanisms through which the rich could "assure undisturbed possession of wealth to their children, however weak or wicked they may be."

Politically impelled opposition to dynasties and the institutions that produced them continued into this century. Efforts to obtain a federal charter for the Rockefeller Foundation in 1910 led to three years of congressional hearings, which ended only when Rockefeller withdrew from the battle. The New Deal's 1935 revision of the tax code was explicitly framed to "soak the rich." And, the Temporary National Economic Committee (TNEC) investigations conducted by Congress in the late 1930s devoted volumes both to the vast size and to the extraordinary influence of the nation's dynastic families. In 1969, a decade of enquiry into the charitable foundations led to changes in the federal tax code affecting self-dealing, excess business holdings, reinvestment of income, and public accountability. These changes came close to eliminating the usefulness of foundations as dynastic mechanisms (Andrews, 1968, 1970; Neilson, 1972, 1985).

Ambivalence

In Europe, aristocratic dynasties were protected by a special legal status. The law of inheritance required lands and titles to be passed undivided to the eldest son. Entail prevented the sale or seizure of dynastic property by nonfamily members, however indebted the family might be. In America, dynasties enjoyed no special standing. That they could exist at all was due to the adeptness of family founders and their successors in preserving and renewing their wealth and sense of special purpose—really the only things that set the so-called "great families" apart from the others.

In the end, the survival of the great families depended on their ability to participate effectively in the capitalist economy and to defend their place in the democratic polity. Neither their own sense of special purpose nor their standing in the eyes of others exempted them from accountability to the marketplace. As one nineteenth-century dynast put it (Hall, 1892, p. 3), "No amount of good blood can make a fool other than he is, but family pride may stimulate a person of respectable origin and but limited capacity to exertions that will bring success in life."

The absence of special legal status meant that the children of dynastic families, like the children of lesser families, had to live in society and exert themselves in order to succeed. These were the only ways of assuring the survival of the dynasty. The rich could be exclusive, but only up to a point. The economic and political skills essential to dynastic survival could not be learned from private tutors; they could only be acquired in schools where merit, not manners, was the standard of excellence. The wealthy in America could not live idly when their self-interest required activity and engagement. They could not set themselves apart, either from society in general or from people like themselves, because the perpetuation of wealth was a matter of collective action to deploy political and economic resources.

However great a family's wealth and however compelling its sense of special destiny, no dynasty could be indifferent to the dominant democratic and meritocratic values of American society. Dynastic survival depended not only on institutional effectiveness in the marketplace but also on the ability of members, who as Americans were influenced by the dominant values, to reconcile the privileges of wealth with social expectations of individual achievement. Because a dynasty is ultimately an affair of persons, its continuation has depended less on its wealth than on the willingness of individuals in each succeeding generation to carry on the family mission. Individual responses to the conflict between dominant values and the family myth ultimately determine the fate of dynasties.

In dealing with this conflict between family and society, each child faces choices about how to use the family myth and the fortune that accompanies it. It can be a source of strength, a crippling burden, or an excuse for failure. The Adams family is a case in point. George Washington Adams (1801–1829), the son and grandson of presidents, lived a short and miserably failed life. He drowned himself in Long Island Sound when, during a psychotic break, he hallucinated that the engine of the steamship on which he was a passenger was speaking reproachfully in his father's voice (Nagel, 1983). In contrast, his brother Charles Francis (1807–1886) accepted both the assets and the liabilities of dynasty and built a brilliant career as a lawyer and diplomat in the mold of his forebears.

Eli Whitney, Jr. (1825–1895), son of the famous inventor and industrial pioneer, represented an interesting variation on this theme in which even children who forge successful careers and fulfill dynastic expectations remain incapable of valuing their achievements. Although his father died when Whitney was an infant, the son spent most of his life in the shadow of the great man's reputation. It was predetermined that he would take over management of the Whitney Armory, which his uncles operated during his minority. Whitney took over the firm shortly after graduating from Princeton. He was phenomenally successful in an intensely competitive industry. But, he was incapable of seeing himself as a success. Through the decade of the 1850s, he kept a diary in which, between notes on spectacular transactions, he endlessly reiterated his sense of personal failure (Whitney, 1852–1860, p. 2): "July 9, 1852: I am very blue and possessed of a feeling of uncertainty as to my future business prospects and standing as a man. . . . I seem to have been continuously putting my hand to the plow and looking back all my life long. My mistakes in life have been many. I am called somewhat energetic but lack energy more than anything else." The tone of the diary begins to change when, in the late 1850s, Whitney becomes involved in the effort to organize the New Haven Water Company. Initially an outsider to the project, he eventually not only became its largest stockholder but built the waterworks itself. What began as an effort to secure a greater power source for his father's factory became in the end a means of creating his own identity as a person and as an entrepreneur. Only by making his work his own could he have a sense that it had any real value. At the same time, it is significant that his self-affirmation came not from rejecting the dynastic burden but from accepting it and building his own life on and beyond it.

As the wealthy in America coalesced into a class at the end of the nineteenth century, the conflict between dominant values and dynastic claims came increasingly to be institutionally mediated. This was no accident, for, as the Holmes quote that began this paper suggests, dynastic families were becoming deeply concerned about their prospects for survival. After the Civil War, private education in America underwent a fundamental restructuring that was largely underwritten by dynastic families. Although they were motivated by the obvious need for an educational system appropriate to a national industrial economy, they were no less concerned with ensuring their own place in that new world.

The keystone of the new elite boarding schools and great private universities was an ethos of public service. This ethos not only legitimated the wealthy as a class but also created a matrix in which members of dynastic families could work to resolve the family-society conflict in a reasonably regulated way. Surrounded by people like themselves who were undergoing the same kinds of stresses, the sons and daughters who filled the prep schools played an especially important role in institutionalizing the intrapersonal struggle and guiding its resolution in socially productive directions. This development probably accounts for the fact that most dynastic families in America ended up accommodating the conflict between dynasty and democracy through public service and philanthropy rather than through exile or Bohemianism.

Conclusion

In spite of the social, economic, and political forces arrayed against them and in spite of individual ambivalence and family conflict, the dynastic process continues. It involves not only the heirs to great eighteenth- and nineteenth-century mercantile or industrial fortunes but any parent who, having succeeded in business, hopes to found a family and any child who faces a future in which expectations and resources garnered in the past have set him apart from his contemporaries.

Although social commentators, from Tocqueville in the nineteenth century through Weber and Parsons in the twentieth, have assured us that the future lay with impersonally and professionally managed bureaucratic enterprises, family firms and the dynastic processes that they often set in motion continue to play a dominant part in American life.

The persistence of family firms suggests that they are not merely holdovers or throwbacks. They can do things that more formally structured business organizations cannot. Proprietors accountable to themselves and their sense of family responsibility can act more flexibly and imaginatively than managers beholden to accountants and anonymous stockholders. The importance of family firms in the newspaper business is not a coincidence. Family control gives editors and publishers the independence of marketplace accountability that permits them to take unpopular or unprofitable stands. And, the family tie to the community makes these stands influential. Family firms have a capacity to make long-term investments and resist the pressure of financial analysts for short-term returns that currently bedevil many publicly held corporations.

The persistence of the family firm, together with evidence of the roles that it plays in industrial innovation, community leadership, and philanthropy, has important implications not only for therapists and management consultants but also for students of economic development and public policy. The larger social, technological, and political forces working against family firms have not been forces of nature but products of legislation and jurisprudence. Investigating them may lead both to a clearer understanding of the dynamics of family firms and to changes that will alter those dynamics.

An earlier version of this paper was presented to the Family Business Conference, the Wharton School, University of Pennsylvania in

October 1986. The research from which this paper was drawn has been supported by the American Council of Learned Societies, AT&T Foundation, the Ellis Phillips Foundation, Equitable Life Assurance Society of the United States, Exxon Education Foundation, General Electric Foundation, the Teagle Foundation, and the Program on Nonprofit Organizations, Yale University.

References

Ames, J. B. *Lectures on Legal History and Miscellaneous Legal Essays*. Cambridge, Mass.: Harvard University Press, 1913.

Andrews, F. E. *Patman and the Foundations: Review and Assessment*. New York: The Foundation Center, 1968.

Andrews, F. E. *Foundations and the Tax Reform Act of 1969*. New York: The Foundation Center, 1970.

Baltzell, E. D. *Puritan Boston and Quaker Philadelphia: Two Protestant Ethics and the Spirit of Class Authority and Leadership*. New York: Free Press, 1979.

Carnegie, A. "The Gospel of Wealth." *North American Review*, 1889, *148*, 653–664, *149*, 682–698.

Collier, P., and Horowitz, D. *The Rockefellers: An American Dynasty*. New York: New American Library, 1976.

Davis, J. S. *Essays in the Earlier History of American Corporations*. Cambridge, Mass.: Harvard University Press, 1917.

Farber, B. *Guardians of Virtue: Salem Families in 1800*. New York: St. Martins Press, 1972.

Folsom, B. W. *Urban Capitalists: Entrepreneurs and City Growth in Pennsylvania's Lackawanna and Lehigh Regions, 1800–1920*. Baltimore, Md.: Johns Hopkins University Press, 1981.

Gray, J. C. *Restraints on the Alienation of Property*. Boston: Boston Book Company, 1895.

Hall, P. D. "Family Structure and Class Consolidation Among the Boston Brahmins." Unpublished doctoral dissertation, Department of History, State University of New York, Stony Brook, 1973.

Hall, P. D. *The Organization of American Culture, 1700–1900: Institutions, Elites, and the Origins of American Nationality*. New York: New York University Press, 1982.

Hall, P. D. "An Historical Overview of the Private Nonprofit Sector." In W. W. Powell (ed.), *The Nonprofit Sector: A Research Handbook*. New Haven, Conn.: Yale University Press, 1986.

Hall, T. P. *Family Records of Theodore Parsons Hall and Alexandrine Louise Godfroy*. Detroit, Mich.: Wm. C. Heath, 1892.

Holmes, O. W. *Elsie Venner: A Romance of Destiny*. New York: Signet, 1957 [1859].

Holmes, O. W. *Autocrat of the Breakfast Table*. New York: Sagamore Press, 1961 [1860].

Jobe, B., and Kaye, M. *New England Furniture: The Colonial Era*. Boston: Houghton Mifflin, 1984.

Koch, A. *The American Enlightenment*. New York: George Braziller, 1965.

Kolko, G. "Brahmins and Businessmen." In B. Moore and K. Wolfe (eds.), *The Critical Spirit: Essays in Honor of Herbert Marcuse*. Boston: Beacon Press, 1967.

Marcus, G. "The Fiduciary Role in American Families and Their Institutional Legacy: From the Law of Trusts to Trusts in the Establishment." In G. Marcus (ed.), *Elites: Ethnographic Issues.* Albuquerque: University of New Mexico Press, 1983.

Middlesex Gazette (Middletown, Connecticut), May 16, 1806.

Miller, H. S. *The Legal Foundations of American Philanthropy.* Madison: State Historical Society of Wisconsin, 1961.

Nagel, P. C. *Descent from Glory: Four Generations of the Adams Family.* New York: Oxford University Press, 1983.

Neilson, W. *The Big Foundations.* New York: Columbia University Press, 1972.

Neilson, W. *The Golden Donors.* New York: Dutton, 1985.

Newhall, G. *Future Interests and the Rule Against Perpetuities in Massachusetts.* Boston: Hildreth, 1942.

Pickering's Reports, Boston, Mass.: 1830, *9,* 461.

Scott, A. W. "Charitable Trusts in New York." *New York University Law Review,* 1951, *26* (2), 251–265.

Scott, A. W. *The Law of Trusts.* Boston: Little, Brown, 1939.

Smith, P. *John Adams.* Garden City, N.Y.: Doubleday, 1962.

Story, R. *The Forging of an Aristocracy: Harvard and Boston's Upper Class, 1800–1870.* Middletown, Conn.: Wesleyan University Press, 1981.

Sweeney, K. M. "Mansion People: Kinship, Class, and Architecture in the Mid-Eighteenth Century." *Winterthur Portfolio,* 1984, *19* (4), 231–255.

Thomas, I. *History of Printing in America, with a Biography of Printers and an Account of Newspapers.* Barre, Mass.: Imprint Society, 1970.

Tocqueville, A. de. *Democracy in America.* New York: Vintage Books, 1945 [1835].

Waters, J. "American Colonial Stem Families: Persisting European Patterns in the New World." Unpublished paper presented at the History Department Faculty Seminar, Wesleyan University, April 1978.

Wharton, E. *Ethan Frome.* New York: Scribners', 1911.

White, G. T. *History of the Massachusetts Hospital Life Insurance Company.* Cambridge, Mass.: Harvard University Press, 1955.

Whitney, E., Jr. "Business Diary. 1852–1860." Whitney Family Papers, Yale University Library, Box 11, Folder 173.

Peter Dobkin Hall is associate research scientist at the Institution for Social and Policy Studies, Yale University.

[7]

PRESIDENTIAL ADDRESS

The Family Business

Wayne Broehl
Dartmouth College

My assignment tonight, one filled so admirably by Mira Wilkins last year, is a nostalgic one, for it calls for the speaker to be autobiographical-- to look backward in one's career over the whole body of research and writing efforts. This generally is a revealing experience, and it was for me, for I realized how centrally my own efforts in the field of business history have been concentrated on family firms.

There are a number of famous family names in American business history-- the Rockefellers, Fords, Du Ponts, Vanderbilts, Watsons-- yes, even the Binghams and the Quayles. In most cases these have been family businesses in the sense that both ownership and management passed from one generation to the next. Yet it is startling to realize how few major American companies which started this way have been able to carry the family management thread much beyond the second generation, let alone the third. The Du Ponts have done so, counting in-laws; Henry Ford II was, of course, the third generation, but that seemed to be the last of the Fords in top management, although a recent set of articles in the press have suggested that the string, although broken, might be mended. Yet the family business has been an enduring American institution and has lessons to relate, both positive and negative.

For a moment, let me use my own work as examples of the family business in the United States. It is a small set but has the advantage of being one of quite varied businesses. Perhaps most important, in most of them I had the special opportunity of being on the scene studying them just at the point of transition from one generation to the next. I will put particular focus on the issue of transition in my remarks tonight.

My first book, also my doctoral dissertation, was a business history of Norwalk Truck Line company, at the time (1954) one of the half dozen large interstate motor carriers. While it was a corporation, it really was the child of one person, the sole owner. A wonderful old man of German extraction, John Ernsthausen, had started the company in 1920 as a produce wholesaler, driving his own truck from the country into Cleveland, Ohio. By sheer persistence and hard work over 35 years he had built it into a major business. Ernsthausen was unsophisticated and had only a primitive view of the management process, but he gave me an acute sense of how important one individual can be in an organization. He had a naivete about business life that was at once both charming and frightening. For example, he made the

BUSINESS AND ECONOMIC HISTORY, Second Series, Volume Eighteen, 1989.
Copyright (c) 1989 by the Business History Conference. ISSN 0849-6825.

2

statement more than once that "I get along with Jimmy Hoffa" (with whom the company dealt throughout its whole system). The "getting along" turned out to be self-deluding; the union ran roughshod over the company. John Ernsthausen had no children, and I witnessed before my eyes an internecine battle among the senior executives as to who would gain control when the patriarch was gone. Sadly, the right combination did not occur at his demise and the whole outfit was swallowed up by a trucking conglomerate. As an equally naive, unsophisticated young academic, I coined my most pretentious title for this book-- *Trucks, Trouble and Triumph*.

Coming to Dartmouth soon after that, I quickly became involved in another business history, once more family-- actually three families in three companies. It was the history of the machine tool companies in Springfield, Vermont. All three had been started in the late nineteenth century by true Yankee tinkerer-inventors. By the time of my story the three companies did well over 10% of the machine tool business of the entire country. Indeed, this small Vermont village was considered by the Defense Department in World War II as being one of the half dozen most important bomb targets in the country.

Each of these was family owned, but with different combinations. In the oldest, Jones & Lamson, a son-in-law had taken over the company and had done quite well until he was elected United States senator. Ralph Flanders became a famous senator, particularly well-known for his courageous battle against Senator Joseph McCarthy, the "red-baiter" of the early 1950s. But Flanders could not pay enough attention to the company and it languished. By the time I was chronicling their history, it had a professional management team, pulling and tugging against each other, and they were not up to the task. Soon Jones & Lamson, too, disappeared into a larger conglomerate.

The second firm, which had a rather strange name, the Bryant Chucking Grinder Company, was also family, just into its second generation of management. In this case there was a single professional manager, for the son of the founder had given up business altogether, becoming a philanthropist and scholar, digging in ancient ruins in Southern Spain. Once more, the professional manager was not suited for the business (though he went on to an outstanding career as chief executive officer of a Canadian company). Was there something especially difficult in stepping into family shoes? I began to suspect so. Finally, this company also was absorbed by a larger enterprise.

The third organization, the Fellows Gear Shaper Company, was in its second generation, too. The family was still in the business, with the chief executive role held by a distant relative of the founder, an outstanding man but quite elderly. Soon he was gone and this company followed the same pattern of being captured by a larger company.

All three companies are still in Springfield but are much smaller, much less effective, and the family links just about eradicated. It was a fascinating study for comparative business history; there were many constants, including the fact that all of the companies were located in the valley of the Black River, where most of the line employees lived. All of the family owners resided on the top of the hills, a telling reminder of late nineteenth century "social

3

Darwinism." Yet the three firms were very different, and I learned more about why family enterprises are so difficult to perpetuate. Many of the difficulties here lay in personal failings of individuals, some family, others from the outside. In most cases the inability of those families to be self-critical was the central problem.

This book had one of my better titles, perhaps because it was picked by my students in one of our Dartmouth morning coffee breaks. It was called *Precision Valley*, and soon there were all sorts of Precision Valley offshoots in Southern Vermont-- Precision Valley Airlines, Precision Valley Motel, etc.

My next endeavor was not strictly a family business history, although one of the entities within it had a unique, quite macabre family involvement. This was my book, *The Molly Maguires*, about a whole set of companies in an industry highly concentrated in one geographical location, the anthracite coal country. The Pinkerton National Detective Agency had made a contract with Franklin B. Gowen, the rail and coal mogul, to infiltrate the Miners' Union with the hidden agenda of picturing them as Molly Maguires, the old Irish secret society that had been brought in by the Irish miners. Allan Pinkerton was the founder and head of the agency, a complex individual, publicly professing righteousness and probity under the rubric "We Never Sleep," but privately planning and executing terrible acts-- and passing on his unethical behavior to his two sons, who were also in the business. Allan Pinkerton's own letterbooks of the agency had remained intact, having been given by later family under restrictions to the Library of Congress, not to be opened until 2025. However, I was able to persuade the fourth generation president of the Pinkertons, Robert Pinkerton, to let me see these, and I soon found some startling evidence in them, particularly an incriminating letter that Allan Pinkerton had been personally responsible for a famous vigilante killing associated with the Molly Maguire story. It had been planned and executed just like the same effort done a few months before by the Pinkerton Agency, in that case an attempt to murder by ambush Jesse and Frank James at their home, planned by Allan Pinkerton but carried out by his eldest son, William. I gingerly extracted from Robert Pinkerton his willingness to have the story told, with no restraints, whatever I happened to find. Later, when the book came out, this story about the vigilante action surfaced and I am sure it must have been a shock to Robert Pinkerton. By this time, in the fourth generation, the company had gone through a complete metamorphosis in company values. Homestead had occurred, Clarence Darrow had made a monkey of Pinkerton agents as he defended Big Bill Haywood and the IWW, the company had been traumatized by the heat of public opinion. The company and the family were now very different and did not want to be reminded of the past.

The next study was family in its most all-encompassing sense. It was done in the late 1960s on the Rockefeller family's international development corporation, the International Basic Economy Corporation. IBEC had been founded by Nelson and Laurance Rockefeller with involvement also from other members of the family to bring socially responsible private enterprise to Latin America and other parts of the developing world. There is probably no family name better known than Rockefeller, as I came to see as I visited

4

the various operations. The name itself opened all sorts of doors, but also was taken advantage of constantly, and always had to be protected. Although designed as a profit-making business, IBEC also took on characteristics of a foundation. It was to carry out a Rockefeller "service to mankind." IBEC was founded in part to "save" the world, not just to produce a service or product. This resulted in a continuing conflict between personal goals and business goals. Often these two are not congruent. In cases where the product or service *is* the goal, this can become a real source of pride for the employees. Being a "missionary," which was IBEC's objective, is a laudatory goal, too, but much more difficult for employees and even management to grasp. And it is much more difficult to assess progress.

This conflict is more frequent than one might guess in the family corporation. One side of the owner-manager is making a personal statement, many times attempting to fulfill family social or personal goals. This lends itself readily to ambivalent leadership.

When Nelson gave up the position as chief executive to go into politics, a professional manager was hired. He was to be an interim until the next generation of Nelson's family could take over. This transition did come to pass but did not last. As perhaps an ultimate irony, IBEC was taken over by a British firm-- a well-known international, colonial company.

My next effort, again international, was *The Village Entrepreneur,* a study of small-scale, rural businesses in South India. My focus was on rice millers and fertilizer distributors, both dominantly family run, the former often into its third or fourth generation, the latter typically a first-generation father/son enterprise. The contrast between IBEC and these firms was striking. These Indian firms were self-serving, narrowly-based entities with little concern for long-range planning. But they *did* know how to make money in the short run. Family succession in India was most often to the eldest son, and my analysis convinced me that such an arbitrary, tradition-bound rule was often unwise.

Next came the John Deere book, published in 1984. Here we have what often is cited as the archetypical family company. The company had been founded in 1837 and there had been a Deere or a Deere in-law in the role of chief executive for five straight generations. Deere & Company had gone public back in the 1920s, but a large bulk of ownership (though not controlling interest) was still held by the family. Three of these five CEO's were, indeed, sons-in-law, and in all three cases were great successes. It is difficult for a blood son to follow a father. A whole set of expectations about adolescence, slips and failures, and sibling rivalry color the case before the fact. The son is being brought up in part to fulfill the father's own self image, and the sons of successful fathers have an abiding, sometimes overweening need to be successful in their own eyes. Few fathers that are powerful, busy, and emotionally involved in their businesses make good mentors. A son-in-law is fresher on the scene, easier to mentor by fathers-in-law or others, and easier to disengage if not up to the job. The son-in-law may carry other disabilities-- his wife has all those family pasts and can slip into mixed loyalties. Still, my small sample of sons-in-law makes the model seem quite attractive, other things equal.

5

Here at Deere I once again had the opportunity to see the revealing transition from the fifth generation leader that represented the family (a son-in-law) to a professional manager. There is no Deere family person in any post of management in the company today. There are capable children, but they have chosen other careers, so this transition is probably final. It has been accomplished by the new CEO with extraordinary grace, due particularly to the qualities of the man, schooled by 32 years as a Deere executive.

My last family company study is still in progress, a business history of Cargill, Incorporated, founded in 1865. In some respects this is even more archetypical than Deere, in that while in its fifth generation of family management, it still remains totally owned by family and privately held, the largest such company in the United States.

This is actually a two-family situation. The Cargills founded the company, but MacMillans became the majority owners. Both families still make up all of the ownership of the company and both families still have several members in top management. Once again I am having the privilege of being in the middle of a transition-- from the fifth generation to the sixth. In this case, however, there are younger members of both families in their 30s and early 40s currently working in the company, with potential to become senior managers, perhaps one of them a CEO. Yet the transition problems are enormous. Whereas the present generation has had only five members in management itself, the next generation has forty-two separate possibilities, only a few of whom are interested in being involved in the company. It makes for a tense and revealing process of interaction and I will be following it with great interest over the next two years or so, before the first volume of the study is completed.

What can be said about family businesses as possible generalizations from which we can learn? My sample is small, so I put the following ideas forward quite tentatively. Let me pose this quest for generalization by asking four questions and attempting some observations about each.

First, are family businesses more oriented toward the long run? By a narrow definition this almost inevitably has to be answered yes. Families do extend over full generations, transitions take into consideration that longer time frame, whereas the transition period for most major corporations with professional management is something in the nature of five to seven years. To be sure, professionally managed companies also are interested in management development and are looking down into the organization for future CEOs, but with a much wider pool and these different time lines. So it is *not* the same process that occurs in the family company.

American business is faulted widely today for being too short-term oriented, too conscious of the quarterly P&L statements, etc. I have not found the family companies that I have worked with any less concerned about these matters, so I suspect that in real terms family companies also must remain interested in these shorter time frames. But the fact remains that there is something very important about trying to plan for an organization to extend into the next generation. It does indeed give a different perspective, and there are more insights that can be drawn from this more complex transition process.

6

A second question that might readily come to mind is this-- are employees of family companies more loyal? There has been much writing recently about the lessening of corporate loyalties, due perhaps to LBOs, the spin-off of corporations, sometimes with loss of employee rights, etc. Company loyalty is critically important and quite ephemeral. Family companies are perhaps in a more exposed position in terms of relations between owner and employee. A family name carries with it certain remembrances from previous generations. These are not always good memories (as can be seen in the Pinkerton saga), and it may be that a poorly-run family company can have more problems here than usual. Nevertheless, I would be willing to postulate that we can learn much from the variegated interactions between a family owner and the employees, an equation that may be rather unique. I felt this strongly in the Deere case, for there was almost a mystical feeling on the part of the employees about their company and about the Deere family. There is something of the same in the Cargill situation, although here it is not directed so much at individual members of either of those two families as it is to the company as a whole. Still, I would guess that much of this high degree of loyalty stems from Cargill's thoroughgoing family influence.

A third question-- are family companies more entrepreneurial? While I hate to sound dogmatic, I believe I can answer this question, out of my own experience at least, with an unequivocal no. Just by the nature of the family at the transition point and the concern about passing along ownership and control, I think it is more likely than not that a family company turns out to be less entrepreneurial than at least some of its more vigorous counterparts among publicly held companies. There is a certain essential truth to the axiom, "from shirtsleeves to shirtsleeve in three generations." Implicit in this belief is the guess that the son cannot live up the father-- and this is often just what happens and is why the third generation sometimes has nothing left over.

There are noteworthy exceptions to this belief. Deere and Cargill are prime examples. Interestingly, both had difficulties in the first generation. John Deere, an innovative genius but untutored and financially inept, had run out on his debts as a blacksmith in Vermont to come to Illinois. When the firm was almost driven to bankruptcy in 1857, his son Charles took over at age 21 and became caretaker to nurse the firm back to strength, and in time to participate in the agricultural expansion and growth of the West. Yet to do this he first had to solve the problem of financial control within the organization, build sound finances, and then introduce new decentralized structures to fit the rapidly-growing business environment.

In the case of Cargill, W.W. Cargill had built a great empire, but built it on shaky financial legs. His view of control was something like this: "I told Hayden I wanted some different accounting but I did not want too much red tape, that things had to be practical rather than system ... the verification of the accounts I told him to drop and call it collecting, and to get around and collect the accounts and not have a whole lot of red tape about verification and two or three bookkeepers and collectors ..." When W.W. died in 1909 and son-in-law John MacMillan, Sr. took over, thorough-going financial controls were desperately needed and MacMillan came down solidly on the side of

7

centralization under a powerful chief executive officer: "there are only two ways I know of, of doing business; one is to trust your men and let them run everything as they please and turn out what results they please,-and the other is to put in an accounting system that keeps you informed as to what is going on everywhere. The latter system is certainly the up to date way of doing, and the only way I can keep track of things. We got a pretty good taste of what it amounts to, to let things drift. The great trouble has been that they do not enter into the spirit of what modern accounting means."

Sometimes a status quo, an inflexibility, can set in. At Deere the management had to force the third-generation family CEO to accept the gasoline engine tractor, and it took fifteen years of arguments to bring him around. Cargill had an interesting transition into the third generation, too. Here the problem was almost opposite. John MacMillan, Jr. was brilliant, creative, arrogant-- moving too fast, so that good financial and administrative controls and ongoing public relations needed to be brought to the organization through other men. The need is always present for a carefully chosen management team to accompany a new president. The family firm has a particular problem here, for it is often difficult to find the right alter egos who can function within the constraints of a strong-willed family CEO.

Sometimes the problem seems to be exacerbated by primogeniture. The question I always asked in my study in India, whether the CEO of those little businesses I was studying was a first son of an entrepreneurial father, gave me real clues to an understanding of entrepreneurship. In most cases the more entrepreneurial were not-- they were sons, but not first sons. I am not certain how I could extrapolate from this to the United States but my guess is that there is some common line running through both.

My fourth question can be answered, I think, with little doubt. Are family companies more idiosyncratic? My answer here is a resounding yes. There is a quite labyrinthine set of nuances operating in most family businesses, and in more cases than not these lead to personalized decisions made only partially on business parameters. I have alluded to some of these earlier (the mixed agendas at IBEC, for example). There may be inter-family or intra-family struggles that add untoward tensions. Idiosyncracies do not necessarily have to be equated with weaker or poorer decisions; sometimes they can provide for a positive thrust, but my guess is that this happens less frequently than the opposite.

If my hypotheses are accurate so far, namely that there are identifiable differences between the family company and the professionally run company, then it should follow logically that there are also differences in writing the business history of the family company. The business historian might find the following in attempting a business history of a family company.

First, I think it is more daunting to persuade a family to have its company chronicled. Just by the nature of the sensitivities of internal family interactions it is difficult to persuade all family members that chronicling the professional growth of a company will be important and valuable to them, rather than keeping family secrets within the family. There have been a number of outside exposés of family business-- the Bingham story being a recent case. There seems to be a great temptation to sensationalize family

8

life. Ralph Nader did a great deal of this in his book on CEOs, *The Big Boys*. For these and other reasons there have been few really good internal business histories of family companies, written with independence and centering on the company rather than family gossip.

Some aspects of management itself are more difficult to assess in a family company. In particular, the question of governance turns out to be highly complex. Even in cases where there is a single owner with "absolute" control there is always a set of governance questions that go beyond those inherent in the professionally managed firm. Governance means just that-- the ability to govern. Sheer ownership alone does not, and should not, guarantee that senior management will willingly follow. The professional senior management always has a stake and a quasi-ownership position that must be recognized. There are often palace intrigues on the part of senior management in family companies about how they might be able to wrest control from the hands of owners who do not seem to have their own goals. I have seen this in operation, at least in an incipient sense in just about every one of the situations I have studied.

In the case of Deere the company solved the problem in part by going public, back in the third generation. In Cargill's case, there is an intricate set of parameters that govern board positions-- a totally inside board-- in order to both represent the two families accurately and to have significant representation (though no ownership whatsoever) by the senior management. In sum, the question of governance has all of the difficulties of the publicly held corporation, plus some further constraints that themselves make for important new problems.

There is an interesting parameter that you might not think of in the family corporation, namely, the presence of adequate records. Solid sets of records always have been the *sine qua non* of good history. In the case of the family company it is likely, first, that the family will have saved more records than would the comparable public corporation. This is not to say that the family is going to be willing to make these available. That is quite another question. Nevertheless, the combination of a family's desire to have its business records preserved, plus the fact that family personal correspondence can mean much more in ferreting out company understandings than it would be in a comparable publicly held corporation makes the question of access to records and the adequacy of them an interesting dimension of writing business histories of family corporations. The Rockefeller enterprises had been beautifully documented. There has long been a formal Rockefeller archives with a professional archivist. Fortunately, too, the Cargill records are outstanding, particularly for the seminal time when the first two MacMillans put the modern corporation together (although archivally they were in terrible shape, much of them stored in the attic of the headquarters in a jumbled mess). Unfortunately, at Cargill, as soon as an inside professional-manager CEO took over in the early 1960s to act as transition until the present family generation again took over, the record keeping became very sparse and limited (though the CEO himself did a superb job of carrying the company through this transition). Sometimes a management throws away not because of lawyers' fears but simply because they lack a sense of history, and that, I think,

9

was true here. Today, once more, this next generation of Cargills and MacMillans is considerably more records oriented.

The business history of a family company also tends to have more than the usual amount of ego built into it. Rather than being the record of a particular CEO and his few years at the helm, here it is a dynasty. Inevitably, there are family icons, and these can become very tricky when trying to get at the truth and in being able to state it. There is a special problem, I believe, in teasing out the full story from a family situation. One is dealing with a range of people all the way from highly professional senior-management family members to the weaker, less interested members from the fringes, sometimes even the "black sheep." Wives are more important than they would be in the professionally run company. And these stories often are not just gossip, but a major source of why certain decisions were made. Yet at the same time the professional historian can sometimes perform a very special, unique role for a family, by putting into factual and historical perspective all of the various pieces of misinformation, prejudice, and various other shibboleths. In Cargill's case, for example, there was a particularly tense battle between the two families over ownership and control back in 1925. This situation has been remembered down to the present, sometimes with less than accurate judgments on the part of each of the groups about the other. In the process of putting together early materials on the Cargill book, I have reconstructed this story in detail and have shown this to all of the family members. I believe this has performed a very useful catharsis for them in the process.

Can we, then, generalize about the family business and the writing of business histories about the family business? My guess is that we can. In the United States, they have been of a particular genre, albeit not a terribly important one. It is revealing that so few American businesses stay within the ownership of a family over any length of time. The second generation seems to be crucial. It puts into place and formalizes the practices giving life to the corporate philosophy. It brings into this process the employees, hopefully with deep loyalties. In this second generation it often seems critical to establish sound financial controls before expansion takes place. Only after this can creativity occur and the broader political and environmental factor be addressed.

Some of the reasons why these transitional crises seem so dominant may lie in our overall history of the country. People came to the United States seeking change. They were willing to break with family and tradition to seek something better for themselves. It would be unusual for Americans to find their outlet just improving things with the status quo-- far better to look for change to solve problems. In Britian's, India's, and Japan's tradition, status quo is far more valued.

This is why comparative business history is most productive here. The lessons from British firms are quite revealing and thought provoking. Patterns of family ownership in India are most pronounced, and my brief brush with this special form of family company begs a comparison both with the British and with us.

10

　　　　Similarly, family business has been vitally important in its impact in Japan over many years. Even today, the family corporation there is one of the dominant forms. They seem to have been able to draw on the best of family values, and actual members of the family, for leadership positions. Yet, when a family member is not up to the task Japanese family companies have quickly moved to professional management. As Tsunehiko Yui, who addressed our meetings last year, has put it, Japanese families have learned well to "reign not rule."

　　　　Why have these examples in other parts of the world been so much more successful than here in the United States? What is there about the family corporation in our own milieu that makes it more difficult to preserve over time, and why is that we have only a few good business histories of American family-held corporations? These are questions that intrigue me. Comparative research on family companies seems to me to be a promising field for further research.

[8]

The Family Firm in Industrial Capitalism: International Perspectives on Hypotheses and History

ROY CHURCH

University of East Anglia

The resilience of family firms, which survive even among the largest companies of the major industrial nations, is commonplace. A survey reported in the *Financial Times* in 1989 concluded that about one in eight of the firms listed in the FTSE largest 100 companies possessed strong family connections. The *New York Times* referred to a growing opinion among management scientists during the 1980s that the management practices and business values associated with family firms, their regard for quality of product, respect for employees, and a focus on 'more lasting concerns than the next quarter's results' offered a model for the rest of American business. Many of the surviving family firms were large, publicly traded companies whose traditional strengths were then becoming acknowledged by an increasing number of large managerial corporations, reflected in their use of advertising and logos to project images linking past long-standing service with present efficiency.[1]

There is also, of course, an extensive literature which emphasises the inherent weaknesses of family firms and their inability to adapt to the pressures of competition and change. The declining numbers of such firms in the twentieth century have been interpreted as evidence of an inability to compete with the large, modern corporations in which widely dispersed shareholding has been combined with multidepartmental or multidivisional organisation and professional, salaried managers working within extensive administrative hierarchies. A similar interpretation, associated particularly with Elbaum and Lazonick, has concluded that from the late nineteenth century successful competitive economic performance in the international arena depended on the replacement of the institutions of traditional competitive capitalism by large-scale corporate enterprise on the Chandler model. From their perspective, the survival of family firms, conservative and resistant in the face of pressures for change, are seen to be both symptomatic and a cause of the institutional sclerosis that afflicted British industry from the late nineteenth century.[2]

18 FAMILY CAPITALISM

This survey considers the historical experience of family and managerial enterprise in Britain, the US, Germany and Japan during the late nineteenth and the first half of the twentieth century, when their role has been a matter of debate. It concentrates on behaviour often considered to be peculiar to family firms, specifically that relating to ownership, control and management; motivation and policy objectives; succession, adaptability and performance. By its very nature a review of the literature virtually precludes the introduction of entirely new evidence and cannot, therefore, aim to present either novel or conclusive observations. There is, nonetheless, room for an adjustment of the perspective from which historians have tended to view family firms. The refocusing resulting from this exercise offers support for the argument that the widespread perception of the role of family firms in industrial capitalism is in need of revision.

II
HYPOTHESES AND GENERALISATIONS

While stressing the tentative nature of his conclusions from a nonetheless extremely valuable and authoritative survey of the role of family firms in the British economy written in 1983, Payne emphasised the importance of adopting a precise definition of the 'family firm' before attempting to generalise. Even in the absence of such a definition, few would challenge the view that, as a consequence of the greater scale and scope of business activities in the eighteenth and nineteenth centuries, family firms were necessarily different in many respects from those which survived into, or were established during, the twentieth century.[3] Yet only if historians focus on the precise characteristics considered to have led family firms to behave differently from other forms of enterprise is it possible to assess the significance of their special role in business history. To this end Chandler has placed the 'personal enterprise', which includes firms which were owned, controlled and managed by families, at the centre of his explanation for the relative decline of British industry beginning at the end of the nineteenth century. A further defining feature of the personal enterprise is the absence of an extensive managerial hierarchy. The entrepreneurial or family-controlled enterprise (entrepreneurial in the first generation) refers to a firm in which the founders and their heirs recruited salaried managers but continued to be influential shareholders, held executive managerial positions, and exercised decisive influence on company policy.[4] All of these conditions are difficult to establish empirically.

There is a consensus concerning the role of family firms during the

THE FAMILY FIRM IN INDUSTRIAL CAPITALISM 19

early stages of industrialisation in the major economies, regardless of chronology. Arguably the most revealing recent detailed analysis of the role of family firms in the process of industrialisation is Scranton's account of the nineteenth-century textile industry of Philadelphia. His stress on the 'matrix of accumulation' and the complementarity of specialised production and marketing functions carried out in an inter-locked set of separate establishments shows family firms to have con-ducted their affairs with an efficiency and success comparable with the precociously corporate, integrated mills of the large Lowell Company.[5] The persistence of the 'proprietary matrix' into the late nineteenth century, represented as much by the formation of new proprietary firms as the persistence of established enterprises, was interpreted as evidence of a continuing vitality and competitiveness of the family firm.[6]

Scranton's study confirms the findings of historians of industries in Europe who have underlined the central role of family firms during the eighteenth and nineteenth centuries. During the early stages of indus-trialisation family firms were appropriate in scale and structure to the size and structure of markets, to contemporary technology, to the level of capital resources required, and to the feasibility of workforce control and supervision. Firms owned, controlled and managed by families provided the kinship network and personal connections which, by offer-ing a basis for mutual trust, helped to offset the uncertainties and risks associated with very imperfect information flows during the early stages of industrialisation.[7] Even so, the high mortality rate of firms and their constant replacement by others was a dominant feature in the nine-teenth century.[8]

With few exceptions, before the second half of the nineteenth century most firms were, in Chandler's terminology, 'entrepreneurial' enter-prises, which only became family firms once the second generation of entrepreneurial families became part of the organisation. The model of the family firm portrayed in the literature is long established and fam-iliar. Family and managerial firms represented contrasting approaches to the conduct of business. Whereas in family firms status tended to be determined by seniority and sentiment, position within the managerial organisation depended on particular skills, knowledge and competence. Motivation within family firms was complicated by non-financial con-siderations, such as family reputation and status within a community, providing employment for family, the enterprise as a store of family wealth, independence, employee welfare and succession. Such diffuse motivation, which in Chandler's model includes a major preoccupation with short-term financial gain, was part of his justification for arguing that entrepreneurial and family firms were unlikely to expand to achieve a scale, scope and performance comparable with the large American corporations that emerged in several sectors of American industry from the 1880s.

Typically governed by extensive managerial hierarchies whose stock options rarely gave managers a significant share of corporate control, American managerial companies have been presented as typically, if not universally, bureaucratic. Professional managers were described as making disinterested decisions in the sense that they were not affected by priorities unrelated to business performance in which efficiency and long-term growth of the organisation were central to the corporate strategy which they determined.[9] Chandler saw the persistence of the traditional, unitary and hierarchical approach characteristic of family firms in Britain as having been a major factor contributing to Britain's industrial decline relative to the US and Germany, and to a loss of international market share before World War II.[10]

Such a view is consistent with, but is stronger than, Payne's conclusion: that whereas the *small* family business positively promotes growth the *large* public company which retains elements of family control probably retards growth. Referring specifically to Britain, Payne asserted that

> if there was any causal connection between the family firm and a loss of economic vitality, it occurred . . . in the inter-war years when a number of holding companies were still sufficiently familial in nature, being essentially federations of family firms, to be reluctant to adopt a centralised structure and to create a managerial staff that would have permitted them to overcome the diseconomies of size.[11]

The failure which this quotation implies is that too many large British firms may have been inhibited by familial influences and priorities to respond to market signals in a way which might have been expected of managerial firms. This is a special case of the argument that institutional rigidities condemned managers to a failure to recognise that a changing competitive environment required diversification, structural adaptation and managerial reform, if organisational capability was to be improved and competitive advantage reestablished.[12]

III
OWNERSHIP, CONTROL AND FINANCIAL POLICIES

Though disputed in detail, the broad contrasts between Britain and the rest of Europe with the United States, in terms of the size of firms, the

THE FAMILY FIRM IN INDUSTRIAL CAPITALISM 21

timing and extent of family control, and influence on company policies, are widely accepted; so, too, is the slower pace of the trend in Europe towards centralised business structures and the adoption of the multi-divisional form of organisation. Central to Chandler's thesis which explains the declining industrial performance of Britain compared with the US and Germany is the persistence until World War II of 'personal enterprises', particularly the family firm, which let the nation down.[13] International comparisons, therefore, must form an important part of the debate over the achievements and failings of family firms.

According to Chandler, 'the goal for family firms appears to have been to provide a steady flow of cash to owners who were also managers'.[14] They preferred short-term income to the long-run growth in assets, which is why dividend payouts were high and retained earnings low by comparison with managerial companies. British industry remained in the grip of 'personal capitalism' long after managerial capitalism came to dominate the US, one consequence of which was decelerating growth in the former. The contrast between growth-oriented managers adopting long-term strategies and dividend-hungry owners preoccupied with short-term reward is asserted but neither explained nor supported by convincing empirical evidence. Within the American economy it has been pointed out that in owner-dominated organisations such as Garrett's Baltimore & Ohio Railroad, Singer, Sears Roebuck, Swift, and Duke's American Tobacco Co., strategies were the outcome of long-run planning. When the Du Pont organisation planned a far-reaching, radical restructuring of the firm's activities the family enjoyed both managerial and financial control.[15]

In the context of Anglo-American comparisons Chandler's forceful restatement of the dichotomy of motives and behaviour is critical to his argument. It also revives in a specific and measurable form a more general thesis concerning the inhibiting effect of family firms on Britain's industrial performance. After its popularity in the 1960s,[16] the widespread conviction that this thesis once enjoyed disappeared.[17] In 1983 Payne's nuanced, though qualified, conclusion on his review of the debate, followed by the unqualified, robust assertions of Chandler in 1990, re-established the issue as alive and lively. The counter-revisionist interpretation presented by Chandler, in particular the dividend–profit hypothesis as applied to Britain, has been challenged elsewhere. By re-examining the limited empirical research on the motor industry, which provided the empirical underpinning for Chandler's assertion, Church revealed flaws which at the very least introduce serious doubts concerning the validity of the thesis.[18]

There is, however, other empirical evidence to support Chandler's

Family Business

conclusion which cannot be ignored. Florence's broader survey of medium and large British companies conducted some 30 years ago found
that dividend-to-profit ratios were higher in small and medium-sized
firms (the category into which most owner-managed, or 'entrepreneurial', and family firms fell) than in large enterprises.[19] This offers support
for the suggestion that the form of ownership and control may have
been causally related to policies favouring lower profit retention and
slower asset growth. The precise explanation for this pattern, however,
is not straightforward. High and stable dividends, the pattern which he
identified, need not necessarily imply short-term income maximisation
at the cost of asset growth of the kind Chandler attributed to family
firms. Florence's hypothesis, based on supposition rather than evidence,
is more subtle, conceding that family business leaders may have been as
concerned with profit retention and long-term growth for their companies as the salaried managers of large corporations, but that the former
were likely to have been more vulnerable to pressure. This was the case,
he thought, in those family firms in which sizeable blocks of shares were
in the hands of distant members of the family, descendants and in-laws
who were more likely, he thought, to favour dividend policies prejudicial to asset growth.[20]

Detailed evidence which might explain dividend policies is scarce. To
some extent Florence's model fits the Kenricks' experience during the
1930s, when in the face of limited profitability the family directors
resisted pressure from a non-family director to raise dividends. The
disgruntled dissident had been given shares from his father, Stanley
Baldwin, after the Kenricks had taken over the Baldwin family's hardware business in 1898 in exchange for Kenrick shares. A.W. Baldwin
received a second batch to enable him to qualify as a director in 1935
from which position he began his solitary campaign to improve the
Baldwin family finances by pressing for managerial changes and for
fresh, non-Kenrick, blood.[21] By contrast, the Colville trustees, the
major shareholders in the large Scottish steel-making company comprised overwhelmingly of members of the Colville family, found their
attempts to secure improved dividend payments blocked by the salaried
managing director, John Craig.[22]

However, public companies were also open to shareholders' pressure
for high dividends. This was a phenomenon which threatened to undermine the early development of the motor industry when venturesome
capitalists, notably du Cros Sr and du Cros Jr, Friswell, and Docker,
were clearly motivated by quick financial returns rather than asset
growth.[23] The Birmingham Small Arms Co., in the management of
which Dudley Docker was involved for more than 30 years, acquired

THE FAMILY FIRM IN INDUSTRIAL CAPITALISM 23

two motor companies, Daimler and Lanchester, on terms which proved to be virtually ruinous to all three. Docker was active as a shareholder and financial manipulator in several industries, and according to his biographer treated them as little more than 'a vehicle to make money from'.[24] This manifestation of short-termism before World War I, according to some interpretations, intensified after World War II as financial institutions emerged as powerful shareholders in large industrial companies both in Britain and in the US.[25]

Dividend policies are difficult to interpret without detailed information from, and behind, company accounts. The common practice of appropriating substantial proportions of net profit to reserves renders a dividends-to-profit ratio read from a balance sheet misleading. So too is the practice, common among family firms since the Industrial Revolution, of leaving declared dividends to accumulate within the company in the form of loans paying four or five per cent interest to partners, and later to shareholders in private companies. Another approach was to distribute low dividends supplemented by an occasional bonus from capitalised reserves and through special payments to working directors.[26] More research is needed on dividend policies and their significance for asset growth.

Although Florence's study is valuable, the criteria he adopted for defining owner-controlled and family firms are now seen to be exceptionally stringent. Whereas he took 20 per cent of voting shares as the minimum figure, later research on American and on British companies adopted a figure of five per cent as the appropriate mimimum proportion to denote ownership and potential control of corporate policy.[27] The appropriate figure may well depend on chronology and the associated pattern of share ownership. In those companies in which owner concentration was high, the 20 per cent figure might have been required to enable a family or an individual to exercise leverage on the board. However, Florence's sample shows that, even in firms with an ownership structure of that kind, family shareholdings were dominant. It seems highly probable, therefore, that Florence's study will have considerably underestimated the number of family firms in his sample of large and medium-sized companies, and that any conclusion concerning the differential patterns of dividends in relation to profit and asset growth is in need of revision. The prospect, however, of establishing an accurate picture of forms of ownership and control and relating these to dividend policies in Britain is bedevilled by the influence wielded by invisible interests in the form of charitable trusts, foundations and nominees.[28]

A further problem is posed by the need to interpret the available

24   FAMILY CAPITALISM

data. First, it is possible that the difference which Florence observed between the dividend profit ratio in small to medium firms compared with larger companies merely reflects the greater risks that affected the former, a probability which is suggested by their high failure rate. Second, it is not clear whether dividends in large companies were lower because salaried managers, rather than families, were in control, or because high profit ploughback proved to be a more successful route to survival and growth.

IV
MOTIVATION

The view that British family firms were preoccupied with short-term rewards is not entirely consistent with the consensus shared by historians that at least until the twentieth century industrial growth was financed largely from profits ploughed back into businesses.[29] In Germany, too, Kocka referred to the classic entrepreneur of the industrial revolution who 'had been ready to accept short term disadvantages for the sake of continuity and security'.[30] The history of Siemens in the nineteenth century is one of resistance against incorporation, until the banks compelled compliance in 1897.[31] Not until after World War I did the legal facilitation of joint stock formation with limited liability result in substantial changes in the ownership structure and managerial control of hitherto family or private partnerships. This was true for Britain and the rest of Europe and Japan.[32] In Germany mergers in the steel and chemical industries had reduced family ownership and control by the 1930s, but it has been suggested that in companies continuing under family control their industrial activities tended to become even more diversified than those of many of the large American organisations.[33]

That family-dominated firms were prepared to accept a trade-off between immediate rewards and long-term ends is suggested by remarks made by Werner Siemens. He referred to money making as 'very pleasant' but offered no guarantee of survival 'as a lasting family institution', which was his ambition.[34] A third generation leader of a British merchant house, Leaf, Sons & Co., Walter Leaf, recalled that paternal expectation brought him into what he described as 'from the first a disagreeable duty'.[35] His father resisted incorporation because 'he could not bear to think of a step which would cut his [elder brothers'] sons out of a career to which they had been devoted'. The independence and 'pride in the achievements of his ancestors and himself in building up one of the finest businesses in the City of London' was another sentiment which in this extreme case led to a decision against incorporation;

THE FAMILY FIRM IN INDUSTRIAL CAPITALISM 25

that was a policy which later imposed heavy financial burdens resulting from the need to pay out capital to the families of deceased partners.[36] Family differences over incorporation were not unusual, and while a squabble at Dalgety may have threatened but did not prevent incorporation in 1884, it has been suggested that many merchant houses, which in a similar position resisted incorporation, did experience disastrous consequences.[37] Just as self-imposed limitations on capital growth might stunt the development of a business, succession could also present problems.

The view that because of incapacity, ineptitude or lack of interest in business, the third generation of a founding business family typically experienced failure or extinction[38] is not now widely shared. Mainly because so few firms survived beyond the first and second generations, historians have generally discounted third generation entrepreneurial weakness as a factor contributing to a significant degree to Britain's relative industrial decline.[39] We know little about family firms that perished, paying the price of failing to strike a successful balance between financial prudence and attention to business on the one hand, with long-term personal aspirations for family and firm, on the other. Those which succeeded have left evidence which suggests that short-term profitability and high incomes should not be assumed to have been the major objective. Unfortunately, the records of companies which did not survive are rare and uninformative with respect to detailed explanations for failure.

Kocka contrasted the motivation represented by Werner Siemens, whose diversification policy in the late nineteenth century was aimed at growth in order to protect the firm's independence, with that of 'salaried entrepreneurs' (senior managers employed by firms in which owners played no managerial role). Kocka had in mind Walter Rathenau, second in command of the large AEG electric company, the growth of which presented Siemens with its major challenge. Yet Rathenau himself drew no distinction between the motives and objectives of founder-owners and salaried entrepreneurs; he maintained that 'much more than profits', business leaders of great companies measured their achievements in terms of the growth and power of their companies.[40]

A handful of major entrepreneurs, Sam Courtauld, Viscount Leverhume, Lord Rhondda, and Sebastian de Ferranti, for example,[41] denied that material reward was the main driving force behind their enterprise-building endeavours. Beyond that there is insufficient information about the motivation of business leaders to permit a comparison between those in family firms and those employed by managerial organisations. The pursuit of market power, however, which enterprise-

26   FAMILY CAPITALISM

building on the scale of these entrepreneurs' activities implied, was also
part of the strategy of General Motors, the managerial enterprise par
excellence, from the 1920s. A policy of costly annual changes in model
style eliminated many of its competitors and created barriers to entry.[42]

A further perspective on the motivation of family-owned firms is
provided by the Japanese experience. Among the entrepreneurial class
as a whole, the elite that emerged in the late nineteenth century
originated from the samurai, a redundant feudal class cut off from its
economic base, whose elevated status within society stemmed from a
traditional dedication to the public interest. In the government-inspired
drive to modernisation through industrialisation, business enterprise
offered an alternative form of endeavour receiving official and public
approval, for in that process entrepreneurial activity assumed an almost
patriotic aspect. The key institutions were the *zaibatsu*. The two defining characteristics of these large business enterprises were high levels of
ownership and control residing within a family or collectively within a
kinship group, and involvement in diversified business activities.
Hirschmeier has described the powerful motive which drove Japanese
entrepreneurs as that of 'national service rather than profit maximization'.[43] The overriding objective was to succeed in the interests of the
nation as a whole, which required profit-making for the purpose of
reinvestment rather than consumption.[44] Hirschmeier's portrayal of the
experience of Japanese business, therefore, is very different from the
widely assumed preoccupation of Western family firms with short-term
financial rewards for material satisfaction. The cultural foundations of
enterprise established in Japan between 1870 and 1900 were powerful
influences on the behaviour of owners and managers in that society at
least until the 1930s.

V

DIVERGENT FORMS OF FAMILY ENTERPRISE

That family ownership and control could be a source of strength even in
large diversified business organisations during the twentieth century is
evident from the history of the peculiarly Japanese corporate form
known as *zaibatsu*. The *zaibatsu* emerged following a long period of
mainly merchant or mining activity during the 1870s and 1880s, when
diversification was undertaken by a number of enterprises owned and
operated exclusively by a family or family groups. The 'new *zaibatsu*',
which were mainly the creation of the samurai, left distribution to the
merchants while establishing new, or acquiring existing, enterprises in
manufacturing, engineering, shipping, banking, and property. These

THE FAMILY FIRM IN INDUSTRIAL CAPITALISM 27

developments intensified after the joint stock form became legal in 1893 when, partly to maintain the value of family properties as well as to avoid tax, the family firms were incorporated as *zaibatsu*, though not as joint stock companies open to share ownership from outsiders.[45]

Like many European family businesses, conversion under company law meant that in reality many firms continued to trade as limited partnerships or private companies, while others continued as unlimited partnerships which maintained exclusive control over financial affairs and safeguarded disclosure of corporate information.[46] The enactment of 'family constitutions' ensured the preservation of family control over subsidiaries either formed or acquired as part of the surge towards diversification. In terms of management policy the function of head office was that of co-ordination rather than deciding strategy for the subsidiary enterprises.[47] By 1920 most of the large diversified *zaibatsu* had adopted the multi-subsidiary structure operating in this way.[48]

Morikawa has revised the traditional view that the *zaibatsu* exercised tight control over subsidiaries, describing the relation between owner-ship, authority and management as one of 'loose control'.[49] Nonethe-less, their role in investment strategy was crucial to the development and performance of the entire organisation. He attributes their strength both to their persistence as family firms 'which did not have to pay profits out in the form of dividends', and to their ability to internalise through inter-subsidiary transactions, thereby increasing profitability. The internally accumumulated funds were then deployed from the *zaibatsu* head office either to promote established, or to create new, subsidiaries.[50]

'Loose control' was an arrangement which depended upon, and received, co-operation between members of the *zaibatsu* family and the top salaried managers responsible for managing the subsidiaries. Apart from the autonomy extended to these managers, another attraction was the career structure thus created, for, despite family ownership, salaried managers were not excluded from the most senior managerial positions within the *zaibatsu*. Morikawa described the 'closed' system character-istic of most of the *zaibatsu* as having maximised the influence of family and patrons, who showed greater concern for achieving long-term growth and development than immediate profits. The 'open' joint stock companies, on the other hand, tended to limit stock offers to a small circle of investors, favouring financial institutions. One consequence of this was the competition among relatively major stockholders for top management posts, limiting the chances for qualified senior managers to advance beyond middle management.[51]

Joint stock companies with dispersed ownership, however, were the

exception in Japanese industry. Data relating to 1935 show that of the
100 largest companies in Japan only 26 could be so described, the
remainder consisting either of family-owned firms or companies in
which other companies held substantial shares. Suzuki's study, therefore, suggests that holding companies dominated Japanese industry and
that families and corporate owners, rather than private shareholders,
were those who determined policy, though by the years immediately
preceding World War II the traditional ownership pattern of big family
business was beginning to change.[52]

Were the financial policies of predominantly family-owned holding
companies significantly different from those of other types of large
business enterprise? Miyamoto's study showed that holding companies
were associated with relatively high payout ratios (which seems to
support the Chandler assertion). However, among the largest 200
Japanese, mainly manufacturing, companies of all kinds only higher
reserve ratios distinguished family from non-family firms; payout rates
and rates of profit were similar in both family and non-family firms. The
inference to be drawn from this is that size and degree of diversification
were more important than contrasting ownership structures in affecting
financial policies and asset growth.[53]

Japan was not the only national economy in which family-owned firms
were a source of strength during the nineteenth and early twentieth
centuries. Co-operation among German industrialists through cartelisation, and between industrialists and bankers, a quasi-business system
described as 'organised' or 'co-operative capitalism', has been seen as a
major contributor to the relative success of the German economy compared with that of Britain.[54] Within that structure, however, family
firms continued to play an important role in Germany, a feature which
Chandler's numerical survey records but which his discursive comparative analysis does not highlight. For nearly 20 years after the 'great
depression' began in 1873, German banks adopted an interventionist
role in industry, in contrast with British banks.[55] During the 1890s,
however, banking influence began to diminish as the family reasserted
its historically important role in affecting the structures and strategies of
German industrial companies.[56]

International differences in relations between businessmen, bankers
and government are not in doubt, nor is the greater diversification and
integration in German business even from the late 1880s compared with
British industry, but these divert attention from the thesis that the
presence or absence of family firms has been fundamental to explanations of comparative growth paths, not only between Britain and the
US but between Britain and Germany. Feldman argued that during the

THE FAMILY FIRM IN INDUSTRIAL CAPITALISM 29

inter-war years managerial enterprise in Germany advanced towards a position of dominance,[57] but other historians have emphasised that the process was slow, gathering pace after German heavy industry had already begun to reveal a growing competitive advantage in some areas. In 1907 the majority of large German enterprises were under family control. It was Kaelble's view that in this respect, as well as the median size of firms and the rise of managerial hierarchies,[58] they probably resembled business enterprises in the other industrial countries of Europe.[59]

Categorisation presents a difficulty for those seeking to generalise, but Brockstedt's examination of German family enterprise concluded that at least until 1914 mining companies were mostly still entrepreneurial enterprises, that families retained a very strong influence in the iron and steel industry and in engineering, and that while in the chemical and electrical industries managerial enterprises had increased in relative importance, entrepreneurial enterprises continued to predominate.[60] Important, too, was the existence of family succession among salaried entrepreneurs, non-share-owning professional managers unrelated to family who played an increasingly important role in Germany's large-scale enterprises until World War II.[61] Family firms declined in importance after 1914, particularly in those industries where the largest companies dominated activity. Unfortunately the paucity of information on firms, notably ownership and the rise of salaried managers, does not permit measurement of the speed with which the trend towards managerial firms occurred. After reviewing the internationally comparative quantitative data which is available, Kaelble concluded in 1986 that 'it would not be astonishing if future, more exact, comparative research should demonstrate that the entrepreneurial or family enterprise retained its position in the prewar and interwar period in Germany about as well as in other European countries'.[62] If, as seems highly probable before 1914 and possibly into the 1930s, family firms were as prevalent in Germany as they were in Britain, then at the level of the enterprise, structural explanations for the contrasting economic performance of these two economies are insufficient.

VI

SUCCESSION

The continuing vigour of family influence on business raises the question of managerial succession; first because in *Scale and Scope* Chandler has identified management skills as among the most important determinants of the strength of organisational capability, and second because management succession has been widely acknowledged to pose particular problems for the longevity and performance of family firms. Rose's examination of management succession, largely based on textile firms in the eighteenth and nineteenth centuries, suggested that the difficulty of securing generational transition helps to explain why the majority of family firms are shortlived. The foundation for successful corporate strategies, she concluded, was stability of leadership through orderly succession.[63]

Family firms are invariably thought to have been vulnerable in this respect. The possibility that family successors might not be forthcoming, or that those who were might lack inclination or interest, is one reason. Another stems from the character of founder, owner-entrepreneurs, whose success in business often resulted, to a considerable degree, from the exercise of strong personalities, for whom retirement represented a personal defeat. This helps to explain a reluctance to withdraw from management until infirmity or death terminated an authoritarian reign. Lever's inability to acknowledge that in his advancing age misjudgement, in part the manifestation of megolomania, were damaging to his company, is well known.[64] Another classic example is that of Arthur Dorman's rule at Dorman Long, the iron and steel-making company which he established as a partnership in 1876 and which by 1914, as a result of growth and acquisition, was the dominant firm on Teeside. In fact in 1902 at the age of 53 he had retired on the grounds of fatigue but was back as chairman and managing director the following year, remaining in those positions until his death in 1931, then aged 84. His successor was Sir Hugh Bell, the deputy chairman, who had joined the board when his own company, Bell Bros., merged with Dorman Long. Sir Hugh, aged 83, died within the year of his appointment, opening the way for the board to promote a much younger manager, an insider but one unencumbered by familial connection with others who remained on the board.[65]

A different set of circumstances at Leyland Motors also meant that on the death, in 1963, of Sir Henry Spurrier III (the third generation of the founding family which had managed the business since its formation in the 1890s), succession presented a problem. Personal differences with the general manager (who was not a Spurrier) led to Markland's resignation when despite a long and successful managerial record he was not appointed to the deputy chairmanship, the key executive position in the company. This post was filled instead by Sir John Black, then aged 70, formerly chairman and managing director of Standard Motor Co. which had been taken over by Leyland Motors. When Spurrier died the same year only one of the four key directors was below 70 years of age, and it

THE FAMILY FIRM IN INDUSTRIAL CAPITALISM 31

was the youngest, the sales manager Donald Stokes, who had worked for the company since he joined as an apprentice, who was appointed as deputy chairman and managing director.[66] The question of succession appears to have been decided by Spurrier alone, influenced by personal prejudices and constrained by a limited choice among internal candidates. When the supply of Spurriers ran out and nepotism was not an option, preferment was based on personal familiarity limited to personnel already within the organisation.

These are not isolated instances. Until the 1930s at least, what Florence called 'leadership by inheritance' is accepted to have dominated much of British industry.[67] But the absence of family heirs or their rejection of a life committed to managing the family business saw the development of variations in the forms of family succession. Family firms were joined by, or metamorphosed into, mixed enterprises in which salaried managers and owning families were involved in policy formulation at board level. Another variant of owner management described by Erickson in the steel and hosiery industries[68] but which is also found in others, was the emergence of 'dynastic management', whereby managerial succession rather than hereditary ownership sustained a continuity not based on ownership. The precise extent of leadership by inheritance, broadly defined, has yet to be documented, but in addition to iron and steel and hosiery similar familial links were probably widespread.[69]

Recent writing on family firms has underlined the importance of planned leadership succession for achieving survival and success, and that enlightened recruitment of senior managers from outside the family can offer major advantages. These might include specialist skills and training as well as an independent perspective on the organisation.[70] This suggests that internal succession and the recruitment of senior managers from within the company may be interpreted as a less effective policy than that which might be expected of large bureaucratic corporations. In search of the exceptional, Chandler applied two tests to family firms. One was whether they introduced extensive managerial hierarchies. The other was whether they recruited professional managers who were not stock-holders to a degree from which control might result,[71] and who, it is assumed, would have accorded to asset growth a greater priority than high levels of dividend. It seems pertinent, therefore, to enquire whether we are justified in assuming that the process of management succession and recruitment in large managerial organisations was necessarily linked to corporate continuity, stability and control; and whether they were characterised by rational, narrowly focused consideration of corporate interest, defined in terms of perceived economic and organisational needs. Or have other influences and loyalties within and outside the organisation created a bounded rationality no less distorting in its effects on management appointments than those affecting decisions made in family firms?

It is clear that in some parts of ICI, acknowledged by Chandler as Britain's outstanding model of corporate organisational capability between the wars,[72] social background, academic honours and a clubable personality were important factors in determining the status of managers. In some parts of the organisation 'gentlemen' were as highly valued at ICI as in Courtaulds, especially if they had grown up with the company, as one manager put it 'man and boy'.[73] The tendency towards internal recruitment to senior positions was not as potentially restrictive in large-scale organisations as in typical family firms, for scale and scope allowed the accumulation of diverse experience within the divisions. There was a tendency, however, for Millbank to incorporate such diversity of managerial experience within its own well-established managerial culture. Insularity was not peculiar to family firms. Management styles also differed from one division of ICI to another, ranging from what managers described as *laissez faire* paternalism and authoritarianism to consensual management. McGowan's autocratic chairmanship during the inter-war years was eventually curbed by the board, just as the vigorous reign of Chambers during the 1960s was succeeded by the re-establishment by the board of a 'smoothing rather than problem-solving culture'.[74] One main board director described the 50-year-old company as 'hierarchical, almost totally inbred . . . very, very conservative'.[75]

Mabel Newcomer's classic study of big business executives in the US between 1900 and 1950 showed that there, too, the most frequent route to the board was through internal promotion; inheritance was the second most common path to top management.[76] The existence within multidivisional firms of a large internal market for managers was no doubt part of the explanation, Newcomer nevertheless emphasised a prevailing preference for the familiar when large American corporations made appointments to the most senior management posts, a selection which was strongly influenced by personal preferences.[77] Clearly, there is a difference between nepotism, which is commonly thought of as the typical practice associated with family firms, and internal recruitment in large managerial organisations, but Newcomer's study suggests that the difference was only one of degree.

As was the typical practice in family firms, even in many of the large industrial companies it was normally left to the chairman or chief executive to initiate the search for his own replacement on retirement.

THE FAMILY FIRM IN INDUSTRIAL CAPITALISM 33

Furthermore, like their counterparts in family businesses, those top executive managers did not always face the problem of succession until the time when retirement was imminent. Evidence of this is the median age of 70 years for the retirement of American top business executives between the wars.[78] Family firms have been criticised for lacking managers who had had experience of other business organisations, yet 25 per cent of American top executives appointed between 1944 and 1953 likewise possessed no experience of management in other firms. Newcomer was critical of the narrow, specialist professional training and background of those appointed. They were lawyers, engineers and accountants, but not necessarily effective administrators or competent in human relations.[79] A comparison between companies in which senior executive positions were held by engineering and law graduates with those in which liberal arts graduates were dominant revealed a lower asset growth in the former category.[80]

VII

ORGANISATIONAL ADAPTABILITY AND BUSINESS CULTURE

The striking resemblances between the successful *zaibatsu* and the family-dominated British holding companies which have attracted such critical comment throw further doubt on the value of the otherwise intuitively persuasive, deterministic analysis which stresses structural characteristics in explaining differential, international industrial performance. How and why did they differ in practice when the family was a dominant presence in both British and Japanese holding companies? Why did the Japanese form of devolved management prove to be successful whereas the British model was largely a failure? One important difference is to be found in the contrasting origins of diversification in the two countries. In Japan, it occurred mainly through the extension of activities from a single organisational base, the *zaibatsu*. In Britain, diversification was often achieved through mergers of existing firms. This meant that the boards of British holding companies were comprised of chairmen and managing directors whose co-directors included former owner-managers and directors of subsidiaries, a formula which tended to inhibit change. By contrast, the *zaibatsu* multi-subsidiary holding company actually created senior management positions. These were attractive not only because of the degree of autonomy with which the chairmen of subsidiary companies were entrusted, but because they were at the same time a part of a very extensive organisation whose long-established history in many cases implied stability, permanence

34   FAMILY CAPITALISM

and prestige. A majority of senior salaried managers recruited to the *zaibatsu* came from the samurai class, others from the civil service and university faculties.[81]

Co-operative relations appear to have been more successfully achieved between Japanese family managers and salaried managers than those between British owner-managers and directors of erstwhile competitive enterprises within the new holding companies. In some of these, *zaibatsu* leaders continued to manage the subsidiaries without the support of a large head office staff,[82] but typically the *zaibatsu* contained a strong autocratic founder whose departure at death or retirement was followed by management shared between family and salaried managers. Until the 1930s, by which time Japan's industrial strength was well established, salaried managers employed by the *zaibatsu* were constrained by rule and custom to respect and show loyalty to the family. For their part, the families either acknowledged their own lack of managerial skills to cope with the increasing complexity of modern business, or in Wiener fashion withdrew from participation from lack of interest ('the sons of the founders tending to invest their energies into arts, politics, and social life'),[83] though even from the late nineteenth century the *zaibatsu* had competed to recruit highly educated personnel, regardless of class or status, to fill managerial positions.[84] While ownership rights perpetuated potential family dominance, for the most part it remained symbolic.[85]

However, Suzuki's wider study of Japanese management structures between 1920 and 1940 suggests that just as owner-managers and salaried 'dynastic' managers were important in British industry during the late nineteenth to the mid-twentieth century, a comparable pattern of internal succession to top managerial positions can be identified in Japan. Suzuki's analysis revealed a continuing preponderance among top management of owner-managers and internal salaried managers, some of whom became owner-managers by acquiring shares after being appointed directors.[86] Two-thirds of the largest firms possessed boards of directors composed entirely of internal senior executives, some of whom, either after initial recruitment or as experienced managers, were supplied to subsidiaries by parent companies, thereby consolidating group identity.[87] In this respect there may have been a similarity to the relative immobility of managers in large British companies. The reasons for this, however, and the significance of managerial continuity, differ internationally and are explicable only by considering the social and cultural origins of entrepreneurs and managers in Japan.

In Britain, America and Germany, merchants, who may be defined to include those who were sometimes engaged in production as well as

THE FAMILY FIRM IN INDUSTRIAL CAPITALISM 35

trading, and who founded family firms during the early stages of industrialisation, were the principal source of entrepreneurship. In Japan, too, merchants played an important role. However, it was the entrepreneurial leadership shown by the samurai, an impoverished and declassed former feudal aristocracy, well educated but cut off from its economic base, which was crucial from the late nineteenth century. By applying their energy and education in support of the government-supported drive towards national modernisation through industrialisation, the samurai re-established themselves as a new business and social elite. Just as status attached to those who were perceived as pursuing business in the public interest,[88] the *zaibatsu* also received social recognition, and the loyalty and effort rendered in their service conferred status upon owners and managers (and upon other workers). Recognition of this kind helped to blur the distinction between self and family and corporate interest: 'On the level of the firm [Japanese entrepreneurs] solidly incorporated the familist mentality and group identity as motives for work and loyalty'.[89] Hazama's elaboration of the importance of group identity, loyalty, continuity and achievement, rather than the focus on self-interest and self-help as in Western individualism, reinforces Hirschmeier's characterisation of the Japanese business ethos during the late nineteenth century and between the wars. Hazama described the prevailing business ideologies among managers as those of 'managerial nationalism' externally and 'managerial familism' internally.[90] Reinforcing the cohesiveness of managerial familism in modern large-scale firms was the introduction of the life-long employment system

The tendency, therefore, for Japanese managers to devote themselves to a single business organisation for life is more likely to have implied dedication rather than a lack of ambition on the part of managers. For their part, owners rewarded and encouraged commitment and loyalty by their willingness to recruit non-family managers, a high proportion of whom were graduates, to the most senior positions.[91]

VIII
THE FAMILY FIRM AND MANAGERIAL CAPITALISM

International comparisons expose the weaknesses of historical explanation based on structural rather than behavioural factors. Payne concluded that in Britain the advantages offered by the family firm before 1914 were probably outweighed by the disadvantages of family holding companies in the period between the wars.[92] Yet in Japan, competing in the same international markets, business families succeeded in exploiting the potential advantages of family ownership and control while minimising the potential disadvantages. The differences appear to have been, first, the mode which diversification took, largely through merger in Britain, whereas in Japan the process was one of organic diversification by which subsidiaries were established by the single family enterprise. The second difference, though more contentious and requiring further research, was the continued willingness of Japanese controlling families to adopt, as an over-riding priority, a policy of profit retention and reinvestment in long-term development, in contrast with the alleged rejection of such a policy by British family firms. The third difference is the acknowledgement by the leaders of Japanese families of the need for the recruitment of well-educated senior managers from outside the family into a corporate culture which rewarded loyalty and efficiency with levels of responsibility and reward hitherto reserved for family members.

It would appear, then, that families in different cultures adopted different priorities for reasons which did not stem, almost deterministically, from the structure of their businesses. Business strategies owed more to contrasting cultural environments which prompted divergent assumptions, aspirations, and the adoption of criteria by owners and managers nurtured within different societies.

There is some justification for concluding that before the late 1930s business structures in Britain, Japan and Germany displayed more similarities than differences; that individual 'actors' (owners and managers) were presented with problems of interpreting the nature of the challenge with which their companies were presented, and that regardless of the structure and organisation of the company for which they acted they could, and often did, take decisions which proved less than optimal.[93] It is true that the corporate culture of family firms often encouraged decisions which might seem irrational by various optimisation criteria, or by the model standards of bureaucratic, functional efficiency. However, the concept of 'bounded rationality' to describe decision-making in large modern corporations is arguably different only in degree from the dysfunctional elements adduced to explain the suboptimal tendencies in family firms.

Should we assume that the priorities, decisions and policies in large family firms are likely to have been less 'rational' or optimal than those of the managerial organisation administered by an extensive professional bureaucracy? There is a literature, beginning with Marris, which suggests that in companies with widely dispersed share ownership managerial discretion has been used to pursue goals other than profit maximisation, in the form of sales volume, growth, management

THE FAMILY FIRM IN INDUSTRIAL CAPITALISM   37

emoluments, or stability and avoidance of risk, for example.[94] Furthermore, a recent study, which included 325 of the largest British industrial companies in the mid-1980s, concluded that ownership control implied a higher valuation ratio, profit margin and return on shareholders' capital as well as higher growth rates of sales and net assets.[95]

It is possible that policies which resulted in these differences were the outcome of managerial discretion concerned with other, less explicit priorities. Organisations have been described as possessing 'logics of action' or rationalities for behaviour and decision-making which develop over time, partly by design, partly spontaneously, the product of corporate, and indeed other, historical experience. The concept of differentiated management spheres has emerged from empirical work carried out on large organisations. That led to the conclusion that the 'logics of action' in an organisation are outcomes of interaction, conflict and negotiation between groups within the organisation, each possessing separate rationalities.[96] This approach contributes to an understanding of how, within such companies, the introduction of, or resistance to, organisational change might depend much upon the power position, education and training (engineering or finance or marketing), and cultural background of business leaders.

It is arguable that their perception of the problems encountered by their companies and of the possible strategies needed to tackle them were influenced as much by strictly non-rational criteria (though rational assessed in terms of any particular sub-group culture) and the observed behaviour of corporate competitors, as by the undifferentiated optimal rationality which the Chandlerian paradigm might imply.[97] In fact, some years ago Chandler acknowledged that even American managers had feet of clay. He observed that policy decisions taken by the head office of multidivisional corporations were based on information originating from divisional sources, and that the reason for this was a partiality which head office senior executives tended to show towards former divisions from which they had been recruited. He concluded 'in reality it is the more aggressive division managers who determine strategy, that is, the investment decisions'. The most senior managers, it seems, rarely responded to deteriorating performance by discontinuing lines or by removing managers.[98] Large-scale multidepartmental and multidivisional companies in the US, therefore, do not seem to have behaved according to the optimal bureaucratic model. Loyalty to managerial sub-groups influenced corporate outcomes.

In Japanese companies the prevailing ideology of managerial familism combined with the perceived primacy of achievements by the group (the business organisation and the national interest) might explain why competing sub-group interests appear to have been relatively unimportant. At the opposite extreme from the managerial familism of Japan, Livesay's evidence from American business prompted his insistence that, regardless of size both in the past and present, entrepreneurial effectiveness has been a more important factor in affecting business performance than the structure of the organisation which entrepreneurs and managers inhabited.[99] This is a view which echoes that of Reader, writing about the history of ICI.[100] The very nature of Livesay's assertion presents problems of testing because it would require a volume of case studies in such a multitude and involving human and financial resources on such a scale as to be beyond the reach of academic researchers. Conceptual and definitional uncertainties and the difficulties of measurement may tempt the historian prepared to challenge the model-based synthesis offered by Chandler to present arguments case by case, but that is a seriously limiting approach. Unless, however, a solution is found to the fundamental methodological difficulties raised by Chandler's work, they will continue to frustrate any attempt to draw confident conclusions concerning the role of family firms after the industrial revolution.

The family firm was different in form and mode of operation over time, the tendency for the structure and organisation of family and managerial firms to converge blurring the distinctiveness of one compared with the other. As a category associated with specific characteristics, therefore, the family firm transcends neither chronological nor national and cultural boundaries. In the search for an explanation for international differences in industrial growth, the generic concept of the family firm and the characteristics which Chandler attributes to it, has little to offer. Nonetheless, the intra- and international diversity of family enterprise, and particularly the absence of systematic quantification of the similarities and differences, clearly justifies further research at the firm and industry level. Two developments in particular, the penetration of industrial companies by financial institutions as major shareholders and the increasing level of industrial concentration, point to the need for historians to examine business institutions within a framework broader than any of the behavioural models of the firm now on offer. They need to be studied as decision-making organisations for reconciling transaction costs, but also as systems of power and networks of association. The dynamics of large, corporate organisations, regardless of ownership, were open to, and could be strongly affected by, political and social as well as financial and economic influences.

Like Payne's survey of the state of the debate over the role of family firms in Britain, this review concludes on a sceptical note. His view was

THE FAMILY FIRM IN INDUSTRIAL CAPITALISM 39

that if a causal connection between the family firm and a loss of economic vitality existed, the damage was done during the inter-war years. In that period, both the adoption of centralised structures and the introduction of professional managerial staff, which he implies were a necessary condition for effective industrial performance, were inhibited by the 'still sufficiently familial' character of major holding companies to have adverse effects.[101] The international dimensions explored above, however, justify a more robust scepticism, for the foregoing comparative analysis finds no justification for interpreting evidence of a greater persistence of family firms as necessarily an important contributory factor in industrial decline. Family firms persisted in Germany probably as widely as in Britain, while in Japan the family enterprise based on a holding company structure was even more dominant than in either country. International differences were observed in the rationalities of business conduct despite some similarities in business structures and the common, widely assumed, dysfunctional influence of family.

The creation of an extensive professional managerial staff, in whom so much faith is placed by the critics of family firms, was no guarantee that the managerial organisation to which they belonged was immune from dysfunctional elements. These may have been different in kind from those arising from family concerns, but the interplay of competing rationalities contained a similar potential for distorting policy away from a notional economic optimality or a standard that might be expected of the model managerial enterprise in a modern corporate economy. Conclusive statements cannot be offered. Nyman and Silberston's analysis of the ownership and control of British industry in the 1970s stressed that their research underlined the limited capacity of information concerning the structure of firms to explain the actual behaviour of corporate organisations.[102]

While it is *possible* that the family firm was a key institutional weakness in the British economy before 1940, we should not accept the *probability* that family firms contained more dysfunctional elements than did managerial enterprises. Furthermore, the case against the family firm *per se*, stressing the institutional rigidity which it represented, cannot be proved convincingly merely by linking a greater persistence of family firms with a relative decline in Britain's industrial performance. International comparisons suggest that greater attention should be paid to the cultural differences which produced contrasting behaviour and performance regardless of the major characteristics of corporate structures.

40   FAMILY CAPITALISM

NOTES

1. S. Rock, *Family Firms* (Cambridge, 1991), p. 21; *New York Times*, 10, 12, 16 June, 1986.
2. B. Elbaum and W. Lazonick (eds.), *The Decline of the British Economy* (Oxford, 1986). See especially the chapters on the textile and shipbuilding industries.
3. P.L. Payne, 'Family Business in Britain: An Historical and Analytical Survey', in Akio Okochi and Shigeaki Yasuoka (eds.), *Family Business in the Era of Industrial Growth* (Tokyo, 1984), p. 196.
4. In several publications, but the thesis has been consolidated with additional evidence most recently in A.D. Chandler, Jr, *Scale and Scope: The Dynamics of Industrial Capitalism* (Cambridge, MA, 1990), pp. 14, 46, 389–92.
5. P. Scranton, *Proprietary Capitalism: The Textile Manufacture at Philadelphia 1800–1885* (Cambridge, 1983), pp. 414–20.
6. Ibid., p. 421.
7. See, for example, D. Landes, 'Technological Change and Development in Western Europe, 1750–1914', in *The Cambridge Economic History of Europe, Volume VI: The Industrial Revolution and After, Part I*, edited by H.J. Habakkuk and M.M. Postan (Cambridge, 1965). Also P.L. Payne, 'Industrial Entrepreneurship and Management in Great Britain', Claude Fohlen, 'Entrepreneurship and Management in France in the Nineteenth Century', and J. Kocka, 'Entrepreneurs and Managers in German Industrialization', in *The Cambridge Economic History of Europe, Volume VII, The Industrial Economies: Capital, Labour, and Enterprise, Part I*, edited by Peter Mathias and M.M. Postan (Cambridge, 1978).
8. Payne, 'Family Business in Britain', pp. 193–7.
9. A.D. Chandler, Jr, *Strategy and Structure* (Cambridge, MA, 1962), pp. 13–15; also *The Visible Hand: The Managerial Revolution in American Business* (Cambridge, MA, 1977), pp. 10–15.
10. Chandler, *Scale and Scope*, pp. 14–46, 240, 389–92.
11. Payne, 'Family Business in Britain', pp. 196–7.
12. Elbaum and Lazonick, *Decline of the British Economy*.
13. Chandler, *Scale and Scope*, p. 294.
14. Ibid., p. 390.
15. R. du Boff and E. S. Herman, 'Alfred Chandler's New Business History: A Review', *Politics and Society*, Vol. 10 (1980), pp. 95–7.
16. C.P. Kindleberger, *Economic Growth in France and Britain, 1851–1950* (Cambridge, MA, 1964), p. 115; Landes, 'Technological Change and Development in Western Europe', pp. 563–4.
17. Payne, 'Industrial Entrepreneurship and Management in Britain', pp. 202–5.
18. R. Church, 'The Limitations of the Personal Capitalism Paradigm', in R. Church *et al.*, 'Scale and Scope: A Review Colloquium', *Business History Review*, Vol. 64 (Winter 1990), pp. 703–10.
19. P. Sargant Florence, *Ownership, Control and Success of Large Companies*, (1961), pp. 140–58.
20. Ibid., p. 304.
21. R. Church, *Kenricks in Hardware: A Family Business, 1791–1966* (Newton Abbot, 1969), pp. 33, 203.
22. P.L. Payne, *Colvilles and the Scottish Steel Industry* (Oxford, 1979), p. 317.
23. S.B. Saul, 'The Motor Industry in Britain', *Business History*, Vol. V (1962), pp. 1–19; R.P.T. Davenport-Hines, *Dudley Docker: The Life and Times of a Trade Warrior* (Cambridge, 1984), pp. 230–35.
24. Davenport-Hines, *Dudley Docker*, p. 230–35.
25. Du Boff and Herman, 'Chandler's New Business History', n. 32; Nyman and Silberston, 'Ownership and Control', pp. 90–102; G. Ingham, *Capitalism Divided? The City and Industry in British Social Development* (1984).
26. T.A. Lee, 'Company Financial Statements; an Essay in Business History' in Sheila

THE FAMILY FIRM IN INDUSTRIAL CAPITALISM 41

Marriner (ed.), *Business and Businessmen: Studies in Business, Economic and Accounting History* (Liverpool, 1980); J.R. Edwards, *A History of Financial Accounting* (1989). I am indebted to Christine Clark of the University of East Anglia for detailed information from her PhD research on the accounting practices of family firms in the malting industry.

27. M. Zeitlin, 'Corporate Ownership and Control: The Large Corporation and the Capitalist Class', *American Journal of Sociology*, Vol. 79 (1974), pp. 1073–101; S. Nyman and A. Silberston, 'The Ownership and Control of Industry', *Oxford Economic Papers*, new series, Vol. XXX (1978), pp. 90–102.

28. Zeitlin, 'Corporate Ownership', pp. 1073–105; Nyman and Silberston, 'Ownership and Control', pp. 90–102.

29. P.L. Cottrell, *Industrial Finance, 1830–1914: The Finance and Organisation of English Manufacturing Industry* (1980), p. 169.

30. J. Kocka, 'Entrepreneurs and Managers in German Industrialisation', pp. 558, 722, n. 149.

31. Ibid., p. 557.

32. Cottrell, *Industrial Finance*, pp. 162–5; J. Brockstedt, 'Family Enterprise and the Rise of Large-Scale Enterprise in Germany, 1871–1914', in A. Okochi and S. Yasuoka (eds.), *Family Business in the Era of Industrial Growth: Its Ownership and Management* (Tokyo, 1984), p. 261; H. Morikawa, *Zaibatsu* (Tokyo, 1992), p. 54.

33. Chandler, *Scale and Scope*, p. 591.

34. Kocka, 'Entrepreneurs and Managers', p. 722, n. 149.

35. S. Chapman, *Merchant Enterprise in Britain from the Industrial Revolution to World War I* (Cambridge, 1992), p. 219.

36. Ibid., p. 219.

37. M.J. Daunton, 'Firm and Family in the City of London in the Nineteenth Century: The Case of Dalgety', *Historical Research*, Vol. LXII (1989), pp. 134–77.

38. Landes, 'Technological Change', pp. 563–4.

39. Payne, 'Family Business', pp. 188–92.

40. Kocka, 'Entrepreneurs and Managers', p. 557.

41. G. Turner, *Business in Britain* (1969), pp. 226–7, 339–41; D.F. Channon, *The Strategy and Structure of British Enterprise* (1971), pp. 96–7; R. Church, *The History of the British Coal Industry, Vol III: 1830–1913, Victorian Pre-eminence* (Oxford, 1986), p. 164.

42. R.P. Thomas, 'Style Change and the Automobile Industry during the Roaring Twenties', in L.P. Cain and P.J. Uselding (eds.), *Business Enterprise and Economic Change* (Kent, Ohio, 1973), pp. 118–37.

43. J. Hirschmeier, 'Entrepreneurs and the Social Order: America, Germany and Japan, 1870–1900', in K. Nakagawa (ed.), *Social Order and the Entrepreneur* (Tokyo, 1977), pp. 33–4, 41; S. Yasuoka, 'Capital Ownership in Family Companies: Japanese Firms Compared with those in Other Countries', in Okochi and Yasuoka, *Family Business*, pp. 1–12.

44. Hirschmeier, 'Entrepreneurs and the Social Order', pp. 13–16.

45. Y. Suzuki, *Japanese Management Structures, 1920–1980* (Tokyo, 1992), p. 48.

46. Morikawa, *Zaibatsu*, pp. 1–2.

47. Ibid., pp. 43, 114, 215.

48. Suzuki, *Japanese Management*, p. 54.

49. Morikawa, *Zaibatsu*, p. 244.

50. Ibid., pp. 210, 244.

51. M. Myamoto, 'The Position and Role of Family Business in the Development of the Japanese Company System', in Okochi and Yasuoka, *Family Business*, p. 66; Morikawa, *Zaibatsu*, pp. 213–16, 245–6.

52. Suzuki, *Japanese Management*, p. 50.

53. Myamoto, 'The Position and Role of Family Business', pp. 85–8.

54. Kocka, 'Entrepreneurs and Managers', pp. 584–9; Chandler, *Scale and Scope*, pp. 587–92.

55. Cottrell, *Industrial Finance*, Ch. 7; M. Collins, *Bank and Industrial Finance in Britain, 1800–1939* (1991), p. 93.
56. Kocka, 'Entrepreneurs and Managers', p. 569; Brockstedt, 'Family Enterprise', p. 231.
57. G. Feldman, *Iron and Steel in the German Inflation, 1916–23* (Princeton, NJ, 1977), p. 25.
58. H. Kaelble, 'The Rise of the Managerial Enterprise in Germany, c.1870–c.1930', in K. Kobayashi and H. Morikawa (eds.), *Development of Managerial Enterprise* (Tokyo, 1986), p. 78.
59. Ibid., p. 83.
60. Brockstedt, 'Family Enterprise', pp. 248–9.
61. Ibid., pp. 249–51.
62. Kaelble, 'The Rise of the Managerial Enterprise in Germany', p. 92.
63. M.B. Rose, 'Beyond Buddenbrooks: The Family Firm and the Management of Succession in Nineteenth Century Britain', Lancaster University Management School, Discussion Paper EC4/91 (1991), pp. 2–16.
64. *Dictionary of Business Biography*, Vol. 3, p. 750.
65. J.S. Boswell, *Business Policies in the Making* (1983), pp. 36–42, 106–9.
66. G. Turner, *The Leyland Papers* (1971), pp. 74–81.
67. P. Sargant Florence, *The Logic of British and American Industry* (1953), pp. 195, 303–4, 320.
68. C. Erickson, *British Industrialists, Steel and Hosiery, 1850–1950* (Cambridge, 1959), pp. 52–3.
69. Florence, *Logic*, 195, 203–4, 320; Payne,' Industrial Entrepreneurship', pp. 201–18; Chandler, *Scale and Scope*, pp. 294–392.
70. Rose, 'Beyond Buddenbrooks', pp. 2–16.
71. A.D. Chandler Jr., 'The United States, Seedbed of Managerial Capitalism', in A.D. Chandler, Jr. and H. Daems (eds.), *Comparative Perspectives on the Rise of the Modern Industrial Enterprise* (Cambridge, MA, 1980), pp. 12–15.
72. Chandler, *Scale and Scope*, p. 358.
73. A. Pettigrew, *The Awakening Giant: Continuity and Change in ICI* (Oxford, 1985), pp. 129, 197–8, 347.
74. Ibid., pp. 71–4, 386–90.
75. Ibid., p. 279.
76. M. Newcomer, *The Big Business Executive, 1900–1950* (New York, 1955), pp. 102–4.
77. Ibid., pp. 134–7.
78. Ibid., p. 110.
79. Ibid., pp. 81–2.
80. Ibid., p. 137.
81. Morikawa, *Zaibatsu*, pp. 46–54, 247; R. Shimuzu, *Top Management in Japanese Firms* (Tokyo, 1986), pp. 245–7.
82. Suzuki, *Japanese Management Structures*, p. 54.
83. Morikawa, *Zaibatsu*, p. 98.
84. Ibid., p. 247.
85. Ibid., pp. 218–20.
86. Suzuki, *Japanese Management Structures*, pp. 51–3.
87. T. Yui and K. Nakagawa (eds.), *Japanese Management in Historical Perspective* (Tokyo, 1984), p. xiv.
88. Hirschmeier, 'Entrepreneurs and the Social Order', pp. 14–15.
89. Ibid., p. 34.
90. Ibid., pp. 14–15; H. Hazama, 'Industrialisation and "Groupism" ', in K. Nakagawa (ed.), *Social Order and Entrepreneurship* (Tokyo, 1977), pp. 212–13.
91. Hirschmeier, 'Entrepreneurs and the Social Order', pp. 16, 23–6.
92. Payne, 'Family Business in Britain', p. 191.
93. D.C. Coleman, 'Failings and Achievements: Some British Businesses, 1910–80', *Business History*, Vol. XXIX (1987), pp. 1–17.

THE FAMILY FIRM IN INDUSTRIAL CAPITALISM   43

94. R. Marris, 'A Model of "Managerial" Enterprise', *Quarterly Journal of* Economics, Vol. 77 (1963), pp. 185–209.
95. D. Leach and J. Leahy, 'Ownership Structure, Control Type Classifications and the Performance of Large British Companies', *Economic Journal*, Vol. 101 (1991), p. 1435.
96. W.M. Teulings, 'Managing Labour Processes in Organised Capitalism: The Power of Corporate Management and the Powerlessness of the Manager', in D. Knights and H. Willmott (eds.), *Managing the Labour Process* (Aldershot, 1986).
97. N. Fligstein, 'The Spread of the Multidivisional Form among Large Firms, 1919–79' *American Sociological Review*, Vol. 50 (1985), pp. 377–91.
98. A.D. Chandler, Jr, 'The Multi-unit Enterprise: A Historical and Interpretational Comparative Analysis and Summary', in H. Williamson (ed.), *Evolution of International Management Structures* (Newark, 1975), pp. 251–2.
99. H.C. Livesay, 'Entrepreneurial Persistence through the Bureaucratic Age', *Business History Review*, Vol. 51 (Winter, 1977), pp. 415–43; idem, 'Entrepreneurial Dominance in Businesses Large and Small, Past and Present', *Business History Review*, Vol. 63 (Spring, 1989), pp. 1–21.
100. W.J. Reader, 'Personality, Strategy and Structure: Some Consequences of Strong Minds', in L. Hannah (ed.), *Management Strategy and Business Development* (1976), pp. 108–29.
101. Payne, 'Family Business', pp. 196–7.
102. Nyman and Silberston, 'Ownership and Control', pp. 91–9.

Part II
Family and Firm:
Theory, Concepts and Culture

[9]

The F-Connection:
Families, Friends,
and Firms
and the Organization
of Exchange

YORAM BEN-PORATH

The family plays a major role in the allocation and distribution of resources. The way in which members of families have dealings with each other, the implicit contract by which they conduct their activities, stands in sharp contrast to the textbook market transaction. Between these two extremes are many other transaction modes and institutions involving elements of both: transactions between friends, business partners, and employers and employees.

The main theme of this essay is that the identity of the people engaged in a transaction is a major determinant of the institutional mode of transaction. Some transactions can take place only between mutually or unilaterally identified parties. Investment in resources specific to a relationship between identified parties can save transaction costs and stimulate trade. Such investment gives rise to what I call specialization by identity—concentration of exchange between the same parties—analogous to specialization by impersonal dimensions of transactions. The organization of activity is determined by the (implicit) attempt to benefit from the returns to scale on the personal and the impersonal dimensions of transactions and the interaction between these returns to scale. The degree to which identity dominates or is subsumed under the impersonal dimensions of specialization shapes the type of transaction or contract. The family is the locale of transactions in which identity dominates; however, identity is also important in much of what we consider the "market," and, in fact, recent developments in economics can be interpreted as a departure from impersonal economics.

1

2   THE ORGANIZATION OF EXCHANGE

In recent years economists have devoted extensive efforts to analyzing aspects of family or household behavior using the ordinary tools of price theory and have emphasized the applicability and transferability of this mode of analysis to the nonmarket sector. I do not wish to abandon this approach but to add to it the transactional characteristics. Within this broader framework, one can analyze the transactions in which families have an advantage over other institutions, the conditions that make families of various types more or less efficient than the alternatives in any given transaction, the sorting of individuals into families, and the implications of family membership for transactions with others.

The main advantages of this approach are:

1. It provides a means of explicitly analyzing the implications on the micro level of various economic and institutional changes that on the macro level are considered as part of processes described as economic development, modernization, or Westernization.

2. Such issues and their bearing on the family tend to be tackled by economists and other social scientists in a nonintegrated fashion—sometimes in terms of "economic" as against "social" or "cultural" variables. The present framework seeks to integrate lines of thought generated in different branches of the social sciences and to link the family more closely with other phenomena studied in economics.

3. Demographers have recently been concerned with family demography. Economists have recently begun to question the decision model in which the household (or the firm) is treated as if it were an individual. I hope to shed some light on the link between individual and group analysis.

The Role of Identity
in Transactions:
The General Framework

Family and Market Transactions   In the broadest sense, a transaction consists of activities or transfers of property rights by or between at least two individuals or groups, the activities or transfers of the participants being interdependent (at least in a probabilistic sense).

Market transactions are a subset of all transactions no matter how one defines the whole set or what language is used to describe nonmarket transactions. Polanyi distinguished between exchange, reciprocity, and redistribution; he and other economic anthropologists oppose the application of economic analysis to social transactions that bear only a superficial resemblance to market transactions (Polanyi et al., 1957; Dalton, 1976; Sahlins, 1965). Others have stressed the similarity to market transactions of affective relationships (Blau, 1964; Homans, 1974) and used the concepts and analytical modes of economics to describe such relationships. Mauss (1954) has stressed the exchange nature of gifts. While I can sympathize with the aversion to superficial analogies and semantic exercises, I believe that economics can be used to provide a framework for analyzing the delimitation of the subsets of transactions and for identifying the determinants of the distribution of transactions by type.

Among nonmarket transactions, those occurring within kinship groups or families predominate. The family is a group of individuals related by blood, marriage, or adoption, but its significance as a social institution comes from the activities it accommodates. The institution takes the form of rights and obligations associated with and defining the roles of the family members, thus forming a comprehensive transaction, or contract, or a set of interrelated contracts (husband-wife, parent-children, wife-mother-in-law, etc.). Terms such as contract or transaction usually connote voluntary association. This seems natural in the case of marriage, where entry into the roles is voluntary on the part of either the spouses or their families of origin. Where the parent-child relationship is concerned, the usage might be objected to because entry of at least one of the parties into the relationship is involuntary. The transformation of the biological event into a social relationship that may extend over several decades, however, involves voluntary behavior of both parties and options on both sides to break away. Parental decisions to have children and how to behave toward them in infancy and early childhood are unilateral but are probably affected by expectations concerning future mutual relationships.

Let us, thus, accept the treatment of the family connection as a transaction or an exchange and consider some of its characteristics:[1] (a) It extends over long periods of time, but the duration is not specified in advance. (b) While the scope and importance of various activities change, the connection generally encompasses a large variety of activities. (c) Not all terms of the contract are specified explicitly—most activities are contingent on events and are decided sequentially; the response to contingencies remains unspecified, guided by general principles or rules of behavior that tend to apply to sets of similar family contracts in the society. (d) The highly interdependent elements of the contract exist as a package; and prices cannot be used as multipliers or weights for adding up all the various elements of the contract. (e) There is generally no explicit balancing of the exchange in terms of a unit of account, although certain money payments (e.g., dowry or bride price) can be interpreted as approximations to the ex-ante differences in the expected value of the packages being exchanged. What is generally true, here too, is that there is no balancing of individual components, there is no running quid pro quo. Instead, large outstanding balances are tolerated; because of the unspecified nature of the contract, when and how these balances are liquidated remains open. (f) Enforcement is mostly internal, although the contract is supported to some extent by the family of origin and by other social forces. (g) To varying degrees, the family contract creates a collective identity that affects the transactions of each member with people outside the family. (h) The most important characteristic of the family contract is that it is

4   THE ORGANIZATION OF EXCHANGE

embedded in the identity of the partners, without which it loses its meaning.
It is thus specific and nonnegotiable or nontransferable. Most of these characteristics are connected with the issue of identity.

Markets involve many (actual or potential) buyers and sellers. Ideally
market transactions are assumed to be perfectly replicable. A market transaction involves a unit price and a value in terms of a common unit of account,
which indicate the opportunities gained and forgone by the transacting parties. In terms of such opportunities, the transaction entails a full quid pro
quo, and there is no left-over business or outstanding balance. The value in
exchange is independent of the identity of the parties; sufficient information
is contained in the price-quantity offers, and nothing else about the transacting parties matters. This is an essential part of the perfect replicability of
market transactions and the essence of perfect transferability. Thus, as it is
pictured through intermediate theory textbooks, economics deals with
agents who are stripped of identity. Faceless buyers and sellers, households
and firms that grind out decision rules from their objective functions (utility,
profits), meet in the market place for an instant to exchange standardized
goods at equilibrium prices.

Obviously, an extreme case in which identity matters is that of affective
relationships: love and care or hate directed at a particular individual, the
desire to be in the company of or avoid certain people, and so on. Such a
relationship has by and large been outside the domain of economics. Some
attempts by economists to explore some of the consequences of such relationships have taken the form of introducing the utility of others in the individual's utility function in the form of "altruism" (Becker 1974a, 1976). The
insertion of the number of children into the utility function in the analysis of
fertility is another expression of affective relationships. But such treatment
cannot provide a satisfactory solution to the general issue that I raise here in
which people are interested in the identity of those with whom they deal for
practical reasons that may be only sometimes intermingled with affective
relationships.

Unlike the textbook view, recent work in economics deals with many
issues in which the identity of the agents and the mechanics of their interaction matter. In order to bring home the general importance of identity, consider the following worlds or models:

A. Every market day people (agents, traders, etc.) change, while the joint
distribution of their endowments and tastes is stationary.

B. People stay the same: they have been present on past market days and they
expect to be present on future market days. They neither recognize anyone nor
expect to be recognized by anyone.

C. People can identify at least some others and be identified by others.

World A is the world of instantaneous transactions, to which much of
general equilibrium theory applies. Moving to world B; in which there are
permanent actors with a past and a future, broadens the range of issues that

can be tackled. Present behavior is affected by accumulated experience and by the expectation that it will have future consequences, so there is room for investment behavior and capital theory. In the absence of identification, however, many activities take a restricted form or do not exist. Obviously there can be no intertemporal transactions; there is room only for the Robinson Crusoe type of capital theory—unidentified individuals cannot take upon themselves obligations for future delivery of goods or money, so there are no financial assets or commodity markets. There is investment in human capital, but only to the extent that the skills acquired can be used or manifest themselves costlessly without resort to identity. People learn the distribution of prices or trading partners confronting them, and they can search for the lowest price, the highest wage offer, or the best quality store, but they will not do so if they cannot identify them for the next transaction. Similarly, there is no incentive to sell more cheaply or to offer higher quality service if one knows one is not going to be identified. It needs but little reflection to realize that giving people an identity (in analysis), in addition to a past and a future, permits the discussion of much that is of interest even in narrowly defined economic activity.

There is a ploy that can solve some of the problem: a Grand Enforcer (sitting next to the Auctioneer and maybe the Invisible Hand) who identifies and is identified by all. He serves as a clearing house—debtors know that because he identifies them they have to pay; by the same token, creditors know they can lend. He declares true quality, he knows all. With free enforcement and free information, identity does not matter. But this is not the world we live in.

Identity and Fixed Transaction Costs The conduct of transactions itself involves a certain class of costs that are part of what the transactors forgo and that differ from other costs only in that they are associated with the exchange. They include the costs of information collection, advertisement, and negotiations, the creation of provisions and guarantees for enforcement, and so on. They arise because the parties to transactions are different individuals with asymmetric information, divergent motives, and mutual suspicions, and because expenditure of resources can reduce the gap in information and protect the parties against each other.

It is important to examine how transaction costs vary.[2] At one extreme are transaction costs that vary proportionately with the volume of goods being traded (e.g., a turnover tax); at the other extreme are the pure set-up costs associated with engaging in any exchange and not dependent on the volume of trade (e.g., a license to trade). Between the two extremes of pure set-up costs and costs that vary proportionately with the volume of transactions lie many possibilities: some costs may be fixed for any volume of trade between given pairs of people only at a point in time or for only one good or type of service. Some costs may serve one party in its dealings with any other party, and some may be fixed only for trade with a given party.

6   THE ORGANIZATION OF EXCHANGE

Insofar as they can serve specific parties for many periods they create capital. This capital is specific inasmuch as the returns materialize only in the exchange between specific parties, the capital stock losing its value when they separate.

The argument that some costs are fixed for fixed trading parties is based on the following factors:

1. Each person has some stable traits—honesty, reliability, skill, etc.—that interest the other and affect his perception of what he is getting or the terms on which he is getting it. The cost of establishing this mutual view is an investment that facilitates future trading between the parties.

2. Parties to a transaction can establish rules or norms for their exchange relationship, a common view concerning contingencies, and procedures for settling disputes that can serve them beyond a single transaction. The cost of negotiating and establishing these rules will have to be incurred again if the parties change.

3. The expectation of continuing exchange has a favorable effect on the behavior of the parties. Abstention from cheating in the present is an investment that will reap the gains of future trade.

We can see clearly how continuity of relationships can generate behavior on the part of shrewd, self-seeking, or even unscrupulous individuals that could otherwise be interpreted as foolish or purely altruistic. Valuable diamonds change hands on the diamond exchange, and the deals are sealed by a handshake. Major transactions are often concluded over the telephone between long-time business associates. Businessmen shun conflict and litigation when they expect continuing relationships (Macaulay, 1963). Members of a robber band must maintain honor among thieves, and needless to say the word "family" has not reached the mafia by accident. On the other hand, tourists are cheated by traders who deal honestly with their local customers; and anthropologists speak about "contextual morality" in primitive societies—ethical codes that forbid internal cheating within a tribe and allow cheating of others (Sahlins, 1965). The following observation by Arrow seems to correspond to many arrangements: "It is useful for individuals to have some trust in each other's word. In the absence of trust it would become very costly to arrange for alternative sanctions and guarantees and many opportunities for mutually beneficial cooperation would have to be forgone" (1969, p. 62).

The confidence of each party in the degree to which he and his trading partners will go on being tied together influences the amount of their investment commitment and the gains. The expected duration is influenced by exogenous factors (e.g., mortality) and by expectations of future changes in conditions (migration, mobility). Contractual arrangements may include provisions that increase the mutual confidence in continued affiliation, even if they are inefficient in a short-run view. Within institutions involving partners with unequal exit opportunities, part of the bargaining may involve the degree to which the parties are tied to the institution. Even the large expenditure associated with weddings has to do with penalties and signals associated with mutual guarantees of continued relationship.

The strategic advantage of expectation of continued contact is analyzed in game theory under the heading of repeated games, or super games (e.g., Luce and Raiffa, 1957). In a single, noncooperative game, parties may fail to achieve a mutually beneficial solution because each party recognizes the opportunities to cheat or to reap a short-term advantage. Adverse selection in the exchange in goods of uncertain quality is an example (e.g., Akerlof, 1970). However, infinite repetition of the transaction (a super game) can induce the parties to give up short-term benefits in order to realize future gains (Heal, 1976). (If the duration of the game is finite and certain and if there is no enforcement by a third party, then in the final game there is no incentive for good behavior; but then this will apply also to the game before the last and so on back to the first game.)

The investment framework ties together in an overall contract transaction that may be unbalanced or unintelligible when observed separately. Even the most extreme instances of seemingly unilateral giving—gifts and favors—are recognized as forms of exchange (see Mauss, 1954). Often they are given in order to create an obligation. They are accepted by those who cannot afford to refuse, or who believe that they will be able to control the repayment, or who believe that they will not be the losers in the implicit contract.[3] The acceptance of a gift constitutes an obligation to repay out of a set of alternatives, which may be defined narrowly or broadly, explicitly or implicitly. The choice within the set will be made by the original "giver" (whether he is Don Corleone or a tribal chief demanding loyalty) or will be left undecided among friends. The tolerance of large outstanding balances signals the presence of trust or implicit threats. The refusal to accept a gift often signals mistrust. A return gift cancels an obligation. Horizontal friendship and vertical loyalty are often associated with a series of gifts and favors.[4]

In addition to affective relationships, the types of transaction in which identity is important include:

1. Transactions in which, because of imperfect information, there is uncertainty about the quality of the object of exchange or the terms of the transaction. The identity of the seller can reduce this uncertainty: a producer's identity can be a signal of the quality of what is produced, and a worker's identity a signal of the quality of his services.

2. Transactions that are not consummated instantaneously and that involve obligations or consequences that extend over time. In one sense this is an important subset of the first category. The quality of promises to pay or deliver depends on the identity of the promise giver. In contracting for an intertemporal transaction between strangers, it is necessary to specify the contract in a manner that would allow a third party to adjudicate in case of disagreement.

Another special class of transactions, insurance transactions, in which a guarantee against future uncertainty is the commodity exchanged, presents problems for buyers and sellers for the solution of which identity is almost a necessary, but not a sufficient, condition. Indeed, transactions in insurance are the classical explanation for the failure of markets and the possible advantage of family contracts. What is known as "moral hazard" comes from the costs associated with making the distinction between the external risk and the incentive effect of insurance; adverse selection is the consequence of the inability of the insurer to assess individual risks. Buyers of insurance also face risks of a transactional nature—the risk of breach of contract in the form of failure to deliver or act and in the form of extortion attempts when the insured is in trouble. When the crop is about to be ruined if it is not harvested immediately, the only workers available can extort most of it; a drowning man or one wounded in battle can be stripped of all his wealth as the price of immediate help. Some risks are thus associated with the insurer's absolute monopoly power, which may allow him to collect not the (ex-ante) expected value of the damage but the ex-post value of the damage to the insured (Landes and Posner, 1978). The deal between Jacob and Esau is a reminder that even within families there is no complete guarantee against such blackmail.

The risks on the two sides do not cancel but add up in generating transaction costs that cause some insurance markets to shrink or vanish. Embedding the insurance contract in a connection between identified parties can provide a partial solution. Of the many examples that one could cite here let me mention the peculiar treatment of food in primitive societies, which put various restrictions on trade and disposal of food even where other items are traded. In one case (an Indian community in Colombia) the researcher notes that trade in food is restricted to trade with special clients: "the individuals must be bound by reciprocal obligation for [an Indian] to consider the transaction worth while, . . . because limiting the exchange in this way has served to minimize the risk of famine" (Ortiz, 1967, pp. 209–210). Special taboos governing food distribution have the same source (Sahlins, 1965, pp. 171–173).

Insurance elements in employer-employee relationships have only recently been mentioned with respect to modern economies but have for long been discussed in connection with the Japanese labor market (see Taira, 1970) and come up in various forms in developing societies. Epstein (1962) describes relationships between peasants and untouchables in Indian villages where the connection is hereditary and remuneration of untouchables by peasants is fixed. In years of famine the peasant receives no more than his worker and by sharing provides subsistence to all. In return, the worker is obligated to be on call: subsistence insurance is exchanged for insurance of labor services. The exchange of mutual obligations to ensure labor supply among farmers is very common.

Specialization by Identity   The approach taken here is that the different modes of transacting—market and nonmarket institutions—can be understood if viewed as the (not necessarily perfect) result of an attempt to minimize all costs, including the costs of transacting. Think of a transaction as the unit of analysis. It can be described in several dimensions—the goods and services being exchanged, the terms, the location, and, what is important here, the identity of those involved in it. The division of labor, or specialization, implies that each individual appears (as a seller) only in those transactions that are similar in most or all of the other dimensions—what is being traded, location, and so on.

In the same way one speaks of specialization by impersonal dimensions of transactions, one can speak of specialization by identity, meaning that individuals deal only with the same person or with small groups.

The Adam Smith tradition links specialization and the division of labor to the presence of returns to scale in production, that is, to the presence of set-up costs that make it cheaper, up to a point, to produce on a large scale. In the preceding section I argued that identity is a form of set-up cost; thus, the rationale for specialization by identity derives from returns to scale. The balance between specialization by identity and other dimensions derives from the minimization of production and transaction costs and reflects the scale economies connected with the different dimensions.

The structure of distribution is sometimes one of a strict hierarchy in specialization with increasingly finer division of labor—each differentiated product being channeled through exclusive wholesalers down to the local store dealing with just one product. But more often, distributors draw from several producers, and the local store draws many products from many producers. This reflects the fact that the economies of scale, or set-up costs, associated with each dimension can often be utilized over more than one dimension, so that at each stage there is a built-in bias toward homogeneity in terms of one dimension and heterogeneity in terms of the other dimension.[5] In buying a used car or taking a personal loan, people often prefer to deal with someone they know well, rather than go to a used car dealer or money lender. When purchasing sophisticated equipment, however, trust in one's friends or relatives cannot compete with the technical know-how of the specialized dealer. A buyer who intends to buy in the future will invest in (search for) a reliable salesman, but the long-term contract will be subsumed under the impersonal dimensions of the transactions. With differences in the importance of identity in various goods and in the specificity of investment of identity to goods or activities, people will be organized in small clusters for some purposes and large ones for others, and these groupings may intersect for different purposes.

Many of the issues that family research is concerned with are associated with specilization by identity. Thus, the class of related individuals engaged in a given set of transactions determines whether we talk about an extended or a nuclear family, and the process of nuclearization is one in which the class narrows until it includes only the spouses and their children.

The range of transactions involving family members has narrowed with modernization. This narrowing has taken the form of a reduction in the range of goods and services supplied within the family; a reduction in the proportion of families acting as producer cooperatives of marketable goods; greater specialization in joint consumption and affective relationships; and changes in the nature of the internal insurance and in capital allocation.

The relevance of household research and the usefulness of the various concepts of the household (Bender, 1967; Laslett, 1972; Goode, 1963) depend on the degree to which coresidence is consistently associated with other family transactions. Caldwell (1976) and others argue against the dominance of the household. Oppong (1976) provides many illustrations from Africa in which individuals are involved with different partners for different transactions and contracts between a pair of individuals defined by kinship differ in content in different settings.

Specialization and Enforcement of Contracts by Competition   The point at which specialization by identity occurs in the flow of transactions matters for the nature of the relationship between the transacting parties. When the permanent trading relationship is subsumed under impersonal specialization, trade is organized around specialized traders or firms each typically facing many buyers and sellers. Firms establish their separate identity via a brand name. This can be done through direct spending on advertising and promotion or by selling high-quality goods for low prices until people learn to recognize the quality.[6] Brand names represent *general* signals directed at potential trading partners of unspecified identity. The trading partners of the specialized trader make some investments that are general—becoming "educated" buyers (or sellers), in effect acquiring information that is of service whomever they deal with. They also make *specific* investments that depend for their value on the specific policies of the specialized trader. Workers who sell their labor services to large employers are in the same position.

On the face of it, the specific investment made by individual buyers in their relationship with each specialized trader gives the latter some monopoly power, a range in which prices change and buyers do not switch. A seller who faces many buyers (or a buyer facing many sellers) in ongoing relationships involving new buyers (or sellers) is, however, restrained from reneging on the contracts with each of his trading partners. What restrains him and provides protection for his trading partners' specific investments in him is the effect that failure to keep his promises would have on the terms at which he could get new buyers (sellers). The cheaper the flow of information among buyers and prospective buyers, the more effective is the self-enforcement mechanism of the implicit contract. An employer who wants to shift the cost of acquiring specific skills on to his workers by paying new employees less than the alternative wage and promising them seniority-linked future benefits above it could subsequently take advantage of them to such an extent that they would go elsewhere. What restrains him is that failure to keep the promises would eventually force him to pay higher starting wages.[7]

This form of social enforcement is the more effective, the finer the specialization by impersonal dimensions, the more standardized the transactions with various buyers (sellers), and the easier the flow of information among buyers (sellers). The more standardized the transactions, the closer we are of course to the ideal market transaction.

In relationships that tend to be exclusive, as in the family, the enforcing power of competition is weaker, and the range for informal bargaining is wide. Parties who have already invested specifically in each other are in a short-run position of bilateral monopoly. If the self-enforcement mechanism is imperfect, trust, or fear, or violence, becomes more important. The thrust of the argument of this section is that specific investment in identity is present also in what is regarded as the market. But where it is subsumed under impersonal specialization, enforcement of an explicit or implicit contract is provided by "the market," and is not internal to the contract.

Collective and Individual Identity   One can view firms (and families) as contracts between identified parties that form units replacing personal identity in transactions between them and the rest of the world. The set of contracts and rules between partners or shareholders, and between them and the hired management and labor that constitute the firm, establishes the extent and limits of individual liability and mutual responsibility vis-à-vis a third party. (Likewise, a family or a tribe may be regarded as a set of contracts that establishes rules of exchange and cooperation internally and allows the appearance of the collective identity vis-à-vis others to replace individual identity.)[8] An organization is a set of contracts and rules defining roles and establishing their relationships, in which individuals assume or leave roles that have been defined for general purposes and permanent use. Investment in identity takes place in the selection for roles and as individuals select the organizations they join.

In standard economic analysis, households and firms exist as collective identities that completely replace the identity of the individuals affiliated with them. For purposes of transactions between households and firms the collective identities exist as atoms rather than molecules.[9] Standard economic theory is concerned only with the transactions between the collective units, while what goes on within them is the subject-matter of other disciplines.

The sharp dichotomy between the external and the internal serves an analytically useful purpose. A more general view of collective and personal identity, however, would be that the involvement of individuals in a set of contracts can affect the cost of their other transactions, either because of the substance of these transactions or because of their value as signals. Sometimes a connection is preferred mostly for its effects on transactions with those outside it: this may be true of some social clubs, law firms, economics departments, and even marriage contracts. In all these cases, there is reliance on what bears a loose resemblance to the transitivity of the brand name—institutions based on personal investment and sorting provide signals that benefit individual members in their dealings with others. The collective name is, in turn, a public good whose value can be diminished by the behavior of each individual and whose survival depends on the internal controls. Internal contracts of the firm that do not provide incentives for (e.g.) quality will damage the brand name. A social club or a university department that does not sort new members carefully will damage its collective name.

The role of family affiliation in the transactions of individuals with those outside the family is particularly evident during the early stages of economic development. Families have played an important part in employment placement (see e.g., Anderson, 1971, on nineteenth-century England and Vogel, 1967, on Japan at the onset of the migration to towns). And family affiliation has also played an important part in the capital market in reducing the transaction costs of individuals (on family capitalism in both Europe and part of the developing world, see e.g., Benedict, 1968). Family relationships also play an important part in the struggle over the establishment of property rights and their physical protection, as is evident in any frontier movie.

The role of family affiliation vis-à-vis others relies partly on its value as a signal of personal traits—honesty, fidelity, skill, and so on—and on the degree to which the family takes responsibility for the obligations and actions of its members. Ascribed status has greater operational significance than achieved status when the family is an important educator and when the set of internal family contracts affects the security of those who deal with family members. Authority, discipline, altruism, and family solidarity affect the value of the signal, "family affiliation," for the rest of the world. The presence of a head of family, serving as director for communication, trust, and redistribution, reduces transaction costs within the family by reducing the need for bilateral relationships.[10] We can speak loosely of transitivity here— the pairwise investment of each member with the center links him to all the others. In his theory of social interaction, Becker (1974a) has shown why a central figure who cares (i.e., has the utility of members at heart, or in his own utility function) can generate socially optimal behavior from all the others, even if they are all egoists.

This concludes the presentation of the general framework. The next two sections of the exposition present, first, a general application of these ideas and, then, an examination of the way the relationship between wealth and family size is related to the functions of the family.

Families
and the Development
of Markets

General Trends   Economic and social development affects the importance of identity in given transactions relative to other elements of the cost structure; the relative weight in all transactions of those in which identity is important; the degree to which specialization by identity is subsumed under impersonal specialization, or investment in identity is specific to some activities; and the ability of the family, compared with other institutions, to provide an efficient milieu for transactions and to affect favorably the transactions of its members with others.

Social enforcement of private contracts, ready access to adjudication, morality, and religious pressure for generalized honesty (in contrast to "contextual morality") all tend to reduce the importance of identity, to facilitate transactions between strangers, and to reduce the need for specific mutual investment by trading parties, allowing people to trade with a wider circle of others and narrowing the range of goods and services in which any pair or small group deals.

Impersonal social institutions provide substitutes for family transactions—sometimes at the price of reducing efficiency (by relieving the individual of the cost of collecting information or by raising the threat of inspection, where from a social point of view it would be desirable for him to internalize these costs). Note, however, that certain types of social action change the types of connections created, but do not necessarily reduce their number or importance. The threat of punitive social action on certain transactions (such as trade in drugs, liquor, or sex) induces connections of mutual dependence between buyers and sellers and distributors at different stages. High penalties on crimes in general increase the mutual dependence of the criminals.

Likewise, money as a social institution reduces the role of identity. Its transactional facility, its liquidity and negotiability, rest on the fact that its value is independent of the identity of the seller. Commodities that served as money have tended to be of a fairly uniform and readily observable quality. Money in the form of coins depends on the identity of whoever mints it or vouches for its content. Paper money depends for its value on the identity of those who issue it. Money in the form of personal checks depends for its value on the identity of the banking concern. People acquire information (at some or no cost) about the identity of the third party who issues money. This serves them in many transactions, saves transaction costs, and makes the identity of the "seller" of money immaterial.

As mechanized production and quality control increase standardization of many commodities, there is a decline in the importance of identity in the trade in tangible commodities.

Transactions in Labor In the exchange of personal services and in capital and insurance transactions, it is more difficult to reduce the relative importance of personal identity than it is in transactions involving produced commodities; but it is, nonetheless, possible. Modern economic growth is associated with the increase in the stock of knowledge and the accumulation of human capital. Information is a consistent source of economies of scale leading to specialization; and behind specialization by identity there is investment in information pertaining to those involved. However, economic development is associated with a greater return to investment in information pertaining to the *impersonal* dimensions, which in turn induces specialized investment in human capital. The transactional advantages of the family cannot compensate for the fact that within its confines the returns from impersonal specialization and division of labor are not fully realizable.

A change in the organization of economic activity that involves a shift from family farm and cottage industry through putting-out system to factory system could be the consequence of purely technological change that increased the advantage of large-scale production, because of economies associated with (e.g.) the harnessing of energy sources. But the emphasis placed on institutional change, at least by traditional economic historians, suggests that institutional innovations may be an important contributing factor, at times even the moving force; the greater efficiency of one organizational structure compared with another is a matter of both technological change in the narrow sense and transactional efficiency, and the two cannot be easily distinguished. Cottage industry, putting out, and the family represent involvement in product markets and division of labor but use mostly the family's own labor and capital or land. The shift to specialized firms, which rests on the concentration of a large volume of labor and capital, means separate sale of labor and capital services in markets that have experienced significant institutional innovations. In labor service transactions (more than elsewhere) buyer and seller differ in the information at their disposal or in the cost of acquiring it; such differences may lead workers to shirk, cheat, or misrepresent their ability. As a result, the use of hired labor has considerable disadvantages over own labor and labor spot markets over the family-type transaction. One (popular) view of the effect of the factory system on the exchange in labor services is that mechanization and automation eliminate the importance of identity in labor transactions. This is the *Modern Times* image of masses of anonymous workers performing mechanical routine tasks requiring little know-how. If this were a realistic image we would find labor spot markets in developed countries. The fact is that such markets exist mostly in less developed countries or sectors. Taira's (1970) interpretation of the emergence of the implicit patriarchal employer-employee contract in Japan is that it provided a solution to the inefficiency of a labor spot market with excessive turnover, rather than being some kind of inert conformity with old customs. Recent studies of the US labor market report on the prevalence of long-term association between employers and employees (Lilien, 1977; Feldstein, 1975).[11] Thus, technological advance and sustained growth have not done away with identity as an element in labor services but, rather, have found ways of dealing with it by permitting increasing interaction between specialization by identity and by impersonal dimensions of transactions.

Another aspect of specialization by impersonal dimensions is the development of standardized (albeit imperfect) signals and certificates produced by organizations specializing in education, sorting, and the production of general signals. Their function is to reduce transaction costs, and one of their effects is to reduce the importance of identity. But increasing complexity of production and fine product differentiation require the services of reliable specialists. The cost of error and the damage that individuals can do both in production and in the financial affairs of large firms, together with the imperfections of the generalized signals, mean that personal identity is still important. Yet clearly, once identity is important mainly when subsumed under impersonal specialization, the family becomes a relatively inefficient institution.

Capital and Insurance Transactions Institutional developments in capital markets have occupied a prominent role in economic historians' account of growth: the emergence of negotiable financial assets and specialized institutions for capital transactions, the rise of the firm as a collective legal identity, and the concept of limited liability. These developments have enabled individuals to separate the sale of their labor and capital services, to separate ownership from operation, and to enjoy the benefits of diversification of ownership; they have enabled firms to mobilize capital from many individuals and to operate on an optimum scale.

The family, particularly in developing countries, often serves as an alternative and very different mode for transacting on the capital account. Thus, a common argument concerning high fertility in developing countries is that children are desirable as partners in capital and insurance transactions and not only as suppliers of labor. The child who receives support is implicitly bound by an obligation to reward his parents by supplying labor and old-age support. These transactions are based on complementarity in the life cycle—children come when they can be provided for and later they assist their parents.

In his pure-loan model, Samuelson (1958) pointed out the inability of a market in pure loans to solve such problems of intertemporal transfers efficiently, in the absence of a general asset. The solution is a "social compact" whereby successive generations implicitly agree not to break the chain of giving and receiving. The absence of general assets is at one end of a spectrum in which assets are partly specific, because of transaction costs, which raise their internal value relative to their market value.

In effecting intertemporal transfers and transacting in contingent claims, the child-parent relationship has the potential advantage that it is reinforced by other transactions and activities. Much of the socialization carried out in the family is concerned with education for roles toward the parents within the family ("Honor thy father and mother" comes before "Thou shalt not kill"). It may be argued that when the family is the major institution for socialization the parents and others have opportunities to invest in family-specific human capital, that is, to create traits that are more valuable within the family than elsewhere, reducing the chances that children will want to leave. Child betrothal serves this function. The cool or even hostile reaction to (even free) schools in some traditional contexts may reflect the objection of the parent generation to the substitution of general human capital for the family-specific human capital and the implied reduction in family attachment (see, e.g., Oppong, 1973).

Investment in family-specific human capital may not be sufficient to insure the bond of obligation. Enforcement of the parent-child contract can be further secured through bequests, giving the parents the last word.[12] Children, for their part, bear the risk that their parents will need more support than the bequest is worth if the parents live "too long." The bequest may not cover the extended support, but once part of the support has been paid, it may be worthwhile to carry on rather than lose the whole bequest. The bargaining position of the parties depends on the size of the estate and on the ability of parents to choose alternative heirs or to secure services from other sources. Bargaining and sometimes written contracts deal with the distribution of the estate, timing of transfer of title and control, the rights and obligations of each side.[13]

Inheritance laws affect and may reflect various trade-offs and assessment of risks. Inheritance practices that keep property intact enhance the ability and willingness of *one* of the children to provide old-age insurance. The timing of transfer of title and the terms of the contract depend on the parties' bargaining positions, which in turn depend on the alternatives available to each, including the presence of other children. Splitting an inheritance between children can secure support from more people but may reduce the probability of support from each. The availability of enforcement of contracts between parents and children makes earlier transfer of title feasible (see Berkner, 1973). Ortiz (1967) mentions children's bargaining over shares in bequests tied to their readiness to provide labor services; Anderson (1971) compares rural Ireland with rural Lancashire in the middle of the nineteenth century and relates the duration of adult children's residence in the parental home to the amount they expect to inherit. Nor is this just a rural phenomenon. Describing family business in East Africa, Benedict (1968) cites examples of parents who finance the education of their children and then make a transfer of part of the family business conditional on the son's readiness to work in it. The supply of labor services by children is thus linked to the transfer-insurance-bequests nexus. The particular form in which parents hold wealth (and in which children accumulate their own) has implications for the demand of parents and children for each other, and the particular choice of assets is affected by returns that reflect both transactional and nontransactional considerations.

It is probably correct to view the changes in the capital market as a reduction in the importance of identity and a corresponding rise in anonymity, so clearly expressed in the French term *société anonyme*. But the importance of identity does not vanish. Investment in identity becomes more specialized for capital or insurance transactions: the village lender represents specialization in intensive investment in identity, and so does his heir, the loan officer in a bank. Note also that there is no uniform monotonic decline in the importance of identity and family-type transactions. The private financing of investment in human capital, which constitutes a significant share of total investment, rests on identity much more than does the financing of investment in tangible capital. Some may describe this as an imperfection in the capital market and others as an imperfection in the labor market, where indentures cannot be enforced (Stigler, 1967). The fact remains that the financing of human capital requires nonmarket substitutes, either a family-type contract or alternatively some kind of governmental intervention.

There is also a scale effect: the development of markets implies that each unit of capital can be traded at a lower cost, and there may be a smaller return to investment in identity from a unit transacted; however, greater wealth and more transactions per unit of wealth may actually raise the total return on investment in identity. Moreover there is some complementarity between market and nonmarket transactions. There are returns to scale in the use of information; the identity of whoever transmits or shares information is important in evaluating it; information is important in doing business in the market—all these elements may increase the returns to cooperation based on family-type contracts. Joint ownership of property has often been part of the definition of the family (e.g., Goode, 1963). Its advantages have ranged from the joint protection and acquisition of property rights to more subtle economic benefits. Business cooperation between the members of rich families continues in highly developed economies. Long-term partnerships with nonrelatives simulate some of the properties of the family-type contract, again mutually investing in identity in order to save transaction costs and reap the benefits of joint action vis-à-vis the rest of the world. The need to invest in identity to operate efficiently even in relatively developed markets is an element in the high salaries of top executives and in the dependence of lonely millionaires on trusty henchmen. (Henchmen become famous by betraying their employer or selling his secrets to magazines, and they do it more often than sons or brothers.)

Transition from Family- to Market-Dominated Transactions   Examples of complementarity between market and family-type transactions abound, particularly in the early stages of development. Parental involvement in the labor market may be combined with an attempt to maintain a family farm as well—certainly prevalent in many developing countries. This is a form of market involvement that increases the domestic tasks of wives and children. This practice is particularly prevalent in early stages of development during which market employment is subject to considerable instability and is essentially a spot transaction. Involvement of mothers in the labor market raises the cost of child rearing. The impact of this change again depends on the context: in a large household there is greater flexibility in allocating members between the labor market and the home—older children take care of younger children and older relatives are sought after for the purpose, temporarily raising household size. The conflict between child rearing and the labor market is more severe once women get into permanent jobs in which on-the-job training and continuity matter.

The employment of children in the labor market can, in the short run, increase family income in periods of slack internal supply of jobs.[14] If employment is uncertain, children will want to remain part of the parental household. Children entering the labor market more permanently may leave the household but may still want the backing of the parental farm and may maintain the implicit contract with parents. If stable employment at a high enough wage is offered, the inducement to break away is greater. We mentioned earlier the traditional objections to education. If, however, both parents work in the market, public education is a social provision of child care and can reduce the cost of children. To the extent that education is offered in conjunction with or as a consequence of the development of a labor market in which education is rewarded, parents may still maintain direct or indirect control of children and may welcome education as an improved investment for their own support and as support for smaller children.[15] This may temporarily increase parental demand for transactions with children; it can at the same time reduce the number of the first vintage to be exposed to education.

The initial entry into a turbulent labor market is associated with increased risks: parents may gamble and reduce risks by pooling the fortunes of several children. The simultaneous entry into the market of several relatives may have the advantage of information and connections that strengthen rather than weaken family ties. No less important, perhaps more so, are the complementarities between the family and the emerging capital market. The role of the family in the history of European capitalism is well-known. There is also some documentation of the role of families in the business world in developing countries, where expansion and credit position depend on the availability of several sons in the various branches of the family business and sometimes in government or banking or elsewhere where connections matter.

Let me conclude this section with a skeleton of a model: The benefits from a family-type connection can be viewed as the savings in transaction cost per dollar transacted times the volume of transaction. The latter rises with wealth. Thus, within one society, for a given institutional setup, the benefit from a connection tends to rise with wealth; the (upward) slope of such a curve rises with the saving per dollar transacted. The development of markets tends to push this curve downward, that is, for any given level of wealth, the benefits from a connection decline as identity becomes less important. The slope tends to decline too. But: economic growth means accumulation of wealth, that is, a move to the right and toward higher benefits to a connection along any given curve for a given institutional setup. Thus, the ambiguity, and even lack of monotonicity, in the relationship between economic development and the benefit from investment in identity can be viewed as the result of two processes—the reduction in the benefit at any given level of wealth and the increase in the benefit coming from the accumulation of wealth.

The Effect of Wealth
on Family Size
and Composition

The relationship between family size and composition, on the one hand, and the level of income or wealth, on the other, has been widely researched. The relatively easy-to-measure variables such as household size and fertility have attracted greater attention, however, than more elusive aspects of family relationships. To some extent there is substitution between intensive relationship in a small family and less intensive involvement with a large family. The balance between intensive and extensive family involvement depends on the functions of the family, on the rate at which internal transaction costs rise with family size, on the distribution of individual traits, and on demographic constraints on the supply of partners of a particular status.[16]

We shall distinguish here between three types of family transactions, namely those involving production, consumption, and insurance. In the standard household production model (Becker, 1965), all categories of household activity are treated uniformly—all involve the transformation of own time and purchased goods into activities useful to the members of the family. This is appropriate if indeed all activities are separable and have constant-returns-to-scale technologies. If some of the commodities produced for own use are semi-public goods, in that there is some indivisibility in their provision, or if there is complementarity in consumption between individuals—in other words, if it is either cheaper or more enjoyable to consume the same things and pursue the same activities—there is some merit in distinguishing between the various activities and between the family as a consumer cooperative (including affective relationships) and as a producer cooperative.

Production   In a production model of the family in which the head of the family possesses tangible capital and in which the operation of factor markets gives an advantage to the family-type contract, we can expect family size to increase with wealth and with the inequality in its distribution between men, women, and children. In the language of production theory, the complementarity between tangible capital and human time means that more tangible capital should work with more labor; that richer men want to "employ" more wives and children within the family. The same will be true if there is gross complementarity between men's human capital and that of children and women. Men with more human capital will demand more complementary services. The same can be said in terms of a trade analogy: diversity in the composition of endowments creates comparative advantage and promotes intrafamily trade (see Gronau, 1973; and Becker, 1974b). So does diversity in tastes. But the gains from trade depend also on the volume of trade—men with a large endowment may need more trading partners to exploit the potential gains from trade.

The greater the advantages of intrafamily over interfamily trade in terms of transaction costs, the more pronounced will be the positive correlation between family size and wealth. The crude association between family size and income in societies with low or declining fertility tends to be inverse, while cross-section studies in peasant societies show a positive association between family size and land holdings. Positive associations between wealth and family size seem also to have prevailed in Europe before the demographic transition. From the demand side, rather than rely on a vague income effect, one could explain these as a reflection of gross complementarity (using a production model) or of the positive association between endowment and gains from trade. The same argument would apply to the positive association between wealth and the number of wives in polygynous societies (see Grossbard, 1978).

Sorting into families is governed by the same rules that determine the sorting of inputs into firms and the selection of partners in trade.[17] Either analogy suggests a positive association between the endowments of men and women who are paired in marriage, that is, complementarity in production, or greater gains in trade. Given that there are fixed costs associated with identity, obtaining complementary services from one person with a large endowment is preferable to obtaining them from several with small endowments. This modifies what was said before about the relationship between property and size. If women and children have a fairly low and uniform endowment, the better-endowed men can satisfy their demand for a larger volume of trade only by increasing family size. But if women's labor endowment is not uniform, the better-endowed will be sought by the better-endowed men, and will substitute for the men's need for a larger family.

Consumption Let us move next to the family as a consumer cooperative and assume that it is based on the joint use of indivisible facilities, cheaper provision of commodities on a larger scale, and the enjoyment of joint activities. One could think here of a family whose members derive their income from the market and spend it together on purchased goods or on recreation activities. Again, we need fixed identity costs to account for the preference for (semi) permanent partners.[18] Several statements can be made on size and composition.

The size of a group cooperating in the consumption of a normal semi-public good will diminish with the income of the members. This is a well-known implication of the theory of social clubs (Buchanan, 1965; and Pauly, 1967), which rests on the statment that, as each individual's consumption rises with income, the range of publicness or declining costs is exhausted with fewer participants. As income rises, an increasing variety of commodities is consumed, which may reduce the sensitivity to income of the size of the sharing group. Still, it is quite plausible that the rich are less in need of partners. Another question that comes up here repeats one raised earlier in general terms: to what extent does specialization by identity dominate other forms of specialization—do people team up as one pair or group for many purposes or do they form specialized groups (clubs), each dedicated to a particular activity? As noted, this depends on the relative personal and impersonal economies of scale. For consumption activities requiring high set-up costs and fewer of the identity-related characteristics, people will join a specialized club. Similarly, when the family is a large kinship group, individual members may team up for special purposes.

While specialized clubs are sorted by the similarity in one activity, multipurpose social clubs, neighborhoods with several public amenities, and, of course, families have to be more uniform in terms of tastes and income.[19] Here the theory of localized public goods is applicable also to families. Affiliation to a firm is dictated mostly by a specialized activity that does not directly satisfy the utility of its members, and this limits the range of utility-satisfying public commodities over which a consensus can be established, such as group health insurance and other fringe benefits in kind (see, e.g., Goldstein and Pauly, 1974). Joint consumption tends to equalize real income in the family and is an incentive for intraclass marriage. Laws or social customs that impose restrictions on the internal distribution of real income and the separate ownership of wealth encourage intraclass marriage. On the other hand the fact that Muslim women keep individual property rights facilitates marriage across classes, as do flexible consumption habits, when husbands and wives do not necessarily share the same consumption level, as is common in Africa (see Oppong, 1974).

Insurance Let us discuss now a third category of family transactions, namely insurance. Here lie all the pitfalls for the operation of markets—moral hazard, adverse selection, the costs or difficulties of explicitly specifying states of the world, and so on. These are some of the reasons why insurance transactions with specialized traders involve specific investment in the identity of the buyer and restrictions on behavior.[20] It is clear why investment in identity is rewarding in these circumstances, why trust is mutually beneficial, why proximity and general involvement create at little expense the information that is lacking among strangers and generate incentives for proper behavior. Typically insurance between family members is mutual, an exchange of promises for aid contingent on the situation of both (or all) parties. Several remarks can be made concerning the sorting of people into groups for mutual insurance.

In discussing the relationship between the size of the coinsurance group and the income of its members, we can begin with some of the club arguments. The security gained by sharing independent risks is analogous to security produced at declining costs. If the size of the group that shares risks is limited, this can be interpreted to mean that fixed identity costs of investing in an additional member just balance the benefits of adding a member. Much of the advantage of risk-sharing can be achieved with fairly small numbers, and the marginal contribution to risk reduction of an additional member declines rapidly. The rich are better able to self-insure against losses of a given size, and a smaller number of coinsurers comes close to exhausting the benefits of the added security. Likewise, if one thinks of a given profitability of default in the face of a given loss, the size of the group and the wealth of its members are substitutes. But "great wealth implies great loss," said Lao-tse (*The Simple Way*, p. 44).[21] The rich can lose more. Note also that the risks that threaten all the units of wealth held by an individual are likely to be correlated—wealth is held in discrete assets, at given locations, subject to risks associated with the identity of the owner. This is by definition true of human wealth and also, but to a lesser degree, of nonhuman wealth. What is clear is that it is worthwhile for the rich to invest significantly in their coinsurers. Beyond this point, statements concerning the connection between size of group and income will have to bring in the connection between income and risk aversion.

The benefits of sharing risks with others are greater the less is the direct dependence of the risks across individuals. Ideally, groups of mutual insurance will consist of people with equal ability to insure each other and with independent or negatively correlated risks.

These observations have several implications for the ability of families to cope with the insurance problem. In insuring, for example, for support in time of sickness or in averaging the randomness of individual incomes, the family can be an effective insurer, and larger families may serve this function either through many children or through ties extending beyond the nuclear family. But it should be noted that if family relationships are intensive, there is also a greater chance that risks are positively correlated across members, that fluctuations in the economy or in other external conditions would hit the coinsurers simultaneously. Of course, pooling the wealth of family members allows greater diversification than in individual portfolios (because of the fixed costs of holding single assets), but the gains from pooling with a close relative on the basis of trust and personal investment in identity have to be weighed against the benefits of doing it with strangers facing independent or negatively correlated risks. This may account for the fact that within kinship networks, groups of coinsurers extend beyond the nuclear and coresident family. The ability of the market to enter into insurance transactions and reap the benefits of sharing between even much larger groups may reflect some success in reducing the fixed costs of investment in additional coinsurers.

The specific investment in relationships with others is subject to risks that affect the choice between concentrating a large investment in a few people and spreading it among many. This is relevant for analyzing the effects of mortality: high mortality means that the expected duration of a relationship between parties is short, and, up to a point, its variance is high. Low mortality increases the returns to specific investment in one or a few individuals, as against the incentive to diversify investment over a broad group of kin. The high risk of investing in a single partner may be behind the observation of anthropologists that in Africa transactions between husband and wife are fewer or less important than those with the families of origin, particularly in regard to property ownership. Even the fact that child-father contracts are much less intensive than the relationships between the children and the family of origin (particularly maternal kin or uncles, as in parts of Africa) may reflect the greater likelihood that a child in a high-mortality and high-fertility environment will have a surviving uncle than a father. This extends the familiar argument that, in a high infant-mortality regime, there may be a tendency to gamble on many children, while investing little in each. The general argument is that reduced mortality intensifies the relationships within the nuclear family and attenuates those with the wider kinship group (see e.g., Shorter, 1975).

We have seen that in different types of transactions the relationship between wealth and family size may differ. It is more likely to be direct in production and more likely to be inverse in joint consumption, while the picture is more complex concerning insurance. Developments in the labor and capital market discussed here and in the preceding section reduce the role of family in production. When families are confined more to joint consumption and affective relationships, there is less reason to observe the positive relationship between wealth and size. On the other hand, joint consumption induces sorting of people with similar tastes and incomes.

Conclusion

Taking a broad view of transactions, I have discussed the role of identity. I sketched a framework in which the opportunity to reduce transaction costs by making specific investment in the exchanges between identified parties affects the organization of social activity, the division of labor, and, in particular, the interaction between specialization by identity and by other dimensions of transactions. This framework provides channels for linking various aspects of economic and social development to changes in the mode of transacting and to the shifts in the borderlines between the various types of market and nonmarket modes.

The motivation for this essay is the study of the family, the most important institution for nonmarket transactions and probably still the least specialized. The general framework is a result of a search for some elements missing from economists' and others' analyses of families and households and the desire to create a bridge between previous analyses. The framework aspires to generality—I do want to point to common elements in transactions that take many institutional forms and to draw examples from many diverse corners of human activity, and the family serves as the chief example.

A Note on Theory

This paper is part of a general attempt to create a new institutional economics. It bears some similarity in approach to Williamson's *Markets and Hierarchies* (1975) and to some extent to Hirschman's *Exit Voice and Loyalty* (1970). This new attempt in contrast to the old institutional school (e.g., Commons, 1924) tries to explain institutions using many developments within economics proper. This was the approach of Coase's (1937) classic work on the nature of the firm, which was maintained partly in the oral tradition at the Universities of Chicago and California at Los Angeles. Some of the theoretical strains underlying this paper are: information economics as positive theory, led by Stigler, and as normative theory (market failure) à la Arrow; the "new" monetarism, which emphasizes the role of transaction costs and institutional constraints (Clower, Leijenhufvud); the implicit contract theory and the theory of agency, starting with Cheung (1969) and elaborated by Stiglitz, Azariadis, Baily, and others; the work on internal labor markets (Doeringer and Piore; Williamson et al.); the theory of repeated games; and the theory of the club. My emphasis on specific investment draws on Oi (1962) and Becker (1964). In the context of the family this approach comes to complement rather than replace the new household economics, as exemplified in the volume sponsored by T.W. Schultz (1974), where again the influence of Becker's work is dominant. Outside the field of economics this paper relates to issues raised by economic anthropologists both in general treatises and in the concerns of many empirical studies (Dalton, Polanyi et al., Sahlins, Firth, Barth). Such issues have also been raised in the demographic work in developing countries (e.g., Caldwell).

Notes

Most of the work toward this paper was done while the author was in residence at the Labor and Population Program of the Rand Corporation and at the Economics Department, University of California at Los Angeles, and completed when he was a fellow of the Institute of Advanced Studies of the Hebrew University of Jerusalem. The work at Rand was financed by a grant from the National Institute of Health.

The author benefited from communications by Peter Diamond, Jack Hirshleifer, Simon Kuznets, Axel Leijonhufvud, T. W. Schultz; comments by William Butz, Robert Clower, Harold Demsetz, Susan Freund, Zvi Griliches, Reuben Gronau, David Harrison, Michael Keren, Ruth Klinov-Malul, Ed Lazear, John McCall, Dale Mortensen, Sam Peltzman, Norman Ryder, Finis Welch, and Menahem Yaari; and seminars at Columbia, Harvard, Jerusalem, the University of California at San Diego, Los Angeles, and Berkeley, and NBER-West.

An earlier, condensed version of this

paper was presented at the 1978 IUSSP conference in Helsinki on Economic and Demographic Change: Issues for the 1980s, and was published in volume 1 of the Proceedings (Liège: IUSSP, 1979).

1. I benefited here from Macneil (1974). Macneil distinguishes between transactional and relational contracts as two extremes of a continuum and suggests their characteristics.

2. For a detailed exposition of this, see Hirshleifer (1973).

3. There is some similarity here to Herbert Simon's description of the implicit employment contract (1951).

4. See, however, Titmuss (1970) for a treatment of anonymous gifts.

5. Contemporary interest in the nature of the division of labor is quite rare. See, however, Stigler (1951) and Leibenstein (1960).

6. These are investments and correspondingly a brand name is an asset that can in part be realized either through deliberate depreciation and debasement (selling bad goods under a good name) or through sale. A brand name is a *specific* asset if its capitalized value exceeds its value in sale. The nature of the information conveyed by a brand name determines whether it can be sold by its original owner at a price equal to the present value of the capitalized services. Franchised names rest on the assumption that there is some monitoring of quality or transmission of patented knowledge. A doctor or a lawyer can sell some of his goodwill, but the trust in his personal knowledge is a *specific* asset (here, it is simply human capital).

7. Thus, the supply function of labor faced by individual employers should include quit rates, layoffs, and discharges in addition to wages. See, e.g., Parsons (1972) and Pencavel (1972).

8. Jones (1976) presents a view of trade within "socially defined enclaves" that is in many respects similar to that presented here.

9. Leibenstein's (1976) first chapter is titled "Atomistic versus molecular economics" and deals with this issue.

10. If the fixed cost of establishing a relationship in a system with m members with a center is F and the cost is F^1 in a system without a center, the former will be superior to the latter in terms of their fixed costs if $(m - 1)F < 1/2m(m - 1)F^1$.

11. The theories of specific human capital, internal labor market, and implicit labor contracts provide various interpretations of this phenomenon. See Oi (1962); Becker (1964); Doeringer and Piore (1971); Baily (1974); Azariadis (1975); Stiglitz (1975); Williamson et al. (1975); and Mortensen (1978).

12. See Hirshleifer's (1977) response to Becker's (1976) handling of altruism. Parsons (1974) interprets old-age support as a contract for income insurance secured by the promise of a bequest.

13. A somewhat extreme example, cited by Anderson (1971), is that of parents losing support once they had "used up" what their children expected to give to them.

14. See the analyses of the relation between child wage and US fertility in Lindert (1974). See also Rosenzweig and Evenson (1977).

15. See, e.g., Caldwell (1965) and Salaff (1975).

16. Thus, for example, the number of brothers who can combine to cooperate in an extended family framework is restricted by the availability of brothers, in turn determined by the mortality-fertility regime. The size of the group participating in such an implicit contract will then depend on the degree to which more distant relatives are good substitutes. [This is the point of the exchange between Levy (1965) and Coale and Faller in Coale et al. (1965).]

17. Becker's (1974b) theory of marriage applies these rules to the sorting of spouses by their traits.

18. In the absence of fixed costs, a semi-public good could be provided by competitive firms (see Berglas, 1976).

19. "It is the wretchedness of being rich that you have to live with rich people" (Logan Pearsall-Smith, *Afterthoughts*), indicating that it is not the pleasure but the cost effectiveness of associating with other rich that causes social stratification.

20. For example, the cost of check-ups for medical insurance, or safety requirements in home insurance; contrast the anonymous sale of in-flight life insurance, where these problems do not exist.

21. Support for this important empirical observation is found in the old Hebrew saying, "He who multiplies assets, multiplies worries," and the presumably independent observations by Benjamin Franklin, "He who multiplies riches multiplies care" (*Poor Richard*) and Periander "The greater your fortune the greater your cares" (Plus est sollicitius magis beatus).

Bibliography

Akerlof, George A. 1970. "The market for 'lemons': Quality uncertainty and the market mechanism." *Quarterly Journal of Economics* 84 (August):488–500.

Alchian, Armen A., and Harold Demsetz. 1972. "Production, information costs, and economic organization." *American Economic Review* 62 (December):777–795.

Anderson, Michael. 1971. *Family Structure in Nineteenth Century Lancashire*. London: Cambridge University Press.

Arrow, Kenneth J. 1969. "The organization of economic activity: Issues pertinent to the choice of market versus nonmarket allocation." In *The Analysis and Evaluation of Public Expenditures: The PPB System*, Vol. 1. Joint Economic Committee, 91st Cong., 1st Sess., pp. 47–63.

Azariadis, Costas. 1975. "Implicit contracts and underemployment equilibria." *Journal of Political Economy* 83 (December):1183–1202.

Baily, Martin Neil. 1974. "Wages and employment under uncertain demand." *Review of Economic Studies* 41 (January):37–50.

Barth, F. 1966. *Models of Social Organization*. Occasional Paper 23. London: Royal Anthropological Institute.

Becker, Gary S. 1964. *Human Capital: A Theoretical and Empirical Analysis with Special Reference to Education*. National Bureau of Economic Research, General Series No. 80. New York and London: Columbia University Press.

———. 1965. "A theory of the allocation of time." *Economic Journal* 75 (September):493–517.

———. 1974a. "A theory of social interactions." *Journal of Political Economy* 82 (November/December):1063–1093.

———. 1974b. "A theory of marriage." In *Economics of the Family: Marriage, Children, and Human Capital*, ed. T.W. Schultz. A Conference Report of the National Bureau of Economic Research. Chicago and London: University of Chicago Press.

———. 1976. "Altruism, egoism, and genetic fitness: Economics and sociobiology." *Journal of Economic Literature* 14 (September):817–826.

———, Elisabeth M. Landes, and Robert T. Michael. 1977. "An economic analysis of marital instability." *Journal of Political Economy* 85 (December):1141–1187.

Bender, D. R. 1967. "A refinement of the concept of household, families, co-residence, and domestic functions." *American Anthropologist* 69:493–504.

Benedict, Burton. 1968. "Family, firms and economic development." *Southwestern Journal of Anthropology* 24 (Spring):1–19.

Berglas, Eitan. 1976. "On the theory of clubs." *American Economic Review* 66 (May):116–121.

Berkner, Lutz. 1973. "Recent research on the history of the family in Western Europe." *Journal of Marriage and the Family* 35 (August):395–405.

Blau, Peter M. 1964. *Exchange and Power in Social Life.* New York: Wiley.

Buchanan, James M. 1965. "An economic theory of clubs." *Economica* 32 (February):1–13.

Burch, Thomas K., and Murray Gendell. 1970. "Extended family structure and fertility: Some conceptual and methodological issues." *Journal of Marriage and the Family* 32, no. 2: 227–236.

Caldwell, John C. 1965. "Extended family obligations and education: A study of an aspect of demographic transition amongst Ghanaian university students." *Population Studies* 19 (November):183–199.

———. 1976. "Toward a restatement of demographic transition theory." *Population and Development Review* 2, nos. 3/4 (September/December):321–366.

Cheung, Steven. 1969. *The Theory of Share Tenancy.* Chicago: University of Chicago Press.

Clower, Robert W. 1971. "Theoretical foundations of monetary policy." In *Monetary Theory and Monetary Policy in the 1970s,* ed. E. Clayton, J.C. Gilbert, and R. Sedgwick. New York and London: Oxford University Press, pp. 13–28.

Coale, Ansley J., et al. (eds.) 1965. *Aspects of the Analysis of Family Structure.* Princeton, N.J.:Princeton University Press.

Coase, R. H. 1937. "The nature of the firm." *Economica* 4 (N. S.; November):386–405.

Commons, John Rogers. 1974. *Legal Foundations of Capitalism.* Clifton, N.J.: A. M. Kelley. Photocopy of New York edition, 1924.

Dahlman, Carl J. 1977. "Transaction costs, externalities and our two paradigms." Workshop in Law and Economics, University of Los Angeles at California.

Dalton, G. 1976. *Economics, Anthropology and Development.* New York: Basic Books.

Doeringer, Peter B., and Michael J. Piore. 1971. *Internal Labor Markets and Manpower Analysis.* Lexington, Mass.: D. C. Heath.

Epstein, T. S. 1962. *Economic Development and Social Change in South India.* Manchester, Eng.: Manchester University Press.

Feldstein, Martin. 1975. "The importance of temporary layoffs: An empirical analysis." *Brookings Papers on Economic Activity,* no. 3, pp. 725–745.

Firth, Raymond. 1967. "Themes in economic anthropology: A general comment." In *Themes in Economic Anthropology,* ed. Raymond Firth. London: Tavistock Publications.

Goldstein, G. S., and M. V. Pauly. 1974. "Group health insurance as a local public good." In *Conference on the Role of Health Insurance in the Health Services Sector.* National Bureau of Economic Research.

Goode, William J. 1963. *World Revolution and Family Patterns.* London: Collier Macmillan.

Gronau, Reuben. 1973. "The intrafamily allocation of time: The value of the housewives' time." *American Economic Review* 63 (September):634–651.

Grossbard, Amyra. 1978. "The economics of polygamy." Ph.D. dissertation, University of Chicago.

Heal, Geoffrey. 1976. "The market for lemons, comment." *Quarterly Journal of Economics* 90 (August):499–502.

Hirschman, Albert O. 1970. *Exit Voice and Loyalty.* Cambridge, Mass.: Harvard University Press.

Hirshleifer, Jack. 1973. "Exchange theory: The missing chapter." *Western Economic Journal* 11 (June):129–146.

———. 1977. "Shakespeare vs. Becker on altruism: The importance of hearing the last word." *Journal of Economic Literature* 15 (June):500–502.

Homans, George Caspar. 1974. *Social Behavior: Its Elementary Forms,* rev. ed. New York: Harcourt Brace Jovanovich.

Jones, J. R. 1976. "Market imperfections in peasant societies." In *Paths to Symbolic Self,* ed. J. P. Loucky and J. R. Jones. Department of Anthropology, University of California at Los Angeles.

Landes, William M., and Richard A. Posner. 1978. *Salvors, Finders, Good Samaritans, and Other Rescuers: An Economic Study of Law and Altruism.* Working Paper No. 227. New York: National Bureau of Economic Research.

Laslett, Peter. 1972. "Introduction: The history of the family." In *Household and Family in Past Times,* ed. P. Laslett. Cambridge, Eng.: Cambridge University Press.

Lazear E. 1978. "The economics of retirement." Unpublished paper.

Leibenstein, Harvey. 1960. *Economic Theory and Organizational Analysis.* New York: Harper & Row.

———. 1976. *Beyond Economic Man.* Cambridge, Mass. and London: Harvard University Press.

Levy, Marion J. 1965. "Aspects of the analysis of family structure." In *Aspects of the Analysis of Family Structure,* ed. Ansley J. Coale et al. Princeton, N. J.: Princeton University Press, pp. 40–63.

Lilien, D. 1977. "The cyclical pattern of temporary layoffs: An empirical study." Paper based on M.I.T. dissertation. Labor Workshop, University of California at Los Angeles.

Lindert, Peter H. 1974. "American fertility patterns since the Civil War." Center for Demography and Ecology Working Paper No. 74-27. Madison: University of Wisconsin.

Luce, R. D., and H. Raiffa. 1957. *Games and Decisions.* New York: Wiley.

Macaulay, Stewart. 1963. "Non-contractual relations in business: A preliminary study." *American Sociological Review* 28 (February):55–67.

Macneil, Ian. 1974. "The many futures of contracts." *Southern California Law Review* 47 (May):691–816.

Makowsky, Louis. n.d. [1977]. "Value theory with personalized trading." Unpublished paper.

Mauss, Marcel. 1954. *The Gift: Forms and Functions of Exchange in Archaic Societies.* Glencoe, Ill.: The Free Press.

Mincer, J. 1977. *Family Migration Decisions.* Working Paper No. 199. New York: National Bureau of Economic Research.

Mortensen, D. 1978. "Specific capital bargaining and labor turnover." Unpublished paper.

Nelson, Phillip. 1970. "Information and consumer behavior." *Journal of Political Economy* 78 (March/April):311–329.

Yoram Ben-Porath 29

Oi, Walter Y. 1962. "Labor as a quasi-fixed factor." *Journal of Political Economy* 70 (December):538–555.

Oppong, Christine. 1973. *Growing Up in Dagbon*. Ghana: Ghana Publishing.

———. 1974. *Marriage Among a Matrilineal Elite: A Family Study of Ghanaian Senior Civil Servants*. London: Cambridge University Press.

———. 1976. "Ghanaian household models: Data for processing by the New Home Economists of the developing world." Paper presented at a Seminar on Household Models of Economic Demographic Decision-Making, Mexico City.

Ortiz, Sutti. 1967. "The structure of decision-making among Indians of Colombia." In *Themes in Economic Anthropology*, ed. Raymond Firth. London: Tavistock Publishing.

Parsons, Donald O. 1972. "Specific human capital: An application to quit rates and layoff rates." *Journal of Political Economy* 80 (November/December):1120–1143.

———. 1974. "On the economics of intergenerational relations." Unpublished paper (revised 1976).

Pauly, Mark V. 1967. "Clubs, commonality, and the core: An integration of game theory and the theory of public goods." *Economica* 34 (August):314–324.

Pencavel, John H. 1972. "Wages, specific training, and labor turnover in U.S. manufacturing industries." *International Economic Review* 13, no. 1:53–64.

Polanyi, Karl, Conrad A. Arensberg, and Harry Pearson. 1957. *Trade and Markets in the Early Empires*. New York: The Free Press; London: Collier Macmillan.

Rosen, Sherwin. 1968. "Short-run employment variation on class-I railroads in the U.S., 1947–1963." *Econometrica* 36 (July–October):511–529.

Rosenzweig, Mark R., and Robert Evenson. 1977. "Fertility, schooling and the economic constitution of children in rural India: An econometric analysis." *Econometrica* 45 (July):1065–1079.

Sahlins, Marshall D. 1965. "On the sociology of primitive exchange." In *The Relevance of Models for Social Anthropology*, ed. Michael Banton. New York: Praeger.

Salaff, Janet W. 1975. "The status of unmarried Hong Kong women and the social factors contributing to their delayed marriage." Paper presented at the Population Research Program Conference at Bellagio, Italy, 2–5 May.

Samuelson, Paul A. 1958. "An exact consumption-loan model of interest with or without the social continuance of money." *Journal of Political Economy* 66 (December):467–482.

Schultz, T. W. (ed.) 1974. *Economics of the Family: Marriage, Children, and Human Capital*. A Conference Report of the National Bureau of Economic Research. Chicago and London: University of Chicago Press.

Shorter, Edward. 1975. *The Making of the Modern Family*. New York: Basic Books.

Simon, Herbert A. 1951. "A formal theory of the employment relationship." *Econometrica* 19 (July):293–305.

Stigler, George J. 1951. "The division of labor is limited by the extent of the market." *Journal of Political Economy* 59 (June):185–193.

———. 1961. "The economics of information." *Journal of Political Economy* 69 (June):213–225.

———. 1967. "Imperfections in the capital market." *Journal of Political Economy* 75 (June):287–292.

Stiglitz, Joseph E. 1975. "Incentive risk and information: Notes towards a theory of hierarchy." *Bell Journal of Economics* 6 (Autumn):552–575.

Taira, K. 1970. *Economic Development and the Labor Market in Japan.* New York: Columbia University Press.

Titmuss, Richard M. 1970. *The Gift Relationship: From Human Blood to Social Policy.* London: George Allen & Unwin.

Vogel, E. F. 1967. "Kinship structure, migration to the city and modernization." In *Aspects of Social Change in Modern Japan,* ed. R. P. Dore. Princeton, N. J.: Princeton University Press.

Williamson, Oliver E. 1975. *Markets and Hierarchies: Analysis and Anti Trust Implications.* New York: The Free Press.

———, Michael L. Wachter, and Jeffrey E. Harris. 1975. "Understanding the employment relation: The analysis of idiosyncratic exchange." *Bell Journal of Economics* 6 (Spring):250–278.

[10]

Journal of Economic Literature
Vol. XXIII (June 1985), pp. 581–608

A Transaction Cost Approach to Families and Households

By Robert A. Pollak

University of Pennsylvania

This research was supported in part by the National Science Foundation, the National Institutes of Health, and the Population Council. My intellectual debts to Oliver E. Williamson are even greater than the references to his work suggest. I am grateful to Judith Farnbach, Claudia Goldin, Vivian R. Pollak, Samuel H. Preston, and Susan Watkins for helpful comments and conversations during this paper's prolonged gestation. I am also grateful to Gary S. Becker, Peter Davis, Stefano Fenoaltea, Janet T. Landa, Marilyn Manser, and Ann D. Witte for helpful comments. The views expressed are my own and the usual disclaimer applies.

FAMILIES ARE FASHIONABLE. Within the last decade, social scientists have rediscovered families and households as fit subjects for serious analysis. Demographers and historians, anthropologists and sociologists have played the major roles; economists, traditionally preoccupied with markets, have been less involved.[1]

The traditional economic theory of the household focuses exclusively on observable market behavior (i.e., demand for goods, supply of labor) treating the household as a "black box" identified only by its preference ordering.[2] The "new home economics" takes a broader view, including not only market behavior but also such nonmarket phenomena as fertility, the education of children, and the allocation of time. The major analytic tool of the new home economics is Becker's household production model, which depicts the household as combining the time of household members with market goods to produce the outputs or "commodities" it ultimately desires.[3]

---

[1] Peter Laslett (1972), Tamara K. Hareven (1977), and John Demos and Sarane Spence Boocock (1978) are collections exemplifying the work outside economics. Gary S. Becker's work over the last fifteen years, culminating in his *Treatise on the Family* (1981), is the leading example within economics. For a legal scholar's enthusiastic endorsement of the power of economic analysis in this area, see Richard A. Posner (1980). Victor R. Fuchs (1983), writing for a less specialized audience than Becker, provides an empirical analysis of "how we live" from an economic perspective and discusses its implications for public policy.

[2] On the theoretical side, see Gerard Debreu (1959) or Kenneth J. Arrow and Frank H. Hahn (1971); on the empirical side, Laurits R. Christensen, Dale W. Jorgenson, and Lawrence J. Lau (1975) or Robert A. Pollak and Terence J. Wales (1978, 1980).

[3] The *locus classicus* of the household production literature is Becker (1965). Robert T. Michael and Becker (1973) provide a sympathetic restatement; Marc Nerlove (1974) and Zvi Griliches (1974) express some reservations; Pollak and Michael L. Wachter (1975) emphasize its limitations. Richard A. Easter-

The new home economics ignores the internal organization and structure of families and households. Although this may surprise noneconomists who tend to believe that the internal organization and structure of an institution are likely to affect its behavior, economists find it natural. For the economist the most economical way to exploit the fundamental insight that production takes place within the household is to apply to households techniques developed for studying firms. Since neoclassical economics identifies firms with their technologies and assumes that firms operate efficiently and frictionlessly, it precludes any serious interest in the economizing properties of the internal structure and organization of firms. The new home economics, by carrying over this narrow neoclassical view from firms to households, thus fails to exploit fully the insight of the household production approach. In this essay I argue that the transaction cost approach which recognizes the significance of internal structure provides a broader and more useful view of the economic activity and behavior of the family.

The transaction cost approach has been primarily concerned with firms and the organization of production.[4] The treatment of vertical integration is paradigmatic. Neoclassical economics explains vertical integration as a response to technological inseparabilities; transaction cost economics explains vertical integration as a response to the difficulties of regulating ongoing relationships by means of

---

lin, Pollak, and Wachter (1980) discuss applications to fertility and provide references to the recent literature.

[4] Oliver E. Williamson (1975, 1979, 1981), building on the older institutionalist tradition, on the work of Ronald H. Coase (1937), and on the "Carnegie tradition" (e.g., Herbert A. Simon 1957), has been primarily responsible for developing the transaction cost approach. Other important transaction cost papers are Victor P. Goldberg (1976), and Benjamin Klein, Robert G. Crawford, and Armen A. Alchian (1978).

contracts.[5] Transaction cost analysis of vertical integration posits a situation in which efficiency requires the use of physical or human capital that is specific to the relationship between a particular supplier and a particular customer; since the value of such "idiosyncratic" capital depends on establishing and maintaining the supplier-customer relationship, the willingness of either party to invest in idiosyncratic capital depends on assuring the stability of the relationship. Firms often avoid using contracts to structure complex, ongoing relationships because doing so is hazardous. Short-term contracting is hazardous because, even when contract renewal is mutually beneficial, one party or the other may have advantages that can be exploited in bilateral negotiations over renewal terms; hence, short-term contracts make it risky to accumulate capital whose value is contingent on the relationship continuing and thus discourage investment in such specific capital. The problems of contract renewal can be avoided or at least postponed by long-term contracts, but only if such contracts are "complete" in the sense that they specify the obligations of the parties under every possible contingency. Complete long-term contracts are costly or impossible to write and enforce, however, a reflection of bounded rationality and asymmetric information; and incomplete long-term contracts which fail to deal with every contingency expose the parties to the hazards of bilateral bargaining. To avoid these contracting hazards firms often rely on some more complete form of integration such as merger. Thus, contracting difficulties—the problems of negotiating, writing, monitoring, and enforcing agreements—are central instances of transaction costs, and transaction cost economics asserts that they are significant determinants of the

---

[5] Time thus plays a crucial role in transaction cost analysis, a point emphasized by Gordon C. Winston (1982, Ch. 12).

organization of production. Since bureaucratic structures have their own characteristic disabilities, internal governance does not eliminate all difficulties associated with a transaction or exchange. Nevertheless, replacing a market relationship by an organization with an appropriate governance structure often safeguards the interests of both parties.

The transaction cost approach focuses on the role of institutions in structuring complex, long-term relationships. Applied to the firm, transaction cost economics studies the boundaries, structure, and internal organization of producing units. To do so, it relaxes the assumption of frictionless efficiency and views the firm as a hierarchical governance structure within which production takes place. By focusing on structure the transaction cost approach provides an alternative explanation of market behavior that traditional economics ascribes to technology, and it illuminates aspects of nonmarket behavior that traditional economics ignores. In many respects the neoclassical and transaction cost approaches are complements rather than substitutes, addressing somewhat different issues and offering somewhat different ranges of admissible explanations.

The transaction cost approach analyzes the "economizing properties of alternative institutional modes for organizing transactions" (Williamson 1979, p. 234). The presumption is that the costs to be minimized include transaction costs, that these costs vary systematically from one institutional mode to another, and that each activity is carried out by the institution that can perform it most efficiently. The transaction cost literature has thus far emphasized production activities and, more particularly, intermediate-product transactions; the central issue has been whether technologically separable activities will be carried out by a single vertically-integrated firm rather than by separate firms dealing with each other through

markets. Addressing the fundamental problems of institutional choice—whether particular activities will be mediated by markets or carried out within families, firms, governments, or nonprofit institutions—requires extending the transaction cost analysis from firms to families and to other institutional modes.[6]

The transaction cost literature has virtually ignored families and households.[7] The

[6] Henry B. Hansmann (1980) provides an excellent transaction cost analysis of nonprofit enterprise. There does not appear to be a corresponding transaction cost analysis of the state, although Goldberg (1976) and Williamson (1976) hint at such a theory in their discussions of regulation. The "Chicago School" theory of economic regulation fails to offer such an analysis of the state. On the contrary, it assumes that such an analysis is unnecessary because the state does not differ significantly from other organizations. Posner (1974), for example, asserts: ". . . no persuasive theory has yet been proposed as to why (government) agencies should be expected to be less efficient than other organizations. The motivation of the agency employee to work diligently and honestly is similar to that of the employee of a business firm" (p. 338).

[7] Transaction cost papers often mention in passing that the analysis applies to marriage or the family. Goldberg (1976, p. 428, fn. 9) does so in a sentence in a footnote; Klein, Crawford, and Alchian (1978, p. 323) devote a paragraph to it; and Williamson (1979, p. 258), two paragraphs. Yoram Ben-Porath (1980) is the only sustained transaction cost analysis of issues related to marriage or the family and in some respects my discussion parallels his. He begins by noting that neoclassical economic theory assumes that economic agents—individuals and firms—transact with "the market" rather than directly with other agents; in this sense, neoclassical theory postulates "anonymous" agents and "impersonal" transactions. Ben-Porath's analysis of the family flows from his more general concern with relaxing this assumption and recognizing that the "identity" of economic agents—their ability to recognize and be recognized by one another—is crucial to many types of economic interactions. His title, "The F-Connection: Families, Friends, and Firms and the Organization of Exchange," is indicative of these broader concerns. Ben-Porath emphasizes the changing role of the family in various stages of economic development and the effect of development on the family. In a review of Becker's *Treatise*, (Ben-Porath 1982), he summarizes his own views:

> The traditional family is the epitome of specialization by identity, based on own use of productive services and on mutual insurance and support . . . Modern economic organization is associated with a market structure based on specialization along the impersonal

neglect of families in Williamson's *Markets and Hierarchies* (1975) probably flows from his assumption that "in the beginning, there were markets" (p. 20). While this assumption is clearly intended to provide an analytical rather than an anthropological origin, it is probably responsible for his neglect of family organization as a theoretical or an actual solution to the incentive and monitoring problems encountered by peer groups and simple hierarchies. The neglect of families and households represents a missed opportunity.

Applied to the family, the transaction cost approach generalizes the new home economics by recognizing that internal structure and organization matter. It treats the family as a governance structure rather than a preference ordering or a preference ordering augmented by a production technology. This has two consequences for the analysis of the family. First, by focusing on the family's ability to provide incentives and monitor performance and on how its ability to do so differs among activities and societies, it clarifies which activities are carried out by the family. Second, by emphasizing the role of institutions in structuring complex, long-term relationships, the contracting perspective of the transaction cost approach elucidates allocation and distribution within the family.

Because of the central role of unobservable variables (e.g., preferences, household technology, genetic endowments), the new home economics view of the family does not lead simply or directly to a model capable of empirical implementation.[8] Unobservable variables also play

a key role in the transaction cost approach; and, even in the context of the firm and vertical integration, the transaction cost approach is often charged with failing to provide a framework for empirical research. Not surprisingly, the offspring of the marriage of the subject matter of the new home economics with the analytical orientation of the transaction cost approach is not a system of equations that an econometrician could estimate. Nevertheless, because the ability of the transaction cost approach to provide a framework for empirical analysis is a crucial issue, throughout this essay I identify topics and areas of research suggested by the transaction cost approach.

My primary purpose, however, is to describe an *approach*, not to specify a *model*. This paper is an essay, not a research program or agenda. The methodological justification for such an enterprise is that an occasional exploratory essay is useful because formal models are self-contained constructs and cannot tell us what phenomena are worth modeling.[9]

---

with the theory." He emphasizes the crucial role of unobserved variables, wonders "whether *any* data could be shown convincingly to be inconsistent with the theory," and hence is "not prepared to agree that the theory has already gained a high degree of empirical verification" (p. 71, emphasis in original).

[9] Critics of the transaction cost approach often object that it is difficult or impossible to test, refute or falsify, claiming that it explains everything and, therefore, explains nothing. Williamson (1979, p. 233) discusses this criticism and argues that carefully formulated versions of the transaction cost approach are not vulnerable to it. We have already seen that this objection is sometimes raised against the new home economics (Hannan 1982, p. 71). The objection is often expressed in the positivistic language that Paul A. Samuelson's *Foundations of Economic Analysis* (1947) has made familiar to economists. Twenty years after Thomas S. Kuhn's *The Structure of Scientific Revolutions* (1962), many philosophers of science are pessimistic about the possibility of "testing" competing theories or paradigms, even in the physical sciences. Closer to home, it is not clear what set of observations would cause economists to abandon the neoclassical theory of consumer behavior, or even to reject the version of it which assumes that preferences (for unobservable "commodities")

---

dimensions of transactions . . . Thus, in a modern economy, the family sheds much of its productive activities and specializes more in affective relationships and joint consumption [p. 61].

[8] Michael T. Hannan (1982), in a review of Becker's *Treatise,* points out that Becker fails "to make clear exactly what kinds of evidence would be inconsistent

The paper is organized as follows. In the first section I examine the advantages and disadvantages of family governance and apply the analysis to two types of economic activity: production for home consumption and production for a market. In the second section I turn to the internal organization of families and households, focusing on allocation and distribution within the family. I begin by analyzing marriage as a "contracting problem." I then argue that the transaction cost approach is broadly consistent with bargaining models of marriage, and examine the roles of marriage-specific capital from a bargaining perspective. Finally, I discuss social exchange theory and its relationship to the transaction cost approach. Section III is a brief conclusion.

I. *The Family as a Governance Structure for Economic Activity*

The advantages of the family as a governance structure for organizing particular activities flow from its ability to integrate those activities with preexisting, ongoing, significant personal relationships.[10] I examine the advantages of family governance and its corresponding disadvantages in Section A. In Section B I discuss the role of transaction cost considerations in the family's production for its own consumption, focusing on the family's role as a provider of insurance, that is, protection against the economic consequences of uncertain, adverse events. The family has been the traditional source of such protection throughout history; even in advanced industrial societies some types of insurance continue to be provided by the family, while others are provided by the market, and still others by the state. In Section

C I examine the role of transaction cost considerations in family governance of market-oriented work by discussing family farms and family-managed firms, that is, firms in which several family members play active managerial roles. Finally, in Section D, I compare the characteristic advantages and disadvantages of family governance with those of market governance and argue that certain identifiable types of activities are more efficiently organized through markets while others are more efficiently carried out by families.

A. *Advantages and Disadvantages*

The advantages of family governance can be grouped into four categories: incentives, monitoring, altruism, and loyalty. All of the family's incentive advantages arise because its members have claims on family resources; some of these advantages can be analyzed in a single period setting, while others depend on the anticipated continuity of family membership. Even in a one-period setting family members have reason to take account of the effects of their actions on family wealth. The strength of this incentive effect depends on the size of the family and on its sharing rule: It is weakest in large families with equal sharing, and strongest in small ones with sharing rules conditioned on individual behavior. Those incentive advantages that arise only in a multiperiod setting and that depend on expectations of lifelong family membership make individuals reluctant to sacrifice long-run benefits for short-run gains. Without such expectations individuals would be less certain that their claims would be honored in the future and, hence, would act to move family consumption or income toward the present. Furthermore, individuals may value family consumption and income beyond their own lifetimes because of their concern for the welfare of their own children or grandchildren. Thus, prudential and dy-

---

are exogenous and identical over time and space (George J. Stigler and Becker 1977). Similarly, it is not clear what set of observations would convince sociologists that tastes are exogenous.

[10] Burton Benedict (1968, p. 2) refers to such relationships as "affectively charged."

nastic considerations combine to give family members direct, long-term interests in the family's well-being.

Because economic relationships are entwined with significant personal ones, the family commands rewards and sanctions not open to other institutions. Severe misconduct involves not simply the risk of dismissal from a job but also the risk of ostracism or expulsion from the family, a penalty drastic enough that it is likely to be an effective deterrent to serious malfeasance.

The monitoring advantages of the family also flow from the entwining of economic and personal relationships. Diligence and work habits, consumption patterns and lifestyles are more likely to be observable because the network of relationships involving "economic activity" and "family" are integrated. The family's informational advantages are greatest when its members live together as a joint or extended family household—a common arrangement in many developing countries. But monitoring advantages, although facilitated by communal living arrangements, do not depend exclusively on them: Social contacts within the family provide information unavailable to outsiders.

"Altruism," based on "love," "affection," and "caring," serves to limit opportunistic behavior within the family.[11] The affectional relationships among family members, whatever their basis, may provide a relatively secure and stable foundation for a wide range of activities.

"Family loyalty" provides a convenient rubric for discussing dimensions of incentives and monitoring that economists are trained to ignore. Although what we call family loyalty may be a consequence of

altruism or of the particular incentive, monitoring, and altruism attributes of the family, it is useful to treat loyalty as a separate category and to examine its social and psychological basis.

The social basis of family loyalty rests on generally accepted norms or standards of conduct regarding the treatment of family members which are enforced through reputation. Individuals perceived as fulfilling family obligations are rewarded with respect and esteem and those perceived as violating them are punished by loss of reputation. The value and importance of reputation varies from one society to another: In traditional societies with little geographical mobility, reputation may be an important factor in personal and business success, and loss of reputation a significant penalty.

The psychological basis of family loyalty depends on individuals' internalizing society's values, standards, and expectations. Fulfilling family obligations becomes a source of pleasure, pride, and satisfaction, and violating them a source of guilt. The rewards and sanctions are thus internalized, incorporated into individuals' preferences and values.

The value of loyalty is not confined to families. Nations, clubs, and firms attempt to instill and foster loyalty in their citizens, members, employees, and managers. Indeed, the language of loyalty itself relies heavily on family metaphors. Citizens are urged to support "Mother Russia" or the "Fatherland"; college students join "fraternities" or "sororities"; workers join labor unions whose names often include the word "brotherhood"; firms like "Ma Bell" have encouraged employees to view them as a family and in doing so claim their allegiance, support, and love. These attempts to encourage loyalty reflect its instrumental value to organizations, as Albert O. Hirschman (1970) and Alchian and Harold Demsetz (1972, p. 790–91) have

[11] Becker uses the term "altruism" to refer to a very special type of interdependent preferences. I discuss Becker's notion of altruism and his theory of allocation within the family in Section IIB.

argued. Almost unconscious reliance on family metaphors to describe or foster loyalty suggests that family ties are recognized as ties that bind.[12]

Notwithstanding its advantages, family governance has four characteristic disadvantages. First, conflict may spill over from one sphere into the other. Although the family may function harmoniously, bound together by ties of affection and interest, even the most casual empiricist must recognize the possibility of discord. The largely anecdotal literature on family firms emphasizes conflicts between parents and children and conflicts among siblings.[13] Conflicts between parents and children centering on the desire of children for independence and of parents to retain control may be continual sources of friction and may pose particularly difficult problems of leadership succession for family firms. Sibling tensions and rivalries whose roots lie buried in early childhood can influence the behavior and relationships of middle-aged men and women as their generation assumes control of the family firm. By linking the firm and the family, the family's stability becomes a

source of strength for the firm, but the family's instability becomes a source of weakness.

Second, inefficient behavior or slack performance may be tolerated because of the difficulty of evaluating and disciplining family members. Objective and dispassionate evaluations of the ability and performance of family members are difficult to make. Furthermore, acting on adverse evaluations may provoke deep-seated resentment persisting through generations. The threat of ostracism gives family firms an advantage in controlling gross malfeasance; but because of its severity and because its use imposes significant costs on others in the family, ostracism is not a credible threat against shirking, slack performance, or minor infractions. The family has available a wide range of social rewards and sanctions that it could in principle use to express its approval or disapproval of an individual's actions or behavior; in practice, however, the family may not be able to calibrate and utilize these rewards and sanctions effectively. It is unclear whether family governance is more or less effective than nonfamily governance in discouraging minor infractions and slack performance. Furthermore, nepotism may prove a serious problem for the family firm.[14]

Third, the capacities, aptitudes, and talents of family members may fail to mesh with the needs of the family's economic

---

[12] Janet T. Landa (1981) analyzes the role of ethnic ties as well as kinship ties and the importance of gradations in these relationships in establishing the reliability of trading partners. Landa and Janet W. Salaff (1982) examine the rise and fall of the Tan Kah Kee Company, a Singapore-based family firm which they describe as the largest Chinese-owned rubber manufacturing and exporting firm in Southeast Asia in the 1920s (p. 21). Drawing on Landa's analysis, they show that kinship and ethnic ties played an important role in the growth of the firm. They attribute the fall of the Tan Kah Kee Company to the collapse in rubber prices during the Depression and the consequent necessity of ceding control of the firm to "outsiders" (i.e., British bankers and their agents). Landa and Salaff provide extensive references to the literature on family firms in sociology, anthropology, and development economics.

[13] Peter Davis (1983) summarizes this literature and presents an analytical framework that is broadly consistent with the transaction cost analysis developed here. An article in *Fortune*, "Family Business is a Passion Play," (Gwen Kinkead 1980) gives the flavor of the popular literature.

[14] Nepotism may be an even more serious problem in other governance structures, and it is likely to be most serious in those that delegate substantial discretionary authority to individuals who lack commitment to the organization's objectives. It is no coincidence that the term "nepotism," from the Italian *nepotismo*, "favoring of 'nephews,'" was first used to describe practices of the pre-Reformation Catholic Church: "A euphemistic use of 'nephew' is that of the natural son of a pope, cardinal or other ecclesiastic; and from the practice of granting preferments to such children the word 'nepotism' is used of any favouritism shown in finding positions for a man's family" ("Nephew," *Encyclopaedia Britannica*, 11th ed. 1911).

activities. The problem is not that certain activities require training; traditionally families have assumed responsibility for children's education and for vocational training. The problem is that certain activities require special talents. Whether the talent mix available within the family in a particular generation meshes well with the requirements of the family's activities depends in part on genetics and in part on luck. When no available family members manifest the required aptitudes, then such activities, if they are to remain within the family, must be carried on without suitable personnel. Whether family governance entails substantial inefficiencies depends on the ability of alternative governance structures to achieve better matches between individuals and activities. Thus, family governance is most efficient in activities requiring talents that are difficult for nonfamily institutions to evaluate and in those not requiring rare or unusual aptitudes.

Fourth, size limitations implied by family governance may prevent the realization of technologically achievable economies of scale. The boundaries of the family or kin group relevant for organizing economic activity are influenced by economic considerations, not rigidly determined by biology. Nevertheless, because expansion weakens the incentive and monitoring advantages of family governance, the family is ill-equipped to exploit scale economies.[15] Insurance, an activity in which limited scale implies limited risk-spreading, provides a range of illustrations, including some in which the balance of advantages and disadvantages favors family governance.

[15] Family firms, if they are to grow in size and complexity to exploit economies of scale, face the problem of integrating professional nonfamily managers with family managers. The growth possibilities of a family firm are severely constrained if it is unable or unwilling to attract and accept nonfamily managers, yet success in introducing nonfamily managers may undermine its character as a family firm.

B. *Family Governance of Production for Home Consumption: Insurance*

Home is the place where, when you have to go there, They have to take you in.

Robert Frost
"The Death of the Hired Man"

The household production approach, with its emphasis on prices and technology, has dominated the analysis of activities in which households or families produce goods for their own consumption. This analysis captures the essence of some household "make-or-buy" decisions, but other household production activities—such as the provision of education, health care, and insurance—are better analyzed from a transaction cost perspective.

Protection against the adverse economic consequences of old age, separation and divorce, unemployment, or the illness or death of an earner can be provided in many ways. In many societies the family is the principal provider of such protection. In advanced industrial societies the family, the market, and the state provide varying degrees of protection against these and other adversities. Market insurance typically provides monetary benefits according to an explicit schedule. The state sometimes provides monetary benefits according to an explicit schedule (e.g., aid to dependent children) and sometimes benefits in kind (e.g., direct provision of care for the sick, handicapped, or disabled); such benefits, whether in cash or in kind, are not always characterized as insurance. The family, in contrast, typically provides benefits in kind rather than in cash and according to an implicit rather than an explicit schedule.

Family provision of benefits often entails restructuring domestic arrangements so that family members who had previously lived in separate households form a single residential unit. Unemployed young adults and recently separated or divorced individuals and their children of-

Pollak: Transaction Cost and Families 589

ten move in with parents; orphans are taken in by relatives; elderly parents often move in with their children. Because the household and the nuclear family tend to coincide, the terms "household" and "family" are often used interchangeably.[16] This usage is misleading even for advanced industrial societies and it is seriously misleading for developing countries. Analysis of household formation—the establishment of separate households by the young and the elderly, or as a consequence of separation or divorce—and, more generally, analysis of the role of kin ties in economic relationships requires maintaining the distinction between households and families.[17] Although the phrase "household production" is too well-established to be displaced by "family production," in the provision of insurance and in many other activities, the fundamental unit is not the household but the family.

The insurance literature identifies two reasons why market insurance may be inefficient: "adverse selection" and "moral hazard."[18] Adverse selection arises when each individual knows his probability of loss better than potential insurers (asymmetric information) and when individuals can opportunistically misrepresent their loss probabilities to potential insurers.[19] This conjunction of asymmetric information and opportunism leaves individuals without credible ways of communicating to a potential insurer their true risk characteristics. Under these circumstances potential insurers find it costly or impossible to distinguish between high-risk and low-risk individuals and, hence, the market must charge everyone the same premium. Low-risk individuals may find this premium excessive and choose to self-insure (i.e., to cover their own losses instead of purchasing market insurance). With a continuum of risk-classes, it may be impossible for market insurance to operate at all: there may be no premium level that would induce purchases by a group of individuals whose total expected losses would be covered by their total premium payments.[20] Moral hazard arises because individuals can undertake activities that alter the probabilities they will suffer losses or that mitigate the magnitudes of losses that do occur. Because insurers cannot easily monitor whether individuals have undertaken such activities and because individuals can opportunistically misrepresent whether they have done so,

[16] For example, Laslett (1972) uses the term "family" to refer to a household—a co-resident domestic group—and much of his work has been devoted to documenting the predominance of nuclear households in Europe during the last three centuries.

[17] Fuchs (1983) provides an overview and references to the literature on many of these issues. On separation and divorce, see Becker, Elisabeth M. Landes and Michael (1977). On the establishment of separate households by the young and the elderly, see Marjorie B. McElroy (1985) and Michael, Fuchs and Sharon R. Scott (1980), respectively. For work emphasizing the strength and importance of kin ties and challenging the myth that the predominance of nuclear households implies the irrelevance of other family relationships, see, for example, Philip J. Greven, Jr. (1970), Michael Anderson (1971) and Hareven (1977, 1978).

[18] Mark V. Pauly (1974), Michael Rothschild and Joseph E. Stiglitz (1976), and Charles Wilson (1977). Two important and widely cited papers going well beyond the insurance issues are Arrow (1963) and George A. Akerlof (1970). Isaac Ehrlich and Becker (1972) discuss the role of "self-protection" as a substitute for market insurance.

[19] Williamson (1975, p. 31–33) terms this conjunction of asymmetric information and opportunism "information impactedness."

[20] In the "lemons" paper (Akerlof 1970) the used-car market serves to illustrate this phenomenon. Sellers know the quality of the cars they are offering for sale, but potential buyers know only the average quality of used cars sold in the market. These circumstances can give rise to two distinct problems. First, as Akerlof points out, "it is quite possible to have the bad driving out the not-so-bad driving out the medium driving out the not-so-good driving out the good in such a sequence of events that" no transactions take place (p. 239)—that is, the only equilibrium may be one in which there is no trade. Second, as Rothschild and Stiglitz (1976) point out, equilibrium may fail to exist. Wilson (1980) shows that price-setting conventions can play a crucial role in markets with adverse selection.

market insurance arrangements may provide protection against the economic consequences of uncertain, adverse events only at the cost of substantial inefficiency.

The state has certain advantages over market insurers in dealing with adverse selection and moral hazard. Compulsory insurance—whether provided by the market, as with automobile liability insurance, or by the state, as with social security—avoids adverse selection by preventing low-risk individuals from opting out. State-imposed standards of conduct can reduce moral hazard, but asymmetric information and opportunism pose problems for the state as well as for market insurers. While state enforcement may be more effective than private enforcement, it is hardly a panacea: Requiring recipients of unemployment compensation to seek work has proved difficult to enforce.

As a provider of insurance, the family has three important transactional advantages over the market and the state. First, adverse selection is limited because outsiders cannot easily join the family nor insiders easily withdraw. Second, information disparities between individuals and their families are generally smaller than those between individuals and nonfamily insurers. Proximity yields substantial monitoring advantages, permitting the family to assess health or intensity of job search more easily, economically, and accurately than the market or the state. Third, both family loyalty and cultural norms limit opportunistic behavior. Virtually every society condemns cheating one's family far more strongly than cheating strangers—blood is thicker than water.

As a provider of insurance the family also has characteristic disabilities. First, conflicts originating in personal relationships can impinge on the insurance arrangement. Such conflicts may make those obligated to provide benefits unwilling to do so, especially when the benefits call for restructuring living arrangements by combining households. Additionally, disputes growing out of the insurance arrangement itself are potential sources of family conflict.

Second, it is difficult to make objective and dispassionate evaluations of risk and of the extent to which individuals undertake to alter these probabilities or mitigate the magnitude of losses. Furthermore, once such evaluations of family members are made, they may be difficult to act on: Poor risks, once identified, cannot easily be excluded from participation in family insurance arrangements.

Third, because the family or kin group is relatively small, risks cannot be spread widely enough to realize fully the advantages of insurance. This problem is most serious in situations involving small probabilities of large losses. Furthermore, when family members face risks that are positively correlated, the family's ability to protect itself through self-insurance is even more limited than its size would suggest. For example, family members working in the same industry or growing the same crops in the same region are poorly positioned to provide each other with unemployment insurance or crop insurance. Thus, since the effectiveness of insurance depends on both the size of the insured group and on the independence of the risks to which its members are exposed, the transaction cost advantages of family insurance are balanced by technical disadvantages.

Insurance is typical of a substantial class of economic activities for which the transaction cost advantages of family governance often outweigh the technical advantages of nonfamily governance. The balance between these advantages and disadvantages is not immutable, as demonstrated by the shifting of some, but by no means all, insurance functions from the family to the market, to nonprofit institutions, and to the state. With insurance, as with the provision of education and health care, market governance entails substan-

Pollak: Transaction Cost and Families 591

tial transaction cost difficulties. Hence, in societies in which these functions are not carried out by the family, they tend to be assumed by nonprofit institutions and the state rather than by profit-oriented firms.

C. Family Governance of Market-Oriented Work: Family Farms and Family-Managed Firms

The family-managed firm and the family farm solve different organizational problems: The family-managed firm is a response to the difficulty of supervising managers, the family farm a response to the difficulty of supervising workers.[21] Despite the differences between supervising managers and supervising workers, the advantages and disadvantages of family-managed firms and family farms are similar, and both illustrate the role of family governance of market-oriented work.[22]

The family farm—typically worked jointly by a married couple and their chil-

---

[21] I distinguish family-managed firms both from firms that are merely family-owned and from those in which only a single family member participates in management.

[22] In both cases the focus on the incentive properties of family governance of market-oriented activity suggests a comparison with consumer or producer cooperatives or labor-managed firms. Jaroslav Vanek (1969) makes strong claims for the advantages of the latter:

> Without any doubt, labor-management is among all the existing forms of enterprise organizations the optimal arrangement when it comes to the finding of the utility-maximizing effort, i.e. the proper quality, duration and intensity of work, by the working collective. Not only is there no situation of conflict between management and the workers that might hinder the finding of the optimum, but the process of self-management itself can be viewed as a highly efficient device for communication, collusion control and enforcement among the participants [p. 1011].

Whether labor-managed firms actually realize these advantages is an open question; Williamson's analysis of the disabilities of peer group organization of production suggests that they may not. Furthermore, the ability of a family to realize these alleged advantages must depend on its internal organization and structure: A hierarchical family (e.g., patriarchal) would not operate in the manner Vanek suggests, although it might offer other advantages for organizing production.

dren or, in many societies, by members of an extended family who live together in a single household—is the dominant form of agricultural organization in the United States and in most developed and developing countries.[23] The family farm can be regarded as an organizational solution to the difficulty of monitoring and supervising workers who, for technological reasons, cannot be gathered together in a single location.

When agricultural tasks can be monitored easily in terms of inputs or outputs, family farms are often overshadowed by other forms of agricultural organization. For some crops and some tasks hired labor can be concentrated into work gangs and supervised directly, so plantation agriculture is possible.[24] For other crops and tasks (e.g., harvesting) output can be measured directly and workers paid on a piece-rate basis. Thus, agricultural wage labor, hired on a daily or a seasonal basis, is important in both developed and developing countries. Nevertheless, since most farm tasks are not susceptible to either of these forms of supervision or monitoring, the family farm is the dominant form of agricultural organization.[25]

---

[23] Family farms accounted for 67.6 percent of the value of farm products sold in the U.S. in 1974, the most recent year for which these data were reported in the *Statistical Abstract of the United States* (10th ed., 1984, p. 653, Table 1143).

[24] Plantation agriculture is sometimes compatible with slavery. Stefano Fenoaltea (1984), in a rich and fascinating paper, argues that the "pain incentives" to which slaves can be subjected make slave labor more suitable for "effort-intensive" than "care-intensive" activities, and that the threat of sabotage makes slave labor more suitable for land-intensive than capital-intensive activities. Thus slave gangs were better suited to the cotton and corn agriculture of the American South than to the vine and olive arboriculture of the Mediterranean.

[25] Discussions of agricultural organization in economics have focused almost exclusively on other issues. The principal focus has been on sharecropping, and while incentive and monitoring issues are sometimes mentioned (along with risk aversion and imperfections in capital and other markets) family aspects of agricultural organization are ignored. In particular, most discussions assume that the sharecropper is an individual worker. Similarly, discus-

592   *Journal of Economic Literature, Vol. XXIII (June 1985)*

Empirical work on agricultural organization has seldom distinguished between family and nonfamily labor, although recent research suggests the importance of doing so.[26] The transaction cost approach draws attention to this distinction by offering two reasons why family and nonfamily labor might be imperfect substitutes: the incentive and monitoring advantages of family organization which I have emphasized in this essay and the idiosyncratic information and knowledge of local conditions that family members are likely to possess.[27] The transaction cost approach generates interesting empirical research projects in this field because it helps to analyze the degree to which family and nonfamily labor are imperfect substitutes in various types of agricultural production and it helps to sort out the roles of incentives and asymmetric information.[28]

Managers in family-managed firms have expectations of a continuing relationship with the firm and claims on its profits and, therefore, are subject to different and perhaps more effective rewards and sanctions than managers in other firms. Both types of firms can reward successful managers with salary increases and promotions, but performance is often difficult to assess and managers may be able to manipulate short-run indicators of performance at the expense of the long-run objectives of the firm. Because family managers expect a continuing relationship with the firm, they are less tempted to sacrifice long-run advantages for short-run gains.[29]

The behavior of family managers can usually be monitored more easily than that of nonfamily managers. The general principle requires no further elaboration, but it must be qualified by the observation that family members living three thousand miles apart may monitor each other less effectively than managers in nonfamily firms located in a small city. Family relationships are not the sole determinant of monitoring costs.

Sally Griffen and Clyde Griffen (1977) emphasize the role of family loyalty and trust in business in nineteenth-century America. Discussing families' use of bankruptcy laws, they write:

> In the Darwinian jungle of small business in the United States, survival frequently involved use of family relationships, founded in trust, to take advantage of loopholes in the law [p. 154].
>
> The family proved most useful in all of these

---

sions of rural labor markets often treat labor as homogeneous, failing to distinguish among men, women, and children and seldom offering integrated models of family labor supply. See Howard N. Barnum and Lyn Squire (1979) and Hans P. Binswanger and Mark R. Rosenzweig (1984). Peter Murrell (1983) offers a transaction cost analysis of sharecropping, although he does not discuss the role of the family.

[26] Anil B. Deolalikar and Wim P. M. Vijverberg (1983a) provide references to the literature and report evidence on the heterogeneity of family and nonfamily labor using district-level data from India. Deolalikar and Vijverberg (1983b) report similar findings using farm-level data from India and Malaysia.

[27] Rosenzweig and Kenneth I. Wolpin (1985), for example, build a model of intergenerational transfers around the "specific experience" hypothesis.

[28] Binswanger and Rosenzweig (1982) view agricultural organization as a consequence of the interplay between asymmetric information and what they term the "material conditions of agriculture" (p. 58). Thus, they argue, differences in the characteristics of the technology from one crop to another have predictable effects on the organization of production. For example, with trees whose continued value depends on pruning and maintenance (e.g., coffee, cocoa, apples) "an owner is unlikely to rent out his trees to a tenant-operator in a contract whose duration is less than the productive life of the tree, given the difficulty of assessing maintenance intensity in the short-run" (p. 47). On the other hand, "coconuts do not require pruning" and "tenancy in coconut trees is quite frequent in India" (p. 49). Although they recognize that family labor has both informational and incentive advantages over non-

family labor (pp. 31–35), they do not systematically examine the family as a solution to the problems posed by asymmetric information in the context of particular agricultural technologies.

[29] Nonfamily firms can and do attempt to provide incentives that bind managers to the firm and induce them to take a long view. Profit-sharing, for example, gives managers an interest in the short-run performance of the firm, while pension plans and stock options represent (among other things) attempts to tie managers' rewards to the long-run performance of the firm as a whole and their interests to the long-run interests of the firm.

Pollak: Transaction Cost and Families 593

legal maneuverings because of trust between its members. Family members could betray that trust—wives could leave their husbands and parents could let their children remain stranded—but the assumption apparently was that they would not or, at least, that relationships outside the family would be even less trustworthy. The same need for trust and loyalty in a mobile society undoubtedly accounts for the frequency of family members in business partnerships in the city. No less than 48% of the firms ever run as partnerships in Poughkeepsie brought together relatives at one time or another [p. 156].

Neoclassical theory obviates the need for distinguishing between family and nonfamily governance by assuming that all firms are frictionless profit-maximizers. Because of this theoretical presumption and the paucity of statistical data, economists have virtually ignored family firms. The major exceptions fall into two subfields—development economics and economic history—but as a consequence of the limitations of theory and data, the treatment of family firms is largely anecdotal.

The transaction cost approach cannot provide the data, but it does provide a theoretical rationale for distinguishing between family and nonfamily firms and it suggests that their behavior might differ systematically. Two behavioral dimensions in which comparisons seems especially promising are efficiency and innovation. Recently developed techniques for measuring the efficiency of firms (Finn R. Førsund, C. A. Knox Lovell, and Peter Schmidt 1980) could be used to compare the efficiency of family and nonfamily firms in particular industries. It is often asserted that family firms are technologically conservative and slow to exploit newly emerging profit opportunities; on the other hand, it is also often asserted that owner-entrepreneurs are more likely than professional managers to be innovators. It would be interesting to know whether, controlling for firm size and for industry, family firms are more or less likely to innovate than nonfamily firms.

Although the transaction cost approach offers a set of reasons why the efficiency and innovativeness of family and nonfamily firms might differ, it does not offer unambiguous predictions about which will be more efficient or more innovative. Hence, a finding that family and nonfamily governance differ systematically in efficiency, innovativeness, or other behavioral dimensions would not constitute a "test" of the transaction cost approach.[30] It would demonstrate, however, its fruitfulness in suggesting interesting topics for investigation.

D. Assessment: Family vs. Nonfamily Governance

Family governance of economic activities is likely to assure loyal and trustworthy performance; nonfamily governance is likely to assure technical competence and skill. The relative importance of these sets of attributes varies from society to society and from sector to sector. The possible combinations are exhibited in Table 1. One would expect family governance to predominate in low-trust environments (that is, in societies in which nonfamily members are not expected to perform honestly or reliably) and in sectors utilizing relatively simple technologies (that is, in sectors using technologies which a high proportion of adults in the society are capable of mastering quickly).[31] Conversely, nonfamily governance would

---

[30] The analysis proposed here is relevant for both family firms and family farms.

[31] Edward C. Banfield's *The Moral Basis of a Backward Society* (1958) explains the economic and political backwardness of southern Italy by "the inability of the villagers to act together for their common good or, indeed, for any end transcending the immediate material interest of the nuclear family" (p. 10). Banfield argues that this cultural ethos, which he terms "amoral familism," with its emphasis on the nuclear family rather than some larger group (e.g., the extended family or nonfamily political, religious or social groups) is pathological (p. 163). He does not, however, discuss the forces that bind the nuclear family together, nor does he offer a convincing analysis of the origins of amoral familism (p. 153–54).

594   *Journal of Economic Literature, Vol. XXIII (June 1985)*

TABLE 1
ENVIRONMENT, TECHNOLOGY, AND ORGANIZATIONAL FORM

	Simple technology	Complex technology
Low-trust environment	family governance	?
High-trust environment	both family and nonfamily governance	nonfamily governance

predominate in high-trust environments and in sectors using complex technologies. In the case of high trust and simple technology, family and nonfamily governance may coexist. In the final case, low trust and complex technology, both family and nonfamily governance encounter serious difficulties, and neither form may be viable. The relative decline of family-based economic activities in advanced industrial societies may reflect a shifting balance between the importance of their characteristic advantages and disabilities—a secular movement from low-trust and simple technology environments favoring family governance to high-trust and complex technology environments favoring nonfamily governance.

This discussion and the corresponding table have focused on only one feature of the technology, its complexity, and only one feature of the environment, the reliability and trustworthiness of nonfamily members, implicitly holding fixed other features of the technology and the environment. Another feature of the technology, the minimum efficient scale of production, and another feature of the environment, the trustworthiness of family members and the stability of family ties, deserve further attention.

Like increases in complexity, increases in minimum efficient scale favor market governance over family governance. Such increases may reflect technological innovations or, as Williamson (1975, Chs. 8, 9; 1981, Section 4) has stressed, organiza-

tional innovations such as the multidivisional or M-form firm, the conglomerate, and the multinational corporation. Technological innovations over the last two-hundred years have increased minimum efficient scale and thus favored nonfamily over family governance. Organizational innovations have also favored larger units by making it administratively feasible to take advantage of technically feasible economies of scale and scope.

Decreases in the trustworthiness and reliability of family ties also favor nonfamily over family governance. Economists have tended to view the family as a harmonious unit and to regard conflict and discord as aberrations of little relevance for economic analysis. In the next section I consider issues related to the causes and consequences of such conflicts.

II. Internal Organization of Families

The family's internal organization is a determinant of its effectiveness as a governance structure for economic activities and for distribution within the family. I begin in Section A by examining marriage from a contracting perspective, emphasizing the difficulties of using contracts to structure complex, ongoing relationships. In Section B I turn to allocation and distribution within the family, bargaining models of marriage, and the roles of marriage- or family-specific capital. In Section C I discuss social exchange theory, arguing that it is broadly consistent with approaches emphasizing bargaining. Section D summarizes the case for bargaining models.

A. *Marriage and Contract*

Individuals desire secure long-term family relationships to provide a stable environment in which to live and to rear children and, in Becker's terminology, to reduce the risks associated with accumulating marital-specific or marriage-specific capital.[32] This requires an institutional structure that is both flexible enough to allow adaptive, sequential decisionmaking in the face of unfolding events and rigid enough to safeguard each spouse against opportunistic exploitation by the other. Marriage is a governance structure which, more or less satisfactorily, accommodates these requirements.

In *Ancient Law* (1861) Sir Henry Sumner Maine identified the progress of civilization with a movement *"from Status to Contract."* He argued that modern society is founded on obligations that individuals create for themselves by voluntary agreements and promises rather than on obligations involuntarily and automatically imposed on them because of their status within the family. Maine's thesis provides a starting point for several recent discussions of marriage. Tony Tanner (1979), for example, begins by quoting several long passages from Maine and views adultery against this background: ". . . adultery can be seen as an attempt to establish an extracontractual contract, or indeed an anticontract . . ." (p. 6) that threatens the

---

[32] Becker uses the phrase "marital-specific capital" to refer to capital that would be "much less valuable" if the particular marriage dissolved (Becker, Landes and Michael 1977, p. 338). "Children are the prime example, especially young children, although learning about the idiosyncrasies of one's spouse is also important . . ." (Becker 1981, p. 224). Becker, Landes and Michael also include "working exclusively in the nonmarket sector" (pp. 1142, 1152), as marriage-specific capital. I return to marriage-specific capital in Section B.

fabric of society. "For bourgeois society marriage is the all-subsuming, all-organizing, all-containing contract. It is the structure that maintains the Structure . . ." (p. 15). For this reason ". . . the problem of transgressing the marriage contract . . . is at the center . . ." of the late eighteenth- and early nineteenth-century novel (p. 12).

Like Tanner, Lenore J. Weitzman (1981) begins with Maine but she denies that his thesis applies to family law: ". . . marriage has not moved from status to contract" (p. xix). The tension between the status and the contract views of marriage is summarized in a recent family law case book by Walter O. Weyrauch and Michael B. Katz (1983):

> *Maynard, Ponder,* and *Ryan* relate to the nature of marriage as seen in the light of Sir Henry Sumner Maine's famous statement, 'that the movement of the progressive societies has been a movement *from Status to Contract.*' In legal practice this statement has never had the same significance it has had for scholarship, but relational and contractual aspects of marriage have lived side by side relatively undisturbed. These cases illustrate that legal practice can live with and accommodate apparent contradictions with ease. *Maynard* stands today for the proposition that marriage is something more than a mere contract, that it is a status or a relationship and, as such, subject to regulation by the government.
>
> *Ponder,* on the other hand, . . . , continues to be relied on for the seemingly opposite proposition that marriage is contract rather than a mere relationship, and that legislation regulating marriage could conceivably impair the obligation of contract if it affects vested rights. . . . *Maynard* can be cited whenever an argument in support of the police power of the state to regulate marriage is made, while *Ponder* can be cited in support of the contractual autonomy of marital parties to regulate their own affairs. In an extreme case this may be done within the same case, and *Ryan* demonstrates this capacity to draw from contradictory sources for support [p. 59].

Firms do not marry, but transaction cost analysis argues that they often resort to merger or vertical integration to avoid using contracts to structure complex, ongoing relationships. Short-term contracts require frequent renegotiation, making it risky to accumulate capital whose value is contingent on the relationship continuing and discouraging investment in such specific capital. Complete long-term' contracts which specify every possible contingency are costly or impossible to write, a reflection of bounded rationality and asymmetric information. Incomplete long-term contracts which fail to specify every possible contingency are perilous because uncovered contingencies must be dealt with through bilateral negotiations under circumstances that may give one party or the other a strategic advantage. While the parties have some control over how complete their contract is to be, more complete contracts are relatively expensive to write and relatively rigid to apply. To avoid these contracting hazards firms often rely on some more complete form of integration such as merger. Since bureaucratic structures have their own characteristic disabilities, internal governance does not eliminate all difficulties associated with a transaction or exchange. Nevertheless, replacing a market relationship by an organization with an appropriate governance structure often safeguards the interests of both parties.

Comparing marriage and merger calls attention to the difference between individuals and firms. When two firms merge, at least one of them loses its legal identity and disappears. When two individuals marry, this is not the case, or, more precisely, this is no longer the case. Sir William Blackstone (1765), describing marriage under eighteenth-century common law, wrote:

> By marriage, the husband and wife are one person in law . . . [T]he very being or legal existence of the woman is suspended during marriage, or at least is incorporated and consolidated into that of the husband, under whose wing, protection, and cover she performs everything; and is therefore called . . . a femme-covert; and her condition during her marriage is called her coverture.[33]

Thus under the eighteenth-century English common law the parallel between marriage and merger was striking: the wife's legal personality was merged with and submerged in her husband's.

Recent legal scholarship that emphasizes the diversity of contracting modes provides a closely related analysis of these issues. Ian R. Macneil (1978) distinguishes among "classical," "neoclassical," and "relational" contracting.[34] The classical paradigm ignores any relationship between the parties other than that established by the contract itself: The parties' identities are irrelevant, since they may be viewed as trading with the market rather than with each other. The classical paradigm thus adopts a discrete transactions view that is very close to the economist's stereotype of contract law. Neoclassical and relational contracting arose in response to the difficulties of using contracts to structure complex, long-term relationships. Neoclassical contracting introduces a governance structure, often involving third-party arbitration, to reduce these hazards. Relational contracting goes a step further in this direction by treating the ongoing relationship between the parties rather than the contract as central. Collective bargaining is the leading example. Thus, the disabilities of contracts for structuring complex, long-term relationships apply to both commercial and personal contracts.

In Macneil's terminology marriage is a relational contract. The feature that

---

[33] After quoting this passage Weitzman (1981) goes on to quote Justice Black: "this rule has worked out in reality to mean that though the husband and wife are one, the one is the husband" (p. 1). U.S. v. Yazell, 382 U.S. 341, 359 (1966).

[34] Williamson (1979) develops the implications of Macneil's analysis for the transaction cost approach. See also Macneil (1974, 1980).

makes classical and neoclassical contracting inappropriate for structuring labor relations agreements—their inability to view specific disputes in the context of a continuing relationship requiring adaptive, sequential decisionmaking—makes them at least equally inappropriate for structuring marriage. Relational contracting provides a more instructive model.

Weitzman (1981) and others have recently urged that privately negotiated marriage contracts be treated like other contracts, enforceable through the courts, but not accorded special treatment.[35] The contracting analysis of Williamson and Macneil draws attention to the range of contracting modes and implies that relational contracts, because they are likely to be less complete than other contracts, are more dependent on legal rules and on institutions for their interpretation and articulation. This dependence on rules and institutions signals a larger role for the state, organized religion, or custom, and a correspondingly smaller role for the contracting parties than is typical in classi-

[35] Weitzman describes marriage as a contract whose terms are imposed by the state rather than negotiated privately by the parties and examines the terms of that state-imposed contract. She then offers examples of privately negotiated marriage contracts and argues that such "intimate" contracts provide a means of redressing the sexual imbalance which she believes remains present in family law and of providing the certainty, clarity, and assurance that are often absent in family courts. Her argument relies heavily on an analogy between personal relationships and business or commercial ones: Our legal system recognizes the advantages of allowing individuals and firms considerable latitude in structuring business relationships by privately negotiated contracts; why not allow individuals similar latitude in structuring their personal, intimate relationships? This analogy provides some support for the use of contracts to structure personal relationships, but it also draws attention to the difficulties of doing so. Privately negotiated contracts can increase individuals' abilities to determine the duties and obligations of their personal relationships. Using contracts to structure complex, long-term relationships, whether commercial or personal, is intrinsically hazardous, however, and certainty, clarity, and assurance are not to be found in relational contracts.

cal and neoclassical contracting.[36] This is evident in labor law, where relational contracting is most fully developed: Special rules and institutions have been created to circumvent the perceived defects of classical and neoclassical contracting.[37] Treating marriage contracts "like any other contract" is to treat them as classical contracts. But marriage contracts, because they are relational contracts, do require "special treatment": Dispute resolution would require special rules and perhaps special institutions.[38] Privately negotiated marriage contracts articulated through public rules and institutions that reflect society's values and mores might yield results not very different from those obtained through a system of family courts.[39]

[36] Because all contracts are subject to certain general rules of law, this distinction is one of degree. Although economists sometimes assume that contracting parties are free to strike any mutually advantageous bargain, this assumption is unwarranted: In the United States some contract provisions are unenforceable because they have been prohibited by statute; others are unenforceable because the courts have held them "contrary to public policy."

[37] These rules affect not only dispute resolution under existing collective bargaining agreements but also the conditions under which collective bargaining takes place in the absence of a prior contract or after the expiration of an existing agreement. Recently some U.S. courts have held that, even absent a collective bargaining agreement or an individual contract, "employers cannot dismiss employees arbitrarily or in bad faith." In Europe protection against dismissal without cause is provided through legislation (William B. Gould 1982, p. 7). Clyde W. Summers (1983) provides a brief overview in his introduction to a recent symposium on "employment at will." Mark R. Kramer (1984, pp. 243–47) summarizes recent developments in this rapidly changing area of the law.

[38] This would be true even absent children and the third-party effects associated with them. The presence of children provides a further rationale for state regulation of marriage and the family.

[39] As Becker (1981, p. 27, fn. 6) notes, Chinese, Japanese, and Christians have generally relied on oral and customary rather than written marriage contracts. In Christian Europe marriage was historically governed not by the state but by the Church through canon law and ecclesiastical courts. The Jewish marriage contract, the Ketuba, is traditionally written. In Islamic law marriage is a civil contract

598   *Journal of Economic Literature, Vol. XXIII (June 1985)*

B. *Allocation and Distribution within Families*

Economists have considered three models of allocation and distribution within families: Samuelson's family consensus model, Becker's altruist model, and recent bargaining models. Although these models usually focus on husbands and wives, they also provide a framework for examining relationships between parents and children. Samuelson's consensus model, explicitly articulated in Samuelson (1956), resolves the problem of intrafamily allocation and distribution by postulating a family social welfare function. Samuelson begins by noting that "the fundamental unit on the demand side is clearly the 'family' " (p. 9), and goes on to pose what he terms the "Mr. Jekyll and Mrs. Jekyll" problem: How can we expect family demand functions to obey any consistency conditions? This question, a crucial one from the standpoint of revealed preference theory, provided the motivation for Samuelson's theory of intrafamily allocation:

> Of course, we might try to save the conventional theory by claiming that one titular head has sovereign power within the family and all of its demands reflect his (or her) consistent indifference curves. But as casual anthropologists we all know how unlikely it is in modern Western culture for one person to "wear the pants." It is perhaps less unrealistic to adopt the hypothesis of a consistent "family consensus" that represents a meeting of the minds

(John L. Esposito 1982, p. 16) but the parties' latitude to specify its terms is circumscribed (N. J. Coulson 1964, pp. 189–91; Esposito 1982, pp. 23–24).

The special legal rules and institutions governing marriage and the family in the U.S. may be viewed as society's response to the difficulties inherent in structuring such relationships. Four features deserve attention. A standard form marriage "contract" is imposed on the parties to avoid problems of overreaching and unconscionability; specialized courts are responsible for administering family law; courts generally refuse to intervene in ongoing marriages; and the legal system provides a complex and unsatisfactory set of rules in the one area in which they cannot escape involvement: marital dissolution.

or a compromise between them. (Perhaps Arrow will produce a proof that such a consensus is impossible.) [p. 9].

Samuelson goes on to consider what he characterizes as "one extreme polar case of family organization":

> This family consists of two or more persons: each person consumes his own goods and has indifference curves ordering those goods, and his preferences among his own goods have the special property of being independent of the other members' consumption. But since blood is thicker than water, the preferences of the different members are interrelated by what might be called a "consensus" or "social welfare function" which takes into account the deservingness or ethical worths of the consumption levels of each of the members. The family acts *as if* it were maximizing their joint welfare function [p. 10].

While Samuelson's approach determines allocation and distribution within the family, this is not his principal concern even in the section of "Social Indifference Curves" entitled "The Problem of Family Preference." His primary point is the logical parallel between distribution in the family and distribution in society. His secondary point, crucial for demand analysis, is that the Mr. Jekyll and Mrs. Jekyll problem can be finessed: The consensus or family social welfare function approach provides a rationale for treating family demand functions as if they were individual demand functions. But because Samuelson's "consensus" is postulated, not derived, his family is simply a preference ordering. Samuelson's concern is to keep the lid on the "black box," not to look inside.

The second model of allocation and distribution within the family is the altruist model articulated in Becker (1974, 1981).[40] Becker, unlike Samuelson, is primarily concerned with intrafamily allocation. He begins by postulating that the

[40] Becker (1973) proposes an alternative model of allocation and distribution within the family in which outcomes are essentially determined by the market.

family contains one "altruistic" member whose preferences reflect concern with the welfare of the others.[41] Becker then argues that the presence of one altruist in the family induces purely selfish but rational family members to behave altruistically and that the resulting intrafamily allocation is the one that maximizes the altruist's utility function subject to the family's resource constraint. He concludes that individual differences can be submerged and the family treated as a single harmonious unit with consistent preferences, those of the altruist, without arbitrarily postulating Samuelson's family social welfare function: "In my approach the 'optimal reallocation' results from altruism and voluntary contributions, and the 'group preference function' is identical to that of the altruistic head, even when he does not have sovereign power" (1981, p. 192, footnote omitted).

Becker's claims have been challenged. Marilyn Manser and Murray Brown (1980, p. 32) argue that Becker's conclusion depends not merely on the presence of an altruist but also on implicitly introducing a particular bargaining rule, the rule that the household maximizes the altruist's utility function. Manser and Brown are correct that Becker's analysis is seriously flawed, although Becker is correct that his result does not depend on the altruist having sovereign power. Neither Becker nor Manser and Brown have analyzed the conditions under which Becker's results hold. In addition to the dictatorial case, it also holds when the altruist is a player in an asymmetric bargaining game in which he can offer the others all-or-nothing choices.[42,43]

---

[41] Becker's use of the term "altruism" differs from its meaning in sociobiology, although Becker (1976) claims they are closely related.

[42] And in which the others are not allowed to form coalitions.

[43] Becker mentions that his result need not hold in the case of "corner solutions" (1981, pp. 191–92). Under my interpretation, corner solutions are rele-

Bargaining models of allocation and distribution within families, developed independently by Manser and Brown (1980) and by McElroy and Mary J. Horney (1981), treat marriage as a cooperative game.[44,45] These models do not require that either spouse be altruistic, although one or both may be. Spouses are assumed to have conflicting preferences and to resolve their differences in the manner prescribed by some explicit bargaining model.[46] The utility payoffs to the spouses if they fail to reach agreement—called

---

vant when the altruist does not have enough resources to move the others to his preferred allocation by offering them an all-or-nothing choice. To see that Becker's solution does not follow from altruism alone, consider a family with two altruists. Alternatively, consider a family with one altruist and one egoist, but suppose that the egoist has dictatorial power or that the egoist can offer the altruist an all-or-nothing choice. Becker's result depends not on altruism, but on implicit assumptions about power or, equivalently, about the structure of the bargaining game.

[44] A cooperative game is one in which "the players have complete freedom of preplay communication to make joint *binding* agreements"; a non-cooperative game is one in which "absolutely no preplay communication is permitted . . ." (R. Duncan Luce and Howard Raiffa 1957, p. 89; emphasis in original). Simone Clemhout and Henry Y. Wan, Jr. (1977) is the only paper I know that models marriage as a non-cooperative game.

[45] Manser and Brown and McElroy and Horney are specifically concerned with marriage rather than the family, but the analytical issues are similar. The differences between models of allocation between husbands and wives and between parents and children are twofold. First, marriage can be treated as a two-person game, while allocation between parents and children may involve more than two players and, hence, raises the possibility of coalition formation. Second, timing issues, which deserve more attention than they have thus far received in models of marriage, become crucial in models involving parents and children.

[46] Alvin E. Roth (1979) provides a survey of alternative bargaining models. Manser and Brown and McElroy and Horney consider the Nash solution (John F. Nash 1950) to the bargaining problem, and Manser and Brown also consider the Kalai and Smorodinsky solution (Ehud Kalai and Meir Smorodinsky 1975). Sharon C. Rochford (1984) analyzes the implications for assignment or matching in the marriage market of a model in which allocations within marriages are determined by Nash bargaining with transferable utility.

600   *Journal of Economic Literature, Vol. XXIII (June 1985)*

"threat points" in cooperative game theory—play a dual role in bargaining models. They are essential both to determining the negotiation set—the set of utility payoffs which are Pareto optimal and individually rational (i.e., better for both parties than failing to reach agreements)—and to determining a particular solution, often a unique solution, within the negotiation set. In some bargaining models the threat point corresponds to the payoffs associated with clearly defined "next best" alternatives for each party; in a bargaining model of marriage, for example, the next best alternative for one or both spouses to remaining in a particular marriage might be becoming and remaining single. Usually, however, the threat point corresponds to the expected utility taken over some set of alternatives, for example, the expected utility associated with leaving the present marriage and searching for another spouse.[47]

Bargaining models of intrafamily allocation, in contrast to Becker's model, emphasize the role played by threat points or alternatives in determining allocation and distribution within the family. Thus, investigating whether threat points or alternatives affect intrafamily allocation and distribution may permit us to distinguish empirically between bargaining models and Becker's model.[48]

Bargaining models explicitly embed the problem of intrafamily allocation and distribution in a game-theoretic context, and therefore they provide an intellectually satisfying framework for addressing these issues. Game-theoretic models serve a similar function in industrial organization: Posing the duopoly or bilateral monopoly problem in game-theoretic terms does not resolve the difficulties inherent in modeling the interaction of two firms that recognize their mutual interdependence. For both families and firms, however, the game-theoretic formulation exposes the fundamental nature of the analytical problem.

The transaction cost approach, although broadly consistent with the spirit of the bargaining models, implies that one-period bargaining models are seriously deficient. Neither adaptive sequential decisionmaking, required to deal with new information and unfolding events, nor a governance structure, required to protect each spouse against changes in threat points that strengthen the bargaining position of the other and leave the disadvantaged spouse vulnerable to opportunistic exploitation, has any place in one-period models. Formulation of multiperiod bargaining models depends, however, on developments in the theory of cooperative games.[49]

Focusing on opportunism and the need for a governance structure that limits its

[47] In bargaining models the threat point almost never involves the threat of physical violence. Economists' models of conflict, whether between husbands and wives or between workers and firms, seldom recognize even the possibility of violence. Ann D. Witte, Helen V. Tauchen and Sharon K. Long (1984) summarize the sociological literature on family violence, which distinguishes between "expressive" violence (i.e., violence as an end in itself) and "instrumental" violence (i.e., violence as a means of coercion). They then propose a game-theoretic model in which violence and credible threats of violence can be instruments of social control and can affect allocation within the family.

[48] This is too simple. In the market-determined model of Becker (1973) alternatives outside the marriage completely determine allocation within marriage. That model, however, implies a negotiation set which reduces to a single point and, not surpris-

ingly, all models give identical predictions in this case. In Becker (1974, 1981) the negotiation set is determined by the alternatives available to each spouse, but the altruist chooses the point in the negotiation set he prefers. Thus, unless the altruist chooses a "corner solution," changes in alternatives which do not eliminate the allocation chosen by the altruist from the negotiation set cannot force him to a less preferred allocation. Finally, there remains the empirical problem of identifying threat points or alternatives.

[49] If marriage is modeled as a non-cooperative game, then the multiperiod formulation is a supergame in which the constituent game changes from one period to another.

scope allows us to understand better the dual role of family or marriage-specific capital. Marriage-specific capital is defined by two characteristics: It increases productivity in the household and it is worthless if the particular marriage dissolves.[50] Thus, other things being equal, an increase in marriage-specific capital widens the gap between remaining in a particular marriage and leaving it, either to become and remain single or to search for a better marriage. By widening this gap the accumulation of marriage-specific capital stabilizes the marriage and reduces the risk of further investment in productive marriage-specific capital.[51]

Becker, Landes and Michael (1977, p. 1142) characterize "working exclusively in the nonmarket sector" as a form of marriage-specific investment. This characterization fails to recognize the two distinct channels through which working exclusively in the nonmarket sector affects both marital stability and intrafamily allocation. Working in the home creates nontransferable skills that increase productivity in the marriage; these skills represent marriage-specific capital which increases the payoff associated with remaining in a particular marriage. But a decision to work exclusively in the nonmarket sector is also a decision not to acquire market human capital. Thus the effects of such a decision on the payoffs are twofold: Because marriage-specific capital has been accumulated, it increases the "married payoff"—the payoff associated with remaining in the marriage; and, because market human capital has not been accumulated, it de-creases the "divorced payoff"—the payoff associated with leaving the marriage and starting work in the market sector.[52]

The relative importance of the married payoff and divorced payoff depends on the rates at which marriage-specific and market human capital accumulate. There are two polar cases. In the first, productivity in the home depends on the accumulation of marriage-specific human capital while wages are independent of experience in the market sector: In this case, working exclusively in the nonmarket sector affects marital stability and intrafamily allocation only by increasing the married payoff; the divorced payoff at a given future date will be the same regardless of whether the intervening period has been spent exclusively in the nonmarket sector. In the second polar case, productivity in the home is independent of experience in the nonmarket sector while wages depend on accumulated experience in the market sector: In this case working exclusively in the nonmarket sector affects marital stability and intrafamily allocation solely by decreasing the divorced payoff; the married payoff will be the same regardless of whether the intervening period has been spent exclusively in the nonmarket sector. In this second case working exclusively in the nonmarket sector involves no accumulation of marriage-specific human capital. Between these poles lies a continuum of cases in which marriage-specific capital and market capital both accumulate at nonzero rates. It is an unresolved and virtually unexplored empirical issue whether

---

[50] In some respects a spouse acquiring marriage-specific capital is analogous to a worker acquiring firm-specific human capital. A major difference is that in labor markets workers are protected by the firm's need to maintain its reputation so it can hire workers in the future, while in marriage markets this protection is attenuated.

[51] Becker is well aware that marriage-specific capital plays both of these roles (Becker, Landes and Michael 1977, p. 1152; Becker 1981, p. 224).

[52] The bases for these comparisons are the payoffs that would be realized at a particular future date in each of the two states—remaining in the marriage and leaving it—if the individual had not worked exclusively in the nonmarket sector. The married payoff refers to the total to be divided between the spouses; in a bargaining model the division of this total depends on the threat point (i.e., the divorced payoff). The "total to be divided between the spouses" is a problematic notion without special assumptions such as transferable utility.

working exclusively in the nonmarket sector increases marital stability primarily by increasing marriage-specific capital, thus increasing the married payoff, or primarily by failing to increase market capital, thus decreasing the divorced payoff.[53]

Becker, Landes and Michael (1977, p. 1152) also characterize children as marriage-specific capital "since one parent usually has much less contact with the children after dissolution."[54] This characterization is misleading for two reasons. First, unlike marriage-specific capital, children do not disappear when a marriage dissolves; typically one parent or the other is granted custody of the children. The observation that one parent usually has much less contact with the children after dissolution suggests that children are like public goods within the marriage, not that they are marriage-specific capital. Second, like working exclusively in the nonmarket sector, children increase the payoff associated with remaining in a marriage and reduce the payoff associated with leaving it.[55,56] Hence, the presence of children affects both marital stability and intrafamily allocation through two distinct channels. The increased payoff associated with remaining in the marriage reflects the "productivity" of children as sources of satisfaction in the intact marriage. The reduced payoff associated with leaving reflects the role of children as "hostages."[57,58]

The transaction cost approach suggests a number of empirically implementable research projects on allocation within the family—between husbands and wives, between parents and children, and among children. Allocation between husbands and wives is difficult to investigate empirically because of the pervasiveness of public goods within the household. Neglecting corner solutions, Becker's altruism model implies that the allocation between spouses depends on the sum of their resources, but not on each spouse's individual wealth, income, and earning power except as they affect this total: The altruist's utility function is maximized subject to the family's resource constraint. The transaction cost approach, like the bargaining models, suggests that the allocation between spouses depends systematically on the individual wealth, income, and earning power of the spouses as well as on their sum. Although the transaction cost approach does not imply a specific

---

[53] Marriage-specific capital is, by definition, idiosyncratic to a particular marriage. The discussion could be generalized, however, to consider the role of human capital which is specific to the household sector but not to a particular marriage. This distinction is analogous to that in the labor market literature between firm-specific and industry-specific human capital.

[54] Becker (1974, p. S23, fn. 36) notes that children "would be a specific investment if the pleasure received by a parent were smaller when the parent was (permanently) separated from the children."

[55] Pollak and Wachter (1975, p. 273–76) criticize the new home economics literature for failing to distinguish between "household production processes" that produce observable and measurable commodities and those that produce "satisfaction" or unmeasurable commodities such as "child services."

[56] Utility payoffs to each spouse in the event of dissolution are conceptually unambiguous. Utility payoffs to each spouse when the marriage remains intact presuppose a particular solution to the problem of distribution within marriage.

[57] Williamson (1983) discusses the use of hostages to lend stability to bilateral governance structures. He argues that reciprocal selling arrangements and product exchanges among rival firms, practices usually condemned as anticompetitive, under certain conditions may represent exchanges of hostages that facilitate socially beneficial trading.

[58] The hostage effect has two components. The first is psychological: Even if leaving a marriage with children entailed no financial obligations, leaving such a marriage would be different from leaving a childless marriage. The second is financial: To the extent that parents retain child support obligations after leaving a marriage, the payoff to leaving a marriage with children is less than the payoff to leaving a childless marriage. These costs may be magnified if there are "economies of scale in consumption" that are lost with dissolution. The financial effect on the payoffs of the parents depends on the extent to which child support is borne by the state and how the portion of it not borne by the state is divided between the parents.

bargaining model, by viewing marriage as a governance structure which permits some flexibility while protecting the parties against the hazards of unconstrained bilateral bargaining, it does suggest that alternatives and threat points affect allocation within marriage.

Direct econometric implementation of any model of allocation within marriage depends on identifying and measuring goods, commodities, or activities desired by one spouse but not the other.[59] For example, contributions of husbands and wives to their respective undergraduate colleges are likely to fall into this category. Or, if either or both spouses have children by previous marriages, then the consumption of these children or expenditures on their education are likely to be of more interest to the children's parent than to the other spouse: An uncluttered case would be one in which a widow with children married a widower with children. Using data from a developing country, one might investigate whether the nutrition of a child in such a family depended only on the family's total resources or whether those of the child's parent had an independent effect on the child's consumption. Using contemporary U.S. data, one might investigate whether the educational attainment of a child depended only on the new family's total resources, or whether the resources of the child's parent had a systematic, independent effect. Although the data needed to estimate models based on the transaction cost approach are diffi-

cult to obtain, in the long run data availability is endogenous. Data collection by government agencies or by individual researchers—a practice less common in economics than in other disciplines—depends in large part on the apparent demand for such data by the research community.

C. Social Exchange Theory

Social exchange theory, a framework developed by sociologists and social historians which draws heavily on economics, has been used to analyze a wide range of social phenomena, including intrafamily allocation.

Greven's *Four Generations* (1970), a study of colonial Andover, explains the changing relationships between successive generations in terms of changing economic opportunities and alternatives:

> With abundant land for themselves and their off-spring, the first generation established extended patriarchal families, in which fathers maintained their authority over their mature sons, mainly by withholding control over the land from them until late in their lives. The delayed marriages of sons testified to their prolonged attachment to paternal families . . . [p. 268].

Greven argues that age at marriage is a sensitive indicator of the assumption of adult status and responsibility (pp. 31–32), that marriage required parental support (p. 75), and that the first-generation fathers retained legal control of their lands until their deaths (p. 78). In the middle decades of the eighteenth century, the fourth generation "married younger, established their independence more effectively and earlier in life, and departed from the community with even greater frequency than in earlier generations" (p. 272). Many sons in the fourth generation acquired land from their fathers by deeds of gift or sale during the father's lifetime, rather than by bequest at the father's death (p. 241).

Greven explains these changes in terms

[59] Empirical implementation need not be either direct or econometric. At least two other strategies are available. The first, which I have already discussed, is indirect and focuses on the implications of the transaction cost approach for marital stability, labor force participation, or other variables for which data are widely available. The second is direct but non-econometric and uses qualitative rather than quantitive evidence. Appealing to narrative case studies does not solve the problem of econometric implementation, but challenges the importance of doing so by implicitly raising the question of what types of evidence are admissible in economics.

generally consistent with a bargaining framework in which threat points (i.e., alternatives or opportunities) play a significant role:

A combination of circumstances probably fostered the relatively early autonomy of many fourth-generation sons and encouraged their fathers to assume that their sons ought to be on their own as soon as possible. The rapid expansion of settlements and the emigration of many third-generation Andover men had amply demonstrated the opportunities which existed outside Andover for those willing and able to leave their families and begin life for themselves elsewhere. The diminished landholdings of many families and the constantly rising prices of land in Andover during the first half of the century also put great pressure upon sons who wished to remain as farmers in Andover and made it imperative that many sons take up trades instead or move elsewhere for the land they needed [p. 222].

If patriarchalism was not yet gone, it had been made less viable by the changing circumstances. The earlier economic basis which had sustained the attempts by fathers to establish and to maintain their control and influence over the lives of their sons no longer was to be found among the majority of families living in Andover. Only the wealthy and only those with sons who were willing to accede to their fathers' wishes regarding the possession and ownership of the land could still consider themselves to be patriarchs [p. 273].

Anderson (1971) utilizes an explicit conceptual framework for analyzing the impact of urbanization and industrialization on family structure in nineteenth-century Lancashire. His framework is an elaboration of "social exchange theory," which postulates that individuals engage in exchange to maximize "psychic profit."[60] Anderson, however, stresses two considerations that exchange theory neglects: whether reciprocation is immediate or in the distant future, and whether reciprocation is certain or uncertain (p. 9). The ex-

[60] The basic social exchange theory framework is borrowed from social psychology. The seminal works are George C. Homans (1961) and Peter M. Blau (1964); for an analytical survey and references to the literature see Anthony F. Heath (1976).

change theory foundation of Anderson's analysis is consonant with a bargaining approach, and the two additional considerations he introduces, timing and uncertainty, suggest modifying social exchange theory in the same general directions as transaction cost analysis suggests modifying bargaining models.

Anderson documents the effect of children's employment opportunities on their relationships with their parents:

. . . children's high individual wages allowed them to enter into relational bargains with their parents on terms of more or less precise equality. If, as was usually the case, a bargain could be struck which was immediately favourable to both parties, then all was well, and the relationship continued, though the degree of commitment to such a relationship must often have been low. If a better alternative was obtainable elsewhere the child could take it. The contrast between the choice element in these relationships between urban children and their parents, and the situation in rural areas . . . is very marked. In the rural areas even in the short run, child and father entered a bargaining situation with the child at a very considerable disadvantage, because the father had complete control over the only really viable source of income [pp. 131–32].

Summarizing his findings, Anderson writes:

. . . one crucial way in which urban-industrial life in the nineteenth century affected family cohesion was by offering to teenage children wages at such a level that they were able to free themselves from total economic dependence on the nuclear family. Because normative controls were weak and because housing, food, and other day to day necessities could be obtained on the open market, many could . . . live as well or better than they could with kin or parents. Some children did desert their families and I have presented some evidence which suggested that even where they did not do so many children were conscious of the existence of this possibility and the alternatives it offered, and used it as a way of bargaining a highly independent relationship with their families [p. 134].

Social exchange theory provides an analytical framework for sociology and social history which appeals strongly to economists; its appeal to sociologists and social historians is somewhat less powerful. For example, Michael Katz (1975), a social historian, contrasts Anderson's work on nineteenth-century Preston with his own analysis of nineteenth-century Hamilton, emphasizing the narrowness of Anderson's exchange theory approach. He argues that it "constricts the range of human motivation," and "it assumes a greater degree of rationality than probably underlies ordinary behavior" (p. 302).[61]

D. *The Case for Bargaining Models*

Even without the contracting problems emphasized by the transaction cost approach, bargaining models would often be required to analyze intrafamily allocation. There are three exceptions: (1) there is a family consensus on resource allocation, (2) some "altruistic" family member has the power to choose an allocation from the negotiation set and impose his choice on the others, and (3) the negotiation set is a single point, so there is no surplus over which to bargain. Virtually any other circumstances require a bargaining analysis to determine an equilibrium allocation within the negotiation set.

The negotiation set corresponding to a particular marriage depends on the next-best alternative of each spouse. When the negotiation set is small, determining an equilibrium allocation within it becomes uninteresting: The well-being of each spouse is essentially determined by the negotiation set, not by bargaining within the marriage to determine an allocation within the negotiation set. In the limit, when the negotiation set shrinks to a single point, the well-being of each spouse is uniquely determined by his or her alternatives outside the marriage.[62]

[61] Katz also argues that Anderson's theory "is not supported by the data in his book" (p. 302).
[62] The limit is a limit for the marriage to continue. If the bargaining set is empty, the marriage will presumably dissolve.

A bargaining approach to intrafamily allocation is required because negotiation sets in ongoing marriages are often large and because intrafamily allocation cannot be resolved at the outset. The emergence of a surplus in ongoing marriages can be ascribed to the accumulation of idiosyncratic or marriage-specific capital or, more simply, to a random process in which marriages with empty negotiation sets dissolve while those with nonempty negotiation sets continue. Because bounded rationality precludes complete long-term contracts which specify intrafamily allocations under every possible contingency, intrafamily allocation must be dealt with in an adaptive, sequential way—in short, through bargaining.

III. *Conclusion*

Although the metaphor of household production can usefully be applied to a wide range of activities, the formal framework of the household production model is best suited to analyzing processes that combine household time and purchased inputs to produce well-defined and measurable outputs. The family's role in many economic activities, however, is explicable not in terms of technology but of governance.

The transaction cost approach provides a new perspective on families and households. Unlike the new home economics, which focuses exclusively on household production, it recognizes the importance of household organization and family structure. The transaction cost approach views marriage as a "governance structure," emphasizes the role of "bargaining" within families, and draws attention to the advantages and disadvantages of family organization in terms of incentives and monitoring, and to the special roles of "altruism" and "family loyalty." It also recognizes the disadvantages of family governance: conflict spillover, the toleration of inefficient personnel, inappropriate ability match, and inability to realize economies of scale. If activities are assigned to institutions in an efficient or cost-minimizing fashion, the balance of these advantages and disadvantages plays a major role in determining which activities are carried out within families and which are performed by firms, nonprofit institutions, or the state.

A principal defect of the transaction cost approach is its failure to provide a structure for rigorous econometric investigations. Developing such a framework requires incorporating the insights of the transaction cost approach into formal models and specifying such models in sufficient detail to permit estimation. The present essay represents a first step toward that goal.

REFERENCES

AKERLOF, GEORGE A. "The Market for 'Lemons': Quality Uncertainty and the Market Mechanism," *Quart. J. Econ.*, Aug. 1970, *84*(3), pp. 488–500.

ALCHIAN, ARMEN A. AND DEMSETZ, HAROLD. "Production, Information Costs, and Economic Organization," *Amer. Econ. Rev.*, Dec. 1972, *62*(5), pp. 777–95.

ANDERSON, MICHAEL. *Family structure in nineteenth century Lancashire.* London: Cambridge U. Press, 1971.

ARROW, KENNETH J. "Uncertainty and the Welfare Economics of Medical Care," *Amer. Econ. Rev.* Dec. 1963, *53*(5), pp. 941–73.

——, AND HAHN, FRANK, H. *General competitive analysis.* San Francisco: Holden-Day, Inc., 1971.

BANFIELD, EDWARD C. *The moral basis of a backward society.* Glencoe, IL: Free Press, 1958.

BARNUM, HOWARD N. AND SQUIRE, LYN. *A model of an agricultural household: Theory and evidence.* Baltimore, MD: Johns Hopkins U. Press, 1979.

BECKER, GARY S. "A Theory of the Allocation of Time," *Econ. J.*, Sept. 1965, *75*(299), pp. 493–517.

——. "A Theory of Marriage: Part I," *J. Polit. Econ.*, July/Aug. 1973, *81*(4) pp. 813–46.

——. "A Theory of Marriage: Part II," *J. Polit. Econ.*, Mar./Apr. 1974, *82*(2), pp. S11–26.

——. "Altruism, Egoism, and Genetic Fitness," *J. Econ. Lit.*, Sept. 1976, *14*(3), pp. 817–26.

——. *A treatise on the family.* Cambridge: Harvard U. Press, 1981.

——; LANDES, ELISABETH M. AND MICHAEL, ROBERT T. "An Economic Analysis of Marital Instability," *J. Polit. Econ.*, Dec. 1977, *85*(6), pp. 1141–87.

BENEDICT, BURTON. "Family Firms and Economic Development," *Southwestern J. Anthro.*, Spring 1968, *24*(1), pp. 1–19.

BEN-PORATH, YORAM. "The F-Connection: Families, Friends, and Firms and the Organization of Exchange," *Population Devel. Rev.*, Mar. 1980, *6*(1), pp. 1–30.

——. "Economics and the Family—Match or Mismatch? A Review of Becker's *A Treatise on the Family*," *J. Econ. Lit.*, Mar. 1982, *20*(1), pp. 52–64.

BINSWANGER, HANS P. AND ROSENZWEIG, MARK R. "Behavioral and Material Determinants of Production Relations in Agriculture." Research Unit, Agriculture and Rural Development Department, Operational Policy Staff, World Bank, Report No.: ARU 5, June 1982. Revised, Oct. 5, 1983.

——. "Contractual Arrangements, Employment and Wages in Rural Labor Markets: A Critical Review," in *Contractual arrangements, employment and wages in rural labor markets in Asia.* Eds.: HANS P. BINSWANGER AND MARK R. ROSENZWEIG. New Haven: Yale U. Press, 1984.

BLACKSTONE, SIR WILLIAM. *Commentaries on the laws of England.* Oxford: Clarendon Press, 1765.

BLAU, PETER M. *Exchange and power in social life.* NY: John Wiley & Sons, Inc., 1964.

CHRISTENSEN, LAURITS R.; JORGENSON, DALE W. AND LAU, LAWRENCE J. "Transcendental Logarithmic Utility Functions," *Amer. Econ. Rev.*, June 1975, *65*(3), pp. 367–83.

CLEMHOUT, SIMONE AND WAN, HENRY Y., JR., "Symmetric Marriage, Household Decision Making and Impact on Fertility." Working Paper No. 152, Cornell U., Sept. 1977.

COASE, RONALD H. "The Nature of the Firm," *Economica, N.S.*, Nov. 1937, *4*, pp. 386–405.

COULSON, N. J. *A history of Islamic law.* Edinburgh: Edinburgh U. Press, 1964.

DAVIS, PETER. "Realizing the Potential of the Family Business," *Organizational Dynamics*, Summer 1983, pp. 47–56.

DEBREU, GERARD. *Theory of value: An axiomatic analysis of economic equilibrium.* NY: John Wiley & Sons, 1959.

DEMOS, JOHN AND BOOCOCK, SARANE SPENCE, eds. *Turning points: Historical and sociological essays on the family.* Amer. J. Soc., Supplement. 1978, *84*.

DEOLALIKAR, ANIL B. AND VIJVERBERG, WIM P. M. "The Heterogeneity of Family and Hired Labor in Agricultural Production: A Test Using District-Level Data from India," *J. Econ. Devel.*, Dec. 1983a, *8*(2), pp. 45–69.

——. "Heterogeneity of Family and Hired Labor in Agriculture: A Test Using Farm-Level Data from India and Malaysia." Economic Growth Center, Yale U., Discussion Paper No. 444, Sept. 1983b.

EASTERLIN, RICHARD A.; POLLAK, ROBERT A. AND WACHTER, MICHAEL L. "Towards a More General Economic Model of Fertility Determination: Endogenous Preferences and Natural Fertility," in *Population and economic change in developing*

Pollak: Transaction Cost and Families 607

countries. Ed.: RICHARD A. EASTERLIN. Chicago: U. of Chicago Press, 1980.

EHRLICH, ISAAC AND BECKER, GARY S. "Market Insurance, Self-Insurance and Self-Protection," *J. Polit. Econ.*, July/Aug. 1972, *80*(4), pp. 623–48.

ESPOSITO, JOHN L. *Women in Muslim family law.* Syracuse: Syracuse U. Press, 1982.

FENOALTEA, STEFANO. "Slavery and Supervision in Comparative Perspective: A Model," *J. Econ. Hist.*, Sept. 1984, *44*(3), pp. 635–68.

FØRSUND, FINN R.; LOVELL, C. A. KNOX AND SCHMIDT, PETER. "A Survey of Frontier Production Functions and of Their Relationship to Efficiency Measurement," *J. Econometrics*, May 1980, *13*(1), pp. 5–25.

FUCHS, VICTOR R. *How we live.* Cambridge: Harvard U. Press, 1983.

GOLDBERG, VICTOR P. "Regulation and Administered Contracts," *Bell J. Econ.*, Autumn 1976, *7*(2), pp. 426–48.

GOULD, WILLIAM B. *A primer on American labor law.* Cambridge: MIT Press, 1982.

GREVEN, PHILIP J., JR. *Four generations: Population, land, and family in colonial Andover, Massachusetts.* Ithaca, NY: Cornell U. Press, 1970.

GRIFFEN, SALLY AND GRIFFEN, CLYDE. "Family and Business in a Small City: Poughkeepsie, New York, 1850–1880," in *Family and kin in urban communities, 1700–1930.* Ed.: TAMARA K. HAREVEN. NY: New Viewpoints, 1977, pp. 144–63.

GRILICHES, ZVI. "Household and Economy: Towards a New Theory of Population and Economic Growth: Comment," *J. Polit. Econ.*, Mar./Apr. 1974, 82(2, Part II), pp. S219–21.

HANNAN, MICHAEL T. "Families, Markets, and Social Structures: An Essay on Becker's *A Treatise on the Family,*" *J. Econ. Lit.*, Mar. 1982, *20*(1), pp. 65–72

HANSMANN, HENRY B. "The Role of Nonprofit Enterprise," *Yale Law J.*, Apr. 1980, *89*(5), pp. 835–901.

HAREVEN, TAMARA K. "Family Time and Industrial Time: Family and Work in a Planned Corporation Town, 1900–1924," in *Family and kin in urban communities, 1700–1930.* Ed.: TAMARA K. HAREVEN. NY: New Viewpoints, 1977a.

_____, ed. *Family and kin in urban communities, 1700–1930.* NY: New Viewpoints, 1977b.

_____. "The Dynamics of Kin in an Industrial Community," in *Turning points: Historical and sociological essays on the family.* Ed.: JOHN DEMOS AND SARANE SPENCE BOOCOCK. *Amer. J. Soc.*, Supplement 1978, *84*, pp. S151–82.

HEATH, ANTHONY F. *Rational choice and social exchange: A critique of exchange theory.* NY & Cambridge: Cambridge U. Press, 1976.

HIRSCHMAN, ALBERT O. *Exit, voice, and loyalty: Responses to decline in firms, organizations and states.* Cambridge: Harvard U. Press, 1970.

HOMANS, GEORGE C. *Social behavior: Its elementary forms.* NY: Harcourt Brace & World, 1961.

KALAI, EHUD AND SMORODINSKY, MEIR. "Other Solutions to Nash's Bargaining Problem," *Econometrica.* May 1975, *43*(3), pp. 513–18.

KATZ, MICHAEL B. *The people of Hamilton, Canada West: Family and class in a mid-nineteenth-century city.* Cambridge: Harvard U. Press, 1975.

KINKEAD, GWEN. "Family Business Is a Passion Play," *Fortune*, June 30, 1980, pp. 70–75.

KLEIN, BENJAMIN; CRAWFORD, ROBERT G. AND ALCHIAN, ARMEN A. "Vertical Integration, Appropriable Rents, and the Competitive Contracting Process," *J. Law Econ.*, Oct. 1978, *21*(2), pp. 297–326.

KRAMER, MARK R. "The Role of Federal Courts in Changing State Law: The Employment at Will Doctrine in Pennsylvania," *U. of Penn. Law Rev.*, Dec. 1984, *133*(1), pp. 227–64.

KUHN, THOMAS S. *The structure of scientific revolutions.* 2nd ed., enlarged. Chicago: U. of Chicago Press, [1962] 1970.

LANDA, JANET T. "A Theory of the Ethnically Homogeneous Middleman Group: An Institutional Alternative to Contract Law," *J. Legal Stud.*, June 1981, *10*(2), pp. 349–62

LANDA, JANET T. AND SALAFF, JANET W. "The Socioeconomic Functions of Kinship and Ethnic Networks in Promoting Chinese Entrepreneurship in Singapore: A Case Study of the Tan Kah Kee Firm." Mimeo. Oct. 1982.

LASLETT, PETER assist. by WALL, RICHARD. *Household and family in past time.* Cambridge: Cambridge U. Press, 1972.

LUCE, R. DUNCAN AND RAIFFA, HOWARD. *Games and decisions: Introduction and critical survey.* NY: John Wiley & Sons, 1957.

MACNEIL, IAN R. "The Many Futures of Contracts," *Southern Calif. Law Rev.*, May 1974, *47*(3), pp. 691–816.

_____. "Contracts: Adjustment of Long–Term Economic Relations under Classical, Neoclassical, and Relational Contract Law," *Northwestern U. Law Rev.*, Jan./Feb. 1978, *72*(6), pp. 854–905.

_____. *The new social contract: An inquiry into modern contractual relations.* New Haven, CT: Yale U. Press, 1980.

MAINE, SIR HENRY SUMNER. *Ancient law: Its connection with the early history of society and its relation to modern ideas.* London: J. Murray, 1861.

MANSER, MARILYN AND BROWN, MURRAY. "Marriage and Household Decision-Making: A Bargaining Analysis," *Int. Econ. Rev.*, Feb. 1980, *21*(1), pp. 31–44.

MCELROY, MARJORIE B. The Joint Determination of Household Membership and Market Work: The Case of Young Men," *J. Labor Econ.*, forthcoming.

MCELROY, MARJORIE B. AND HORNEY, MARY J. "Nash-Bargained Household Decisions: Toward a Generalization of the Theory of Demand," *Int. Econ. Rev.*, June 1981, *22*(2), pp. 333–49.

MICHAEL, ROBERT T. AND BECKER, GARY S. "On the New Theory of Consumer Behavior," *Swedish J. Econ.*, Dec. 1973, *75*(4), pp. 378–96.

_____; FUCHS, VICTOR R. AND SCOTT, SHARON R. "Changes in the Propensity to Live Alone: 1950–1976," *Demography*, Feb. 1980, *17*(1), pp. 39–56.

MURRELL, PETER. "The Economics of Sharing: A Transactions Cost Analysis of Contractual Choice in Farming," *Bell J. Econ.*, Spring 1983, *14*(1), pp. 283–93.

NASH, JOHN F. "The Bargaining Problem," *Econometrica*, Apr. 1950, *28*(1), pp. 155–62.

NERLOVE, MARC. "Household and Economy: Toward a New Theory of Population and Economic Growth," *J. Polit. Econ.*, Mar./Apr. 1974, *83*(2, Part II), pp. S200–18.

PAULY, MARK. "Overinsurance and Public Provision of Insurance: The Roles of Moral Hazard and Adverse Selection," *Quart. J. Econ.*, Feb. 1974, *81*(1), pp. 44–62.

POLLAK, ROBERT A. AND WACHTER, MICHAEL L. "The Relevance of the Household Production Function and Its Implications for the Allocation of Time," *J. Polit. Econ.*, Apr. 1975, *83*(2), pp. 255–77.

——— AND WALES, TERENCE J. "Estimation of Complete Demand Systems from Household Budget Data: The Linear and Quadratic Expenditure System," *Amer. Econ. Rev.*, June 1978, *68*(3), pp. 349–59.

———. "Comparison of the Quadratic Expenditure System and Translog Demand Systems with Alternative Specifications of Demographic Effects," *Econometrica*, Apr. 1980, 48(3), pp. 595–612.

POSNER, RICHARD A. "Theories of Economic Regulation," *Bell J. Econ. Manage. Sci.*, Autumn 1974, *5*(2), pp. 335–58.

———. "Anthropology and Economics," *J. Polit. Econ.*, June 1980, *88*(3), pp. 608–16.

ROCHFORD, SHARON C. "Symmetrically Pairwise-Bargained Allocations in an Assignment Market," *J. Econ. Theory*, Dec. 1984, *34*(2), pp. 262–81.

ROSENZWEIG, MARK R. AND WOLPIN, KENNETH I. "Specific Experience, Household Structure and Intergenerational Transfers: Farm Family Land and Labor Arrangements in Developing Countries," *Quart. J. Econ.*, forthcoming.

ROTH, ALVIN E. *Axiomatic models of bargaining.* Lecture Notes in Economics and Mathematical Systems, No. 170. Berlin: Springer-Verlag, 1979.

ROTHSCHILD, MICHAEL AND STIGLITZ, JOSEPH E. "Equilibrium in Competitive Insurance Markets: An Essay on the Economics of Imperfect Information," *Quart. J. Econ.*, Nov. 1976, *90*(4), pp. 629–49.

SAMUELSON, PAUL A. *Foundations of economic analysis.* Cambridge: Harvard U. Press, 1947.

———. "Social Indifference Curves," *Quart. J. Econ.*, Feb. 1956, *70*(1), pp. 1–22.

SIMON, HERBERT A. *Models of man: Social and rational.* NY: John Wiley & Sons, 1957.

STIGLER, GEORGE J. AND BECKER, GARY S. "De Gustibus Non Est Disputandum," *Amer. Econ. Rev.*, Mar. 1977, *67*(2), pp. 76–90.

SUMMERS, CLYDE W. "Introduction. Individual Rights in the Workplace: The Employment-At-Will Issue," *U. of Michigan J. Law Reform*, Winter 1983, *16*(2), pp. 201–05.

TANNER, TONY. *Adultery in the novel: Contract and transgression.* Baltimore, MD: Johns Hopkins U. Press, 1979.

VANEK, JAROSLAV. "Decentralization under Workers' Management: A Theoretical Appraisal," *Amer. Econ. Rev.*, Dec. 1969, *59*(5), pp. 1006–14.

WEITZMAN, LENORE J. *The marriage contract: Spouses, lovers and the law.* NY: Free Press, 1981.

WEYRAUCH, WALTER O. AND KATZ, SANFORD N. *American family law in transition.* Wash., DC: The Bureau of National Affairs, 1983.

WILLIAMSON, OLIVER E. *Markets and hierarchies: Analysis and antitrust implications.* NY: Free Press, 1975.

———. "Franchise Bidding for Natural Monopolies—in General and with Respect to CATV," *Bell J. Econ.*, Spring 1976, *7*(1), pp. 73–104.

———. "Transaction-Cost Economics: The Governance of Contractual Relations," *J. Law Econ.*, Oct. 1979, *22*(2), pp. 223–61.

———. "The Modern Corporation: Origins, Evolution, Attributes," *J. Econ. Lit.*, Dec. 1981, *19*(4), pp. 1537–68.

———. "Credible Commitments: Using Hostages to Support Exchange," *Amer. Econ. Rev.*, Sept. 1983, 73(4), pp. 519–40.

WILSON, CHARLES A. "A Model of Insurance Markets with Incomplete Information," *J. Econ. Theory*, Dec. 1977, *16*(2), pp. 167–207.

———. "The Nature of Equilibrium in Markets with Adverse Selection," *Bell J. Econ.*, Spring 1980, *11*(1), pp. 108–30.

WINSTON, GORDON C. *The timing of economic activities: Firms, households, and markets in time-specific analysis.* Cambridge: Cambridge U. Press, 1982.

WITTE, ANN D.; TAUCHEN, HELEN V. AND LONG, SHARON K. "Violence in the Family: A Non-random Affair." Working Paper no. 89. Dept. of Econ., Wellesley College, Oct. 1984.

[11]

The Effect of the Nigerian Extended Family on Entrepreneurial Activity

E. Wayne Nafziger[*]
Kansas State University

Security against economic loss resulting from sickness, accidents, death, old age, poverty, and unemployment is valued highly by most societies. Social security, provident funds, old age pensions, life insurance, unemployment insurance, accident insurance, medical insurance, and welfare programs instituted by government (and business) provide much of this function of security in economically advanced countries. In contrast, this function is supplied by the institution of the extended family in many of the less developed countries such as Nigeria.

It would be useful, though difficult, to compare the costs and benefits of providing the security through government on the one hand, and the extended family on the other. However, the problem under consideration in this study is more specific.

Many development economists emphasize the importance of sociocultural variables as partial determinants of the supply of entrepreneurs and the rate of economic growth. This study analyzes the effect of one of these variables, family structure, on entrepreneurial activity.

Development economists generally contend that the institution of the extended family is a major barrier to entrepreneurial activity.[1] The joint

[*] The author, assistant professor of economics at Kansas State University, is indebted to the Midwest Universities Consortium for International Activities and the Economic Development Institute of the University of Nigeria for the funds and facilities to undertake a year of research on Nigerian entrepreneurship. He is also grateful for the helpful comments of John F. Due, Clinton L. Folse, John R. Harris; colleagues at Kansas State University, the University of Illinois, and the University of Nigeria; and members of his Ph.D. thesis committee at the University of Illinois. However, any errors are solely the responsibility of the writer. The article is based on parts of the author's Ph.D. dissertation written at the University of Illinois.

[1] Charles Wolf, Jr., "Institutions and Economic Development," *American Economic Review* 45 (December 1955): 872–73; Adamantios Pepelasis, Leon Mears, and Irma Adelman, *Economic Development: Analysis and Case Studies* (New York: Harper & Bros., 1961), p. 170; Benjamin Higgins, *Economic Development: Principles, Problems, and Policies* (New York: W. W. Norton Co., 1959), pp. 255–56; and Charles P. Kindleberger, *Economic Development* (New York: McGraw-Hill Book Co., 1965), pp. 21–22.

Economic Development and Cultural Change

family is thought to dampen incentives to achieve, deter risk taking, and impede the mobilization of capital. For example, Wolf writes:

> The joint or extended family system provides another example of institutions deterring economic growth. . . . The joint family . . . involves a system of shared rights and obligations encompassing a large number of near and distant relatives. One characteristic of these relationships is that the individual family member receives the right of support and security from the group in return for the obliga- tion to share his wealth to provide support and security for other members of the group. Where an individual member of the group contemplates a wealth- increasing activity, e.g., through investment in a productive asset that will yield future returns, he must bear all the costs associated therewith. Such costs are not a levy on the group since they are not essential to the individual's support or security. However the fruits or returns from his investment are subject to sharing among the other members of the extended family. Because of the differentiation between responsible and benefitting economic units, what may appear objectively to be strong incentives to invest are not subjectively so regarded by the potential entrepreneur.[2]

The purpose of this study is to examine the effects of the extended family on capital formation and entrepreneurial activity in small manufacturing firms in Nigeria. After a discussion of definitions, sources, methods, and procedures of the study, the paper considers the effects of the extended family on apprentice training for prospective entrepreneurs, the establishment of firms, and the growth of firms. The conclusion suggests further questions for researchers studying the relationship between the extended family and entrepreneurial activity in less developed countries.

A. Definitions

The entrepreneur of a firm is the person with the principal responsibility for making the decision about the level of capital stock for the firm.[3]

Small firms are those with an average net worth of £3000 or less.[4]

Profit is defined as revenue plus changes in inventory minus costs. Costs include, *inter alia,* implicit returns to all the businessman's own factor resources except capital.

[2] Wolf, pp. 872–73.

[3] Other concepts of the entrepreneur with more theoretical appeal are not sufficiently concrete so that entrepreneurs can be identified in an empirical study. See E. Wayne Nafziger, "Nigerian Entrepreneurship: A Study of Indigenous Businessmen in the Foot- wear Industry" (Ph.D. diss., University of Illinois, May 1967), pp. 9–12. The initial entrepreneur, a special case of the entrepreneur, is the person exercising the initiative for bringing the firm into existence. That is, the initial entrepreneur is chiefly responsible for making the decision to increase the level of capital stock from zero to some positive amount.

[4] The exchange rate is £1 = $2.80.

E. Wayne Nafziger

The smallest family unit, the nuclear family, consists of the father, mother, and offspring.[5] The joint or extended family consists of two or more nuclear families in which the resources of its members are pooled for consumption.[6]

B. Sources, Methods, and Procedures

This study is based upon a sample of twenty-eight small indigenous[7] manufacturing[8] firms in Nigeria prior to the January 1966 coup d'état.[9] The firms examined are small enough so that, in general, the same person exercises both the entrepreneurial and capitalist functions.[10]

C. Apprentice Training for Prospective Entrepreneurs

Most entrepreneurs of small firms are trained in the indigenous apprentice system. Under this system, a boy, usually fourteen to eighteen years old, enrolls for a two- to five-year course with a proprietor of a small firm. Over a period of a few years, the boy learns the craft on the job.

The supply of entrepreneurs of new small firms is basically a function of the supply of apprentice-course graduates. It is very rare for a small firm to survive for more than three years if the entrepreneur

---

[5] For an elaboration of the concept of the nuclear family, see M. F. Nimkoff, *Comparative Family Systems* (Boston: Houghton Mifflin Co., 1965), pp. 14–17.

[6] A two-generation polygynous household would not be considered an extended family, while a consumption unit consisting of a father and mother with a married son, wife, and children would (see Nimkoff, p. 19).

[7] Indigenous firms are those in which at least 50 percent of the capital is Nigerian. "Nigerian" includes only: (1) Nigerian citizens of African origin, and (2) regional statutory corporations.

[8] "Manufacturing" includes the making of goods and articles, either by hand or with machinery.

[9] The firms comprise those from a universe of thirty-six firms from which the author could obtain reasonably reliable data. The universe includes all indigenous footwear manufacturing firms, listed in the ten 1964–65 federal and regional directories, which had, in 1964, an average of eight or more persons working and an average net worth of less than £3,000. There is no reason to believe that the effect of the extended family on entrepreneurial activity in small footwear manufacturing firms differs significantly from that in small manufacturing firms as a whole in Nigeria. In addition to interviews conducted in firms of the universe, the author interviewed representatives of fifty-three other indigenous firms. (See Appendix for more information on the sources, methods, and procedures of the study.)

[10] In twenty-two of the twenty-eight firms, the person owning the majority of the capital in 1964–65 was also the entrepreneur. The entrepreneurs of three firms are close relatives of those with a majority of the ownership capital. In two instances, the entrepreneur is co-owner of the enterprise. Finally, in one firm, a cooperative, the entrepreneur is the secretary, who is one of twelve members with equal shares in the business.

27

Economic Development and Cultural Change

lacks apprentice training. For example, all the initial entrepreneurs of the twenty-one sample firms more than three years old (on January 1, 1966) had been trained in the apprentice system.[11] As Callaway indicates, "Almost all the proprietors of the few Nigerian-owned and managed modern small [industrial firms] . . . began their business lives [as apprentices]."[12]

As a result of the scarcity of capital and highly skilled manpower in Nigeria, small firms can compete in a number of industries by using very intensively the abundant factor, labor—especially unskilled apprentice labor, where the receipts from apprentice fees may exceed wages. However, these labor-intensive techniques demand designing skills and craftsmanship on the part of the prospective supervisor-entrepreneur that can only be acquired from a long period of training, supervision, observation, and practice.

Consider the expenditures required for apprentice training for prospective entrepreneurs of small firms. Total apprentice fees for a two- to four-year course usually range from about £17 to £40. In addition, subsistence costs in Onitsha, for example, amount to about £25–£30 a year. Since individual youths can rarely obtain access to credit or raise the funds themselves, the resources of the extended family may be required.

Callaway's study of apprentices in 5,135 Nigerian firms found that 96 percent of the apprentice sponsors are members of the extended family.[13] In addition, family members provide or finance the apprentice's room and board.

Moreover, the prospective apprentice may be dependent upon the extended family for initial contacts with capable apprentice instructors.

In rare cases, the extended family may prevent a youth from obtaining apprentice training.[14] The person who might otherwise be able to afford apprentice training may have to forgo it as a result of the demands on his income by the extended family.

D. The Establishment of the Firm

Raising the initial capital of the firm is one of its major problems. The outlay needed for the establishment of even a small firm is £25 at a minimum, and perhaps more than £150.[15] Most prospective small entre-

---

[11] The only sample firm three years old or less in which the initial entrepreneur was not trained in the apprentice system recorded a loss of £900 (on a net worth of £850) in 1964.

[12] Archibald Callaway, "Nigeria's Indigenous Education: The Apprentice System," *Odu: University of Ife Journal of African Studies* 1, no. 1 (July 1964): 4.

[13] Ibid., p. 8.

[14] Paragraph 7 of section D, below, explains why these cases are rare.

[15] See Peter Kilby, *Development of Small Industries in Eastern Nigeria* (Enugu: Ministry of Information, 1963), p. 9.

E. Wayne Nafziger

preneurs in Nigeria do not have access to funds from organized financial institutions.

The extended family, because of its age composition and size, may be able to mobilize funds that the prospective entrepreneur would not have available, especially if he is young. When asked for the sources of initial capital for the firm nineteen of the twenty-eight entrepreneurs in the sample indicated that at least part was raised from other members of the extended family (see table 1). Even though the median initial investment was no more than £200, only eight of the twenty-eight entrepreneurs obtained all the initial capital from their own resources.

TABLE 1

INITIAL SOURCES OF CAPITAL FOR SAMPLE FIRMS

Source	Total
Personal savings*.	8
Family savings†	13
Personal and family savings	4
Inheritance of business	2
Government loan	1
Total	28

    * Two entrepreneurs received part of their capital from the master of their apprentice course.

    † Extended family savings.

On the basis of evidence from our sample and other studies,[16] it seems reasonable to conclude that small Nigerian industrial entrepreneurs are very dependent upon the extended family for their initial capital.

Usually the entrepreneur does not have a formal obligation to repay family members the money expended on his training and the establishment of his firm. The lack of formal repayments may be very advantageous to the enterprise in its early years when liquid funds may be scarce. However, as funds permit, the businessman is expected to contribute to the subsistence, education, training, and establishment of firms of other family members.

The extended family may reduce the entrepreneur's initial outlays

[16] Archibald Callaway, "From Traditional Crafts to Modern Industries," *Odu: University of Ife Journal of African Studies* 2, no. 1 (July 1965): 42–45; and John R. Harris, "Industrial Entrepreneurship in Nigeria" (Ph.D. diss., Northwestern University, August 1967), chap. 8, p. 36.

29

Economic Development and Cultural Change

in other ways. Family members may provide room and board, and/or building space and tools needed for the enterprise.

The family may also help the fledgling entrepreneur obtain access to suppliers, merchants, creditors, market authorities, local officials, and persons with economic power and influence. For example, suppliers may extend credit to the entrepreneur only if a member of the extended family guarantees payment.

In a few cases, however, the extended family may impede the establishment of a firm. Income which a person might have otherwise used for investment in training or in the establishment of an enterprise may be allotted by the family for other purposes, such as consumption expenditures.[17]
On the other hand, the family may allot the funds for investment in the training, education, or enterprise of another family member whose investment project is expected to yield higher returns. This transfer of funds to other family members by prospective entrepreneurs occurs only rarely, however, since most of them are young and unlikely to have income and wealth to divert.

Finally, the associations of the extended family in the home village affect the businessman's acquisition of labor and apprentices. Most small firms obtain more than half of their labor force from the entrepreneur's home city or village, even when the firm is located in a different city.

It is not surprising that a large percentage of the labor force of the firm is drawn from the entrepreneur's home district. Over a period of years, the extended family of the entrepreneur has incurred a number of (social) claims and obligations which can be satisfied in part when selecting a labor force. In some instances, the entrepreneur may be pressed to hire a laborer or train an apprentice from some family to whom his family is obligated. On the other hand, it may be difficult for the entrepreneur to find persons to evaluate applicants outside his home village.

Frequently workers from the village take their positions for granted and do not work as hard. However, it may be easier to instill a high *esprit de corps* in the work force if the entrepreneur and most of the laborers are from the same district.[18] Thus, on balance, the entrepreneur probably benefits at least as much as he loses from the fact that a large percentage of his labor force is drawn from his home district.

E. The Growth of the Firm

Entrepreneurs from seventeen of the twenty-one firms acquiring additional capital raised at least 50 percent of the funds from profits retained in the enterprise. Part of the expansion of two other firms was financed through

---

[17] See section E, below.

[18] Theodore Geiger and Winifred Armstrong, *The Development of African Private Enterprise* (Washington, D.C.: National Planning Association, 1964), p. 134.

E. Wayne Nafziger

profits. In no case did the entrepreneurs report that new capital had been received from members of the extended family[19] (see table 2).

In fact, the demands of the extended family curtail the use of profits for the expansion of sample firms. As the income of the entrepreneur increases, the number of dependents he is required to support also increases.[20]

TABLE 2

SOURCES OF EXPANSION CAPITAL FOR SAMPLE FIRMS

Source	Total
Profits*	15
Profits and savings†	2
Profits and government loans	1
Profits and loans other than government	1
Savings†	2
No additional capital	7
Total	28

* Profits include those realized from the enterprise in question.

† Savings include those from income of the entrepreneur realized outside of the footwear firm.

Among thirteen sample firms on which reliable data on profit were available, there is a strong positive relationship between the profit of the firm and the number of dependents[21] of the entrepreneur.[22]

This evidence is reinforced by a finding of the Harris study. "It seems clear that family obligations [on the part of entrepreneurs] require substantial amounts of current consumption expenditure, some of which might otherwise be saved and reinvested. . . . The number of dependents is positively correlated with income."[23]

[19] *Inter alia*, entrepreneurs were asked the following questions: Where did you obtain new capital (after the firm had been established)? From retained earnings (or profits)? From relatives? What were their relationships to you? Were they members of the extended family (i.e., from the same household or consumption unit)?

[20] In some cases, relatives of the entrepreneur would withdraw funds from the enterprise exceeding its profits. (See the definition of profit used above.)

[21] A person who receives more than one-half his support from an entrepreneur is a dependent of the entrepreneur.

[22] If X equals the 1964 profit of the firm (in pounds) and Y the number of dependents of the entrepreneur in 1964, $Y = 8.12 + .0039X$. If the t-test is used, the regression coefficient is a significant at the 0.5 percent level.

[23] Harris, chap. 8, p. 36.

Economic Development and Cultural Change

It seems reasonable to believe, though, that the prestige and power afforded the successful entrepreneur by the extended family may provide an important incentive for entrepreneurial activity which may at least partially offset the disincentive effects of sharing income and wealth.[24]

Finally, as indicated in the discussion of the establishment of the firm, the extended family can affect the acquisition of labor and apprentice supply, and assist in obtaining useful contacts with business and persons with economic power.[25]

G. Conclusion

On the basis of this study, some generalizations about the effect of the extended family on entrepreneurial activity in small Nigerian industrial firms can be made. This section summarizes the influence of the institution of the extended family on apprentice training of prospective entrepreneurs, the establishment of firms, and the growth of firms.

Almost all prospective entrepreneurs have been students in an apprentice course, which in virtually all cases is sponsored by members of the extended family. Only rarely does a potential entrepreneur forgo the necessary apprentice training as a result of demands on his income by the extended family. Clearly the effect of the extended family is to augment the number of students taking apprentice courses, which increases the supply of entrepreneurs.

Small entrepreneurs are very dependent upon the extended family for capital to establish a firm. Only rarely is the income of a prospective entrepreneur diverted from the establishment of a firm to consumption expenditures of other family members. Thus, *in toto,* the extended family increases the establishment of firms by entrepreneurs.

Entrepreneurs wishing to expand their firms lose more than they benefit from the institution of the extended family. Although entrepreneurs rarely receive funds from the family for expansion of the firm, the family does

[24] This point was mentioned to the author by John R. Harris.

[25] The effect of the extended family on entrepreneurial activity probably varies from region to region. Several social scientists lend support to the view that the Ibo families (mostly from eastern Nigeria) have a higher percentage of income invested in physical and human capital than families from other Nigerian socioethnic groups. Peter Kilby, "Nigerian Industry in the Northern Region" (unpublished report submitted to the United States International Cooperation Administration, April 1961), p. 8; Robert A. LeVine et al., *Dreams and Deeds: Achievement Motivation in Nigeria* (Chicago: University of Chicago press, 1966), pp. 12, 74, 78–79; Peter T. Bauer, *West African Trade* (London: Routledge & Kegan Paul, 1963), pp. 30–31; James S. Coleman, *Nigeria: Background to Nationalism* (Berkeley and Los Angeles: University of California Press, 1958), p. 333; Victor C. Uchendu, *The Igbo of Southeast Nigeria* (New York: Holt, Rinehart & Winston, 1966), p. 36–37; and Callaway, "Nigeria's Indigenous Education: The Apprentice System," p. 12.

E. Wayne Nafziger

require resources for current consumption which might otherwise have been reinvested in the business.

Is the institution of the extended family a major barrier to entrepreneurial activity, as many development economists contend? The extended family hinders the expansion of the firm by the entrepreneur, but facilitates the entrepreneur's training and establishment of a firm. Without further evidence, there is no longer reason to believe that the extended family has, on balance, a negative effect on entrepreneurial activity. It is quite conceivable that, in many cases, the positive contribution of the extended family to the training and firm establishment of the entrepreneur exceeds the negative effect on firm expansion.

Although it has been possible to ascertain the effect of the extended family on the supply of apprentices, the establishment of firms, and the expansion of firms in Nigerian small industries, it has not been possible to find out the effect of the extended family on Nigerian entrepreneurial activity *in toto*. Further research is necessary to assess the relative significance of positive and negative effects of the extended family on entrepreneurial activity.

Appendix

Over a period of twelve months in 1965, the author spent about 105 hours interviewing representatives and observing operations in the twenty-eight sample firms. The accuracy of the information obtained was checked by examining the internal consistency of the answers and by utilizing oral and written information from government officials, civil servants, officials in statutory corporations, and management and training centers, bankers, suppliers, customers, competitors, and employees acquainted with the firm.

The 1964 data on profits in thirteen of the sample firms, referred to in section E, were based on firm accounting statements obtained from government agencies and/or the enterprises in question.

See Nafziger, pp. 6–15, 20–22, 192–223, for a detailed presentation of the method of the study; the sources of information on sample firms; sources for data on profits; adjustments to the data to insure comparability; interviewing problems, procedures and response; and the structure and use of the questionnaire.

[12]

THE FAMILY AS A FIRM AND
THE FIRM AS A FAMILY IN JAPAN:
THE CASE OF KIKKOMAN SHŌYU
COMPANY LIMITED*

W. Mark Fruin**

Family and Firm in Japan:
The Basis for the Analogy

It is argued often that the key relationship in Japanese social structure and psychology in both preindustrial and industrial periods is that of kinship. This assertion follows from the observable preference of the Japanese to work out their deliberations and aspirations in small groups which often have family-like characteristics. It does not hold logically, however, that small groups are synonymous with families or that groups described as "family-like" are indeed like families. One of the most frequent uses of the analogy involves the relationship between family and firm. On one hand, management writings often allege that Japanese firms behave like families, while on the other, anthropological works report that families in Japan function like firms.

My contention is that the family-firm analogy in Japan is often misleading and generally overworked; its character is usually symbolic or ideological rather than descriptive. I would like to examine the relationship between family and firm in light of the history of one of Japan's larger and older enterprises, Kikkoman Shōyu Company Limited, which is known in Japan as a "family firm" and which offers for our examination a nearly three-hundred-year history of the combined efforts of family and firm for entrepreneurial success.

In discussing the "family as a firm" or "the firm as a family," it is necessary to distinguish between the nuclear family (conjugal family unit), which is not the basis for the analogy, and the stem family, which is. The nuclear family, known in Japanese as *setai* or *kazoku*, is limited in size, scope, and space-time, while the stem family or *ie* is a descent group considered to endure forever. *Ie* persists by virtue of the continuity of property and genealogy through current family members with past and future generations. A *dōzoku* is a large lineage or clan composed of several *ie*, with a main household and a number of branch households where descent from the main house is traced through males (Befu, 1971: 38-46).[1]

*Mark Fruin, a Stanford Ph.D., is associate professor of history at California State University, Hayward. Currently, he is a Senior Research Associate in Business History at the Graduate Business School of Harvard University where he is writing a history of the Kikkoman Shōyu Company Limited.

**The author would like to thank Professors Richard M. Abrams, Alfred D. Chandler, Jr., Thomas G. Hall, and Tsunehiko Yui for their helpful comments on earlier drafts of this essay. He is appreciative as well for a small grant from the Committee on Research, California State University, Hayward, which underwrote a portion of the research contained in this paper and for the institutional support of the Harvard Graduate School of Business Administration in preparing a final version of the article.

[1]Probably the best historical work in Japan on the changing structure and function of *ie* over time

Winter, 1980   JOURNAL OF FAMILY HISTORY   433

According to Smith, a leading expert on Japanese kinship, the residential unit of the *ie* or stem family

> . . . consists of a senior married couple and a married child with his or her own spouse and children. Such a family unit may include as many generations as are alive, but there can be only one married couple in each generation. . . . Among the sacred duties of the head, who controlled the destiny of its living members, was that of preserving the descent line unbroken. He was responsible for passing on, enlarged if possible, the goods and property that he had inherited, and it was his task to see to the proper veneration of the ancestors. . . (Smith, 1978: 45-46).

It should be clear already that the *ie*, the "family" in the Japanese family-firm analogy, is not the family with which we in Western Europe and North America are familiar. Contemporary American family households are not formed primarily to preserve continuity of property and genealogy through time. Marriages are alliances based partly on affection and partly on implicit contractual obligations to share in housework, child rearing, and breadwinning. When one says that the firm is a family or the family is a firm in Japan, however, the metaphor does not refer to the family as a volitional or even contractual alliance. Instead, as most often conceived, the family is a kin-based unit where property ownership and descent relationships are exclusively male-centered and where power and dignity are enjoyed preponderately by male heads of household. As a result, the *ie* apportions obligations and concentrates authority hierarchically by sex and descent.

This characterization is clouded by the existence of family members in the *ie* who

are not biologically related to the household head. The distinction between kin and nonkin, often so important in the Chinese and Western family, is not always emphasized in the Japanese stem family; and as a result nonkin and fictive kin, most often the adopted, have frequently constituted a substantial part of the total household membership. Rather than a genealogical or biological definition of family, *ie* is often determined by who contributes to the economic welfare of the group. Usually the nucleus of such economic groups are kinsmen in the genealogical sense, but kinship is neither the absolute nor exclusive criterion of membership. Logically, therefore, the *ie* is not purely a kinship unit, but often an economic organization dressed up in family trim (Befu, 1971: 39). It is useful, then, to conceive of the Japanese *ie* in terms of concentric circles of "kinsmen": an inner core of consanguines where genetic descent is presumed and an outer core of consanguines where genetic descent is implied but not required.

Such variations in the composition and structure of *ie* and *dōzoku* have fascinated and puzzled many. This has been reflected in a continuing debate among social scientists as to whether kinship in Japanese stem families and lineages should be defined *primarily* by descent or by contributions to corporate property, tools, and knowledge. Most often, *ie* and *dōzoku* are viewed as patrilineal descent groups where economic ties have frequently overshadowed genealogical relationships (Ariga, 1956:199-207; Nagai, 1953). Other scholars, however, have emphasized the genealogical relationships over economic ties, arguing that households come together typically in times of crisis and emergency, and do so on the basis of kinship (Kitano, 1962; Brown, 1966). Moreover, one well known Japanese social scientist has taken the extreme view that *ie* and *dōzoku* are not

---

is being done by Professor Akira Hayami of Keio University in Tokyo. For a seminal study of Japanese lineage and enterprise development, see Nakano, 1964. Most students of *ie* and *dōzoku* emphasize patrilineal descent, but Keith Brown does not. He argues instead for cognatic, not agnatic, descent; see Brown, 1966.

patrilineal descent groups at all, but instead groups based solely on residence and locality (Nakane, 1962: 133-67). Examples of households organized around common residence and occupation may be found in traditional Japan, as they are for that matter in modern America, but such households are the exception, not the rule.

Most social scientists, therefore, have recognized the importance of both genealogical relationships and economic ties in defining *ie* and *dōzoku*, although each researcher tends to emphasize one or the other in practice. Apparently both views have validity, depending on what part of rural Japan is studied. The northeast in particular is noted for a strong economic content in kinship relations, so strong in fact, that genealogical ties are sometimes created to buttress established economic dependencies. The northeast is an area of limited economic resources, single rice cropping, and skewed personal income. The southwest, by contrast, is characterized by a more highly developed commercial economy, double rice cropping, agricultural land reclamation, and more evenly distributed personal income. In the southwest, the kinship relationship normally overshadows the economic content of household composition and structure.

Economic geography, therefore, helps to clarify the nature of membership in Japanese stem families. It is also useful conceptually to separate the question of the family as a descent group from the question of the family as a corporate group, for it is this distinction which so often puzzles non-Japanese. Yet there is really no need for the perplexity since most institutions have multiple purposes, and Japanese households are no exception. Where a variety of tasks are required, different sets of rules can be created to achieve different goals within the same institutional framework. Rules for the maintenance and continuity of kinship relations defined by descent can be

sustained in the face of rules for the maintenance and continuity of kinship defined by property relations.

In short, the Japanese household can be both a descent and a corporate group although in practice, I suspect, one is emphasized over the other. The latter concept and practice undoubtedly have many origins, most of which are lost to historical documentation. I will attempt to sketch the barest historical justification here in order to make the practice more comprehensible. From the thirteenth to the seventeenth centuries, the country passed through a period of internecine warfare and economic disruption. If one was a soldier, a violent and early death was likely. If a cultivator, the prospects were often not better, given the dangers from malnutrition, epidemics, and tyrannical government. Among warriors and peasants alike, a rule of primogeniture evolved during this era as a means of preserving family and property.[2] However small an inheritance, chances for survival and perhaps for eventual accumulation and transmission to future generations were enhanced when the inheritance remained intact and was passed to and through the head of the household, the socially and legally designated heir.

Often in such turbulent times inheritances must have gone unclaimed. Property outlasted its possessors and pursuers, in the sense that property did not pass in an orderly fashion between parties, be they related or not through descent. To circumvent this, the household head was thought to occupy a kind of office, the functions of which outlasted the individual occupant. Over many years of civil and economic turbulence, then, the idea of the house-

---

[2] Primogeniture was modified to the degree that, although one son and only one son inherited, he was not necessarily the eldest son or even one's natural son.

hold as a corporate group, distinct but not necessarily different in personnel from the household conceived as a kinship group, was joined with the concept of the office of household head. In this case, *ie* and *dōzoku* were corporate entities managed by a household head who was nominated to that office on the basis of merit and promise rather than descent. The head was usually referred to by that title, "household head," and this position, indeed that of membership in the corporate household itself, could exist without any current incumbents.[3] The household was, in this sense, a legal fiction awaiting the appointment of an executor to carry out its corporate functions, primarily the maintenance and continuity of property and genealogical office.

In short, the traditional stem family in Japan was and is now a flexible institution. While it could be solely focused on genealogical descent, it could be partially or even wholly concerned with corporateness, that is, with property and its management, independent of kinship. Since anthropologists have done most of the research on Japanese households and since their field work has taken them to various parts of Japan, they tend to emphasize one side or the other of the household equation depending on where their research was done. Those going to the southwest find relatively egalitarian villages where agnatic, and occasionally cognatic, descent defines the character of family groups. Sojourners to the northeast, by contrast, find an area of relative economic backwardness where households are often linked more by economic than by kinship ties. Since the Japanese household, it would appear, can

be either a kinship or a corporate group, or both, an historical approach to *ie* and *dōzoku* in Japan would permit the unveiling of family strategy and structure over time in response to those features, internal as well as external, which permit and at times compel a household to act as if it were a kinship group at one moment and a corporate group at another.

Thus, the broad definition of family and household in Japan is very different from that in the West, and this elasticity of concept and meaning is one reason why the Japanese have effectively handled the management of single firms and groups of firms within a "family" context. Needless to say, such malleability in the definition of who belongs to a family contributes to the inconsistent use of the family-firm analogy in Japan.

The Family-Firm Analogy

If kinship in the *ie* or *dōzoku* is to be determined principally by descent, a number of anomalies immediately appear in the case of those families most closely associated with the Kikkoman Shōyu Company Limited or its antecedent enterprises. Although traditional Japanese households practiced single son inheritance, it was not always the eldest or even one's natural son who inherited. Adoption was widely practiced in order to provide male heirs when none existed, to substitute a more promising male heir when one's own did not measure up, or to attract a husband for a nubile daughter. In this last case it was common to adopt a son for the combined purposes of marrying one's daughter as well as providing a household successor.

Given the flexibility of recruitment and membership in households provided by adoption, it would be accurate to say that, in the case of households and lineages associated with Kikkoman, economic considerations sometimes overwhelmed

---

[3] I owe a great deal of my thinking on the office of the household head, and on Japanese household more generally, to an unpublished paper by Laurel Cornell, "Patterns of Succession to Household Headship in Japan." (October 20, 1976), Dept. of Anthropology, Cornell University.

Figure 1. Branching Relationships in Mogi, Takanashi, Ishikawa, and Horikiri Dōzoku

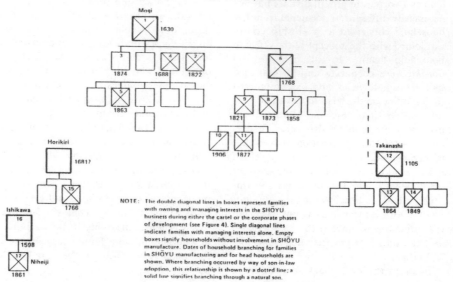

NOTE: The double diagonal lines in boxes represent families with owning and managing interests in the SHŌYU business during either the cartel or the corporate phases of development (see Figure 4). Single diagonal lines indicate families with managing interests alone. Empty boxes signify households without involvement in SHŌYU manufacture. Dates of household branching for families in SHŌYU manufacturing and for head households are shown. Where branching occurred by way of son-in-law adoption, this relationship is shown by a dotted line; a solid line signifies branching through a natural son.

kinship considerations. This can be seen most clearly when households divided or branched for the purpose of initiating a new economic venture. (Branching was a device wherein a main household would establish a separate related household with its own genealogical and corporate identity.)   In only one of six cases of adopted son-in-law marriage did the adoption and marriage coincide with a household branching for the purpose of founding a new *shōyu* enterprise (shown in Figure 1 by a dotted line connecting the households involved).   In the five other cases, however, adopted son-in-law marriages sustained the continuity of family ownership and control in a *shōyu* enterprise.   In the case of male adoption and marriage, therefore, economic considerations, namely the founding and organizing of branch households in the *shōyu* business, appear to have directly dominated kinship decisions involving household division about 17 percent of the time (1 out of 6 cases of adopted son-in-law marriage).   Where household division was

not the concern but household maintenance and continuity in *shōyu* manufacture were, 83 percent of son-in-law adoptions were linked to economic concerns (five out of six cases).

The use of kinship for economic ends is apparent in other ways as well.   The following is a summary of a larger figure detailing kin exchange within 18 families which were involved for nearly three centuries, 1688-1978, in one way or another in the Noda soy sauce business.[4] In order of frequency, the summary lists:

    25 daughter marriages
    11 son branchings
     6 son marriages
     3 son adoptions
     3 daughter branchings
     2 daughter adoptions

---

[4]Noda is located in Chiba Prefecture at the confluence of the Edo and Tone Rivers about one day's sailing distance from Tokyo. Access and ease of river transportation proved to be an important factor in the success of the soy sauce industry in Noda.

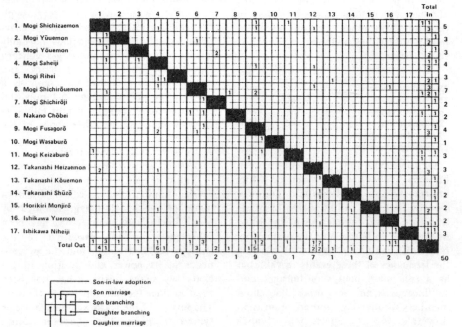

Figure 2. Kin Exchange, 1688-1978

It is immediately apparent that more than half of these events are female centered. Combining marriages and adoptions (adoptions are really a form of betrothal) by sex, we find 27 such events for women and only 9 for men. This difference in frequency is highly significant statistically, indicating that the imbalance was planned and not accidental.[5] I am not implying that the frequency of these events should coincide with the sex ratio of the general population. Far from it. These tallies were taken from family tablets maintained at local Buddhist temples; they were kept not to inform government officials but to record family relationships that were considered significant to the *ie* in either

its genealogical or corporate manifestation. That the imbalance should be so striking is intriguing, and the reasons for it, I believe, have to do with political and economic considerations in the exchange of kinsmen for enterprise development.

Why would families choose to record female-centered events so frequently? These families, it should be emphasized, recorded these activities for their own purposes and from their own points of view, and herein lies the key. A marriage of a daughter involved neither power nor property in a formal or institutional sense. In a patriarchally organized society, power was a privlege of men, notwithstanding occasional deviations from the rule. Likewise property was concentrated, by custom, in the hands of men. Female marriages, therefore, risked neither power nor property and so were ideally suited to

---

[5]Using a chi-square test, the difference in frequency was significant at the 99.99 confidence level.

the initiation and maintenance of family alliances within the soy sauce business. In the same way other sorts of family-to-family interactions might be analyzed, as shown below:

	Property	Power
25 daughter marriages	no	no
11 son branchings	yes	yes
6 son marriages	no	yes
3 son adoptions	no[a]	yes
3 daughter branchings	yes	no
2 daughter adoptions	no	no

Of these 50 events, 14 occur between lineages, 19 within the extended Mogi lineage, 3 within the Takanashi, and only 1 in the Ishikawa. Additionally, 13 events transpire within sublineages of the Mogi lineage and do not involve the main Mogi house of Mogi Shichizaemon. Reviewing the frequency of these events reveals that as a rule main houses of lineages and sublineages send out more household members for marriage and adoption than they take in. In effect, main houses implant their offspring in subsidiary houses. Between *dōzoku* the same rule applies. In fact, the number of women a house is successfully able to offer out for marriage may be interpreted as a measure of dominance, gauged by the genealogical rank order of donor and recipient households and the frequency of in- and out-marriages. This may be related to the desire of main houses to keep their children close to home and the willingness of subordinate houses to take in family members from genealogically prior and therefore socially superior households.

Within *dōzoku*, male rather than female placement in subordinate households assumes importance. This makes sense given the desire of main houses to control

the timing and number of minor houses established within its own line through branching principally and through marriage secondarily. Branchings normally involve "sons," while marriages concern "daughters." If this summary and analysis of kin exchange may serve as a guide to the role of biology in family and enterprise development, then the following epigram may capture the essence of the relationship.

It's better to give than receive,
Between *dōzoku*, dispatch daughters,
Within *dōzoku*, secure sons.

One family, the so-called Kashiwa house of the Mogi lineage founded by Mogi Shichirōuemon in 1768, has been conspicuous in the execution of the strategy outlined above; and the preeminence of its power and position in the Noda soy sauce business has not been equaled since the mid-nineteenth century. The success of the Kashiwa house must be viewed in perspective, however. Since different development strategies have been pursued by other lineages associated with the soy sauce industry in Noda, the wisdom of their investment choices should be weighed against their probable success in the manufacture and marketing of *shōyu*. The sublineage headed by Mogi Saheiji, for example, diversified into local commercial and professional endeavors. Although the main house of the Mogi Saheiji *dōzoku* continued to work successfully in the soy sauce business, sub-houses moved into such occupations as cereal commodity sales, pharmacy, optometry, jewelry, and watchmaking. Although these endeavors have certainly been less financially rewarding than management in the *shōyu* enterprise, working within the community has provided economic security, civic respectability, and personal satisfaction for many members of the Mogi-sa lineage.

The Takanashi lineage's move into the Tokyo warehousing and distributing busi-

---

[a] In the case of son-in-law adoption, even though he brought little property with him, he soon became the heir apparent of the house into which he was adopted and married. This is a case, then, of delayed property transfer.

ness offers another example of diversification outside of *shōyu* manufacture which, on the whole, has compared favorably with the economic success of Kikkoman. A considerable portion of the canned food as well as the alcoholic and carbonated beverages destined for Tokyo is handled by Takanashi branch households. *Shōyu* producers located in Choshi, another well known site of *shōyu* manufacture in Chiba prefecture, have diversified in much the same manner. One of the two Hamaguchi households making *shōyu* in Choshi established a branch household in Edo (Tokyo) in 1645 for wholesaling *shōyu* and marine food products. This branch of the Hamaguchi family, along with the Tokyo branch of the Takanashi family from Noda, account for a large share of the *shōyu* sold and distributed in Tokyo today.

The success and failure of any family strategy of either diversified or concentrated investment, however, depends in large part upon luck; and it was bad luck in the form of two disastrous fires in 1871 and 1908 which has accounted for the declining fortunes of Mogi Shichizaemon, head of the oldest Mogi lineage and once the principal investor in the Noda soy sauce industry (Ichiyama, 1968: chronological appendix 3, 5). But such misfortune was not unique. Earlier in the mid-nineteenth century, for example, bad luck, including successive years of poor harvests, declining business, and famine from 1836 to 1838, reduced the number of soy sauce breweries in Noda from eighteen to eleven (Ichiyama, 1975: 41).

Understandably in an era when raw material availability, the fermentation process, and even transportation were to a considerable degree dependent on weather, climatic fortune was a crucial concomitant of enterprise success. The unpredictability of weather, harvests, commodity markets, and consumer demand cautioned against too great an investment in any one line of endeavor, like *shōyu* manufacture. Yet the costs of making *shōyu* were

considerable, for the most part fixed in the form of fermentation tanks, brewing and extracting equipment, storage and shipping facilities. Moreover, the fixed nature of this rather large investment in plant and equipment did not facilitate either production at the plant or turnover in the marketplace. Fermentation required eighteen to twenty-four months for completion, and market sales were controlled by the *tonya* system of wholeselling and distributing which denied manufacturers direct access to consumers. Accordingly, Noda *shōyu* manufacturers were presented with a difficult investment decision, namely, how much to invest in manufacturing capacity given the lumpiness of investment and the unpredictability of supply and demand markets. Too little invested might result in insufficient capitalization to take advantage of a rise in prices, whereas too much invested might lead to an inadequate return in a poor market and possible bankruptcy as a result.

In this context, the advantages of a large kinship network to support business activities become immediately obvious. In addition to opportunities for sharing information concerning raw material costs, labor availability, and production know-how, kin support in financing *shōyu* manufacturing and shipping facilities was a noteworthy advantage of the Mogi-Takanashi group. Not only did they aid each other in the establishment of enterprises, but they frequently sold and traded all or part of their operations to each other. They also stood ready to purchase the facilities of non-kinsmen in the Noda area. Although such financial dealings were not handled in a formal sense by the combined Mogi and Takanashi families until the days of cartel and incorporation in the late nineteenth and twentieth centuries, such deals were struck informally most often between the head and branch households of a single genealogical line. Where intermarriage and adoption may have created strong ties between households of different lines of descent, close business dealings could be expected to develop over time.

Further examination of the pattern of marriages, adoptions, and household branchings within the four main Kikkoman lineages reveals another way in which the organization of economic relationships and the promotion of social solidarity were primary ends to which the kinship system was employed. The histogram or bar graph which summarizes the frequency of kin exchange between and within the Mogi, Takanshi, Horikiri, and Ishikawa *dōzoku* discloses that the frequency of such events increased regularly until the end of the nineteenth century, at which point a noticeable drop occurs; in the twentieth century, interlineage alliances almost disappear (see Figure 3).

The decline in frequency coincides directly with the formation of a *shōyu* manufacturing cartel in 1887 and the founding of Noda Shōyu Company Limited in 1918, the precursor of Kikkoman Shōyu Company Limited. In other words, once the organization and regulation of economic relationships and activities could be handled by formal institutions designed for such purposes, the kinship system essentially gave up such

functions. The promotion of social and economic solidarity, the protection of property, and the continuity of family enterprise were turned over to the cartel and eventually to its corporate successors, with the result that non-economic matters became more salient for descent groups: children married out of the business; natural offspring, and not adopted scions, assumed family headships; affection and attraction played a greater part in courtship and marriage. Families were less economic and calculating, and they cultivated more personal and emotional matters instead.

Although interlineage alliances in the form of *dōzoku*-based marriages, adoptions, and household branchings no longer play a dominant role in the organization and operation of Kikkoman, family as opposed to lineage membership continues to count for a great deal within the company. Kinship is now employed not for interfamily cooperation but for interfamily rivalry. Household membership has become all important in determining access to the upper reaches of corporate power. Consider the following statistics on family membership and corporate power and privilege. There are 28 main and branch households in the three Mogi, Takanashi, and Horikiri *dōzoku*. Of these 28 households, 3 (11 percent) were of the Horikiri lineage, 6 (21 percent) of the Takanashi, and 19 (68 percent) of the Mogi. Within each *dōzoku*, 13 percent of the Horikiri households engage in *shōyu* manufacture, 50 percent of the Takanashi and 53 percent of the Mogi.

Clearly the Mogi lineage has spawned the largest number of households and spurred the highest rate of participation in the soy sauce business. But within the Mogi clan a main and two branch households contend. The importance of the subdivisions within the Mogi lineage is revealed by the fact that, although all eight of the company presidents to date have

Figure 3. Historical Frequency of Marriages, Adoptions, and Household Branchings 1688-1978

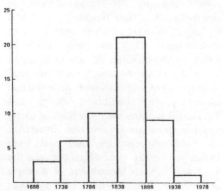

been Mogis (to the exclusion of Horikiri and Takanashi aspirants), within the greater Mogi lineage 63 percent of the company presidents can be traced to the Kashiwa branch household of Mogi Shichirōuemon, 25 percent from the Mogi-sa group of Mogi Saheiji, and only 12 percent from the main house of Mogi Shichizaemon. Household hegemony was reflected as well on the first Board of Directors, with 67, 22, and 11 percent representation for the households of Mogi Shichirōuemon, Saheiji, and Shichizaemon, respectively.

The reasons for differential success rates within the firm according to family membership have been discussed earlier. In sum, the position and privlege of the main house were consumed by conflagration; the Mogi-sa and Takanashi households have chosen to diversify family investments outside of the firm, while the Kashiwa family has plowed back human and capital resources into the *shōyu* business. The Horikiri group was never committed to the soy sauce enterprise in a major way, and it has not played an important owning or managing role in the firm. Likewise, the Ishikawa family has not been active in *shōyu* manufacture since the early twentieth century; it did not continue its representation with the corporation after the cartel was relinquished.

Thus, if one looks at the three *dōzoku*— those of Mogi Shichirōuemon, Mogi Saheiji, and Takanashi Heizaemon— which were most directly associated with Kikkoman or its antecedent enterprises, the analogy between the family and the firm describes accurately the priority sometimes given to social and economic cooperation for enterprise development within the kinship framework. This was most true in the eighteenth century, when in the absence of other devices, the family was institutionalized as a social and economic control group in the management and maintenance of *shōyu* manufacture. Since that time, however, the analogy has become less and less appropriate as individual families have come to pursue social and economic advancement *within* the framework of the corporation.

The family no longer behaves like a firm because the corporation's characteristics of limited liability, perpetual succession, organized and concentrated management, and standard operating procedures make the functioning of a kinship system in these areas redundant. Families now rely upon the firm, rather than vice versa, for economic security and advancement; and enterprise endogamy which once decided the compatibility of interfamily alliances no longer determines the choice of marriage partners.

The Firm-Family Analogy

The three-hundred-year history of the manufacture of soy sauce by Kikkoman Shōyu Company Limited or its antecedent enterprises may be divided into four major phases, each characterized by different styles of ownership and management and by different levels of suitability in using the firm-family analogy. The first phase, the longest, lasted from the late seventeenth through the nineteenth century, and was characterized by the nearly complete separation of ownership and management. Such a seperation is usually considered a unique feature of modern managerial capitalism, which boasts a high level of specialization in functions and consequently the divorce of ownership from professional management. Yet in this early modern period, overall management was divided between separate spheres of ownership, general management (sales, finance, and purchasing), operations management (the production process itself), and labor management (the hiring and contractual conditions of workers). In effect, four different kinds of authority

Figure 4. Organizational Change and Enterprise Development

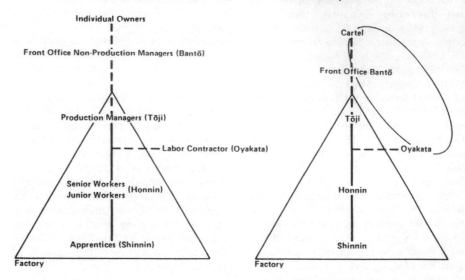

I. 17th Century to 1887

II. 1887 to 1917

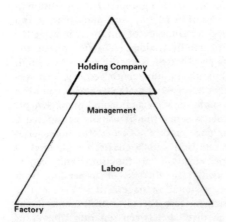

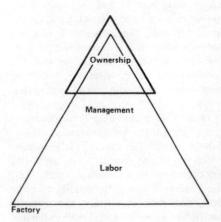

III. 1918 to 1946

IV. 1947 to Present

existed—one financial and three managerial—each distinct and relatively independent of the others. This complex managerial system evolved when the sizes of various facilities producing soy sauce were small, on the order of several hundred full- and part-time workers per factory (*Noda shōyu kumiai shi,* 1919: 16-19).

The separation and specialization of functions, such as sales, personnel, and production, had less to do with the size of the firm or the speed of production than with the failure of owners to manage. Owners did not actually operate or even oversee their production facilities. By custom, they entered their plants no more than twice a year, and on such occasions, they entered in full ceremonial dress and ritually inspected the soy sauce brew in various stages of fermentation. Otherwise, they stayed out of the way, far from production.

Owners in a real sense did little more than finance the operation and "supervise" the front office. They could, if they wished, inspect the books, but records, such as they were, constituted listings of what goods were bought and sold by *bantō*, the office managers and personal retainers of the owning families. It was not possible to calculate costs of unit production, profit margins, or any other refined measure of efficiency or profitability from such records. To consolidate what information was available could prove difficult, moreover, for owners would have to petition their *bantō, tōji* (factory foremen), and *oyakata* (labor recruiters) to pull their lists, journals, and notebooks together. And such an effort on the part of owners would have been entirely out of character, even if it had been possible.

With so little direct involvement on the part of owners and with so many separate yet equal spheres of management, workers suffered. *Oyakata* benefited mainly by fees paid for placing workers, *tōji* concerned themselves with technique and not with industrial relations, and *bantō* were in the front office where they never worried about workers' welfare. The only hint of worker identification came through an association with a production plant based on a particular patrilineal organization. But since owners involved themselves

so little in the actual operation and no one else assumed overall responsibility for enterprise management, a sense of association felt by workers rarely matured into an identification with family and enterprise. Obviously, at this stage of development, no firm-family analogy would appropriately describe an enterprise so fragmented and divided.

A second phase of growth began with the banding together of owners in order to reduce risk and uncertainty. Diverse and separately owned enterprises, numbering as many as 19 different production facilities, were joined together for the purchase of raw materials, the standardization of wages, and the distribution and shipping of finished goods. The owners, in effect, formed in 1887 a cartel, the Noda Shōyu Manufacturers' Union; and during the next thirty years met regularly twice a year, and irregularly more often, to buy raw materials and to fix costs and shipping schedules (*Noda shōyu kumiai shi*, 1919: 11, 19). The regularly scheduled meetings on January 8 and June 20 coincided roughly with the traditional dates of ritualized inspection of factory facilities. Although the tour of the breweries was largely ceremonial, the cartel meetings were not. The January meeting was concerned with fixing labor costs and estimating production levels, while the June assembly set the amount and cost of raw material purchases.

Administrative coordination, in the sense of combining and rationalizing processes internal to the enterprise, was not a cause of the cartel. The reasons for collaboration were almost all external to the actual manufacture of *shōyu*. The functions of the *bantō, tōji*, and *oyakata* changed not at all as a result of the cartels. The chasm between owners and workers remained vast, and it was not alleviated by paternal concern. Workers lacked job security and their wages were arbitrarily set by cartel agreement. When prices fell, so did wages. Wage manipulation was one of the most obvious means to control costs and owners took full advantage of it. Owners did not yet enter the factories that they owned, except upon the New Years and All Souls celebrations, and they continued to leave day-to-day management to others. Thus, even though enterprise-owning families were collaborating to a degree, family operations remained distinct in what counted the most: internal costs of production.

The formation of a cartel, in an important sense, represented the communal regulation of an already existing competition over production costs and production levels between individual *shōyu* makers; these, as pointed out already, the cartel left alone. What it did was to combine the separate factories, really family-owned breweries, into a collusive network to fix some but not all their shared costs, thereby mitigating but not eliminating the competitive struggle. Nevertheless, the cartel forced families of owners to assume some managerial functions themselves, such as the purchasing of raw materials, the setting of wages, the sorting out of distribution and shipping channels, and the determining of marketing territories in the countryside but not in the cities. The latter was left to the *tonya* for determination. In short, in this phase, although families began to cooperate in certain important aspects, they still remained relatively competitive with each other and uninvolved in the internal operation of their own enterprises. As a consequence, the family analogy could not be fairly applied to the collection of enterprises manufacturing *shōyu* in Noda; the families of owners were still quite distinct in organization and operation from their own breweries, those of their associates, and from men who labored in them.

In 1918, a third period of enterprise development unfolds. That year a joint stock company was formed through the merger of some but not all of the cartel members and their assets. At first, eight and then nine families joined to form the Noda Shōyu Company Limited, named for the town in Chiba Prefecture where most of the facilities were located. All nine families were related through descent or marriage; previously all had been independent manufacturers of *shōyu*, *miso*, or *sake*, products made from fermented soy beans or rice. For the first time, owners became managers. Owners made up the majority of senior company officers and members of the Board of Directors. Through the mechanism of a holding company, actual ownership of the firm remained somewhat distinct from the operation of the enterprise, yet ownership and management were merged as never before. The disarray of managerial interests was finally ordered within the structure of the firm. Although it would be wrong to suggest that the new structure was easily accomplished, given the long standing tradition of independent organization and operation on the part of the families concerned, within a decade consolidation and coordination characterized the management of the greatly enlarged enterprise.

Only at this point does the firm-family analogy begin to be truly appropriate. Most top managers in the firm were "family," that is, they were from the firm's founding *dōzoku*; and many middle managers, who were the *bantō* of individual entrepreneurs in prior phases, now came into the newly established corporation along with their family enterprise heads as "lifetime employees" (Fruin, 1978: 273-274, 289). In other words, the firm's management was composed largely of family members and family followers. Accordingly, the appropriateness of the firm-family analogy at this point is mainly biological, or perhaps, genealogical, in view of the importance of

Winter, 1980   JOURNAL OF FAMILY HISTORY   445

adoption in Japanese kinship. Eighty-five percent of the Board of Directors were family, and 63 percent of the first 80 managerial employees came to the company tied to individual family members on the Board.

Of course, it was possible for the firm-family analogy to be valid without Kikkoman's genealogical underpinning. Especially in joint stock companies which were independent of any *zaibatsu* association, it was rather common to have both dispersed ownership and paternalistic management. In fact, the lack of concentrated ownership in such cases probably inclined professional managers toward paternalistic management as a means of securing worker compliance. The best examples of this sort of firm-family analogy come from the textile industry where firms like Kanebo Spinning were well known for paternalistic management (of a largely female work force) and widely dispersed stock ownership. Thus, in the early twentieth century, it was possible to have a paternalistic firm with a "family-style" but without family management or even closely held ownership. Such firms were more the exception than the rule, however, in the view of the prevalence of family-owned and closely-held enterprises in prewar Japan.

In the case of Kikkoman, the suitability of the analogy in the genealogical sense soon faded, as the firm grew in size and as nonkinsmen came to outnumber kinsmen in management. Within a decade of incorporation, the number of employees doubled from one to two thousand; sheer size dulled the aptness of the genealogical analogy. Then an extraordinary thing occurred which made the family-firm analogy even more appropriate than previously.

In 1927-28, a strike of 218 days, the longest labor strike in prewar Japan, erupted at Noda Shōyu Company. The strike was not only long, it was bitter,

politically motivated, and received national attention. It took an appeal to the emperor himself, among others, to bring the strike to settlement.[7] In the end, 1,300 employees were fired, although two-thirds eventually came back, and the company was faced with the need to rebuild its public image and its internal morale. The firm-family analogy was employed to these ends.

The first public announcement of the firm-family *ideology* which I have been able to find occurred within weeks following the strike settlement. The company began a campaign of employee education which preached that all employees, from Board members to shop sweepers, were members of one "family" (*ikka*) united in a spirit of industry and common purpose. For Kikkoman, spiritual kinship, as symbolized by the firm-family analogy, was the road to company rejuvenation following the labor strike of 1927-28.

The transmutation of a biological or genealogical analogy into an ideological one at Kikkoman was not an isolated event. It happened commonly at other companies in the country generally. Kikkoman's analogical transformation coincided with efforts of the Japanese government to instill in all citizens the belief that Japan was a patriarchical state, whose people were related to one another and to the emperor, the supreme father of the nation. The theory of the patriarchical state with the emperor as father is usually known as *kokutai*, and it became the central belief of modern Japanese ideology from the late 1880s until 1945. The thesis of Hozumi Yatsuka (1860-1912), who is credited with being the chief architect of the state-as-household ideology, was simple and direct: the state is the household writ large; the household is the state in microcosm; they

---

[7] The emperor became involved, in part, because Kikkoman had been a supplier of *shōyu* products to the Imperial Household.

Family Business

differ only in size, and they are made one through the medium of ancestor worship (Duus, 1976: 118).

More precisely, that part of the *kokutai* theory concerned with the identity of state and household was known as *kokka*. This concept stressed the equivalence of state and household in both a biological as well as an ideological sense. Officially, the correspondence of state and household was not made by way of any intermediary institution. Nevertheless, firms like Kikkoman sought to juxtapose themselves between the state and household with the following construction: state ↔ firm ↔ household. In spite of the attempts of many enterprises to provide a bridge between state and household in their programs of employee education and socialization, the state never sanctioned their efforts, and many right-wing groups were publicly critical of such endeavors. But concepts of *kokka* and *kokutai* remained extremely useful to enterprise owners and managers in their efforts to secure the loyalty and the labor of their employees.

Insofar as businessmen were effective in their use of the firm-family analogy, it was largely because officials at all levels of society were employing the ideas of *kokka* and *kokutai* to counter the growing political and economic unrest which disturbed Japan from the first decade of the twentieth century onward. In 1906, the government began its "Every Village a Family" campaign to consolidate the deities worshiped on the local level into one shrine. About the same time, slogans like *kigyō-ikka* or "the enterprise as family" became widely current. Kikkoman's employee education program in the aftermath of the great Noda strike was representative of a national effort to enshrine the family ideologically (Hirshmeier and Yui, 1975: 206-211). Unlike a biological or genealogical analogy, an ideological analogy is infinitely expand-

able in space and time, since it is symbolic rather than substantive. This accounts in part for the enthusiasm with which Japanese leaders pressed such family-based political and ideological analogies on their own as well as on colonial peoples before and during the Pacific War period (Maruyama, 1963: 1-24).[8]

Since World War II, Kikkoman has entered a fourth phase of enterprise growth where the legal, ideological, and even genealogical foundations of the firm-family analogy have disappeared. Holding companies, which provided the device by which family ownership in the firm was concentrated and protected, have been abolished legally. The emperor has been demythologized, no longer providing the essential element in the ideological analogy. The household, *ie*, is no longer a legal entity, and its head has been stripped of his power and authority. As a result, firms today cannot presumptuously appropriate power among kinsmen, be they real, fictive (adopted), or symbolic, as in the case of the emperor. A new egalitarian ethos of democracy undercuts the traditional partriarchal attitudes and policies. It coexists surprisingly well with a host of paternalistic benefits which Japanese firms provide for their regular employees. But such benefits as medical plans, housing subsidies, annual pay

_____

[8] The patriarchal authority of the family and state could be transferred to the corporation because the distinction between government and household (public and private), so basic to modern Western European thought, was undeveloped in Japan. As a result, Japanese managers enjoyed an authority which derived from more than their economic and managerial responsibilities; their positions carried moral weight and great social and political importance as well. Accordingly, the divisiveness which characterized labor conditions and colored labor-management relations in the West could only be repeated superficially in prewar Japan because managers, as heads of enterprise, combined the private authority of owner-operators with the public power of state officials.

increases, and job security should not be misunderstood. They derive from postwar employee rights, not patriarchal or even paternalistic gratuity. They are as much in evidence in large American and European companies as they are in Japanese firms (Taira, 1970: 184-203).

Though large companies may continue to espouse managerial ideologies that speak vaguely of "the firm as a family," the legal, political, and biological-genealogical scaffold behind the analogy is gone. Without formal underpinning, the firm-family analogy no longer requires respect or even lip service. Yet, as a cultural ideal and as a characterization of the flexibility in *ie* structure and membership, the analogy remains viable. A genealogical basis for the analogy continues to be found in the prevalence of family-based enterprise in Japan even today. Ninety-nine percent of Japanese firms, by absolute number, are classified as small- and medium-sized enterprises. They continue the tradition of family identification with enterprise, since the core of self-employed and nonpaid family members in such operations amounts to 15 percent of all gainfully employed Japanese (Small and Medium Enterprise Agency, 1975: 50; Chūshō Kigyōchō-hen, 1975: 337-347).[9] In these firms, size, control, and management make the firm-family analogy apt, just as it was appropriate in the earliest days at Kikkoman following incorporation. For Kikkoman today, however, its four thousand employees, performing mostly specialized and professional jobs, make even an unofficial and

informal use of the firm-family analogy inappropriate.

Yet problems of interpersonal relations and organizational behavior are most salient in large firms. As a result, they devote a far larger share of their earnings for employee socialization and corporate welfare programs than do small firms. They can, of course, more easily afford to do so, but size of enterprise rather than per capita cost seems to determine the necessity of such efforts. Paradoxically, therefore, it is in large Japanese firms rather than small ones that the firm-family analogy has greatest currency today. In use, however, it is less an analogue than a simile. The prewar analogy of genealogical and ideological equivalency of firm and family has been transformed into a postwar simile of cultural proclivity. That is to say, the firm has become like a family in an emotional sense because company employees in Japan tend to identify themselves emotionally as well as intellectually with their firms or, more accurately, with their work mates. This tendency is understandably more evident in firms that provide more extensive in-company training and fringe benefits. The Japanese display a cultural preference for affective as well as instrumental work commitment which large firms are more easily able to take advantage of through their considerable emphasis on corporate welfare and paternalism. In this cultural sense, therefore, the firm *as* a family when used to describe the spirit or feeling of a firm has a certain validity in postwar Japan (Marsh and Mannari, 1976: 199, 202, 213, 253).

Finally, in a more subtle way, the "firm-family" analogy mirrors the continuing competition among the Mogi and Takanashi families for position and prestige within the corporation. Since World War II the competition is not carried out under the guise of cartels, *kigyo-ikka*, or any other firm-family

---

[9] A delightful description of the family character of small industry in Japan may be found in Olson, 1963: 13-33. It should be noted that the official definition of what constitutes a small- and medium-sized enterprise in Japan has changed. Before World War II, a firm with less than 100 employees fell into the category; from 1945-65, the cutoff grew to 300 employees, and since 1966, the upper limit has been moved to 500 employees.

analogy. As employment and promotion within the firm for family members are no longer patriarchal duties or rights, families have had to become more frankly competitive with each other within the context of the corporation. By agreement, only one son—most often, the eldest—from each family in each generation has been allowed to join the company in the postwar period (although two out of nine families have managed to circumvent this rule). As a result, families carefully groom that scion, for a family's corporate prospects are anchored on his future. Recently, a prestigious postgraduate education in business and economics from the finest universities of Japan and the United States has been commonly added to a son's natural talents. The competition among families has produced what has been called in other situations "whiz-kids," and it is through the extraordinary socialization as well as the abilities and efforts of such sons that family stakes within the firm are maintained and, if successful, advanced. In short, since the Pacific War, the firm is no longer an extension of family property and pride; instead, families have come full circle to rely upon the firm for purpose and direction. In this sense families follow the firm, and the firm-family analogy has a certain authenticity for the relatively few Mogi and Takanashi family members in Kikkoman today.

Conclusion

Comparisons are odious and analogies are never perfect—or so we are told. But there is no denying the close and constant interaction of family and firm for over three centuries in the case of Kikkoman Shōyu Company Limited. And yet in spite of the plasticity of form and function displayed by the traditional Japanese stem family, family and firm were and are different and distinguishable. The genea-

logical, the ideological, the cultural, and the socio-economic uses of the family analogy in Japan must be descriptively and conceptually separated. Otherwise, reliance on the family analogy by Westerners and even Japanese to describe small and occasionally large group behavior in Japan will result in ambiguity and imprecision. Such analogizing has been historically inappropriate in most cases when applied to Kikkoman, and accordingly it is particularly misleading and misinformed when aimed at the larger, more mature, more diversified, and internationally-minded firms which characterize Japanese enterprise in the world today.

BIBLIOGRAPHY

Ariga, Kizaemon
1956 "Introduction to the Family System in Japan, China, and Korea." Transactions of the Third World Congress of Sociology 4:199-207.
Befu, Harumi
1971 Japan: An Anthropological Introduction. San Francisco: Chandler Press.
Brown, Keith
1966 "Dōzoku and the Ideology of Descent in Rural Japan." American Anthropologist 68:1129-1151.
Chūshō Kigyōcho-hen
1975 Chūshō Kigyō Hakushō (White Paper on Small and Medium Enterprise). Tokyo.
Duus, Peter
1976 The Rise of Modern Japan. Boston: Houghton-Mifflin Company.
Fruin, W. Mark
1978 "The Japanese Company Controversy." Journal of Japanese Studies 4-2:267-300.
Hirschmeier, Johannes and Yui, Tsunehiko
1975 The Development of Japanese Business. Cambridge: Harvard University Press.
Ichiyama, Morio
1968 Kikkoman shōyu shi (A History of Kikkoman Shōyu). Tokyo.
1975 Noda no rekishi (A History of Noda). Nagareyama.

Kitano, Seiichi
  1962 *"Dōzoku* and *Ie* in Japan: The Meaning of
        Family Genealogical Relationships." In R.
        J. Smith and R.K. Beardsley, eds. Japanese
        Culture: Development and Characteristics.
        Chicago: Aldine.
Marsh, Robert and Mannari, Hiroshi
  1976 Modernization and the Japanese Factory.
        Princeton: Princeton University Press.
Maruyama, Masao
  1963 Thought and Behavior in Modern Japanese
        Politics. London: Oxford University Press.
Nagai, Michio
  1953 "Dōzoku: A Preliminary Study of the
        Japanese Extended Family Group and its
        Social and Economic Functions." Interim
        Technical Report No. 7. Columbus: Ohio
        State University Research Foundation.

Nakane, Chie
  1962 "Analysis of Japanese *Dōzoku* Structure."
        Toyobunka Kenkyūjo kiyo 28:133-167.
Nakano, Takashi
  1964 Shōka dōzokudan no kenkyū.   Tokyo:
        Miraisha.
Noda Shoyu Kumiai shi
  1919 (n.p.) Noda Shōyu kumiai-shi. Noda.
Olson, Lawrence
  1963 Dimensions of Japan. New York.
Small and Medium Enterprise Agency
  1975 The Shift to an Economy of Slow Growth
        and Small Business. Tokyo.
Smith, Robert J.
  1978 Kurusu: The Price of Progress in a Japanese
        Village, 1951-1978.   Stanford: Stanford:
        University Press.
Taira, Koji
  1970 Economic Development and the Labor
        Market in Japan. New York: Columbia
        University Press.

[13]

THREE TYPES OF THE MARWARI FIRM

THOMAS A. TIMBERG
American University, Washington D.C.

No institution has been as important in traditional Indian commerce or in traditional commerce in general as the family firm. The varying contours of that firm in the pre-modern period determine to a considerable extent the development of the firms that emerge to take part in modern economic activities, especially industry. The varying types of the traditional firm are in themselves crucial institutions in the traditional economy. Because of the persistence of features of that economy into the present, they even help in understanding aspects of the present-day Indian economy.

Materials for this particular study are primarily the individual Marwari family/firm histories, more than 1000 in number, which I gathered for use in my doctoral dissertation.[1] The Marwaris, whom these histories represent, were an emigrant group, numbering perhaps 300,000 by 1921, composed of the members of several commercial castes originally domiciled in Northwestern Rajasthan and its environs. They spread throughout India at an accelerated pace in the eighteenth and nineteenth century, and constituted one of the major elements in the trading class in that period and today. It can further be argued that the organizational details of all the major North Indian commercial communities, and their historical experience are sufficiently similar, that the Marwaris may illustrate many characteristics of other segments of the Indian trading class as a whole.

Some parts of this consideration appeared in more extended form in an earlier issue of this journal and the section on "Speculators and Industrialists" was presented in somewhat different form at the

---

1. Thomas A. Timberg, "The Rise of Marwari Merchants as Industrial Entrepreneurs to 1930," Ph.D. Dissertation, Harvard University (Cambridge, Mass., 1972).

2   THOMAS A. TIMBERG

March 1971 session of the Association of Asian Studies in New
York City.[2]

The Family Firm

The traditional family firm takes deposits and makes loans, collects
and transfers government funds, engages in retail and wholesale
trade as the opportunity offers itself, opens first processing (ginning,
milling), then manufacturing factories, transfers funds for its clients
to distant cities, and opens branches as the numbers of sons,
nephews, and trustworthy clerks permits. A single day's transactions may include futures, large scale encashment of bills of trade,
insurance, commission purchases for export, and household expenses. Gadgil quotes from Moreland, a historian of the Mughal
era (1525-1775):

> Virji Vora was eminently a merchant, that is to say a buyer
> and seller of commodities, and his business extended to any
> class of goods in which there might be hopes of profit; but
> at the same time he freighted ships, he acted as a banker, he
> received deposits and he arranged remittances by means of
> bills or letters of credit to his branch houses. The activities
> of the firm of Malaya were equally multifarious, and I have
> not noticed any record of a banker as distinct from a mer-
> chant, or of a prominent merchant confining his transactions
> to a particular line of goods.[3]

Those whose primary business was "shroffing" narrowly defined, that
is banker on the indigenous model, also served as intermediaries for
the joint stock banks, taking their money, as they did that of the
general public, as demand deposits. All enterprises, however, in-

---

2. Thomas A. Timberg, "A North Indian Firm as Seen Through its Business
Records, 1860-1914: Tarachand Ghanshyamdas, A 'Great' Marwari Firm," *The
Indian Economic and Social History Review*, VIII (September 1971), pp. 264-283.
3. W. H. Moreland, *From Akbar to Aurangzeb* (London,1923), p. 158 cited in
D. R. Gadgil, *Origins of the Indian Business Class*, N. Y. (1959), page 29.

volved elements of moneylending.[4] The family firm readily took on the function of "peak" firm in an industrial combine, of the managing agency for newly founded industries. The "peak" firm serves a central function analogous to that of the managing agent for a wide variety of subordinate enterprises. Its legal relationship to them may be that of a banker or consultant, managing agent, selling or purchasing agent, large stockholder, or simply protective aegis.

Though the family firm appears at first undifferentiated, I will suggest three types of Marwari firms—the "great" multi-branch trading firms, the banians and brokers in the major export and import markets, and the speculators in futures.

The following sections show that the activity of each of these types of firms, though multi-faceted, usually had one or another central thrust, or function, which played a different part in accelerating the progress of the Marwari emigrant community as a whole and in determining the further evolution of the firms themselves.

A. Great Firms

Of the three "ideal types" of firms we will consider, the "great firms" are the first in point of time. I dealt at length with these great firms in a previous article in this journal and need now only summarize their functions.

"The Great Firms", were possessed of large resources disposed of through a large number of branches scattered through India, and occassionally abroad, and involved simultaneously in a large number of lines of trade and economic endeavor. They were important to the other Marwaris as customers, commission agents, bankers, employers and principals as well as providing much of the commercial infrastructure on which migrant Marwaris relied.

It is perhaps best not to think of them as single firms, since typi-

---

4. The profits to wholesalers lie, not as in the United States in a margin given by the factory to wholesale customers (this may not exist or is nominal), but in the interest paid by retailers on advances to them, often 9-10% per annum. Those who perform the wholesale function often also receive the 1-1 1/4% brokerage and banian's commission I refer to later. Of course, this refers to firms in the period of which I speak, before 1930. Many firms now use a system similar to that in vogue in the U.S.

4 THOMAS A. TIMBERG

cally they were a congery of interacting firms belonging to closely related members of one family. Just as Bhagoti Ram Poddar, the founder of Tarachand Ghanshyamdas (the main "great firm" dealt with in my previous article) had many descendents—and his descendents spawned many large related firms, so also was the case with many other large firms. The descendents of Sargandhas Dadda of Phalodi (who lived in the mid-17th century) in Jodhpur, also founded numerous firms.[5] Like the Poddars in Ramgarh, the Dadda's created a merchant's city state in Phalodi.[6] The senior branch was connected with the Bikaner court from 1767 onward. Another branch had a firm, Udaymal Chandmal, with branches in Hyderabad, Deccan, and Calcutta and yet another was a leading banker in Indore.

Many of the largest firms were primarily bankers. With headquarters at Ajmer or in Bikaner they were initially moneylenders to the Rajputana rulers. The Dadda's were especially prominent in Jodhpur, Bikaner, Indore, Hyderabad, and Jaisalmer; the Bapnas of Pathua in Indore, Kotah, and Jaisalmer; the Lodhas in Jaipur, Jodhpur, Kishengarh, and Shahpura; and the Pittys and Ganeriwalas in Hyderabad.[7] Bhagoti Ram, too, was supposed to have been treasurer to a Nawab, and his descendents', Mirzamal's, business included moneylending to the rulers of Bikaner and the Punjab. Like Tarachand Ghanshyamdas, too, the owners of the large firms often remained at their headquarters in Rajasthan long after the bulk of their business was conducted through their chain of branches outside, and the leading branches were often operated through clerks. However, the proprietors of most of these firms

5. S. R. Bhandari, *Oswal Jati ka Itihas* (Bhanpura, Indore, 1934) hereinafter *Oswal*, pp. 265-276; Balchand Modi, *Desh kee Itihas mee Marwari Jati ka Sthaan* (Calcutta, ?), pp. 500-501; Umraolal Dadda, Interview in Ajmer, 1971.

6. A. H. E. Boileau, *Personal Narratives of a Tour through the Western States of Rajwara in 1835* (Calcutta, 1837), p. 99.

7. For Daddas see Note 5 supra; for Lodhas see *Oswal*, pp. 247-250 and Sampatmal Lodha, Interview in Bhilwara, Rajasthan, 1971 and Kundanmal Mehta, Interview in Calcutta, 1971; for Bapnas see *Oswal*, pp. 197-210 and the memorial volume for Sir Wazir Bapna, Om Prakash Sharma, *Eek Yug, Eek Purush* (New Delhi, 1969), for the Pittys and Ganeriwalas see S. R. Bhandari, *Aggarwal Jati ka Itihas*, Vol. I (Bhanpura, Indore, 1937) hereinafter *Agg. I*.

were more actively involved in their management than those of Tarachand Ghanshyamdas and more likely to send their sons out to actively run their branches.

Bankers with headquarters in Rajasthan like the Poddars and Daddas bargained for and received from the princely state rulers criminal and civil jurisdiction over their own employees—both to protect the employees from harassment and to strengthen their own control over their firms. Returning clerks might be closely questioned or even imprisoned in the proprietor's dungeons for suspected embezzlement. These two concerns—for control over the firm's personnel and autonomy from vexatious harassment—seem to have been keynotes of great firm organization.

Some of the great firms like Bansilal Abirchand of Nagpur and Tarachand Ghanshyamdas tried to have each branch operate independently—and balance its books on its own. These naturally had more rudimentary central books. The branches of Bansilal Abirchand by the 1880's sent only semi-annual statements to the proprietors. This lack of centralized control is somewhat unusual in Marwari firms and especially contrasts with the practice of Seth Goculdas Malpani of Sevaram Khushalchand of Jabalpur.[8] Goculdas would spend nine months of the year on the road meticulously checking the books of his clerks. He transferred the clerks frequently and without warning, so that they would not have time to "cook" the books before they left. He made a policy of never putting relatives together in the same branch firm.

To secure their headquarters from vexations, many of the larger banking firms decided to shift them to safer ground. For the Poddars and the Daddas with their protected merchants' city states—there was no need to move. But other firms found Ajmer, an enclave of British territory, provided a physical security still lacking in the princely states. The Muhnots of Riyan (the famed Riyanwala Seths—who were reputed by folk-saying to own "The Maharaja and half of Marwar"), and a branch of the Daddas

---

8. Assaram Rathi, Interview in Nagpur, 1970; see J. Mukherjee, *Raja Gokuldas Jivan Charitr*, (*Biography of Raja Gokuldas*) (Bombay, 1929), pp. 45-49.

6   THOMAS A. TIMBERG

moved to Ajmer.[9] Two other prominent firms of bankers—the
Lodhas and the Sonis—made their fortune in Ajmer as it became a
national center for state banking and an entrepot for trade.

The early gazetteers indicate that because of the Maharajas' protection equally important banking centers had emerged in Bikaner
and Jaipur. Jaipur's leading bankers were reported to have a
capital of seven million pounds sterling in 1879.[10] Bikaner's bankers
were supposed to have 55 million Rs. in capital in 1930.[11]

As Marwari businessmen moved out of Rajasthan, the great
banking firms extended their branches to serve them. The Jora-
warmal Gambhirchand Soni firm of Ajmer was founded by Jora-
warmal (died 1858) on the proceeds of some successful opium
speculations in the late 1820's.[12] By 1850, it opened an office in the
banking center of Jaipur. In 1855, another branch followed in the
opium mart of Mandsour in Malwa, followed by another in 1862 in
nearby Kotah, and finally by a branch in 1866 in Calcutta.

The marauding armies of the late eighteenth century, too, often
required their treasurers to keep branches to serve them all over
India. Thus we notice the Daddas moved to Indore and the Riyanwala Seths to Poona to serve various Maratha clients. The British
government made much the same demands—and the heir of the
Riyanwala Seths, Hamirmal, added interests in the Punjab to those
he had accumulated in Central India because of his connections
with the Gwalior court, when he accompanied Henry Lawrence's
invading armies into the Punjab in the late 1840's.

The choice of fellow community members as staff was a normal
device to assure loyalty to the firm. Hanna Papanek notes in a
study of the Memons, a Muslim trading group from Gujarat, a

---

9. Vallabhdas Riyanwala, Interview in Bhilwara, Rajasthan, 1971; Surajmal
Riyanwala, Interview in Ajmer, 1971; Shivdutt Tiwari and Nauratanmal Riyanwala,
Shri Gulabh Darshan (Ajmer, 1930); *Oswal*, p. 74.

10. J. Digges La Touche and Captain C. E. Yate, *Rajputana Gazetteer*, Vol. II
(Calcutta, 1879), p. 150.

11. Bikaner Banking Enquiry Committee, *Report of Bikaner Banking Enquiry
Committee* (Bikaner, 1930).

12. Sir Bhagchand Soni, Kt., Interview in Ajmer, 1971. Sir Bhagchand was kind
enough to allow me to inspect some of the older records of the firm.

strong preference for better known fellow community members as employees.

This limitation does not extend to business partners. Tarachand Ghanshyamdas seems to have traded with the entire spectrum of contemporary Calcutta business. As Hanna Papanek reported in her study of the Memons, her respondents were surprised at the notion that community considerations would affect brokerage—an impersonal relationship—though they found such considerations normal in the question of employment.

The extensive business and organizational sophistication of Tarachand Ghanshyamdas were not exceptional for a firm of this "great firm" type. Another of the large firms, Bansilal Abirchand, had major centers in Bikaner (where its proprietary family had been located since 1598), Nagpur, and Indore. The firm was of assistance to the British during the revolt in 1857 and was rewarded with numerous government treasurerships, contracts and so forth. By 1908, the firm owned 17 villages, two cotton textile mills, 20 cotton gins and presses, and a multi-branch banking business, complete with deposit facilities. British officers in the smaller towns often kept their accounts with it. One of the firm's regular projects in the period 1919-1939 was the seasonal transfer from Central India and back of 3 million Rs. to cover its trading operations in Burma.

Each branch of the firm functioned as a separate unit—though several branches in the same town might be under the general supervision of a senior clerk. Each branch manager had full authority to run his branch as he saw fit. Though Nagpur's four branches, for example, were nominally specialized in banking, gold, grain, and cloth all were empowered to do any sort of trading. Each branch manager was, in later years, supplied with a wide ranging power of attorney for the firm. Centralized bookkeeping was rudimentary, as we noted previously. But as with Tarachand Ghanshyamdas there seem to have been few cases of embezzlement—though one clerk is reported to have fled Nagpur with 30,000 Rs. during the interwar period (1919-1939).

Relevance

The great Marwari firms formed both the meshwork on which

8   THOMAS A. TIMBERG

the Marwari emigrants spread themselves through the country and exemplified the steps by which the Marwari businessman progressed. In the former role, they provided credit, information, and initial employment to Marwari emigrants. In the latter role, the great firms moved into commercial line after commercial line to forward their business fortunes, to turn a profit where it might be turned. First wool, then opium and imported cloth, jute and cotton, and finally industry marked the steps in their and the general Marwari community's evolution.

B. Banians and Brokers

Lineaments of a System

The bulk of Marwaris were originally engaged as intermediaries between domestic producers and consumers and foreign exporters and importers. No matter what the commodity, by the midnine-teenth century the final stages of this intermediation usually had some common features.

Local retailers and purchasers operated on perhaps six month credit of a limited amount from "wholesale" storekeepers in the larger market towns (themselves sometimes the clerks or branch managers of larger firms). The term "wholesale" must be qualified since all firms from the lowest to the very highest in the pyramid would often sell directly to final consumers at the same rate, or almost the same rate, as to "retailers."[13] Further, even the smallest village storekeeper might create another stage by sharing his small profit with yet lower level peddlers or purchasing agents.

The market town stores purchased and sold through their branches or commission agents in the port cities. The actual extensions of credit were undoubtedly an important element in these hinterland port city connections and the extension probably went both ways, depending on the relative financial position of the two parties. The commission agents may have dealt directly with the European firms (read also Parsee, Jewish, Armenian firms) or they used the services

---

13. A. Cohen, "Tradition, Values and Inter-role Conflict in Indian Family Business," D. B. A. Thesis, Harvard Business School (Cambridge, Mass., 1967).

of a broker, or they had to use the services of another firm which may have had the restricted privilege of dealing with a given European firm. Some European firms, especially those purchasing raw jute or cotton or importing cotton piece goods, did not restrict their dealings in this way. The European importers often appointed a guaranteed broker, colloquially "banian", usually remunerated with a 1% commission on sales, who had to guarantee the trustworthiness of other Indian businessmen who dealt with the firm. Simple brokers (in the cloth import trade) were often given 1/4% on their dealings. In the jute trade, too, the European sellers with whom the Calcutta firms dealt directly received a $1\frac{1}{4}$% commission—of which they passed on 1/4% to their Indian underbrokers.[14] The relations of the "guaranteed broker" and his firm were usually far closer than this simple relationship would imply. The guaranteed broker's approval was necessary for sales, and he could thus allocate the stock among the various dealers. Sir Badridas Goenka in his *Memoirs* mentions that brokers used to come to visit his brother, Sir Hari Ram Goenka, in his garden on Saturdays to get allocations of packets of piece goods. Sir Hari Ram was guaranteed broker to Ralli Bros.—sole broker, as the Thacker's of 1915 reports it—and Ralli Bros. was the greatest of the cloth importers (at least by the time of the First World War).[15]

Originally banians had much wider responsibilities than seem to have been imposed at the turn of the century.

A banian is a person by whom all purchases and sales of goods, merchandize, and produce are made and through whom all shipments are made on account and on behalf of the merchants or mercantile firm in whose establishment he is banian. Such a banian is therefore responsible for the quality and quantity of the goods, merchandize, produce and shipments made through him or his Sircars or servants whom he employs. He has to make good any deficiency in weight

---

14. S. C. Mitter, *A Recovery Program for Bengal* (Calcutta, 1936), pp. 74-96.
15. B. D. Goenka, *Mere Sansmaran* (Calcutta, n.d.), p. 15.

10   THOMAS A. TIMBERG

or quality, to make compensation for any fraud in shipment
of such goods or produce.[16]

As British firms began to own their own warehouses and apparently
were able to oversee the care of their goods themselves, the banian's
role apparently evolved into that of the guaranteed broker. In
many cases, he may still have also looked after the goods. The
role, however, seems to have diminished over time. S. B. Singh
asserts that the importance of the banians for British firms began
to decline even before 1810.[17]

The guaranteed broker was responsible for disposing of the firm's
goods at the highest possible rates, and if he failed could be replaced. He usually supported his European principals with a large
interest free or low interest loan and introduced them to the complexities of the Indian market.[18] Besides cloth, guaranteed brokers
seem to have been regularly employed in the opium trade, sometimes in raw cotton, and by banks. They were sometimes found in
gunny and jute.[19] The banks dealt with Indians in foreign exchange, by buying bills on foreign importers of Indian goods from
various Indian brokers. Some of the banks also appear to have
purchased hundis, and extended margin credit to the larger Indian
businessmen. Perhaps it is to approve Indian brokers for this
purpose that they used their banians.[20]

The device of a sole selling or purchasing agent seems to have
been most common in manufacturing industries such as cotton textiles and sugar, where financial participation in the firm's initial
equity was often rewarded by an agency. Thus the Singhanias in
Kanpur were major financiers of the early Kanpur mills and receiv-

---

16. N. K. Sinha, "Indian Business Enterprise: its Failure in Calcutta (1800-1848),"
Bengal Past and Present : Diamond Jubilee Number (1967), pp. 112-113.

17. S. B. Singh, *European Agency Houses in Bengal* (Calcutta, 1966), pp. 8-9.

18. Hukumchand v. Radhakrishen, Calcutta 916 *All India Reptr.* in 1925 refers
to such a deposit.

19. Rishi Gemini Kaushik Barua, conversation in Calcutta.

20. S. M. Edwardes and R. E. Enthoven, *Gazetteer of Bombay City and Island*,
Vol. I (Bombay, 1907), p. 297, and following.

THREE TYPES OF THE MARWARI FIRM   11

ed sole selling agencies for them.[21]   Even today, as indicated in a study by Leon Hirsch of the North Indian sugar industry, deposits by those with sole selling agencies are important sources of capital.[22]

The jute industry seems to have been more reluctant than cloth importers to make Indians guaranteed brokers—perhaps because it had less use for their capital or market connections. [23] The mills apparently purchased three months futures contracts through their European agents and these in turn must have developed means of certifying brokers' reliability. Indians did not deal extensively in the hessians market, until the First World War. The 1915 Gazetteer of Hissar district already notes emigrants from Bhiwani among the more prominent poineer hessians traders. The poineers in hessians include Lakshmi Narain Kanoria, closely connected with McLeod and Co. from 1887, and M. D. Somani and G. D. Birla, who are already noted as hessians traders in 1915. The entry of Indians into the hessians market may have required the exercise of the new power accumulated during the First World War.

Naturally enough, the "banians", the guaranteed brokers to the largest firms, were the leaders of the community of Shekhavati Aggarwals in Calcutta—to which they belonged and whose members largely relied on their patronage. This was even true to some extent of the Bengali banians before 1850 in regard to the larger Bengali community[24].

Exchange of Roles

As we noted, the banians of the larger European firms were initially Bengalis. An exhaustive list in 1863 shows one non-Bengali firm.[25] Later, the Bengalis were displaced to some extent by Khatri

21. Lakshmi Narain Tripathi and Narain Prasad Arora, *Kanpur ka Itihas*, part II: *Udhyog aur Byavsay* (Kanpur, n. d.), p. 285.

22. Leon Hirsch, *Marketing in an Underdeveloped Economy* (Englewood, N. J., 1961), pp. 167-168.

23. Mitter, *A Recovery Program*, pp. 76-94.

24. S. N. Mukherjee, "Class, Caste and Politics in Calcutta, 1815-1838," S. N. Mukherjee and E. Leach (ed), *Elites in South Asia* (Cambridge, 1970), pp. 44-45.

25. *The New Calcutta Directory for 1863*, compiled by A. G. Roussac (Calcutta, 1863), VII, pp. 35-41.

THOMAS A. TIMBERG

merchants from the Punjab. Finally, the Khatri merchants declined in face of the Marwaris and remained only as banians to the importers of woolen cloth. Like the Bengalis before them, the Khatris apparently suffered from an insufficient network upcountry (i.e. the lack of a "resource group") and high overheads.[26] India is not the only country where such networks were relevant. A similar lack of a "resource group" explains the difficulty the denizens of the rich Southern Fukien province experienced in becoming comparadors (Chinese agent generals) to European firms in nearby Hong Kong.[27]

The leading banians to European business houses in Calcutta were quickly recognized by Marwaris as their communal elite. Like the Chinese compradors, to whom they were often compared, the leading banians were closely related to one another by ties of patronage and marriage.[28] Though closely related by marriage to the great firms, too, their fortunes were more often founded in Calcutta itself.

Some of the first firms to undertake the banian role were from among the great firms. Devkararandas Ramkumar Chokhani of Nawalgarh is listed as a banian to Ludwig Duke in 1878.[29] Gursahaymal Ghanshyamdas (an earlier name for Tarachand Ghanshyamdas) was apparently banian to Crook and Rowe before 1860, and Sevaram Ramrikhdas (a Singhania firm of Mirzapur and Kanpur) to Ralli Brothers before 1880.[30] Tarachand Ghanshyamdas itself became banian to Shaw Wallace and Sevaram Khushalchand Malpani was eventually banian to Jardine Henderson.[31]

---

26. "Lala Babu" Damodardas Khanna, Interview in Calcutta, 1971; Modi, *Desh kee Itihas*, pp. 414-418.

27. Yen-Ping Hao, *The Comprador in Nineteenth Century China* (Cambridge, Mass., 1971), pp. 173-177,

28. Hao, *op. cit.*, pp. 172-173.

29. *Thacker's Indian Directory for 1878* (Calcutta, 1878), p. 288 and thereafter.

30. Modi, *Desh kee Itihas*, pp. 414-418; Sir Padampat Singhania, Interview in Kanpur, 1970.

31. Seth Gobind Das, Interview in Delhi, 1970.

THREE TYPES OF THE MARWARI FIRM   13

Some Exemplars

Saraf and Musuddi

Tradition reports that Nathuram Saraf of Mandawa, the first Marwari banian, moved to Calcutta in the late 1830's as a super-cargo on one of Sevaram Ramrikhdas' goods boats from Mirzapur, a river port roughly 500 miles from Calcutta.[32] He got his initial employment under Ramdutt Goenka, then Sevaram Ramrikhdas' chief clerk in Calcutta. He became, again according to tradition, banian to Kinsell and Ghose (a Bengali European partnership of the sort that declined radically after the 1848 panic). According to tradition, he displaced Nikkamal Khatri, then one of the leading Khatri banians. Later, and here our sources are firmer, he became banian to Hoare Miller, one of the leading European firms. Saraf's business expanded so rapidly that he called a large number of relatives and associates from Mandawa—our source names 11. He opened separate "basa" for Brahmins and Bania immigrants—to accommodate those he called. In 1870, he retired to his home in Mandawa and to Jaipur city, where he lived out his days as an important banker to the princes of Rajasthan.

The banianship was given to his head clerk, Ganeshdas Musuddi (died 1882), whose family continued it for many years.[33] The Musuddi family firm was still banian to Hoare Miller in the 1930's as well as a jute and oil seeds broker to them, and running its own shop for imported cloth in Calcutta.

Goenka

Most banians did not retire to become court bankers. They employed their resources to consolidate their position as heads of the Calcutta Marwari community and extend their contacts in the European business community. Occasionally, one family would provide banians to several British firms. The descendants of Ramdutt Goenka, Nathuram Saraf's first boss, provided several such banians.[34]

32.. Modi, *Desh kee Itihas*, pp. 439-448.
33.   Modi, *Desh kee Itihas*, p. 500; *Agg. I*, pp. 535-536.
34.   Modi, *Desh kee Itihas*, pp. 473-479; Sir Badridas Goenka, *Sansmaran*.

14   THOMAS A. TIMBERG

Ramdutt continued his duties as chief clerk for Sevaram Ramrikh-das, but his brothers are reported to have started, immediately on their arrival in Calcutta, as commission agents and brokers, assisted by his patronage.   At first, Ramdutt had special relations with Kinsell and Ghose.   After the demise of that firm, he resigned his post with Sevaram Ramrikhdas and became an independent cloth broker to Kettlewell Bullen.   At about the same time, he founded his own firm, Ramdutt Ramkissendas (circa 1848).   Apparently the family had early connections with the Greek firm founded by Alexander Ralli.   Sevaram Ramrikhdas was supposed to have been the Ralli banian first.[35]   Shivbaksh, Ramdutt's nephew, was already employed in a responsible way by the Ralli firm before his uncle's death in 1864.   One source reports that he was the actual executive of the firm.[36]   In any case, when Shivbaksh resigned as banian because of some differences with the Rallis in 1880, they were insistent on a Goenka replacement.   Ramchandra, Ramdutt's grandson, was made the Ralli banian and the relationship continued.

Ralli was the largest importer of cotton piece goods and among the leading exporters of raw jute and hessians.   This position was to no small extent attributable to the Goenkas' efforts.   The same seems to have been the case with Surajmal Jhunjhunwala's relation with Grahams.   Apparently, the new Marwari banians rose more by the progress of the firms with which they were associated than by the initial act of getting their banianships.

The Goenka firm retained its association with Kettlewell Bullen— and after the turn of the century actively entered the jute trade. Both Hari Ram and Badridas were recognized leaders of the Marwari community and sat as its representative on the Calcutta local government and later in the central legislature.

Jhunjhunwala

Often linked because of its importance with the Goenkas was the Jhunjhunwala firm at Grahams'.   Lalchand Kayan had arrived in Calcutta in the 1830's from Surajgarh and established a firm, Lal-

---

35. Sir Padampat Singhania, Interview in Kanpur, 1971.
36. Modi, *Desh kee Itihas*, pp. 473-479.

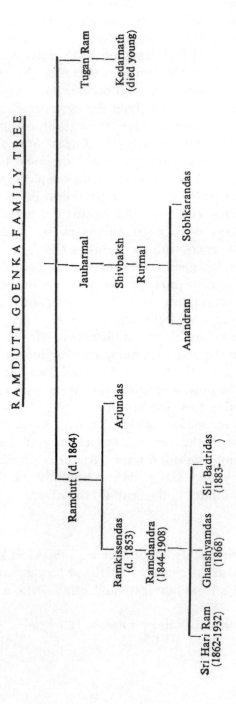

RAMDUTT GOENKA FAMILY TREE

16 THOMAS A. TIMBERG

chand Baldevdas, in opium and cotton, with branches all over eastern India.[37] He died in 1875 and his sons continued his business. One branch of the family entered the stock market in 1915 and established a series of lead and canning factories in the 1920's.

Lalchand's son-in-law, Surajmal Jhunjhunwala (1850 [?]-1894) arrived in Calcutta in 1867 and by January 1868 had become a metals broker to the large Bengali-owned firm, Pran Kissen Law.[38] He soon transferred to the firm's piece goods section and then left the firm entirely to work with Smellie and Co. In April 1868, we find him back with Law as "Senior Broker." He was also made a broker to another firm owned by the Law family, headed by Abhoy Charan Law. A decade later, in March 1879, Pran Kissen Law became piece goods banian and Surajmal, sole piece goods broker to Graham and Co. Somewhat later, Surajmal seems to have taken over the banianship himself as well as handling for a period the banianships of Hoare Miller (Musuddi) and Gladstone Wright while the heirs to those banianships were minors. He died in 1894 and his leadership role and banianship were inherited by his son, Shivprasad (1878-1935).

Jatia

Luckily we have extensive material on the large firms like Tarachand Ghanshyamdas. The Goenkas and Jhunjhunwalas are listed in several biographical dictionaries and I have read memoirs of some important members of those families. The other leading banian who would complete the picture of the four fiirms we named, Sir Onkar Mal Jatia (1882-1938) has left less of a record—though I understand a biography is in preparation for him, too. Unlike Hari Ram Goenka (1862-1932) or Surajmal Shivprasad Jhunjhunwala (1878-1935), his contemporaries, he was not an active leader of

---

37. Modi, *Desh kee Itihas*, p. 431; *Agg. I*, pp. 509-510.

38. *Rai Surajmal Jhunjhunwala Bahadur* and *Rai Bahadur Shivprasad Jhunjhunwala*, typescripts, n.d.; Modi, *Desh kee Itihas*, pp. 490-494; Kumud Lal Dey, *The Law Family of Calcutta* (Calcutta, 1932); listed in Jnanendra Nath Kumar, *The Genealogical History of India*, Part I (Calcutta, n.d.).

the Marwari community.[39]   Sir Hari Ram prevailed upon him to
make donations and attend key public meetings but his primary
orientation was toward the European business community.   Though
impeccably orthodox in matters of food and worship, he preferred
western clothes and lived in a Victorian garden house on the
Howrah side of the Hooghly River, across from Calcutta.

His grandfather, Mahaliram, had been a partner in the firm Sadhuram Ramjidas, based in Khurja (80 miles from Delhi and more
than 1000 from Calcutta), one of the "great firms" we referred to
earlier.   He probably moved to Calcutta to oversee some of its
operations, or else after that firm's partition in 1838.   The Jatia
firm maintains a large and old establishment in Khurja, an area
with a large grain surplus and which used to have a large cotton
crop.   The firm presumably shipped much of this wheat and cotton
especially after the opening of the railroad in the 1860s, for export
to Calcutta.   I should add that three large firms of Khurja, all
founded by former partners of Sadhuram Ramjidas, continued to
dominate Khurja—till its recent decline as a grain market.

The origin of the relation with the Yule firm (founded 1863), to
whom they became banians has been, at least for me, shrouded in
mystery.   The connection dates from the time of Ramjidas, Onkar-
mal's father.   Tradition records particularly strong personal ties
between Sir David Yule (1858-1928) and Sir Onkar Mal (1882-1938).
There are also suggestions that the Jatia firm had helped David in
his youth when he was cut off financially by his father because of
some differences between them.   In any case, by the 1880's the
relation seems to have been firmly established.

Yule himself identified with India and Indian businessmen in a
unique fashion.   He was often called "the white bania."[40]   His
office was one of the few in Calcutta in which Indian businessmen
did not have to accept racial slights such as separate entrances,

---

39. Modi, *Desh kee Itihas*, pp. 424-426; Murlidhar Jhunjhunwala, Interview in
Calcutta, 1970.

40. George Slater, *South India, Its Political and Economic Problems* (London,
1936), p. 227.

18 THOMAS A. TIMBERG

"Europeans only" benches, and so forth. David Yule's donations to public causes were significant enough to be singled out as unprecedented—for a European businessman. The commercial community of Calcutta rarely left much to Indian charities. Even his widow continued his connections. She returned in the early 1930's to use her wealth to assist a Marwari firm, Harisingh Nihalchand, in severe financial difficulties.[11]

In Bombay

European firms in Bombay, too, employed banians, mostly Parsees and Bhatias (two of the more prominent commercial communities there). The Parsees and Bhatias did not abandon commerce, however, as had many successful Bengalis. Only a few Marwari firms like the Ruia's and Cheniram Jesraj Poddar adopted these banian roles in Bombay. As in Calcutta, these Marwari Bombay banians, too, came almost exclusively from Shekhavati.

Impact

The banian relationship and the subordinate distributing network, along with that of the "great" firms, provided the economic basis of the Marwari diaspora. On the basis of these networks arose the speculative markets which are responsible for considerable income redistribution in the community. Even more generally, the profits from these networks represented a capitalization fund that was used in the stage of Marwari entry into industry.

On the other hand, these banian relations were essentially conservatizing ones, in that the banians' identification and subordination to British firms kept them from an independent commercial policy of their own. The large banian firms did not move into direct import and export trade on their own; they did not start industrial

---

41. Murlidhar Jhunjhunwala, Interview in Calcutta, 1970.

enterprises; and they opposed social reform and the nationalist movement, at least in the early 1920's.

The banians' commercial position was dependent on their good relations with the British mercantile community in Calcutta; their social position within the Marwari community would have been threatened by the perturbations and fights reform entailed. In any case, the banians having prospered under the old order, human and divine, were reluctant to challenge it. Any reformist urges had to be sub rosa, until the reformist strength was clear. In the early 1920's, the reformers were opposed by an almost solid phalanx of the leading firms in Calcutta. Nationalist sympathies, which were natural in the traditionalist frame of reference many Marwaris held, had to be pursued discretely. When a court case threatened to reveal secret donations by leading banians to the Congress in 1930, one of them committed suicide.[42]

On the other hand, the role of a broker to Europeans, the necessity of continuously confronting their economic overlordship, meant that some felt more strongly the need to compete with them. G. D. Birla notes of his first experience with the English:

> When I was 16 (1908) I started an independent business of my own as a broker, and thus began my contact with Englishmen who were my patrons and clients. During my association with them I began to see their superiority in business methods, their organizing capacity and their many other virtues. But their racial arrogance could not be concealed. I was not allowed to use the lift up to their offices, nor their benches while waiting to see them. I smarted under these insults, and this created within me a political interest which from 1912 until today I have fully maintained.[13]

In the case of Chinese compradors, to whom the banians have been compared, close contact with British businessmen sometimes caused

---

42. Prabhudayal Himmatsinghka, Interview in Calcutta, 1971.
43. G. D. Birla, *In the Shadow of the Mahatma* (Bombay, 1933), p. xv.

20   THOMAS A. TIMBERG

a nationalist reaction—and a desire to compete with the foreigner economically.[44]

The conservatism of the banians began to change during the thirties, at the same time that the traditional cloth dirtribution network collapsed as a result of the development of the domestic textile industry and the boycott of foreign cloth.

It is not clear that any group within the Marwari community's elite (the leading bankers and banians) with the possible exception of some of the new speculators like G. D. Birla, were strongly nationalist before 1930. The nationalist and reformist movements seem to have been initially supported by those whose interests tied them less closely to the British—and one or two scions of old aristocratic banking families. Those who were less explicitly nationalist or reformist like Sarupchand Hukumchand and Sadhuram Tolaram Goenka were, however, sometimes early entrants into industry.

The complexity of the leadership of nationalist movements—the combination of pro-industrial and anti-reformist attitudes—suggest some problems in applying theory to the phenomenon of the banians.

A Theory

One theoretical apparatus which exists to deal with groups like the banians is that used by Soviet scholars.[45] They characterize businessmen of this sort as compradors (from the Portuguese compradores)—applied to those Chinese merchants who dealt for the European houses on the Chinese market. As an almost perfect counterpart of Sir Onkar Mal Jatia we have Sir Robert Ho Tung (1862-1956) of Hong Kong, associated with Jardine Matheson and the only Chinese readily admitted to the English inner circle in that Crown Colony.[46]

---

44. Yen Ping-Hao, "Cheng Kuan-ying; The Comprador as Reformer," *Journal of Asian Studies* XXIX (November 1969), pp. 15-22.

45. Shirokov and Reisner, *Sovremennaya Indiiskaya Burzhuaziya* (Moscow, 1966).

46. Hao, *"Cheng Kuan-ying"*.

The Chinese compradors were apparently employees—employed on contract to handle the "Chinese side of the firm"—not independent businessmen working on commission. In this way the Indian compradors differ from the Chinese prototype which the Soviets use. The functions they performed were often analogous, however. They were responsible for any defalcations by the businessmen and employees for whom they stood guarantee.

In the Soviet framework these compradors are distinguished from national bourgeois involved in trade and industry independently of European firms. More generally the compradors are oriented toward foreign commerce, the national bourgeoisie toward the internal market, "the basic economic interests of which demand the independent capitalist development of the country."[17] The British it is alleged could not meet their demands and they were thus led to support the nationalist movement. From this distinction flows some crucial generalizations: compradors will support imperialism, and the national bourgeoisie, the nationalist movement; the compradors will oppose indigenous industrial development, and the national bourgeoisie support it.

The causation may well work in the other direction. The leading English firms may have discriminated in favor of those known to be especially favorable to British rule. As Blair Kling argues, this may have been a factor favoring the Marwaris in the period 1880-1920, when they were still relatively quiescent, politically, as compared to the Bengalis.[48]

Amalendu Guha suggests that the lack of connection between Parsees and previous regimes argued their loyalty to the British—and made them favored economic collaborators. The growing militancy of Bengalis would have helped disqualify them. On the other hand, there is little indication that the progressive group within the Parsee community was discriminated against commercially

---

47. Amalendu Guha, "The Comprador Role of Parsee Seths, 1750-1850, " *Economic and Political Weekly* V (November 28, 1970), pp. 1933-36.

48. Blair Kling, "Entrepreneurship and Regional Identity in Bengal," in David Kopf, (ed), *Bengal Regional Identity*, (East Lansing, Michigan, 1970).

(Guha grants this in a footnote)—or that specific Bengali firms were let go for their political deviations. Bengali businessmen such as Pran Kissen Law remained relatively conservative, too.

But reality is complex, and Soviet scholars now focus on the dynamics of the comprador's role. In the early period comprador economic activity may be the only one possible. Those with commercial ability may move into comprador functions. As other functions become possible the former compradors may transfer their capital and their interests into new lines of endeavor—or they may be tied to the nascent national bourgeoisie in a fashion which transfers their gains, as through a speculative market.

Shirokov and Reisner in a recent Soviet study on the subject see this transformation as having occurred as early as 1918—and as confirmed in the period 1929-33.[49] My own data would indicate the persistence of many externally oriented firms into a later period.

Hao even grants that the very differentiation of the comprador role may be impossible:

> The distinction between comprador and an independent merchant is usually blurred. . . a "national" capitalist might end up a comprador. . . a prominent comprador frequently became a *bona fide* merchant and competed vigorously with his foreign counterpart.[50]

The ideological effect of working with a foreign firm may be radicalizing (as with Birla) as well as conservatizing. The gains from compradorship may enable opposition as well as collaboration.

While some of the impact of the banian relation on elements of the Marwari community impeded them from undertaking industrial entrepreneurial roles—the total impact of the experience is ambiguous. It is not clear that the banian phase was not a necessary if not sufficient one in their development.

---

49. Shirokov and Reisner, *Sovremennaya*, pp. 5-9.
50. Hao, *The Comprador in Nineteenth Century China*, p. 112.

C. Speculators and Industrialists

Nature of the Data

Unlike other episodes in Indian economic history, the speculative activities during and after World War I have left little in the way of records behind them. Of the ledgers kept by the participants, most turn out to have been destroyed or are unavailable. Any account must rest primarily on the memories of the participants. Of all potential sources these are the most imprecise and hard to verify. Only the crucial role of this speculation in Indian economic development justifies an attempt on such a sketchy basis. One can hope that researchers, over the next few years, will uncover primary sources to add to our knowledge of this period—such as the "vahis," old style ledgers, of participant firms or businessmen's diaries.[51]

The amounts recorded are large and approximate. It might be worthwhile remembering that they represent many times the purchasing power that similar sums would represent today. The Indian rupee, especially in regard to staple commodities, has not been exempt from the inflation that has characterized the world economy since 1940.

The Speculative Market

The futures markets of Calcutta in opium, specie, and later hessians and raw jute were started by Marwaris.[52] Marwari firms record opium futures transactions in several ledgers I examined— one from as early as 1791. Several firms are noted in their firm

---

51. One of the unexplored resources for this study are the diaries of leading merchants of the period—three of which are available in the Fatehpur, Shekhavati area. Other sources which I was not able to use in my thesis study, but which are in existence, are the estate records of the various Shekhavati "thikanas". The records of two of the most important Marwari family/firms—the Chamarias and the Lodhas—are in the possession of the Calcutta High Court while litigation continues over their settlement. The Raja of Santosh is the court appointed overseer for these estates, whose records are apparently not now available for public inspection.

52. *Agg. I.* , pp. 74-88.

24 THOMAS A. TIMBERG

histories as having proceeded to Bombay from Malwa in the 1860's to take part in the opium futures trade.

The prominent Soni firm of Ajmer made its start with a successful opium speculation in the 1820's.[53] A group of Ramgarh bankers failed, apparently in 1859-60, because of an unsuccessful opium corner, though the details of this corner seem obscure.[51]

The rapid oscillations in opium prices, compounded by the unstable conditions of exchange between India and China, where the opium was sold, rendered the opium market particularly unstable— and thus gave it the potential for producing speculative coups. Regular Marwari opium futures trading in Bombay seems to have started in the 1840's—in Calcutta it dates from the 1860's.[55]

It was in the opium futures trade that several earlier Marwari fortunes were made. The leading Marwari opium speculators included J. K. Birla, a founder of the largest industrial house in India today, and several figures such as Harduttrai Chamaria, Nirmal Lohia, and Sir Sarupchand Hukumchand. Chamaria and Hukumchand were "kings" of the speculative markets in their day—and deserve some attention as "types" of the successful speculator. Contrary to one myth, both were born, so to speak, in comfortable circumstances. Harduttrai Chamaria's (1872-1916) father came from Fatehpur in Shekhavati to Calcutta in the 1840's.[56] By the time we are able to follow his family's career, they were brokers to the prominent Bombay firm of Currimbhoy Ibrahim's Calcutta office. By the 1880's, they were able to buy some Calcutta real estate. Harduttrai partitioned the family estate with his brother, Ram Pratap, in 1903— and the partition deed already included a considerable number of large buildings. Hukumchand's family owned one of the largest state banking firms in Indore.

Both Chamaria and Hukumchand engaged in a wide range of enterprises. Chamaria dealt in salt, gold, silver, and opium—as well

53. Sir Bhagchand Soni, Inerview in Ajmer, 1971.

54. Modi, *Desh kee Itihas*, pp. 419-421.

55. *Agg. I*, pp. 74-88; H. L. Dholakia, *Futures Trading and Futures Markets in Cotton*. . . (Bombay, 1942), p. 29.

56. Keshavdeo Chamaria, Interview in Calcutta, 1971; Modi, *Desh kee Itihas*, pp. 553-556.

as conducting a large-scale banking and real estate business. He
organized the first silver futures market in Calcutta. Similarly,
Sir Sarupchand (1874-?) was a major factor in opium, cotton, state
finance, jute, gunny and hessians, specie, and latterly industry.

It was opium, however, that established Sarupchand and Chamaria
as major financial powers. Chamaria's fortunes were established
quite early. The honors and recognition accorded to the wealthy
came to him. By 1900 if not before, he was a regular invitee to the
Viceroy's levees and had been given the title of Seth by the Maharaja
of Jaipur.[57] Chamaria suffered some reverses at the end of the first
decade of the twentieth century. But he and Sarupchand regained
their position in the dizzying speculations of 1909-1913—when the
British policy of curtailing opium exports and the Chinese Revolution helped opium speculation reach its crescendo. During 1909-10,
when the British started restricting the number of opium boxes
permitted for export, the Indian market weakened. Hukumchand
bought 2-2.5 million Rs. of opium on bills of credit ("hundis"). The
price skyrocketed ten times and Hukumchand cleared 20 million
Rs.[58] Then in 1911, Chamaria was the key organizer in the syndicate,
including inter alia, J. K. Birla, which organized the entire opium
trade, and reaped rich profits.

The stockmarket was a second major speculative market. The
Calcutta stock exchange met informally from 1850.[59] The original
brokers were mostly Bengali. In 1863, a list of "Native Share-
brokers" shows few Marwaris; by 1900, there were ten on a comparable list.[60] Babulal Soonee of Didwana, Jodhpur, had been a
merchant in Mirzapur U.P., before 1857.[61] During the revolt of that
year he is reported to have helped an Englishman, who later, as
a highly placed banker, encouraged him to enter the stock market in
Calcutta—possibly around 1870. The firm was formally founded as

---

57. *Englishman*, Dec. 20, 1900; Dec. 24, 1903, p. 7.

58. S. Vidyalankar (ed.), *Hukumchand Abhinandan Granth* (Delhi, 1951), p. 58.

59. A. K. Sur, *Diamond Jubilee: The Calcutta Stock Exchange, 1908-1963* (Calcutta, 1968), pp. 41-43.

60. *New Calcutta Directory for 1863* (Calcutta, 1863), p. 49; *Thacker's Indian
Directory for 1900*, (Calcutta, 1900), p. 361.

61. Shreenarain Soonee, Interview in Calcutta, 1971.

26   THOMAS A. TIMBERG

Babulal Gangaprasad Soonee in 1892 (but I have found references
to Gangaprasad Soonee as a stockbroker from as early as 1872).[62]

Many of the most prominent figures in the market such as Magniram Bangur, Babulal Soonee's son-in-law, arrived a little later—
mainly during the boom in coal shares, 1904-1908.[63] By 1905, more
than one-fourth of the firms in the Calcutta Stock Market were Marwaris.[61] Press lists of attendance at shareholders meetings show
Marwaris in a small minority.[65]

The *Bombay Gazetteer* of 1909 discusses several of the city's speculative markets. The *Gazetteer* notes, with typical British disapproval,
the widespread existence of futures market—"gambling on the
differences in rates"—in various commodities.[66]

The Mercantile and Moneyed classes in the city perform an
enormous amount of speculative business on behalf of up-

62. In a rokarvahi of Tarachand Ghanshyamdas for 1872-1873.

63. Sur, *The Calcutta Stock Exchange*, pp. 43-44.

64. Sur, *The Calcutta Stock Exchange*, p. 117.

65. From time to time stockholders lists appeared in the press in connection with
shareholders meetings. It is possible to allocate the attendants to the various communities roughly on the basis of their names. This does not insure the completeness of
the lists or tell us anything about the size of the shareholdings they represented. For
example:
Capital, Dec. 24, 1888, p. 169—there were three Marwaris and three Bengalis listed
at a meeting of the Indian General Steam Navigation Co.
Capital, Jan. 8, 1889, p. 214—at another company meeting most of those listed
were Bengali, but ten Marwari shareholders were represented by a Bengali attorney.
Capital, Feb. 5, 1889, p. 303—The Shibpur Jute meeting listed: nine Armenians,
nine Jews, twenty-nine Europeans, six Bengali Hindus, two Muslims, and fourteen
Marwaris (represented by a Jewish sharebroker).
Capital, April 9, 1889, p. 501—The Bowreah cotton textile meeting notice listed:
eighteen Muslims, twenty-one Europeans, one Parsee, eight Bengali Hindus, one Gujerati, and twenty-five Marwaris [including Nirmal Lohia (1804-1889), a leading Mar-
wari speculator].
Capital, April 30, 1889, p. 566—Nirmal Lohia is also listed at a Fort Gloster Jute
mill meeting.
Englishman, Sept. 12, 1890, cited by R. S. Rungta, *op. cit.,* p. 164—reports five
Marwaris out of twenty-seven listed at a Fort Gloster meeting.
Englishman, Jan. 19, 1905, p. 15—among listed shareholders at Fort Gloster Jute
are Magniram and Ramkumar Bangur (Ramkumar was Magniram's brother).

66. S. M. Edwardes, *The Gazetteer of Bombay City and Island,* I, p. 299-300.

country constituents . . . in Government Promissory notes . . .
the shares of joint companies, in cotton, in oil seeds, . . . in
wheat, in Rangoon rice, in Calcutta-made gunny-bags and in
gold and silver,"[67]

—as well as in opium.   Marwaris were early participants in these
Bombay markets though their number remained relatively low.
The dominant Bombay speculators were Gujerati Hindus, Parsees,
and Muslims.

The brokers in Bombay were responsible for any defaults by
their principals.   Standard contracts seem to have been the rule
and informal panchayats existed to arbitrate intra-market disputes.
Formal organized markets, partially because of the British view that
futures were illegal gambling transactions, came much later.

The first of the markets to be organized in a formal way was
apparently that in shares.   The Calcutta Stock Exchange was formally organized and provided with quarters in 1908.[68]   A jute
exchange had existed under European auspices since 1892, but one
dominated by Indians was formed in 1906.[69]   The Bombay Stock
Exchange was founded in 1875 and reorganized in 1909.[70]   Other
futures markets remained informal—until the period during and
after the First World War.[71]

Why the Shekhavati migrants showed such aptitude for these
markets is not clear.   Their home areas—Shekhavati and Bikaner—
did have vigorous speculative markets as early as the 1870's.[72]

---

67. *Ibid., loc. cit.*

68. Sur, *The Calcutta Stock Exchange,* pp. 44-45.

69. Thomas Timberg, "The Origins of Marwari Industrialists," in Robert
and Mary Beech, (ed.) *Bengal: Change and Continuity,* Occasional Paper No. 16,
Asian Studies Center, Michigan State University South Asia Series (East Lansing,
Michigan, 1971), pp. 162-163.

70. G. D. Binani and T. V. Rama Rao, *India at a Glance* (Bombay, 1954), p. 930
and others.

71. Rishi Gemini Kaushik "Barua", *Ramdev Chokhany* (Calcutta, n.d.), p. 45. The
old opium panchayat in Calcutta, for example, included Harduttrai Chamaria, Binjraj
Choudhry, Vishveshvarlal Chitraria, Chunnilal Binani, and Shivnand Rai Tiwari.

72. P. W. Powlett, *Gazetteer of the Bikanir State* (Calcutta, 1874), p. 93.

28   THOMAS A. TIMBERG

There is no reason to suppose that these did not represent traditional institutions there. One of the most common forms of speculative transactions were what were called "rain bargains"—
wagers on what day the first rains would arrive. These bargains
because of the relationship of the timing of the rains with the grain
crop may be seen as futures operations. A more familiar type of
bargain was the "teji-mundi" transaction, essentially an obligation
to pay the difference between a stated amount and the market price,
and the Tarachand Ghanshyamdas books for the 1870's refer to
several such transactions in opium. An older ledger from another
firm in the 1790's reports what is apparently a transaction of this
sort.[73] The fact that fellow Marwaris were already doing a considerable ready opium business in the Malwa area, made the opium
futures operation a natural extension for Marwari businessmen,
and one for which they had superior access to commercial intelligence. The sophistication of the Marwari banking system and their
system of accounting also provided the possibility for coordinated
speculation.[71] The Marwari migrants from Jodhpur state, who were
far more numerous in the hinterlands of Bombay than those from
Bikaner and Shekhavati, did not enter speculative markets to any
considerable extent—possibly reflecting their lack of an indigenous
speculative tradition. They had access to the same sort of large
scale banking and commercial intelligence infrastructure as the
Shekhavati firms, as represented by the large firms of Ajmer. Perhaps the orientation of these Ajmer firms, as the century went on to
more honorific forms of commerce like state banking partially
explains the absence of Jodhpuris in the speculative field. Speculation was, however, considered disreputable, even by the established
Shekhavati firms—and the very fact that the Shekhavati Marwaris
were often latecomers to the big cities may partially explain their

73. James Cambell, *Gazetteer of the Bombay Presidency*, Vol IV: *Ahmedabad*
(Bombay, 1879), pp. 66-67; Powlett, *op. cit.*, p. 145.
    74. Thomas Timberg, "A North Indian Firm as Seen through its Business Records,
1860-1914".

option for this route.[75]   More reputable branches of trade had been pre-empted by early arrivals.

Besides the factors of propensity and infrastructure, the Shekha-vati speculative brokers had access to large accumulations with with which to work—the accumulated capitals of the large firms from that area established in inland trade and in intermediary trade in the ports.   In addition, their involvement with the intermediary role also gave them considerable access to the capitals possessed by private Europeans, particularly for speculations on the stock market.

The First World War

The speculative markets of Calcutta were closed at the beginning of the First World War and their participants fled.[76]   Then slowly, with the developing defence demand for sandbags, the lagging jute industry received a fillip.   Most of the major jute shares increased three times in value from 1915 to 1921.[77]   The price of a seat on the Bombay Stock Exchange went up from Rs. 2,900 in 1914 to Rs. 48,000 in 1921.[78]   Speculations based on these developments in jute reflected themselves on both the ready and futures markets for jute shares, raw jute, and manufactured jute products such as gunny and hessians.   Profit possibilities in the import of cement and refined sugar were opened up by the cutting off of former sources of supply like Austro-Hungary and the shortage of shipping.   Grain, cotton, and specie markets also fluctuated and provided speculative oppor-tunities.   Marwaris were able to reap the rewards of speculation on all these markets.

Among them, Keshoram Poddar (1883—1945), the great grandson of one the earliest Marwari traders in Calcutta, Soniram Poddar, specialized in the shares of the New Empire and Clive jute mills managed by McLeod and Co.[79]   He had started in business, while

75. Modi, *Desh kee Itihas.*
76. *Capital*, October 29, 1914, pp. 459-460.
77. Sur, *The Calcutta Stock Exchange*, pp. 46-48.
78. Binani, *India at a Glance*, p. 931.
79. Modi, *Desh kee Itihas*, pp. 576-579; Nagarmal Keria and Purshottomlal Poddar, Interview in Calcutta, 1970 and 1971.

30   THOMAS A. TIMBERG

in his teens, as under-broker to Mitsui—the leading Japanese firm
in India. Next he went into the umbrella and umbrella cloth business. Finally, he became a sugar broker, especially to Rallis, the
pre-eminent European firm in Calcutta. By 1909, he could afford to
build his own house and by the outbreak of the war was already a
prosperous merchant.

When the First World War broke out, Keshoram Poddar rapidly
became a leading stock market speculator. Poddar used his stock
holdings as leverage to be admitted to the restricted circle of firms
permitted to deal directly in hessians and gunny bags with the big
British firms.[80] At the same time, Poddar started the import of
sugar and cement from Java and Japan, to supply the wartime deficiencies.[81] He developed close relations with various Japanese firms
—to the extent that he was able to draw eight million rupees on his
account with the Yokohama Specie Bank in 1918 to complete a
purchase.[82] He became a major Calcutta real estate owner, especially of the blocks of luxury flats for Europeans which had been
constructed over the previous few years primarily by Jewish and
Armenian businessmen.[83] He ventured into the taxi business, ran
ferries on inland waterways, bought a colliery and a flour mill, and
loaned the capital to start the Hindi daily, *Vishvamitra*. At one
time, he dabbled in brick kilns, and was rumored to be cornering
the brick market. At his height, Poddar was supposed to have
been worth thirty million Rs.—but his book-keeping was rudimentary and his approach to business carefree. The reverses he suffered
in the post-war crash turned out to be irreversible.[84]

---

80. Murlidhar Jhunjhunwala, Interview in Calcutta, 1970.

81. Confirmed in an interview with Ezekiel Jacob (Calcutta, 1971) who worked
with E. Meyer, through whose firm the sugar purchase was made. Apparently both
Meyer and Poddar thought they made a good transaction.

82. Purshottomlal Poddar, Interview in Calcutta, 1971.

83. Poddar, Interview above.

84. The judgements given in his decline turn out to be considerable. Keshoram sued his stockbroker for five million and settled out of court for three million. Rs.
In 1926, we see a Lloyd's firm suing Keshoram for 1.8 million Rs. (*Englishman*, March
7, 1962, p. 6).

THREE TYPES OF THE MARWARI FIRM 31

Baldevdas Dudhwawala, another leading World War I speculator, had an uncle who entered the stock market in 1880. After a period working in Mirzapur and Kanpur, Baldevdas and his brother, Basantlal, entered the stockmarket in Calcutta around the turn of the century, presumably with their uncle's sponsorship. Baldevdas controlled trading in Kamarhatti Jute shares during World war I.[85] At his height, during the war, he was making five million Rs. a year from the dividends on the stocks he controlled. many of them purchased on bank credit. Baldevdas apparently had particularly close relations with the British owned banks.

A third prominent wartime speculator was the firm of Vishveshvarlal Hargovind, owned by Vishveshvarlal Halwasiya (1870-1925) and Hargovind Rai Dalmia (both from Bhiwani in Hissar District, adjoining Shekhavati).[86] The firm was active both in shares and gunny (a Bhiwani specialty). Vishveshvarlal's father had been a jeweller in Hyderabad, his uncle had a prominent firm in Calcutta and Lucknow. Hargovind Rai's father had established a firm in Calcutta in 1866. Established in 1890, when the firm Vishveshvarlal Hargovind was partitioned in 1921 each partner took away 25 million Rs.

G. D. Birla and M. D. Somani made sums in the gunny and stock markets as well. G. D.'s brothers (with a separate firm) also did well in various speculations in several different markets. An informant estimated that the total Birla worth rose from 2 million to 8 million Rs. over the war years.

Sir Sarupchand Hukumchand, whom I referred to earlier as an opium speculator, extended his activities into many of the other speculative markets during this period. When he opened his Calcutta office in 1915, it did five million rupees of business on its first day.[87] Hukumchand's specialty, however, was cotton.[88] Sir Sarupchand made 10,000,000 Rs. in the accounting year 1914-1915 and

---

85. *Agg. I*, pp. 363-367; Harish Sharma, *Nathany Smriti Granth* (Calcutta, 1966), p. 54; Modi, *Desh kee Itihas*, pp. 514-515.

86. Modi, *Desh kee Itihas*, pp. 524-525; *Agg. I*, pp. 23-24 and 31-33.

87. Harish Sharma, *Nathany Smriti Granth*.

88. *Ibid.*

32 THOMAS A. TIMBERG

7.5 million in 1918-1919 on the basis of successful cotton corners.[89]

Primitive Accumulation

The mastery of capital these sums represent can be discussed in Marxist terms as "Primitive Accumulation." It is in this light that Amalendu Guha views the opium trade as a key element in enabling further Parsee growth in Bombay. Guha argues:

> "Under colonial constraints, the shipwrights and other artisans could not emerge straight as independent capitalist shipbuilders from their handicraft base—as has been explained earlier. It was necessary for them to enter the lucrative field of export trade in raw cotton and opium for primitive accumulation under British patronage."[90]

Guha had demonstrated in a previous article that British policy was a major cause for the decline of the formerly prosperous Western Indian shipbuilding and shipping industry. The accumulations of funds in the hands of various Marwari merchants during the First World War period would seem to represent precisely the same phenomenon as that of the Parsees accumulation in raw cotton and opium.

Marx's classic formulation of "Primitive Accumulation" at the end of the first volume of *Capital* emphasizes rather different aspects of this concept than would be represented by such an accumulation.[91] Unlike many other concepts in that work there does not seem to be a single general definition of "Primitive Accumulation". Rather it seems to be a description of the period which preceded the era of industrial capitalism, particularly in England. The con-

---

89. I found no press notes on Hukumchand's cotton operations mentioned in his biography. The cotton corners of 1915 and 1914 are the only ones of the various speculative episodes on which I have found press notices. (*Capital*, April 1, 1915, pp. 728-729). The corners were led by Ramchandra Dungersidas (of Fatehpur, Harduttrai Chamaria's hometown) and Ramdayal (manager of the firm Balchand Agarchand).

90. Amalendu Guha, "The Comprador Role of Parsi Seths, 1750-1850."

91. Karl Marx, *Capital*, translated by Samuel Moore and Edward Aveling, ed. Friedrich Engels (Modern Library edition) (N. Y., 1906), pp. 784-848.

THREE TYPES OF THE MARWARI FIRM 33

crete character of the treatment continues in some later work.[92] The emphasis is on the preparation of the proletariat through depriving them of independent means of subsistence and driving them into the labor market. The preparation of the class of capitalists draws less attention.

The lack of a generalization by Marx may indicate his peculiar openness to variations in form at this stage—the stage in which some are enabled to offer employment and some to seek it.

The size of the national product being determinate at any given point, the major task in starting the process of the creation of industrial capital is the diversion of claims over that product to those parties who will use it for productive investment. In the societies with which we are familiar, these claims are usually expressed in monetary terms, and the moneys involved can be stockpiled, in a way that few other goods can. Thus these monetary claims could be accumulated in the hands of potential industrial investors over a long "Primitive Accumulation" period, as a pre-requisite to industrialization itself. But they can equally well be transferred to such investors by sudden speculative episodes, or any other transfer of claims—and even by state fiat. In speculation, unlike some other forms of economic activity, someone's loss is immediately someone else's gain (disregarding the question of hedging services). The possibility of substituting a "period of accumulation" by a shorter episode is one of the ways in which what former writers characterized as "pre-requisites of industrialization", may be mere historical accidents of certain paths toward industrialization.[93]

Given this possibility for the "substitution of pre-requisites", it is not surprising, especially in colonial situations where accumulations may already exist in some hands, if speculative markets serve as a major way to equip the indigenous businessmen with the money they need to transform into industrial capital.

---

92. L. S. Feuer (ed.), *Marx and Engels: Basic Writings on Politics and Philosophy* (N. Y., 1959), pp. 438-441 (letter to editor of *Otechestvennyi Otpiski*, Nov. 1877).

93. W. Rostow, *The Stages of Economic Growth* (Cambridge, England, 1960); Alexander Gerschenkron, *Economic Backwardness in Historical Perspective* (Boston, 1962); Gerschenkron, *Europe in the Russian Mirror* (London, 1970).

34   THOMAS A. TIMBERG

The acceptance of this concept of "capital accumulation" is particularly important because of its implications for the theory of the
entrepreneur.   Many approaches to development emphasize the role
of the entrepreneur as the active agent in economic development.
A focus on capital accumulation countervails the entrepreneurial
emphasis by seeing it and other so-called pre-conditions of economic
growth as a by-product of capital accumulation.[91] This pure capital
accumulation focus, however, neglects the "who-whom" aspect of
capitalist accumulation.   The important thing is not that just any
group gets possession of the societal surplus, but one that will invest
it in socially preferred lines of endeavor.   Whether the beneficiaries
of a given device for capital accumulation will invest that accumulation in industry is uncertain.   That industrial investment must be
doubly determined by the investment possibilities the economy
presents to them and the skills and orientations the owners of the
accumulated capital bring into the industrial period.

The Fruits of Speculation

In any case, it was the speculative gains received by various Marwari businessmen that enabled some of them to start industries
right after the First World War.   In particular, both Sarupchand
Hukumchand of Indore and G. D. Birla started jute mills in 1918-
1919.[95] These were the first large Indian-controlled jute mills.   In
the latter case, however, the equity was widely dispersed among
other businessmen than the Birlas.   In the case of Hukumchand
Jute, the bulk of the capital was provided by Sir Sarupchand himself.   Keshoram Poddar bought a cotton mill from Andrew Yule
for 8 million Rs. in 1918.   Hukumchand proceeded to start an insurance company, a steel rolling mill, and added to his chain of
cotton textile mills.   His first two mills were acquired in 1909 and
1913—both in Indore.   He added one in Indore in 1916, and took
over the management of another in nearby Ujjain from his son-in-

94. Sayre P. Schatz, "The Role of Capital Accumulation in Economic Development," *Journal of Developing Societies* V (October 1968), pp. 49-53.
95. Thomas Timberg, "The Origins of Marwari Industrialists," pp. 164-166.

law in 1918. Hargovind Dalmia bought the Mathuradas Mills for 500,000 Rs. in 1921. Harduttrai Chamaria's children set up two jute mills in the early 1930's. In 1921, the Birlas floated a 1.8 million Rs. equity textile mill in Gwalior, concessions by the Maharaja having determined the shift of its site from Delhi where they already had a mill.

Other commercial innovations were enabled by the speculative gains. In 1917, Birla Bros., in the person of Sonny Gubbay, a Baghdadi Jew from Calcutta, became the first Indian owned Calcutta firm with its own export office for jute in London.[96] The office had to fight hard to get into the market and was not admitted to the "official" Baltic Exchange for several years—but its establishment coincided with the rapid rise of Birla Bros. into the group of the top three exporters of raw jute—where it is to be found by the mid-1920's.[97]

Others used their funds to invest in urban real estate and obtained the position of banians to British firms.[98] Some of the funds were spent on charities—including the bulk of the funds (10,000,000 Rs.) collected in the Tilak Memorial Fund Drive by the Congress, the first major fund raising attempt by the Congress. The period after the war, as I note elsewhere, also covered a sudden explosion of social reformist and nationalist activity in the Marwari community.[99]

Conclusion

Without being dogmatic it seems that the speculative firms were particularly successful as entrepreneurs in the modern period. The great firms, with the notable exceptions of the Jatias and the Singhanias, have receded relatively—the banian firms, again excepting the Jatias and the Goenkas have receded absolutely.

In one sense, each type of firm belonged to a certain epoch. The great firm was most prominent in the era of state finance and con-

---

96. L. N. Birla, Interview in Calcutta, 1970.

97. Various listings in the Calcutta edition of *Commerce* in the 1920's.

98. Poddar and Dudhwawala were most prominent in real estate. Harduttrai Chamaria, himself, started as a banian to James Taylor and E. D. Sassoon before his death. His sons became bank banians and continued in that line.

99. Thomas Timberg, "The Origins of Marwari Industrialists," pp. 166-170.

36 THOMAS A. TIMBERG

voy trade (with private guards and political protection) before the establishment of British rule in India. The banian firm belonged to the apogee of that rule. The speculative firms rose as the British economic dominance fell relative to the Indian. The political and social accidents of these firms corresponded to the necessities of the era to which they properly belonged.

In another sense, all these types of firms were reifications of the same plasma, capital, and all can and did transform themselves one into another. They all belonged to a common commercial culture.

Much as the three persons of the Christian trinity are described as having separate identities but a common essence, so these three types functioned differently, but on common principles.

The organizational mastery this institutional variety suggests was itself a prime advantage to the rise of Marwari merchants in the modern period.

Part III
Training and Organization of Work

[14]

Learning Manufacture: Education and Shop-Floor Schooling in the Family Firm

PHILIP SCRANTON

On September 8, 1902, a young man "21 yr. 5 mos. old" commenced work in the machine shop at James Doak, Jr.'s, yarn factory, a worsted spinning mill in the Kensington section of Philadelphia.[1] The Doak Company was fairly typical of the local textile manufacture, a proprietary firm located in a substantial brick building, employing about 200 workers in the production of specialty textiles, in this case a variety of yarns for men's suitings and fine carpets. Hundreds of such firms operated similarly in the various industrial trades in the nation's greatest manufacturing center, engaging the talents of over 60,000 workers on textiles alone.[2] Yet this young man was special, if not unusual. He was Charles Doak, son of the proprietor, and he, like hundreds of others, was being groomed to succeed to a family business through embarking on his manufacturing apprenticeship, a shop-floor education in the social and technical relations of production. Aided by the diary young Doak kept from 1902 to 1906, we may reconstruct his experiences and come to understand their role in the factory culture of the private firm. Situating this tale within the larger context of industrial (and educational) development will help expose the rarely glimpsed imperatives of proprietary businesses, long overshadowed by historical attention to mass-production corporate enterprises.

DR. SCRANTON is associate professor of history, Rutgers University, Camden, N.J. An earlier version of this article was presented at the 1983 Washington, D.C., conference of the Social Science History Association. The author wishes to acknowledge the helpful critiques offered by Fred Rosen and Steve Meyer and by the *Technology and Culture* referees and to thank the Doak family for their donation of Charles Doak's journal to the Pastore Library of the Philadelphia College of Textiles and Science, the Pastore Library staff, and the Rutgers Research Council, which provided funding to assist revision and publication. He is currently at work on a study of the 20th-century fate of the textile trades in the Philadelphia region and (with Walter Licht) has completed *Work Sights: Industrial Philadelphia, 1890–1950*, forthcoming from Temple University Press.

[1]Charles Doak, Journal, 1902–1906, Archives, Philadelphia College of Textiles and Science, Philadelphia, p. 1 (hereinafter cited as Doak, Journal).

[2]John J. MacFarlane, *Manufacturing in Philadelphia, 1683–1912* (Philadelphia, 1912), pp. 98–99.

©1986 by the Society for the History of Technology. All rights reserved.
0040-165X/86/2701-0003$01.00

Charles Doak represented the third generation of a Scots-Irish family in the Philadelphia textile manufacture. His grandfather, James Doak, Sr., had emigrated from Londonderry, Ireland, in 1844. Initial stays in New York, Newark, and Fall River were followed by permanent settlement in the Quaker City, "where he commenced the manufacture, by hand, of checked cotton goods" around 1847. Handweaving had a durable presence there that would continue (on carpets and fancy goods) well into the 1880s. However, the cotton craft shops were hard pressed by competition from powered mills, and by 1850 the elder Doak had migrated to the Manayunk factory district where "the whole family found employment in the mill of Joseph Ripka."[3]

His namesake, James, Jr., had earlier worked in two city steam mills, first (at age 10) in a picker room preparing cotton for carding and later for a weaving firm. In a decade's labor at the Ripka Mills, James Doak, Jr., rose to a position as a power-loom boss, overseeing production of the cotton pantaloon stuffs that were a specialty of the firm. With the onset of the Civil War, he joined the 23d Pennsylvania Regiment and served through the Peninsular Campaign, when "illness obliged him to enter the army hospital." Discharged from the land forces, James joined the navy in the last year of the war, recovering his health in the bargain. Though mill labor had left him with at best a spotty education, Doak was able to secure postwar employment as a clerk in the insurance office of William Arrott.[4] His return to the mills would be, not as a laborer, but as Arrott's partner in a new enterprise in 1866. Moreover, his entrepreneurial venture would prove far more successful than that launched by his father a generation earlier.

The Civil War, and the cotton shortage that attended it, brought a wool boom to the textile mills of Philadelphia. The profits from weaving millions of yards of army cloths, carloads of blankets and stockings, were funneled into factory construction at an unprecedented level.[5] With the wool tariffs of the war and postwar Congresses providing ample protection, new firms sprouted and rooted in all local trades based on wool use. One of these was the carpet manufacture, in which the construction of plain and figured ingrains[6] was a specialty both of

[3]D. Robson, ed., *Manufactories and Manufacturers of Pennsylvania in the Nineteenth Century* (Philadelphia, 1875), p. 82 (hereinafter cited as Robson, *M&MPa.*).

[4]Ibid.

[5]Emerson Fite, *Social and Industrial Conditions in the North during the Civil War* (New York, 1916), pp. 114–16.

[6]Ingrains were flat, rather than pile, carpets, using two sets of warp and filling, the warp often flax or cotton, the filling wool. All-wool or worsted ingrains were rather fine goods, while the mixed-fiber products were commonly used in working-class homes. See John Ewing and Nancy Norton, *Broadlooms and Businessmen* (Cambridge, Mass., 1955), chaps. 1–3.

42   *Philip Scranton*

Philadelphia handshops and "Eastern" power-loom firms.[7] Renting part of a Frankford mill, Doak and Arrott began with "sixteen [hand] looms," the former overseeing manufacturing and the latter handling commercial details. In the next five years, they moved twice to larger rented quarters as their trade expanded. Though burned out in Christmas week, 1872, they were thoroughly insured (remembering Arrott's background) and used the proceeds to buy the property and erect a new building with equipment for preparation, spinning, and weaving.[8] In his spare moments, Doak enrolled at "night schools and commercial colleges" to upgrade his practical education, and at thirty-four he married Annie Wallace, a niece of a Manayunk textile manufacturer.

The partnership lasted until Arrott's death in 1889, at which time Doak paid the estate "$80,000 for his half interest"[9] and continued as sole proprietor. The value of the Arrott share bespeaks the prosperity enjoyed by the firm but tells little of the strategy that brought such accumulation. During the depressed 1870s, the carpet trades were fairly resilient at Philadelphia,[10] but competition from Eastern power-loom firms drove prices downward. Local manufacturers faced stiff resistance to wage cuts in Kensington; strikes multiplied, and in response James Doak, Jr., and Co. altered its production orientation from carpets to worsted yard goods. By 1880, the firm retained only eighteen carpet handlooms but had added 120 power looms for "worsted coatings" and a new factory building to house them.[11] These goods were becoming a local specialty; as high-ticket and fashionable items, they promised sizable profits if designs capturing the market's fancy could be created.

The firm responded to the great depression of the 1890s by dropping weaving entirely and specializing in fine yarn manufacture. This move both cut the work force by more than half (from 282 in 1893 to 132 in 1895) and allowed the proprietor to focus on servicing regional weaving firms as a manufacturer of producers' goods rather than confront uncertain fashion demand directly.[12] By the end of the

[7]Ewing and Norton, chap. 1; Nancy Levine, "Their Own Sphere" (Ph.D. diss., City University of New York, 1979).

[8]Robson, *M&MPa.*, p. 82.

[9]Charles Doak, Miscellaneous Papers, Archives, Philadelphia College of Textiles and Science, unpaged.

[10]Philip Scranton, *Proprietary Capitalism: The Textile Manufacture at Philadelphia, 1800–1885* (New York, 1983), chaps. 9–10.

[11]Lorin Blodget, *The Textile Industries of Philadelphia* (Philadelphia, 1880), p. 11.

[12]*Fourth Annual Report of the Factory Inspector: Pennsylvania—1893* (Harrisburg, Pa., 1894), p. 122; *Sixth Annual Report of the Factory Inspector: Pennsylvania—1895* (Harrisburg, Pa., 1896), p. 76; *Tenth Annual Report of the Factory Inspector: Pennsylvania—1899* (Harrisburg, Pa., 1900), p. 159.

decade, Doak had his 6,000 spindles humming, employment had rebounded to 225, and his three sons, James, Charles, and Samuel, had
begun their trek toward proprietary succession.

This half-century of a family's involvement in textile entrepreneurship exemplifies the most common form of manufacturing
organization in 19th-century America, for the private firm—either sole
proprietorship or partnership—was far more prevalent than corporate forms. Though the pioneering efforts of New England textile
companies, railroads, and others may have been the harbingers of
"modern business organization," the plain fact remains that before
1900 most industrial workers toiled in shops and mills with whose
owners they had direct face-to-face relations, often on a daily basis. As I
have argued elsewhere,[13] within the cultural boundaries of proprietary
capitalism, manufacturers placed a high value on direct participation
in and supervision of the production process, distrusting management
by hired parties who were not financially "interested" in the business.
To be a "practical" manufacturer, a proprietor had to know not just the
outlines but the intimate details of the materials and machinery his
firm used *and* had to negotiate the commercial and financial mazes of
uncertain markets. To address this latter puzzle (credit and marketing), firm heads either enlisted the services of sales agencies or commission houses or else became partners with individuals with commercial
experience. Such partnerships were codified in the textile and apparel
trades as "Mr. Inside/Mr. Outside" teams, dividing production and
sales responsibilities in the fashion of Doak and Arrott.

The role of family relationships in the private firm was significant at
all stages in the "life cycle" of the enterprise. In Philadelphia, the bulk
of postbellum textile proprietors had fathers who had been textile
workers or shop/mill operators.[14] Marriage was on occasion partly a
device for capital raising or the cementing of trade connections. In the
junior Doak's case, it was deferred until the fledgling firm had passed
its initial crises, signaling the achievement of a level of solidity that
allowed the assumption of family responsibilities. Skilled factory workers starting their own firms tended to be somewhat older than proprietors' sons when commencing on their own account. As a result, the

---

[13]Scranton, *Proprietary Capitalism*, chap. 4.

[14]From a review of 300 firms profiled in Robson, *M&MPa.*, the following information
was gleaned. Of the 300, 276 were proprietary or partnership ventures, twenty-four
incorporated. Among the proprietary group, 368 owners were listed, with biographical
details provided for 289 of these (78 percent). Two-thirds of this pool (197) had learned
manufacturing in the shops, a sixth (fifty-three) had commercial backgrounds. These
figures are suggestive only, for they are by no means a reliable sample of all firms active,
given that Robson treated only persistent firms (80 percent had been ten years or longer
in business in 1875) and that Robson had to rely on voluntary responses to his inquiries.

unpaid labor of their offspring was frequently blended in with that of regular employees, both preserving a family labor system and easing the cash-flow demands of newly started enterprises. Nevertheless, given the small capitals initially mobilized by private firms, even the best attention of their masters could not prevent frequent failures, which drove proprietors back into others' mills and shops either to nurse their discouragement or to spend years in the search for funds and partners with which to start afresh.[15]

If a proprietary firm survived its first few years, adult kinsmen (brothers, cousins, nephews) could be brought in, or brought across, in the case of immigrant family firms, to serve as workers or partners. Ultimately, the mature firm and its aging operators had to face the issue of succession, the admission of sons to partnership that laid the foundations for a generational transition.[16] Clearly, only a minority of private firms lasted long enough to be passed into the hands of the founders' sons, yet the practice was common enough[17] to be worth some exploration. It represents a dimension of that late 19th-century factory culture so ably profiled by Patrick Joyce for the Lancashire and Yorkshire textile industries,[18] in which the firm stood both as an economic enterprise and as a family legacy. As yet we know little of the interior process by which sons were schooled for succession, the activities and relationships inside the mill. With some additional background on the mechanics of transition (ca. 1840–80), an exploration of Charles Doak's turn-of-the-century journal will open the door for a glance at the business of "learning manufacture."

Given the gradual and uneven displacement of craft workshops and their hand labor by factory and powered production, the training of sons in their fathers' trades altered as well. Though the pace of this change was quite different across industrial sectors—in part a function of varied rates of changing market scale, transport costs, and technological development—a broad pattern is evident. Roughly, in the antebellum years, on completion of basic schooling (or, more rarely, high school), sons entered an apprenticeship with their fathers, spending long hours in the shop which ended with elevation to partnership on or after their twenty-first birthday. In later decades, as firms

[15]Scranton, *Proprietary Capitalism*, chaps. 6–10.

[16]For a case study of this sequence, see Philip Scranton, "An Immigrant Family and Industrial Enterprise: Sevill Schofield and the Philadelphia Textile Manufacture, 1845–1900," *Pennsylvania Magazine of History and Biography* 106 (1982): 365–92.

[17]Of partners added to the private firms mentioned in n. 14, three-fifths (129 of 207) were sons of proprietors and another sixth (thirty-five) were kin by descent or marriage.

[18]Patrick Joyce, *Work, Society, and Politics: The Culture of the Factory in Late Victorian England* (New Brunswick, N.J., 1981).

Education and Shop-Floor Schooling in the Family Firm 45

reached beyond local markets, and as the division of labor and powered production altered the manufacturing process, proprietors' sons
were sent to commercial or technical "colleges" (rather than liberal arts
schools), returning to commence their apprenticeship, or, in more
complex firms, to "tour" the rooms of the mill, spending a few months
at each stage of the production sequence. In such circumstances, the
transmission of industrial skills was no longer direct from father to son,
as in the craft shop or small foundry. Instead, sons had to learn from
other workers, whose role as educators was hardly free from ambiguity.

The Bromley clan of Philadelphia nicely captures the older pattern.
The father, John Bromley, a handloom carpet weaver, emigrated from
England in 1841 with his wife and sons, setting up a tiny manufactory
in Philadelphia's Kensington district. Two sons, George and James,
worked for him; the first "assisted his father in the factory until the age
of twenty-one," the second "served an apprenticeship to his father at
carpet weaving" during the 1840s, being made "superintendent of the
factory in 1850." The course followed by a younger son, Thomas
(b. 1835), suggests the awkwardness of transitions. Thomas Bromley
was permitted to continue his formal education until he finished work
at "the High School" in Philadelphia, then entering the factory for the
full course of his apprenticeship. Given this delay, his reception as a
partner came not at age twenty-one but three years later, "at the
commencement of 1860." A further sign that his majority was acknowledged on joining the firm (rather than at an age boundary) was his
marriage (January 10, 1860) immediately following elevation to
partnership.[19]

The same sequence was traced a decade earlier for the Philadelphia
firm of Charles Abbey and Sons, dentists' gold-foil manufacturers.
Here the elder son entered the shop at fourteen (1839) and "after
having served the regular apprenticeship . . . finally became associated
with his father as a partner" following his twenty-first birthday. A
younger son and the founder's namesake graduated from "the Central
High School" and "became an apprentice . . . the same year" (1847).
He was welcomed to membership in the firm six years later, aged
twenty-three.[20] Elsewhere in the city, education through high school
also delayed Isaac Williams's entry at his father's tannery until his
nineteenth year and his partnership until his twenty-fifth (1858).[21] The
value to a firm of a son with "advanced" skills in calculating and reading
was increasingly recognized, but as yet the full apprenticeship term

[19]Robson, *M&MPa.*, p. 43.
[20]Ibid., p. 98.
[21]Ibid., p. 56.

(five to eight years) could not be abrogated. Thus young men were drawn in the late antebellum years into an extended adolescence within the culture of the family firm.

Of course, the mathematical benefits of formal schooling could also be secured through outside experience in the commercial trades or, more traditionally, within the firm under the tutelage of a family member. The external path is exemplified by the experience of John Clapp, who left school at fourteen to work in his father's woolen mills. In 1855, after four years, he departed to "engage in mercantile pursuits," returning at the close of the Civil War to succeed to the business on his father's retirement.[22] For Albert Mershon, the internal path was adequate. Beginning labor in the family furnace manufactory at an "early" age, he progressed to positions of "bookkeeper, superintendent of the works and, at the age of twenty-one, received an interest in the concern" (ca. 1859).[23] Before the war, customary apprenticeships, education through high school, and hands-on experience in merchandising were the three paths which, in various combinations, dominate accounts of the succession practices of proprietary manufacturing firms.

In later decades, with changing dimensions of national markets, appropriate technology (the increasing use of steam power), more clients, more workers, and more paper, the business of learning manufacture became even more problematic. The increased complexity of expanded operations brought two broad tensions to family firms, firms that were most often centered on what we would now describe as "batch" rather than "mass" production formats. On one hand, practical familiarity with the techniques of manufacture was essential to the management of production, to the development of new outputs, the solution of shop-floor problems, and the control of the work process. The young Bromleys' handweaving apprenticeships may have well fitted the world of antebellum treadle looms, turning out sturdy but fairly plain goods. For the postwar world of powered manufacture, their own sons would need more: an understanding of mechanical principles, capacity to innovate in design, an ability to coordinate production on a grander scale. On the other hand, commercial skills were increasingly vital for the management of sales and distribution. If the firm were not to place its market fate in the hands of distant and possibly indifferent "selling agents," its members had to understand credit, sales, discounting, and advertising, as well as the customary bookkeeping techniques. A son could be sent through high and/or

[22]Ibid., p. 395.
[23]Ibid., p. 51.

commercial school, be put through six years of craft apprenticeship, and be farmed out to a commercial house, but he would be nearing thirty by the time the job was done, his father aging all the while. The increasing demands of learning manufacture pressed against an actuarial as well as a psychological barrier. How long would the old man live? How long would his son remain an industrial minor? How was one to define an optimal path for succession that dealt with family dynamics as well as the future of the firm?

To the extent that status mobility was a concern of proprietors, they might well ship their sons off to the University of Pennsylvania or Haverford College, aim them toward the professions, sell their firm to nonkin successors, and retire to dabbling in local politics or community/religious affairs. This surely happened, but it was relatively rare before the First World War, at least in the textile trades (with whose development I am most familiar). If instead the firm was regarded as both a source of profit and pride *and* as a legacy for the next generation, that option was foreclosed for it represented, in precisely the contemporary sense, "selling out." Rather, a redefinition of learning manufacture took shape in the last third of the 19th century. It involved the reconstruction of apprenticeship into the "tour of the mill" and the creation of new institutions for specialized education germane to the needs of proprietary firms.

At this juncture, it is useful to stress the differences between proprietary batch firms and corporate mass producers, for the trajectories of each sector had quite different implications for education, in or out of the factory. As Alfred Chandler and others have documented, for the great firms built or merged in the Progressive Era, problems of coordination and control tested the ingenuity and resources of corporate leaders. The standardization of outputs, complexities of finance, and creation of hierarchical managerial systems that facilitated increasing efficiency and scale of mass operations necessitated the training of ranks of middle-level specialists. While internal and interfirm recruiting of promising individuals was clearly important, the development of institutions fostering sophisticated business education embellished this process. The evolution of the University of Pennsylvania Wharton School (and of the business schools at Harvard, Chicago, and elsewhere) contributed to the solution of the managerial dilemmas of corporate enterprise.[24] Their emphasis on establishing broad, generally applicable principles spoke to the issue of creating order out of the chaos of huge firms. In such schools, one did not learn production as it

[24]Steven Sass, *The Pragmatic Imagination: A History of the Wharton School, 1881–1981* (Philadelphia, 1982); David Noble, *America by Design: Science, Technology, and the Rise of Corporate Capitalism* (New York, 1977).

48   *Philip Scranton*

was practiced in a particular industry, for the grit of manufacturing was abstracted away or filtered through the medium of case studies.

However valuable for mass-production sectors, these educational experiments held little magnetism for the proprietors of batch-productive firms. Throughput refinements and the law of trusts were of little relevance to firms whose viability depended on their capacity to adjust production rapidly to market shifts and whose individual scale was trifling in comparison with the steel or chemical giants. For "practical manufacturers," a particularistic, shop-centered education that systematically exposed the techniques of their trade was mandatory. Such schooling would broaden their sons' experience beyond current practice at the family mill and would compensate for the assuredly uneven quality of their stints as learners in its various departments. With an industrial school at hand, sons might well slog their way through the "rooms" of fathers' factories, but two or three years, not six, would be devoted to such labor.

The creation of industrial schools overlaps with the inauguration of engineering education in the latter 19th century, but there are notable contrasts. Lehigh commenced in 1871 through a half-million dollar grant by railroad magnate Asa Packer, offering a "School of General Literature in addition to four scientific schools of, respectively, civil engineering, mechanical engineering, mining and metallurgy and analytical chemistry."[25] Similarly, the Drexel (1891) and Carnegie Institutes (1901) were opened through the benefaction of vastly wealthy individuals to promote the application of science to technical problems arising in the dynamic corporate sectors. How different were the origins of the Philadelphia Textile School (1884), launched in rented quarters with $35,000 secured from two dozen of the city's 800 textile firms. Through alliance with the Pennsylvania Museum (now the Philadelphia Museum of Art), earnestly solicited donations of equipment, and a politically negotiated annual grant from the state government, the school by the early 1890s offered a composite production-centered three-year course in cotton and wool manufacturing. Students worked hand and power looms, spinning frames, cards and combs from a variety of machinery firms, learned the mechanics of fabric design and card punching for jacquard specialties, and were drawn into the mysteries of dyeing and finishing. The goal was not the mastery of engineering principles but the broadest possible exposure to the practicalities of manufacturing practice. Ideally, these skills

[25]G. L. Beezer, ed., *Lehigh University Catalog, 1979–81* (Bethlehem, Pa., 1979), p. 5.

would be translated into productive innovations when graduates turned from the mill school to the mill proper.[26]

The experiment in textile education mounted at Philadelphia was quickly copied elsewhere in the nation. Textile schools were initiated in the 1890s at Lowell, New Bedford, and Fall River, in Massachusetts, and thereafter in Southern states. By the turn of the century, at least in Philadelphia, a sound solution to the succession problem in proprietary firms had been devised, the marriage of the mill tour and the textile course that together would occupy at most a half-dozen years after completion of high school. Young Charles Doak participated in a variant of this scheme, three years of mill learning, three years of technical education to which were added night courses at the Textile School, leading to his elevation to the position of factory superintendent in 1904, aged twenty-three. After fifteen months in charge of manufacturing, Charles commenced specialty work for which he was now fully prepared, running quality- and cost-control tests throughout the mill, a critical function in a firm whose prowess rested on a capacity to meet exacting standards for batch-produced worsted yarns.

Born April 24, 1881, in Philadelphia, Charles Doak entered the family mill at seventeen, following his 1898 graduation from the city's Manual Training School. He was initially placed in the "Wool Room,"[27] where he spent one year, likely as a helper/learner for the wool sorters, highly skilled men who separated baled fleeces into different grades for use in later production steps. Though his journal refers but once to this stint, the initial placement and the full year he spent there are indeed significant. To the outsider, many industrial raw materials may well appear homogeneous, but for the production process, the varieties and gradations of iron ore, coal, cotton, or wool are a critical and often problematic dimension of manufacturing. As the varieties of sheep and fleece are enormous, and the quality of raw wools varies with climate and region, the complexities of wool buying and processing are vast. In addition, within a single clipped fleece, the fibers will be of quite different production value. The critical role of the wool sorters

---

[26]Though regional proprietors' sons made up a major proportion of PTS enrollment, some of the students were young men seeking entry to textile employment as designers or overseers, perhaps envisioning proprietorship at a later time. Others came from merchant families to learn the manufacturing basics for careers in the commercial end of the trade. In addition, night classes, from the first year, drew skilled workers from the city's textile districts and satellite manufacturing towns and a handful of owners' offspring already involved in mill work. See Catalogs and Annual Reports, Philadelphia Textile School, 1886–1900, Pastore Library, P.C.T.&S.

[27]Doak, Journal, p. 1.

50   *Philip Scranton*

follows directly: "Each fleece is carefully opened and an expert grader pulls the fleece apart and sorts the fibers according to fineness or width and length of fiber, and sometimes according to strength . . . . Fine fibers that are relatively long are reserved for sheer wool fabrics and worsteds; . . . coarse fibers, both long and short, go into rough fabrics and carpets. The best-quality fibers come from the sides and shoulders of the sheep."[28]

Sorting by "feel" takes years to learn; Doak in twelve months would be barely initiated into the craft. However, he would come to appreciate the work habits of the sorters, a notoriously independent-minded crew over whom the mill superintendents had no authority. Though gathered together in the wool room, sorters worked individually "at the board" and were hardly welcoming to outsiders' curious questions about their steady handling of the fibers. Jeff Tattersfield, who passed through an analogous "tour of the mill" at a Germantown worsted yarn firm a generation later, pointed out that his months in the wool room were a misery. The sorters ignored all inquiries and railed when the young Tattersfield was slow in carrying fleeces to their boards. What he learned was secured by watching the work and through talking with the few apprentice sorters in off moments.[29]

Sorters were among the highest paid workers at the Standard Worsted Mills; Doak's discussion of a "Task" and bonus system installed in 1904 gives their hourly wage at 25¢, or $15.00 a week for the sixty hours then in force. The *bosses* of combing, drawing, and spinning rooms earned the same rate, but ordinary help could expect from 15¢ to 7¢ an hour, the latter for spinning "boys." Only the machinist made more than sorters on an hourly basis (26⅔¢), with the mill "Super" receiving a flat $23.00 weekly.[30] Under the bonus system, wool sorters would be expected to handle 5,500 pounds weekly, with a penny premium paid for every 8 pounds over the Task. While no records of the impact or effectiveness of this incentive tactic have survived, some recognition of the sorter's status is evident in Doak's comment that should a week's work fall below the 5,500-pound level, "nothing is deducted."[31]

After his year with the wool sorters, Charles was dispatched to the Drexel Institute for a three-year mechanical course, during which he

[28]Marjorey Joseph, *Essentials of Textiles* (New York, 1976), p. 138.

[29]Interview with Jeffrey Tattersfield, Philadelphia, November 18, 1981. The mill Mr. Tattersfield "toured" was the Dearnley Worsted Spinning Co., located on Chelten Avenue in the city's Germantown district. Still standing, it is currently used as a furniture salesroom and warehouse.

[30]Doak, Journal, pp. 41, 105–6.

[31]Ibid., p. 41.

mastered the principles of steam power. Doak completed this in 1902, and the precise drawings and testing charts that dot the journal testify to the competence with calculations and compass that he developed there. His return to the mill full-time came in September of that year, but formal education continued through night classes at the Philadelphia Textile School, then located in central Philadelphia at Broad and Pine Streets. There his Drexel training and mill experiences were drawn together in courses on the mechanics of worsted production. (Class notes crowd the back section of the journal.) Doak regularly carried puzzles from the shop floor to his instructors and noted their responses, occasionally adding room bosses' criticisms of this advice.[32]

Beginning at the heart of the mill, in the machine shop and engine rooms, Doak moved step-by-step through the full production sequence over the next two years. His journal became a reference volume on the minutiae of worsted manufacture, topic headings in the left-hand margin, dates of conversations and tests scattered throughout, the whole meticulously indexed. While he rarely noted his own activities, it is difficult to imagine him perpetually standing at the side of others' labors. Most likely he served as a variety of "spare hand," available to help smooth the room bosses' tasks each day in a dozen tiny ways. (The tidiness of his entries, including testing charts, suggests that he scribbled in a notebook through the working hours and transferred the more salient points at intervals to the journal.)

The machine shop was located at the southwest corner of the original factory building, on the second floor above the two "Dynamos" and immediately adjacent to separate structures for the engines, pumps, and boilers. It held, among other equipment, two lathes, a grindstone, a drill press, and a "vertical engine."[33] Doak noted: "All the repair work of the mill was done as far as the machinery would permit. Patterns were made and sent out to be cast."[34] Capacity to fashion replacements for worn parts of cards, combs, and spinning and twisting frames of different ages and sources was of special import for a firm meeting specialty, time-critical demands. With a skilled machinist always on hand, long waits for parts could be short-circuited by their on-site manufacture or through having shop-made patterns cast at nearby Kensington foundries.[35]

---

[32]Ibid., pp. 160 ff. For consultations with instructors see pp. 28, 44, 54, 79, 81; on steam, see pp. 111–12.

[33]Ibid., p. 206.

[34]Ibid., p. 1.

[35]The Doak firm's Westinghouse steam engine was a constant source of trouble in this period (1902–6). Major parts could not be locally secured and the suppliers were "very slow." See ibid., p. 147.

52   *Philip Scranton*

After two months in the machinist's shop, Charles spent three weeks in the scouring building. There raw wool was washed in soapy hot water to remove the "grease," animal oils that made up a substantial but variable amount of its weight. There too, after a week's introduction to the machinery, Charles assembled his first production chart, tracking the hourly output of the room through the next twelve workdays. As "the grade of the wool running through determines the speed of the . . . feed," it is no surprise to find wide variations in the amounts of wool scoured daily, from a low of 6,100 pounds to a high of 7,700. The flexibility in the length of the lunch break is more intriguing, for the machinery was "down" at midday for periods ranging from forty to ninety-five minutes over the two-week span.[36] Though the mill's production depended on a set of sequenced steps, there clearly was no fixed "line" that started and stopped in unison. Intermediate products had to be moved from building to building and among floors, allowing a certain softness to time discipline.[37]

At the close of November 1902, James Doak, Jr., directed his son to the carding room, where eight engines raked thousands of tiny teeth-wires over the scoured wool, pulling out burrs and "vegetable matter," straightening the mass into a broad "lap," a blanket-like web 4 feet wide and under an inch in thickness. The eight machines came from four different manufacturers—three cards were English, five of U.S. make, with four of these purchased from Philadelphia textile machinery firms (James Smith, Merill Furbush). In addition to noting the nickname of the largest card (Jumbo) and drawing a scale plan of the workroom, Charles penned extensive notes on the problems that arose in carding (six causes of imperfections in the output, details of adjustments needed when the grade of wool used was altered).

Issues of quality versus volume production surfaced as well, as for example when he noted "the less wool fed to the card, the better it will be carded and the less fly [waste] will be made." Reducing the waste proportion of overall production through slowing down the rate of feed could have significant financial benefits, as the "fly" sold as waste brought 2½¢ a pound, but "if it went on through the card it would be worth 40 cents at the least."[38] When, at the start of February 1903, Doak

[36]Ibid., pp. 2–3.

[37]In this regard it is worth noting that start-up times ranged from 7:10 in the morning to 7:25 and that the end of the workday in scouring varied between 5:30 and 6:00 P.M., the latest time coming on the long-lunch day. Doak made no comment on these matters but did complain in his first critical note that "the temperature of the [scouring] water . . . is given very little thought, and thus is away off" (p. 2). Water too hot increased fiber shrinkage and that too cool impeded the soap's grease removal.

[38]Doak, Journal, pp. 4–8, quotation from p. 8.

was moved to the combing room, that special area in which wool becomes worsted,[39] he took the occasion to calculate the weight loss in scouring, carding, and combing from the previous year's work, an effort which adds depth to the waste issue. Of 1.427 million pounds of raw wool processed, 38.5 percent (547,000 pounds) was "dead loss," grease, sticks, leaves, and other trash, 4.1 percent was "waste," 9 percent second-quality fibers (noil), and 48.6 percent first-quality fibers (tops) for worsted spinning.[40] The reduction by .5 percent of the waste in the total would add 7,000 pounds to the latter categories, and $2–$3,000 to the year's product value. Keeping the cards at a moderate speed, preventing the stuffing of feedboxes, and keeping the teeth sharp, both generated "better" quality work and would be worth $10 a day to the firm.

The richness of the detail Doak provides about the worsted process, only glimpsed here, continues throughout the journal, but in the early months he wrote hardly a line about the specific individuals from whom he drew these guidelines for practical manufacturing. This silence continued through his five months in the combing room, but ended in June 1903. Thereafter, extended accounts of conversations appear with regularity. This textual transition indicates Charles's development of a more personalized relationship with the room bosses with whom he worked. Certainly it is of some significance that he had been circulating through the mill for the best part of a year, as the passage of time might gradually ease the ambiguity of his role as present student and future master in the shop. But the key to the timing of this stylistic break lies in the great crisis of June 1903, a general strike of unprecedented dimensions in textile Philadelphia.

The overture to the citywide walkout was played crosstown near the Schuylkill River at another worsted yarn firm, S. B. and B. W. Fleisher. There on May 6, seventy-five women walked out demanding a reduction in their sixty-hour work week, and were joined quickly by 225 others from the nearby Caledonia Worsted Mills of Alexander Crow, Jr. With the revival of the economy from the depths of the 1890s, textile work was plentiful in Philadelphia, but the return of prosperity had brought no easing of the eleven- to twelve-hour days in the Fairmount district's mills. The Fleishers had expanded their labor force by a third since 1900 (to 1,200) and continued unaffected by the strike of a small proportion of their spinners. Crow's smaller firm, which spun yarns to feed its own carpet looms, closed entirely.[41]

[39]See Howard Priestman, *Principles of Wool Combing* (London, 1904).
[40]Doak, Journal, p. 25.
[41]*Philadelphia Evening Bulletin*, May 6, 1903, p. 3; *Davison's Textile Blue Book 1899–1900* (New York, 1900), pp. 217, 219–20.

54   *Philip Scranton*

Though most mill operatives were unorganized, there were thirty-four independent and AFL textile unions active in the city. The sudden walkout in Fairmount spurred them to action. Meetings between the Central Textile Workers Union and the separate Ingrain Carpet Weavers Union produced a broad demand for shorter hours, though no strikes would be authorized until June 1. For their part, the Manufacturers' Protective Association (a descendent of the Philadelphia Textile Association which had warred with the Knights of Labor in the 1880s) declined to act, citing the loss of production that shorter weeks would entail. Though a few firms locked their workers out or were struck in the final May days, Monday, June 1, brought a massive shutdown. About fifty firms (with 15,000 workers) had individually granted the fifty-five-hour week to avoid closure, but nearly 600 others were struck, press reports estimating that 85–95,000 hands had abandoned their frames, looms, and dye vats. Issues of whether or not shorter hours were acceptable if they meant shorter pay (shades of Lawrence in 1912) lay unresolved, but the dyers, highly skilled and heavily unionized, held a picnic and parade to celebrate the general strike.[42] The MPA wailed that, should the hours be lessened, the workers' "success would simply cost this city its supremacy as a textile manufacturing center."[43] Nonetheless, the struggle had commenced.

The public drama of the strike makes an impressive panorama, including the figure of Mother Jones, who headed a march of child laborers to New York in an appeal for presidential intercession.[44] But through Charles Doak's journal, we may gain a rare interior view of the impact of the walkout on one firm. Kensington, the region's textile hub, was nearly stilled, and the Doak Company was no exception. Charles noted: "On June the first the mill ran up to ten o'clock when a very large majority went out, (none of the combers came in at all) and the mill shut down." When the strikers returned on Friday the fifth to collect pay for their last week of work, the firm posted a notice: "These mills will start up Monday the eight [sic]. Any concessions made by the Manufacturers Protective Association will be given by us." As an attempt to "get the hands in," this formalized effort proved a failure,

[42]*Philadelphia Record*, May 25, 1903, p. 6; *Manayunk Sentinel*, May 28, 1903, p. 1; *Record*, May 30, 1903, p. 1; *Philadelphia Public Ledger*, June 1, 1903, p. 2; *Bulletin*, June 1, 1903, pp. 1, 2, 6.

[43]*Bulletin*, June 1, 1903, p. 1.

[44]Philip Foner, ed., *Mother Jones Speaks* (New York, 1983), pp. 100–103, 487–88; *Bulletin*, June 17, 1903, pp. 1–2; *Ledger*, July 7, 1903, p. 2.

for on the eighth only "a few hands come in [*sic*] but not enough to start up the machinery, and at ten o'clock the engine was stopped again."[45]

With the mill silent, Charles and the room bosses spent their days together doing maintenance work, as "there are a great many things that can be seen and need attending to when the machinery is stopped." They discovered a major cause of bad yarn resulting from flaws in leather-covered rollers in the spinning rooms, repair of which "entail[ed] a heavy expense for supplies and labor."[46] These weeks of undistracted contact, involving the shared tasks of tuning the mill and devising a means to bring back its work force, seem to have lessened the distance between Charles Doak and his father's core supervisors (superintendent John Vogelman and spinning room overseers Bill Blair, Tom Miller, George Sax, and Bill Taylor). Accounts of their opinions, notes of formulas, and "tricks" given him fill Doak's journal thereafter. Close interactions during the walkout served to integrate Doak with the cadre of "bosses."

The 1903 textile strike was a disaster for most workers. Though the solidary dyers held out until mid-October, some slippage—gradual erosion of the strike force by trickles of returnees—was apparent by the end of June.[47] The Doak mill was one of the first to get back into production. Instead of threatening to seek an entirely new work force, as some proprietors did,[48] James Doak sent his bosses into the neighborhood to talk individually with striking operatives. The result: "On Monday June the fifteenth a few hands were persuaded by J. Vogelman and T. Miller to come in. Each succeeding day of this week more came in, till on Monday the twenty-second a large majority started up (all the combers . . . except the Johnsons)."[49] No trace of violence or even sharp words was reported by Charles, but his one mention of "trouble" reveals something of the informal bonds among even unorganized workers when their sense of right behavior was violated. "Trouble was just avoided at one stage. Bill Anderson [an engineer]

[45]Doak, Journal, p. 150.

[46]Ibid., p. 151. Another task undertaken during the shutdown was installation of new clothing (sets of wire teeth) on three of the cards. Doak then ran a test to see if this change reduced the fly, which it did, by about one-third (p. 23, June 10, 1903).

[47]*Bulletin*, June 20, 1903, p. 1; June 25, 1903, p. 2; July 8, 1903, p. 2.

[48]Ibid., June 4, 1903, pp. 1–2; July 15, 1903, p. 2. The threat to fire all strikers came from James Dobson, long one of the most tenacious opponents of unions in the textile industry. Dobson, partner with his brother in the city's largest cloth, blanket, and carpet firm, supervised a set of mills at the Falls of Schuylkill, near Manayunk, employing 4,000 workers. For all but a few other firms the issue was not whether but *when* their old workers would return and on what terms.

[49]Doak, Journal, p. 150.

56   *Philip Scranton*

came in on Friday the nineteenth and was told that his job was given to the fireman, but tha[t] he could work on the dryer. [H]e left and the combers who had promised to come in Monday threatened to stay out. Anderson was pacified, and promised his old job back, if he would take the dryer, till everything was settled, at no monetary loss to himself. This brought him in together with the combers."[50] With this compromise, forced by the combers' solidarity, Anderson was satisfied, for his skilled worker's rate was assured during the face-saving interval until the fireman could be returned to his original duties.

Crucially, the management option that was forgone must be stressed, for it indicates quietly the strength of workers' shop culture. Anderson, protesting, was not fired. Such an act would have shuttered the mill a second time, wrecking a week's patient persuasion and demonstrating bad faith on the Doaks's part. His demotion in favor of the fireman who had broken ranks early (to start "the engine" the Monday after the posted notice) was rescinded, but in a fashion which minimized the social damage all around. With Anderson "pacified," the combers kept their "promise" and the mill got under way after a three-week stoppage.

On June 29, 1903, Doak commenced five months' work in the drawing and spinning rooms. During July he summarized an example of shop-floor problem solving, detailing the opinions of room bosses Blair and Sax and that of "Priestly, the machinist." A yarn order was running poorly on one set of frames, a "bad spin" with frequent breaks. After some discussion, an adjustment of the frames was engineered. Blair, "who had suggested it in the first place," was dubious about the results; Priestly thought it would "do more harm than good"; Sax "didn't want the change made as [Sup't.] Vogelman was away at the time and he did not wish to make any change in his absence." But Charles pressed forward and noted after the alteration that "the yarn seemed to spin better." This early effort at exercising a measure of authority did not work out, for the breakage resurfaced, and the room was "shut down soon after this." After the spinning frames had been leveled in September, the adjusted mechanisms "were restored to their original position."[51]

More confident if not yet competent, Doak continued this varied pattern through the fall, sometimes working the machinery ("Tried bundling for the first time, did 14 Bs. 355 lbs, in 4 hrs."),[52] monitoring the output with tests and tables, conversing with the bosses, and giving

[50]Ibid.
[51]Ibid., pp. 76–77. On drawing and spinning, see Howard Priestman, *Principles of Worsted Spinning* (London, 1906).
[52]Ibid., p. 75.

them credit for solutions to knotty problems in his journal. His relations with the rest of the work force appear only in the form of criticisms of the shortcuts and inattention to detail of the "girls" and "boys" who fed the cards and combs and doffed the spinning frames.[53] As regarded his father, there was a similar distance, but one rooted in the formalized respect appropriate in a patriarchal family. When Charles mentions James Doak, Jr., there are no traces of the casual familiarity that developed vis-à-vis the "hands." (The elder Doak appears always as "Father" or "Mr. Doak," never as "Dad.")[54]

Shortly after being "given charge of the top making" late in 1903,[55] Charles was for the first time drawn into a family conference regarding a troublesome customer, a small sign of recognition that his capacities were maturing. Earlier, during the general strike, J. S. Keim's Shackamaxon Mills had booked a large order and demanded "immediate delivery," a request that was met by subcontracting the job to a nearby spinner who had avoided the strike.[56] Now, the firm had run a sample yarn lot to hook another sizable order from Keim, only to find that the grade of wool used in the sample had vanished from the market. The conferees, "Father, Joe, and myself," agreed to substitute a comparable staple which would yield "good yarn but a shade darker." The switch worked, as Charles later reported that "there has been no kick on this yarn."[57]

Making samples to meet a buyer's needs was a component of the specialty trades, a continuous and contingent expense of competition at the quality end of the textile industry. The subcontracting of work under emergency or rush conditions was another feature, a common pattern of 19th-century proprietary Philadelphia textile firms.[58] One of the spatial advantages of operation in the crowded Kensington district was the availability of nearby firms to handle such tasks, networks of personal contact between their owners being facilitated by propin-

[53]Ibid., pp. 7, 11, 50.
[54]Ibid., p. 13.
[55]Ibid., p. 9.
[56]Ibid., p. 151.
[57]Ibid., p. 60. The firm was not so lucky with another Kiem order, which was returned as not up to standard (p. 79).
[58]Small mills were both more threatened with collapse by strike-induced shutdowns and more eager to seize opportunities to run while others were stopped, filling market vacancies to the advantage of their firm's life chances. Likewise, firms with seasonal demands were poorly placed to resist timely strikes; such diverse "placements," structural locations in space and market, were chinks in the solidarity of the body of local textile capitalists. Only with a congruence of industrial form and function (integrated, standardized corporations) would the basis for unified resistance to labor be strengthened. Equally, these variations posed nearly insuperable problems for the regional textile workers' unity, the rapid deterioration of which doomed the 1903 general strike.

quity, by common productive orientations, and by association in the manufacturers' leagues.[59] The final phase of Charles's manufacturing apprenticeship began early in the new year, soon after veteran superintendent John Vogelman resigned on January 16, 1904. When his replacement, H. H. Rawnsley, "took charge" as "superintendent of the entire mill, the sorting room excepted,"[60] Charles commenced the task of pulling together his individual "room" experiences of the previous year. For the next seven months, he ranged throughout the factories, accompanying Rawnsley on his rounds, filling page after page in the journal with notes on "Rawnsley's Alterations." From the room-by-room technics, Charles had progressed to learning operation of the system of production as a whole.

Rawnsley's remarkable talents soon had an effect on the shop floor. On February 12, Doak recorded: "Talking to Bill [Blair], he said Rawnsley had made several changes in the Drawing Room, sacrificing production to quality." For example, "every lot of wool that came up was looked over carefully by Rawnsley and the whole Drawing set accordingly."[61] With this attention to detail, errors and waste were minimized. For a specialty firm, such care often proved a matter of greater importance than speeding production.[62]

That Charles closely attended the superintendent's travels, and that the proprietor too had noticed his capacities, is indicated by a conversation reported at mid-month. "Father in speaking to me 2/15/04 said that since Rawnsley was here the yarn seemed nearer the count." That

[59]In the 1890s, the Manufacturers Club undertook to develop penalties (fines) for firms which broke ranks and settled during sector-wide strikes, thereby setting the pattern of the terms for resuming work and encouraging strikers at other mills. See Manufacturers Club of Philadelphia, *Members List, 1895* (Philadelphia, 1895), p. 3.

[60]Doak, Journal, p. 83. Vogelman became "super" at Thomas Wolstenholme's Kensington spinning mills, a much larger worsted yarn firm (35,000 spindles and 700 workers). Unlike Rawnsley, he remained as employee throughout. Vogelman had become superintendent for the Doaks in the early 1890s and remained at Wolstenholme's at least through 1922. (See James Doak, Jr., Journal, 1888–92, Pastore Library, Philadelphia College of Textiles and Science; *Official American Textile Directory: 1916* [New York, 1916], p. 293; *OATD: 1922*, p. 447.)

[61]Ibid. Rawnsley proposed other later changes to reduce the amount of "Twitty" (poor quality) yarn. These too "would cut down the production" (p. 84).

[62]Charles's ambivalent relation with Rawnsley is suggested as well in his use of the super's last name only. Doak's more relaxed interactions with the drawing room boss, Blair, are evident from his regular references to him as "Bill." But Rawnsley stays Rawnsley, never "Mr.," never a mention of a first name, a form which may express Charles's balancing between acknowledging the super's mastery of production and his own position as a proprietor-in-waiting, as if reminding himself that Rawnsley is a family employee but one already possessed of the authority and technical prowess to which Charles aspires.

is, the varied outputs were closer to the standard weights (counts) than hitherto. "He told me to see how Rawnsley worked this."[63] The secret, of course, was not this adjustment or that, but the skills, mechanical and personal, that Rawnsley had honed in his years in the trade. Such long accumulation of capacities, at least within the factory culture of proprietary capitalism, had a specific goal, the establishment of one's own firm. To just this end, "Rawnsley left our employ on Saturday Aug. 20, 1904," closing seven months of work during which he contributed one "very good idea" after another to Standard Worsted Mills.[64]

Charles's account of the departure fully expresses an awareness of his own shortcomings and a suspicion of his mentor's motives, for, on Rawnsley's recommendation, young Doak became his successor. "He suggested that I be given the job, and Father gave it too [*sic*] me. I believe that R. suggested this plan as he seemed rather expectant of coming back at some future date, and thought he would have more chance if I were Super and not some outsider." Then follows a penciled addition: "This must have been an erronenous [*sic*] impression of mine for most of the time R. was with us he had been planning to start a mill of his own which he did as soon as he got through here. He started the Lyon Mill at Angora [in West Philadelphia] with Mr. Binder, called the Lion Worsted Co. making floss yarn for a N.Y. commission house. Binder is late of Tracey's."[65] No longer an employee, he had commenced on his own account, retracing the path to proprietorship so often followed by 19th-century shop and factory veterans in Philadelphia.

Following Rawnsley was a staggering assignment for the twenty-three-year-old Doak. During the first twelve months, Charles's problems with machinery and personnel were substantial. Pages detailing "Bad Spins" and speculations about their causes (September–November 1904) are succeeded in 1905 by the firing of the comb room boss and "at Father's instigation" a change in a spinning boss.[66] An early sign that production had lagged with Rawnsley's departure was the restoration of the bonus system in spinning, after Charles had been "Super a

[63]Doak, Journal, p. 81.
[64]Ibid., pp. 84–86.
[65]Ibid., p. 86. R. C. Binder had been secretary of the Tracey Worsted Mills Co., another yarn specialist located on the western edge of downtown Philadelphia (see *Davison's Blue Book 1899–1900*, p. 228). Capitalized at $300,000, the firm was most likely an incorporated partnership, closely held as were so many regional textile mills. Tracey could be expected to be the commercial, capital-bringing, partner in the new firm, with Rawnsley directing production.
[66]Ibid., pp. 23, 37, 87–89.

60   *Philip Scranton*

month at Father's request."[67] The ensuing series of "Bad Spins" suggest that Charles had not the skills to duplicate Rawnsley's adjustments of machine settings and speeds to the changing grades of wool. To compensate for his son's inexperience as superintendent, James Doak altered the supervisory hierarchy in 1905, first hiring a man to oversee all preparatory processes after sorting and in November adding a second super for all stages "after the Combing."[68] Thus ended Charles's manufacturing apprenticeship. With these changes, he was freed for such tasks as monitoring production and testing for cost and quality, tasks he seems to have continued through 1910.[69] His entry into partnership came in 1905, five years before the firm incorporated "with paid-in capital of $300,000."[70]

*   *   *

This extended chronicle of a manufacturing son's introduction to the production processes and shop-floor relations of a proprietary firm has provided a detailed view of a customary practice among family businesses. The earlier format of direct apprenticeship and rudimentary schooling have been superseded here by a more complex preparation for entrepreneurship appropriate to the level of manufacturing development achieved by the turn of the century. Whereas James Doak, Jr., son of a failed handweaver, matured as a factory worker before finding a commercial backer for his entry to the proprietor's world, his own son was carefully prepared for the role of "practical manufacturer."

Though the conformation of the manufacturing apprenticeship varied in other textile families,[71] other regions, and other trades,[72] it

[67]Ibid., p. 70.

[68]Ibid., pp. 23, 96.

[69]Charles Doak's continuing role as an early "quality assurance" supervisor may provide an interesting counterpart to the contemporary production engineering commonly referred to as Taylorism. However, rather than being concerned to measure and modify workers' activity to press for maximum *output*, Doak focused on refining the technical aspects of manufacturing to stabilize or increase product *quality*. Given the variety of machinery in place at Standard Worsted Mills, many of his tests and calculations seem oriented toward the problem of producing yarn counts of comparable quality on frames from different manufacturers (Hall and Stell, Farrar, etc.). Charles also experimented with new oil mixtures (for wool) and lubricants (for machines) rather than make notes about the task performance of individual workers. See Doak, Journal, pp. 36–39, 93.

[70]Communication from Elizabeth Doak Tarnay (Charles Doak's daughter), September 27, 1983.

[71]For a contemporary textile case, see R. Chase Whitaker, *Grampa's Stories* (Philadelphia, 1976). Whitaker, scion of a Philadelphia textile family active since 1813 in the cotton sector, was completing his engineering course at Princeton University in 1921 when the combination of his father's illness and a major fire at the family mills forced him into a radically shortened apprenticeship in the factory.

[72]For a case from New York boot and shoe manufacturing, see William Inglis, *George F.*

functioned generally to serve both sons as prospective owners and firms as family-based productive systems. For heirs apparent who had the benefit of technical or trade education (Drexel, Textile), their "tour of the mill" provided both the opportunity and the necessity to apply in practice such principles as had been learned in classrooms and labs. Further, in the context of variable-output batch production, their stints at each stage of the total process enabled them to appreciate the nuances of "flexible-system" manufacturing and to appreciate the skills involved in generating quality products. Shop-floor experience had, however, much more than technical proficiency as its object, as sons also found themselves immersed in the social relations of factory culture: the sorters' independence, shopworkers' solidarity, the varied styles of "bossing," formal and informal means to problem solving. The astute apprentice proprietor would learn to root leadership or superintendence both in mechanical competence and in cultural fluency. If it was signally important for David Montgomery's skilled machinists to display a "manly bearing" toward the boss,[73] it was equally important for the apprentice proprietor to learn the meanings of such behavior, to "read" worker caution or bravado in a fashion that smoothed the flow of goods and contributed to the accumulation process.

For the firm as a manufacturing enterprise and a family legacy, the apprenticeships of sons served additional, related ends. Fathers could evaluate their sons' prowess and potential, their effectiveness and aptitude for directing the firm. In the worst case, a decision to "sell out" might be reached as an alternative to certain ruin of the business by an inept successor. More concretely, the tour laid the basis for buttressing the authority of blood lines with that derived from comprehension of the production system as an entirety (materials, processing, production, sales, repairs), something that neither workers nor room bosses were afforded the chance to learn. Although the retention of several sons, and later of *their* sons, could produce a firm top-heavy with lifelong rivals (such a problem surely sped the bankruptcy of Philadelphia's toy-making giant, the Albert Schoenhut Company),[74] when

---

Johnson and His Industrial Democracy (New York, 1935), especially chaps. 5 and 6. George F.'s two sons both worked their way through "all the departments" before taking on managerial responsibilities (ca. 1900–1905), as did his grandson, "right after graduation from high school in 1930" (p. 72).

[73]David Montgomery, *Workers' Control in America* (New York, 1980).

[74]U.S. District Court, Eastern District, Pennsylvania, Bankrupt Files, Docket no. 18421, National Archives and Records Service, Philadephia Branch. These bankruptcy records are an untapped source for business and local history, according to Archivist Robert Plowman. Many files contain extensive, typed hearing transcripts that identify contributing causes of regional manufacturing crises. Seven Schoenhuts were on the payroll when their firm collapsed in 1934.

the succession was "clean," proprietary firms could move forward with confidence.[75]

For batch manufacturers of skill-intensive quality goods, booklearning was only a preface to hands-on experience of production. The capitalism they practiced was a world apart from that of the throughput architects of capital-intensive, low-skill manufacture. As the latter were erecting graduate business education for the "modern business organization," industrial proprietors blended technical schooling and shop-based learning into the manufacturing apprenticeship, a means to extend the lineage of the customary private firm in a changing economic environment.

[75]James Doak, Jr., and Co. survived its founder's death in 1916 to endure through the Second World War. During the 1920s, Charles Doak became secretary to the Worsted Spinners Association of Philadelphia and, as president of the firm, managed the Standard Worsted Mills through the Depression. In 1940, on its original site, the mill had 199 workers producing fine worsted yarns (*Tenth Industrial Directory of the Commonwealth of Pennsylvania* [Harrisburg, 1941], p. 508). For a recent review of family enterprises that touches on this and other issues, see Pamela Hollie, "On 7th Avenue, It's All in the Family," *New York Times*, June 26, 1983, sec. F, pp. 1, 8–9.

[15]

Introduction: the political economy of the small firm in Italy

Edward Goodman

The fastest growing economy in Europe in the first half of the 1980s was the Italian. Figures from the OECD indicated that by 1986 Italy's GDP at $673 billion was higher than that of the UK. Later estimates from the Italian Institute of Statistics put the Italian figure below the British. But the difference is slight, and it is not a matter of doubt that an 'economic miracle' took place. In a surprisingly short space of time a relatively backward economy was transformed and Italy emerged as a major industrial power. As in Britain, the resultant prosperity was more evident in one half of the country than the other – in Italy's case, the north. The role of the small firm in the Italian success story has been crucial; in the area of central and north-east Italy, known as the *Terza Italia*[1] where the small manufacturing firms are concentrated, the increase in the rate of production has far outstripped that of the rest of the country.

To those accustomed to thinking of Italy as the home of a happy-go-lucky, at times irresponsible life-style, with shabby workshops and an electoral system incapable of producing stable government, the figures on industrial production may appear surprising. But appearances are deceptive. True, the workshops are shabby, and the electoral system throws up many more parties and coalitions that are candidates for government than does the British system; true, too, these are engaged in constant debate that reflects the ever-changing climate of opinion and fashions of intellectual dilettantism as well as the continuous emergence of new critical issues. Yet the system has shown itself to be capable of a kind of long-term economic stability, and the changes in direction of public policy since the war have been less erratic than those brought about by the first-past-the-post method of registering electoral success in Britain.

It has to be remembered that Italy has been a unified nation-state for less than 130 years and that it was much later than most other European countries in developing an industrial economy. The boundaries

1

Small firms and industrial districts in Italy

of the medieval city states remain amongst the hills and plains, crossed as they are by the efficient communication-network of the modern autostrada; but within these boundaries are still autonomous, purpose-bent groups, assertive, and immensely confident of themselves and of the smaller communities to which they belong. Evidence of these different cultures remains in the distinctive architecture and other art forms for which each of the cities or regions has become renowned.

At a less exalted level, each has still its characteristic commercial achievements in the crafts and urban skills that derive from the practical traditions going back into the remote past and continuing in modern forms, some within the confines of the industrial districts that have become one of the principal features of present-day Italy's industrial economy. Right at the heart of these are, as ever before, the really vital entrepreneurial groups of ten workers or fewer.

It is the visual image of Italy's industrial performance which has given confidence to the OECD's assessment of her achievements and to the prediction that better is to come. This is a picture of fickle markets, constant innovation and the fusion of art with high technology resulting in beautiful new forms and highly saleable and ada,table designs of swift appeal to the world of fashion. Beneath these are cleverly conceived prototypes that are quickly converted for mass markets and then broken down into small batches of customerized production and a plethora of low-cost, eye-catching items, useful, but intentionally not lasting. This is a market which understands itself well: a 'Janus-type market', a fragmented market, able to respond almost instantly to fashion and changed demands, alert to quick openings, with flexible programmes and short production runs, what Giacomo Becattini calls the 'amoeba like ability of the Italian small firm to respond to changing demands'.[2]

How does this image of brittle success and disposable production square with the more ordinary picture of the run-of-the-mill Italian small business? The fact has to be admitted that small firms are not inherently smart, nor are they run by a set of temperamental genius-designers, but by steady inventive entrepreneurs with a feeling for aesthetic values and a flair for knowing where to buy and where to sell, and often with the tenacity to perfect their own skills and to adapt them to the tasks in hand rather than to be forced into paying high prices for new tools and technology. If an image is required, it is of the converted makeshift workshops abutting on to narrow streets with hardly room for a van to turn, cheek by jowl with residential accommodation; or the new, small, cramped trading estate built on to the dirt roads, and the family-based group of six or seven talkative workers grouped round one of the older craftsmen, whilst

2

the quick-thinking entrepreneur listens at a desk of his own, making notes and determined to get on.

Beneath the surface of both these images – the highly polished one and rougher one – are the most important achievements of the Italian economy to which thousands of small firms contribute in quality markets, where well-tested traditions of individual workmanship as well as good looks and unique design are hallmarks, and the very label 'Made in Italy' attracts custom.

A question of style

In all these achievements style is an important ingredient, uniquely and conspicuously Italian; a style that is rooted in the self-confidence of the individual workman and of the entrepreneur himself. Brought up in the security of family and community relationships and in a set of cultural assumptions resting upon instinctively shared values, no job is too menial for him and all jobs are worth doing well.

How is it that these very likeable personal qualities have been incorporated into an impersonal commercial economy and what are the mechanisms through which the values contained in these images have been transmitted to world markets? And how is it that the Italian Lilliputian firms have stood up to a world of giants?

It is tempting at this point to give reasons for the declining influence of the economies of scale based on extensive production lines, and to introduce the concept of the model of flexible production together with that of the division of labour according to firm specialization. The large manufacturing firm, according to this argument, is out of date and its machinery is as obsolete as the steam engine. The numerically controlled tool and the computer have transferred the ability to meet demand promptly, cheaply and efficiently from the large to the small firm. Customerized production in small batches is here to stay and the market likes it. There are several disadvantages in continuing to argue in this way. For example, one could counter-argue that the recent success of the small firm will be short-lived and that the large multi-product undertaking will make a comeback, that its financial power will enable it to organize the setting-up of a variety of interdependent units of production, sharing the same economies of scale and fitting into an overall pattern of organization. Or it can be suggested that the innovative skills and adaptability of the small firm will be more than offset by the greater resources of the giant firm when it comes to exploiting the next wave of high technology. There is a third view, not incompatible with the first, which sees the success of the small firm in modern Italy as stemming from the explosive power of the

3

Small firms and industrial districts in Italy

values of the craft firm and of the self-employed worker based, as they are, on family and community. According to this view, the ability to introduce new technology stems also from the same set of values: and this makes it necessary to discuss at least part of the Italian industrial success in terms of what one may simply call the political economy of the small firm.

In such a discussion, by way of leitmotif, it is helpful occasionally to make comparisons with England's experiences at similar stages of development. The most conspicuous differences between the two countries lie historically in their attitudes to trade and money-making and the importance they attach to design and ordinary good appearance. This second is noticeable in everyday things, such as the wrapping up of a parcel or the design of a five-bar gate. Good design and a quality of thought-out artistry have always formed the essential basis of authentic Italian workmanship. Men of every trade seem to possess a good eye and a sense of acceptable appearance. In considering what design and ornament are appropriate, the craftsman has to take into consideration what his customer can afford just as much as what exactly he wants the appearance to be. Whenever there is a gap between the two, he is trained to evolve new techniques to abridge it. This is the basis of much of his capacity to adapt and innovate. Sebastiano Brusco says, for example, 'the tools used by traditional artisans are in general simple and multi-purpose. The skill of the artisan lies here: in being able to cope in complex situations working with few tools, often with unsuitable material.'[3]

The idea of money-making is not disreputable nor trade a dirty word, and they have never been looked down upon socially as they have been in England. In Italy it has always been thought legitimate for the dealer and tradesman 'to make a turn' and for the man with entrepreneurial spirit to be one of the most admired in the local community; indeed, success as an entrepreneur has always been regarded as at least a rung on the ladder to social recognition. For the same reason, the earning of money as a means of securing positional goods has never been discouraged. Display and ornament associated with wealth have been from the earliest times implicit in the ambition of almost every talented person who has had the opportunity to succeed. In the Middle Ages, as the merchant classes grew rich, some cities became something like plantations of towers attached to the largest houses as signs of prestige. Armour and weapons of war were finely ornamented, and of course the dresses of both men and women were beautifully designed and richly embroidered. The courts of the city-states and the merchants themselves were the patrons of the crafts and of good design.

4

All this of course was reflected in the nobleman's palaces and the town houses of merchants. Much of the furniture and tapestry were made *in situ*; so also the paintings – for example, in the Ducal Palace at Urbino, where a Raphael portrait of a lady is still on the easel where he painted it. At the time of the Renaissance, painters and architects had no separate status; they were superior dignified decorators or designers, and it was in these roles and belonging to teams of equally talented colleagues that they designed the courtyards and decorated in fresco the walls of cloisters and the interiors of churches, palaces, and large houses alike. It was to this tradition that the artist and the skilled tradesmen belonged. Their contemporary conventions and social attitudes go back to these roots.

In order to obtain their original stock of wealth, the merchants had to display something similar to what centuries later was identified as the entrepreneurial spirit. At first they were little more than dealers, buying and selling commodities that were quickly resold in the market places. However, in time their biggest profits came from international trade, and soon after they became lenders of money; the merchant bankers of today are derived from them.

When life in the cities became orderly and trading on a wide scale became possible, the growth of the entrepreneurial spirit provided one of the first pieces of evidence of the Italian admiration of commercial skills and of the ability to make use of an idea, show initiative and maintain control of undertakings. But historically Italians do not have a taste for large-scale administration, nor do Italian men of spirit like being organized, or being obliged to obey superiors without question.

Because of the entrepreneur's reluctance to administer large organizations, the businesses organized by him tend to remain small. Expansion for him means the possibility of allowing things to develop beyond his control. Though he takes risks, his key role is to be in control of things and to keep intact his own independence and powers of initiative. He is the ideas man searching out new niches in the markets of today. He is accustomed to ducking authority and getting by on his own. The local market is important to him both as a means of selling his goods and of learning what the public wants and what designs are coming into fashion. The ultimate of his ambition is not growth, but recognition.

There are other visual images of modern industrial Italy besides those that derive from the small firm's successes in the *Terza Italia* and the prestigious consumer goods and design centres of the north-eastern industrial triangle; and some of these other images are not only unattractive but lead one to wonder, if they do indeed represent a reality, how Italy has managed to appear in the industrial league

Small firms and industrial districts in Italy

table at all. Its bureaucracy has a reputation for being, with the exception of the Russian, the most cumbersome in Europe. With feet of stone and head of ancient iron, and with a file of forms in quin-triplicate, it is a monster from Byzantium that has long held Italy in its claws: a cumbersome spirit of delay and obstruction, it sometimes seems to drag upon every transaction. The postal service is surely the most unreliable in Europe, so secure in its bad ways that it seems incapable of making any improvement.

Yet another image of Italy is the poverty of many areas in the south; it is only in the centre and north that prosperity reigns. Finally, there is the very recent expansion of the large private companies, with an era of mergers and takeovers already begun. But none of this is part of the present volume.

The *artigiani* and the family firm

The merchant and the entrepreneur are the two figures who, larger than life, stand in the background of Italian small-firm development. In the foreground is the master craftsman, the *artigiano*. Pre-eminently a man of skill and sensitivity, he is also independent, and in order to stay so he has to economize on tools and almost every-thing else he needs. It is this which gives him the impetus constantly to sharpen his repertoire of skills with new techniques and to improvise. A passion for detail and a flair for design run in his blood. He is not well educated and his class, the artisan class, is not far up the social hierarchy, but he is inventive and he believes in himself and in his craft. He likes solving problems in his work, but he does not like the solutions that the big firm offers. It is for him to use the machine and not for the machine to rule him. It is love of work that explains the pleasure he takes in life, and this provides a strong contrast to the British utilitarian idea that all work is painful and has to be endured to gain the needs of existence. The Italian craftsman delights in pleasing his customers and unashamedly wants to see their appreciation of what he does for them. He likes display and to have social confirmation of his mastery of craft skills and his ability to run a small firm successfully – but no more than a small firm, just the number of people whom he can know intimately and whose work he can criticize and control. Above all, he has an eye for relevance; his life is one which cannot afford mistakes. It is a combination of these qualities which has kept the *artigiano* firm in business for so many centuries and made it a model of nearly all Italian small businesses from the earliest times down to the high-technology small firm of the *Terza Italia*.

6

The role of the family

Underpinning the entire *artigiano* economy is the family. The firm is rooted both in the family and in the *artigiano*'s exceptional personal skills. This creates a more or less permanent tēnsion. The family is a conservative force depending for its effectiveness on its solidarity. Members of the entrepreneur's own family work in the business, as well as the in-laws (*cognati*). Many of them may live in residential quarters attached to the workshop. In times of economic recession it is usually found that employment in *artigiano* firms increases as young members of the family can now find a place of some sort working in the family business. Starting-up capital is usually found in the family before the entrepreneur goes to the local bank. In contrast to the conservatism which such a structure creates, is the colourful individualism and single-mindedness of the entrepreneur himself and of his most-talented craftsmen. It is remarkable that with contradictions such as this at their core such firms survive year after year and generation after generation. That they do is due to the fact that the family itself is the breeding ground of strong character and has its own rules of give and take, which assert that, to be productive, all differences must be exercised within commonly accepted limits. It follows also that there must be limits to the size of the firm.

To the observer what seems even more surprising is that into this conservative structure of a family conducting its affairs in a manner resembling a small debating society have been successfully introduced the tools and equipment of sophisticated modern technology. The enthusiastic reception of new technology by traditional industries is one of the most promising features of the *Terza Italia*.

Characteristics of the small firm

Since very early times there have been two main categories of *artigiano* firm. The first was very small, centred around the personality of the master craftsman himself, doing purely craftwork. The second was somewhat larger and, under the leadership of a more entrepreneurial type of craftsman, produced goods for wider sale in the retail market; for example the small shoe firms of northern Italy or the makers of ceramics around Deruta. The larger firms might make use of sub-contracting or putting out to home-workers. In recent times, especially since the trade unions tended to make life difficult for managers and skilled workers in large firms, new types of *artigiano* firm have grown up in industries using high technology. Two are of chief importance and have been selected, together with the traditional *artigiano* firm, by Brusco as the

7

Small firms and industrial districts in Italy

archetypes of the genre. One is the dependent subcontractor and the other the small specialist firm, usually employing flexible production methods. Both types flourish in the industrial districts of the *Terza Italia* and are described in subsequent parts of this book.

There are many factors to be taken into account in order to understand what it really is that makes the Italian small firm a stimulating place to work, and how, in the modern world, it has come to produce goods that attract a world-wide reputation. The Italian craftsman's capacity to adapt and innovate has already been noted (to quote Brusco again, it is 'an integral part of his own make-up'), and one of the secrets of Italian success has been the ability to revive traditional industries by the careful application of new technology. Equally significant is the urge to compete and the entrepreneur's intense awareness of his competitors. These are fundamental characteristics of the protagonists in this remarkable economy.

The size of the typical *artigiano* firm varies from about five to ten persons. Limitation of size has been, and in many circumstances still is, an important consideration for the small firm, since it gives exemption from certain legislative requirements and local authority controls and regulations. It is also, by virtue of the small numbers employed, easy for the firm to avoid trade union pressures and many of the more vexatious items of the rule book. Perhaps most important of all, size is very much a function of the style of the firm and relationships which characterize it. These relationships include those between the owner or the entrepreneur and those whom he employs. Ideas flow freely in the workshop, and those participating often include the customer who may be waiting for his work to be finished. There may be buyers anxious to see what the next year's fashions are likely to be or to ask for modifications to suit their own requirements. Their comments will often provoke a general discussion. The entrepreneur will rarely comment, except to make notes of the suggestions he likes or to smile at justified criticisms. At the end of the week or month these will be incorporated into new models which will be put on display whilst the old ones will be sold off cheaply. This example shows that smallness of both firm and factory is indeed one critical factor, not only because of the close relationships that it fosters between the workers but also for two other reasons: it makes possible an unacknowledged system whereby each worker tends to monitor and encourage the other according to a tradition of workmanship and design to which they all belong; and it stimulates the discussion of new ideas in a wider circle. In these ways it leads to flexibility and innovations, small and large. These advantages can be seen equally well in one of the small ceramic workshops described by Margherita Russo or in one of Italy's most

8

sophisticated fashion houses. They are not just the standards of a particular craft; they are part of the intrinsic qualities of the Italian tradition of workmanship that govern the small-firm economy.

What matters eventually, however, is not so much the exact numbers of employees working in a given firm as the fact of whether or not a project or plan can be understood, shared and worked upon as an act of collaboration by a group of the size chosen by the entrepreneur. How does an idea travel between its members, how easy do they find it to identify problems they encounter and to devise innovations – perhaps no more than little improvements and original ways of doing things better? How, too, does the firm react to the society around it? It is their interest in each other's work and the means they adopt for fulfilling their role in the common project that renders unnecessary detailed surveillance and other associated costs. (In the United States, according to Samuel Bowles, these costs in large firms are usually as great as the annual net profits.[4]) The Italian small firm is thus more of a cultural entity than the English equivalent. It has familial, social and artistic aspects as well as economic, offering its workers a wide range of satisfactions besides that of earning a living. Its standards are those of excellence.

There are no sleeping partners or equity shareholders in the *artigiano* firm. Thus right at the beginning the idea of a takeover is made unlikely and small Italian firms cannot be regarded as fodder for the larger growing firm to feed on and eventually completely devour, which was the prevalent view in Britain in the 1960s and early 1970s.[5] Thus too, neither growth nor profit maximization for capital value purposes can be regarded as the raison d'être of the *artigiano* firm.

The Italian small firm has one other advantage: because of the absence of class barriers, it has few of the communication problems that can beset the larger hierarchical firms. Indeed, it is this lack of hierarchy and the very informality of the boss–worker relationship, often accompanied by a certain untidiness of procedure, that stimulates the flow of invention from the small workshops.

This, then in outline is the *artigiano* firm which dominates the traditional industries such as fabrics and clothing, shoe-making and leather goods, ceramics, carpentry, and furniture. There is much common ground, of course, between the traditional *artigiano* firm and the new high-technology firm which began to emerge in the late 1960s; for example, in the contemporary engineering industries the ancient idea of bespoke production for individual customers has been transformed under the impact of modern technology into the concept of 'customerized production'. Bespoke production is the habit of the traditional craft firm serving either a particular customer or the local

9

Small firms and industrial districts in Italy

market. Such a firm is always on the lookout for small differences in design that may constitute novelty and frequently uses its customers' ideas as its own inspiration. When the design is judged to be successful, the entrepreneur first tries out no more than a dozen or so copies of it on his local market. In his workshop, he aims to be one or two steps ahead of fashion and to avoid producing long runs of anything which would have to be destroyed were new designs to be adopted. In the high-technology *artigiano* firms using the most up-to-date equipment, short runs are nearly always favoured. The difference is, of course, that they have the advantage of computers which forecast demand and of numerically controlled tools which give expression to it quickly in economically regulated batches.

Where there has been a changeover in production methods from those based on craft traditions to those of high technology, the character of the working lives of many of the workers has also changed. Automation has taken away the skills from the hands of some of them and in doing so has created a new type of worker whose skills are mental and conceptual and whose main value to the firm is often his judgement rather than his manual dexterity.

In 1985 it was estimated that small firms employing fewer than ten workers made up 80 per cent of all Italian manufacturing firms, and they comfortably outperformed the larger firms in the same industrial sector; moreover, their wages at that time were significantly higher. Guido Rey in Chapter 2 gives plenty of evidence to put this achievement into perspective, suggesting that there is no need to make a fetish of small numbers of employees. There is no magic number. The point is that the ethos of the *artigiani* firm is not simply valuable in its own context but also as a wider influence on Italian industry.

The community and a concept of freedom

The *artigiano* firm, as well as being rooted in family, is grounded in community. This familiar statement has, of course, cultural and political implications, besides economic and organizational.

The word 'community' gives rise to a wide range of interpretations. For the moment, suppose five sets are taken:

(1) An aggregate of individuals but not a collective, who live in the same territory, who also know each other by name, speak the same language, have a common history and, in some minimal sense, share the same interests.

10

(2) Values, beliefs, loyalities or interests held in common; this
    gives rise to the idea of people sharing these things and having
    aspirations and projects in common, so that they identify with
    each other and work together to achieve common goals.
(3) More abstract and metaphysical meanings which include (2) but
    go beyond it: the community is an organic entity and has a
    value independent of those who compose it. This meaning is
    derived from times when communities were autonomous and
    self-contained and geographically cut off from each other; they
    each had an idiosyncratic sense of justice which they
    administered.
(4) Union of separate peoples or states, as in European Community.
(5) A concrete legal entity with interests to protect and functions to
    carry out. The Italian word *comune* can be used in several
    general senses, but its specific meaning is the administrative
    organization of the district, that is the local authority.

All five usages of 'community', although quite separate, give a
particular intellectual flavour when taken together. However, (1) and
(2), when combined with the values encapsulated in the claim for the
artigiani to be rooted in community, yield valuable insights into the
nature of personal liberty that underpins the Italian small-firm
political economy. This commences with the idea of freedom as
related by, for example, Simone Weil: 'Freedom is not to be defined
in terms of a relationship between desire and its satisfaction', but by
a relationship between, on the one hand, thought, judgement, and
imagination and, on the other, the action and sequence of means
needed to achieve the images so constructed. 'The absolutely free
man would be he whose every action proceeded from a preliminary
judgment concerning the end which he set himself and the sequence
of means suitable for attaining this end.'[6]

In order to achieve the co-ordination between the workers needed
to carry out a given project, each worker would have to employ
methodical thought and to have the same mental blueprint in his head
and this blueprint would need to give clear ideas of all the
specialized procedures needed for its exact execution.

The *artigiano* version of freedom in activity also starts with the
need of a shared image of the end to be achieved, but in place of
Weil's methodological co-ordination through mental and manual
discipline, it relies for its realization upon the knowledge each
worker has acquired of the other workers through his life in the
community and upon the skills and spontaneous forms of co-
operation which the community, through tradition and practice, has
shaped for all to use. The family and the community also provide

Small firms and industrial districts in Italy

necessary resources, which on occasion may be capital or institutional support. This view of liberty emphasizes the individual's desire to be free and to attain his freedom through the realization of consciously formulated mental blueprints; but at that point it leaves Weil's Cartesian description of methodical thought and its specialized procedures, and substitutes one that is less static. This version of freedom involves an on-going interaction, a negotiation as it were, between the craftsman and the tools he uses, and it is sustained by an actively participating community in which the individual lives and works. (In Chapter 6 Sforzi takes up a similar point in his identification of industrial districts.)

What is really being described is the working-out in real situations of 'freedom as integrity'. It is the freedom of the whole man, and what makes the man whole is his establishing his identification with the plans and projects of others (though his ability to identify with his own plans and projects is of course crucial). The important metaphors are those of wholeness, community, integrity: freedom in activity is not solely J.S. Mill's freedom as autonomy, but freedom as integrity. This emphasizes both the need of the individual to be true to himself – to fulfil his own plans and projects – and the need to be true to a common project, to perceive and recognize the aspirations and needs of those with whom he is working. Also, it gives a new slant on the concept of 'alienation', since alienation constitutes an attack on the integrity of the individual, fragmenting his own life and at the same time his relationships in the rest of the community.[7]

This description of freedom in the small-firm economy relies on two conditions. The first is a decentralized economy and the second is a small-sized working group, which Weil's description fits: 'collectives should never be sufficiently vast to pass outside the range of the human mind'.[8]

These reflections provide the basis of the distinction between a first and second tier of the modern technological economy, which, as already noted, underlies the current studies by the Acton Society.

The *comune* and political subcultures

The family and communal characteristics which make for small entrepreneurial firms coincide with another set of notable features of contemporary Italian life: the strength of the traditions and tendencies directed towards decentralization. These tendencies are not solely political; they also arise spontaneously from the vitality and self-interest of local communities and the common life and beliefs of those living in them. The geography of the country is also a factor,

12

and features of the terrain which in the past have isolated the regions and cities from each other still help to preserve some ancient differences.

The origins of the tradition of decentralization are to be found in Italy's peculiar history. After the break-up of the Roman Empire it eventually emerged as a country made up of city-states, with hinterlands of rural communities, that were almost self-contained. Not surprisingly they each developed distinctive characteristics, heightened in some cases by different ethnic mixes. At the end of the first millennium some cities in central and northern Italy were electing consuls and by the twelfth century the prototype of what was to be the *comune* was well established. The cities of Tuscany were among the first to be self-governing. By the end of the fifteenth century the great city-states had absorbed many smaller towns and had themselves been converted into duchies or principalities, later to be ruled by foreign powers or by the Vatican in the extensive Papal States. But certain functions and, in some cases, rights were retained by the *comuni*, even if their role was confined to the more pedestrian administrative work.

In these respects it is important to separate two entities: first, the local authority, the *comune*, with its mainly administrative functions, and second, the community itself, which has a past and present identity, and consists of individuals, who can at least recognize each other, and who, more often than not share values, attitudes, and priorities. The common life tends to be closer than that lived in a territory of similar size in England, and in comparatively recent times this has spurred on the *comune* to attempt to take political initiatives in furtherance of the collective interest or the interests of particular groups of citizens, such as the unemployed.

As the *comune* developed, the ideas it represented tended to be radical and republican. For example, during the period when these states fell under Vatican or foreign rule, the *comune* functioned as the egalitarian organ of local administration directly under the occupying powers. Both the Vatican and the Habsburgs are known to have encouraged a sense of responsibility in those they ruled, and hence *comuni* in territories in the north and centre occupied by either of these powers would have gained experience in local government earlier than those elsewhere. However dependent upon the occupying powers' connivance such a form of local participatory government had to be, it gave the local citizens political maturity and a confidence in their decision-making abilities.

It was thought that the unification of Italy would abridge the role of the *comune* but this is not what happened. In time the *comune* became a very important feature of social and industrial life, filling

Small firms and industrial districts in Italy

some of the gaps left in default of central government action. Local interest groups also began to thrive and helped to create a movement towards decentralization. As Carlo Trigilia shows in Chapter 7, new political forces developed within the boundaries of the old allegiances and adapted the old social habits to modern economic and industrial conditions.

It is within this context of political and economic decentralism that a new philosophy of localism emerged in the nineteenth century, to be revived with renewed vigour in the 1970s. Following the unification of Italy the two most intellectually vigorous and socially dedicated political cultures in the *Terza Italia* were effectively exiled from political life: the Catholics because of Leo X's vendetta against them for their part in the expropriation of the Papal States, and the Socialists because in the public mind they had come to be associated with anarchists and other revolutionary forces. As a result, Catholics with abilities well-suited to public life were left without roles to play, and instead of contributing to the new politics of united Italy, they joined the Socialists in giving their talents to the public life of the region in other ways. For example, together they helped develop new co-operative movements throughout the territory; others turned to forming a strong local banking system to absorb the savings of local people and to channel them into *artigiano* firms and the new forms of enterprise beginning to grow up in the neighbourhood. New forms of political organization were created, some of them deriving from municipal socialism, some from what became the Catholic Action movement, which helped to form associations in order to further particular communal activities. These various structures provided niches for men of ability to occupy. In this way the community mobilized local wealth for the development of businesses, and out of all this eventually grew up the mid-twentieth-century movements which are the principal subject of this study. Another local activity of much significance for the future was adult education, especially technical and professional education. The movement was particularly strong in Emilia-Romagna, Tuscany, Friuli and parts of the north-west. No less important than these practical activities was the discussion of intellectual and ideological issues. This increased in intensity after the turn of the century when the issues themselves became more timely. The expression which gave the whole movement significance was the somewhat rhetorical one 'in defence of local society'. This not only voiced a virtuous form of local patriotism and crystallized local feelings of caution towards the new centralized government of united Italy, but also expressed the misgivings of many politically conscious Italians, the Socialists especially, about economic developments which they saw as

14

manifestations of social disintegration: the mass-based markets and industrialization coming from Anglo-Saxon societies. There was also considerable agreement with the critique of the capital-investment process made by Marx and Engels. A perception of 'exploitation' was certainly shared by both parties and has survived into recent times. In looking for a method of investment that did not rely upon equity capital sharing the profits, these thinkers drew upon the experience of the *artigiani* who managed to build up their enterprises without having to raise capital in this way.

Was there not a Christian or Socialist alternative to the hard-faced mechanized society that seemed fast approaching and about to pour the culture of northern and central Italy into its mould? This question persisted, and many who asked it saw in co-operatives and small-scale enterprises a sound moral alternative to capitalism. It may even be that the development of an industrial society in Italy was delayed two generations by these misgivings. The keynote sounded in both Socialist and Catholic cultures was the virtue of conserving local society and the values that they believed it embodied. It was in a world of this intellectual and moral quality that the new spirit of localism found expression.

Later, after the interregnum of Fascism and the Second World War, two political movements (or subcultures, as Trigilia describes them) came to dominate the regions of central and north-east Italy: the Italian Communist Party (PCI) and the Christian Democrats (DC), the former more powerful in the centre (the red areas), the latter in the north-east (the white areas). Different as they were, they both inherited the spirit of localism and began to develop economic policies which in various ways, and often in co-operation with local interest groups, helped to stimulate industry in their areas. This ensured that the communes devoted their available resources to supporting the infrastructure of local industry and also that the trade unions co-operated. As Trigilia's chapter explains, these two political parties 'favoured a localist regulation of the small firm economy through their influence on industrial relations and the activity of local governments. On these bases a social compromise was reached which brought about high levels of economic flexibility.'

This compromise brought about the paradox of Prato – the small-firm area perhaps best known outside Italy – where a Communist local authority presided over an industrial district which exemplifies in extremely efficient form all the characteristics of a capitalist system described by the classical economists: some thousands of small textile firms (many of them employing fewer than ten people) competing with each other, producing high-quality goods, achieving remarkable success in export markets and bringing great prosperity to the district.

15

Small firms and industrial districts in Italy

Reserves of labour: leaving the land

Between 1945 and 1960 Italy seemed set to be well on the way to becoming a successful industrial nation following the models of American capitalism and the British mixed economy. The war was over and the post-war recession in Italy had left behind no marks of permanent damage. Industries that had been nationalized for wartime production were being dismantled to make room for efficient peacetime enterprises; others returned to their previous owners to meet the demands of new markets. Heavy industry was being methodically built up in what has since become known as the northern industrial triangle – based on Turin, Milan, and Genoa. Into this triangle would soon be drawn an army of migrant workers from the south. Light industry, mostly engineering, was beginning to be attracted into adjoining areas and the infrastructures of many cities in the north and centre of the country were being improved. As employment and investment increased, the need for subsidiary and secondary industries arose, and these were developing in districts where there had been industrial establishments before: engineering for example, in and around Bologna and Modena; textiles in Prato; refrigerators, furniture, and other consumer durables in the region of Venice and the northern part of Tuscany. The labour situation at that time seemed likely to remain particularly favourable. As the mechanization of agriculture got under way, so it was argued, there would be released in the north and centre of the country large reserves of skilled and experienced labour.

It is worth having a look at a sample of the small farmers and agricultural workers that made up this reserve. They were hardworking and knowledgeable people versed in the many skills needed for success on the hillside farms: grapes and olives to cultivate and harvest; corn between the rows of vines to grow; sheep and oxen to care for as well as the dozen or so subsidiary occupations that helped to make a living in winter. The men were also able to repair equipment and knew enough about the petrol engine to keep their vehicle on the road. The women, besides making the family's clothes, and probably the linen too, collected and prepared the orris roots to take to the perfume factories, made the honey and vinegar and preserved the fruit and still had time to box and tan the animal hides for leather for sale or their own use. The family was not only skilled in all these land-based occupations, but it had also, over the centuries, acquired hard-headed business experience. The agricultural system which they worked and which survived in parts of central and northern Italy until after the Second World War was the *mezzadria*. The land was worked by extended families, and the head of the

16

family would be experienced at organizing the varied operations, in negotiating with the *fattore* (the land agent or estate manager) and in selling the produce in the local market. Here in fact was a flexible division of labour practised in the countryside. The houses stood together in groups by the side of their ample barns in a way that suggests a small industrial complex. Moreover, as Becattini has pointed out in relation to Tuscany, many of the agricultural units were related to each other and bound together by having a common landowner in a system that had characteristics later to be found in the industrial productive process.

This labour force of multi-purposed skills would be redeployed as machines came to take on many of the burdens of its heavy work. It was only a matter of time before Lamborghini and Fiat tractors would become commonplace. Most of the workers when they left the land, it was believed, would adapt their repertoire of skills to enable them to meet the newly articulated needs of the northern triangle or go into the traditional industrial areas as they developed new ranges of consumer goods. There were other options: some abandoned manual work and became stall-holders or dealers in one of the markets of nearby cities. In any event, they took with them a basic entrepreneurial ability.

At the same time as the *contadini* in the north were leaving their farms, workers from the south were coming to the north-eastern industrial triangle in search of work in the factories. Permanent employment in the prosperous factories did not easily come to them, and when it did, they discovered that the work itself bore little relation to that to which they were accustomed. They felt themselves regarded as unskilled and resented strangers who were putting pressure on the already scarce stock of housing resources. They wanted to be accepted and to have some kind of social standing which at that time no union or political party offered them. They needed to make a convincing gesture to show that they were willing to take on the values of the northern industrial proletariat, and to do this they adopted a militancy and a trade-union loyalty not known in the north before. They followed four aims. The first was to become accepted by the northern workers as good union members, and in the course of a few years they led many of the strikes. Second, they agitated for better working conditions and better housing. The third aim was to remove what was for them the wounding distinction between skilled and general work; at least the money value of the distinction could be progressively whittled away; time after time they successfully proposed to union leaders the same wage increase for all grades of workers irrespective of skill differentials. Their fourth aim was to ensure that their wages were high enough for them to make

Small firms and industrial districts in Italy

generous allowances to their families still in the south, and the way to do this was to make themselves a militant force to be feared. They were the first to occupy the factories where they worked, on a 24-hours-a-day basis. Another feature of their radicalism in the late 1960s was their desire to be involved in new forms of political action, alongside the students. This they believed would create a new political force that would take in much besides the conventional list of Marxist grievances. Eventually, political and economic objectives combined to create demands in an atmosphere which intimidated management and alarmed skilled workers, whose wage differentials were already threatened. As a result, the power of the general workers' unions dramatically increased. One of the fruits of their success was the 1970 *Statuto dei Lavoratori*, the first of a series of legislative measures which provided almost cast-iron security of employment and also gave the unions the right to organize elections in the factories and to establish factory councils. It seemed as though the unions would take full control when factory councils were given additional powers in 1972 and 1973. A policy of radical action continued to be pursued by the unions, though by the beginning of the late 1980s their strength was diminishing.

In a comparatively short time this unrest and its aftermath came to play an increasingly decisive part in a nation-wide debate on decentralization. It challenged many of the ideas of the left and centre-left concerning the nature of collectivism and the desirable qualities of working life. Localism once again became a strong force. Discussion centred on the objectives of local policies and how the ways of perceiving them differed from those of central government. The doctrine of popular participation also became the subject of debate. This was a new concept, and as it developed it became part of the political vocabulary of the left as well as of others, finding a place alongside the traditional ideas of decentralization. Finally, decentralization crossed into the economic and industrial vocabulary and gave yet another boost to the small firm rooted in the fertile ground of local community.

The small firms had in fact benefited from the *Statuto dei Lavoratori*. During the debate leading up to the legislation, the associations of small business had exerted the maximum political influence to persuade the political parties of the need for concessions in their favour, which the statutes duly embodied. Small firms, defined first as having fifteen members or fewer (later increased to twenty) were exempted from the principal provisions of the *Statuto dei Lavoratori*, especially those concerned with trade-union representation in factories. In addition, they were given fiscal concessions, such as exemption from VAT up to a generous limit, and they were

18

also exempted from social security payments. A third privilege
which they shared with the *contadini* was to be assessed for local
taxes at a lower rate. The central government also enabled local
authorities to build trading estates where small factories could be
built or let at advantageous terms to small firms wishing to have
better working space or to come out of their back garden, garage,
or kitchen-workshop. Another legislative measure authorized local
authorities to denote certain areas within their boundaries as
'depressed zones' and to provide subsidies or other forms of special
treatment to those starting new businesses there.

The role of the small firm in the local economy became an important issue which was heightened by the wave of unemployment in the
wake of the oil crisis of 1973. This was supplemented by a renewal
of interest in the need for a more active and concerned local government. The pressures that were exerted by interest groups and local
institutions resembled the scene at the beginning of the century when
localism first became an issue. This time, however, the pressures
had very much greater practical content: there was a consensus on
the need for local economic development and the capital expenditure
to accomplish it. The *comuni* became aware of the need to find
employment for those who had lost their jobs as a result of the oil
crisis. The *artigiano* firms themselves formed pressure groups which
were well received by the leading political party in the *comuni*,
whether the DC or PCI. They were concerned to fill, in practical
ways, the gaps they believed central government had left in their
political attitudes to local economic issues. Thus, as Trigilia points
out, in a great many different and distinctive ways, Communist and
Catholic local parties (PCI and DC) 'fostered a localist regulation of
the small firm economy through their influence on industrial
relations and the activity of local government'.

At the same time, the general unions themselves recognized that
they were losing their bargaining power, because of technical
developments which enabled management to abandon the assembly
line and to use instead new, flexible methods of production, and
because of rising unemployment.

Even before this, the owners and managements of many large
firms, especially in the northern triangle, had begun to extend the
practice of subcontracting important pieces of work; and this process
was taken further by encouraging their skilled men, sometimes the
entire workforce of a crucial department, to turn themselves into
independent specialist firms under separate management. In order to
be exempt from further union pressure and from the provisions of
union-instigated legislation, these new firms had to be seen to be
independent of any outside ownership. They were then able to enter

19

Small firms and industrial districts in Italy

into contractual relationships with their previous employer, who often helped them by making loans as starting capital. Some remained in the area and can be recognized as dependent subcontractors. Others moved further afield. The alternative for some large firms was liquidation, so the arrangement had some guarantee of permanence; and so it has proved. However, the small firms had to face the danger of being dependent on a single, large client who would find it easy to exploit them, and therefore they had to develop relationships with other customers. Eventually, the number and variety of their customers became a measure not only of their independence but also of their commercial solidity and viability. This was the origin of that particular characteristic of the high-technology *artigiano* firm, namely that it was not only highly specialized but also flexible. Each contract it made was for a different product demanding from the workers skills in different sequences of work.

The industrial district

Four tendencies have been discussed above: localism, participation; resistance to the organized pressures of the unskilled workers; and the formulation of a new type of skilled industrial enterprise. Together these factors generated the force to create a distinctive type of manufacturing complex which has been identified as a contemporary form of the 'industrial district'. It may be too early to judge the success of the Italian industrial district in meeting the needs of modern society or how permanent a social and economic structure it will prove to be. But even with this reservation and the added one that the area of the *Terza Italia* where it has been created is but a small part of Italy and a tiny part of the industrial world, it is yet clear that the high-technology industrial district is an innovation of great importance in the realm of ideas which carries with it few of the moral objections to capitalism and few of the political objections to communism.

Since a large part of this book is involved with industrial districts, the notes that follow are designed to introduce the English reader to the modern Italian concept of what has previously been described mainly in terms of British nineteenth-century experience. It will be seen that there are broadly two types of industrial district, one conventional and, in economic terms, classical, and the other with certain collectivist features. Roughly speaking, the former tended to evolve naturally; the latter was more positively encouraged and more systematically supported by local interest groups.

The term 'industrial district' is a concept made familiar by the English economist Alfred Marshall. The division of labour which

20

characterizes the area is not by individual workers in a single factory but by different highly specialized firms which both compete with each other and complement one another. The ultimate refinements are the flexible use of resources, including manpower, and a specialized vertical production process. The more specialized the process the fewer the firms in the pyramid. This is illustrated by Brusco's maxim that in an industrial district only one type of specialist firm corresponds to each stage of production. The definition of the industrial district is at present a subject of debate, especially in Italy, among economists and industrial sociologists. Initially, it can be said that an industrial district is an 'exclusive and restricted locality which has both industrial and residential characteristics'. The classic type described by Marshall had a number of features that still have validity today. Two of Marshall's comments are worth quoting for the flavour they give: ' "The Mysteries of Industry" that children learn unconsciously and others breathe in through the air'; 'Workers by associating with one another teach one another'. A third is worth summarizing: opportunities for innovation are enhanced when small firms operate within industrial districts and can draw on the pooled resources and the generational accumulation of skills that are stored there. Innovations are born in this industrial atmosphere and the harder the challenge, the more likely it is that simpler and more efficient ways of responding to it will be found.

The industrial district is essentially a territorial system of small and medium-sized firms producing a group of commodities whose products are processes which can be split into different phases. This definition was given by Becattini.[9] Other authors refer to it as a system of firms rather than as an exact geographical concentration. It is interesting that in this connection they do not think it impossible for two or three industrial districts to thrive in the same geographical area, or in overlapping or contiguous areas. Where a given area of specialization in interrelated forms of production lacks some of the features of an industrial district, it is convenient to call it a 'product specialist area', a label which points to the continuation of craft traditions, as in some parts of Tuscany or in the south of Italy.

Fabio Sforzi follows a meticulous path, seeing the industrial district as a well-defined part of a particular kind of geographical system. For him it is 'an organised complex of local interdependence within which the interrelations between family systems and firm systems takes place'. Its primary purpose is as a local labour market, where 'the majority of the local population can find work or change jobs without having to change their place of residence'. He infers that there is a strong relationship, almost by definition, between

21

Small firms and industrial districts in Italy

social class and industrial district. He quotes Marshall as saying that an industrial district has to be organized as 'a totality of integral parts' and also that its population has to have social characteristics, just as the manufacturing firms it includes have to have 'productive characteristics' and to be specialized in different phases of production. For him, an industrial district is a predominantly working-class area where most wives go out to work, and he tends to reject candidate-areas for inclusion on the grounds that they have too many white-collar workers. His point about the class basis of the industrial districts opens up many topics of discussion, and, of course, begs the question of white-collar workers in areas such as machine-tool making, where an educational qualification and white collar or similar symbol of class may be very nearly inevitable.

From these remarks it ought not to be inferred that in modern Italy class distinction is an important factor. In fact, it should be stressed once again that the Italian small firm has few of the communication problems that beset larger hierarchic firms in many parts of the world. What is significant about an industrial district, and often other kinds of industrial areas too, is that its inhabitants tend to be homogeneous. Living and working together is a precondition of specialization.

Becattini claims that the basic unit of economic analysis should be the industrial district or industrial area and not a particular firm or industry. He likes the expressions 'systems of firms' and 'network of firms', which make the system of industrial districts themselves seem a more flexible and adaptable idea. Moreover, the concentration of skills and the rapid circulation of ideas within these areas, and the constant experimenting with new practical forms of them, leads to innovation, which is especially important in businesses committed to high technology. What holds together the firms in an industrial district, according to Becattini, is 'a complex and tangled web of economies and diseconomies, of joint and associated costs, of historical and cultural vestiges, which envelop both inter-firm and interpersonal relationships'. Russo's fascinating study of the ceramic tile makers, introducing innovations made by their neighbours the machine-tool makers, is an example ready to hand to illustrate Becattini's point.

Central to the understanding of the industrial districts is the notion of internal and external economies of scale. An internal economy of scale is, of course, an economy organized and achieved within a firm for the benefit of all its parts: a typing pool, an accounts department, a drawing office and sometimes, a research department, perform the functions of internal economies. Other examples will be obvious. An external economy arises where it is cheaper for an external firm or agency, and sometimes an institution, to carry out specialized work for all the firms in an industry, rather than for each of the constituent firms to do it in-house. In general terms, therefore, it can be said that in an industrial district, economies of scale are internal to the district but external to the firms that make it up.

The unique feature of an industrial district is that by one of two methods it carries out the external economies for all the firms in the district. These two methods correspond to the type of industrial district they serve. In the first, the classical type of district with its strong historical traditions and other features very much resembling Bellandi's account of the Marshallian system, there is no collective provision of external services. (This type prevails in Tuscany, for example.) Instead, the external economies of scale here are provided through specialist firms and through one or two large firms that existed in the district before the small firms came and which now act as training centres for workers and transmitters of old skills and traditions.

By contrast, in the red areas (dominated by the PCI) a collectivist model of the industrial district is the more usual form, and the method of providing common services is through centralized agencies. This system can be quickly comprehended in Chapter 3, by Ash Amin. It is as though an entire industrial district specializing in one type of production had become a kind of corporation housing a number of independently owned, interlocking small firms.

Competition in industrial districts, especially in the engineering sectors, is exceptionally severe, because each firm is very specialized, and the smaller and more specialized, the more determined are its members to win the contract. Having won a contract, a firm may subcontract parts of it to other even more specialized firms, all of which collaborate with each other to complete it with maximum efficiency. Moreover, many of these specialist subcontractors may again subcontract to yet other specialized firms. This holds especially true of the Emilian industrial districts. Any individual firm may enter into any number of contracts during the course of a year: between twenty and thirty is normal. The firms sell their products either to the local market or, more usually, to each other. The more specialized the product, the more likely it is that the sale will be to another specialist firm. Eventually, of course, the completed product reaches the national or international market.

These remarks point to the significance of the dualism of competition and collaboration in the modern industrial district. The firms may work together to find new techniques or devise new tools, but competition remains fierce. They may pass to another firm, orders

23

Small firms and industrial districts in Italy

they cannot fulfil; and the relationship may become contractual, which justifies the reference to some small specialist firms as subcontractors.

In his idealized model Amin describes even closer collaboration by a 'cluster' of small firms making up integrated production units and then selling their finished goods to 'strategic entrepreneurs composed of other small firms from provincial cities'. These latter firms come from different family units and share the bargain of the strategic entrepreneur on a contractual basis. All contracts are short term and can be adjusted to actual market conditions. This leads Amin on to the subject of flexibility of contracts, which he sees as the logical and symmetric counterpart of flexible production.

Flexible production is the second most conspicuous feature of the industrial district which has attracted public attention. It can be regarded as the Italian industrial district's unique contribution to lowering the cost of modern technology. In mass production specially designed plant and machinery is used to achieve the economies of scale, but the plant is costly and needs a very long series of production to justify it. The use, instead, of flexible methods of production – in the deployment of labour and the use of tools – makes possible short series of production in batches. It also gives scope for customized production. Modern technology, in particular the computer and numerically controlled tools, makes small-scale production possible and leads to variations in output which would not have been possible in systems of production based on the conventional economies of scale and conventional production plans. Such flexibilities are particularly appropriate for markets concentrating on quality-based products the demand for which fluctuates, sometimes dramatically, in terms of both quality and design. The adaptability of the labour force, a salient characteristic of the *Terza Italia*, is of course crucial to flexible production methods.

The financial backing for small firms in Italy shows a sharp contrast to the contemporary British banking system, dominated as it is by a few centralized national banks. A significant part of the Italian system is formed by local banks, often called savings banks or artisans' banks. They have counterparts in Germany, variously called co-operative, savings, or *Handwerk* banks, and bear some resemblance to nineteenth-century British provincial banks before the amalgamations took place. These Italian banks derive their funds from local sources and lend to local firms. Their directors and managers have a close working relationship with the firms in their area and a personal knowledge of anyone setting up in business and needing to borrow money to do so. In some cases the bank may be involved in the decision-making of the business and may even lend

24

staff. Some banks subsidize centres for providing specialist services
to small firms. But equally important is the fact that the decisions
of the bank will be based on an understanding of the economy of the
district rather than on rules laid down by a distant head office.
Another institution, called *Intermediatore con l'Estero*, provides help
to small firms in import–export business. It is a private-enterprise
common-service agency performing the function of intermediary
between producer and buyer. Sometimes, in the case of long-term
contracts, the *Intermediatore* is in a position to vary the contract
(e.g. to initiate changes in price) when it seems realistic to do so.

The difference that the existence of an industrial district makes to
the success of the small firm is illustrated in two other chapters: the
one on Ravenna by Mario Pezzini and the one on Naples by Ash
Amin. In Ravenna the small manufacturing firms hardly get off the
ground, or if they do there are few others with whom they can
develop markets and trade-offs, and there are no reserves of trained
and experienced labour. In Naples there certainly are small manufacturing businesses, but few of them flourish. Amin describes some
really excellent firms of shoemakers, but they enjoy neither the
growth nor the profits of the firms in the industrial districts of the
north.

Summing up

Brusco's chapter introduces comments on two justly celebrated
pieces of economic literature which give a perspective on our present
study of the small firm economy in Italy. One is Adam Smith's
maxim that the division of labour is limited by the extent of the
market, and the other is George Stigler's article in the *Journal of
Political Economy* in June 1951 which refers at length to the book
by G.C. Allen, *The Industrial Development of Birmingham and the
Black Country 1860–1927*.[10] This latter opens up the vista of that
part of Birmingham centred around St Mary's Church, where two
industrial districts coincided: that where jewellery was manufactured
and where the specialist parts of guns were assembled and the gun
finished. Stigler's comment is as appropriate today as it was in 1951
when his article was first published. 'The division of labour is not
a quaint practice of eighteenth-century pin factories: it is a
fundamental principle of economic organisation.'

This is not, however, the primary reason for bringing up again
Stigler's discussion of the specialism carried out in the Birmingham
small arms industrial district in 1860. The intention was rather to be
able to add, 'So we have all been here before!' The population of
this particular small firm economy was as skilled, as knowledgeable

Small firms and industrial districts in Italy

and as productive as that of any Italian district now; yet in the 1920s it disappeared. The mass-production motor industry took its place, drawing on its reservoir of skilled workers. There are of course important differences of tradition and culture, especially the important role of family and community. Nevertheless, on first rereading the passage from G.C. Allen's book quoted by Stigler, a chill goes down the spine of any of us who are concerned about the future of the Italian small firm: history may repeat itself.

With their familial relationships, their generational build up of skills, their asymptotic dependence upon both competition and co-operation, their obvious sense of community and camaraderie, the industrial manufacturing districts of Italy are important cultural entities. What we have been describing, and the chapters in this volume refer to, is not only a small-firm economy. It is a polity as well, and if British economic history were to be repeated, this might soon be in jeopardy from monopolies and conglomerates.

Yes, we have been here before. Consider the small-arms industry in 1860, when Birmingham was still the leading production centre of the world:

Of the 5,800 people engaged in this manufacture within the borough's boundaries in 1861 the majority worked within a small district round St Mary's Church. . . . The reason for the high degree of localisation is not difficult to discover. The manufacture of guns, as of jewellery, was carried on by a large number of makers who specialised on particular processes, and this method of organisation involved the frequent transport of parts from one workshop to another. The master gun-maker – the entrepreneur – seldom possessed a factory or workshop. Usually he owned merely a warehouse in the gun quarter, and his function was to acquire semi-finished parts and to give these out to specialised craftsmen, who undertook the assembly and finishing of the gun. He purchased materials from the barrel-makers, lock-makers, sight-stampers, trigger-makers, ramrod-forgers, gun-furniture makers, and, if he were engaged in the military branch, from bayonet-forgers. All of these were independent manufacturers executing the orders of several master gun-makers. Once the parts had been purchased from the 'material makers', as they were called, the next task was to hand them out to the 'setters up', each of whom performed a specific operation in connection with the assembly and finishing of the gun. To name only a few, there were those who prepared the front sight and lump end of the barrels; the jiggers, who attended to the breech end; the stockers, who let in the barrel and lock and shaped the stock; the barrel-strippers, who prepared the gun for rifling and proofing; the hardeners, polishers, borers and riflers, engravers, browners, and finally the lock-freers, who adjusted the working parts.[11]

History may not repeat itself, and there is much in the Italian tradition of small firms that will delay whatever ineluctable economic forces there may be. Let's try to be clear about what some of its advantages are: intimate-sized working units based on family and community relationships between men and women who traditionally support each other; the relentless pursuit of skill both as a means of maximizing economic gain and of the individual's response to the challenges set out by his work; no need for surveillance, no free riders, and the rich opportunities for improvization and the discussion of technical problems that so often result in innovation. All these provide economic advantages to the firm as well as satisfaction to the workers.

One needs to refer again to Brusco's work and to Stigler's article to put this optimism to the test and discover the real threats to the small-firm economy. In 1951 Stigler pointed to one threat and in 1986 Brusco took it up: vertical integration. Specialist small firms develop a new high-technology product which becomes indispensable to a large manufacturer, the raw material, as it were, of the essential output of the large firm. It is assumed that sooner or later the small firms will be taken over by the big manufacturer, giving it vertical economies and adding to its size and security.

However, Brusco is confident that this is a situation with which a well-organized industrial district can deal successfully. Specialization takes the place of vertical integration, 'thus enabling the industrial district to have at its disposal high level skills'.

Brusco's main fear seems to be whether the system of disintegrated firms will be able to survive the introduction of new electronic technologies. Will the small manufacturer be able to develop new products in competition with giant firms which can devote massive resources to research and development? His solution is a much more systematic provision of central services in industrial districts, with both public and private support. Some degree of collectivism is of course implied.

Brusco relates two views of technical progress: one from Schumpeter, the *élan vital* which sees progress created by intuitive leaps occurring in daily experience in the workshop, the other a more institutional approach, associated with the name of Rosenberg, whose advance is by small successive steps. There can be little doubt that those who believe in the small firm economy will find the creative theory of technical progress more attractive. Nevertheless, progress of this nature would be well served by the underpinning that a solid

Small firms and industrial districts in Italy

institution could give. Leaps forward are safer in the light than in the dark, and research and scientific expertise can provide the light. So it may be that these are not two contradictory models, and that there is a role for specially designed centres for common services in the patient and systematic follow-up of innovative ideas. It needs to be said that a danger for the future of industrial districts is that those responsible will imitate more closely the blueprint efficiency of the large firm and reinforce the collectivist trends, already strong in the institutions of the high-technology districts. ' The superiority of the small *artigiano* firm has been founded on the belief in the efficacy of the 'bottom-up' form of organization, and on the ability of these firms to handle the tools of high technology. Why diminish these strengths? A debate on this issue might illuminate the problem of how better these industrial districts may be supported.

At the immediately practical level it seems obvious to suggest that if the causes for sounding the alarm are the predatory noises, still some way off, coming from the centres of international capital, the most effective safeguard is to make sure that the money supply line to the constituent firms is at least as effective as it would be if international capital were actually to take them over. Statistics show that wages in some of the districts of the *Terza Italia* are falling below the level of a year or two ago, and this may indicate a levelling off of the upward curve of prosperity.

Is it realistic to expect the present structure of the industrial district to remain intact in the face of the financial pressures and inducements that are likely to come? These are issues the EEC might address itself to. For one of the threats to the political economy of the small firms comes from developments in the EEC itself. Among the changes under the single market in 1992 will be the removal of the current restrictions in Italy which prevents a foreign company owning more than 49 per cent of an Italian business. Possibly more alarming is the prospect of foreign banks freely entering the Italian market, since, as we have seen, the Italian local banks give vital support to the small firms. The Italian central bank has already let it be known that the arrival of European competition will necessitate bigger banks.

The question above all that the chapters of this book invite to be asked is this: are these small independent craft firms simply efficient agents of economic purpose at this particular time in Italy's industrial history or do they also embody important human values which might well cease to find expression if the firms were to suffer the fate of their counterparts in the industrial districts of England in the time of Alfred Marshall? This is a question addressed to the

28

Introduction

political theorist and the educated public as well as to the economist and the industrial sociologist. Possibly enough has been said to show that the Italian small-firm economy offers at least one approach to the liberal dream of free and creative work as an essential part of liberty.

As the work on this book progressed, it became more and more evident that the distinction implied in the title of the Acton Society's continuing study of the two-tier economy has a reality and perhaps a universal significance. The first tier is defined as the sphere of the large-scale organization, of mass production and the unskilled worker, of the vertical division of labour and hierarchical relationships, and inevitably, of impersonal and bureaucratic systems of control. The second tier is the tier of skill, imagination, and adaptability, where production is for the market-place where people's needs differ; the sphere of worker satisfaction and personal service, involving a type of work that has to be done on a human scale and where relationships operate *al livello umano*. It is clear that the first and second tiers have separate characteristics, not only in economic terms but in social, cultural, and political terms as well; and it may be that they should be governed by quite separate rules. It may also be true that these considerations apply as strongly to Britain as to Italy. The belief that the interests of economic and political liberalism are identical, that economic progress by whatever means achieved is political progress, and the belief that there is only one way to a desired economic or political end – these false theories are refuted in this book, which points to an industrial future that will preserve and extend the human as well as the economic values enshrined in these small firms and the complex of relationships that bind them together.

Notes

1. The term *Terza Italia*, the third Italy, distinguishes the area of north-central and north-east Italy from the south of the country and from the area of heavy industry in the north-west. It consists of the regions of Tuscany, Emilia-Romagna, Umbria, Marche, Veneto, Friuli-Venezia-Giulia and Trentino-Alto Adige. Arnaldo Bagnasco is credited with inventing the term.
2. Professor Becattini is a distinguished economist and an authority on the subject of this book. See, for example, his *Mercato e forze locali: il distretto industriale*, Bologna: Il Mulino: 1987 and 'Dal settore industriale al distretto industriale', in *Rivista di Economia e Politica Industriale*, no. 1, 1987.
3. Professor Brusco is the leading authority on the Emilian economy. See, for example, 'The Emilian model: production, decentralisation and

Small firms and industrial districts in Italy

social integration', *Cambridge Journal of Economics* 6, 1982; 'Small firms and industrial districts', in D. Keeble and E. Wever (eds.) *New Firms and Regional Development*, London: Croom Helm, 1986.

4. At an Acton Society seminar in Florence, 1987.
5. See *Bolton Committee of Inquiry on Small Firms*, Cmnd 4811, HMSO, 1971.
6. S. Weil, *Oppression and Liberty*, London: Routledge & Kegan Paul, 1958.
7. I owe much of the insight in this section to discussions with Dr Susan Mendus of York University. See her 'Liberty and autonomy', *Proceedings of the Aristotelian Society*, 1986.
8. Weil, op. cit.
9. In an address to an Acton Society seminar at Eynsham Hall, Oxford, October, 1987.
10. G.J. Stigler, 'The division of labour is limited by the extent of the market', *Journal of Political Economy* 59 (31), June 1951.
11. G.C. Allen, *The Industrial Development of Birmingham and the Black Country 1860–1927*, quoted in Stigler.

30

Part IV
Diversification

[16]

The Large Family Firm in the French Manufacturing Industry

Maurice Lévy-Leboyer
University of Paris X-Nanterre

Even though there is a general tendency to look upon all family firms as very much alike—and so they probably are in terms of life-time employment, career opportunities, zeal and loyalty of their officers to the company—one should keep in mind that historical factors in France, more specifically the great depression that held down industry in the latter part of the 19th century, have contributed to shape its business institutions in ways that may have proved detrimental in the long run. Quite apart from technological change and market development which no doubt had an immediate impact on policies and structures, the fact that growth had been deficient for some twenty years or so meant that, in the many sectors which they came to dominate, the large corporations based on family ownership and management did not make up a group of homogeneous and mature enterprises. All these firms had been launched over a long period of time, before and after the beginning of the depression, and they reacted therefore to its adverse effects in two opposite ways. Most of the older concerns that had managed to survive the period of difficulties were prevented from expanding and diversifying their production; very few among them, even after the 1914–18 war, were able to adopt the multi-line, multi-market strategies that were characteristic in other industrial countries of modern corporations branching out into new ventures.[1] While the more recent ones, having often started their operations at the turn of the century, in what were years of slow revival, hence from a narrow basis and with limited outside finance, were still striving in the 1920s to establish themselves. The paradox of French large family firms, in the early part of the 20th century, is that the great majority were considered as having had long years of experience and capital accumulation—some textile mills and ironworks, in fact, had been under the control of the same families for six or seven generations and sometimes even longer in the North and Eastern France— although only a limited number, as a few instances will show, had reached a position of financial autonomy and a secure basis.

A. The *older group*, dating back for many of its members from Napoleon's days, included in its formative years large mercantile houses that had entered industry. It is an original feature of the country that Swiss, German and of course French merchant bankers, located in the out-ports and in Paris, were among the prime movers of the first industrial revolution, supplying them with capital, information, managing partners and even correspondents to develop the works they had contributed to create. However, in spite of these past achievements and of their long standing position among the French business elite—some of their descendants were still holding directorships by the 1920s in railroad companies, banks and leading industrial firms—their influence had been on the wane all through the 19th century, for reasons that may be perceived by examining briefly the example of the Rothschilds as a case in point.

The house, originating from Frankfurt in the 18th century, included five brothers and five banks spread over the main European cities, though with business centered first in London, up to the 1840s, and then in Paris, until the death of James de Rothschild in 1868. Their success, exemplified by their multiple business initiatives and accumulated wealth,[2] may be partly ascribed to the constraints that a strongly knit family could assign to its members. According to the deeds of settlement, revised every three years or so from 1818, there was to be among them a community of capital: balance sheets had to be consolidated each year into one single account, all profits being retained and cumulated, after deduction of fixed family expenses, interest charges, etc.; all books were to remain secret and closed to the children after the death of a partner; no arbitration was allowed, out of the family circle, in case of litigation between members, etc. There was also to be a community in ways of life and ideas regulated by written rules (each partner being required to give all his time to the house, to circulate information by weekly letters, to make frequent visits to his parents); and it was further strengthened by family customs that were then traditional in Jewish communities (James de Rothschild, for instance, married one of his nieces in 1824, and marriages between cousins were to follow in the third and fourth generations).

But these were abstract principles easy to apply only up to the second generation. With the passage of time, there was a risk that the family's initial cohesion might be undermined because of the unequal success of the different houses, and further because of a change in business orientation, the firm having moved from bills of exchange and specie (the main Frankfurt and London trade), first, into the financing of post-war indemnities and government debts, and then—at least so far as the continental houses are concerned—into railroad building and industrial investment, that made them more dependent on local economic conditions. Of course equality had been very much on the mind of the founder and his sons; they had devised schemes that entitled each of the partners to a share in profits that was adjusted periodically to their capital (in the consolidated balance sheet) and to their own responsibilities (in each of the individual houses). But the system, quite complex, tended in practice to reduce the share of the London partners, who withdrew from the association when the third generation came of age, and it was finally given up in the 1850s with the decline of the Vienna and Naples houses, the latter being liquidated in 1860–63. Solidarity was upheld, but between what had become *de facto* independent firms, endowed with great prestige, but having no more resources than the big deposit banks of the day: the Paris house, still the most powerful, had a capital of 40 million francs in 1868 (50 million in 1880 divided equally between James' three sons), so that, with the partners accounts (assessed to 30 or 40 million) and those of the public, the house's total liabilities were of the order of 280–300 million francs, that is, one-half the total held by the other private bankers, but only one-fourth of those of the four big deposit banks in Paris.[3]

This could not maintain the Rothschilds in the lead, overcommitted as they were with capital invested and to a certain extent frozen in steel plants and coal mines (in Belgium) and in railroads (in France, Northern Italy and Spain). They had given up a project, studied in 1849 by a junior partner, of enlarging their foreign trade operations and of opening a sixth house in New York; they renewed their attempt in the 1860s, then giving precedence to the oil and metals trades. But they had to wait until the pre-1914 war recovery in the stock market and in raw material prices to have enough funds released and reassert themselves. And the outcome was not dissimilar with the other merchant bankers in Paris: they had to cope with the country's territorial dismemberment and monetary inconvert-ibility in the 1870s, and later with the displacement of railroad traffic to the Gothard and with the industrial slowdown; some succeeded in protecting the name of their family, but they did not regain much of their former influence.

B.   *New developments*, though, became possible with the reform of company laws (limited liability being instituted in 1863–67), with the rise in stock market operations (and a shift in savers' demand from bonds to equities after the 1890s), and with the entry of a new generation of entrepreneurs and engineers eager to use new tech-nologies and market opportunities to build what became for the first time large-scale production units. Major increases in business' annual turnover were reported after the beginning of the century. Earlier in the past a 100 million francs sales per year was a limit that had been seldom achieved except by the big department stores and textile chains; it had remained out of reach among manufacturing firms before 1900: 15–20 million F was the range that pioneers had set in chemicals, when successful; 20–30 million was not unfrequent in the steel industry, 40–55 in coal mining and in the automobile sector. But with the revival of activity in the pre-war years and with the war orders, the whole economy was set in motion: the 100 million F mark was passed by Saint-Gobain (the leading chemicals and glass manufacturer) as early as 1910, 200–300 million by firms in the mechanical industries (Renault reached 350 million turnover in 1918, almost seven times the firm's pre-war figure); 400–450 million were often registered in steel, metals and engineering—one billion at the Schneiders' works in 1918; and the trend was to con-

TABLE 1 Securities Issued by Private Corporations on the Stock Exchange, 1900–1939 (average annual value in millions of 1913 francs).

	Shares	Bonds	Total	Percentage shares	Share Bonds
1904–13	650	460	1,110	58%	42%
1920–29	1,700	615	2,315	73	27
1930–34	840	610	1,450	58	42
1935–39	300	210	510	59	41
1900–39	935	490	1,425	66	34

Source: *Annuaire statistique de la France* (Paris, 1966), pp. 352–53. The railroad companies are not included in the table.

tinue with the 1920s inflation that multiplied prices by a factor of five: although they tried to rationalize their production and hold down costs to bolster their sales, the three leaders in the automobile sector were heading for 740 million at Peugeot, and 1.4 and 1.8 billion at Renault and Citroën, respectively, in 1929–1930.

This major increase in the level of business operations caused acute financial problems: firms had to build up new plants in their own product line; some moved back from the assembly of parts to that of their manufacturing and into more basic sectors, to overcome supply shortages. Further, since industries could no longer rely on the assistance of old-established trade houses and on that of the State (as during the war), many entered marketing or enlarged their commercial operations, all steps that were even more demanding both in capital and credit facilities. A shortage of liquid funds therefore developed that was most serious in the automobile industry: an old and experienced firm like Peugeot kept on the average 100–120 million francs of net cash assets through the 1920s, i.e. the equivalent of one year's sales immediately after the war; but the ratio very soon fell to much lower levels—to one-fifth in 1927—as a consequence of the company's rising activity; at André Citroën's, who had started his car plant only after the war, the firm reported in 1927 a short-term liability position of 100 million francs against a turnover that had passed one billion. It is this imbalance between cash funds and the flow of current operations that became the concern of all the large industrial companies and made it necessary for them to appoint bankers on the board (sometimes for a few

months) and to call on the securities market, first, to issue new
shares—bonds being unsaleable in the 1920s, since people had lost
four-fifths in real value on their past bond holdings (Table 1)—and,
second, to do so on a scale that had never been registered before:
in 1913, capital stocks had seldom reached 30 million francs per
firm (coming from 0.6–0.8 million in the mid-1890s for new firms
in the modern sectors); but they increased by five and even ten
times in the 1920s: Edouard Michelin, the tire manufacturer, was
able to raise his capital, in two issues, up to 150 million by 1924;
Robert Peugeot to 250 million, in four steps, by 1930; André Citroën
was already at 400 million in 1928 (against 50 million in 1924 when
his firm had become a public company), etc. Some of the older
firms that were carrying on a policy of diversification, for instance
in the chemicals industry, were heading for half a billion F capital,
sometimes after twelve or thirteen stock issues.

If bonds had been still in use—and firms frequently turned back
to them after 1930—the danger would have been minimal. But with
the fall in the level of equities that individuals or families could hope
to keep in industrial companies, it was to be doubted that family
firms would last very long. In point of fact, two waves of mergers in
the 1920s brought to the fore a new generation of engineers who
had access to the Paris financial market, to State orders, and so
were able to take over large sectors of production in the more
capital-intensive parts of industry. The threat of a separation between ownership and management thus had become an actual
issue. Some family firms, though, held on to their past structures,
through one of three main devices.

(1) *Financial holdings:* In a few sectors, where manufacturers
had to carry on their usual production, and at the same time
finance and often conduct the operations of a customer or a subsidiary company—e.g. when some industrial plant had been erected
by an engineering firm, or when streetcars, generating power
stations or other public utility companies were set up by a more
specialized concern—it had become customary, even before the
war, to incorporate a holding company that would act as a financial
intermediary, i.e. to issue, buy, hold or sell stocks for the account of
the mother firm, using as cash reserves the spare funds held by the

sub-companies and co-partners. The *Centrale de Dynamite* had acted in such capacity for the Nobel trust from 1887, the *Société parisienne pour l'industrie électrique* in 1900 for the group headed by Edouard Empain, the *Union européenne industrielle et financière* in 1920 for that of Eugène Schneider II, etc. Their primary aim had been to procure external funds and allocate them between the members of the industrial group. And they were later used in practice by its founder (who maintained a majority share in the holding) to keep some influence over the affiliated companies: indirect financial controls were thus being used to protect individuals' or families' interests.

(2) *Family trusts:* Many firms in the 19th century were managed under the influence of some inside group having a substantial, but not always a majority, share in the capital: Eugène Schneider I, for instance, who built the country's largest industrial company, had started his career at the Creusot plants with a small capital share limited to 5%, but with the backing of two substantial shareholders whose descendants were still present a century later in the company's executive committee. In a similar way, members of the board at St-Gobain, who were recruited for some four generations in the same narrow circle of ten old families, held together 4% or 5% of the equities as an outside limit but enjoyed throughout the confidence of two or three parties whose influence was decisive in the 19th century when the company had a limited number of shareholders (375 in 1862, less than 1,400 in 1907), and after the war, thanks to the wide dissemination of the stock. In the 1920s, however, with the massive sales of equities by companies which were then only medium-sized family firms, some of the directors felt that they were at the mercy of bankers, collecting blank votes in the public at large, and that they could no longer be content with tacit and informal pacts. They organized new trust companies on a family basis—such as *Progil* (1919) in the man-made textile industries, *Filor* (1924) in the foundry and metals sector, etc.: they were in charge of holding the shares individual members had transferred to them, of raising the extra funds necessary to subscribe to new issues and of protecting their position in the company.

(3) *Preference shares:* On the assumption that the public was more interested in cashing dividends than in having a say in a busi-

ness firm's policy, many companies had issued just before the war
and in the mid-1920s passive shares (*parts de fondateur*), i.e. stocks
with no stated value, no right to take part in the shareholders' general assemblies, but entitled to some 15 or 20% of the net profit;
they were distributed as a kind of indemnity to their shareholders
by Dollfus-Mieg and other Alsatian cotton firms, Michelin, Peugeot,
Citroën and many others, when the capital of these companies was
opened to outside subscribers. The same proceeding was adopted in
a slightly amended form, again in the 1920s, to market further stock
issues: shares labelled "A", with a plural vote, were assigned to the
older members of the company, while shares "B", with a one vote
each, were being issued to the public at large. This gave rise to a
wide variety of schemes: some firms, like Michelin in 1928, had the
passive shares listed on the stock exchange to the exclusion of the
active ones—probably for arbitrage purposes; others tried to hold on
to those that had a greater voting power—all the 20,000 "A" shares
that had been issued in 1928 were back into the hands of the Peugeot
family by March 1931—they amounted to a fraction of the 500,000
shares then in circulation, but to 29% of the votes; André Citroën
in 1934 also held 50,000 "A" shares in his company (with six votes
each) and 104,000 "B" shares and was entitled to 22% of the votes,
against a lesser portion of the capital stock, etc. All these and other
measures, such as a right of preemption that some firms had reserved
for themselves over their own shares, were devised in a pragmatic
way to strengthen the authority of managers having to supervise
the activities and coordinate the resources of what had become,
probably in too short a time, large-scale organizations.

These, however, were but temporary devices that could not stop
the slow erosion of families' influence over business activity: new
company laws, destructive of artificial majorities, were passed in
1933–35—they brought to a par all types of equities in terms of
voting power; freedom of sale was claimed in courts by shareholders;
economic setbacks and fiscal reforms seriously curtailed individuals'
incomes, contracting further the means that could be allocated to
holding companies, etc. Still, the large family firms held their sway
in the 1930s, keeping a real power of attraction and a true resilience
through the depression, in contrast with many overgrown enter-

prises that had captured the public's attention but had made wrong market forecasts. This was no doubt because of the major success they had achieved in the earlier part of the century, and also because of the social environment they were able to maintain, financial and majority problems being only a minor factor compared to the human relations some of these firms had built and preserved. It is therefore logical, first, to determine the factors that may explain their performance up to the 1930s depression, their contribution to the country's economic growth, and, second, to ascertain the forces that made their decline foreseeable in the near future.

I. Hierarchical Structures and Personnel Management

French large corporations did not differ in their institutional setting from those one finds in most European countries: with a large labor force per firm and with closely integrated production units to service the market, they had to be managed under elaborate hierarchies, strongly structured, made up of two different sets of personel and objectives, one for general management and external relations, and one for more routine and concrete duties. These two were to be found as early as the 1850s in the six railroad companies which had built the great trunk lines and kept henceforth the task of their management. At the Compagnie du Nord, the Rothschilds' main line, the board of directors was made up of men of finance (including members of that family) and officials from the State, Chambers of Commerce and other local authorities; their office was to negotiate with outside parties (including the State) and to review the whole operation at regular intervals, while the actual task of operating the lines was left to the care of a staff of engineers who had an organization of their own within the company and enjoyed a fair measure of autonomy. This dual system was extended to new sectors in the latter part of the 19th century for the reason that big manufacturing firms like St-Gobain, the Schneiders' works, the main machine and repair shops, as well as iron-works in Eastern and Central France, ran across serious difficulties: they met falling markets in the 1880s and faced serious competition from firms having access to superior technology and cheaper resources; and their proprietors were therefore compelled to transfer much of the business duties to engineers and high ranking officers who took it upon themselves to enter new markets and to experiment with new products that proved successful (fertilizers at St-Gobain, ordnance and engineering at the Schneiders' works, more elaborate products in the Lorraine works, etc.).[7] The same dual structures applied in many of the new family firms after the turn of the century, even though they had taken initially single-product lines that did not require extensive planning and supervision. But growth in their case was achieved rapidly and, given the constraints of modern industries, they had to depend on the close cooperation of an active staff—teams of three, five or even ten people from the start, and not one single entrepreneur working in isolation were to be found running most firms[8]—and also on the assistance of personalities recruited from the public and the private sectors who entered the board (and sometimes assumed its presidency) to hasten its social and financial establishment. All large-scale enterprises thus had central executive offices working in a highly cohesive way with the board of directors, a system in keeping with the idea of authoritarian command that was a key to the management of all French companies, family and non-family alike.

These two sets of authority did not remain closed to each other. In the past century, it is true, the recruitment of directors tended to be rather restricted because the boards were limited to a few members and also because family nominees belonged to a small elite. At St-Gobain, according to an analysis of the pre-1870s personnel, they were all men of distinction, by birth or through scientific achievements; many had served as civil servants or members of the government before entering the board. And so, they were fully prepared to run the affairs of the company and to keep aside the officers in the staff who had the training, the experience and often the revenues of high-ranking officials—with much higher salaries than those allocated to the board—but who remained in a subordinate position, in particular because they could be dismissed and had never (except two in a century) the opportunity of being called to the board.[9] But with the change in the scale of operations that new technologies and the integration of production had brought about, barriers to mobility were partly removed, first, because the personnel in the central offices assumed a new dimension: staff members at St-Gobain who had been in the order of 65–100 in the 1880s were to reach 350 in 1910, and their numbers trebled in the inter-war years, their increase in number and greater specialization opening new ways to career mobility. Second, the mere experience gained in business life became a decisive element: as has been shown by various studies of corporations, officers unrelated to business families or influential circles who had followed ordinary business careers and who were called to a board of directors secured a significant proportion among managers; they accounted over the 1912–1973 period for one fourth of the larger corporations' executives.[10] These are general trends that apply to all companies. While there is no sample study restricted to family firms that might help to differentiate their case, on the basis of a number of historical records, two further points may be worth mentioning.

1. In conformity with a tradition firmly rooted in the eastern and some of the more central regions of calico printing, clock and machine manufacturing industries, firms under family control had always been attentive to the problem of training their work force. This attitude had mixed origins, partly religious (a minimal level of literacy being the concern of Protestant minorities in the North-East), and partly technical (mills being opened in rural areas where labor had to acquire new skills and be upgraded). Eugène Schneider, for instance, on the very first year of his appointment to le Creusot in 1837, had set up an elementary school for his workers' children. That was followed within ten years by a second, more technical "école spéciale préparatoire," to train foremen, mechanics, drawers and accountants, and prepare the better ones to enter a provincial engineering school. These local institutions that existed in many plants all through the country were eventually transferred to the State for political reasons, and also because of the increased attendance of pupils that gratuity had brought to the educational system in the 1870s: at le Creusot, the student body jumped from 600 to 2,200 in 1873, and had trebled by 1878, the schools being made public in 1882. But the Schneiders still maintained control over the special preparatory classes with 400–500 students in the 1890s, to

prepare middle ranking personnel as in the past and to help the most eligible who wished to complete their studies in one of the engineering schools, including those in Paris, and return to the works fully equipped with higher degrees.

This policy which was duplicated by many companies answered two purposes: to raise the technical ability of the staff and to strengthen its authority. (1) After an ill-fated attempt in the 1870s and 1880s at intensifying work, capturing markets by sales-drives or simply sharing them through cartels, manufacturers had turned to new sectors that required centralized offices, research divisions, as well as a network of plants and subsidiary companies. Hence the sharp increase of engineers working for industry: some 13,000 in the 1870s, 28–30,000 at the turn of the century and easily twice that number in 1930, the old family firms taking the lead, because of their past traditions, in calling on their services.[11] (2) All firms in allocating young people when they entered industry had a well-known bias in favor of graduates from the higher engineering schools ("les grandes écoles"); they were given precedence and quicker promotions irrespective of their age and experience; the heads of classes from Polytechnique, for instance, held one-fifth of the presidencies of the large corporations in the 1912–1973 period, although they accounted for less than one percent of the engineering profession. This policy expressed on the part of employers a true respect for fundamental sciences, but even more so their will to give a new spur to authority by having business responsibilities entrusted to individuals whose qualifications were undisputed. Wrongly or not it was felt that the hierarchical structure would be better accepted if ranks and merits were made to coincide.

2. School facilities were only one part of the services that manufacturers, when located in remote areas, had been induced to offer. There were many in the 19th century who had set up—leaving aside wage schedules which were more or less regulated by regional customs—elaborate systems of social benefits, i.e. cheap housing facilities, family allowances on a per-child basis, health care at the shop floor (and in hospital at le Creusot), accident and old age pensions; and, as additional incentives, to ensure the stability of the work force, bonuses that were awarded on a fixed rate (a thirteenth

month after five years or service at the de Wendel's works, in Lorraine), or in a more flexible and personal way at St-Gobain, where such indemnities amounted to 5–7% of the nominal wages in the 1870s but almost ten per cent in 1912 (for a total wage bill that increased in that period from 8 to 20 million F).[12] These highly paternalistic measures, which were clearly aimed at fixing and disciplining the work force, explain that few employees were tempted or enticed away: to take a job with a family firm in the country was something of a lifetime decision; according to samples taken in the 1860s and 1880s, laborers entered rural mills at less than 20 years of age and remained on the average for 33 to 37 years at work with the same company.

But, once urbanization had opened up new job opportunities, the lifetime employment system came to an end, labor turnover developing in proportion to wage competition and loss of involvement in work: in Paris, the ratio for semi-skilled workers was of 100:23 per year (one hundred hands to be taken in to keep 23 at work) at the *Bon Marché* in the 1870s; and it increased to 100: 17 during the 1914-war at the Renault plants; in the country, the same outflow was reported, but at the level of trained personnel (two out of five engineers leaving the company, at St-Gobain, every ten years in the pre-war period). Against this turnover, the response of manufacturers was of course to broaden up the range of social services, join building societies, press for reductions in the price of public utilities for the benefit of their employees, and also to devise more specific measures. The most simple one, when vacancies could be filled by promotions from the ranks, was to structure the careers of individuals so that they would perceive their future through the company; this induced firms to create intermediate levels in the first line staff, broaden the dispersion of wages, reward seniority especially during periods of full employment, etc.[13] But the most pressing problem for provincial companies was that of the drift of engineers to Paris and the northern industrial region. This was due to low salaries (young graduates who had just come out of school were being paid the equivalent of an overseer's wage), the absence of self-fulfillment in work (during the transition period from school to work), and to uncertain career prospects. These were questions that family firms, given their concern for their employees, could handle efficiently. From 1891, after a review of their alumni's position by provincial engineering schools, new rules were applied at le Creusot and extended to other companies: young engineers were offered standard wage rates that were to be steeply increased during their first years of tenure (by fifty per cent in four years), to impose a true penalty if they left the company; wage structures were revised upward to bridge the gap between middle and higher ranking management; reasearch divisions were instituted as intermediary stages between school and practical work; new rules for promotions were introduced, etc. Beyond these individual measures, quite in line with 19th century paternalism, it should be kept in mind that the absence of information, lack of the personal relationship that exists in human-sized enterprises and loss in the quality of life, which are the penalties of size, could be better obviated in large family firms, for they offered some participation in decisions and rewards, a true concern for the quality of products and pride in the name and repute of the company. It is not surprising that an old engineer at the Schneiders' works still remembered in the 1970s the firm as "a magnificent instrument for social promotion."[14]

II. Two Limits to Business Families' Influence

Large firms that had been under family control for a number of generations remained somewhat immune to the social strife that plagued the 1930s: no strikes were reported in the major provincial works, in particular at le Creusot (in contrast with the mass movements that had cost the company some 15% of its labor force who had left the city in 1899–1900); unemployment was contained, in part because firms were situated in progressive sectors that were among the first to recover (Peugeot in 1935–37 reported substantial increases in its work force and wage rates); and, although the drying up of profits meant that investments were halted, very few casualties were registered in their ranks. This might lead one to imagine that these firms still had the power to ward off outside difficulties and that they would later revive unchanged. But a closer analysis of their social and financial structures shows that their position was precarious and their future uncertain.

First, the legitimacy of family leadership was unquestioned in the 1920s. This was due not only to the family element that pervaded all businesses, but also to the prestige of some key business families. According to traditions that had been laid down during the first industrial revolution, their members had been submitted, before entering practical life, to a formal training, at school and in business, that had made them equal—leaving aside all questions of ownership, experience and personal character—to any member on their staff. This had been true of the generation of founders in the early part of the 19th century (Eugène Schneider, for instance, had graduated as an engineer, together with a great many Alsatian manufacturers); it was so of the heirs to older family firms, dating back from the 18th century, who were educated at Polytechnique or at the Ecole Centrale and held prominent positions, such as the de Wendels who developed the Thomas steel patent in the 1880s, or the Peugeots and Bréguets who pioneered the automobile and aircraft industries. After the turn of the century, the same constraints were reinforced; and it was only logical that, among the large corporations' executives who had business family ties over the 1913–1972 period, one finds 58% were engineers, 15% lawyers, 10% university graduates, etc.

Still, leadership tended to depend much more upon the institutional framework and less upon individual characteristics and kinship. The broadening of functions assumed by large corporations meant that new lines of authority, new decision centers—and so counter-forces—were created that would limit in time the power formerly held by business families. Changes, of course, were slight in the textile and metal industries, since low technology, single-product lines and mutual trust were still of paramount importance: Pont-à-Mousson in the 1920s, to take the case of a prosperous family firm in the foundry business, had only two managers, both of the family in control, two main departments (for sales and production), and standing committees to maintain contacts with the personnel and initiate research. Many firms in Alsace and northern France divided their operations between smaller independent units to maintain this simple functional organization, in keeping with family means. But in the chemicals, engineering and other growth sectors, where sizable firms were accumulating profits (during the recovery

TABLE 2   Four Family Firms: Main Items from the Balance Sheets, 1899–1938 (millions of current francs).

	Assets					Liabilities					Total Annual sales
	Buildings and plants	Stocks	Cash, bills	Other credits	Shares[a] held	Capital reserves	Bonds	Cash debts	Other debts	Balance	
Michelin (Clermont-Ferrand)—rubber											
1899	1.1	2.9	0.1	0.6	—	2.2	0.7	0.2	1.2	0.3	4.6
1919	20	1		174	—	107	—	71	—	17	195
1928	78	253		360	343	427	75	256	172	119	1050
1931	123	164		547	303	586	296	101	138	32	1153
1934	113	201		385	229	457	279	57	144	6	942
1935	120	171	109	234	325	459	273	69	141	31	973
Peugeot (Sochaux)—automobiles											
1899	1.1	2.9	0.1	0.5	—	2.9	—	0.1	1.2	0.3	2.9
1919	45	47	29	52	—	93	9	64	—	6	120
1924	62	163	19	63	—	116	53	136	—	5	295
1930	235	223	86	154	68	394	181	199	50	44	740
1934	431	144	41	36	50	448	174	26	23	51	606
1935	420	146	41	49	44	460	160	19	—	60	668
Dollfus-Mieg (Mulhouse)—cotton											
1919	5	50	10	5	2	43	10	18	—	3	73
1929	16	52	221	25	6	172	—	118	—	29	319
1935	11	30	237	14	29	180	—	99	—	48	322
1938	10	36	104	144	32	180	—	99	—	44	326
A. Prouvost (Roubaix)—wool											
1920	4	17	1	21	3	10	4	21	11	—	46
1931	78	68	37	29	17	85	25	89	23	7	210
1938	31	78	60	27	26	85	25	77	30	6	222

Total Annual sales (additional column, right): 2.9 | 120 | 295 | 740 | 606 | 668 (Peugeot); — | — | — | — (Dollfus); — | — | 280 (Prouvost); Michelin: — | 3250[b]

Source: *Bilans annuels, présentés aux Assemblées générales d'actionnaires.*
On the asset side, buildings and plants are presented in gross value at Peugeot (the depreciation charges being added to the capital and reserve accounts), and net of depreciation at Michelin, Dollfus-Mieg and A. Prouvost. The item "shares held" (a) includes securities and participations in subsidiary firms. The balancing items are not detailed Separately in the assets. Sales at Michelin (b) are a press estimate.

period) and had started raising capital in the stock market from about 1905, the scale of operations of the parent firm and the management of its subsidiary companies—Schneider and St-Gobain had accumulated each 170–180 such companies by 1930–brought new problems that could not be solved without a true reallocation of authority between branches, departments and the central office. The tendency, in practice, for the larger corporations still under family influence or control—e.g. Kulhmann, les Aciéries de la Marine, those of Longwy, the Schneiders' group, etc.—was to let the company transform itself into a loose federation of semi-independent units with a holding organization at the top, probably for the reason that it answered two purposes: one, to maintain in function the board of directors or the supervisory committees, as in the past, with their family element; and, two, to appoint a general director, who was brought in at first as representative or advisor to the shareholding families, but who had assumed by the 1920s a position of real autonomy, being recruited in one of the State engineers' corps and being as such acceptable to the staff.

The case of St-Gobain, then the largest corporation in the country, was somewhat different. It had followed policies similar to those of other firms, entering foreign markets through branches and subsidiaries, and steadily diversifying its production through the 1920s under the lead of its departments' directors. Perhaps to too great an extent, for the company found itself with falling sales and uncompleted investments in 1932–33, when the boom came to an end. This made its reorganization a more urgent matter. One obvious solution, in line with past policies, was to strengthen the authority of the board by calling in new recruits and setting up a new executive sub-committee, restricted in number and reinforced by a consultant engineer, to review current policies and offer new lines for action. But, in the mid-1930s, as the depression was deepening, an alternative solution was taken up: an officer, who had set in order one of the subsidiary companies was called to the presidency, with the task of building up a central executive office and a divisional organization that were to supercede the functions formerly held by the board. This reform—which did not do away with family tradition in the company[15]—was a further sign of the greater weight inside officers had won in large corporations and of the need to find a new balance between inside officers and family representatives.

The second limit was financial. There was a general feeling that the wealth of business families made their firms safe and secure, whatever the state of the market. This belief came from a wrong assessment the public had made of the amount of funds all firms had accumulated in the 1920s inflationary period, price rises relieving them for a while of the necessity of clearing up their debts, and again in 1928–30, once inflation had abated, when active, but obviously exaggerated campaigns were organized in the press to prepare their introduction on the stock market and to float new issues. Further, most family firms, especially in the provinces, had kept to the same old amortization rules that were used in the 19th century—they still depreciated their capital investment as fully as possible each year—so that their rise in market value, when they were first quoted on the stock exchange, uncovered what appeared at the time as hidden resources, but amounted simply to the substitution of inflated replacement costs for old depreciated values. It may be recalled that fixed assets at the Michelins' company were entered in 1928 accounts for less than 80 million francs (Table 2), although they included sales agencies (at home and abroad), plants (with a capacity equal to 40% of the French tire production), workers housing facilities and rubber plantations (still unproductive); these two last items alone were valued in financial reports for half a billion F, six times more than all the company's depreciated assets taken together. In the same way, Dollfus-Mieg & Cie maintained at 12–15 million francs—the figure at which they had been appraised in the 1890 accounts—the net value of their plants, although some 225 million F, almost six million a year, had been invested in the intervening forty years, etc. When companies remained unlisted, as the majority were, State officials' interventions often brought about the same impression, for they had the power to revise upwards—for tax purposes—the companies' balance sheets. For instance, the gross value of the plants, at A. Prouvost's textile mills, in Roubaix, was raised in one stroke in the 1931 accounts from 100 to 150 million F, and other cases of similar magnitude were many. Besides the same conservative methods of valuation applied to inventories of imported

raw materials whenever the French currency fell on the foreign
exchanges, price rises were being under-reported in the accounts
for fear of a possible reversal of the market. In 1929–30, at the time
of the Wall Street crash, this procedure was extended further to other
items in certain firms' accounts to hedge against foreseeable losses.
As one could read in the late 1920s reports to the shareholders at
the Dollfus-Mieg company:

> all financial elements, bank accounts, in France and in foreign
> countries, debts to be cashed in, bills receivable and securities in
> the company's portfolio, have been entered with important depre-
> ciation charges to guard against any contingency.

But these and other measures were to prove defective under the
impact of the depression, because it was most severe in the modern
sectors where firms had built vertically integrated units, combining
production and marketing, highly vulnerable to changes in
demand; and because the length of the debt-deflation process,
once the collapse of the stock market had closed a major source of
capital, and the long deferment of replacement orders, meant that
no one could remain unscathed. Contemporary observers tended
to draw a distinction between the old conservative families, who
were supposed to hold financial reserves, and the more recent ones
who had built excess capacities with borrowed capital, more particularly in the automobile sector, where, in contrast to his competitors, André Citroën, who had redesigned his production lines
and made large investments in response to the crisis, was forced to
suspend his payments in December 1934, with more than 900
million in debts unprovided for. But this presentation is unacceptable
as it does not give a fair account of facts.

Two concrete cases may be recalled. First, that of the Peugeots.
They are said to have pursued a most uneventful course, keeping
their output equal to one-fifth of the market, extending and specializing their production and sales facilities, ear-marking each year
large sums for depreciation charges and issuing new stocks ahead of
the crash to keep out of debt. The firm, though, was unexpectedly
caught short in October 1930 when the two bankers who had been
admitted to the board to organize the company's financial operations

went bankrupt (the first in a long list), leaving unpaid the last of the company's capital issue and costing thereby three-fifths of its cash accounts. The accident was overcome by writing off the 1930 profit, deducting the balance from the reserves and drawing in almost all outstanding credits. But at a cost: sales were cut by a third in 1930–32, and remained for three years at 80–85% of their peak level, at half of what was technically the potential output.[16] The Michelins' firm was never in such a predicament, thanks to their large reserves and net short term assets; they remained all through the 1930s among the ten largest industrial firms listed on the exchange.[17] But they could not escape losses. These came from the depreciation of their raw materials' stocks (profits were already down by 30% in 1926–28); the contraction in sales turnover and bad debts—250 million F were written off in 1933 to cancel part of the credits left unpaid by Citroën, the firm's main customer, and last, from the fall of this firm, since the Michelins had to reduce the value of the shares they still held in the company and to subscribe most of the new stock that was issued in 1935 to absorb it, Citroën becoming a subsidiary that had to be kept running.[18] Inflation had produced fictitious profits, but the depression did cost large capital outlays to cover hidden, but genuine, losses.

This is not to say that family firms had no cards to play: they still had the power to command sacrifice from their shareholders in the shape of foregone dividends (through most of the 1930s); their affiliated companies were able to raise new credits from local banks, using the parent firm's old reputed name; they proved more sensitive to changes in consumer demand (market studies conducted in 1935–36, when demand at last revived, led Peugeot and Citroën, under its new direction, to start manufacturing economy cars).[19] But the new trends that have been examined—the greater autonomy of the firms' managerial structures and the loss of capital resources during the 1930s—were two adverse forces that could not be remedied.

To sum up the main points, the large family firm, i.e. a firm in partial control of a market, which had remained for two or three generations or more in the hands of the same family, did not play in France the role that might have been expected from the country's past technical achievements. As it was recalled, the great merchant banking houses did not regain after the 1860s their former position, and in 1929, family firms were few to have reached a scale of operations that would have made them competitive by international standards.[20] Economic factors—the sluggishness of the domestic market, a great vulnerability of the export trade, concentrated as it was on products with high skilled labor and technical content, and two sharp depressions in the late 19th century and in the 1930s— were among the causes of this disappointing performance. But it may well be that the family system as such was not economically viable. This is not to say that it did not deserve consideration and esteem. The idea that family capital could be substituted to outside finance, business responsibilities should be allocated according to school achievements and the building of a community based on the forbearance and dedication of the work-force, in short that family firms could ward off market forces, had much to commend in a country of small entrepreneurs who were still living by these principles. But this is no proof that they were well adapted to the requirements of large-scale production and mass markets, the priority given to the upgrading of the work force, the selection of high ranking engineers and paternalistic measures being no substitute for long-term planning and managerial efficiency.

NOTES

1. M. Lévy-Leboyer, "The Large Corporation in Modern France," in A. D. Chandler, Jr., and H. Daems, ed., *Managerial Hierarchies. Comparative Perspectives on the Rise of Modern Industrial Enterprise* (Cambridge, Mass., 1980), pp. 118–ff.
2. High estimates of the capital that belonged to the five Rothschild houses have been made: £2–4 millions in 1818–25, 22 in 1863 and 35 million in 1875, i.e. equivalent to 900 million francs. Cf. B. Gille, *Histoire de la Maison Rothschild* (Genève, 1965–1966), t. I, pp. 450–1, and t. II, p. 571.
3. A. Plessis, *La Banque de France sous le Second Empire* (Université de Paris-I, unpubl. Pd. D. thesis, 1982), pp. 428–ff.

4. B. Gille, *Les Rothschild, op. cit.*, II, pp. 539–64 and 579–89.
5. On the role of the Neuflize and Seillière families at le Creusot, cf. J. A. Roy, *Histoire de la famille Schneider et du Creusot* (Paris, 1962). An analysis of the shareholders at St-Gobain—150 in 1830, and 60,000 in 1900—has been sketched by J. P. Daviet, "La direction des affaires de la Cie de St-Gobain, 1830–1872," paper presented at the 2nd Congrès national de l'Association française des Historiens économistes, Paris, 1980; and "Les problèmes de gestion et d'organization de St-Gobain entre les deux guerres mondiales" (unpubl. paper, 1981). Cf. also M. Lévy-Leboyer, "Hierarchical Structures and Incentives in a Large Corporation: the Early Managerial Experience of St-Gobain, 1872–1912," in N. Horn and J. Kocka, *Recht und Entwicklung der Grossunternehmen im 19. und frühen 20. Jahrhundert* (Göttingen, 1979), pp. 451–ff.
6. P. Cayez, "Une explosion du capitalism urbain: La naissance de la société Progil, 1918–25," in *Colloque franco-suisse d'histoire économique* (Lyons, 1977); A. Baudant, *Pont-à-Mousson, 1918–1930. Stratégies industrielles d'une dynastie lorraine* (Université de Paris-I, Unpubl. Ph. D. thesis, 1979), which presents an account of the Financière Lorraine, the holding trust of the Cavallier family, who dominated Pont-à-Mousson.
7. F. Caron, *Histoire de l'exploitation d'un grand réseau. La compagnie du chemin de fer du Nord, 1846–1937* (Paris, 1973), *passim;* M. Lévy-Leboyer, *St-Gobain, 1872–1912, op. cit.*; F. Crouzet, "Essor, déclin et renaissance de l'industrie française des locomotives, 1838–1914," in *Revue d'histoire économique et sociale*, 55e vol. (1977), n° 1–2, pp. 112-sqtes.
8. P. Lanthier, "Les dirigeants des grandes entreprises électriques en France, 1911–1973," in M. Lévy-Leboyer, ed., *Le patronat de la seconde industrialisation* (Paris, 1979), pp. 101–36. In the automobile industry, small teams of 3–5 fellow-workers helped Louis Renault, from the opening of the shop in 1899, André Citroën when he left the Mors company to start on his own, and Robert Peugeot, in 1922, when he modernized the Sochaux plants; cf. G. Hatry, *Louis Renault* (Université de Paris-I, unpubl. Ph. D. thesis, 1982), p. 120; J. L. Loubet, *Histoire d'une entreprise automobile, Citroën, 1919–1939* (Université de Paris-X Nanterre, unpubl. Ph. D. thesis, 1978); and Ph. Girardet, *Ceux que j'ai connus* (Paris, 1952), on the Peugeot company.
9. J. P. Daviet, *La direction de la Cie de St-Gobain, op. cit.*
10. M. Lévy-Leboyer, "Le patronat français a-t-il été malthusien?"

Le mouvement social, nº 88 (1974), pp. 3–ff; G. Ahlström, *Engineers and Industrial Growth* (London, 1982), p. 38.

11. M. Lévy-Leboyer, "Le patronat français, 1912–1973," in M. Lévy-Leboyer, *Le patronat, op. cit.*, p. 174; and P. Lanthier, *Le patronat électricien, art. cit.*

12. Besides J. A. Roy, *Les Schneider, op. cit.*, cf. P. Fritsch, *Les Wendel, rois de l'acier* (Paris, 1952), and M. Lévy-Leboyer, *The Managerial Experience of St-Gobain, op. cit.*

13. Pioneers of these policies were the managers of department stores in Paris, the Boucicaut (le Bon Marché) and the Congnacq-Jay (la Samaritaine); cf. M. B. Miller, *The Bon Marché. Bourgeois Culture and the Department Store, 1869–1920* (Princeton University Press, 1981). The same ideas, within the constraints of an entirely different environment, were applied in the automobile industry, in particular at Peugeot in the 1920s and the late 1930s, when seniority and fidelity bonuses were reenacted.

14. Speaking of the Schneiders' works as they were in the 1930s, at a meeting of former students of the Ecoles des Arts et Métiers in October 1979, Pierre Chaffiotte, president of the Association, who had made his career with the firm, after his father, praised the company as "un magnifique instrument de promotion sociale, donnant à tous l'égalité des chances"; cf. Cl. Beaud, "Les ingénieurs du Creusot à travers quelques destins du milieu du 19e au milieu du 20e siècle," in *Ingénieurs et Société* (Colloque, le Creusot, October 1980), p. III-2.

15. The Baron Pierre Hély d'Oiseel, who was elected president in 1936, was the fifth man in the family to hold either a seat on the board or the presidency (since 1830), and he succeeded to his father-in-law, president Roederer, himself of a family who had been for many generations on the board. P. Hély d'Oiseel came from the Ecole des Mines, while Alphonse Gérard, president of the company from 1917 to 1931, again the fourth member of the family on the company's board, was a Polytechnicien ingénieur du Corps des Mines.

16. Peugeot's loss with its bankers, A. Oustric and Gualino, amounted to 61.4 million F, the equivalent of the cash balance they had left with them, their condition for issuing the last capital increase had been that the funds would be drawn monthly. The firm had to reduce their short-term commitments from 263 to 31 million F in 1936, forcing its agents to assume a more independent position and to find credits with local banks.

17. E. Michelin had partly refunded the company's capital so that it had 350 million F of reserves and amortized capital and 700 million F of short-term net assets in 1928, 535 and 965 million in 1932.

18. Out of 400 million F capital, 325 were cancelled and transfered as passive shares (parts de fondateurs) to the creditors for half their claim, the other half being covered, for the same nominal amount, by new bonds at 3.25% interest. And 135 million F of new shares were issued, making in all (with the 75 million F left to the older share-holders) a new capital of 210 million F; J. L. Loubet, *L'entreprise Citroën*, pp. 143–46.

19. *Automobiles Peugeot. Rapport aux actionnaires*, 18 March 1937; J. L. Loubet, *op. cit.*, pp. 166–68.

20. The very large firms—St-Gobain, with 3.7 billion F market value in 1929, and Citroën, then with 1.9 billion market value—realized $50–75 million annual turnover, i.e. only a fraction of 3–5% of the large American oil and automobile companies, 12–15% of the leaders in electrical industries.

[17]

By *Hidemasa Morikawa*
PROFESSOR OF BUSINESS HISTORY
HOSEI UNIVERSITY

The Organizational Structure of Mitsubishi and Mitsui Zaibatsu, 1868-1922: A Comparative Study

❧ *As their enterprises expanded at the turn of the century, the leaders of two of the most famous Japanese* zaibatsu *worked continually to maintain the delicate balance between centralization and decentralization so essential to continued growth. Professor Morikawa chronicles and analyzes the most important organizational developments in these gigantic family firms.*

The *zaibatsu*, which was such a unique and prominent feature of pre-World War II Japan, can be defined as a business entity composed of diversified enterprises owned and exclusively controlled by a single family. Investigation of the larger *zaibatsu*, which were dissolved after the end of the war, shows that their basic strategies were invariably aimed at maximizing expansion for their constituent enterprises regardless of differences in the processes by which these strategies were implemented.

But, obviously, the expansion and coordination of vastly diversified enterprises required an appropriate management organization. Usually, the simple *zaibatsu* comprised a set of "divisions" or autonomous "companies" with a central headquarters which exercised overall control.[1] As the enterprise became more diversified, and as each product division expanded, the total *zaibatsu* organization became increasingly gigantic and the management system more complex.

Whether simple or complex, however, the management organization of the *zaibatsu* was always a delicate combination of centralization and decentralization of authority. Divisions or companies naturally exerted pressure for decentralization because they aspired

Business History Review, Vol. XLIV, No. 1 (Spring, 1970). Copyright © The President and Fellows of Harvard College.

[1] Central headquarters of the *zaibatsu* took various forms (committee, company, etc.). It controlled departments, divisions, companies, or joint-stock corporations. In this last instance, the central headquarters became a holding company.

to autonomy with regard to the management of the part of the enterprise for which they were responsible. On the other hand, in order to preserve the integrity and superiority of the *zaibatsu* and confine the activities of the divisions or companies within the strategies mapped out for the *zaibatsu* as a whole, substantial powers of control were retained in the central headquarters.

In short, the basic structure of *zaibatsu* could be described as a combination of centralization and decentralization of authority; but the relative proportions could vary in many ways. There were situations in which decentralization of authority was sought in order to avoid disadvantages found in extreme centralization of power. There were also situations in which centralization of authority was attempted in an effort to remedy inefficiencies found to be inherent in extreme decentralization.[2]

There was noticeable contrast, for example, between Mitsui and Mitsubishi, which were the two giant *zaibatsu* in prewar Japan. The Mitsui Zaibatsu, after the Meiji Restoration, was comprised of three business fields: banking, trading, and mining. The individual fields were operated under the exclusive control of subsidiary companies which were given autonomous authority, namely, Mitsui Ginko (Mitsui Bank, established July 1, 1876), Mitsui Bussan (Mitsui Trading Co., established July 1, 1876), and Mitsui Kozan (Mitsui Mining Co., established April 23, 1892 as a limited partnership). As the subsidiary companies were formed out of firms of long standing, and because they enjoyed an overwhelming influence in their respective fields, they were able to assume the right to act at their own discretion in their dealings among themselves as well as with the central headquarters.

The Mitsui Bank, in particular, took a very aggressive posture in competing with its fellow subsidiary companies following Hikojirō Nakamigawa's assumption of its directorship in 1891 and his introduction of drastic changes in management. This reflected the trend toward decentralization characteristic of the earlier days of Mitsui's post-Restoration history. In endeavoring to stop and reverse such a trend toward excessive decentralization of authority among the subsidiary companies, however, it became necessary for the central headquarters to strengthen its power. As a result, assertion of control by the central headquarters has consistently been pursued.

The Mitsubishi Zaibatsu in the Meiji era, on the other hand, had

---

[2] A clear contrast can be seen in the United States during the 1920's in the case of Du Pont and General Motors who played the role of pioneers in the development of the multi-divisional organization. Alfred D. Chandler, Jr., *Strategy and Structure: Chapters in the History of Industrial Enterprise* (Cambridge, Mass., 1962), chaps. 2–3.

MITSUBISHI AND MITSUI ZAIBATSU   63

management divisions covering extensively diversified fields such as metal mining, coal mining, shipbuilding, banking, and so on. All the divisions were placed under the centralized management of a single headquarters and were not given independence. With the expansion of the diversified enterprises, however, a gradual trend toward decentralization appeared.

The theme of this article is to identify and explain differences in these two *zaibatsu* by reviewing the course of development of their management organizations. But as the details of Mitsui's management have already been discussed in another article,[3] this article will concentrate mainly upon the process of development of Mitsubishi's management organization with a comparison with Mitsui to follow. The period of time to be reviewed herein will be between 1886, when Mitsubishi reorganized its management following elimination of the shipping business, the principal concern of Mitsubishi up to that time, and the beginning of the Taishō era, since adequate historical data is available for a proper comparison with Mitsui during this time period.

Mitsubishi Before Decentralization of Authority

Establishment of Mitsubishi-sha and its Management Structure

Yatarō Iwasaki, the founder of Mitsubishi Zaibatsu, died in February 1885.[4] Shortly before his death, the internecine struggle between Mitsubishi and the Kyōdo Unyu Co. (Kyōdo Shipping Co.), established under government sponsorship in order to counteract Mitsubishi's monopolistic position in the shipping business, had reached its climax. The two competitors had fought each other savagely by rate-cutting, and, as a result, their business had suffered grave losses. After the death of Yatarō, the two competitors merged through pressure from the government, and a new company called Nippon Yūsen Kaisha (NYK, Japan Mail) was incorporated in September 1885.[5]

Yanosuke Iwasaki, the younger brother of Yatarō, had to confront the critical situation in Mitsubishi's business brought forth by the

[3] Hidemasa Morikawa, "The Organizational Structure of the Mitsui Zaibatsu: Analysis of the Historical Materials Concerning the Mitsui Trading Co. during the Meiji Era," *Keiei Shirin* (The Hosei Journal of Business), VI (1969).

[4] For the entrepreneurial activity of Yataro Iwasaki, see Kozo Yamamura, "The Founding of Mitsubishi: A Case Study in Japanese Business History," *Business History Review*, XLI (Summer, 1967), and *Life of Yataro Iwasaki* by a Biography Compilation Committee for Yataro Iwasaki and Yanosuke Iwasaki, 2 vols. (1967).

[5] Mitsubishi transferred 515 of its 2,200 employees to the newly formed company. *History of Mitsubishi*, XII, 441ff.

illness and death of Yatarō and Mitsubishi's loss of major involvement in the shipping business. Yanosuke had worked in the Japanese shipping business and studied in the United States for two years (1872–1873) and, on his return to Tokyo, became the vice president in order to assist his brother. As Yatarō was an invalid for most of his last years, Mitsubishi in those days was much more dependent on Yanosuke for its management than has been described in the historical literature.

On March 29, 1886, Yanosuke established Mitsubishi-sha (Mitsubishi Co.) with himself as its president and concentrated his efforts on the reconstruction of Mitsubishi based upon formerly secondary activities – the Takashima Coal Mine, the Yoshioka Metal Mine, the Nagasaki Shipyard, the 119th National Bank, and the Senkawa Water Supply and Service Co.[6] The establishment of Mitsubishi-sha was accompanied by the promulgation of a new set of Company Regulations which established the unlimited authority of the president. But Mitsubishi had not yet reached the stage of establishing a full-fledged central management organization.[7]

A memorandum entitled "Acting Principles of Mitsubishi-sha" issued on November 9, 1888, included interesting and more specific provisions regarding management structure.[8] The business of the company was divided into three sections: mining, accounting, and general affairs, and a section manager was appointed over each. Secondly, the function of the mining section was clearly specified to encompass the following three affairs: management of mines, sales

---

[6] *Ibid.*, XIII, 28.

[7] The company regulations of the new Mitsubishi-sha were as follows:

"Title of the Officers and Rank: President, General Manager, Manager, Assistant Manager, Officer in Charge of Office Work, and Officer in Charge of Miscellaneous Work. Regulations: (1) The subject company which is owned by the family of Iwasaki shall be called 'Mitsubishi-sha.' (2) Appointment and resignation of the officers, and any problems pertaining to proper execution of the business concerned, regardless of importance, shall be settled by the instructions, decisions, and approval of the president, and shall in no case be governed by any other officer. (3) The general manager shall see to the task of properly controlling and fairly evaluating profits and losses of the business and the ability and diligence of the company employees. (4) The manager shall see to the due performance of the internal and external business respectively assigned." (*Ibid.*, XIII, 28–29.)

The characteristic which one would first notice is the enormous authority of the president. As described in Article 2, the president was fully empowered to give orders with respect to personnel affairs and business operations, no matter how trivial the matter might be. Such a centralized management organization survived in fact from the time of Yatarō Iwasaki's presidency of Mitsubishi-Kaisha, as is stipulated in the company regulations of his time:

"Although this company has the stature of a corporation with its registered company name, it is completely a family company in its management and shall remain distinct from those of joint-capital or joint-partnership. Accordingly, all matters pertaining to the company including personnel affairs such as rewards, discipline, promotion and demotion shall be subject to the decisions and approvals of the president." Also, in the regulations, the general manager seems to have played the role of "general staff," but neither his duties nor his authority were clearly specified.

[8] *Ibid.*, XV, 213–15.

of mine products, and procurement of materials. Thirdly, the authority and functions of a general manager were specified for the general control of the three sections' business activities. Judging from the stipulation that the "three section managers should refer their affairs to the general manager and execute their offices at the order of the president," it is surmised that they were able to execute their offices within the order of the president by only obtaining the approval of the general manager.

Comparing this memorandum with the regulations issued at the time of establishment of Mitsubishi-sha, we notice the delegation of certain powers from the president to the general manager. In 1886, the main business activity of Mitsubishi-sha was metal and coal mining. By the end of 1888, Mitsubishi had already procured many metal mines such as Yoshioka, Osarizawa, Komaki, Omodani, and Kuromori, and a coal mine, Takashima. The geographical dispersion of these operating units was considerable, and the immediate establishment of a formal management structure for mines was necessary. This is the reason for the establishment of the mining section first during the revision of the management system in November 1888.

About half a month later, it was decided that the Takashima Coal Mine (Nagasaki Prefecture) should be placed under a separate line of control from that under which the various metal mines were operated. Thus, it was decided "the general manager shall be placed in Nagasaki and shall have the general control of affairs concerning the coal mine and shipyard." [9] This new system was aimed at the management of the Takashima Coal Mine, and that of the Nagasaki Shipyard was regarded as secondary. In June 1887, Mitsubishi-sha had bought the government-owned Nagasaki Shipyard, but the shipyard was mainly engaged in repair work and its scale of business was small. In later days, the shipbuilding industry became the core of the Mitsubishi Zaibatsu, but their advance into the field of large-sized steel shipbuilding was not to come until 1896 when they undertook the building of Nihon Yūsen's *Hitachi Maru*.[10]

In 1889 and 1890, Mitsubishi-sha acquired more coal mines, such as Namazuda, Shinnyu, Kogayama, and Usui in the Chikuhō coal field. As a result, in December 1890, the Mitsubishi Coal Mining Office was established in Nohgata (Fukuoka Prefecture) and the Takashima mine and the coal mines in Chikuhō were put under the

---

[9] Masakatsu Yamawaki was appointed as general manager. In December, Nagasaki Shipyard was renamed the Mitsubishi Shipyard, and Yamawaki became the head of the shipyard in addition to serving as general manager.

[10] Yōichiro Inoue, "The Nagasaki Shipyard and the Establishment of the Modern Shipbuilding Industry," *Keiei Shigaku* (Japan Business History Review), III (1968).

control of this office. The general manager (formerly stationed in Nagasaki) was also transferred to Nohgata and, consequently, Mitsubishi Shipyard was put back under the direct control of the head office in Tokyo.[11] Finally, the Mitsubishi Coal Mining Office and the post of general manager were abolished at the end of 1893, and in October 1894, all the coal mines and branch offices selling coal came under the direct control of the head office. Metal mining remained under its section manager.

Establishment of Mitsubishi & Partners, Ltd. and the Products Department System

In December 1893, Mitsubishi & Partners, Ltd. was established to succeed Mitsubishi-sha, effective January 1, 1894. The amount of capital was 5,000,000 *yen* which was divided between Yanosuke Iwasaki and Hisaya Iwasaki, the eldest son of Yatarō Iwasaki. Hisaya assumed the office of president.

The first major change in business after the establishment of Mitsubishi & Partners, Ltd. was the addition of banking to the articles of association and the establishment of a banking department in October 1895. The new department took charge of the management of the 119th National Bank which had already been under the indirect control of Mitsubishi-sha.[12] This dual system of a central banking department and the relatively autonomous 119th National Bank continued until the expiration of the bank's charter in December 1898.[13]

Following the establishment of its banking department, Mitsubishi established a coal sales department in February 1896, in response to the expansion of the coal market following the outbreak of the Sino-Japanese War. Also, a mining department was established to consolidate the management of metal and coal mining in October of the same year. The expansion of the coal sales business was so great that it required a single department, but the remainder of the coal mining business was put together with metal mining business within the mining department.

The heads of each department were given the title of assistant managers of the company. By the end of October 1896, Mitsubishi & Partners, Ltd. had one manager (Heigorō Shōda) and four assis-

---

[11] *History of Mitsubishi*, XV, 222, XVII, 220–22.

[12] Mitsubishi-sha or Mitsubishi & Partners, Ltd. could not obtain governmental approval to incorporate the 119th National Bank under its direct control, but they issued the announcement of appointment of the directors and officers of the bank. This was not the case with Senkawa Water Supply and Service Co. which was dissolved in 1908.

[13] *History of Mitsubishi Bank* (1954), 64ff.

tant managers: banking, coal-sales, mining, and general affairs. These departments, however, were quite different from what was to be called the multi-divisional system established by Mitsubishi after 1908. All that had happened was that management functions which had been previously carried out by the head office were merely divided among the four departments. Accordingly, neither decentralization of authority nor central budgetary control existed. Only the Bank Department, for example, paid part of its net profits to the head office (after 1897).

In July 1906, a Mining Department (*Kōgyō-bu*) was formed by combining the Sales Department (Coal Sales Department renamed) and the Mining Department (*Kōzan-bu*). This change was regressive because the products department system had been designed to meet the diversified expansion of the enterprise. On the other hand, a Shipbuilding Department was established in March 1907.

Those who made strategic decisions for the enterprises of Mitsubishi as a whole were the president, Hisaya Iwasaki, and the manager, Heigorō Shōda. The latter seems to have played the key role. In June 1897, the general manager system was revived and Shōda, previously called the manager, was renamed the general manager. Furthermore, at the same time he assumed the position of manager of Mitsubishi Shipyard as an additional post. These moves were designed by Shōda himself. It was his plan to modernize and expand the Nagasaki Shipyard by accepting an order from NYK to build the *Hitachi Maru*, a large, modern steel ship. The ex-manager of Mitsubishi Shipyard, Masakatsu Yamawaki and others, who attached more importance to Mitsubishi's coal mining business, took a negative view of Shōda's plan. But Shōda was determined to build up Mitsubishi's shipbuilding capacity and reputation. As a result, he moved to Nagasaki and he lived there until May 1901.[14]

Upon Shōda's appointment to the office of general manager, four assistant managers of the company were promoted to the rank of manager. This left no top-executive except the president who could devote himself to making strategic decisions over the business as a whole, since Shōda, the general manager, was actually spending his time as manager of the shipyard. Ryōhei Toyokawa, Shin Uryu, and Kyugo Nanbu were appointed managers of the banking, coal sales, and mining departments, respectively. The remaining manager, Masamiki Kawabuchi, took charge of general affairs (account-

[14] *Life of Hisaya Iwasaki*, by Biography Publishing Committee for Hisaya Iwasaki (1961), 384–87. Concurrently with the beginning of modernization of Nagasaki Shipyard, Mitsubishi & Partners, Ltd. decided to build the Kobe Shipyard which was completed in July 1905.

ing, personnel, correspondence and documents, and real estate).

But President Hisaya Iwasaki was not competent enough to take responsibility for over-all decision making by himself. This situation continued until December 1906, when Heigorō Shōda relinquished his post as manager of Mitsubishi Shipyard and began to take his responsibilities as general manager seriously. Hisaya Iwasaki's weakness and Shōda's preoccupation, however, had meant that Mitsubishi's top management during the period of the products department system had been ineffective.

FOUNDATION OF THE MULTI-DIVISIONAL SYSTEM AND ITS PROBLEMS

In the years from 1906 to 1908, some important changes occurred in Mitsubishi's central headquarters. In 1906, Koyata Iwasaki, eldest son of Yanosuke, who had been in England for five years and had obtained a B.A. at Cambridge University, returned to Tokyo and took the office of vice-president.[15] Koyata Iwasaki was such an aggressive and able man that he was regarded as a reincarnation of his uncle, Yatarō. By comparison, his cousin, Hisaya, was more gentle in nature and lacked qualities of leadership. On February 15, 1907, Mitsubishi & Partners, Ltd. increased its capital by 10,000,000 *yen* following the investment made by Hisaya Iwasaki, and, thus, the total capital became 15,000,000 *yen*. On the following day, Koyata Iwasaki joined the limited partnership by inheriting 1,000,000 of his father's share of 2,500,000 *yen*. When Yanosuke died in March 1908, Koyata succeeded to all of his father's share. He used his new power swiftly to restructure the enterprise.

In October 1908, the mining, banking, and shipbuilding departments were made self-supporting "divisions" to which authority was delegated by the central headquarters. The following are the main points of the reform: [16]

(1) Amount of capital of each division was set as follows:

Mining Division	15,000,000 *yen*
Banking Division	1,000,000 *yen*
Shipbuilding Division	10,000,000 *yen*

Payment of a part of net divisional profits to the head office was put into practice in mining and shipbuilding in 1909; the banking division had started this practice in 1897. Explicit provisions relating to these profit payments were made in later years.

[15] Koyata Iwasaki went abroad after having graduated from the First Senior High School (Dai-Ichi Kōtōgakko) and having spent a year at the Imperial University of Tokyo. *Life of Koyata Iwasaki*, by Biography Publishing Committee for Koyata Iwasaki (1957), 56–69.

[16] *History of Mitsubishi & Co., Ltd.*, XV, 1096–1098.

(2) If the mining or shipbuilding division wished to invest an amount which exceeded their own capital, they could do so and carry a temporary debt with the president's approval.

(3) Regulations and procedures that were specific and limited to each division could be set and practiced at each division's initiative, however, the president's approval was to be sought with regard to important issues.

(4) The personal affairs of each division were to be reviewed within the division itself with a report to the president including the comments of each division chief.

(5) Expenses for operations, entertainment, contributions, salaries and allowances, and bonuses for the staff below the chief of the division were to be borne by the respective divisions. Special bonuses, pensions, and annuities were to be borne by the head office.

(6) All the memoranda and reports which had previously been sent between the head office and each operating unit were to be continued between the head office and each division.

(7) Affairs concerning real estate and buildings which did not come under the direct control of the head office but which belonged to the respective divisions were not to be handled and reported by or to the head office.

Mitsubishi's products department system had shown no evidence of decentralization. But now, its new divisions could invest within the limits of their capital, set regulations and business procedures within their own boundaries, manage their own personnel affairs, and maintain communication with other operating units — all with considerable divisional discretion. The most significant characteristic of the new structure was the level at which the major divisions were capitalized. The combined capitalization of the mining and shipbuilding divisions was 10,000,000 *yen* more than that of their parent, Mitsubishi & Partners, Ltd. The fact that both divisions were able to invest such large amounts at their discretion suggests the abundance of Iwasaki's financial resources, but at the same time reveals the extent of authority delegated to the divisions.

In comparison, the diversified enterprises of the Mitsui Zaibatsu — banking, trading, and mining — were organized into independent general partnerships in July 1893; further, in October 1909, each general partnership was incorporated into a limited liability company. But none of the Mitsui companies was given investment authority equal to that enjoyed by Mitsubishi's divisions. Mitsui's subsidiaries had no discretion over investment decisions or affairs concerning organization, contribution, and the handling of intangible assets. They were required to submit such matters for the approval of the head office.

After the reform of 1908, the number of Mitsubishi's divisions was increased. In December 1910, the Mining Division was divided into two new divisions — Mining and Sales. Further, in October 1912, a Coal Mining Division was created. The activities of the sales division were limited to the sale of mining products and it did not yet have as many business activities as it did later when it developed into Mitsubishi Shoji (Trading Company). Concurrent with the separation of the Sales Division, a Real Estate Division and an Internal Affairs division were also established. Thus, the technical problems of synthetically managing and effectively coordinating numerous divisions were increased.

The head office, of course, sought the power to control the divisions and pursued a more effective means of control than it had previously enjoyed, particularly, with the establishment of inside rules for employment and a standardized accounting system. A first step was the establishment of a division chief's meeting, on January 13, 1911: "In order to facilitate communication and consolidation among divisions, a division chiefs' meeting will be held three times a week. The vice president shall be appointed the chairman and the division chiefs shall report the business affairs of their respective divisions." [17]

Three days following the establishment of the division chiefs' meeting, a memorandum on the function of the general manager was issued: "The general manager shall hold a meeting at the vice president's office at a set time every day in order to discuss employees' employment, corporate planning, and other important issues. . . . The general manager shall exert efforts to maintain communication and business contact among each division and between the head office and operating units." [18]

Thus, a system was established wherein authority concerning the management of each enterprise was transferred to the divisions and the top management of the head office concerned itself with the planning, coordination, and appraisal of divisional activity (from the standpoint of the Mitsubishi Zaibatsu as a whole). It is also important to mention that a Research Section was set up in the Internal Affairs Division in June 1911, so as to keep top management well informed.

These changes indicate what an important role the vice president, Koyata Iwasaki, played among the top management of the Mitsubishi Zaibatsu. In January 1911, the office of general manager was jointly occupied by Ryōhei Toyokawa and Kyugo Nanbu (Heigorō Shōda having resigned the position in the previous year). Toyokawa

[17] *Ibid.*, XVIII, 1302.
[18] *Ibid.*, XVIII, 1303.

retired in 1913. The successive retirements of Shōda and Toyokawa, who had contributed so much to the foundation of Mitsubishi, made the role of Koyata Iwasaki all the more important in the decision making of the Mitsubishi Zaibatsu.[19]

MITSUBISHI ZAIBATSU TRANSFORMED INTO A FINANCIAL *Konzern*

On July 1, 1916, Koyata Iwasaki assumed the office of president of Mitsubishi & Partners, Ltd. He devoted himself to expanding the diversified enterprises of the Mitsubishi Zaibatsu — especially in the field of heavy industry — and, even more energetically than before, to establishing an organization appropriate for its management. For the next thirty years, until the *zaibatsu* were split up by order of the occupation forces after World War II, Koyata Iwasaki and Mitsubishi Zaibatsu were synonymous.[20]

As soon as Koyata entered the office of president, he executed an important reform in organization: each division became an independent joint-stock corporation and Mitsubishi & Partners, Co. Ltd. became a holding company. In the first place, Mitsubishi Zosen K.K. was established on October 8, 1917, to succeed the Shipbuilding Division. The other corporations were incorporated in succession as listed below:

Name of New Company	*Date of Foundation*	*Capital*
Mitsubishi Zosen K.K.		
(Shipbuilding)	October 8, 1917	50,000,000 *yen*
Mitsubishi Seitetsu K.K.		
(Iron Manufacturing)	October 15, 1917	30,000,000 *yen*
Mitsubishi Soko K.K.		
(Warehouse)	March, 1918	
Mitsubishi Kōgyō K.K.		
(Mining)	April, 1918	50,000,000 *yen*
Mitsubishi Shōji K.K.		
(Trading)	April, 1918	15,000,000 *yen*

[19] See Jūichi Shukuri, *Life of Heigorō Shōda* (1932), and Kumakichi Usaki, *Life of Ryōhei Toyokawa* (1922).

[20] The fields of heavy industry of Mitsubishi Zaibatsu included iron and steel (Kenjiho iron works, in Korea), aircraft, automobiles (obliged to be suspended in 1921), and electric appliances (which was derived from the shipbuilding industry). Coal, chemical, and petroleum refining were newly born in that Koyata's era and enjoyed brilliant success. A study of these newly born industries, however, has to be omitted in this article because of the limited space. (*Life of Koyata Iwasaki*, 220ff.) A comprehensive study of the diversified enterprises of the Mitsubishi Zaibatsu will require that space be given to the accounts of such related companies as Nippon Yusen K.K. (Shipping), Tokyo Marine & Fire Insurance Co., Meiji Life Insurance Co., and some railway companies, i.e., Sanyo and Kyushu, of which Mitsubishi & Partners Co., Ltd., were principal shareholders, and also of Mitsubishi Paper Mills, Kirin Brewery Co., Koiwai Ranch (in all of which Hisaya Iwasaki and his family had an interest), and Asahi Glass Co. (in which Koyata Iwasaki and his family had an interest) but those accounts have been omitted in this article.

Mitsubishi Ginkō K.K.		
(Banking)	August 15, 1919	50,000,000 *yen*
Mitsubishi Nainenki Seizō K.K.		
(Internal Combustion Engine		
Manufacturing)	May 15, 1920	5,000,000 *yen*
Mitsubishi Denki K.K.		
(Electric Appliance		
Manufacturing)	January 15, 1921	15,000,000 *yen*

Some explanations of the above companies are necessary. Mitsubishi Kogyo K.K. combined the Mining and Coal Mining divisions. Mitsubishi Shoji K.K. was formed by making the Sales Division independent. Previously, in October 1915, it had been decided to add commission sales to the business activities of Mitsubishi & Partners, Ltd., and in September 1917, in this context, Zakka-ka (Other Firms' Products Section), had been set up within the Sales Division.[21] Thus, Mitsubishi launched into trading activities on a full scale aiming at taking advantage of the world market conditions during World War I. As a result, the Sales Division had completely changed its original character which had been as an agency for selling only Mitsubishi's mining products. With this background, Mitsubishi Shoji K.K. was established with the goal of becoming a general trading company dealing in all kind of goods. Mitsubishi Nainenki Seizo K.K. (Internal Combustion Engine Manufacturing) later developed into Mitsubishi Kokuki K.K. (Aircraft) and, in 1934, Mitsubishi Kokuki K.K. and Mitsubishi Zosen K.K. (Shipbuilding) were combined to form Mitsubishi Jukogyo K.K. (Heavy Industry). Divided into three parts by the order of the occupation forces for a while after World War II, Mitsubishi Jukogyo K.K. was revived as an integrated organization in 1964, and today it has made striking achievements, holding first rank among all manufacturers in Japan.

With its development into a financial *Konzern*, Mitsubishi & Partners, Ltd. doubled its capital to 30,000,000 *yen*, in May 1918, which consisted of Hisaya's investment of 25,000,000 and Koyata's 5,000,000 *yen*. In April 1922, the capital was further increased to 120,000,000 *yen*, of which Hisaya's holdings were 90,000,000 and Koyata's 30,000,000 *yen*.

After 1918, agreements were made concerning the relations between Mitsubishi & Partners, Ltd. and its new subsidiary companies which were significantly different than the previous relations with them as divisions. The divisions had had the power to enact and

---

[21] *History of Mitsubishi & Co., Ltd.*, XXII, 2601, XXIV, 3937.

carry out regulations and business procedures at their own option, except in regard to very important issues, but as subsidiary companies they were unable to exercise such power without the president's approval. Moreover, all the regulations and private rules of Mitsubishi & Partners, Ltd. were applied to the subsidiary companies. These changes might indicate that the Mitsubishi Zaibatsu was following a retrogressive course to centralization but, on the other hand, each subsidiary company did gain the right to make a budget. During the period of the division system, the general affairs division of Mitsubishi & Partners, Ltd. had formed a budget plan for all divisions, except banking which was under the command of Vice President Koyata Iwasaki.[22] However, when the subsidiary companies were established, they were given the authority to make their own budget plans, which were then submitted to the president for his approval.

But in spite of the changes described above, Mitsubishi's administrative policies, which had governed the division system starting in 1908, survived even after the firm became a financial *Konzern*. The subsidiary companies inherited a considerable amount of the authority of the divisions, except in regard to the enacting regulations, personal matters concerning executives, raising funds, approving budgets, and settling accounts which remained in the hands of Mitsubishi & Partners, Ltd. By exercising this authority, the *Konzern* managed to contain the decision-making of each subsidiary company within the framework of Mitsubishi's overall strategy in order to appraise the performance of each and coordinate the activities of all the subsidiary companies. In other words, the same combination of centralization and decentralization that had existed between Mitsubishi's head office and its divisions was brought in between the holding company and subsidiary companies. The division and subsidiary company held almost the same status as far as the authority delegated to them was concerned. Intrinsically, Mitsubishi's *Konzern* system which started between 1917 and 1919 was no more than multi-divisional system.

What then was the motive for Mitsubishi to incorporate the divisions into independent joint-stock companies? It was not the managerial motive, because the division system met the requirements of systematically controlling diversified enterprises. Rather, it was that Koyata Iwasaki anticipated that an enormous amount of capital would be needed for the direct management of Mitsubishi's diversi-

[22] *Life of Kazuo Funada,* by Biography Publishing Committee in Honor of Kazuo Funada (1953), 255.

fied enterprises, and he prepared for procurement of additional funds from the public capital market. The joint-stock company form enabled each former Mitsubishi division to offer its stock for subscription and thus obtain funds from the public capital market. In fact, Mitsubishi Kogyo K.K. (mining) offered some of its stock to the public in 1920.

Koyata Iwasaki played a leading role in the process of transforming each division into a joint-stock company. Koyata, head of Iwasaki's branch family, who took a minor share of the capital of Mitsubishi & Partners, Ltd. seems to have not had as strong an adherence to the exclusive ownership and control of the whole enterprise by the Iwasaki families, as Hisaya, leader of the Iwasaki head family, who invested a major amount of the capital.

In December 1919, the new company regulations of Mitsubishi were enacted which stipulated the establishment of board of directors as a top management organization. Until this time the general manager system had remained under the holding company form. The new company regulations provided the constitution and authority of the board as follows: [28]

III. Board of Directors

[Article] No. 5: Mitsubishi & Partners, Ltd. shall set up a board of directors. The board of directors shall deliberate on any important matters concerning Mitsubishi and its subsidiary companies and shall provide advice and suggestions on the matters inquired by the president.

No. 6: The board of directors shall consist of the following:
(i) Representative directors.
(ii) Managing director.
(iii) Special appointees from among managing directors of subsidiary companies.

No. 7: The matters to be deliberated on by the board of directors shall be the following in principle:
(i) Enactment, revision, and abolition of important regulations.
(ii) Budget, settlement of accounts, and handling of profit and loss.
(iii) Large scale new ventures, investment, financing, and other related matters.
(iv) Important internal and external strategic policies.
(v) Important matters concerning operational policies.
(vi) Disputes between Mitsubishi and subsidiary company, or among subsidiary companies, and important matters concerning external negotiations.
(vii) Important personnel matters.
(viii) Any important matters concerning both Mitsubishi and subsidiary companies other than those specified above. . . .

[28] *History of Mitsubishi & Co., Ltd.*, XXVI, 4964–966.

No. 9: The important matters of Mitsubishi and subsidiary companies shall be carried out after they are taken into deliberation by the board and have obtained the president's approval.

No. 10: Urgent or confidential matters, if the board could not take them into deliberation for any reason, may be carried out with only the president's approval. In that case, the summary of the matters shall be reported to the board immediately after the fact.

No. 11: The matters, in case that the president's approval could not be obtained because the matters were of great urgency or for any inevitable reasons, may be carried into effect only with the deliberation by the board. In that case, the president's ex post facto approval shall be obtained immediately after the fact.

The members of the board under the new company regulations were appointed on the 1st of January 1920, and consisted of:

Representative Directors
  Kusuyata Kimura (chairman of Mitsubishi Seitetsu K.K. and Mitsubishi Kogyo K.K.)
  Teijo Eguchi (auditor of Mitsubishi Zosen K.K., director of three subsidiary companies)
Managing Director
  Kikuo Aoki (representative director of administrative division, auditor of six subsidiary companies)
Directors
  Hideo Takeda (chairman of Mitsubishi Zosen K.K.)
  Manzo Kushida (chairman of Mitsubishi Soko K.K., managing director of Mitsubishi Ginko K.K.)
  Hyakutoro Miyagawa (managing director of Mitsubishi Seitetsu K.K.)
  Hirokichi Ohishi (managing director of Mitsubishi Shoji K.K.)
  Yoji Shigematsu (managing director of Mitsubishi Kogyo K.K.)

In comparison with the general manager system, the board of directors as a top management organization seems to have been well qualified for the coming expansion of Mitsubishi's diversified enterprises from the viewpoint of the number and the status of the constituent members. Since the board of directors included the chairman (at this time, the head of a subsidiary company was called chairman) and managing director of each subsidiary company, it had the advantage of exchanging information between Mitsubishi & Partners, Ltd. and the subsidiary companies without delay and interruption. However, there was also the offsetting disadvantage that the interests of each subsidiary company might possibly clash. Consequently, the decisions made by the board could become the products of maneuvers and compromises among subsidiaries so that the board of directors as the overall decision making body for the Mitsubishi Zaibatsu as a whole might lose its proper position in the end.

In order to eliminate such evils, Mitsubishi & Partners, Ltd. was very cautious in selecting the members of the board. While five directors were chairmen or managing directors of the subsidiary companies, the representative director and managing director were not representatives of any subsidiary company. Representative director Kusuyata Kimura had held a post in both the general affairs division and the coal mining division. Thus, he was not an individual who would represent any one of subsidiary companies. In addition, he resigned the post of chairman of Mitsubishi Seitetsu K.K. and Mitsubishi Kogyo K.K. immediately after he assumed an office on the board of directors. Teijo Eguchi, another representative director, was a former representative director of the research division in charge of the auditing of subsidiary companies. Managing director Kikuo Aoki was representative director of the administrative division which was independent of the other line divisions. Both of them were not in a position to commit themselves to any line division. As far as these three executives and Koyata Iwasaki were concerned, the unfavorable propensity that the board might have the character of a representative committee of subsidiary company would not be allowed to develop.

In July 1922, the company regulations of Mitsubishi & Partners, Ltd. were revised to change the constitution, authority, and function of the board. The following are the main points of the revised regulations: first, the number of the representative directors on the board was limited to one; second, it was specified that the purpose of the board was to deliberate on any matters *inquired by the president* and make efforts to establish better understanding among Mitsubishi and subsidiary companies; third, all the chairmen of the subsidiary companies were specifically added to the membership of the board; and finally, article No. 7 referring to the matters to be deliberated on by the board of directors and articles No. 9 to 11 referring to the president's approval in the original regulations were omitted.[24]

These points of revision may first bring us to the conclusion that great emphasis came to be laid on the function of the board of allowing smooth liaison and coordination between Mitsubishi & Partners, Ltd. and each subsidiary company and among the subsidiary companies themselves. It seems that for these reasons, the chairmen of the subsidiary companies were joined to the membership of the

[24] *Ibid.*, XXIX, 5882–883.

board. The diversified expansion of Mitsubishi Zaibatsu had made
the function of liaison and coordination more important than ever.
The second is that the board of directors had become an advisory
body to the president. Instead of the principle in the original company regulations that the decisions produced from the deliberation
at the board should be authorized as the formal policy of Mitsubishi
by the president's approval, "one-man control" by the president seems
to have been established even more systematically than ever. In
other words, this revision completely eliminated the unfavorable
propensity of the board of directors toward becoming a representative committee of subsidiary companies. A system within which the
strategic framework of the subsidiary companies' activities could
be set up under the one-man control of the president, Koyata Iwasaki, had been finally established. On the other hand, the board of
directors as an organ for liaison and coordination was intensified
to complement the one-man control system of the president.

Many people who had been associated with Koyata talk about
how his "one-man control" used to operate. For example, Mr. Ko-
shiro Shiba, ex-chairman of Mitsubishi Jukogyo K.K. (heavy industry) recollects by saying, "There were many management systems
in the Mitsubishi Zaibatsu in the prewar era, but in reality, all the
final and supreme decisions were made only by Mr. Koyata Iwasaki.
As a matter of fact, he was a big figure of large caliber, of excellent
talent and of comprehensive knowledge, and well qualified for such
dictatorial control." [25]

CONCLUSION

In 1908, the management structure of the Mitsubishi Zaibatsu
changed from a centralized to a decentralized structure. As a result of the development of product diversification, a multidivisional
system took the place of the prior system of multiproduct departments. At the end of the 1910's, each division came to be organized
as an independent joint-stock company and the *zaibatsu* as a whole
took the form of the so-called *Konzern*. In the case of Mitsubishi,
which experienced reorganization toward the decentralized form
as a direct result of product diversification, the principle of decentralization was found to be rather compatible with the principle
of centralization. The power of the head office (or mother company)

[25] Kazuo Noda, "Managers in the Past 50 Years," *Seisansei* (Productivity), Series 11,
No. 7 (1964). Other changes occurred in the top management of Mitsubishi & Partners,
Ltd. at the beginning of the Showa era not only because of the unusual economic conditions but also due to Koyata's sickness. The study on this point, however, is beyond the
scope of the subject of this article.

for confining the activities of divisions or subsidiary companies into a certain strategic framework was quite strong, but it was never exercised to an undue extent. The top management was wholly under the command of Koyata Iwasaki after he became president and reorganized the whole structure of the Mitsubishi Zaibatsu, succeeding in fencing off the disturbing effects grown from the interests of the subsidiary companies that might otherwise have affected the quality of the entrepreneurial decision-making by the head office.

In contrast with this, the Mitsui Zaibatsu was founded after some of its principal subsidiary companies had been established. Each of them, being a leading enterprise in its own field with a long business history behind it, had a strong inclination to stand on its own and show a conspicuous trend toward decentralization. Therefore, the head office of the Mitsui Zaibatsu had to establish an extremely centralized system in order to control the subsidiary companies.

In case of the Mitsui Zaibatsu, the head office, as an organ for control of the diversified enterprises, first materialized in 1891 as a provisional board of trustees of the Mitsui family. Before that, the enterprises related to the Mitsui family included Mitsui Bank, Mitsui Bussan (trading), both established in July 1876, Miike coal mine and some other mines, and also a kimono store that had survived from the Edo era. It was, however, only Mitsui Bank that had been under the direct management of the Mitsui family. Mitsui Bussan came to be directly controlled by the Mitsui family at the same time that the provisional board of trustees was established in 1891. The various mines came to be directly run by the Mitsui family in 1892 (Mitsui Kozan), and the kimono store, in 1893. Previously, there had been no need for the Mitsui family to have any head office as a comprehensive control center of diversified enterprises.

However, it is to be noted that diversified enterprises of the Mitsui family were all full-fledged, powerful entities which had been in existence for a considerable length of time, especially Mitsui Bank and Mitsui Bussan (trading), both of which had established a strong domain of their own by that time. Thereafter, Mitsui Kozan (mining) had grown rapidly and the three subsidiary companies soon formed a triangular relation of brotherhood under the head office of the Mitsui Zaibatsu.

The head office was not strong enough to control these three powerful divisions during the period of the provisional board of trustees and the years which followed when Mitsui's enterprises

MITSUBISHI AND MITSUI ZAIBATSU   79

were directly controlled by a family council which replaced the board of trustees in November 1893. This can be illustrated by the fact that in April 1892, Mitsui Bussan established a branch office in Bombay without the sanction of the head office and executed all transactions but those on consignment without its approval.[26] The authority of the head office, however, became remarkably stronger after the Mitsui Shōten Rijikai (board of directors) was established in August 1896, and began to control all Mitsui activities. This change was reflected in the increase of the number of items submitted to the head office for approval. The centralization tendency after the establishment of the Mitsui Shōten Rijikai, resulted from the failure of "industrialization of the Mitsui" that Hikojirō Nakamigawa had advocated from his base as director of Mitsui Bank.

Thereafter, the structure of the head office of the Mitsui Zaibatsu went through a number of changes but never lost the strong, centralized power over its subsidiary companies. The items to be sanctioned by the head office included such various problems of subsidiary companies as personnel affairs of executives and senior officers, organizational change, budgets, settlement of accounts, purchase, disposal, construction and modification of fixed assets, contracting with other companies, holding of shares of other companies, dispatch of directors to other firms, and non-operating expenditure (contributions, etc.).

Especially in the case of Mitsui Bussan, the approval and the decision on alteration of the maximum point of business activities, except for transactions on consignment (loans in advance, hedging, forward contract, sales, and purchase on contingent), all had to be all sanctioned by the head office after the establishment of the Mitsui Shōten Rijikai. Therefore, the president of Mitsui Bussan was unable to approve the above-mentioned activities' plan submitted by a branch or detached offices without referring to the head office. However, after Mitsui Gomei Co. (general partnership) was founded as the head office in 1909, some authority was delegated to the board of directors of Mitsui Bussan. This included the right of sales and purchase on contingent which was delegated in October 1913, and the right of hedging which was approved in November of the same year. Nevertheless, the right to lend in advance and to make a forward contract was in the hands of the head office, namely Mitsui Gomei Co., as late as January 1922, which is the most recent year that it is possible to follow the fact with historical materials.[27]

[26] Chandler, *Strategy and Structure*, chaps. 2–3.
[27] *Ibid.*

In the Mitsubishi Zaibatsu, the head office was not in a position to have the right, as did Mitsui, to decide on the kind and extent of the activities of its subsidiary companies. Moreover, as was explained earlier, after the multi-divisional system came into existence, all the activities concerning investment within the limits of the subsdiaries' capital amounts, minor organizational changes, contributions, and dealings with fixed assets (excluding those under the direct control of the head office) were all outside the realm of the head office.

The centralization of authority in the head office of the Mitsui Zaibatsu tended to become excessive with the expansion of the diversified enterprises and inevitably resulted in the lack of fast and dynamic managerial decision making on the part of the Mitsui's entrepreneurs. Furthermore, excessive centralization of authority prevented the top management of Mitsui's head office from concentrating on strategic planning and decision making.

Incidentally, the strong board of directors in the Mitsui head office was usually composed of directors representing subsidiary companies. For instance, the Mitsui Shōten Rijikai consisted of seven representatives, besides family members, who were on the board of subsidiary companies: Torashiro Nishimura (banking), Takashi Masuda (trading), Hikojirō Nakamigawa (banking), Takuma Dan (mining), Yasusaburo Ueda (trading), Eiji Asabuki (industrial dept.), and Yoshio Takahashi (kimono store). The same can be said of other forms of the head office, Mitsui Eigyōten Jūyakukai (the board of directors) and the Management Department of the Secretariat of the Family Council. Therefore, the head office of the Mitsui Zaibatsu was the place where each representative insisted on his own interests and was confronted with those of other representatives. The subsequent ill-effect was that the strategic decisions of the head office were rarely made from the point of view of the Mitsui Zaibatsu as a whole, and this accounts for the successive changes in the structure of the head office. The Management Department of the Mitsui Family Council was established because members of Mitsui Eigyōten Jūyakukai "were too much intent on expressing opinions only from their own one-sided standpoints and tended to forget their duty not to be prejudiced in favor of any particular field but to see things from the over-all viewpoint of the well balanced business management of the Mitsui family."[28] The motivation of the foundation of the Mitsui Gomei Co. was also to prevent the three rival subsidiary companies from going any further

[28] *History of the Mitsui Head Office,* II, 426.

in the "deplorable practice of each representative being too much
independent, . . . and adhering without reconciliation to their
own stands on the occasion of the directors' meeting." [29]

It was a natural result of the tendency of decentralization within
the subsidiary companies that the head office of the Mitsui Zaibatsu
turned itself into a committee of representatives of the subsidiary
companies. Mitsui Gomei Co. was also unable to avoid the above-
mentioned tendency. It was first headed by Takashi Masuda (trading) in the capacity of an advisor, and later by Takuma Dan
(mining) as representative director from 1914 until 1932 when he
was assassinated. The assistant to Dan, the vice-representative
director, was Senkichiro Hayakawa from the Mitsui Bank, and
most of the directors were also experienced career men from the
subsidiary companies. In this respect, too, the top management of
the Mitsubishi Zaibatsu showed a remarkable contrast with its counterpart of the Mitsui.

Another difference was that, in case of the Mitsui Zaibatsu, official members of Family Council or partners of Mitsui Gomei Co.
came from the heads of as many as eleven families, while the partners of Mitsubishi & Company, Ltd. were confined to the heads of
two families, namely, Hisaya Iwasaki, and Yanosuke and Koyata
Iwasaki. The top management of the head office of the Mitsui
Zaibatsu had to spend considerable time and energy to merely
coordinate among eleven partners (family heads).

The top management of Mitsui undoubtedly had an exceptionally
hard time with the many delicate organizational problems on their
hands, the excessive centralization of authority in the head office,
and the conflicting interests among the subsidiary companies and
eleven heads of families. The activities of Takuma Dan during his
twenty years as representative director often lacked dynamism
because of the hindrances surrounding him. Born in the family
of an ex-*samurai* and trained as an engineer at MIT, Dan was often
referred to as "Tan instead of Dan" (*tan* means guts in Japanese)
in his younger days. However, while he was the representative
director of Mitsui Gomei Co., he was criticised for his fascilation.
People called him "Dan of Yujufu*dan*" (*yujufudan* means fascilation
in Japanese).[30] A really marked contrast existed between Dan and

    [29] *Ibid.*, 460.
    [30] *Life of Baron Takuma Dan*, by the biography Publication Committee for the Late
Baron Dan (1938), II, 221; Kazuo Noda, "Managers in the Past 50 Years," *Seisansei*
(productivity), Series 1, No. 5 (1963); Hidemasa Morikawa, "The Diversified Development
of Heavy Industry of the Mitsui Zaibatsu," *Keiei Shirin* (The Hosei Journal of Business),
IV (1967), V (1968).

the top manager of the Mitsubishi Zaibatsu, Koyata Iwasaki, noted for his one-man management.

The structural difference between Mitsui and Mitsubishi was that the former's subsidiary companies were much older than the head office and therefore had already established their own independent empires with a strong inclination toward decentralization, while the Mitsubishi went through a different process of forming its organization. Its centralized structure delegated some authority in response to the actual needs of subsidiary operation, establishing decentralized "divisions" or developing joint-stock corporations. In the former case, excessive decentralization brought with it excessive centralization and turned the top management at the head office into a committee of representatives. In the latter case, however, decentralization developed moderately in response to managerial needs and functioned so as to check an expansion of centralized control at a certain limit, thus enabling the top management at the head office to keep itself aloof from interests of subsidiary companies. This certainly helped make it easier for President Koyota Iwasaki to display a one-man control.

[18]

By Wellington K. K. Chan
ASSOCIATE PROFESSOR OF HISTORY
OCCIDENTAL COLLEGE

The Organizational Structure of the Traditional Chinese Firm and its Modern Reform*

¶ *Whatever economic growth and development took place in nineteenth-century China, it was by no means an expansion highlighted by a commercial and industrial revolution comparable to that which occurred in Great Britain, the United States, and Japan. While many factors accounted for these alternative paths of change, one element was clearly the differing organization of business enterprise. In this essay, Professor Chan examines the organizational structure of the traditional Chinese firm during the nineteenth century. Then he presents two case studies, one of which illustrates how an enterprise developed an innovative strategy of growth based upon traditional Chinese methods, and a second that illustrates how a company wedded western managerial practices to the Chinese model with spectacular results. While it would be dangerous to generalize about the entire Chinese managerial experience from such a limited number of firms, their successful, though divergent paths of development do indeed suggest the role that traditional Chinese organizational methods had in stifling modern development as well as the influence that western practices and techniques would have on China's growth in the early to middle years of the twentieth century.*

Recent studies analyzing the development of the Chinese economy from the sixteenth to the early twentieth century have revealed a very high level of economic activity based upon sophisticated business practices. This activity included the growth of cash crops and the rise of a cottage industry in rural areas, the stimulation of foreign trade in several coastal towns, and the increase in elaborate contractual arrangements for land use and investment properties. Nonetheless, although these and other developments allowed the Chinese economy to grow in size and complexity, they did not give rise to a commercial or industrial revolution similar to that which occurred in the West. The question is why not?[1]

Business History Review, Vol. LVI, No.2 (Summer, 1982). Copyright © The President and Fellows of Harvard College.

* The author gratefully wishes to acknowledge the support of the American Philosophical Society during the writing of this article.

[1] Albert Feuerwerker, *The Chinese Economy ca. 1870-1911* (Ann Arbor, Michigan, 1969); Evelyn S. Rawski, *Agricultural Change and the Peasant Economy of South China* (Cambridge, Mass., 1972) Fu-mei Chang Chen and Ramon Myers, "Customary Law and the Economic Growth of China during the Ch'ing Period," *Ch'ing-shih wen-t'i* (Problems in Ch'ing History) 3:5 (November 1976), 1-32 and 3:10 (November 1978), 4-27.

The lack of basic, large-scale changes in the Chinese economy led earlier historians and economists to underestimate the dynamism of the traditional Chinese economy, while more recent scholars have advanced a host of historical factors and socio-cultural theories as their favorite explanations for the incongruity between this newly discovered economic activity and persistent underdevelopment in general. We need a fresh perspective, however, if we are to gain a better understanding of why there were no revolutionary breakthroughs in the commercial and industrial development of China during the crucial four hundred years from the early 1500s to the early 1900s. This article represents a preliminary effort to do this from the perspective of Chinese business management history.[2]

It is generally assumed that the traditional Chinese firm maintained the same basic organizational structure and managerial practices. What has not been explored, however, is whether in fact it remained unchanged, and with what consequences. Alfred D. Chandler, Jr., in his two seminal studies, *Strategy and Structure: Chapters in the History of the American Industrial Enterprise*, and *The Visible Hand: The Managerial Revolution in America*, has demonstrated graphically how structural changes in business organizations in response to ever-evolving new strategies have contributed most decisively to the unprecedented growth in American corporate enterprise since the 1850s. In this light, an exploration into whether or not there was a relative lack of change in Chinese management practices takes on particular significance in evaluating the Chinese experience. As this essay will show, Chinese enterprise did undergo some remarkable changes at about 1900. Inspired by Western organizational models, a number of Chinese entrepreneurs began to introduce some innovative managerial techniques in organization and operation, techniques that paved the way to the future.[3]

THE TRADITIONAL FIRM

The ownership of the traditional firm was vested in either sole proprietors or a number of partners. If singly owned, the proprietor would either manage it himself or more likely, he would hire an experienced manager to run it for him. Such a manager

[2] See, for example, John K. Fairbank, Alexander Eckstein and L.S. Yang, "Economic Change in Early Modern China: An Analytic Framework," *Economic Development and Cultural Change* 9:1 (October 1960), 1-26; a good summary of the various factors and theories is found in Frances V. Moulder, *Japan, China and the Modern World Economy: Toward a Reinterpretation of East Asian Development ca. 1600 to ca. 1918* (Cambridge, England, 1977), 1-23.
[3] *Strategy and Structure* (Cambridge, Mass., 1962) and *The Visible Hand* (Cambridge, Mass., 1977).

would be paid a salary plus a fixed percentage, ranging from about 10 to 40 per cent of the net profit. The actual proportion, often referred to as *jen-li* shares (literally, "human labor" shares), was clearly spelled out in the contracts between owners and managers. In the case of real partnerships in which each partner put in capital, the number of partners and the size of the capital contribution of each varied widely. Usually, one or more of the partners contributing smaller amounts would also serve as manager. Otherwise a manager would be hired to take charge of the business. In either case, the active partners, managers, or hired executives would also receive *jen-li* shares in addition to salary.[4]

The manager (*chang-kuei*, or literally "holder of counter") hired assistants, selected and supervised apprentices, and submitted accounts only once every one, two, or even three years, depending on contract, to the sole proprietors or the several partners for approval. Minority partners might recommend their friends and kinsmen for employment, represent the company, or participate in some particular business project. But they did so with the manager's consent, for the latter had complete authority over the management of the business. His only restraints were that he would be liable for losses if found negligent or dishonest, and that he was usually not allowed to do similar business of his own on the side.[5]

In urban areas, each business establishment was opened for fourteen or more hours each day: from between 5 and 7 in the morning (depending on the season) to about 9 at night. There were few holidays: the first fifteen days of each new year, plus four or five others for major festivals during the rest of the year. Since there was but one work shift, all clerks had to work excruciatingly long hours. For apprentices, who still had to put the shops back in good order after they had been closed for the day, practically all waking hours were devoted to work duties. Partly because of these long hours, but more because the managers expected total loyalty and dedication from the staff, practically everyone excepting the very senior members roomed and boarded in the shops. This practice was also facilitated by the custom of hiring only those who came from the same county or village as the owners and managers. Most establishments had a rule forbidding families of the staff from taking up residence in town. The clerks were allowed home leave whose length varied by

---

[4] Wu Kuei-ch'ang et al., *Chung-kuo shang-yeh hsi-kuan ta-ch'uan* (A Complete Handbook on Chinese Commercial Customs) (Shanghai, 1923), section 7, pp. 1-24.

[5] For a number of such partnership contracts, see *Shindai keiyaku monjo shokambun ruishu* (A Collection of Contracts of Ch'ing Dynasty), annotated by Yamane Yukio (Taiwan, 1916), esp. 80-83.

firm, ranging from about one to over two months each year. Most leaves appear to have been unpaid, although travel expenses were provided. During the nineteenth century the wages of the average clerk were uniformly very low: a base pay of 2 or 3 taels of silver each month in the larger establishments, with some fringe benefits, such as bonuses that increased the base pay by as much as 50 per cent, free room and board, paid medical bills, one or two sets of work clothes each year, pocket money for haircuts, and an occasional theatre ticket.[6]

Apprentices had the harshest working conditions. Both large and small establishments offered apprenticeships that usually lasted three years. As a rule, larger establishments had a more rigorous selection process and a more systematic program, but in all cases there was no formal training. An apprentice learned by observation and by task assignments that ranged from the most menial, such as, sweeping floors, cooking, cleaning spittoons and toilet buckets, to learning about business etiquette, merchandise, sales, and, if greatly favored, correspondence and bookkeeping. The discipline was strict: no fancy brocade garments, no absence from the business premises except for major festivals and on two evenings to the theatre, no home leaves, no pay excepting some pocket money, and during the first year, no sitting down while on duty.[7]

Yet in spite of these restrictions, apprenticeships were sought after, especially if they involved reputable firms. To be a serious applicant, one had to come from the same native place as the manager or owner and be properly equipped with recommendations. The applicant's family was probably moderately well off, for he was expected to have received some formal schooling and been able to provide for his own clothes and shoes. Indeed, several were sons of managers and proprietors who did not want their offspring apprenticed in their own shops for fear that they might receive preferential treatment. Their reward came later: only those so apprenticed could hope to rise to senior positions, and if the firm was expanding, to the post of branch manager. As "housemen," they enjoyed higher status and greater consideration than those hired part time or on term. Some might be given permission and monetary support at the end of their apprentice-

---

[6] *Chiu Shang-hai Hsieh-ta-hsiang ch'ou-pu shang-tien ti "tien-kuei"* ("Company Regulations" of Hsieh-ta-hsiang Piece Goods Company in Former Day Shanghai) (Shanghai, 1966), 6-10, 14; *Pei-ching Jui-fu-hsiang* (The Jui-fu-hsiang Company of Peking) (Peking, 1959), 41. The 2-3 taels, or approximately 3-4.50 Chinese dollars, in basic monthly wage is an estimate based on several texts. By 1912, Hsieh-ta-hsiang was paying 5 Chinese dollars.

[7] *Hsieh-ta-hsiang*, 67-68; *Jui-fu-hsiang*, 31-42; Wu Kuei-ch'ang, *Chung-kuo shang-yeh*, section 4, pp. 1-5.

ship to set up their own shops, often in related lines so that in
this way, supplies and sales outlets would emerge as the parent
firms laid out a network of lateral, backward, and forward integration.[8] The establishment of new shops seems to have been
especially prevalent among handicraft apprenticeships. Nineteenth-century contracts are full of printers, carvers, and other
craft apprentices who spent three years in a master's shop and
were then given a nominal bonus to help them buy the tools of
their craft to start new businesses.[9]

THE JUI-FU-HSIANG OF PEKING

Under such a general format of organization and management
practice, there could be several modifications within traditional
boundaries, which resulted in considerable growth in size and
further sophistication of practice. This is reflected in the well
preserved record of one major traditional commercial establishment, the Jui-fu-hsiang of Peking.

Begun in the seventeenth century in a district township in
Shantung province, this firm was owned by a Meng family. It
served as a wholesale and retail outlet for native cloth. Sometime
in the eighteenth century the fortune of the Jui-fu-hsiang declined, and its revival did not begin until the 1870s, about the
time Meng Lo-ch'uan (ca. 1850-1939) began to assume control.
An able entrepreneur, Meng seems to have combined an un-
wavering sense of traditionalism with an uncanny ability to take
advantage of changing market conditions. He maintained into the
1930s the same traditional layouts for all his shops: a warehouse
in the back; cheaper quality goods by the front counter on the
ground floor for less wealthy customers; and silk, brocade and
other refined merchandises on the second floor where wealthy
clients and socially prominent personages were invited.

In his personal lifestyle, throughout his life Meng was a model
of the traditional merchant: hardworking, conservative, and fru-
gal. His pastime was to read and re-read his company's books and
records that filled the shelves of his bedroom and study. His
children and grandchildren were not allowed to attend modern
schools; he hired established scholars who held degrees from the
imperial examination system to tutor them and their cousins at
home. He never retired; even in his eighties he took his title as
chief manager (*tsung ching-li*) seriously, and remained in charge.[10]

[8] Gary G. Hamilton, "Nineteenth Century Chinese Merchant Associations: Conspiracy or Combination,"
Ch'ing-shih wen-t'i (Problems in Ch'ing History) 3:8 (December 1977), 50-71.
[9] For an example, see *Shindai keiyaku monjo*, 156-157.
[10] *Jui-fu-hsiang*, 3-5.

Until 1893, Meng's native cloth business was still known only as a prominent local establishemnt in Tsinan, the capital of Shantung province. In that year, however, through the encouragement of his manager Meng Chin-hou, Meng the owner began to take advantage of imported goods and started branching into imported fabrics, cosmetics, and other foreign luxuries new to the Chinese market. He also set up branches in Peking, where he soon had five stores, and then in Tsingtao, Cheefoo, and Shanghai. He diversified into pawnshops, Chinese pharmacies, and handicraft weaving. At its height around 1925, his chain of some twenty-six shops employed about 1,000 men and grossed over 600,000 taels in sales annually. It was one of the eight largest piece goods establishments in Peking.[11]

Even though the Jui-fu-hsiang was owned solely by the Meng family, and Meng Lo-ch'uan served as chief manager, 30 per cent of the profit was set aside as *jen-li* shares for his hired assistants. According to company records, the *jen-li* share had in fact been higher, at 40 per cent before the 1870s, when they were reduced to 30 per cent. One can only conjecture that before the 1870s hired managers had run the family firm. After Meng Lo-ch'uan assumed control, he could not break the contract with his hired partners. Later on, as the firm expanded, he stopped the practice of signing contracts with his senior managers. Instead, he turned the 30 per cent profit into 300 bonus shares (*fen-tzu*). Out of this pool, between 220 and 240 shares were assigned to some seventy-five members of his senior staff, i.e., about 7 per cent of his employees. Meng himself, in addition to the 70 per cent profit belonging to his family, took 10 shares for being an active manager; his chief assistant, Men Chin-hou, also received 10 shares, while lesser managers received anywhere from 1 to 8 shares each, with most of them getting only 1 or 2. Altogether there were about seventy-five senior members who received shares (known as "*ch'ih fen-tzu*" or "*ch'ih ku*", literally, eating shares). The number of senior members was fixed so that others with ability would not be promoted into their ranks until openings occurred through death or retirement. It is not clear how the remaining 70 or 80 shares were divided. It seems that they became a part of the general pool that supplemented regular staff salaries as periodic bonuses. We do know that the average clerk's monthly income of 3 to 5 taels in the early years of the twentieth century was generally increased by 25 to 50 per cent through bonuses.[12]

[11] Ibid., 3, 9-11, 43, 98.
[12] Ibid., 20-22, 41.

CHINESE MANAGEMENT STRUCTURE   223

Because of their strong and able personalities, Meng Lo-ch'uan and Meng Chin-hou developed a highly personalized form of management that was quite successful in achieving centralization and coordination of their enterprise. The problems of coordination were compounded by rapid growth — from one to about twenty-six branches in less than two decades — and by the lack of a central office. Moreover, each branch was treated as a separate unit with its own account of profits or losses. Each one had a branch manager and four assistant managers to handle the four departments: front counter (selling inexpensive goods), brocade and silk, imported goods, and accounting. There were thirteen piece-goods stores in five cities, and they were grouped into three or four districts. Each morning, managers of the various branches within each district would go to the home of the district manager to discuss the sales, business accounts, market conditions, and personnel matters of the previous day. The district manager would then make a tour of the stores in his district. His responsibility was to report his observations and discussions to the two Mengs, coordinate supplies and sales in his district, meet financial obligations, and prepare statements of accounts. The district manager, who also served as manager of one of the branches in the area, left the day-to-day routine of his own shop in the care of the assistant manager in charge of accounts.[13]

Meng Lo-ch'uan maintained his centralized control through a personalized network of trusted subordinates and a formal structure of meetings and written reports. Meng selected two kinds of officers for each of his shops: one on the basis of talent, the other on the basis of personal loyalty. He required formal reports in writing from each district manager once every five days. He also used his own home to hold two major meetings each year attended by all the district managers and his chief assistant, Meng Chin-hou. The first one at mid-year was to assess conditions, plan strategies, and write interim reports. The second at the end of the Chinese year was to present accounts, check inventories, and decide on dividends, appointments, promotions, and other personnel matters. Meng Lo-ch'uan was assisted by his own family accounting office whose staff handled both his private estate and his business accounts. Meng Chin-hou, officially the district manager of Peking, had the added responsibility of touring the different cities to gain a broader understanding of market trends and inspect all the thirteen branches dealing in cloth and im-

---

13 Ibid., 45-47.

ported goods. But Meng Lo-ch'uan's chief assistant, Meng Chin-hou, was not given responsibility to look after all of Meng's stores. The pawnshops, pharmacies, tea houses, and so forth had their own chain of coordination. In this way, Meng the owner alone retained command of his total empire.[14]

The Jui-fu-hsiang was therefore managed by and large in the traditional way. Meng Lo-ch'uan continued to treat his business accounts as part of his private estate. Coordination of business and the planning of strategy were done in highly personalized ways, largely in the homes of senior managers. Moreover, Meng continued to diversify in traditional types of enterprises. Indeed, he balked when invited to modernize his old-fashioned weaving looms into a machine-operated weaving factory. He pleaded that as an outsider (*wai-hang*) to machines and the factory system, he could not understand the technicians needed to run the machines.[15]

This firm's ability to achieve fast paced growth, however, also resulted from innovations that included a conscious strategy not only to come to terms with changing market conditions but also to turn those new conditions to its own advantage. Thus, its management seized upon new products to branch out into new lines, and it turned the traditional *jen-li* shares for the hired manager into a system of bonus shares to reward some seventy-five members of its senior associates. Its system of coordination among the several branches was also a marvel of adaptation upon the traditional structure. Some managers saw to the day-to-day affairs while others planned, coordinated, and assessed the efforts in a manner suggesting some understanding of the distinction between line and staff practiced in modern management.

The Jui-fu-hsiang's pattern of high growth ended rather abruptly. Decline set in from the late 1920s. Even though the enterprise retained its size and a considerable number of branches, decline began in the late 1920s and continued until the firm was nationalized by the Communist regime in the early 1950s. This decline was due to a deterioration in management as the two Mengs grew old and died, Meng Chin-hou in 1936 and Meng Lo-ch'uan in 1939. The highly personalized part of the system of coordination and control could not survive their deaths. The more formalized part involving reports, meetings, and inspection tours became a ritual. The district manager's daily rounds to the

---

[14] Ibid., 43-45.
[15] Ibid., 6.

CHINESE MANAGEMENT STRUCTURE   225

branches were no longer taken seriously, co-workers used the telephone to announce his arrival in advance.[16]

A secondary reason for the decline was political. The Meng family had cultivated friendship with the warlords; Meng Lo-ch'uan himself had been befriended by Yuan Shih-k'ai, and Meng's children and grandchildren had married into the families of several Peiyang warlord leaders including those of Ts'ao K'un and Hsu Shih-ch'ang. But Meng did not apparently cultivate any relationship with members of the Nationalist Party, which was coming to power. The loss of political patronage during the 1930s further weakened the declining leadership, and the fortunes of the company fell even more precipitously as a result.[17]

British and American Comparisons

The general lack of structural changes in the organization of the Chinese firm stands out in sharp contrast to that of British firms during the late eighteenth and early to mid-nineteenth centuries. In Britain, the social gap between owners and managers narrowed as the latter received proportionately higher wages than the average clerk. Hired managers were also allowed to turn their bonuses into capital stock so that, over time, more and more managers became partners. Those partners who worked as managers and who, as in China, usually started out with fewer shares than the inactive partners, were allowed to plow back more of their earnings until their capital shares equalled or exceeded those of their inactive partners. By contrast, Chinese managers, though still maintaining their full authority in running the business, could not turn their *jen-li* shares into regular capital, much less increase them. Their social status was still dependent on the owners. In the case of the Jui-fu-hsiang, where the owner returned to become the chief manager, the hired managers lost ground. Meng Chin-hou and the other senior managers served without contract. Profits from the *jen-li* shares were turned into bonus shares and divided up. Although still very well paid and powerful compared to the average clerk, these senior managers had in fact lost ground socially and economically in relation to the owner.[18]

---

[16] Ibid., 46.

[17] Ibid., 6.

[18] Sidney Pollard, *Genesis of Modern Management: A Study of the Industrial Revolution in Great Britain* (Cambridge, Mass., 1966), 144-147, 150-151.

Another area of contrast between the British and Chinese firms was in the use of accounting methods. While there was dramatic improvement in the way that nineteenth-century British firms kept their accounts over the simple double-entry method first introduced by Italian merchant houses a few centuries earlier, there was no appreciable change in bookkeeping procedures in China. Even the large-sized Jui-fu-hsiang used the time-honored *"ssu-chu chang"* (literally, four-column accounting) method as late as the 1930s.[19] Newer and more sophisticated accounting techniques substantially minimized errors or embezzlements, facilitated the growth of complicated business transactions, and improved the control over distant agents. They also added another dimension of rationality and assurance into business management.[20]

Finally, the increasing importance of managers in Britain suggests the rise and development of a managerial class skilled in technical and managerial functions. In America, such a class emerged even more dramatically as small, owner-operated personal enterprises with perhaps a few hired managers blossomed by the late nineteenth century into large operations with thirty to fifty salaried managers. At this level of development, the American owners continued to have a major say in selecting the managers and in making long term overall policies. In this sense, they still played a role comparable to Meng Lo-ch'uan, who by the late 1920s was chief manager and chairman of the board to his twenty-five managers and eighty assistant managers. To the extent that the American managers owned only a minimal amount of company stock, most of which was still retained by a few owners, such a pattern of ownership was not unlike that of Jui-fu-hsiang. But the parallels ended here. American managers continued to expand in number, in the variety of their skills, and in the areas of responsibility. At the same time, the continuing growth of the American corporation demanded a constant influx of new capital that in turn led to a wide scattering of stock ownership. By about World War I, the original owners, like the newer investors, became rentiers with interest in dividends, while the corporations became totally managed by full-time salaried managers owning little or no stock. Such a progression into truly managerial enterprises did not take place in China.[21]

[19] *Jui-fu-hsiang*, 52-55.
[20] Pollard, *Modern Management*, 209.
[21] Alfred D. Chandler, Jr., *The Visible Hand: The Managerial Revolution in American Business* (Cambridge, Mass., 1977), 1-12.

CHINESE MANAGEMENT STRUCTURE   227

ADAPTING WESTERN MODELS

Beginning in the first years of the twentieth century, China saw the formation of new companies that had a decidedly different structure in mind. The founders invariably were Chinese who had returned after trading overseas. Their starting point was to use as a model some organization that they had seen abroad, but if they were good entrepreneurs, they soon realized that any model, in order to be successful, had to be adapted to suit Chinese conditions.

Borrowing from overseas dated back to the 1860s, first by the Ch'ing government in order to start a modern armaments industry. Several other ventures followed, organized by both officials and private entrepreneurs. All, however, dealt with modern industry, for the consuming interest was with Western mechanical superiority and the utilization of new kinds of energy—steam, electricity, and finally, internal combustion. But the organization that managed the modern industry remained traditional, with only minimal adjustments made in the work rules and the arrangement of plant workers. In fact, in most cases, such as at the Kiangnan Arsenal (1865), the Foochow Shipyard (1866), the China Merchants' Steam Navigation Company (1872), and the Hupei Cotton Cloth Mill (1889), officials managed bureaucratically in much the same way as the traditional state monopolies.[22]

Private entrepreneurs appear to have been more flexible. We do not know anything about the organizational structure of the first privately owned enterprise, a steam-powered silk filature organized by Ch'en Tsu-yuan in Nan-hai (just outside of Canton) in 1872. But Ch'en had been a merchant in Southeast Asia where he discovered in Thailand a silk factory using imported French machines. Ch'en's company was apparantly successful. In the 1880s he developed a modified machine that was much smaller, could be run by one worker, and was thus inexpensive enough for individual farm families to own and run as part of the cottage industry. It seems, however, that the pressure for this adaptive change did not come from managerial imperatives; several of the larger machines had been wrecked by angry local silk workers who feared that the more efficient machines would drive them out of work. Nonetheless, Ch'en's ability to adapt technology to

---

[22] The bureaucratic nature of the China Merchants' Steam Navigation Company's organizational structure is discussed in Li Ku-fan, *Chao-shang chü san-ta-an* (Three Major Cases involving the China Merchants' Steam Navigation Company) (Shanghai, 1933), 53-55, 137-141. For a general treatment, see Wellington K.K. Chan, *Merchants, Mandarins and Modern Enterprise in Late Ch'ing China* (Cambridge, Mass., 1977).

suit his own needs suggests a supple mind able and willing to innovate.[23]

The first entrepreneur who, in borrowing from foreign models, was more interested in the managerial than in the manufacturing process was Ma Ying-piao, founder of the first modern department store in Hong Kong. Ma had worked as a small importer-exporter in Sydney, Australia, during the early 1890s. Among his clients was a very successful Australian entrepreneur who in thirty years had risen from a mere peddler to the owner of a large department store employing thousands of workers. Ma studied this organization and was impressed by its many features that were in striking contrast to Chinese setup and practice. In 1894, he returned to Hong Kong and began to interest his friends in a similar venture. But it was not until 1899 that he got sufficient support. When his company, the Sincere Company, finally opened on January 8, 1900, there were twelve partners: four Chinese merchants from Hong Kong, six from Australia, and one from the United States. They put up a capital of $25,000 with Ma as general manager.

After renting a three-story building in the central business district on Hong Kong island, Ma introduced several strikingly novel features. Instead of setting up an apprenticeship program and hiring those who had experience, he hired twenty-five young men and girls who had come fresh from his home village without any previous experience in sales. They were simply given on-the-job training, emphasizing courteous service and orderliness. He also established a one-price policy for each item to be sold. He set up displays and conducted sales on all three floors, without the traditional distinction of storing quality goods on the upper floors only. Ma followed the modern department store's practice of making the displays and the interior decor as attractive as possible so as to encourage customers to browse around on all display floors. To that end, he spent $20,000 on glass windows, comfortable furniture, and other pleasant decor in his store, leaving only $5,000 for merchandise. He issued individual receipts to customers on all sales and purchases and provided copies for his own accounting department. Finally, he closed his store on Sundays in order to allow his employees to attend Christian gospel meetings.[24]

Ma Ying-piao's partners were bewildered by all these inno-

---

[23] *Chung-kuo chin-tai kuo-ming ching-chi-shih chiang-i* (Lectures on the National Economic History of Modern China) (Peking, 1958), 234, 236.

[24] *Hsien-shih kung-ssu erh-shih-wu chou-nien chi-nien ts'e* (The Sincere Company: Twenty-fifth Anniversary) (Hong Kong, 1925), section on "Record," 1-3.

CHINESE MANAGEMENT STRUCTURE   229

vations. They objected especially to the hiring of salesgirls. In response, it seems that Ma proposed to compromise by offering to hire a few experienced salesmen in foreign goods, but he could find no takers because the men refused to work for a company with so many new ideas. So conservative were those salesmen who supposedly were experts in foreign goods.

Ma's partners tried to terminate the business one month after it opened, but he prevented them from doing so because of the terms in the partnership contract. They feared that the company would lose heavily, a fear that almost came true in August 1900 when a severe typhoon brought the upper floors down. An effort to rebuild ran into trouble with government regulations. It was not until 1904 that the Sincere Company was able to resume business.

During the next three years, profits rose quickly. In 1907, the partnership was changed into a corporation with limited liability. New capital came in from eight new investors, some of whom were Chinese returned from Australia. Paid-up capital reached $200,000. With new capital and good business came the need to expand space for displays. Ma solved this problem in his characteristic, daring manner. He decided to build a new store along the outskirts of the business district where he was able to buy six adjoining lots. His gamble paid off. By the time the new store opened for business the following year, the area was becoming commercially active as more stores and offices were moving in. Profits doubled, tripled, then increased five-fold in each of the succeeding years.

Ma and his associates developed a new strategy for further and bigger growth for the second decade of the company. They built an ultra-modern emporium five-stories high on two acres of land. It had a garden and an entertainment park on the roof. It also introduced new departments for its store: a tea house, a bar, a restaurant, a photo studio, a cinema, and a Western-style barber shop. The Canton branch went on to open a hotel and several subsidiary factories for making shoes, cookies, soft drinks, glass, and cosmetics. In 1914, yet another new branch with similar setups was established in Shanghai. Further diversifications followed: an insurance and investment company in 1915, and a life insurance company in 1923.[25]

Ownership, however, remained largely in the hands of the original partners. Ma and his fellow directors decided that they should have the option to buy up to 80 or 90 per cent of each

[25] *Hsien-shih kung-ssu*, section on "Record," pp. 3-5, 15-16.

Ma Ying-piao.
The founder of the Sincere Company, Ma bewildered his
partners who opposed his innovations in management and
merchandising.

new capital stock before anyone else. As the size of the needed
capital grew beyond their own private resources, however, the
management experimented with limited sales of company stock
to the public, but in fact, even in these limited sales, most of the
stock was sold to friends and relatives of the original investors.
For example, when the initial $600,000 capital of the Shanghai
branch was raised to $2,000,000 within the first two or three years,
the management explained that it was swamped by friends and
relatives who clamored to buy shares.[26]

By 1918, with paid-up capital reaching $7,000,000, a general
meeting of all the shareholders of the Hong Kong, Canton, and
Shanghai stores decided to consolidate the financial and administrative organization of the company by merging the three separate boards of directors into one, with Hong Kong serving as
headquarters. All the stock from the three places was pooled. The
administrative chain of command was also made more explicit:

[26] *Hsien-shih kung-ssu*, section on "Shanghai Branch Company."

from Ma Ying-piao now serving as superintendent (*chien-tu*) and chairman of the board, to chief and associate managers for each of the three branches, assistant managers, Chinese and English secretaries, and department heads. In each branch there was also a group of inspectors, who were probably "censors" adapted from Chinese official administrative practice.

Another important innovational aspect of the Sincere Company was that it combined both traditional Chinese moralistic and social concerns with the modern techniques of organization. In 1907, the Sunday gospel service was organized into a Bible study group for moral education. Ma personally assumed the role of preacher and Sunday school teacher until heavy administrative responsibilities forced him to hire a minister. In 1911, an evening school was added to teach English, Chinese, and commercial mathematics. Finally, in 1922, a social club was formed for social mixing and to raise money for sick and indigent workers.[27]

In 1925, as the Sincere Company celebrated its twenty-fifth anniversary, the enterprise noted that it had grown from $25,000 in capital, 12 partners and 25 employees into one with $7,000,000 in paid-up capital, 3,000 shareholders, over 2,000 employees, and several thousand factory workers. The Sincere Company had overtaken the Jui-fu-hsiang many times over in terms of annual gross sales, number of employees, and types of businesses. The same year also marked Jui-fu-hsiang's peak while the Sincere enterprise would keep on growing for decades to come.

There were a few others about this time who were making similar managerial innovations and achieving equally spectacular success. The two Kuo brothers, Kuo Lo and Kuo Chuan, who like Ma were Chinese returned from Australia, had started a department store, the Wing On Company, in Hong Kong in 1907, seven years after the Sincere. During the 1910s and 1920s the Kuo brothers also made similar diversifications that eventually would overtake the Sincere group of enterprises in size. But it was Ma Ying-piao who had led the way. There is no question that the Sincere Company owed its impressive and fast paced growth to Ma's foresight and exceptional entrepreneurial skills. He borrowed, he adapted, he dared to take risks, and he branched out from one kind of new business to others equally new. Both the Sincere and the Wing On Companies also benefited greatly from the British legal system and the political stability provided by Hong Kong during those years.[28]

[27] *Hsien-shih kung-ssu*, section on "Record," pp. 5, 9.
[28] *Hsiang-kang Yung-an yu-hsien kung-ssu erh-shih-wu chou-nien chi-nien lu* (The Wing On Company Ltd. of Hong Kong: In Commemoration of the Twenty-fifth Anniversary, 1907-1932) (Hong Kong, 1932).

CONCLUSION

A number of scholars have advanced various historical and cultural explanations to account for the lack of major changes in the Chinese economy. Albert Feuerwerker has emphasized the corruption and obscurantism of an overpowering bureaucratic elite in repressing the spirit of enterprise. For Marion Levy, the more pernicious influence came from social institutions—family, clan, native district, or guild. What is often forgotten or minimized when arguing in this manner, however, is the continued presence of considerable entrepreneurial activities in the midst of bureaucratic domination. There was in fact a good deal of symbiotic relationship between merchants and officials. Moreover, a reliance on kinship ties and common place origins need not be detrimental to economic development. Scottish agency houses in the Far East, such as the Jardine Matheson and the Butterfield & Swire companies, owed their phenomenal success to the use of similar clan and regional connections.[29]

Evelyn Rawski has argued that traditional China's domestic commerce grew too slowly, especially in areas that had already been commercialized since the Sung dynasty (960-1279). The addition of foreign trade, however, might not have made the difference for, as G. William Skinner has shown, the increase in the size and number of markets that foreign trade stimulated did not necessarily lead to any basic change in the market structure. Indeed, Frances Moulder has blamed world trade and the unfavorable terms it imposed on the Chinese economy for China's economic underdevelopment.[30]

One argument that Frank King and others have put forth has particular relevance for this article. King contended that there was no development of an economic infrastructure such as an efficient network of transport or a rational system of public finance with uniform taxes and annual budgets. This line of argument suggests not only the government's ideological preference for a self-sufficient and subsistence economy, but also the persistence of a type of economic structure that would not permit sustained economic growth. The latter is crucially important because, while Chinese merchants have won many battles in different historical periods challenging such an official ideology, they have never

[29] Albert Feuerwerker, *China's Early Industrialization: Sheng Hsuan-huai (1844-1916) and Mandarin Enterprise* (Cambridge, Mass., 1958). Marion J. Levy, Jr., "Contrasting Factors in the Modernization of China and Japan," in Simon Kuznets, W.E. Moore, and J.J. Spengler, eds., *Economic Growth: Brazil, India, Japan* (Durham, 1955).
[30] Rawski, *Agricultural Changes*, 97; G. William Skinner, "Marketing and Social Structure in Rural China," *Journal of Asian Studies* 24:1 (November 1964), 3-43; 24:2 (February 1965), 195-228; (May 1965), 363-399; Moulder, *Japan, China and the Modern World Economy*, 48-50, 83-84.

圖面門店酒亞東及行行粵

The Sincere Company completed this department store and hotel building in Canton in 1912.

won the war because they did not understand what had to be done with the economic structure in order to achieve their goals of larger enterprise and greater wealth.[31]

The traditional Chinese merchants' ignorance of the broad economic structure in the public domain paralleled the ignorance of how they might make use of their own private firms' organization to realize their goals. This became the major reason why the Chinese economy went through periods of growth and stabilization, but achieved no revolutionary breakthroughs. As indicated in this article, the traditional Chinese firm remained fairly constant in its organizational layout. Thus, in the case of the Jui-fu-hsiang, much of the innovations advanced by Meng Lo-ch'uan and Meng Chin-hou were in the area of strategy, including their ingenious method of profit sharing and their new lines of merchandise. Their strategy allowed the company to achieve considerable growth in the years between the 1890s and 1920s. But the Jui-fu-hsiang's organizational structure remained very much within the confines of traditional formats. Meng Lo-ch'uan continued to hold exclusive ownership and absolute authority through a highly personalized system of administrative control, personnel management, and finance. The limits of such an institutional structure were fully exposed when the company began to decline because the two Mengs grew old and died.

By contrast, Ma Ying-piao's success with the Sincere Company came from his ability to adopt Western organizational models creatively. He did away with the apprenticeship system; he introduced several modern concepts for his department stores, such as the one-price policy, an attractive window and counter display of goods, and a more efficient system of bookkeeping. He also diversified into several modern fields of enterprise—modern manufacturing, investment banking, and insurance. Although Ma and his original partners continued to own a majority of the company's stock and to dominate the senior management of the company, the Sincere Company became incorporated in 1907, increased the number of shareholders to 3,000 by 1925, and, in the intervening years, took on a number of professional managers. By 1925, the Sincere Company, in both its organizational structure and operational strategy, was an institution quite unlike the Jui-fu-hsiang or any other traditional company. The Sincere's reforms were followed by others. And it was this group of modern enterprises that would eventually modernize the Chinese economy.

[31] Frank H. H. King, *Concise Economic History of Modern China* (New York, 1969), 17-21, 47-50.

CHINESE MANAGEMENT STRUCTURE 235

[19]

Build a Firm, Start Another: The Bromleys and Family Firm Entrepreneurship in the Philadelphia Region

PHILIP SCRANTON

Rutgers University, Camden, and Center for the History of Business, Technology and Society, Hagley Museum and Library

From the mid-nineteenth century, industrial Philadelphia's prosperity centred on the elaboration of speciality manufacturing. Overlapping complexes of firms, especially in textiles, metalworking, and machinery, vitalised the city's neighbourhoods, employing a quarter of a million operatives by 1890 and sustaining an infrastructure of working-class home-ownership and commercial, financial and technical institutions. Linked by proximity, contract and collective activities, networks of flexible enterprises sent forth a striking diversity of intermediate and final goods crafted for style or precision. Still, the vagaries of market demand entailed that while hundreds of small and middle-sized companies thrived and expanded, thousands failed, scattering their founders and workers. In this process, an atypical minority of firms became immense, regionally or nationally prominent employers: Baldwin Locomotive, Disston Saw, Campbell Soup, or, in textiles, J. & J. Dobson and the Bromley carpet and lace mills. Among the textile operations, family ownership prevailed, and indeed was common elsewhere, as at Disston or Campbell. This essay offers the Bromleys' business chronicle, spanning five generations from the 1840s past the mid-twentieth century. Sketches of family business practice at Disston and Campbell follow the main discussion, providing contrasts that introduce a closing assessment of venues for research in American family business history.

Philadelphia textile firms most often sprang from a proprietary base, when an entrepreneur commenced production on his 'own account' in rented premises, often with both used machinery and the aid of kinfolk. The strategic challenge was to capitalise on technical and trade experience specific to a product range (worsted spinning, carpets), to recruit a cadre of skilled and auxiliary workers, and to forge profitable links with nodes of wholesale demand. With such initiatives, a pattern of 'separate establishments' materialised, each firm specialising in a discrete stage of textile processing, thereby duplicating the *dis*integrated structure of the UK textile trades that had sent forth as emigrants so many of

Philadelphia's enterprisers.[1] Such operations became family firms if and when two or more kinsmen worked therein, and more visibly, when relatives were brought in as partners.[2] The Bromleys exemplified these practices as fully as any clan in the mid-Atlantic textile trades.

In 1800 John Bromley was born to a wool weaver's family at Hanging Heaton, near Leeds, Yorkshire. His father routinely carried blankets and army clothes to the Leeds Cloth Hall for sale. 'Educated to the business' as a lad, John worked inside a family economy until his marriage in 1827, when he started on his own as a handloom weaver, placing his 'pieces' in northern and Scottish markets.[3] Soon he joined his father and 22 others in commencing a 'joint stock' steam powered carding mill at nearby Batley Carr. In this co-operative, the elder Bromley served on a rotating committee of managers. Carded wool was shared out among the partners and 'taken home' for hand-spinning and weaving.[4]

By 1835 John and Elizabeth Bromley were parents to three sons and two daughters. George Bromley led the parade in 1828, followed by James the next year, Mary (c. 1831), Ellen (1833) and Thomas (1835). Charles (n.d.) and Edward (1840, died young) also arrived before the family's 1841 departure for the United States. The carding mill having failed in 1837, and with hand-weaving prospects ebbing, John gathered his small resources and sizeable brood, embarking from Liverpool for Philadelphia. Finding work, then a partnership, in a New Jersey woollen spinning mill, Bromley endured the death of his wife and a child and remarried (in 1843 to Lucinda Smalley), but returned to Philadelphia when the spinning venture foundered in 1845. After paying a veteran to teach him the trade, he commenced carpet hand-weaving on a single loom in rented quarters north of the city centre.[5]

Though Lowell's Erastus Bigelow had pioneered carpet power-weaving, the early technology's slow diffusion left ample room for skilled handwork through the 1870s.[6] Bromley's rise was gradual, paralleling the expansion of his family. By 1860, when he purchased a disused dyehouse for $10,000 (on a ten-year mortgage) and installed his 37 hand-looms, he had fathered four more children, John H. (c. 1845), Phoebe (n.d.), Anne (n.d.), and Joseph H. (1857), and Lucinda was pregnant with the second Edward (1861). When the Civil War commenced, John Bromley was master of a modest factory, father to six sons (the three eldest would be 'admitted to' the firm by the war's end), and valuably connected with local carpet distributors. His religious heritage as a birthright Quaker had proved an asset in the Quaker City (and may have occasioned his return there), as Friendly contacts through the local Yearly Meeting helped him gain the attention of wholesalers who marketed his ingrain carpeting,[7] provided advances that eased cash flows and assisted purchases of additional looms, and 'recommend[ed] him to the favorable notice of other large carpet dealers'. One of the latter invited him to 'match their foreign colors in carpets', inducing him to experiment with style and enter into the weaving of Venetians, a step up-scale. Without such support, the firm's upward course would certainly have been less assured.[8]

The Civil War and its aftermath brought swift changes. Aided perhaps more by inflation than profits, Bromley paid off his mill mortgage in 1865, and invested in more looms and building improvements. In 1868, he supported the elder sons, nearing middle age, in inaugurating their own carpet firm, Bromley Brothers. This move, first, eliminated any potential succession crisis, for all three were married with children, and appreciably older than their half-brothers, for whom their departure created room to grow.[9] In the 1870s, John H., Joseph and Edward Bromley worked their way through factory apprenticeships and became junior partners in the original firm. Second, it left the still-vigorous founder in charge of an expanding enterprise, which took full advantage of burgeoning Gilded Age demand for fashionable carpeting.[10] This was a cordial and well-financed parting, for the brothers located their new four-storey, 12,000 square foot factory immediately opposite their father's Kensington district mill.[11]

John Bromley promptly began another transition, installing power-looms for ingrains. Power carpet looms were double-edged innovations, for, once incrementally refined, they generated higher weekly yardage yields than their hand- (or more precisely, foot-) operated predecessors, but threatened to deliver both job losses for male weavers and price-damaging overproduction at firms that chose to run yardage in advance of confirmed orders. Nonetheless, by 1875 32 Murkland models stood beside 100 Bromley hand-looms and total employment passed 200, 'one fourth of whom [were] women'.[12] Initially Bromley Brothers had a rougher time, for within three years their new mill burned down, destroying all 'machinery, raw material, and manufactured goods'. Still, 'the next day' the trio rented temporary quarters nearby, ordered looms, and 'resumed active operations' while their mill was being rebuilt on the original site. Five months later, they reopened at a new five-storey factory, geared up its 100-horsepower engine, and commenced production with 120 looms, 3,600 mule spindles, carding engines, and an adjacent dyehouse. Employment shortly matched that of Bromley & Sons, and together by 1875 the two mills manufactured nearly $1 million in ingrain, Venetian and 'patent Imperial Damask' carpets.[13]

The independent sons departed from John Bromley's practice along three tracks. They integrated all stages of production, which created potential internal bottlenecks but offered the chance to manage production costs more consistently than was plausible with outside contractors.[14] Second, they chose to sell direct, bypassing jobbers and commission agents. This became a widely adopted tactic among textile specialists seeking the custom of expanding department stores and other retailers who could be approached by 'road men' to order from seasonal samples at prices above those quoted to middlemen. Third, the brothers divided their responsibilities functionally. James, the 'senior partner', had 'sole superintendence of the manufacture'. George managed finances and the office, while Thomas handled marketing from a downtown sales centre.[15] These tactics may have been responsible for their rapid success, but an expanding market and the Bromleys' local reputation for quality doubtless played telling roles as well.[16]

Sons James and George had experience that informed their managerial responsibilities. James was apprenticed at the loom, and had superintended weaving at J.B. & Sons since 1850. George had had a Friends' school education in Yorkshire, but after four years' work in the patriarch's Philadelphia firm, he left to join a milk company, starting his own commercial operation four years later, soon after marrying. Following his first wife's death (1862), George returned to carpeting with a decade's experience in commercial relations. Thomas, the youngest immigrant son, had completed his studies at the Central High School, graduating to the Bromley factory in 1851. How he developed selling skills is unknown.[17]

Both firms became major figures in the carpet industry's largest manufacturing constellation by the early 1880s. However, John's company responded more rapidly to demand mutations than did its offshoot, which soon split in a parting of partners. At Bromley & Sons, as governance passed to the founder's second trio of sons, a decisive product strategy shift arose. Recognising that the technical adoption of power-looms for flat ingrains threatened to overload the market and demoralise prices, the original firm invested during the late 1870s in 20 power-looms for pile Brussels carpeting, a complex, high-end fabric for which demand appeared to be growing. Ingrain prices had dropped 40 per cent in the 1870s and would continue to decline, so the American sons began disposing of their ingrain capacity. In 1880 only 82 ingrain looms remained, 20 of which were reportedly operated only to give employment to aged, long-service weavers. In place of the discarded looms, Bromley & Sons had also installed 104 Smyrna carpet looms, which created a mid-price, weft-inserted floor covering distinct from either Brussels or ingrains. The shift toward upmarket goods roughly doubled total product value over the five years after 1875.[18]

Meanwhile, Bromley Brothers followed a different track. They adapted some of their ingrain looms to weave other flat carpetings, damasks and Venetians, making no technical shifts comparable to those attempted at Bromley & Sons. In consequence, though their monthly output was rated 8,000 yards higher than their father's firm, Bromley Brothers earned appreciably less per yard in the trade's most over-crowded sub-sectors.[19] It is not difficult to imagine the Yorkshire-born trio's unease as their half-brothers moved assertively with market and technical trends. In 1881, unable to resolve strategic disagreements, they ended their partnership and divided its assets. From the outcome, it appears that Thomas, the marketeer, had pushed for investment in new machinery for novel product lines, echoing the steps of Bromley & Sons, but his elder brothers, then in their fifties, resisted. The settle-ment gave them the mill and its existing equipment, but Thomas retained the firm name plus an unknown financial settlement. With this stake and additional funds secured from members of Bromley Brothers' wholesale house, Boyd, White & Co., Thomas created a new Bromley Brothers that by 1882 reported 170 looms and 350 workers making 'Wilton, Brussels, Ingrain and Venetian Carpets'. George and James operated the renamed Albion Carpet Mills, with 140 looms and 305 operatives on ingrains. Thomas had not discarded the family's original craft, but his move toward diversification was obvious. Following his brother James's death in 1884, a year after John Bromley's demise, George held on to ingrains at Albion for the rest of his career.[20]

John Bromley's direct successors strode forward. Running 303 looms on three classes of carpets in three Kensington mills in 1882, they abandoned ingrains and doubled their loom count to 650 by 1885, a step that entailed constructing additions to their main factory. Scrapping the ingrain machinery cleared part of the space needed for roughly 400 new looms, chiefly hand-looms for Smyrnas, whose curious fabric structure had long resisted full mechanisation. By 1890, Bromley & Sons would operate 750 Smyrna looms, making it the largest employer of hand-weavers in the United States and doubtless the last posting for ingrain hand-loom refugees. It also had invested in 162 first-generation Smyrna power-looms, whose crucial mechanism had been devised by Thomas Bromley Jr (b. 1864) while he was 'farmed out' to the American sons by his father, their half-brother. Eighty-two huge Brussels looms com-pleted Bromley & Sons' weaving equipment, and constituted a fifth of those active in Philadelphia's carpet industry. The firm's shift from the slipping ingrain trade to lines that constituted the market's strongest growth poles had been accomplished with aplomb.[21]

At the same time, the younger sons were striking out into new terrain. In 1888, John H., Joseph, and Edward Bromley formed the Bromley Manufacturing Co. for the manufacture of curtain and upholstery fabrics. Initially sited near the brothers' carpet plant, BMC added a second facility some blocks to the north within two years. Drawing on a familiarity with chenille gathered through work on Smyrnas, they started with 125 hand-looms for chenille curtain fabrics, then added 217 power-looms for upholsteries. As they were experimenting with pile textiles, it is probable that these furniture coverings were plushes and velvets, rather than the flat Jacquard cottons and silks that other neighbourhood firms favoured. As in the carpet shift, profits were being recycled into new capacity to reap benefits from being at the cutting edge of technical and style trends. The American Bromleys would repeat this 'build a firm, start another' strategy across the ensuing half-century, a performance unmatched in the nation's speciality textile sectors.[22]

Thus, by 1890, two distinct family firm processes had matured. John Bromley had helped his elder sons create a spin-off firm in 1868, but after his death, the Yorkshire group split that enterprise while retaining an exclusive focus on carpeting. The founder's American-born successors, however, took a wider view of the whole field of styled fabrics. They ventured both into new carpet constructions and stretched out into related lines of house furnishing textiles that engaged their technical experience and could be marketed through familiar channels.[23] Iterations of practice based on these separate visions would open an enormous gap between the two wings of the Bromley family. Both would prosper, but only one branch would bank millions.[24]

By 1890, four of the five surviving sons had families of their own. George Bromley's daughter Susanna (1852) had already married Frank Birch, who was later drawn into the firm, as was son James A. (1861), named for his uncle. Thomas had a bigger pool of candidates for succession at Bromley Brothers – four sons: John H. Jr (1862), named for his American-born uncle, Thomas Jr (1864), Schuyler (n.d), and Howard (1878). All would eventually become junior partners after working both for their father and for Bromley & Sons. Among the Americans, John H. Bromley had two sons, William and John E. By 1889, William, then in his early twenties, was installed as manager at BMC. In the early 1890s, John E. joined the carpet mill team and moved in with his bachelor uncle Edward, who looked after his widowed mother, Lucinda, in a 'millionaire's row' mansion on Philadelphia's new money boulevard, North Broad Street, roughly a mile west of the factories. Joseph and Emily S. Bromley had three young sons in 1890: Joseph Jr (1881), Charles (1883), and Henry (1887). A fourth, John, was born three years later. Edward remained single and host to divers sisters and cousins until his death in 1915.[25]

Both branches were blessed with a profusion of third generation sons, the necessary condition for further successions given contemporary mores, and relations between the branches were fraternal, as nephews had working apprenticeships with uncles in the different mills and in several cases took up residence in their homes. These crossovers would not, however, be repeated after 1900, as the two groups' production orientations and fortunes diverged. In addition, city directory entries indicate that as their wealth increased, the Bromleys unsurprisingly migrated away from the factory district. Whereas in the 1880s five of John Bromley's six sons lived a few minutes' walk from their factories, in the 1890s only John H. remained in central Kensington. Yet the relocators did not scatter randomly. In 1901, four Bromley households clustered near Edward's manse, and two third generation sons lived a short tram-ride away. None moved to the city's famed Main Line railway suburbs; even Edward's summer house lay within the city limits. The extending Bromley family evidently re-created an older residential constellation that mediated between the appeals of privacy and family contact. This too would change in the new century.[26]

At first glance, the depression decade seems to have little damaged the Bromleys' prosperity. Despite shrunken sales, the partners conserved sufficient resources to add selectively to mill technologies, spin off two more textile firms, and purchase or erect new homes. Yet by 1899 the earlier differences between the Yorkshire and American branches had sharpened. At Albion, though employment had rebounded from a depression trough to 260, new investment was minimal. With increasing shares of a decaying ingrain trade that others were abandoning, the family firm became simply a livelihood – a source of current income without efforts at retooling for product shifting. Past 70, George Bromley remained in charge until his death in 1902. His son James and son-in-law Frank Birch divided the company, literally, two years later, setting up as independent operators of the mills' spinning and weaving floors, so that Birch could bring *his* son into a separate proprietorship. Both folded in 1912. At the end, James sold his few wide ingrain looms to employees, who thus bought back their jobs, and devoted his attention to a catalogue sales, home furnishings business he had started in 1907, perhaps in recognition of the mill's impending liquidation. Thus did textile manufacturing terminate for the family of John Bromley's eldest son.[27]

Bromley Brothers had been more imaginative in its timely shift toward pile carpets, but its collapse preceded Albion's and was tinged with scandal. In the later 1890s and early 1900s, Thomas Bromley, who 'was never satisfied with doing things on a small scale', made a serious business misjudgement and then botched the succession transition. The firm was to outlive him by less than two years. Having incorporated (1891), brought his sons in as partners and officers (1894–97), and bought out his non-family investors (1897), Thomas controlled a closely held family enterprise with a 'very excellent body-brussels and Wilton capacity', plus several hundred looms for ingrains and Smyrnas. However, deciding that the pile carpet section would have to be 'much larger to be profitable', he sold off this high-end market capacity and moved heavily into Smyrnas, Thomas Jr's speciality. In 1902, he rein-forced this dubious search for scale by purchasing a nearby 125-loom mill making wide ingrains, just as that trade segment was enjoying a brief final boom.[28] His death came near the peak of this surge, and his heirs shortly faced ruin.[29]

In May 1905, Thomas Jr bought out his brothers' shares in the firm, becoming sole proprietor, and shortly sold off the 1902 mill acquisition, perhaps to secure the liquidity necessary to assume full control.[30] It soon became clear that he had no capacity to manage the company his father had left behind. Thomas had been a proprietor-in-waiting for 15 years, but at the age of 41 he was both clueless about speciality textiles as a business and hamstrung by a mill equipped for production in two of the trade's fading divisions. Thomas Sr may have well understood the incapacities of his designated successor, for his will placed the mill buildings in a family trust, transferring title only to the firm's machinery, supplies, and the smaller, second mill to his sons. During 1905, Thomas invested most of his available funds in the speculative LaLuz Mining & Tunnel Co., in an attempt 'to make money quickly'. This futile gesture went hand-in-hand with curtailed production, marketing 'conducted in a desultory way' and the quietly desperate issuance of $20,000 in commer-cial paper early in 1906. The firm collapsed a few weeks later, owing $100,000 in liabilities against pitiful assets that netted creditors five cents on the dollar. In and out of court over the next several years and twice jailed amid charges of fraud and malfeasance over unpaid commercial notes, Thomas Jr's 'career' degenerated into farce. Partly supported by the family trust, he drifted into real estate sales, and became tabloid fodder for a series of affairs and noisy divorces, complete with private detectives and court battles. He died in 1934, long after the Yorkshire branch's dedication to the carpet trade had been all but forgotten.[31]

Press accounts of his 1906 bankruptcy took care to assure the trade that the rest of the Bromley clan was unaffected by Thomas Jr's plight.

By that time, the American wing was operating seven companies: Bromley & Sons, Smyrna and Axminster carpets; BMC, in lace curtains and upholsteries; National Lace, owned by B&S; Joseph H. Bromley, lace; Lehigh Manufacturing, lace curtains; North American Lace; and Glenwood Lace Mills, both lace and curtains. All were local, family-owned plants, and 'all of unlimited credit', the trade journals announced.[32] Their route to this stature is worth recounting.

The family flagship, Bromley & Sons, had also departed from the Brussels game, which was dominated by the firm of Hardwick and Magee, led by the Bromleys' former employee Harry Hardwick. Hardwick had combined scale and scope advantages to create a huge, integrated carpet firm with mules for spinning, dyehouses, and hundreds of jacquard Brussels looms capable of weaving thousands of style varieties. Shying away from this axis of competition, Bromley & Sons committed all its 1,000 looms in 1899 to Smyrnas, soon adding Axminsters, which echoed them in technique and fabric structure, early in the new century. Still and crucially, by 1906 carpets were no longer the American wing's main interest. In the 1890s BMC more than doubled its curtain and upholstery capacity (to 800 looms), employing 1,225 workers in 1899. Both Bromley & Sons and BMC by then sold direct through their own travellers, yet retained some connections with New York jobbing agents. In the same years, the younger brothers started both Lehigh (c. 1897), which first operated on Belgian-style lace curtains in a section of Bromley & Sons' factory, and Joseph H. Bromley's separate Nottingham lace mill (c. 1898), a new plant some blocks distant. As Nottingham machines were 30 feet wide and 15 high, initiating this trade demanded new construction. Each loom cost $4,000 (compared with about $500 for ordinary weaving), plus duty, for all lace machinery was made in Britain. In Nottinghams, one started large or not at all; and in Philadelphia, the Bromleys had the resources and vision to start large.[33]

By 1900, the American wing was in full flight, operating four firms with 2,600 employees, making hundreds of fabric styles in eight textile lines: two sorts of lace, nettings, chenille and tapestry curtains, and two forms of carpets. In carpets, a later price list showed that each design could be produced in 63 rug sizes spread across six grades with prices ranging from $1.75 for a hall mat to $106 for a 12' by 18' room size. Full-time designers were kept busy. In 1904 BMC offered 'all new' patterns in mercerised and untreated heavy cotton draperies, styled for current vogues in 'bagdads' [*sic*] and 'ottoman reps', plus French, Oriental, and Egyptian designs in table and couch covers, piece goods in 'stripes [and] small-figured patterns', and 'heavy fabrics for furniture coverings, Gobelin tapestries, etc.'. Bromley lace curtains featured a 'point de Venise line' with 'many . . . Arabian patterns and numerous fillet effects', along with 'fillet Brussels, Marie Antoinette, Cluny, and Irish point styles', some with 'stained glass effect', or 'flower centers, renaissance effects, imitations of Mexican drawn work . . . as well as heavier designs', and a 'full assortment of bed sets'. A common strategy informed the Bromleys' product planning: profusion in design and an emphasis on creating goods finished for retail sales. Though yard lace and piece goods were offered to downstream 'makers-up', selling direct to stores was eased by marshalling capacity to market ready-to-use covers, curtains, tablecloths and bed sets.[34]

Between 1904 and 1906, the younger trio expanded production facilities and founded three new companies. The $1 million North American Lace mills and the adjacent Glenwood Lace plant were finished by 1904, and the former commenced an addition within months of its opening, doubling its initial size. BMC built new quarters to house 250 lace curtain operatives, and Lehigh Manufacturing moved out of the cramped Bromley & Sons buildings in 1906 to a $2 million factory covering a full city block half a mile west of Edward Bromley's Broad Street household hub. As this was to be solely a Nottingham lace mill, the Belgian lace machinery at Bromley & Sons was left behind to be operated under the guise of the National Lace Co. By 1912 the BMC lace curtain addition was hived off as the Bromley Lace Co., the eighth outpost of a family empire that represented the largest concentration of lacemaking in North America.[35]

As their lace mills constituted 95 per cent of local capacity, state government statistics on the Philadelphia lace trade effectively profile the Bromley companies' course, 1906–9 (Table 1).[36] Several stories are embedded in this bundle of data. First, with earnings averaging 15 to 30 per cent above the citywide manufacturing mean, experienced male lace twisters were among the region's highest paid skilled workers. Women's earnings, however, were unexceptional, for they were tasked to winding, sewing and finishing, and were readily replaceable. Second, operating days dropped sharply in 1907, as did earnings. This was not centrally due to that year's market panic, but instead derived from a male-unionist-led, 39-day strike for a 15 per cent advance in piece rates (settled at seven per cent). Transferred from Britain, the lace workers' union would be a durable presence. Third, 1908 was even more messy; for though employment and operations rebounded, worker earnings declined. Here the problem was the exhaustion of the local pool of skilled operatives, for lace was twisted, not woven or knitted, and the skills transfer from other sectors was limited. The Bromleys hired

BUILD A FIRM, START ANOTHER 125

TABLE 1

THE PHILADELPHIA LACE SECTOR, 1906–9

	1906	1907	1908	1909
Product value (millions)	$2.8	2.0	2.7	3.9
Workforce	955	942	1,626	1,877
Days of operation	296	249	267	264
Working week (hours)	56	n.a.	n.a.	51
Yearly earnings				
Men	$763	680	437	627
Women	$403	352	233	320
Minors	$332	194	142	80
Product value/worker	$2,915	2,122	1,641	2,064

Source: Commonwealth of Pennsylvania, Secretary of Internal Affairs, *Annual Reports: 1906–1909*, Part III: Industrial Statistics, Harrisburg, P A, 1907–10.

hundreds of learners and recruited quietly in Britain, while efficiency sagged. Piece rates displaced much of the expansion's disruptive costs onto workers, but by 1909 the lace mills were up to speed again. Adult earnings rose substantially despite a shortened working week, due to adopting a Saturday half-holiday, and output reached record levels.[37]

Rapid growth was supported not only by style shifts favouring lace and consumers' rising real incomes, but also by a heavy tariff (70 per cent *ad valorem*) on imports that set market prices high enough to cover advances in skilled labour rates and leave a solid profit margin. Though exact figures are lacking, the Bromleys' labour costs were but 20 per cent of each sales dollar, compared with 25–30 per cent at other Philadelphia fabric mills, creating a payout differential of $125–200 thousand annually for the lace operations. Though part of this sum was offset by the need to import costly high-count and oblate lace yarns, the potential for rapid accumulation was substantial. In addition, despite brief 'grievance' stoppages that were common before World War One, there was but a single, strike-producing labour relations impasse in the next 30 years. Veteran lace twisters demanded and received a measure of autonomy and respect that assured labour peace for decades. However, the multiplication of companies stretched the core group's managerial capacities to the limit and complicated marketing and accounting. Here there would have to be changes.[38]

Organisationally, four of the lace firms were merged into two. In 1907, the Bromleys notified the public that North American and Glenwood had been joined. Late in 1911, Joseph H. Bromley announced the combination of his namesake mill and Lehigh Manufacturing. The new corporation adopted the brand name, Quaker Lace, that had been used in marketing since about 1904. Equally important, for the first time nonfamily managers were given leadership responsibilities. In 1907, William Turner, who had served as production manager at Lehigh and supervised construction of its huge new plant, was transferred to become president of North American, with J.H. Dalrymple brought in as treasurer. After the Quaker Lace merger, Turner was appointed first vice-president there as well, and became the principal spokesman for the family enterprises in subsequent years. Whereas once the Bromleys had themselves travelled to testify at tariff hearings, after 1910 Turner spoke before Chambers of Commerce, congressional committees, and the federal Commission on Industrial Relations (1914). John H. and Edward Bromley were more visible at the Philadelphia Yacht Club, where John was six times elected commodore, or at bank and trade association board meetings. The senior trio increasingly took long European trips, summered at coastal resorts, and participated in society affairs. William H. Bromley ably handled the BMC and carpet matters, but Turner served as a bridge figure until Joseph's sons accumulated enough experience to take charge of the lace complex.[39]

By 1913, the Bromley group employed over 4,000 workers, operated more than half the Nottingham lace machines in the United States (251 of 487), and enjoyed annual sales nearing $10 million, according to a trade journal report.[40] Control over and returns from this aggregation rested in a small set of hands, enabling decisive investment when opportunities opened. Their rapid response to a duty-free 'window' for lace machinery created in the 1909 Tariff Act is a good example. Perhaps a calibrated response to the Bromleys' long activism on behalf of protectionist Republicanism, this provision suspended the statutory 45 per cent duty for 18 months. When it took effect, Lehigh instantly ordered 49 Levers lace outfits from the UK, saving $150,000 in tariff charges, a sum augmented by machinery orders from the other Bromley firms.[41] More than a dozen other firms grabbed this chance to initiate lace production, and a total of 400 sets worth $2.9 million were imported before the window closed. Competition soon tightened and capacity use slipped to 60 per cent by 1913, but the war and ensuing depression brought a sectoral shake-out. Most of the new mills failed; none of the Bromleys' plants did.[42]

Quaker Lace made another assertive move in 1912, this time in marketing. To enhance brand name promotion, it began circulating by mail and through retailers annual style books displaying classic and novel designs and their uses for women's wear and 'colonial' home furnishing. Moreover, the firm leased a large, street-level showroom on Broadway in New York, open both to the trade and the public. Commercial clients could view samples in private rooms, whereas individuals could meet their needs from a full stock kept ready on a lower floor. Thus Quaker established both a highly visible presence in the nation's central fashion market and a 'listening post' to monitor signals from its most discriminating customers, Manhattan women from the privileged classes. Selling direct to an estimated 1,700 commercial accounts entailed a sizeable Philadelphia office staff. Numbering 103 at Quaker and North American in 1916, this white collar group represented six per cent of employees, double the proportion employed by other local manufacturers. Given increased selling and administrative expenses, intensified competition, and decreased capacity use, short-term profits may have been elusive, but these tactics solidified an already substantial base for long-term accumulation.[43]

The war years had a mixed impact on the Bromley network. Carpet wool and dyestuff prices rocketed, both being imports, the latter chiefly from Germany; and high-count cotton yarns for the finest laces dropped from the market. Still, war also eliminated the threat of mass impor-tations under lower tariffs that the new Democratic administration had secured in 1913, and brought government contracting into play, with the lace mills making tons of military nettings. They at least were immu-nised against the dye crisis, for their goods only required bleaching, and bleaching agents were in plentiful supply. Cotton yarn prices rose dramatically, to the delight of planters and spinners, but users passed these increases along to clients without evident difficulty. In 1916, reports for all but one of the Bromley mills totalled just under 3,000 operatives and 138 office staff, a fairly healthy showing. If not unaffec-ted, Bromley companies came through the war unscarred.[44]

Between 1918 and 1920, Joseph H. Bromley, his sons, and Turner made two strategic gambits, one a dead end and the other of lasting significance. As tariff-window lace startups began folding, North American bought two of them, a 15-machine plant near the city and a slightly larger operation in Rhode Island. These purchases were not repeated, for by the early 1920s the great lace boom was clearly ending as style trends moved toward high-gloss modernism in dress and furnish-ings. Augmenting the Bromleys' 30 per cent share of national pro-duction through adding capacity in a mature market was a strategy which was quickly dropped. Instead, as the second generation made way for the third, a second product line shift would be the key mechanism for transition.[45]

How the decision to invest in full-fashioned silk hosiery was made is unknown, but two factors surely were salient. Women's stockings were another mill-finished product that could be marketed directly to retailers, and their appeal as a semi-luxury item was rapidly spreading from the elite to the middle classes, especially among fashion-conscious, employed young women. By 1919, 24 Philadelphia firms had installed the huge German-designed machines for knitting and joining tapered leg and foot sections, machines then being produced and refined by an immigrant partnership at nearby Reading, PA. Moreover, though a thousand leggers and footers were already active in the city, there was no trace of a glut. Demand raced ahead of capacity and labour supply. Thus, the Bromleys experimented with the Quaker Hosiery Co. in 1919, placed machinery orders, and doubtless paid a high salary to lure a veteran production manager from cross-town Kensington to space within Quaker Lace's plant, a necessity given that they were devoid of experience with both silk and knitting.[46]

Clearly this technical ignorance carried risk. Earlier Bromleys had learned their craft at the loom or combined factory work with schooling, including time in business academies. Yet the craft-centred focus of the Yorkshire sons had not attuned them to wider sectoral dynamics, whereas the American group had reaped riches from its attention to fashion and marketing, while hiring and relying upon first skilled workers, then production managers for the lace mills. These business sensibilities, fostered by Joseph's sons' education at the University of Pennsylvania, would become keys to the next generation's vitality. Moreover, creating Quaker Hosiery gave Charles, Henry and John Bromley a means to make their own mark, just as had John H. and Edward with BMC and their father with his curtain ventures in the 1890s. Joseph Jr, the fourth son, would remain with Quaker Lace, but his brothers, amply funded, renewed the family vocation for entrepreneurship.[47]

Within a year, Quaker Hosiery's first 166 workers struck, refusing a 15 per cent piece rate reduction during the post-war 'inventory' depression. For nine months, the brothers and their associates in a 14-firm local full-fashioned trade group resisted bargaining with the American Federation of Hosiery Workers, but they could not prevent non-member companies eagerly hiring skilled strikers to run full while their competitors' frames were idle. Defeated in the rate cut effort, which became irrelevant as markets revived strongly, the Bromleys capitalised on their locational advantage and devised a new production and wage payment strategy.

First, as their incubator site far from the conflict's Kensington centre had insulated them from the strike's nastiest confrontations, they targeted it for future hosiery investments rather than relocating to the core knitting district when expanding. Indeed, they invested heavily in a nearby full-fashioned startup, John Bromley becoming an officer in the

Rodgers corporation, as a step toward creating a development pole west of Broad Street. Thereby, they evaded the main unionisation thrusts through the early 1930s. Second, Quaker offered sizeable cash compensation to knitters who would ignore the union's 'one machine rule', which attempted to conserve room in the expanding trade for graduating three-year apprentices and which frustrated companies taking delivery on machines they wanted up and running right away. At Quaker and other open shop firms, qualified knitters were assigned two machines and a helper for each, paid hourly by the company.[48] Knitters' piece rates were set a bit below the one machine rate at unionized mills and guaranteed, so as to maximise output and worker earnings. As silk hosiery boomed, two machine knitters banked wages of $90–100 weekly, triple the wages of typical skilled factory workers. The Bromleys prospered far more; Charles' 'net income' for tax purposes stood at $84,000 in 1927, and Henry's was $93,000. At the lace mills, Joseph Jr made do with $53,000. Instead of slipping into a Buddenbrooks malaise, the third generation hammered home another round of adroit profitability.[49]

By 1925, Quaker Hosiery and Rodgers employed 720 workers who operated 100 multiple-section full-fashioned leggers and footers as well as a new bank of 'single-head circulars' knitting seamless cotton hose. North American and Quaker Lace's labour totals, 1,090, were well below pre-war levels, but overall the Joseph Bromley group, including hosiery, roughly matched its 1909 workforce. John E. Bromley had fallen heir to the carpet and curtain firms (Bromley & Sons, BMC) long managed by William H. Bromley. Having dropped upholsteries and tapestries, they nonetheless provided 1,538 jobs for a family-wide total of 3,347. Within five years of the hosiery start, a fifth of the Bromley workforces were generating silk and cotton stockings.[50] Three years later knitting's impact could be more fully gauged.

In 1928, Quaker Hosiery held 193 full-fashioned machines and 900 workers, with 410 more at Rodgers, an 82 per cent increase. Meanwhile, both the lace mills and the carpet/curtain complexes had shed 19 per cent of their employees (Table 2). With little new technologically and their carpet and lace lines sliding out of the style mainstream,[51] these Bromley mills seem to have been managed for survival or as 'cash cows' for building hosiery capacity. By contrast, the full-fashioned trade *was* technically dynamic in the 1920s. Wider, faster, and higher-gauge machines succeeded one another rapidly, making possible the knitting of high-style, finer, sheerer hosiery. In 1929–30, Quaker Hosiery sold its first complement of machines, invested about $1 million in new leggers and footers, while Rodgers opened a branch plant in a similar expansion and updating move. The timing could hardly have been worse, but the technical logic of these steps was impeccable. Dozens of sectoral firms that failed to invest in new technology failed during the 1930s; others that borrowed heavily to upgrade fell into creditors' hands. Neither fate awaited the Quaker interests, though the depression was a time of endless troubles.[52]

Joseph H. Bromley, the second generation's most aggressive entrepreneur, died in 1931, leaving an estate assessed at $6.5 million, $2 million in cash and blue chip securities, $3.7 million in six per cent preferred Quaker Lace shares, and the balance in real estate, other textile stocks, and a $500,000 trust for his four sons, created in 1923. The lace company holdings alone were entitled to over $200,000 of the company's annual profits, providing of course that there were profits to distribute. The probate report confirmed that Joseph had completely separated the hosiery operations from his properties and had previously turned over North American to his heirs. In its gradualism, this succession process was superior to Thomas Sr's effort. It spanned two decades from Joseph's sons' initial entry at the lace firms, through his sponsoring of the hosiery venture and the trust fund, relinquishing common stock control of Quaker Lace and ownership of North American, to his will's final disbursements.[53] Yet even a skilful transition carried no guarantees for the future.

In the 1930s, Charles Bromley headed Quaker Hosiery, adding his son Charles Jr as treasurer in 1934, the first entry of the fourth generation. Joseph Jr chaired the Quaker Lace board; John was president and also active in managing Rodgers Hosiery. Henry led North American, and John E. Bromley ran the original John Bromley & Sons in Kensington, bringing in his son as treasurer. No residential anchor remained, for family homes and estates were scattered across elite suburbs, but overlapping ownership shares brought Joseph Sr's successors into close and regular business contacts. There would be new ventures during the 1930s, but none would match the earlier successes.[54]

First was the North American Knitting Mills, an attempt to make 'Knitted Ties and Scarfs' on jacquard-like Raschel machines and the second new start on the Quaker Lace premises. Though consistent with the clan's finished goods strategy, it foundered early in the depression, being revived as Mayfair Mills in 1933. Expanding its equipment to 60 machines, Mayfair soon offered knitted ties, sweaters, headwear, and novelties, in cotton, silk, rayon, and worsted. The Bromleys' trend sensors here worked smoothly, for knitted outerwear would become regional textile specialists' last expansive subsector. Ultimately, the third generation quartet failed to bankroll its timely departure.

BUILD A FIRM, START ANOTHER 131

Distracted by their commitment to silk hosiery, they let this one get away.[55]

Having retooled to chase the high-end hosiery market, Quaker was unworried by the post-1928 price-cutting wave in medium grades of silk stockings. In 1930 employment there and at Rodgers reached 1,600. A year later, with the accelerating slump, a thousand of those workers had been dismissed, and the Hosiery Workers union commenced a fierce organising campaign to balk corellate rate slashing. As two of the area's largest open shop mills, Quaker and Rodgers were prime targets; but Charles and John locked out workers at Quaker, secured an injunction to block obstructions at Rodgers, and left for widely publicised Florida vacations, a set of hard-nosed manoeuvres that broke the union drive. Once the economy's pulse quickened in 1933, they responded by calling back 700 workers, then signed a 1934 Quaker Hosiery union agreement that averted further labour conflict and soon extended to the rest of the 'Bromley chain'.[56]

Mention of the 'chain' heralds the brothers' larger strategy. Appreciating that silk hosiery was tending toward standardisation, they sought to achieve a scale comparable to that of the industry leaders, Gotham and Berkshire, each of which had over 3,000 workers. Hence after 1930 they acquired controlling interests in the local Windsor and Berger plants, which when fully engaged and added to Quaker and Rodgers, accounted for 2,800 production jobs. Unionisation precipitated a spatial course change after 1934, but the search for scale continued. Over the next years, the four brothers reprised their father's brief post-war lace acquisitions on a grander scale, starting or purchasing five full-fashioned mills, all outside Philadelphia's increasingly unionised environment. Adding output from about 750 additional workers, these plants in five states brought the Bromleys' the capacity to match full-fashioned leaders.[57]

For the first time, however, the American branch had made a gross miscalculation. Neither of the city mills proved viable; both closed by 1937. Quaker and Rodgers ended operations by 1940, the former being merged on paper with Quaker Lace as a distributor for the group's Tennessee startup. This southern mill lasted through 1943, as did one other outside plant, but the others shut down permanently. What had gone wrong? Joseph's successors had erred triply. They had undervalued the potential of knitted outerwear and let Mayfair lapse, in all likelihood due to a growing shortage of funds and a concern about the Amalgamated Clothing Workers' effectiveness in that sector. Second, they failed to appreciate the implications of sharp price competition in relatively standard hosiery lines, a different game from the familiar

132   FAMILY CAPITALISM

TABLE 2

EMPLOYMENT AT BROMLEY COMPANIES, PENNSYLVANIA, 1925–40

	1925	1930	1933	1937	1940
Quaker Lace	536	418	437	675	524
North American Lace	553	352	303	546	500
Quaker Hosiery	547	988	1,273	922	–
Windsor Hosiery	–	(612)[a]	555	–	–
Rodgers Hosiery	173	597	601	260	–
Berger/Bromley	–	–	284	156	–
Mayfair Mills	–	–	10	–	124
Joseph H. branch total	1,809	2,355	3,463	2,559	1,148
John Bromley & Sons[b]	1,538	9,45	709	781	956
Family total[c]	3,347	3,300	4172	3,340	2,104

Notes: [a] when independent, not included in total. [b] includes Bromley Manufacturing Co.
and Bromley Lace Co. [c] out of state employment not included.

Sources: *Fifth, Seventh, Eighth, Ninth, and Tenth Industrial Directories of Pennsylvania,
1925–41*, Harrisburg, PA, 1926–41, Philadelphia County, Textile and Clothing
Industries. (The 1941-dated directory reported data gathered for 1940
operations.)

pattern and style dynamics of lace, curtains, and carpets. Third, they
overestimated the abilities of the core group and their managers to coordinate scattered operations profitably. The wage advantages derived
from being one-quarter non-unionised were a weak reed as the gravi-
tational centre of hosiery manufacturing shifted to the open shop South.
Thus did the third generation heirs squander a large portion of Joseph
Bromley's legacy. Importantly, the damage was done well before World
War Two cut off silk supplies and caused the collapse of the full-
fashioned trade, devaluing what was left of the family hosiery assets.
The fault lay in strategic misjudgement, not the war crisis.[58]

The hosiery debacle broke the Bromleys' growth momentum, but all
was not lost. The lace mills chugged along at or above mid-1920s levels;
Bromley & Sons was evidently still able to make saleable curtains and
carpets. As Table 2 indicates, the lace companies flowed with the 1930s'
business cycle, before falling in employment as war matters dampened
remaining enthusiasm for speciality textiles. The carpet/curtain operations followed a similar ebb and flow, but their 1940 peak was far below
the 1925 showing, a pattern that continued as decline advanced. Hosiery
died, and with knitted outerwear abandoned, the burnt brothers and
their sons abjured further ventures, shifting to survival management in
later decades. Entrepreneurship's magnetism had vapourised and did
not reappear.[59]

BUILD A FIRM, START ANOTHER 133

TABLE 3

EMPLOYMENT AT BROMLEY FAMILY COMPANIES, 1945–63

	1945	1949	1952	1956	1960	1963
Quaker Lace	432	574	404	391	294	266
North American Lace	359	533	456	417	143	82
John Bromley & Sons	408	845	452	352	122	–
Totals	1,199	1,952	1,312	1,160	559	348

Sources: Eleventh, Twelfth, Thirteeth, Fourteenth, Sixteenth, and Seventeenth Industrial Directories of Pennsylvania, Harrisburg, PA, 1947–65. Directory listings cover employment for the years given in the table, but were published, on average, two years later.

As hosiery contracted, so too did openings for fourth generation successors. Charles Jr shifted to Quaker Lace, which he headed for 17 years after 1939. Henry Jr completed college in 1933, joined North American in 1936, and followed his father into the chief executive's post 20 years later. His brother Richard finished undergraduate work in 1937 and joined Quaker Lace, becoming vice-president in 1940, succeeding his cousin Charles as president on the latter's death in 1950. Edward Bromley, Henry's third son, later served Quaker Lace as vice-president. Several other men from this generation left the family businesses or never played any role in them as they declined, but all moved up the educational hierarchy, taking degrees from Harvard, Yale and Princeton, and became active in local elite society's institutions and festivities.[60]

Post-war contraction appears in Table 3. All outside branches were liquidated by the early 1950s, only North American's 22-machine Rhode Island branch surviving into the next decade. The surge of home construction after 1945 brought a last burst of sales for John Bromley & Sons, but the 1950s proved less favourable, and decline became inexorable once southern carpet firms supplied mass demand for cheap, synthetic fibre floor coverings. The lace mills again reached 1920s-scale employment in 1949, but tailed off thereafter. Quaker and North American combined their marketing efforts in 1957, sold a section of the latter's plant in 1960, and squeezed free publicity out of the Eisenhower White House's order for a custom tablecloth. The bottom dropped out of the lace trade in the 1960s, as the volume of cheaper imports grew and homemakers became increasingly unwilling to shoulder the maintenance demands of lace goods *vis-a-vis* synthetic curtains and covers 'that could be washed and dried without being stretched out on cumbersome, skin-pricking' frames.[61] North American tried relocating part of its equipment to a suburban mill, but expired nonetheless. At its lowest point, Quaker Lace retained fewer than 100 workers, but development of a permanent press process for lace and a stylistic turn toward 'nostalgia' brought enough of a revival to sustain a rebound to 250 operatives in 1980. A fifth generation took charge at the Bromleys' surviving company, but in 1992 long-standing rumours of a final shutdown of the Philadelphia mill at last proved accurate.[62] Clearly, the once-supple network of family textile enterprises was eroded once each of its product lines met inter-regional or import competition, fibre substitution, or a growing uninterest in style profusion.[63] The hosiery disaster simply wrecked any opportunities for creative response to these 'structural' shifts.

For a century, the Bromleys had benefited from access to numerous heirs capable of managing and expanding operations, one of a family business's most critical assets. Moreover, the American wing created new firms to sponsor entrepreneurial departures from existing product lines, a strategy that spurred innovation along the leading edges of stylistic and technical development. Though not every successor was able, nor every venture profitable, the clan's cumulative trajectory was expansive, until, in a burst of collective lack of wisdom, the third generation cohort committed the double gaffe of seeking scale and spatial diffusion in full-fashioned hosiery while failing to pursue knitted outerwear's potential. Yet, lest it be concluded that family managers were peculiarly vulnerable to such errors, it must be noted that professionally managed speciality textile corporations (Gotham, Berkshire, American Woolen) endured serial disasters after 1930 and that the Bromleys persevered in reduced circumstances long after those giants were liquidated.[64] Across the generations, the Bromley companies cycled from being means for getting a living to being large players on a national scale, before returning to their early survival strategies. Despite the reverses of the late 1930s and 1940s, the fourth generation did not sell or shutter the mills and retire to country club life. Instead, it manufactured fabrics, provided inner-city jobs, and scrambled after clients. As economists and business historians turn away from the stylised rationalities of 'economic man' toward appreciating institutions and culture, their experience is well worth our attention.[65]

This is all the more the case because the Bromley pattern was hardly unique in Philadelphia, where many multi-generational textile companies can be documented, some with product line shifts and spin-off firms.[66] Instead of further exploring textiles, however, two contrasting examples of durable family firms in metalworking and food processing will be briefly introduced to suggest other ways in which long-term vitality was conserved in, respectively, speciality manufacturing at

Disston Saw and mass production at Campbell Soup. Disston, like the Bromley firms, grew out of the efforts of a British immigrant. It remained in family hands into the fourth generation until its sale to a conglomerate in the 1950s. Campbell was a late nineteenth-century corporation 'taken private' by John Dorrance, a partner's nephew who invented condensed soup and transformed the firm into a family company. His heirs retain majority ownership today.

Henry Disston was the son of a Nottingham metalworker who in 1833 accompanied his father to the United States. Intending to initiate lace manufacturing in Philadelphia, using a new machine he had devised, Thomas Disston died soon after arrival. Placed in a sawmaking apprenticeship with three English-born craftsmen, Henry emerged as a journeyman in 1840 with $350 in savings that he promptly invested in opening his own shop. After a decade squabbling with landlords and shifting sites, Disston built his first works, 20 yards square, in 1850. Four years earlier, he had brought across the water two younger brothers as apprentice sawmakers and a sister (to keep house?), while a third brother remained in Britain until 1868 to attend their widowed mother. Disston imported English crucible steel for his saws until he erected the first American melting shop in 1855, issuing that year his initial catalogue offering 'twenty-one different saws, four types of knives, [various] trowels, gauges, slaw cutters, many kinds of springs, steel-blade squares, and bevels'. The Civil War brought an array of military contracts as well as a stiff tariff that created hazards for rivals who were still dependent on imported materials. Disston expanded, adding a rolling mill, widened his product range and commenced a speciality jobbing works. Soon after the war, he invested a portion of his profits in riverside land north of his city-centre location and began a 15-year process of gradual relocation to enlarged quarters. He also began national marketing, using splashy multi-page displays in industrial journals to supplement catalogues.[67]

Disston included each of his brothers in the firm through individual 'sub-partnerships' that provided them with profit shares yet preserved succession for his own sons. Upon the brothers' deaths, the firm repurchased their interests, paying sizeable sums to their heirs. Each of Henry's five sons joined the company, beginning in 1865. Hamilton, Horace, and William worked their way through the factory, whereas Albert and Jacob were schooled for accounting and financial tasks. Henry Disston died at 59 in 1878, and Hamilton, carefully groomed, succeeded him without a mis-step. In his 17 years at the helm, Hamilton pursued technological improvements, added to the family's saw patents, incorporated the firm (1886), and completed the plant relocation, which included constructing hundreds of homes and auxiliary community facilities as a means to retain Disston's skilled workforce. At Hamilton's death (1896), brother William took charge of the United States' most prominent saw manufactory. Employment topped 1,700 in 1890, double the 1870s level. By the time William retired (1913), nearly 3,000 operatives produced and marketed the output of this closely held, highly diversified saw and tool concern.[68]

Five third-generation kinsmen then assumed control at Disston, which had become Philadelphia's fourth largest metal trades firm, after Baldwin Locomotive, the Cramp shipyards and Midvale Steel. Like his forebears, vice-president William D. Disston was intimately involved with shop practices and in 1919 instituted a 'co-operative management system' anchored by a foremen's General Factory Committee 'to oversee the interrelationship of departments and its effects on product quality and production'. Despite attention to quality and flow, contraction followed in the 1920s. The workforce was pared down to well below 2,000 and equipment updating lagged. When depression brought further cuts, Disston's once-hearty labour relations soured, and union organisers found a ready audience. The Disstons acceded to their employees' desire for union recognition and signed contracts with American Federation of Labor locals. A heart attack short-circuited William D.'s succession to the presidency, and his cousin Horace assumed the post in the late 1930s. Never production-oriented, Horace distanced himself from the shopmen and their concerns. Unanswered grievances accumulated, and workers struck at Disston in 1940, the first walkout in half a century. Soon after its settlement, war demands delivered a rush of business – millions in contracts for tools and speciality steel. But by 1945, having run round the clock for years, Disston's equipment was worn out, while sizeable government loans for installing arms-specific capacity lay on the books, and inflation-pressed workers called for pay increases. Serious trouble loomed.[69]

By the early 1950s, promising post-war export markets ebbed. This disappointment combined with costly contract agreements that secured labour peace and defeat in a $2 million lawsuit to create 'an unprecedented profits squeeze'. In addition, dispersion of Disston shares among third generation family members meant that a largely female cohort of family members uninvolved in the business relied on dividends for the bulk of their personal income. Though Horace relinquished the presidency to his cousin Jacob in 1950, fresh leadership seemed mandatory. Thus, in 1953, the company hired its first outside president, John Thompson of Roebling Steel, and borrowed $3 million to develop a portable power chain saw engine and facilities to manufacture it. Family managers had simply missed the potential significance of hand-held power tools; the future of the firm depended on the speed and skill with which this error could be corrected. As with the Bromley knit goods venture, a crucial error followed. Pilot models were designed, crafted, and tested successfully; dies for production runs were soon cut. However, an internal marketing report forecast sales potential inadequate to generate profits. Panicking, the leadership team cancelled the project.[70]

This stunningly foolish move brought into force a clause in the loan agreement that had funded the venture, a provision the management team either had forgotten or thought they could work around. If the chain saw effort were cancelled, the bank could (and did) demand prompt repayment, all dividend payments being suspended until the debt was cleared. In the 1890s a tight group of owner-managers had declared a moratorium on profit distributions to eliminate debt, but dividend-dependent cousins would not accept a repetition in the mid-1950s. As word spread of the company's financial straits in 1955, acquisitions-minded Thomas Evans of H.K. Porter Co. began quietly purchasing the holdings of a number of women Disstons. Though several family managers fought to the end, other Disston men accepted Evans' terms for a buyout: exchange of $6 million in Porter preferred stock for all shares he did not yet own, plus acceptance of all obligations. Liquidating aggressively, Evans eradicated debts within a year and reduced H.K. Porter's tax liabilities by $3 million through applying Disston losses and depreciation to its corporate returns. The dismantling of the company and later transfer of manufacturing to Virginia deeply divided family factions. Wounds from the collapse of family control remained obvious in interviews conducted a generation later, yet one must agree with the historian Harry Silcox that managerial obtuseness and a 'lack of family commitment to operate the firm' were core contributing factors. As well as this, the Disstons' failure to create non-voting preferred shares for kin inactive in the company cannot be overlooked as an organisational foundation for the 1955 debacle.[71]

The Campbell Soup story was quite different. John Dorrance's empire derived not from immigrant craftsmen and speciality production, but from classic 'second industrial revolution' techniques: applied chemistry, flow production, and mass merchandising. In 1869, fruit merchant John Campbell and icebox maker Abram Anderson started a canning factory in Camden, New Jersey, directly across the Delaware River from downtown Philadelphia. Thirteen years later, Arthur Dorrance bought in as a third partner and shortly became president of the jams, pickles, and canned fruits and vegetables firm.

His nephew John joined in 1897, bearing an MIT chemical engineering degree and a Göttingen doctorate at age 24. John accepted a nominal $7.50 weekly salary in order to prosecute his key idea, extracting the water from canned soups, then selling it in quart containers whose weight/value ratio made shipping costs a major expense. If bulk-produced soup could be condensed to a third its original volume, the price could be halved, and markets and profits thereby expanded. Once he had mastered the technique and his employers authorised wide advertising, sales surged dramatically.[72]

John Dorrance was rewarded handsomely for his innovation, and the firm dropped other lines to focus on soup. Yet his goal was control, not promotion within the company, and by 1910 he reportedly threatened to pull out and create a rival firm unless the partners, including his uncle, sold him their shares on reasonable terms. By 1915, this process was completed with acquisition of Arthur's holdings for $5 million; John became sole proprietor. Devoted to detail, he 'delved into every phase of production, from advertising to cultivating varieties of tomatoes', and the firm prospered marvellously. A 1920s buyout offer of $120 million was rejected summarily; but, entering his fifties, Dorrance faced a problem chemistry and marketing could not master. Of his five children only one, the last-born in 1919, was a son. Correctly anticipating an early death, Dorrance devised a will that would avert a succession crisis. It placed the entire firm in a trust, one third to his son, a sixth to each daughter. Dividends would be paid regularly, but assets were only to be distributed to *their* heirs upon their individual demises. Professional managers would govern the firm's daily and strategic practice. Thus did John Dorrance reach beyond the grave to control the third generation and influence the fourth. At his death in 1930, Campbell Soup was appraised at $79 million.[73]

Through the trust, family ownership endured, but the company was completely insulated from family influence. Young Jack Dorrance went to Princeton during the Depression (and was appalled at newspaper revelations that he was provided $20,000 monthly by the estate), then served in military intelligence during World War Two. He joined Campbell in 1946, but could never 'live up to his highly motivated and highly successful father'. The company roared ahead, but Jack played a featured role only in local philanthropy. None of the five siblings' children entered Campbell, but one incoming husband did climb the managerial hierarchy. In the 1980s, once a series of third generation deaths released blocks of shares, he promoted merger deals with Quaker Oats and Scott Paper, precipitating an intra-family conflict that lasted three years. When the merger drive failed and he departed, new top management repositioned Campbell in the convenience foods sector. Profits and share values rebounded, and the family resumed its accustomed marginality.[74]

John Dorrance's legacy is a rough inverse of the Bromleys', for he divided family from firm decisively, and distinct from that of the Disstons, where provision for family created too porous a barrier between active and non-contributing kin. Yet these three cases suggest that specifics of age and family structure were critical to organisational outcomes. Dorrance's trust scheme derived from the late birth of a single son, whereas Henry Disston, who died at roughly the same age, had worked for decades with several of his sons in the saw shops and was partner with the eldest for 13 years. The Disston and Bromley first generational family settings were also distinctive. Disston started in business at the age of 21 and involved three same-generation kin in his efforts,[75] while watching over his five sons' maturation. Here the sub-partnership approach drew on and rewarded the brothers' abilities, yet its buyout feature blocked dilution of his direct descendants' inheritance. Bromley was over 40 when he started carpet weaving, and had two sets of children from his successive marriages to contend with. Providing a legacy for each group, without abandoning the younger to the good will of their half-brothers inside the original firm, led him to commence the supported spin-off tactic that was re-used in later entrepreneurial initiatives. Dorrance, by contrast, was an inside manipulator obsessed with achieving control. He conquered his employers and uncle, dominated every aspect of Campbell's operations, and made certain none of his heirs would tarnish the perfection of his achievement. Only formally was his a family firm.

Given these differences in initial conditions, relational contexts, and sectoral environments, each trajectory has a certain logic. Yet collectively they suggest how complex any effort to theorise about the family firm must be and how thin is the base of organised information, at least in the United States, upon which to begin to seek patterns of practice. Clearly, none of the three was a 'typical' family firm, but, firstly, we have not at present sufficiently broad studies to establish empirically at particular places and junctures what *was* typical, and secondly, even if 'typical' means only a nuclear family ideal type,[76] these three cases diverge so far from it as to make one wonder how useful a simplified conceptual model would be. Nevertheless, these firms rose to positions of industrial leadership in a shared regional environment strongly supportive of family enterprises. In the Philadelphia district, family and locally owned firms dominated the roster of leading industrial employers until the Second World War,[77] long after they had been

Family Business

eclipsed elsewhere by managerial, publicly traded corporations or peripheralised into small business manufacturing and service sectors. Clearly, chain migration from the United Kingdom played a substantive role in transferring a cultural template for family entrepreneurship to Philadelphia. Doubtless, networks of contact mediated by religious and ethnic organisations provided additional reinforcement. Yet the place and significance of other institutions, ranging from legal structures to banking/credit systems and trade associations, has yet to be gauged. If we widen our focus from the firm to the district, we might profitably inquire why particular locales proved hospitable to durable constellations of family firms, and where, beyond Philadelphia, similar patterns took shape in the industrialising United States.[78]

What is certain is that neither the Bromley nor the Disston approaches created a continuing upward glide toward bigger operations and better returns. For them, critical errors rooted in their individual family histories brought crises and contraction. On the other hand, it is arguable that Campbell's success derived not so much from excluding family as from relentless promotion of 'soup for lunch' at a time when food consumption patterns were dramatically changing.[79] Twenty years ago, the negative outcomes were described as inherent to the pathologies of family firms by scholars who regarded 'the presence of the family . . . as an impediment to the accomplishment of business goals'.[80] More recently, perceived shortcomings in managerial theory's formalism and quantitative methods have yielded a revaluing of the invisible assets family firms may bring to bear on business decisions. All organisational forms embody structural tensions, are prone to failure under particular situational stresses, and have a greater or lesser capacity to respond to environmental shifts.[81] The challenge is to identify at what scales, in what sectors, and within what arenas of problem stating and solving do different forms of family and professional management, and differing amalgamations of the two, operate more or less effectively. Such efforts must, in my judgement, resist the effort to define effectiveness along a single, necessarily arbitrary parameter (net asset growth, ROI, inflation-adjusted sales). Not only does such a step conflate uneven sectoral opportunities and technological or market trends with organisational formats, it fails to acknowledge that the actors themselves had patterned, but highly varied and rational notions of what effectiveness meant.

Focusing on family firms, it should be useful to inquire if speciality manufacturing (or service) is more congenial to realising the potentials of family enterprise than mass production (or routine service); to seek more systematically for clues as to whether they are more prone to misread market and/or technological signals than managerial operations (consider New England textile companies after 1900 or American auto makers in the 1970s); and in each case to establish when, how, and why. Is there a theoretical stance, perhaps from life-cycle or family system perspectives, that offers provocative leads for understanding their long-term dynamics?[82] Finally, given the 'externality' of the research undertaken here, how are scholars to penetrate into the decision-spaces of family firms making choices?[83]

The family business profiles examined here exemplify differing practices in separate trades across more than a century of American economic activity; but until the historical study of family firms is better grounded in concept, method, and theory it is uncertain what their experience implies for the continuing reassessment of business development in the United States. If family business history is to step beyond being interestingly anecdotal or a foil for the triumph of managerialism, its practitioners will need to postulate and debate frameworks for systematic investigations. Undertaking to determine whether 'family business' is; in Joan Scott's telling phrase, 'a useful category for analysis' stands as a worthy, perhaps overdue project.[84] The revival of business historians' concern for family firms is yielding multiple and fascinating studies of clans and companies, like the Bromleys. But, without such 'theory work', it will not generate lines of analysis that either integrate their histories into the dominant organisational synthesis or differentiate them from it creatively and critically, thus provoking fresh thinking about the canons of significance in business history more generally. In the interplay between empirically informed conceptualising and theoretically informed research lies the promise of family business history.

142   FAMILY CAPITALISM

TABLE 4

Bromley Firms and Business Strategies

Firm Name	Date(s)	Strategic Orientations(s)
John Bromley	1845-60	Quality, low-end, handloom ingrain carpeting; space leasing; agent sales.
	1860-68	Midprice carpets added; independent mill ownership; elder sons trained and admitted to partnership, then supported in new venture (Bromley Brothers, 1868)
John Bromley & Sons	1868-83	Wider product/style ranges; transition to power looms; training/admission of second group of sons; mill expansion, but continued focus on weaving.
	1883-97	Move to top-end carpetings and increase in weft-inserted lines; departure from ingrains; shift toward powerlooms on weft-inserted goods; spin-off firms: BMC (1888), curtains and upholsteries; Jos. H. Bromley (1894), lace; training of third generation sons and admission.
	1898-1920	Focus on mid-price weft-inserted goods; emphasis on finished rugs; brief effort spin-off worsted weaving.
	1920-50s	Survival mode; gradual contraction.
Bromley Brothers	1868-81	Integrated production; direct sales; functional division of management; product emphasis on low- and mid-price carpets. (Partnership split in 1881).
	1881-97	Up-market product line additions; agent sales; entry of sons; buyouts of non-family partners.
	1897-1906	Discard of high-end lines; mill purchases to add capacity; following founder's death, successor buy-out of kin; speculations/debt yield failure.

BUILD A FIRM, START ANOTHER   143

TABLE 4 cont.

Albion Carpet	1881-99	Ingrain focus; agent sales; integrated production.
	1900-12	Curtailments; partnership split into seperate spinning/weaving firms; failure of both enterprises.
Bromley Mfg. Co.	1888-end	Focus on mid- to luxury market home furnishing fabrics; agency sales; training site for successor managers.
Jos. H. Bromley & early lace companies	1894-1912	Mid- and up-market styled lace fabrics, also plain laces, curtains and nets; no integration; mix of direct and agent sales; acceptance of unions.
North Am. Lace Co. & Quaker Lace Co.	1912-92	Results of mergers; direct sales at NY showroom (through 1950s); finished styled curtains, tablecloths & yardage; kin and non-kin managers trained within the firm.
Quaker Hosiery & subsidiaries	1919(?)-43	Top-end full-fashioned silk hosiery; constant technical updating; investment in expansion and capacity acquisition; direct sales; solid anti-union policy into mid-1930s, spatial evasion there-after; defeated by increasing standardization of product markets and consequent price-based competition.
North Am. Knit./ Mayfair Mills	1928-43	Product focus on styled knit outerwear; starved of expansion investment due to family commitment to silk hosiery efforts.

144   FAMILY CAPITALISM

Appendix: John Bromley and Descendants

John Bromley, b. Yorkshire, 1800, d. Philadelphia, 1883.

I. Married Elizabeth Day, c. 1826, Hanging Heaton, Yorkshire.

- George Day, 1828-1912

- James, 1829-1884

- Mary (Stewart), ?-1891

- Ellen, 1833-1936

- Thomas, 1835-1905

- Edward, 1840-1841?

Elizabeth Day Bromley, d. 1841, near Paterson, New Jersey

II. Married Lucinda Smalley, c. 1843, New Jersey

- John H., c. 1844-?

- Phoebe, n.d.

- Anne, n.d.

- Joseph H., 1857-1931

- Edward, 1861-1915

Three second generation families:

I. George D. Bromley, married Letitia Arthur (1852)

- Susannah, 1852, m. Frank Birch, who joined firm as partner

- George A., 1854-?

- Ella, 1857-?

- Elizabeth, 1859-?

- James A., 1861-?, joined firm as partner.

Letitia A Bromley d. 1862; George D. remarried to Margaret Rushton, who reportedly

bore him one child, no name or dates. Margaret R. Bromley died in 1912.

BUILD A FIRM, START ANOTHER 145

II. Thomas Bromley m. Eliza Hendrickson (1860), d. 1886.

- John H, Jr., 1862-1937 m. Cora Lunger

- Thomas, Jr., 1864-1934 m. Lydia Rodear (div. 1900), m. Annette Hanson

    (1913), div. 1914, remarried, 1930.

- Schuyler C., n.d.

- Howard H. 1878-1911 m. Mary Sipple, 1899.

III. Joseph H. Bromley m. Emily Sawyer (c. 1880), d. 1928.

- Joseph H. Jr., 1881-1947 m. Bonnie Smith (1908), d. 1953

- Charles S., 1883-1950 m. Dorothy Wilmsen (c. 1905), d. 1970

- Henry, S., 1887-1973 m. Margery Nell (c. 1910), d. 1956

- John, 1893-1962, m. Helen Kingsley (1913).

146   FAMILY CAPITALISM

NOTES

1. P. Scranton, *Proprietary Capitalism* (New York, 1983). It should be noted that in the American legal system, state-level legislation governed matters of business registration and incorporation. During the nineteenth century, Pennsylvania was slow to authorise general incorporation outside the realm of functions directly related to public services (e.g. transportation companies), contributing strongly to manufactures' widespread use of partnership forms. The state did have statutes regularising practices regarding term or limited partnerships and their renewal or dissolution (generally after five years), further enhancing the prevalence of proprietary-style institutions. When obstacles eased in the 1880s, many private companies incorporated as closely held firms, in considerable part to simplify generational transitions.
2. There is some debate about how best to define the family firm. See W. Handler, 'Methodological Issues and Considerations in Studying Family Businesses', *Family Business Review*, Vol. 2 (1989), 257–76. Here I employ a common definition that excludes sole proprietorships lacking kin efforts or ownership shares. It is still far from adequate, as, for example, a corporation in which a shareholder's relative worked would technically become a family firm. Thus a minimal amendment would restrict corporate discussion to closely held companies with kin employment and/or majority ownership shares. This too is imperfect, as a moment's reflection will show, but definitional issues plague family business studies. Still, the 'corporation' or even the 'managerial corporation' is a blunt analytical instrument as well.
3. This may suggest decline in trade at the Cloth Hall or a choice to make different fabrics than those locally demanded (or both, in some combination, of course).
4. D. Robson (ed.), *Manufactures and Manufactories of Pennsylvania* (Philadelphia, 1875), pp. 259–60.
5. Ibid., p. 259.
6. Dunwell, *The Run of the Mill* (Boston, 1978), p. 60; S. Levine, *Labor's True Woman* (Philadelphia, 1984).
7. Ingrain was a flat, double- or triple-weave fabric floor covering that, with Jacquard attachments to looms, could be produced in almost unlimited pattern variations.
8. Robson, *Manufacturers*, p. 259; *Philadelphia Record*, 5 Nov. 1910.
9. George had married Letitia Arthur in 1852, with whom he had five children by 1868. James wedded Elizabeth Humphrey in 1862 (one child) and Thomas took Eliza Henderson as his wife in 1860 (two children by 1868). In order of age, the three brothers were then 40, 39, and 33.
10. See K. Greer, *Culture and Comfort* (Rochester, NY), 1988.
11. Robson, *Manufacturers*, pp. 42, 259.
12. On women carpet weavers, see Levine, *Labor's True Woman*.
13. Ibid., p. 42. There may have been a mix of power- and hand-looms, as at Bromley & Sons. Given hand-loom output levels of 100 yards/week, and the trade's standard 40 week yearly production schedule, 120 hand-looms would have yielded 480,000 yards in 1875, the year Bromley Brothers reported output of 500,000 yards. However, as power-looms then generated about 140 yards weekly, some admixture of them is entirely plausible. On carpet types and early power-looms, see C. Kendrick, 'The Carpet Industry of Philadelphia', Part D of PA Bureau of Industrial Statistics, *Seventeenth Report* (Harrisburg, PA, 1889).
14. The modest spinning complement may indicate that Bromley Brothers was pursuing a partial integration strategy, for three mules might well have been hard pressed to supply yarn for 12,000 yards of carpet weekly.
15. Robson, *Manufacturers*, p. 42.
16. See *Philadelphia Record*, 5 Nov. 1910, for an appreciative review of how the family's reputation was built on conscientiousness 'about the quality of everything that was used in making [their] carpets', leading to 'the name "Bromley" [being] a synonym for reliability'.
17. Robson, *Manufacturers*, p. 43.

18. Kendrick, 'Carpet', pp. D34–D35, D39–D44. This report includes photographs of men and women working on Smyrna rugs at Bromley & Sons around 1888. See also L. Blodget, *The Textile Industries of Philadelphia* (Philadelphia, 1880), p. 5. Smyrnas were 'heavy reversible tufted' fabrics for which pile loops were cut to create a chenille effect through an intricate series of both hand and powered operations. Brussels weaving was yet more complex, needing four to six yarn frames each holding 260 spools whose feed into the warp shed was controlled by overhead Jacquard card mechanisms.

19. Blodget, *Textile Industries*, p. 45.

20. Bloget, *Census of Manufactures of Philadelphia for the Year 1882* (Philadelphia, 1883), pp. 160, 162; *Textile Manufacturers' Directory of the United States and Canada* (Boston, 15th edn. 1885), pp. 193, 198. The principals in the new Bromley Brothers firm were John White (president), James Boyd, and Thomas Bromley. (See *City Directory of Philadelphia for 1884* (Philadelphia, 1884), p. 234 (hereafter *CDP*).) Wiltons were another variety of pile carpet whose weaving demanded complex machinery different from that for ingrains or Smyrnas.

21. *Kendrick's Directory of the Carpet and Upholstery Trades* (Philadelphia, 1890), pp. 210, 214; Kendrick, 'Carpet', p. D45. Philadelphia was then the nation's largest carpet production centre, having more than half of total capacity. See Levine, *Labor's True Woman*, and P. Scranton, *Figured Tapestry* (New York, 1989).

22. *Kendrick's Directory*, p. 217; *The Blue Book: A Directory of the Textile Manufactures . . . for 1889* (New York, 1889), p. 197.

23. For example, carpeting, drapery and upholstery fabrics were all heavily purchased by urban department stores and 'comprehensive' furniture retailers. The three lines had their own trade directory and trade journal as well, edited in Philadelphia by the above-cited James Kendrick.

24. The 1890 reports already showed this gap. Albion employed 300 workers, half of them women, but only seven of its 108 ingrain power-looms were the new nine-footers that obviated sewing together four 27″ carpet strips. Thomas' mill engaged 500 workers, again half of them women, across a wider fabric range, but 1,100 employees (600 men, 500 women) reported daily to Bromley & Sons while another 500, four-fifths of them female, made curtain and upholstery goods at BMC. Compared with 1875 figures the American clan's rate of growth doubled that of the Yorkshire sons. See Commonwealth of Pennsylvania, Secretary of Internal Affairs, *Annual Report*, Part III: Industrial Statistics (Harrisburg, PA, 1890), pp. 31, 37, 51, and *Kendrick's Directory*, p. 207.

25. *CDP: 1884*, p. 239; *CDP: 1889*, p. 254–5; *CDP: 1894*, p. 249; Viola Bromley, *The Bromley Genealogy* (New York, 1911), pp. 337–8. See also, *CDP: 1901*, pp. 311–12; *CDP: 1904*, pp. 323–4; *CDP: 1908*, p. 159; *CDP: 1912*, p. 282; *Philadelphia Bulletin*, 15 May, 8 Oct. 1917 (hereafter *PB*).

26. *CDP: 1184–1901*, pages as cited in n. 27.

27. Commonwealth of Pennsylvania, *Tenth Report of the Factory Inspector: 1899* (Harrisburg, PA, 1900); *Textile World Directory . . . for 1899* (Boston, MA, 1899), p. 191; *Official American Textile Directory: 1906–07* (hereafter *OATD*) (Boston, MA, 1906), p. 263; *OATD: 1910*, p. 285; *American Carpet and Upholstery Trade* (hereafter *ACUJ*), Vol. 22 (Sept. 1904), p. 87, (Oct. 1904), p. 73; Vol. 31 (April 1913), p. 85; *Carpet and Upholstery Trade Review* (hereafter *CUTR*), Vol. 43 (1 Feb. 1912), p. 79; Vol. 44 (1 March 1913) p. 85, (15 March), p. 83. At George Bromley's death, his estate was estimated at $273,000, but 85 per cent of this represented his interest in the carpet factory (*ACUJ*, Vol. 22 (Oct. 1904), p. 73). James A. Bromley's catalogue sales firm failed in 1916. Its assets of $6000 faced liabilities five times greater (*ACUJ*, Vol. 34 (Feb. 1916), p. 67).

28. Ingrains were sold chiefly to working-class and farm households. Trade journals at the time accounted for the brief flurry of demand by suggesting that these families, after several years of prosperity, were replacing flat carpets bought before the depression. After 1904, ingrain sales collapsed as capacity for cheap pile carpets was augmented.

29. *Tenth Report: Factory Inspector; Textile World Directory: 1899*, p. 191; *OATD: 1906–07*, p. 263; *ACUJ*, Vol. 22 (February 1904), pp. 72–3; *CDP: 1884*, p. 234; *CDP: 1897*, p. 249, *CDP: 1901*, p. 311–12.
30. Howard relocated to Virginia and John H. Jr took up brokering insurance for merchants and physicians. Nothing is known of Schuyler. Their posts at the firm seem to have been largely honorific.
31. *ACUJ*, Vol. 24 (Feb. 1906), p. 91; *Philadelphia Inquirer*, 14 Sept. 1907 (hereafter *PI*); *Philadelphia Public Ledger*, 30 April 1908; *Philadelphia Press*, 15 June 1908; *PB*, 1 May 1908; 19 April, 24 Sept. 24–25 Oct. 1913; 2 June 1914; 11 Oct. 1930; 3 March 1934.
32. *ACUJ*, Vol. 24 (Feb. 1906), p. 91. Alert to decaying interest in Smyrnas, Bromley & Sons added capacity for Axminsters, another variety of weft-inserted carpets.
33. In 1899, Joseph H. already employed 620 workers. See *Tenth Report: Factory Inspector; Textile World Directory: 1899*, pp. 191, 193, 204; *OATD:1906–7*, pp. 263, 279, 283; and Scranton, *Figured Tapestry*, p. 262.
34. *CUTR*, Vol. 43 (15 June 1912), p. 107; *Upholsterer*, 15 June 1904, P. 86; *ACUJ*, Vol. 25 (May 1907), p. 85.
35. Scranton, *Tapestry*, p. 260.
36. The few non-Bromley firms made lace edgings and trims, and typically were capitalised at about $15,000 and employed 10–20 workers. For details on one of these small operations, see *ACUJ*, Vol. 25 (June 1907), p. 75. After 1909, the state ceased gathering and printing details of lace manufacture.
37. PA Internal Affairs, *Report: 1907*, p. 136; G. Palmer, *Labor Relations in the Lace and Lace Curtain Industries*, US Bureau of Labor Bulletin, No. 399 (Washington, DC, 1925). Recruiting had to be indirect, for under American law it was illegal to guarantee positions to foreign nationals to encourage their emigration.
38. PA Internal Affairs, *Reports: 1907–1909*; Scranton, *Tapestry*, p. 278; *CUTR*, Vol. 44 (1 Feb. 1913), pp. 100–101
39. *ACUJ*, Vol 24 (May 1906), p. 79; Vol. 25 (Nov. 1907), p. 101; Vol. 31 (Oct. 1912), pp. 81–2; Vol. 32 (Feb. 1914), p. 81; Vol. 33(Feb. 1915), p. 74; *CUTR*, Vol. 43(1 Jan. 1912), p. 108; Vol. 44(1 Feb. 1913), pp. 100–102; Vol. 45(15 July 1914), p. 71; Scranton, *Tapestry*, p. 278. No information on Turner's background was discovered, but neither it does not appear that he or Dalrymple had married into the family. Such weddings would have had press coverage. Joseph's sons, Charles, Henry, and Joseph Jr, all then served in various managerial roles in the lace mills.
40 *CUTR*, Vol. 43(15 Jan. 1912), p. 84; Vol. 44(1 Feb. 1913), pp. 101–2; *OATD:1916*, pp. 274, 288.
41 Only records on Lehigh's orders are available, but the other mills most likely did not let this chance slip by. Including auxiliary equipment, Lehigh spent just under $400,000 on duty-free machinery. See Lehigh Manufacturing Co. Invoice Book, 1908–11, in possession of the Quaker Lace Co., Philadelphia. The absence of access to extensive personal and family papers entails using disparate 'external' sources, and a fair measure of inference, to reconstruct the Bromley chronicle. A considerable quantity of materials on the American wing's businesses since the 1890s are held by the Quaker Lace Co. Discussions about their deposit at the Hagley Museum and Library finally bore fruit in the fall of 1992, though these records will not be open for inspection until processed.
42 Scranton, *Tapestry*, pp. 261–2; Palmer, *Labor Relations*; *CUTR*, Vol. 45(1 April 1914), p. 60; (15 Oct.), p. 78; (15 Nov.), p. 77; (15 Dec.), p. 76.
43. *CUTR*, Vol. 43(15 July 1912), p. 86; Commonwealth of Pennsylvania, *Industrial Directory of Pennsylvania: 1916* (Harrisburg, PA, 1916), (hereafter *IDPA*), pp. 1304, 1322; *PB*, 15 May, 1917. At Edward's death in 1915, the estate transferred to sisters Phoebe and Anne was valued at $2.85 million in real estate, cash, and shares in four family companies. At Anne's death in 1935, $400,000 in cash was distributed, in addition to shares bequeathed to nephews and grand-nephews (*PB*, 4 Oct. 1935). Phoebe died in 1941 with assets of $382,000 (*PB*, 25 Nov. 1941).

44. Palmer, *Labor Relations*; *IDPA: 1916*, pp. 1304, 1322; *OATD: 1918*, p. 316; *OATD: 1919*, p. 330. William H. Bromley's National Lace was omitted from the *IDPA*'s 1916 compilation.

45. Palmer, *Labor Relations*; *OATD: 1919*, pp. 330, 358. Hard-finished mercerised cottons and glossy silks were supplemented by the vogue for shimmering rayons in women's wear, draperies, and upholsteries. Lace still had appeal at the market's top end, among certain ethnic groups, and in rural areas, but it had become a conservative fabric choice, not a style leader.

46. Scranton, *Tapestry*, 362–4; Textile Machine Works Papers, Accession No. 1304, Archives, Hagley Museum and Library, Wilmington, DE; *OATD: 1919*, pp. 315–46.

47. *PB*, 25 Oct. 1906; 4 Dec. 1929; 8 Aug. 1950.

48. In some settings helpers were paid by knitters out of their earnings. Whether this was Quaker's practice before 1922 is not known, but if so, the change represented a burden lifted. Again, knitters often chose their own helpers; if this custom was not continued, that change represented a liberty lost.

49. Scranton, *Tapestry*, pp. 363–6; G. Taylor, *Significant Post-War Changes in the Full-Fashioned Hosiery Industry* (Philadelphia, 1930); *PB*, 6 Aug. 1929; *Hosiery Worker*, 7 Jan., 7 and 19 April 1921. John H. Bromley's descendants remained involved with carpets and curtains, and from available records, never took up knitting.

50. *OATD: 1923*, pp. 441, 457, 461; *OATD: 1925*, p. 470; *OATD: 1928*, p. 488; *IDPA:1925*, passim.

51. Increasingly, mid-price carpeting was trending toward plain weft-inserted Axminsters, though fine and figured Brussels and Wiltons still prevailed in the high-end trade. The great home, office, movie house, and hotel construction wave of the 1920s sustained many a regional carpet company that foundered during the ensuing depression. See Scranton, *Tapestry*, Chap. 6.

52. *IDPA: 1928*, passim; *OATD: 1928*, pp. 477, 481, 494; *OATD: 1930*, pp. 470, 482; Taylor, *Significant Post-War Changes*.

53. North American had been handed over to Henry and John by 1928, possibly at Turner's retirement (*OATD: 1928*, p. 467; *PB*, 30 Nov. 1931). See also *New York Times*, 30 Nov. 1931; *PB*, 29 Nov. 1932; 9 July 1950.

54. *OATD: 1934*, pp. 315, 323, 325; *PB* 17 June 1931; 5 Sept. 1947; 8 Aug. 1950; 6 May 1962.

55. *OATD: 1930*, p. 467; *OATD: 1934*, p. 322; Scranton, *Tapestry*, p. 497; *IDPA: 1933*, p. 599; *IDPA: 1940*, p. 502. Mayfair employment grew from ten in 1933 to 124 in 1940, but the firm was abandoned during World War Two.

56. Taylor, *Significant Post-War Changes*; Scranton, *Tapestry*, pp. 427–50; *IDPA: 1930*, p. 563; *IDPA:1933*, pp. 598–9; *PB*, 4 June 1931; 15 May 1934.

57. The acquisitions were mills in nearby Riverside, NJ and in central New York, whereas Rodgers' branches were started in Laurens, SC and Athens, GA, and a Quaker subsidiary, Smoky Mountains Hosiery, commenced in Kingsport, TN, for which the latest machinery was ordered from Reading. See *PB*, 15 May 1934; *OATD: 1934*, pp. 195, 325, 329; *OATD: 1935*, pp. 314, 329, 326; *Davison's Knit Goods Trade: 1937* (New York, 1937), pp. 116, 148, 224, 230, 246, 252. Managers at Quaker Hosiery and North American Lace became officers at Windsor, as overlapping managerial jobs were increasingly assigned to non-family members.

58. *Davison's Knit Goods: 1937*, p. 224; *Davison's Textile Blue Book: 1939* [(hereafter *DTTB*)] (Ridgewood, NJ, 1939), 522–3; *DTTB: 1943*, pp. 437, 458, 511–12, 534. Later the firm that bought the Bromleys' Riverside, NJ, mill, also purchased Rodgers' Athens, GA, plant (*DTTB: 1956*, p. 446.). For the war's effects on silk hosiery firms, see A. Ellis, 'A Study of the Raw Materials Problems Caused by the War in the Women's Full-Fashioned Hosiery Industry' (unpublished MBA thesis, University of Pennsylvania, 1943).

59. No textile firms were created by family members after 1940, insofar as trade directories provide information, though other businesses may have been undertaken. Only access to personal papers would permit documentation of such initiatives.

150   FAMILY CAPITALISM

60. Charles, Jr. and Henry's three sons carried on the lace businesses, but John's son, a decorated World War Two pilot, and Charles Jr's brother Brooke were the most prominent socially. See *PB*, 16 Nov. 1942; 27 April 1944; 9 Oct. 1949; 8 Aug. 1950; 22 Feb. 5 June 17 Aug. 1956; 6 May, 24 June, 1962; *PI*, 23 Feb., 6 June, 1956.

61. *PB*, 16 Aug. 1954; 15 March 1957; 8 Feb. 1960; 17 Nov. 1980.

62. *PB*, 17 Nov. 1980. The family seems to have retained control of a small lace plant in north-eastern Pennsylvania, but its production manager has relocated to Maine to join a competitor. Family members are reportedly culling documents being deposited at the Hagley Museum and Library to remove items that deal with intra-family matters. This understandable, but unfortunate, effort may sharply limit the value of the collection for a more thorough analysis of family dynamics.

63. Both the narrowing of styles and fibre substitution struck the full-fashioned hosiery trade as the Bromleys were leaving it. Fancy pattern hosiery was acclaimed in the 1920s and 1930s, but gave way first to standard gauges dyed in multiple colour effects during the Depression, then to plain hose in a small number of hues by 1940. Nylon, once freed from wartime commandeering by the War Department, displaced silk, and given its elasticity, displaced full-fashioned technologies for a revival of seamless techniques in the 1950s, devaluing thousands of knitting frames and pushing Reading's Textile Machine Works toward liquidation. Trade journals credited the pressure for style narrowing as coming from distributors and chain retailers. See Scranton, *Tapestry*, Ch. 7, and J.D. deHaan, *The Full-Fashioned Hosiery Industry in the United States* (The Hague, 1958).

64. Some of the most successful American textile corporations combined family leadership and professional management, however, as with the Loves at Burlington and the Millikens in South Carolina. See J. Hall *et al.*, *Like a Family* (Chapel Hill, NC, 1987).

65 G. Hodgson, *Economics and Institutions* (Philadelphia, 1988); F. Block, *Post-Industrial Possibilities: A Critique of Economic Discourse* (Berkeley, CA, 1990); P. Scranton, 'Understanding the Strategies and Dynamics of Long-Lived Family Firms', *Business and Economic History*, 2nd series, Vol. 21(1992), pp. 219–27.

66. These would include the Globe Dye Works, Whitaker Cotton Mills, the Chesterman-Leeland Co., and, at nearby Wilmington, the Bancroft mills, each of which operated for over 100 years under family control. The Whitaker and Bancroft papers are conserved at the Hagley Museum and Library's archives in Greenville, DE.

67. H. Silcox, 'Henry Disston's Model Industrial Community', *Pennsylvania Magazine of History and Biography*, Vol. 114 (1990), pp. 483–516. For a wider view of the trade, see G. Tweedale, *Sheffield Steel and America* (Cambridge, 1987), esp. pp. 147–52, 175.

68. Silcox, 'Henry Disston', p. 493 (n. 21); Tweedale, *Sheffield*; W.D. Disston, H.W. Disston, and William Smith, 'The Disston History', typescript, 1920, Hagley Library, pp. 51–6, 69–71; *Tenth Report: Factory Inspector*, p. 66; *IDPA: 1916*, p. 1221. The 1902 workforce was totalled 2,425 (*Twenty-Second Report: Factory Inspector*, p. 114).

69. Silcox, *Disston and Tacony* (University Park, PA, forthcoming 1993), Ch. 6; 'Disston History', pp. 101–4; *IDPA: 1928*, p. 474.

70. Thompson had long experience steel and wire management, but was not a 'tool man' and thus apparently placed excessive faith in the negative marketing estimate. The managerial cousins were themselves divided on the wisdom of the power chain saw venture. See Harry Silcox, 'The Selling of Henry Disston and Sons', unpublished paper, 1990, pp. 1–15, and the shortened version in *Disston and Tacony*, Ch. 7

71. Silcox, 'Selling', quotation from p. 16. As a counter-example, the Textile Machine Works founders created preferred shares for their daughters, a separate trust fund of blue chip bonds and securities (fuelled by profit distributions as high as $600,000 semi-annually to the two partners in the 1920s), and, as they aged without sons to succeed them, transferred common stock to a trust controlled by veteran managers and an incoming son-in-law. See Textile Machine Works Papers, Accession 1904, Directors' Minute Book, Box 22, Hagley.

72. *PI*, 18 March 1991. The fourth-generation family struggle over whether to sell off

BUILD A FIRM, START ANOTHER 151

large blocks of company shares and diversify the heirs' holdings triggered an extensive historical investigation by the *Inquirer* staff. Company archives are not open to researchers.

73. Ibid. 17–18 March 1991.
74. Ibid.; *Business Week*, 17 June 1991, pp. 56–7; *Fortune*, Vol. 124 (9 Sept. 1991), pp. 142–8; *Financial World*, Vol. 161 (31 March 1992), p. 16.
75. William in England tracked steel supplies, British patents, and eventually sought markets for Disston saws there, successfully enough that his son returned to Britain after the brothers were reunited in Philadelphia to serve as the firm's overseas agent. Silcox, *Disston*, and Tweedale, *Sheffield*, p. 148.
76. Founder, spouse and offspring engaged in a sole proprietorship, facing across time decisions about expansion, product development, kin provision, and succession to leadership.
77. See P. Scranton, 'Large Firms and Industrial Restructuring: The Philadelphia Region, 1900–1980', *Pennsylvania Magazine of History and Biography*, Vol. 116 (1992), pp. 419–65.
78. My locational 'candidates' at this point would be secondary industrial cities with strong commitments to product-diverse manufacturing, such as Newark, NJ, Providence, RI, or Grand Rapids, MI. Family firms also predominated in particular trades at sites that also held leading managerialist operations, as in printing and publishing or apparel in New York or machine tools at Cincinnati, OH.
79. See H. Levenstein, *Revolution at the Dinner Table* (New York, 1987).
80. B. Hollander and N. Elman, 'Family Owned Businesses: An Emerging Field of Inquiry', *Family Business Review*, Vol. 1 (1988), pp. 145–64, quotation from p. 147. See also R.G. Donnelley, 'The Family Business', *Harvard Business Review*, Vol. 42 (1964), pp. 93–105, and H. Levison, *The Great Jackass Fallacy* (Cambridge, MA, 1973), Ch. 8.
81. For an instructive reading of the psychodynamics of organisations, see H. Baum, *The Invisible Bureaucracy* (New York, 1987).
82. Hollander and Elman, 'Family Owned', 152–61.
83. For a rare example that exposes these processes, see the father–son letters in the Beetem Carpet Papers, Accession No. 1176, Hagley Museum and Library Archives, Series I, Box 9, discussed at some length in Scranton, *Tapestry*, 247–59.
84. Scott, *Gender and the Politics of History* (New York, 1988), Ch. 2. See also P. Scranton, 'Small Business, Family Firms, and Batch Production: Three Axes for Development in American Business History', *Business and Economic History*, 2nd series, Vol. 20 (1991), pp. 99–106, and Scranton, 'Understanding the Strategies and Dynamics'. The reference to Scott's work is not incidental, for family firms are vivid sites for the intersection of gender and economic relations and can illuminate the ways in which 'manhood' is constructed and reproduced in different configurations. Moreover, historically daughters were at times objectified and 'capitalised' as means to attract incomer talent through marriage, but recently have joined the succession order, creating a restructuring of gender expectations. All this bears closer scrutiny. On issues of manhood in industry during the Second Industrial Revolution, see P. Scranton, 'Where's Poppa?', paper presented at the Montreal Industrial Paternalism conference, Oct. 1992.

[20]

The Dutch Family Firm confronted with Chandler's Dynamics of Industrial Capitalism, 1890–1940

KEETIE E. SLUYTERMAN and HÉLÈNE J.M. WINKELMAN

Erasmus University, Rotterdam and Netherlands Economic-History Archives, Amsterdam

In his book *Scale and Scope*, Chandler compares patterns of industrial growth and competitiveness in the United States, Germany and Great Britain. In his view, the ability of a nation to create an international competitive industry depends, to a large extent, on investment in managerial capabilities. In the US a business system developed where decisions were made by salaried managers not owners. This system was highly competitive and Chandler therefore describes the US industrial capitalism as 'competitive managerial'. In contrast, British industrial capitalism is found to be 'personal', because the British held on to their family firms and failed to invest in managerial capabilities, as well as in production and distribution. As a consequence, the British failed in the core sectors of the 'Second Industrial Revolution'. By attempting to maintain market power solely through use of patents, advertising, cartel arrangements and mergers, the family firms lost competitiveness, concludes Chandler. The Germans were more similar to the North Americans in that they created large companies and large managerial hierarchies. However, according to Chandler, they differed from the US in their preference to cartel agreements. Their capitalism is termed 'co-operative managerial capitalism'.[1]

The Netherlands are geographically situated between Germany and Great Britain and have maintained close commercial relations with both countries. In this article we will explore whether the Dutch industrial capitalism can be characterised as 'personal' or as 'co-operative managerial'. Having reached a conclusion about the typology of the Dutch industrial capitalism, we will study the performance of the Dutch firms in regard to the industries of the Second Industrial Revolution. Chandler's generalisations suggest there is a causal connection between the adherence to personal capitalism and the family firm and a poor performance in these sectors. In conclusion we will compare and contrast our findings with Chandler's harsh judgement on the family firm.

II

The first step in our analysis of Dutch industrial capitalism was to draw up a list of the 100 largest Dutch industrial enterprises in 1930 (see Appendix 1).[2] Following Chandler, we used assets employed as the ranking criterion.[3] This exercise was not without major problems, because it was easy enough to trace the assets of listed companies, but very difficult to discover those of partnerships or unlisted limited liability companies. This meant there was the danger of underestimating the importance of family firms. We tried to trace as best as we could the major family firms to prevent under-rating the extent of personal capitalism. Nevertheless, the family firms are probably under-rated for another more subtle reason, to do with the financial policy of family firms. Dutch family firms were in the habit of writing off buildings and machinery more quickly than was necessary, as long as profits permitted. In this way they kept profits in the company and built up large hidden reserves to use in adverse economic circumstances.[4] This policy explains why family firms often appeared smaller than listed companies when ranked by assets, but showed a remarkable resilience in depression periods.

To assess the size of the Dutch companies, we have compared Dutch assets with those of the American and German companies using the currency exchange rate of 1930.[5] Comparison with the British companies was not possible, because in the British case Chandler used the market value of shares instead of assets employed as the size criterion. Comparison with the American companies reveals that the top four companies of the Dutch list, the well known Royal Dutch Shell, Unilever NV, Philips and AKU, would have appeared on the American top 200 list, while only the first two (Dutch/Anglo) companies were within reach of the American top 100.[6] The 100th German company would have ranked 14th on the Dutch list and the 200th would have come in 36th place. As was to be expected, the Dutch companies were much smaller than those of the USA and Germany. We also compared the combined assets of the top 100 companies in Germany and the Netherlands. The combined German assets were four times larger than those of the Netherlands. As the German population in 1930 was eight times larger than the population of the Netherlands,[7] the amount of capital collected in Dutch industrial companies does seem to have been considerable. This observation is in line with earlier conclusions that the Dutch had a relatively strong position in foreign direct investment.[8]

Considering the small scale of Dutch industrial companies, managerial structures of the American type are not to be expected.[9] Of the top

100 companies, 14 were still family partnerships with ownership and management united. Another 17 started as family partnerships but had been turned into listed companies by 1930; 30 more started as family partnerships, but changed over the years towards less family-oriented managerial structures. This happened by seeking access to the capital market, by mergers and/or by appointing salaried managers. In most of these companies, family influence was still noticeable. Of the remaining 39 companies, five were co-operatives and 19 can be characterised as entrepreneurial, in the sense that one or two persons decided to start a business and succeeded in raising funds within an informal circle of acquaintances. Even if the initiators themselves were salaried managers, it often happened that their sons followed them into management. The other 16 companies were on their way to develop more objective means to attract professional management and capital. Even in these cases, personal connections remained important, and finance, or at least part of it, came more often from other companies than from banks. Except for a short period from about 1910 until the 1922/23 crisis, bankers kept away from long-term financing industrial enterprises,[10] while transport and trading companies were more inclined to support promising new ventures in industry. Thus, if British industrial capitalism can be classified as personal, this applies even more to Dutch industrial capitalism.

Were cartel agreements in the Netherlands as important as they were in Germany? Until the First World War, industrial cartels were the exception rather than the rule in the Netherlands. Dutch family firms might be relatively small, but they invested enough in marketing to find valuable outlets in foreign markets before 1914. With a small home market and large foreign exports, a policy of free trade was the obvious choice. Nor did the many scattered production units help Dutch industries to come to cartel agreements. The Dutch were reluctant to take part in foreign cartels as they did not want to be left with their home market only. Occasionally a Dutch company participated in a German cartel, as was the case with Philips. However, the First World War brought many difficulties in the supply of raw materials and export of finished products. These problems, and also the unexpected opportunities offered by war, brought Dutch industrialists closer together and changed their attitude towards communities of interest.

By 1930 about a third of the top 100 companies was involved in some kind of national gentlemen's agreement or international cartel. It was not until the 1930s that co-operation between companies became really *en vogue*. The agreements restricted, but did not eliminate, competition, since agreements often related to specific products, while other products remained unregulated. To prevent unreasonable price-cutting,

THE DUTCH FAMILY FIRM 155

TABLE 1

THE TOP 100 COMPANIES IN 1930 (BRITAIN AND THE NETHERLANDS) AND 1929 (GERMANY), ARRANGED BY INDUSTRIAL SECTOR

	Britain	Netherlands	Germany
Food and tobacco	35	24	9
Textiles	13	16	10
Paper and printing	7	5	5
Chemicals	5	17	15
Petroleum	4	1	4
Primary metals	11	3	23
Fabricated metals	4	2	2
Non-electrical machinery	2	8	7
Electrical machinery	5	6	6
Transportation	7	8	13
Various	7	10	6
Total	100	100	100

Sources: Appendix 1; A.D. Chandler, Jr., *Scale and Scope: The Dynamics of Industrial Capitalism* (Cambridge, MA, 1990), pp. 673–9, 704–13.

prices and sales conditions were arranged. Sometimes areas of interest were agreed upon or cartel members' clients respected.[11] The Dutch government did nothing to hinder cartelisation, but neither did it coerce outsiders into participating in national cartels. The government's attitude to looser entrepreneurial agreements was more supportive. Measures to restrict competition at home were often a prerequisite for import restrictions. In this way, the government hoped to fight unemployment and loss of production capacity.[12] Once having tasted the advantages of restricted competition, Dutch business developed an attitude of close co-operation.[13] Thus Dutch industrial capitalism became co-operative, but much later than Germany.

Before investigating the Dutch performance in the sectors of the Second Industrial Revolution, we will compare the Netherlands, Germany and Britain with regard to the distribution of the top 100 companies into different industrial sectors. We have taken the top 100 companies out of the 1929 (Germany) and 1930 (Britain) lists Chandler presented and put these figures alongside our own figures.

In Table 1 the number of companies in the various sectors is represented; Table 2 shows the relative importance of each sector, according to the total amount of assets employed (German and Dutch case) or the market value of shares (British case). These figures do indicate that in some respects the Dutch economy was more like the British economy, while it was complementary to the German. Both the Netherlands and Britain were strong in food, textiles and petroleum. On the other hand, the Germans led in chemicals, whilst the British had few large-

TABLE 2

THE MARKET VALUE OF SHARES IN THE TOP 100 BRITISH COMPANIES AND THE ASSETS EMPLOYED OF THE TOP 100 DUTCH AND GERMAN COMPANIES (% BY SECTOR)

	Britain (1930)	Netherlands (1930)	Germany (1929)
Food and tobacco	31	24	4
Textiles	11	12	6
Paper and printing	5	2	2
Chemicals	17	5	25
Petroleum	14	33	4
Primary metals	5	2	34
Fabricated metals	2	1	1
Non-electrical machinery	1	5	3
Electrical machinery	3	9	11
Transportation	5	4	7
Various	6	3	3
Total	100	100	100

Sources: As Table 1.

scale chemical companies and the Dutch had many small-scale chemical firms. In primary metals the Germans were absolute leaders, while the Dutch were nowhere and the British in between. In electrical machinery, however, the relative position of the Dutch was nearer that of the Germans and better than that of the British. Of course, these conclusions must remain tentative, since it is debatable whether these figures are accurate enough to make such comparisons.

We will now turn to the question of how the Dutch performed in the sectors of the Second Industrial Revolution. We have chosen chemicals, petroleum, and electrical machinery for closer scrutiny. An ideal way to assess performance would have been to compare the profitability of Dutch and foreign companies. However, we lacked time and data for such a complicated exercise. Therefore, we have taken into consideration factors such as the export position of companies, the possession of foreign subsidiaries and the participation in international cartels.

III

Out of the 100 largest Dutch companies in 1930, 17 can be classified as being within the chemical industry, with only the food sector having more firms. Yet, counted in assets, the performance of the chemical industry was not impressive. Most firms were small scale but long lived: 11 dated back to the nineteenth century, three were set up between 1900 and 1914, and only four were set up in the 1920s. With only one exception, all the 1930 companies still existed in 1950. Though many merged several times over the years, all these companies can be followed up to the present time.

At the beginning of the twentieth century, the manufacturers of superphosphate comprised the most important sector within the Dutch chemical industry. The large domestic demand for fertilisers and the geographically favourable trade position of Holland made this line of business attractive. Money for the new ventures was raised in various ways. M.H. Salomonson came from a wealthy family of textile mill owners, and when his firm was first set up it had a link with the textile industry.[14] In 1895 the partnership was transformed into a limited company: II Centrale Guano Fabrieken NV. The relation between transport and the production of bulk product superphosphate was evident in the creation of the Internationaale Guano- and Superphosphaat Werken in 1895. The Board of Directors consisted of three members of Rotterdam trading partnerships and one banker. The finance for the Amsterdamsche Superfosfaat (ASF), established in 1906, was found from amongst the Amsterdam business elite. A. Waller, a cousin of W.A. Waller, the managing director of the Nederlandsche Gist & Spiritus Fabrieken (NG&SF), became its manager.

Together, the Dutch producers controlled 27 per cent of world trade in superphosphates in 1913. For a short time between 1900 and 1914 Belgian and Dutch producers had formed a cartel, but real co-operation among Dutch producers was achieved during the First World War. Three producers merged into the Vereenigde Chemische Fabrieken (VCF) in 1915. The initiative to merge seemed to have come from a bank, which, after a merger of its own, served three producers of superphosphate. With the fourth producer, de ASF, a pooling agreement was reached the following year. Initially intended to regulate exports, co-operation went further with an exchange of managing directors and directors. As a reaction to this concentration movement, the first co-operative manufacturer of fertilisers, ENCK, was set up in 1920. During the crises following the First World War, the VCF/ASF took drastic measures to rationalise by concentrating production in the most suitable units and the number of managing directors declined. Though the combined firms were listed companies, the familial element in their management remained strong. Two sons and one son-in-law of the managing directors found their way into top management. In the inter-war years, several foreign subsidiaries were set up in co-operation with the British firm Fisons Fertilizers. The VCF/ASF was a member of the International Superphosphate Manufacturers Association. Of the total

Figure 1 Cover of the memorial volume, published by the Nederlandsche Gist & Spiritusfabriek, Delft, in 1930. This volume is one of many company histories consulted for this article. (Collection NEHA)

Dutch production, 68 per cent was exported in 1929, rising to 86 per cent in 1938, the Dutch share in world exports being 40 per cent in that year.[15]

The other chemical companies before the First World War manufactured 'traditional products': oils, soap, candles, glue, gelatine, yeast and paint. Relatively large firms were the NG&SF, the Lijm- en Gelatine Fabriek Delft and Kaarsenfabriek Gouda. The three firms were all listed companies in 1913, but their management hierarchies were small and the personal element was still strong. They all worked a great deal for foreign markets. Though the manufacturing of lead-white was once an important activity, the initiative to manufacture the higher quality zinc-white came from Belgium. Belgian finance and Belgian management were responsible for the development of the Maastrichtsche Zinkwit Maatschappij, which began in 1870 as a partnership. It is not quite clear whether the firm was in fact a Belgian subsidiary. The founder, G. Rocour, certainly possessed other companies there. In this case as well, two sons succeeded their fathers. In the inter-war years several foreign subsidiaries were set up and a large part of the production was exported.[16]

At the beginning of the century, techniques to bottle oxygen and other gases were developed. The Dutch soon followed the foreign example. W.A. Hoek succeeded in making a business out of this new technique. This family firm began by producing gas cylinders, and later supplied the gases themselves. The firm had a subsidiary in the Netherlands Indies. For the rest, it concentrated mostly on the home market.[17]

Between 1913 and 1930, an essential broadening of chemicals production took place, which eventually resulted in a strong international position in intermediate chemicals. The First World War had shown the Dutch the disadvantage of dependence on foreign producers in times of crisis. For that reason, the Dutch government together with several leading industrialists made plans to further the national production of raw and intermediate materials. This had important implications for the chemical industry, because it meant the introduction of a large-scale processing industry. The Staatsmijnen (State Mines) set up a coke factory; when the Haber-Bosch patents expired, the State Mines could carry out a downstream integration by adopting the Haber-Bosch ammonia synthesis. The result was the Stikstofbindingsbedrijf.[18] Hoogovens, established to make the Dutch less dependent on foreign steel, also commenced the synthesis of ammonia together with Royal Dutch Shell.[19] This co-operation began with one managing director of Royal Dutch Shell, J.B.Aug. Kessler, brainstorming with his brother, D. Kessler, the managing director of Hoogovens. Even in companies of this size, family links thus played an important role. The Royal Dutch Shell entered this field on strategic grounds, to familiarise itself with gas processing techniques. As IG Farben seemed to threaten the oil market with synthetic oil, it seemed wise as an oil company to experiment with chemicals. The ammonia was used for the manufacture of nitrogenous fertilisers, which were mostly exported, in the same way as superphosphates.[20] A special place was occupied by the Stikstofbindingsindustrie Nederland. It prided itself on having succeeded where even the German chemical firms had failed, in making nitrogen fixation with the cyanide process into an ongoing process. This business was still in the entrepreneurial stage.[21] The Dutch companies were newcomers in the market of nitrogenous fertilisers, and disturbed the existing cartel agreements between German and British producers. Dutch producers were therefore included in the 'Convention Internationale de l'Azote' in 1930, though this fell apart in 1931. As prices went down rapidly, a second agreement was reached in 1932, which lasted until the war.[22] The expansion of the nitrogenous fertilisers encouraged the manufacturers of sulphuric acid. Ketjen, a family firm dating back to 1834, when it was among the first Dutch producers of sulphuric acid, extended its operations in scale, but not in scope.

The field of electro-chemicals was entered in 1931, when the Koninklijke Nederlandse Zout (KNZ) diversified its operations. The KNZ was built up with state money after the First World War to provide the Dutch market with salt. Solvay, ICI and IG Farben tried to drive the Dutch electro-chemical works out of business by setting up a competing firm in the south of the Netherlands. This firm prospered, but did not achieve its initial aim.[23]

Besides intermediate products, Dutch manufacturers produced a whole range of fine chemicals. Here we come to the group of firms where the family element was strongest and the scale of operation smallest. Oldest in the group is the pharmaceutical company Brocades-Stheeman. Started as one of many chemist's shops, it went into the production and sale of packaged medicines at the end of the nineteenth century. Through the use of foreign agents a considerable level of exports was achieved. Exporting to many less-developed countries like Poland, Turkey and the countries of South America suggests that the firm sought countries where competition might be weakest. However, the establishment of a sales agent in Germany is not in accordance with this supposition. Brocades Stheeman took over several small firms and merged in 1927 with Pharmacia, another pharmaceutical firm which combined trade with production. After the merger, rationalisation took place, but the family influence continued.[24] The other pharmaceutical firm in the 1930 list, the Amsterdamsche Chininefabriek, owed its success to the Dutch Indies monopoly position in regard to *chinchona* (bark).[25]

Noury & Van der Lande is an interesting example of a successful family company. The firm started with an oil-mill in 1838 and extended its operations to a flour-mill at the end of the century. The first step towards chemicals production was the employment of an English chemist in 1917. The result was a product to bleach flour, followed by other chemicals to improve the quality of flour. In relation to its size, the firm invested heavily in research and worldwide marketing, some of its products being protected by patents. The firm had subsidiaries in

THE DUTCH FAMILY FIRM 161

Germany (1889), France (1931) and Britain (1937). A production unit in the US was also considered in 1926, but instead the patents were sold to the US firm Agene. Over the years, the firm tried its luck in several directions, using links between raw materials or new discoveries in their chemical laboratory. Formally separate companies were established to undertake new activities.[26]

Another family firm in the food sector which diversified into chemicals was Zwanenberg, a meat producer. The founding of the subsidiary Organon was steeped in the nineteenth-century tradition of agrarian feedstock and extractive processes. With a licence from the University of Toronto, Organon began the manufacture of insulin in 1923 and the production of synthetic hormones followed in later years. The managers attached great value to chemical research. The strong German influence on research and the nearness of leading German firms did not dampen all initiative; on the contrary, its example inspired, as did the favourable intellectual surroundings. Organon employed German and Dutch chemists who had studied in Germany. To penetrate the German market a sales agent was appointed in 1923, and this agency was taken over a few years later. Subsidiaries in Britain and France followed in the 1930s. Nearly half the production was destined for foreign markets. Clashes with the German pharmaceutical companies were unavoidable, and this led to a mixture of cartel agreements, licensing and exchange of patents.[27] Together with Hoffman-La Roche, a subsidiary was set up in the USA.[28]

Patents stimulated the start of Norit, set up in 1908. It was a listed company with two chemists as managing directors, one of whom was the inventor of the first patents. Methods were devised to bleach sugar, and active carbon appeared to be very useful. Wood was used to produce active carbon. When wood became scarce during the First World War the firm searched for an alternative source of raw materials, and found it in peat. With plenty of peat nearby, the firm could produce carbon relatively cheaply, and built up a strong position in foreign markets. Later research revealed that active carbon had many other commercial uses. In 1927 an alliance (*Interessengemeinschaft*) was formed with the German Verein für Chemische Industrie AG, which took part in a cartel agreement (the Carbo-Norit Union) with four other European producers in 1930. The cartel lasted until 1939. Norit established one foreign subsidiary in the inter-war years, the American Norit Co. Inc.[29]

Of course, all these firms were too small to threaten the position of the international first movers, but they succeeded in creating a place for themselves alongside them. The German firms might be leading, but they could not crush every competitor, even if they wanted to. These small firms not only succeeded in home markets, but were also internationally competitive, exporting part of their output and setting up foreign subsidiaries.

IV

Measured by assets employed, the Dutch position in the petroleum sector was exceptionally strong. Two factors played a part in the rise of the Dutch oil industry: the presence of oil in the Dutch East Indies and the interest of the Dutch capital market in oil companies. At the end of the nineteenth and the beginning of the twentieth century, three areas caught the attention of Dutch investors in oil companies: the Dutch Indies, Romania and the USA.[30] One of these companies was Royal Dutch, which started in 1890; it was not the first oil company in the Dutch Indies,[31] but it brought its competitors one after the other under its influence, until the company was strong enough to challenge the first mover in this field, the Standard Oil Co. The Dutch entered the field after the Americans, but well ahead of the Germans.

Royal Dutch started its activities in oil at the beginning of the production chain with small-scale exploration. When the results proved promising, the production of crude oil was taken in hand and a new limited company, Royal Dutch, was floated in 1890 and succeeded in raising the necessary capital at the Amsterdam capital market. No special link between management and ownership existed. As there was practically no home market in Sumatra, it was necessary to invest in marketing from the start. While J.B.Aug. Kessler organised the production, H.W.H. Deterding was appointed to set up a marketing organisation. The sale of lamp oil in the Asian markets went so well that, when production stagnated in 1897, oil was brought in from Romania to keep the customers well provided. After the unpleasant experience of failing oil wells, Royal Dutch extended its interest in prospecting and the production of crude oil. A formally independent production company was set up with money from Royal Dutch and under the direction of a brother of Kessler. Delivery contracts with other companies were signed, which often was the first step towards a takeover by Royal Dutch. It is interesting to note that Standard Oil was still hesitant to tie up money in the less profitable production of oil at that time.[32]

The position of Royal Dutch was considerably strengthened by the well-known merger with the Shell Trading Co. in 1907. It was a perfect match, because the Dutch company was strong in exploration, production and refining, while Shell possessed a well-developed trading and transport organisation. This merger was preceded by a combination of the sales activities of both companies in the Asiatic Trading Co., which had operated under the direction of Deterding since 1903. The Dutch company had the upper hand in the merger and got a 60 per cent share against a 40 per cent share for Shell in the working companies that were set up in the merger process. To produce and refine oil nearer the European market, Royal Dutch Shell turned to the Romanian oilfields. Several of the Dutch companies already active there were brought together in a new holding company. Next, oilfields in Russia were bought. The decision of Standard Oil to challenge Royal Dutch Shell in its home base in 1910 made a counter-attack inevitable. Royal Dutch Shell already possessed a sales organisation in the USA, but now Deterding was determined to start production there also. A few Dutch companies, working in Oklahoma, tried to get Deterding interested in their oilfields, but his experts advised him otherwise. The fields that were being offered were unsuitable as a basis for the enterprise Deterding intended to establish. Indeed, these Dutch companies did not prosper, were sold to a French company and later vanished from the market. The companies Deterding did buy in Oklahoma were not so impressive either, but the goal of entering the USA had been achieved. In 1913 there followed the takeover of the California Oilfields Ltd, and the oilfields in Mexico were entered with a newly established company, the Petroleum Maatschappij La Corona.[33]

While deliberating in 1910 over confrontation with the Standard Oil in the USA, Deterding had launched a plan for a 'defensive concentration'. The programme comprised of improving the apparatus of management and the strengthening of the bonds which held the group together. Central departments had to be set up under professional leadership to keep top management informed and ensure that the experience gained in one country was applied in another. This reorganisation was still being implemented in 1914. The method adopted in the reorganisation of the sales division was just the opposite: a large measure of decentralisation was introduced in bookkeeping. The various sales areas were more sharply defined than before and in each area a legal entity was set up according to the law of the land, each such legal entity constituting an independent administrative unit. The separate accounts and balance sheets of the local companies helped to avert double taxation. Managers of local companies were made responsible for the profit.[34]

Chandler remarks that in 1914 Deterding, who was still involved in building his giant empire, had as yet given relatively little thought to managing it.[35] This conclusion is somewhat surprising. The company structure, which left much opportunity for local initiative, cannot have

Figure 2 Henri Deterding, director of the Royal Dutch Shell, inspecting the subsidiary Astra Romani Romania. Date unkown. (Collection Royal Dutch Shell)

worked too badly, given the fact that the company so successfully challenged the Standard Oil Company worldwide. In any case, the stress on local responsibility proved an advantage when the First World War broke out. During the war, the procedures for central monitoring of the company's activities had to be changed. The relationship between Royal Dutch and the British-based Asiatic Trading Co. was severed to secure the imports from the Dutch Indies in the Netherlands. The Russian subsidiaries came under British control, while the German and Austrian subsidiaries remained with Royal Dutch. In 1917 the important Russian possessions were lost without compensation. Works in Romania were severely damaged, and the company's fleet was diminished. Thus, a great deal of reconstruction and repair was needed after the return of peace. However, the American subsidiaries had flourished during the war.

The expansion policy was continued in the 1920s, new companies being added to the group. As described in the preceding section, Royal Dutch Shell took the important step of entering the world of chemicals by taking in hand the synthesis of ammonia in the 1920s. A second factory for the manufacture of nitrogenous fertilisers was set up in California, which became the first factory of the Shell Chemical Co., and other developments continued the diversification into chemicals in the USA.[36] Although a large part of Royal Dutch Shell activities took place outside the Netherlands, there was a positive influence on the other Dutch industrial sectors. For instance, Royal Dutch Shell orders stimulated Werkspoor to invent a diesel engine for seaworthy ships.[37] The Dutch shipbuilding industry no doubt profited from the many tankers Royal Dutch Shell needed. The tin producers found in the company a ready customer. And last, but not least, the ample yearly dividends brought the Dutch capitalists money to invest in industrial activities.

V

In non-electrical machinery, eight firms worked their way into the top 100 industrial companies in 1930. Compared with the two British and seven German machinery companies in the respective British and German top 100s, this performance does not look bad. In the German and British cases, however, part of the machinery production was probably concealed in the primary metals sector.

In the nineteenth century, foreign machine building companies were already far ahead of the Dutch. Most of the machinery needed in the Netherlands was imported, but repairs had to be executed locally as well as adaptation to local production conditions and raw materials. The Dutch machine building industry grew from small repair shops which undertook a great variety of activities. In the process of adapting foreign machinery to local conditions there was more ingenuity involved than is sometimes realised. In polder drainage, for instance, the Dutch became specialists. Foreign inventions could be copied and adapted freely in the Netherlands between 1869 and 1911. Nevertheless, it was often preferable to acquire a licence because of the complexity of the machinery. Sometimes, Dutch research in this field was original enough to patent the results, although working with foreign licences was more normal. There was no mass production, but manufacturing according to the product specifications of the individual client. Very large companies that covered the entire range from blast furnaces to finished products never existed.[38]

The Dutch machine building industry lacked the stimulating influence of a primary metal industry. In comparison with Germany, and to a lesser extent Britain, the Dutch position in primary metals was very weak. This is easily explained by the lack of mineral ores and the late exploitation of coal. In 1900 one small iron foundry, erected in 1851, took the important step of experimenting with cast steel manufacturing. After achieving some success, this family firm, De Muinck Keizer, decided to install a Bessemer convertor in 1911, and in this way created the first modern steel works in the Netherlands. Its most important customers were the Dutch ship and machine builders.[39] The Kempensche Zinkfabriek was a Belgian initiative. The Belgian government had refused to give its founders a concession in Belgium, and for that reason they had crossed the border and set up a zinc production unit in the Netherlands. The company was, strictly speaking, not a family firm, but the Dor family provided the technical know-how and played an important role in the management of the production unit. The company proved that successful processing of primary metals was possible within Dutch borders.[40]

Lack of iron ores, indeed, may not have been the only reason why the Dutch lagged behind in primary metals. It took nearly half a century before the exploitation of tin mines in the Dutch Indies encouraged the Dutch to set up tin works.[41] It is not chance that this decision was taken after the First World War. Until then, the Dutch relied on their trading position, and were not so inclined to integrate production vertically. It required wartime isolation to demonstrate the hazards of this policy. In this period plans were made to set up a large Dutch steelworks. During the war the demand for steel exceeded the capacity of De Muinck Keizer. Capital was needed to extend the works and the owners turned

Figure 3 Regarding machinery, the Dutch were successful in a few niches, poldar drainage being one of them. This picture shows centrifugal pumps for polder drainage ready for delivery, at Werkspoor, Amsterdam, circa 1910. (Collection NEHA)

the firm into a listed company in 1917. At the same time negotiations started between industrialists and the Dutch government to establish a large steelworks. This resulted in the establishment of Hoogovens. An agreement was reached between Hoogovens and De Muinck Keizer in 1919, by which Hoogovens took a large financial interest in De Muinck Keizer and production was divided between mass steel manufacturing (Hoogovens) and specialities (De Muinck Keizer). However, Hoogovens did not start production until 1924; even then it could only manufacture to a few specifications, and therefore could only serve part of the home market. In fact, most of its products were exported. The project probably lost most of its urgency after the war ended and, instead of striving after an independent Dutch position, co-operation with the German industry was advocated.[42] It is unlikely that the Dutch failure in primary metals was the result of a lack of capital. In some trade and transport companies far more capital was brought together than was needed for Hoogovens.[43]

The Dutch probably trusted their ability to make profit out of trade or transport but felt insecure about the metal industry. In the fabricated metals sector, the Dutch position was equally weak; thus this sector could not inspire the machine building industry either. Only two companies appear in this section. The older one, Lettergieterij Amsterdam, a family firm turning slowly into a professionally led company, combined a type foundry with trade in printing machines and also occasionally supplied the wholesale paper trade. Part of its competitive strength may well have come from the trade department. The firm had one speciality: printing machines for Javanese script. In the 1920s, the firm acquired a German subsidiary and several 'foreign interests'.[44] The other company in this sector, De Vereenigde Blikfabrieken, had a link with the food sector and was the result of concentration in the tinplate industry in 1912. Three family firms had expanded at the end of the nineteenth century as a result of the blossoming food industry, which needed tins to preserve biscuits and cocoa. One of these companies specialised in high quality tins, a second in printing tins and the third in mass production. After concentration in 1912, family leadership persisted until the mid-1920s. In these years the firm turned to the manufacturing of tins for oil and paint. Rationalisation of the production and concentration of printing also took place. A small financial interest was taken in a Belgian firm in 1929 to underpin a co-operative venture. The Vereenigde Blikfabrieken produced mainly for the home market and about half of this market was in its hands.[45] Thus the primary and fabricated metals sectors did very little to stimulate machine building.

The only sector that really contributed to the development of machine building in the Netherlands was shipbuilding. Of the large firms engaged in machine building, the majority were closely connected to shipbuilding, and often both activities were carried out by the same company. The oldest company on the 1930 list, Werkspoor, had such an origin. It started in 1829 by repairing steamships, and broadened its range to building machinery for the sugar industry as well as several locomotives and steam engines. During the late nineteenth-century depression the company ran into difficulties and had to be liquidated in 1890, but was resurrected a year later with capital from D.W. Stork and the Dutch railway companies. The shipbuilding department was closed down, though the other activities were continued. Furthermore, in 1902 the manufacturing of diesel engines was taken in hand, when a licence was acquired from the German MAN (Machinefabrik Augsburg-Neurenberg). A whole range of diesel motors followed. As well as machinery for the sugar industry, some machines for palm oil production were developed, but there were no other capital goods.[46] The German and American position in production of capital goods was so dominant that the Dutch could not penetrate this market, whereas in the field of engines the Dutch did have some success.

Kromhout Motorenfabriek was an example of a family firm of shipbuilders which erected a separate motor factory to exploit its patents in marine diesel engines.[47] The firm of P. Smit Jr was a combination of ship and machine building, set up by the shipbuilder Fob Smit for his cousin P. Smit.[48] Burgerhout's Machinefabriek en Scheepswerf, also a family firm, was a shipbuilding company which diversified into machinery. Among the shipbuilding companies in the transportation equipment sector, De Schelde manufactured steam engines and turbines and Wilton diesel engines, and its designs were original enough to encourage some foreign producers to obtain licences to copy them.[49]

It could have been expected that the Dutch cotton industry would have encouraged machine building. The family firm Stork, founded in 1859, developed in the environment of the Dutch textile industry, but did not produce textile machinery until 1900, because British competition was too strong. Instead, Stork manufactured steam engines, boilers and polder pumping engines. When the sugar cane plantations in the Dutch Indies expanded in the 1880s, Stork recognised the potential of this new market. Over the years, the company specialised in machinery for sugar factories and could deliver complete production units. For these products a foreign outlet could be found. Most other products were destined for the home market and Dutch Indies. Stork often made use of foreign technology by way of licence agreements.[50] Within the Dutch machinery industry, Stork had a central position. Members of the

Stork family turned up everywhere to encourage and finance new ventures. The Machinefabriek 'Reineveld', set up in 1893, was one such firm. It started with general machine building, but specialised in steam pumps for sugar factories. These pumps went well with the sugar machinery Stork built.[51] The firm worked for the international market.

The Machinefabriek Breda, a partnership turned into a listed company in 1884, specialised in steam engines and followed foreign inventions closely. Between 1882 and 1920 the firm built more than 200 tramway locomotives, about 30 per cent of the Dutch market of tramway locomotives. In 1910 a German engineer was employed to develop a diesel engine.[52]

A rather exceptional company within the Dutch machine building industry was Van Berkel's patent, established in 1898. It was exceptional because it specialised in a few products, and the foreign market was much more important to it than the home market. The company was based on W.A. van Berkel's invention and subsequently patenting of a slicing machine. It successfully tapped the capital market, thanks to the strong support of the important Dutch transport company Phs. van Ommeren. In 1918 another product for the same market was invented: automatic scales. Subsidiaries were set up in many countries, initially probably mostly sales organisations, but in the inter-war years Van Berkel owned one factory in the USA and seven in Europe.[53]

During the First World War, the Dutch machine building industry was temporarily freed from foreign competition. This led to several new initiatives. After the war, however, competition returned and was stronger than before because of weak foreign currencies and recession. Many new activities disappeared again. In the mid-1920s the world economy recovered, but it was only a temporary relief. It is in periods of crisis that the competitive strength of companies is most clearly revealed. One of the eight machinery firms from the top 100 list failed this test: Burgerhout closed down the shipyard first and the machinery department later on. P. Smit Jr was taken over by the shipbuilders RDM and Wilton-Fijenoord. The others continued, though not without considerable losses and reduction in capital.[54]

On the whole, the Dutch performance in metal manufacturing and machine building was not impressive. Dutch firms were competitive in a few niches, but the sector was mostly characterised by small-scale, borrowed technology and production for the home market.

Figure 4 Festivities in the docks of the firm Wilton-Fijenoord, Rotterdam, circa 1930. Directors, the brothers Bartel and William Wilton, are standing in the middle. (Collection NEHA)

VI

The Dutch performance in electrical machinery compared quite well with the German performance, if the difference in total assets employed is taken into account. This was the result of one top-flight company, Philips. Here we encounter a family firm making the Chandlerian three-pronged investment in production, marketing and management.

Philips was not a prime mover, not even at home. Therefore, Philips had to face strong competition from the start. Several foreign producers had settled in the Netherlands, because patents were not protected there before 1911. This patent situation also enabled Philips to make extensive use of foreign inventions. Gerard Philips started in 1891 in the traditional way with family capital (in this case earned in the tobacco trade and banking) and production on a small scale. After a process of trial and error, he began large-scale industrial production. In later years he followed the same course with new products and processes. Great value was attached to remaining in the forefront of scientific developments and to manufacturing quality products. The firm invested in research and was prepared to obtain licences from elsewhere if this was necessary to speed up development work.[55]

Philips was not prepared to restrict itself to the home market. The importance of investing in marketing was recognised early. Gerard's brother Anton joined the firm in 1895 to promote sales worldwide with a team of sales agents. This brought Philips into contact with foreign competitors, especially the Germans. Philips took an active part in negotiating the creation of a carbon filament bulbs cartel in 1902. The firm was also included in later cartel arrangements. These arrangements reduced price-cutting, but did not rule out competition. Often, foreign producers claimed the right to serve their own home market exclusively, but this was not an attractive proposition for Philips, which found the Dutch market too restricted. Foreign sales were actively promoted by setting up sales companies. The first two were set up in 1912, one in France and the other a joint venture in the USA.

The First World War brought problems but also new opportunities. It became difficult to get certain materials, such as argon gas and glass bulbs. These problems were overcome by integrating vertically. New opportunities arose where German competitors lost their markets and Philips could step in. The policy of vertical integration was supplemented by horizontal integration.[56] The US sales company had brought Philips into closer contact with General Electric, which resulted, after litigation and prolonged transactions, in closer co-operation in 1920. Both companies agreed to exchange patents and know-how, Philips paid a licence fee to General Electric and the latter took a 20 per cent share in Philips. The agreement was reaffirmed in 1929. Due to its own research, Philips now had sufficient to offer to make a free exchange of patents and know-how attractive to the Americans.[57] The international incandescent lamp cartel, the Phoebes-cartel, in 1924 meant a further, worldwide consolidation of the lamp market. It enabled its participants, Philips among them, to concentrate on new developments.

In the 1920s Philips diversified its production into consumer electronics, especially electron tubes, followed later by complete radio sets. Technically related to the electron tubes were X-ray tubes, which provided an entry into the production of medical equipment. A rapid expansion in the manufacture of radio sets, components and semi-finished articles took place in the second half of the 1920s. Philips entered this field sooner than its competitors, RCA, Marconi, Telefunken and Compagnie Générale de Télegraphie sans Fil. The family firm was flexible enough to grasp the new opportunities by directing capital and energy into this new field, while the decision-making process in large integrated companies such as RCA and Telefunken was slower. With a network of foreign sales organisations and, later on, foreign production units, Philips could expand world exports of its products.[58]

However, the economic crisis of the early 1930s revealed the organisational weakness of Philips. Financial control and direction of activities had not kept pace with rapid expansion. The members of the family firm were wise enough to understand the need to invest in new management structures, but by doing so the firm lost much of its family character. However, father, son and sons-in-law remained prominent in top management for a long time.[59]

In comparison with Philips, the other electrical firms in the top 100 were of minor importance. These companies were established at the end of the nineteenth and the beginning of the twentieth century with family finance. Scientific knowledge was borrowed from neighbouring countries, often by way of working in foreign companies, though imitated technology was supplemented by in-house research. The First World War opened up new horizons. NKF could furnish the Dutch market with endless high voltage cable for underground power transmission. DRAKA achieved access to the British cable market.[60] HEEMAF diversified its activities from the building and administration of power stations and the manufacturing of electrical appliances into the manufacture of electric motors and dynamos. The supply of many intermediate products halted, generating other new opportunities. Smit & Co. Transformatorenfabriek, for example, started the manufacture of

Workers coming out of the factories.

Figure 5 Philips employees leaving the factories at the end of the working day,
Eindhoven 1929. (Collection Philips /Electronics NV)

THE DUTCH FAMILY FIRM 175

dynamo cable when supplies grew short. By and large the business expanded during this period, but the backlash came in the years immediately after 1920. Competition from countries with weak currencies, especially Germany, threatened the Dutch products in foreign as well as home markets. Lost ground was recovered after 1925.

In the 1920s, HEEMAF, Hazemeyer and Smit & Co. Transformatorenfabriek made use of foreign licence agreements, but also possessed patents of their own. HEEMAF, for instance, had an arrangement with Westinghouse for diesel engines, with A.G. Brown Boveri & Co. for switch gear, and with Siemens & Halske for telephone apparatus. On the other hand, HEEMAF erected a German subsidiary in 1927 to manufacture its patented SKA motor. This motor was also an important export product. Hazemeyer developed low voltage switch gear of its own and worked together with the British company Reyrolle & Co. to produce high voltage switch gear. Hazemeyer founded foreign subsidiaries in Belgium and France in 1931. The activities of Smit & Co. Transformatorenfabriek were mainly restricted to the Netherlands and Dutch Indies. For specific products the firm acquired licence from the American company Union Carbide and the German company Otto Junker. So it seems that many links existed between the producers of electrical machinery. Draka participated in a German cartel by way of a financial interest in a German company. Whether the other minor electrical companies were involved in cartel agreements, however, is not clear.[61]

VII

The family firm and personal relationships played an important role in Dutch industrial development. It was not until the 1930s that cartels and entrepreneurial agreements became important in the Netherlands. Therefore, Dutch industrial capitalism can be characterised as personal capitalism, just as in Britain. This conclusion is not really surprising, as the Dutch and the British shared a long trade tradition and both had a colonial empire. Was the adherence to personal management structures a sign of weakness, as Chandler suggests? In his view, personal capitalism is not simply a way of managing a small company, or any company; it stands for a *failure* to grasp the opportunities of scale and scope. In this, we disagree with him. Our evidence shows the continuing vitality of more traditional forms of business organisation. Creating large, integrated companies and managing them with a managerial hierarchy was a viable option, but not the only way to run a business successfully.

Large integrated companies were rare in the Netherlands, but this did not necessarily mean lack of efficiency or competitiveness. Well developed international trade diminished the necessity for forward and backward integration. It was not evident that internalising was cheaper than using the market, except in war circumstances. Furthermore, the many personal, and sometimes financial, links between firms worked to a large extent as an alternative to integration or diversification. Family firms often entered new fields by setting up a new, separate company. Our survey of the various sectors showed that many industries of the Second Industrial Revolution were set up by family firms working in the traditional sectors. Chandler clearly undervalues the strength of the family company. Concentrating on a few products, the family firms were able to compete successfully with large, diversified companies which had to divide their attention over many products and markets. Many of the small Dutch firms competed successfully in foreign markets. Some even built up foreign subsidiaries.

The weak Dutch position in primary metals is in accordance with Chandler's supposition that personal managerial structures were unsuited to the exploitation of economies of scale and scope. However, in the Dutch case, the opposite can also be argued. With strong German competition and without indigenous supplies of ores, there was little incentive for the Dutch to start up a metal manufacturing industry and therefore no need for large-scale production and managerial hierarchies.

Chandler suggested that owner-managers might have been more hesitant to deprive themselves of short-term income in order to invest in long-term growth.[62] This suggestion has already been severely attacked in the British case.[63] Similarly, in the Dutch case there is little evidence that family firms extracted more profit from the business than listed companies. From the many firm histories we studied, we obtained the strong impression that family firms were prepared to invest heavily in the company and to bear its losses longer than may have been economically justified, in order to hand over the company to future generations. The family often thought very long term, because the company must be kept going for the next generation. In fact, the listed companies were more in danger of handing out too much profit than the family firms, because they had to pay a regular dividend to keep the capital market content.[64]

The personal approach was indeed a different approach to management in industrial companies. It is interesting to note that, despite their personal management culture, the Dutch and British succeeded in building up together two very successful, large, worldwide companies: Royal Dutch Shell and Unilever.[65] After having succeeded, it was necessary to build up managerial hierarchies in accordance with what had been achieved. Philips followed the same route. What we would like to stress is that the first achievement was reached within the personal management culture Chandler dismisses as a failure.

THE DUTCH FAMILY FIRM   177

APPENDIX I
THE TOP 100 DUTCH INDUSTRIAL COMPANIES IN 1930, RANKED BY
ASSETS EMPLOYED (MILLION GUILDERS)

1 Rank	2 Company Name	3 Assets	4 Source	5 Type	6 SIC Code
1	Koninklijke (Royal Dutch Shell)	790.9	B	M	291
2	Unilever NV	353.8	B	F-M	202
3	Philips Gloeilampenfabrieken	188.5	B	F-M	364
4	Algemeene Kunstzijde Unie	163.5	B	P-M	228
5	Centrale Suiker Maatschappij	55.4	B	P-M	206
6	Hoogovens	35.2	B	M	331
7	Ver. Kon. Papierfabrieken Van Gelder Zonen	32.7	B	Fl	262
8	Van Berkel's Patent	31.6	B	P	355
9	Werkspoor	31.0	B	F-M	351
10	Nederlandsche Scheepsbouw Mij. (NSM)	26.1	B	P	373
11	Koninklijke Maatschappij De Schelde	24.6	B	F-P	373
12	H.J. van Heek & Co.	24.4	A	F	221
13	Machinefabriek, Gebr. Stork & Co.	22.7	B	Fl	351
14	Ned. Gist- & Spiritusfabriek (NG&SF)	22.0	B	P	286
15	Maastrichtsche Zinkwit Maatschappij	21.8	B	F-P	285
16	Beiersch-Bierbrouwerij 'De Amstel'	19.1	B	P-M	208
17	Hollandsche Kunstzijde Industrie (HKI)	18.0	B	Fl	228
18	Hollandsche Beton Maatschappij	17.9	B	P-M	327
19	Dok- en Werf-Maatschappij Wilton-Fijenoord	17.7	B	F-P	373
20	P. de Gruyter & Zn	16.8	B	Fl	209
21	Erven de Wed. van Nelle	16.0	E	F	209
22	Heineken's Bierbrouwerijen	16.0	E	F	208
23	Nederlandsche Linoleum Fabriek	15.4	B	Fl	227
24	Arnold I. van den Bergh's Emballage Fabrieken	14.9	B	Fl	242
25	Wessanen's Koninklijke Fabrieken	14.0	E	F	204
26	Vereenigde Touwfabrieken	13.8	B	F-P	229
27	Stikstofbindingsbedrijf	13.5	B	M	281
28	Hollandsche Fabriek van Melkprodukten 'Hollandia'	12.7	B	F-P	202
29	ENCI	12.7	B	M	324
30	VCF/Amsterdamsche Superfosfaat	12.0	B	P-M	287
31	Rotterdamsche Droogdok Maatschappij (RDM)	11.8	B	P-M	373
32	Kempensche Zink Maatschappij	11.4	B	P	334
33	Nederlandsche Kabelfabriek	11.0	B	F-M	361
34	Zuid-Hollandsche Bierbrouwerij	10.5	B	F-P	208
35	H.P. Gelderman en Zonen	9.9	A	F	221
36	Stoom Chocolade- en Cacaofabriek 'Kwatta'	9.6	B	P	206
37	HEEMAF	8.8	B	P	361
38	Lijm- en Gelatinefabriek Delft	8.6	B	P	286
39	Meelfabrieken der Nederlandsche Bakkerij	8.5	B	C	204
40	De Vereenigde Blikfabrieken	7.7	B	F-M	346
41	Van Vollenhoven's Bierbrouwerij	7.3	B	F-P	208
42	P.F. van Vlissingen & Co.'s Katoenfabrieken	7.1	B	Fl	226

178 FAMILY CAPITALISM

1	2	3	4	5	6
Rank	Company Name	Assets	Source	Type	SIC Code

43	H. ten Cate Hzn en Co.	7.0	E	F	221
44	Bierbrouwerij 'De Drie Hoefijzers'	6,9	B	F-P	208
45	Coöp. Beetwortelsuikerfabriek 'Puttershoek'	6.8	B	C	206
46	Machinefabriek en Scheepswerf P. Smit jr.	6.8	B	F-P	351
47	Stoomspinnerijen en -weverijen v/h S.J.Spanjaard	6.6	B	Fl	221
48	Ned. Staalfabrieken v/h J.M. De Muinck Keizer	6.5	B	Fl	332
49	Lettergieterij Amsterdam/Tetterode	6.3	B	F-M	349
50	Hollandsche Draad- en Kabelfabriek (DRAKA)	6.2	B	P-M	364
51	De Sphinx v/h Petrus Regout & Co.	6.2	B	Fl	326
52	Ind. Maatschappij v/h Noury & Van der Lande	6.1	E	F	286
53	Burgerhouts' Machinefabriek en Scheepswerf	6.1	B	Fl	351
54	Koninklijke Stoom Weverij	6.1	A	F	221
55	Amsterdamsche Chininefabriek	6.0	B	P-M	283
56	Kon. Ned. Papierfabriek	5.4	B	F-P	262
57	Société Céramique	5.2	B	P	326
58	Kon. Stearine Kaarsenfabriek Gouda	5.0	B	P-M	289
59	Coop. Beetwortelsuikerfabriek Dinteloord	5.0	B	C	206
60	Rubberfabriek 'Vredestein'	5.0	E	Fl	301
61	ENCK	4.9	B	C	287
62	Zwanenberg-Organon	4.9	A	F	202/283
63	Ned. Vliegtuigenfabriek	4.8	E	P	372
64	Stoommeelfabriek Holland	4.7	B	P	204
65	Utrechtsche Asphaltfabriek	4.7	B	F-P	295
66	Edelmetaalbedrijven v/h Van Kempen, Begeer & Vos	4.6	B	F-P	391
67	Kon. Pharm. Fabr. Brocades-Stheeman en Pharmacia	4.6	B	F-P	283
68	Kromhout Motorenfabriek D. Goedkoop Jr.	4.4	B	F	351
69	Papierfabriek Gelderland	4.3	B	P	262
70	Kon. Vereenigde Tapijtfabrieken	4.3	B	F-P	227
71	Kunstzijdespinnerij Nyma	4.3	B	M	228
72	Leeuwarder IJs en Melkproductenfabriek 'Lijmpf'	4.1	B	C	202
73	Internationale Gewapend Betonbouw	4.1	B	F-M	327
74	Vereenigde Hollandse Sigarenfabrieken	4.0	B	F-P	212
75	Stikstofbindingsindustrie 'Nederland'	4.0	B	P	281
76	J.A. Carp's Garenfabrieken	4.0	B	Fl	228
77	Mij. voor Zwavelzuurbereiding Ketjen	3.9	B	F-P	281
78	Koninklijke Nederlandse Zout (KZN)	3.8	B	M	281
79	Machinefabriek 'Reineveld'	3.6	B	P	355
80	Stijfselfabriek 'De Bijenkorf' (Honig)	3.4	A	F	209
81	U. Twijnstra's Oliefabrieken	3.4	B	Fl	207
82	Carton- en Papierfabriek v/h W.A. Scholten	3.3	B	F-P	263
83	Blijdenstein en Co.	3.3	A	F	221
84	Glasfabriek 'Leerdam'	3.2	B	F-P	321
85	Allan&Co's Fabr.van Meubelen en Spoorwegmaterieel	3.0	B	Fl	374
86	Twentsche Stoombleekerij	3.0	B	P	226
87	Brood- en Meelfabrieken Mij. 'De Korenschoof'	3.0	B	P	204
88	W.A. Hoek's Machine-en Zuurstoffabriek	3.0	B	Fl	281

THE DUTCH FAMILY FIRM 179

1 Rank	2 Company Name	3 Assets	4 Source	5 Type	6 SIC Code
89	Fabr.v. Electrische Apparaten v/h Hazemeijer & Co.	2.9	B	P	361
90	Kon. Ned. Katoenspinnerij	2.9	B	F	228
91	Algemeene Norit Maatschappij (Norit)	2.9	B	P	289
92	Drukkerij De Spaarnestad	2.9	B	P	272
93	Machinefabriek 'Breda'	2.7	B	F-P	351
94	Nederlandsche Springstoffenfabrieken	2.7	B	F-M	289
95	Verkade's Fabrieken	2.7	E	F	209
96	W. Smit & Co.'s Transformatorenfabriek	2.6	B	F-M	361
97	Amsterdamsche Droogdok Mij. (ADM)	2.6	B	P	373
98	Verschure & Co.'s Scheepswerf en Machinefabriek	2.6	B	Fl	373
99	W.A. Scholten's Aardappelmeelfabrieken	2.6	B	F-P	204
100	Vereenigde Ned. Rubberfabrieken	2.6	B	F-M	301
	Total Assets	2,419.4			

Notes: In column 5 the companies are classified as follows: F = family partnership; Fl = family firm turned into a listed company; F-P = family firm turned into a listed company and accepting outside managing directors; F-M = family firm turned into listed company with rising influence of professional managers; P = listed company in its entrepreneurial phase, in which family links still play a decisive part in succession to management positions; P-M = personal company with rising influence of professional management; M = listed company with professional management, in which impersonal considerations regarding financing and succession to leadership are dominant; C = co-operative. Column 6 shows the Standard Industrial Classification (SIC Code) for the firm's major product line(s).

Sources: B = balance sheets found in *Van Oss' Effectenboek* and in the NEHA collection of published balance sheets; A = unpublished balance sheets found in company archives, E = estimate based on assets in nearby years or on issued share capital (assets 2x share capital): *Mrs. Van Nierop & Baak's Naamlooze Vennootschappen,* 1922-1931.

NOTES

1. A.D. Chandler, Jr., *Scale and Scope: The Dynamics of Industrial Capitalism* (Cambridge, MA, 1990), pp. 3–13, 235–7, 391.
2. We are very grateful to Dr J. Kok, who was drawing up similar lists at the same time and who was kind enough to share his findings with us. We also wish to thank Dr B.P.A. Gales for his helpful comment on an earlier draft.
3. This criterion is arbitrary, because each company could present its balance sheets in the way it chose in the Netherlands. A difference in presentation could make a great difference in total assets. Therefore, the comparison between the companies can be no more than an indication of their relative importance. We realise that the total assets depended greatly on the valuation and depreciation policy the firm followed, but we share this problem with Chandler. Dutch or foreign subsidiaries are not included in the top 100 list, with the one exception of the chemical company of State Mines (Stikstofbindingsbedrijf), because in this case the State Mines is not included. Foreign subsidiaries are also excluded. Companies which were independent but financed with foreign (Belgian) capital are included, while companies working in the Dutch colonies only are not included.
4. Examples of family firms with this kind of financial policy were, to name a few, Heineken, Honig, Ned. Linoleum Fabriek and Zwanenberg.
5. We used the following exchange rates: US $ = f 2,49 and DM = f 0,593.
6. To avert an exaggeration of the Dutch assets, we have taken the Dutch part of Unilever, the Unilever NV, only. The assets of the Koninklijke (Royal Dutch Shell) represent the 60 per cent share of the Dutch in the combined Royal Dutch Shell.
7. A. Maddison, *Dynamic Forces in Capitalist Development: A Long-run Comparative View* (Oxford/New York, 1991) p. 198. In 1930 the German population was 65.1 million, the Dutch 7.9 million.
8. B.P.A. Gales and K.E. Sluyterman, 'Outward Bound: The Rise of Dutch Multinationals', in G. Jones and H.G. Schröter (eds.), *The Rise of Multinationals in Continental Europe* (Aldershot, 1993), pp. 65–6.
9. To assess the financial and managing structures of the top 100 firms, many company histories, too many to name them all, were consulted. A useful survey of Dutch company histories can be found in P. Dehing and C. Seegers, *Katalogus van de kollektie gedenkboeken van ondernemingen en organisaties in de Economisch-Historische Bibliotheek* (Amsterdam, 1988). Information is also available in a database 'Business Archives Registration' (BARN) in the NEHA, Amsterdam.
10. J. Jonker, 'Sinecures or Sinews of Power? Interlocking Directorships and Bank–Industry Relations in the Netherlands, 1910–1940', *Economic and Social History in the Netherlands*, Vol. 3 (1991), pp. 119–31.
11. A. de Graaff, 'De industrie', in *De Nederlandse volkshuishouding tussen twee wereldoorlogen*, Vol. VIII (Utrecht, 1952), pp. 36–9, 80–93, 114–39, 176–204.
12. J.H. Gispen, 'De practijk van de wet op het algemeen verbindend en onverbindend verklaren van ondernemersovereenkomsten 1935', *Antirevolutionaire Staatkunde*, Vol. 14 (1938), pp. 75–88, 128–46.
13. H.W. de Jong, 'Nederland: het kartelparadijs van Europa?', *Economisch-Statistische Berichten*, 14 March 1990.
14. E. Homburg, 'The History of the Dutch Chemical Industry', in *The Anatomy of Chemical Holland: Special Issue of Chemisch Magazine* (Rijswijk, 1986), pp. 16–22.
15. E. Bloembergen, *75 jaar Superfosfaat; Gedenkboek ter gelegenheid van het vijfenzeventigjarig bestaan van het superfosfaatbedrijf in Nederland* (Utrecht, 1958).
16. A. Smeets, *90 Jaren zinkwitindustrie in Nederland, 1870–1960* (1960).
17. R.M. de Vries, *135 millioen Kub.m. zuurstof in een halve eeuw* (Schiedam, 1957).
18. This subsidiary was the beginning of DSM.
19. This subsidiary, Mekog, is not included in the 1930 list, because we have excluded subsidiaries in cases where the holding company is included.
20. Joh. de Vries, *Hoogovens IJmuiden 1918–1968. Ontstaan en groei van een basisindus-*

THE DUTCH FAMILY FIRM 181

trie (n.p. 1986), pp. 320–8. See also E. Hexner, *International Cartels* (Chapel Hill, NC, 1946), pp. 313–21.

21. *25 Jaar stikstofbindingsindustrie 'Nederland' NV, 1918–1943* (Dordrecht, 1946).
22. J.H. van Stuijvenberg, *Het Centraal Bureau. Een coöperatief krachtveld in de Nederlandse landbouw, 1899–1949* (Rotterdam, 1949), pp. 237–9.
23. E. Homburg, 'De overgang naar een moderne chemische industrie', *Chemisch Magazine* (Dec. 1989), pp. 741–3; (Jan. 1990), pp. 31–4.
24. D.A. Wittop Koning, *NV Koninklijke Pharmaceutische fabrieken v/h Brocades-Stheeman & Pharmacia, 1800–1950* (Amsterdam, 1950).
25. Hexner, *International Cartels*, pp. 336–9. There were inadequate data to draw any informed conclusions about this firm.
26. A. Leemans, *Van molen tot moleculen, van Noury tot AKZO* (Amersfoort, 1988).
27. Hexner, *International Cartels*, p. 312. Another example of a small firm (too small to figure in the 1930 list), which competed successfully with a far larger German firm, was the family firm Océ-van der Grinten. Eventually, the German firm Kalle & Co., a part of IG Farben, found Océ's research interesting enough to come to patent agreements. K.E. Sluyterman, 'From Licensor to Multinational Enterprise: Océ-van der Grinten in the International World, 1922–66', *Business History*, Vol. 34 No. 2 (1992), pp. 28–49.
28. M. Tausk, *Organon. De geschiedenis van een bijzondere Nederlandse onderneming* (Nijmegen, 1978).
29. *Activiteit in Zwart. Vijftig jaar Norit* (Amsterdam, 1968).
30. *Van Oss' Effectenboek*, 1904–1914.
31. The oldest petroleum company in the Dutch Indies was the Dortsche Petroleum Maatschappij. A Dutch mining engineer, A. Stoop, began prospecting in Java. Production was taken in hand in 1887 with family and acquaintances providing financial means. Two years later a refinery was set up under the direction of A. Stoop's brother. When larger amounts of money were needed, the company was successfully introduced at the Amsterdam Effectenbeurs. Dortsche became part of the Royal Dutch Shell group in 1911. F.C. Gerretson, *History of the Royal Dutch*, Vols.I–IV (Leiden, 1953–57); about Dortsche, see in particular Vol. II, pp. 202–27.
32. Ibid., Vol. II, pp. 60–1.
33. Ibid., Vol. IV, pp. 229–57.
34. Ibid., Vol. IV, pp. 1–2, 56–8.
35. Chandler, *Scale and Scope*, p. 440.
36. H. Gabriëls, *Koninklijke Olie: de eerste honderd jaar 1890–1990* (Den Haag, 1990), pp. 52–3.
37. Gerretson, *History of Royal Dutch*, Vol. IV, pp. 54–5.
38. W.H.P.M. van Hooff, *In het rijk van de Nederlandse Vulcanus. De Nederlandse machinenijverheid 1825–1914. Een historische bedrijfstakverkenning* (Amsterdam, 1990), pp. 357–60.
39. J.C. Westermann, *Geschiedenis van de ijzer- en staalgieterij in Nederland in het bijzonder van het bedrijf van de Nederlandsche Staalfabrieken v/h. J.M. de Muinck Keizer N.V. te Utrecht* (Utrecht, 1948), pp. 197, 207, 266.
40. W. Blom, *100 Jaar zinkproduktie in Nederland* (Eindhoven, 1992) pp. 5–18.
41. In 1930 this subsidiary had just come into production, but its assets were too small to include the company in the top 100; Joh. Visser and J.F.M. Vet (ed.), *25 Jaar tin in Arnhem* (Arnhem, 1953), pp. 7–22.
42. Westermann, *Geschiedenis van de ijzer- en staalgieterij*, pp. 104, 307, 344–50; De Vries, *Hoogovens IJmuiden*, pp. 233–7, 347–65.
43. There were several transport and trading companies that would have ranked immediately after the first four industrial companies of the top 100 list, as was the case with the transport companies Stoomvaartmaatschappij Nederland, Koninklijke Paketvaart and Rotterdamsche Lloyd with assets of 141, 119 and 97 million guilders respectively, and the trading and plantation companies Handelsvereeniging

182 FAMILY CAPITALISM

Amsterdam, Deli Maatschappij and Internatio with assets of 118, 74 and 55 million guilders respectively. The last one, Internatio, had the same amount of assets as the fifth industrial company.
44. G.W. Ovink, *Honderd jaren lettergieterij in Amsterdam* (Amsterdam, 1951), p. 52.
45. J.C. Westermann, *Blik in het verleden. Geschiedenis van de Nederlandsche blikindustrie in hare opkomst van gildeambacht tot grootbedrijf* (Amsterdam, 1939), pp. 307–72.
46. *Werkspoor 1827–1952. Gedenkboek uitgegeven ter gelegenheid van het honderd vijf en twintig jarig bestaan op 9 februari 1952* (Amsterdam 1952), pp. 9–30, 50–52; *Machinefabriek Gebr. Stork & Co., opgericht 1868* (Hengelo, 1922), pp. 11–12.
47. J.C. Westermann, *Kagen, clippers, werven en motoren; geschiedenis van een geslacht van schippers, reeders, scheepsbouwmeesters en motorenfabrikanten te Amsterdam* (Amsterdam, 1942), pp. 164–70, 203–4.
48. S.G. Steenwijk, 'Machinefabriek en Scheepswerf van P. Smit jr.', *Contact* (Dec. 1971).
49. *De schepen die wij bouwden 1875–1950; gedenkboek van de n.v. Koninklijke Maatschappij 'De Schelde' Vlissingen* (Haarlem, 1950); M.J. Brusse, *Wilton 1854–1929: vijfenzeventig jaar: geschiedenis van Wilton's Machinefabriek en Scheepswerf* (Rotterdam, 1929).
50. For steam turbines Stork obtained a licence from the German/Swiss Zoelly-syndicate and for water pipe generators from the British company Babcock & Wilcox Ltd. *Tachtig jaar Stork* (Hengelo, 1958).
51. Van Hooff, *Vulcanus*, pp. 108, 238; *Machinefabriek Gebr. Stork*, pp. 15, 19; J.J. Middelkoop, *60 jaar Reineveld 1893 – 29 juni – 1953* (Delft, 1953) pp. 25–9.
52. Van Hooff, *Vulcanus*, pp. 206, 220; L. Huizinga, *Janus van Breda; uitgegeven naar aanleiding van het 85 jarig bestaan van de n.v. Machinefabriek 'Breda' voorheen Backer en Rueb* (Breda, 1956).
53. A. Glavimans, *Een halve eeuw Berkel; gedenkboek, uitgegeven ter gelegenheid van het 50-jarig bestaan der Maatschappij Van Berkel's Patent N.V.: 1898 – 12 October – 1948* (Rotterdam, 1948).
54. *Van Oss' Effectenboek*, 1930–1939.
55. A. Heerding, *Geschiedenis van de NV Philips' Gloeilampenfabrieken; Vol. I, Het ontstaan van de Nederlandse gloeilampenindustrie* (Den Haag, 1980), pp. 310–1, 336–8.
56. A. Heerding, *Geschiedenis van de NV Philips' Gloeilampenfabrieken; Vol. II, Een onderneming van vele markten thuis* (Leiden, 1986), pp. 27, 413–4. By 1920, Philips possessed the majority of shares in the Vitrite Works, Volt's Metaaldraadlampenfabriek and Pope's Metaaldraadlampenfabriek, the three most important Dutch competitors.
57. *Van Oss' Effectenboek*, 1925, 1932.
58. I.J. Blanken, *Geschiedenis van Philips Electronics N.V.; De ontwikkeling van de N.V. Philips' Gloeilampenfabrieken tot electrotechnisch concern* (Leiden, 1992), pp. 322–4.
59. Blanken, *Philips Electronics*, pp. 413–20.
60. After its start in 1911, *Draka* caught the attention of Anton Philips, which considered setting up a cable manufacturing unit itself. *Draka* tried to prevent the entry of such a potential strong competitor in the Dutch market and started negotiations. In the end, Philips decided to take a majority interest in the share capital of *Draka* in 1913. *Veertig jaar DRAKA, 1910–1950*, pp. 10–24.
61. *Willem Smit & Co.'s Transformatorenfabriek NV* (Nijmegen, 1938); *Gouden Schakel: uitgegeven ter gelegenheid van het 50-jarig jubileum van de NV Hazemeyer te Hengelo* (Deventer, 1957); *HEEMAF NV Hengelo* [1958; *NV Nederlandsche Kabelfabriek NKF Delft 1904–1954* (Delft, 1954); *Veertig jaar DRAKA 1910–1950* (Amsterdam, 1950).
62. Chandler, *Scale and Scope*, pp. 236–7.
63. L. Hannah, 'Scale and Scope: Towards a European Visible Hand', *Business History*, Vol. 33 (1991), p. 302; R. Church, 'The Limitations of the Personal Capitalism

Paradigm', *Business History Review*, Vol. 64 (1990), pp. 706–8.
64. Evidence in figures is difficult to provide, since comparing profits and the distribution of profits is even more precarious than comparing assets.
65. For the managerial development of Unilever see Chandler, *Scale and Scope*, pp. 378–89. We did not discuss Unilever, because the food sector was not included amongst the chosen sectors.

Part V
Co-operative Behaviour and Groups

[21]

Industrial Organization and Entrepreneurship in the Developing Countries: The Economic Groups

Nathaniel H. Leff*
Columbia University

I. Introduction

The subject of industrial organization has not received much attention in the analysis of postwar economic development. This neglect has occurred despite the importance of industrial organization for such questions as efficiency in production and investment and, especially, for transmitting the external economies which are believed to play a central role in the development process.[1] By contrast, the topic of entrepreneurship in less-developed economies has been discussed extensively, if not always in satisfactory theoretical terms.[2] As William Baumol expressed it a decade ago, despite the entrepreneur's "acknowledged importance . . . [he is] one of the most elusive characters in the cast that constitutes the subject of economic analysis . . . [and has] virtually disappeared from the theoretical literature."[3] This conceptual elusiveness is especially unfortunate for the analysis of the developing economies, in which entrepreneurship is likely to be more necessary for output expansion and structural change than in the more developed countries.

* I am grateful to Tuvia Blumenthal, Neil Chamberlain, Frank Edwards, Ronald Findlay, David Felix, Harvey Leibenstein, Richard Porter, Frederic Pryor, Kazuo Sato, and Julian Simon for helpful comments on an earlier version of this paper. I also thank the Faculty Research Program of the Columbia Business School for financial support; and the Department of Developing Countries of Tel-Aviv University, where the first draft of the paper was written, for the use of its research facilities. I bear sole responsibility for any deficiencies in the paper.

1 Paul N. Rosenstein-Rodan, "Problems of the Industrialization of Eastern and South Eastern Europe," *Economic Journal* 53 (June 1943): 202–11.

2 For an indication of the large volume of professional literature addressed to the subject of entrepreneurship and economic development, see the bibliography in Flavia Derossi, *The Mexican Entrepreneur* (Paris: OECD Development Centre, 1972), pp. 409–28.

3 William Baumol, "Entrepreneurship in Economic Theory," *American Economic Review* 58 (May 1968): 61–71; quote from p. 64.

© 1978 by The University of Chicago. 0013-0079/78/2604-0001$01.30

661

Economic Development and Cultural Change

Industrial organization and entrepreneurship are of course related.[4] Accordingly, this paper attempts to make some analytical progress by considering these two subjects together. We will proceed by drawing attention to and analyzing a pattern of industrial organization in the developing countries which has important effects on the functioning of these economies, particularly on the conditions which affect investment and production decisions. This pattern of industrial organization, which I shall call "the group," is distinct from other forms of capitalist organization in the less developed countries which have been more widely noted and discussed; for example, the public sector corporation, the broadly held public company, the family owned company, and the multinational corporation. Despite its existence as a phenomenon which appears in many developing countries and despite its pervasive economic effects, which we shall discuss below, the group has received surprisingly little generalized analysis. Some aspects of the group phenomenon have been noted before, usually in observations for individual less developed countries. Also, most observers have focused on one or two features of the groups, such as their monopoly power or their political connections. However, relatively little effort has been directed to conceptualizing the groups in more general analytical terms, and analyzing the implications for economic development, industrial organization, and entrepreneurship.[5]

II. The Economic Groups

In many of the less developed countries a significant part of the domestic and privately owned industrial sector, and particularly the activities which use relatively modern and capital-intensive techniques, is organized in a special institutional pattern. Following the Latin American term, we may call this structure the "group," although this pattern of economic organization is also common, with different names, in Asia and Africa. Documentation on the structure and scale of group activities in many less developed countries is sparse. This is not surprising, for collection of data on a phenomenon usually requires that its existence first be noted in the professional literature and a conceptual framework be developed to analyze it. Such a general framework has previously not been developed for the groups. Nevertheless, on the basis of presently available materials, the following generalizations can be advanced.[6]

4 Cf. the comment by W. A. Lewis: "We have no good theory of entrepreneurship because we have no good theory of monopoly," cited by Baumol, p. 68.

5 The present paper concentrates on the causes of the group structure and on its positive effects on the functioning of the less developed economies. Pernicious effects and their policy implications are discussed in my "Monopoly Capitalism and Public Policy in the Less-developed Economies," mimeographed (1978; available from the author).

6 For some published sources which discuss aspects of the groups (often in different terms), see, e.g., W. Dean, *The Industrialization of São Paulo* (Austin:

Nathaniel H. Leff

The group is a multicompany firm which transacts in different markets but which does so under common entrepreneurial and financial control. More generally, this pattern of industrial organization has two essential features. First, the group draws its capital and its high-level managers from sources which transcend a single family. The capital and the managers may come from a number of wealthy families, but they remain within the group as a single economic unit. The group's owner-managers typically include some (but by no means all) members of the family within which the group's activity originated. However, what distinguishes this institution from the family firm and what gives it the resources for greater scope is the fact that owner-managers from other families also participate. Participants are people linked by relations of interpersonal trust, on the basis of a similar personal, ethnic, or communal background.[7]

Second, somewhat like the *zaibatsu* in pre–World War II Japan, the groups invest and produce in several product markets rather than

---

University of Texas Press, 1969), pt. 1; A. Lauterbach, "Management Aims and Development Needs in Latin America," *Business History Review* 42 (Winter 1968): 558–59; Derossi, esp. pp. 97–115 and 158–93; François Bourricaud, "Structure and Function of the Peruvian Oligarchy," *Studies in Comparative International Development* 2 (1966): 1–15; Robert T. Aubey, "Entrepreneurial Formation in El Salvador," *Explorations in Entrepreneurial History*, vol. 6 (November 1969), esp. pp. 272–76; D. W. Stammer, "Financial Development and Economic Growth in Underdeveloped Countries: Comment," *Economic Development and Cultural Change* 20 (January 1972): 318–25; Andrew J. Brimmer, "The Setting of Entrepreneurship in India," *Quarterly Journal of Economics* 69 (1955): 553–76; G. Rosen, *Some Aspects of Industrial Finance in India* (Glencoe, Ill.: Free Press, 1962), chap. 1; E. K. Hazari, *The Corporate Private Sector* (Bombay, 1966); Gustav Papanek, *Pakistan's Development* (Cambridge, Mass.: Harvard University Press, 1967), pp. 67–68; Thomas A. Timberg, "Industrial Entrepreneurship among the Trading Communities of India," Harvard University Economic Development Report no. 136, mimeographed (Cambridge, Mass.: Harvard University, July 1969), pp. 1–126; Hannah Papanek, "Pakistan's Big Businessmen," *Economic Development and Cultural Change* 21 (October 1972): 1–32, esp. 17–32; Lawrence J. White, *Industrial Concentration and Economic Power in Pakistan* (Princeton, N.J.: Princeton University Press, 1974); and Harry Strachan, *The Role of Family and Other Groups in Economic Development: The Case of Nicaragua* (New York: Praeger Publishers, 1976). (The page references cited below to Strachan's work refer to his D.B.A. thesis, Harvard University, 1972.) I have also been informed by Steven Resnick, K. S. Lee, and Jose Buera that a similar pattern exists in the Philippines, South Korea, and the Dominican Republic, respectively. Also, on the basis of his field experience in Asia and Africa, Richard Porter has written to me that the groups are common in other countries of Asia and Africa. These materials, as well as my own interviews conducted in the course of fieldwork in less developed countries, constitute the basis for the statements advanced in the text.

[7] The groups I am discussing are, for reasons of their comparative advantage and private returns, largely in the "modern" sector of the economy. Another type of group, often purely ethnic and without capabilities in modern technology, sometimes operates as an informal financial intermediary in activities where "organized" sources of finance are scarce in less developed countries (see, e.g., William Baldwin, "The Thai Rice Trade as a Vertical Market Network," *Economic Development and Cultural Change* 22 [January 1974]: 179–99).

Economic Development and Cultural Change

in a single product line. These product markets may be quite diverse, ranging, for example, from consumer durables to chemicals to steel rolling. These activities have sometimes been selected on the basis of forward or backward integration. In other cases, new investments have been made in product markets which are unrelated but in activities where the group's technical and managerial capabilities are applicable as inputs.[8] Large groups have also established banks and other financial intermediaries to tap capital from sources outside the immediate members of the group.[9] Finally, the groups usually exercise a considerable degree of market power in the activities where they operate.

In some respects the groups' diversified activities obviously resemble the American conglomerates. However, for microeconomic reasons discussed below, they developed indigenously and independently in the less developed countries.[10] It is also important to note that in many less developed countries the assets of the larger individual groups run to tens of millions of dollars. Taken together, they comprise a significant perecentage of the modern industrial sector, particularly of that portion which is not owned by public sector firms or by multinational corporations.

Reliable documentation on the extent of group activities is not available for many countries; and in developing countries with a substantial stock of direct investments by multinational corporations it would be easy to underestimate the groups' quantitative importance. This is because their investment strategy involves portfolio balance through diversification in different activities; consequently, they do not concentrate their investments in a single industry. By contrast, foreign-based multinational corporations can also diversify their portfolios interna-

[8] For a similar pattern in more developed countries, see Edith T. Penrose, *The Theory of the Growth of the Firm* (New York: Basil Blackwell, 1959), chaps. 5 and 7. Cf. also with G. B. Richardson's distinction between expansion into activities which are "complementary" to or "similar" to a firm's initial activities (see his paper, "The Organization of Industry," *Economic Journal* 82 [September 1972]: 887–92).

[9] In some cases, the reverse sequence has occurred: from a group's establishing a bank to entry into nonfinancial activities. Derossi (p. 178, n.) remarks that in addition to the banks which belong to industrial groups in Mexico the same can be said of 41 of the country's 44 *financieras* (investment banks).

[10] In some respects these reasons are similar. Thus the groups' pattern of diversifying to utilize slack resources is similar to the expansion path documented by Alfred D. Chandler for American firms (see, e.g., his *Strategy and Structure: Chapters in the History of Industrial Enterprise* [Cambridge, Mass.: M.I.T. Press, 1962], pp. 102–3, 432, 448). By contrast, the emergence of the groups in the less developed countries owes less to the conditions of tax and capital-market legislation, which were important in the United States. On the latter, see Jon Didrichsen, "The Development of Diversified and Conglomerate Firms in the United States, 1920–70," *Business History Review* 46 (Summer 1972): 202–19. Didrichsen has also emphasized the importance of economies of scale to imperfectly marketed skills (see the discussion in Sec. III below).

Nathaniel H. Leff

tionally.[11] Because of the groups' interactivity diversification, multinational corporations are often the largest firms within specific industries. The foreigners' position as the dominant firm within individual industries may divert attention from the groups' large overall assets within the industrial sector as a whole.

Despite data limitations, some figures convey an idea of the groups' scope. In Nicaragua, Strachan reports that in the early 1970s four groups accounted for 35% of all loans and investments of the total financial sector and a much larger share of loans and investments in the private financial sector.[12] In Pakistan in 1968, 10 groups controlled 33% of all assets of private, Pakistani-controlled firms in the modern manufacturing sector; and 30 groups controlled 52%.[13] These assets were held in a wide range of diversified activities.[14] Similarly, in India the largest four groups held 17% of the assets of public and private companies in 1958 and the largest 20 groups, 28%.[15] As regards diversification, data for 37 of the largest Indian domestically owned groups show an average of five activities per group.[16] Excluding the two largest groups (Tata and Birla), the average was still four activities per group.

A more detailed picture of the size and diversification of groups in a developing economy is available from a 1962 study in Brazil.[17] These data on the assets and diversification of Brazilian groups in 1962 are presented in table 1. Although these data convey an idea of the size of groups in Brazil, for a number of reasons table 1 tends to understate the importance of the groups. First, the study considered only the groups' own capital, excluding external resources which they could mobilize. The balance-sheet data utilized may also underreport true asset values, both to reduce tax payments and because of accounting lags during inflation. The study was also confined to the four most industrialized states of Brazil's south, thereby omitting groups located elsewhere in the economy. Finally, the data of table 1 relate to 1962, before the large economic expansion which began after 1967. An update of these data

[11] In some cases where multinational corporations operating in developing countries have generated cash flow in excess of profit-remission constraints, they have also followed a pattern of interactivity investment within the local economy. This behavior reflects the same causes as those affecting the groups (see Sec. III below).

[12] Strachan, pp. 80–81.

[13] White, p. 65.

[14] Letter from Gustav Papanek, May 6, 1969.

[15] Hazari, chap. 2, as cited in White, p. 71.

[16] These figures on group participation in different activities were computed from data presented in Timberg, pp. 88–104.

[17] Maurício Vinhas de Queiroz, "Os grupos multibilionarios," *Revista do instituto de ciências sociais* (Rio de Janeiro) 2, no. 1 (January 1965): 47–77; Luciano Martins, "Os grupos bilionarios nacionais," ibid., pp. 79–115. I am grateful to Marcio Teixeira for bringing this data source to my attention.

Economic Development and Cultural Change

TABLE 1

OWN ASSETS AND DIVERSIFICATION OF PRIVATE, LOCALLY OWNED GROUPS
IN FOUR STATES OF BRAZIL, 1962

	ASSET CLASS ($ MILLION)		
	2.5–10	>10	>25
Groups (N).................	144	24	5
Average companies per group (N)	8*	21	N.A.

SOURCES.—Maurício Vinhas de Queiroz, "Os grupos multibilionarios," *Revista do instituto de ciências sociais* (Rio de Janeiro) 2, no. 1
(January 1965): 47, 50, 64; Luciano Martins, "Os grupos bilionarios
nacionais," ibid., p. 86.
NOTE.—The asset figures are in 1962 dollars, converted from cruzeiros
at an exchange rate of 400 cruzeiros per dollar. N.A. = not available.
* Sample estimate.

would undoubtedly show a much larger scale for the assets of groups in
Brazil.

Bearing in mind the size and diversity of groups and their importance in the private, domestically owned modern sector of the economy,
we will consider and discuss below the effects this feature of industrial
organization has on the functioning of the developing economies. First,
however, let us analyze the causes of the group structure.

III. Causes of the Group Pattern of Industrial Organization

The group pattern of industrial organization is readily understood as a
microeconomic response to well-known conditions of market failure in
the less developed countries. In fact, the emergence of the group as an
institutional mode might well have been predicted on the basis of familiar
theory and a knowledge of the environment in these countries.

The group can be conceptualized as an organizational structure for
appropriating quasi rents which accrue from access to scarce and imperfectly marketed inputs. Some of these inputs, such as capital, might be
marketed more efficiently, but in the conditions of the less developed
countries they are not. Some of these inputs are inherently difficult to
market efficiently; for example, honesty and trustworthy competence
on the part of high-level managers.[18] Finally, substantial private gains
can accrue from *not* marketing some inputs, for example, information
generated in one group activity which is relevant for (actual or potential)
investment and production decisions elsewhere in the economy.

The absence of markets for risk and uncertainty also helps explain
another feature of the groups' pattern of expansion—their entry in diversified product lines. This pattern may appear to be due exclusively to
the relatively small size of the domestic market for many manufactured

[18] Harvey Leibenstein, "Entrepreneurship and Development," *American Economic Review* 58 (May 1968): 72–83.

Nathaniel H. Leff

products in the less developed countries. More important, however, for reasons of portfolio balance, diversification has an obvious appeal in economies subject to the risks and uncertainties of instability and rapid structural change. The groups' practice of choosing new investments on the basis of backward and forward linkages also stems in part from an effort to alleviate risk and uncertainty. Vertical integration has been sought to avoid being dependent on a monopolist or oligopolist for materials inputs, or on an oligopsonist for the group's output. In conditions where both parties must make specific and long-lived investments, bilateral oligopoly involves serious risks and uncertainties concerning future quantities, qualities, and prices for inputs and for outputs. In addition, vertical integration can avoid the transactions (bargaining and enforcing) costs which intricate arm's-length negotiations would entail.[19]

These conditions which lead to gains from vertical integration are well known from the more developed countries.[20] They are likely to be more severe, however, in the less developed countries. The probability of having to confront strong market power is greater in these economies whose domestic markets are often too small to accommodate more than a few sellers and buyers for many intermediate products.[21] Also, in relatively large and open economies such as those of the more developed countries random fluctuations in the components of overall market demand for specific intermediate products may be offsetting. The less developed economies, however, are too small and often too closed to enable the law of large numbers to have this smoothing effect, and make more predictable the total market demand for individual intermediate products.

The institution of the group is thus an intrafirm mechanism for dealing with deficiencies in the markets for primary factors, risk, and intermediate products in the developing countries. In this perspective, the group pattern of industrial organization fits closely into the theory of entrepreneurship and development formulated by Harvey Leibenstein.[22]

Leibenstein has suggested that entrepreneurship in less developed countries involves the opening of channels for input supply and for marketing of output in situations where a routinized market mechanism does not exist. In the absence of such "intermarket operators" some input and/or output quantities, qualities, and costs would be so beclouded by risk and uncertainty that investment and production in these activities

[19] Oliver E. Williamson, "The Vertical Integration of Production: Market Failure Considerations," *American Economic Review* 61 (May 1971): 112-23.

[20] George J. Stigler, "The Division of Labor Is Limited by the Extent of the Market," reprinted in his *The Organization of Industry* (Homewood, Ill.: Richard D. Irwin, Inc., 1968), pp. 136–38.

[21] Reliance on international trade to complement the domestic market might be another possibility. However, in addition to problems often posed by overvalued exchange rates, foreign trade often involves—or is perceived to involve—substantial risks and uncertainties of its own in the less developed countries.

[22] See n. 18 above.

Economic Development and Cultural Change

would not take place. With their access to nonmarketed inputs and with their pattern of vertical integration, however, the groups create a channel both for mobilizing and for allocating such inputs and outputs. In fact, the group can perhaps best be understood as an institutional innovation for internalizing the returns which accrue from interactivity operations in the imperfect market conditions of the less developed countries. What has happened in effect is that the groups have appropriated as gains the quasi rents of the output which Leibenstein envisaged would otherwise be foregone due to imperfect factor markets and insufficient entrepreneurship.

Not only does the group pattern of industrial organization provide the "real life" correspondence to Leibenstein's theory of entrepreneurship, but it also suggests some analytical extensions. First, the group constitutes a pattern of industrial organization which permits *structure* rather than gifted individuals to perform the key interactivity function of entrepreneurship. Another departure from earlier theoretical expectations is that with the institution of the group some factors and products flow within the *firm* rather than through the market.

IV. Other Explanations

The preceding discussion has explained the group pattern of industrial organization largely as an institutional innovation for overcoming—and reaping the benefits from—imperfect markets in the less developed countries. We must also consider some other interpretations of this phenomenon.

Thus it has been suggested that the group structure arises mainly because of political connections which permit special access to government dispensations of, for example, import licenses.[23] Groups undoubtedly do benefit from government largesse in the form of import licenses, bank charters, and tax and investment credits; but this is hardly an "alternative" explanation. For one thing, the groups' entrepreneurship and the externalities which they internalize (see below) help explain why particular government favors may have higher present value for groups than for other firms and, consequently, why the groups can outbid others in acquiring political favors and connections.[24] More generally, I do not believe that political influence per se is a *sufficient* reason for the emergence of the group pattern of industrial organization.[25] If the reader

---

[23] See, e.g., White, p. 17.

[24] For a more general framework on this topic, see my "Corruption and Economic Development," *American Behavioral Scientist* 3 (December 1964): 8–14.

[25] Cf. Hannah Papanek's comment: "Although political influence obviously played an important role in the development of the Big Houses, it was not in itself sufficient for large-scale growth of the enterprises" (p. 17).

Nathaniel H. Leff

judges otherwise, however, political connections can readily be conceptualized as an imperfectly marketed input.

It may also be suggested that the group structure is due to no more than imperfect access to capital and that the highly skewed distribution of wealth common in less developed countries simply means that the very rich take a pervasive role in industrialization. I find this explanation insufficient on a number of grounds. First, it fails to explain why only a small percentage of individuals and families in the traditional wealthy class establish groups. Also, some groups have been founded by individuals who were initially not in the high-wealth brackets.[26]

The emphasis I have placed on the importance of conditions other than preferential access to capital alone as an explanation for the groups[27] is supported by other features of their structure.[28] The groups do not operate simply as financial trusts or holding companies; rather, they maintain active entrepreneurial participation in their manifold activities. The existence of structures similar to groups in the public sector of some less developed countries provides further evidence that more than imperfect access to capital underlies the group pattern of industrial organization. Public sector companies in the less developed countries generally face less stringent conditions of capital supply than do private firms. Nevertheless, where legislation has permitted, some public sector companies have also operated with diversified investment and production activities similar to those of private groups.[29]

V. The Groups and Entrepreneurship

The existence of large-scale, diversified firms is a familiar phenomenon in advanced capitalist economies. What have we gained from noting that a similar phenomenon, in the special form of the groups, is also present in the developing countries?

First, the group pattern of industrial organization has helped relax entrepreneurial constraint which, in the first postwar decade, many observers expected would limit the pace of economic development in the

[26] Hannah Papanek (ibid.) has also noted the "modest antecedents of some of the big businessmen in Pakistan today."

[27] Cf. George Stigler's comment that the phrase "imperfections in the capital market" has too often been employed as a substitute for analysis of other relevant conditions (see his "Imperfections in the Capital Market," *Journal of Political Economy* 75 [June 1967]: 287–92, reprinted in *The Organization of Industry*).

[28] Strachan (p. 111) reports that in the Nicaraguan groups people who can contribute only capital but not special management skills to group activities are gradually excluded from participation. He has also noted another piece of information which reduces the importance of preferential access to capital as a sufficient condition for the group structure. He points out that Costa Rica, where the banking system has been nationalized since the late 1940s, has groups which operate in modes similar to those of Nicaragua, with its privately owned banking system.

[29] An example is the Pertamina company in Indonesia.

Economic Development and Cultural Change

underdeveloped countries. Thus, this institution has permitted "pure" Schumpeterian entrepreneurship to become effective. This is because the group provides the capital and the technical and managerial resources which are necessary to transform "innovativeness and alertness to opportunities"[30] into actual investment and production decisions. The institution of the group also facilitates economies in the use of scarce entrepreneurial resources. Economies of scale to entrepreneurship can be appropriated as able individuals are utilized to their full potential in the group's large and diversified activities. In addition to such "central office" effects, the groups increase entrepreneurial mobility, for they can deploy entrepreneurial resources to specific intragroup companies as opportunities arise.

Perhaps even more importantly, the group *structure* itself reduces the amount of enterepreneurial capacity which is required per unit of innovative decision making. Thus the groups' partcipation in many different activities increases information flows and reduces uncertainty surrounding investment and production decisions.[31] More generally, the groups embody in their structure and expansion path a number of suggestions which have been advanced on theoretical grounds for economizing on entrepreneurship in developing countries. As noted earlier, the group performs the Leibenstein entrepreneurial function of overcoming deficiencies in important factor and product markets. In addition, as we have seen, the groups expand along a path of backward and forward linkages, with investment decisions taken in function of economic and technological complementarities. Thus the groups have in effect implemented at the micro level the development pattern which Albert Hirschman proposed as an optimizing *macro* strategy for economies where entrepreneurship is scarce.[32]

Note finally a subjective, motivational feature which also increases the groups' orientation toward the investment and economic expansion aspects of entrepreneurship. The groups' top managers are often aggressive "empire builders." However, these managers lack some standard criteria for evaluating their performance, either for purposes of their own self-assessment or, perhaps even more important subjectively, for com-

[30] For a discussion of these aspects of entrepreneurship, see I. M. Kirzner, *Competition and Entrepreneurship* (Chicago: University of Chicago Press, 1973), pp. 39–57.

[31] In terms of John Harris's decision-theory conceptualization of entrepreneurship, the reduced uncertainty caused by the group pattern of industrial organization leads to a shift of the action set toward the origin and a rise in the probability that a given profitable investment will be implemented. For Harris's model of entrepreneurship, see his paper, "Entrepreneurship and Economic Development," in *Business Enterprise and Economic Change: Essays in Honor of Harold F. Williamson,* ed. Louis Cain and Paul Uselding (Kent, Ohio: Kent State University Press, 1973).

[32] Albert O. Hirschman, *The Strategy of Economic Development* (New Haven, Conn.: Yale University Press, 1958), pp. 42–43.

Nathaniel H. Leff

parison with rival groups. Thus, the deficiencies of formal capital markets in the developing countries prevent the use of share-prices in the stock market as an evaluative mechanism. And problems of accounting in these inflationary environments also preclude utilizing the group's overall rate of return on capital as a yardstick. In this context, two figures which are more readily available take on a special appeal as a performance measure: the size of a group's turnover and, relatedly, the rate of sales growth over time. This approach leads to a bias toward sales maximization, subject to a profit constraint, in the group's operations. The inefficiencies associated with such a management orientation are well known.[33] In the present context, however, this orientation also reinforces a group's propensity for entrepreneurial expansionism.

VI. Other Beneficial Effects on the Developing Economies

In addition to entrepreneurship, the group pattern of industrial organization also makes a difference in terms of other positive effects on the functioning of the developing economies. Not only does the group provide an institution for mobilizing capital from a pool which extends beyond the resources of a single family, but it performs a similar function for higher-management personnel as well. Such an enlargement of the base from which human resources can be recruited is especially important in the less developed countries. This is because mobilization and utilization of these human resources is in any case severely limited, due to the fact that top management is often selected only from within the circle of people who have at least some participation in ownership. The separation of ownership from control has not occurred on a large scale in the indigenous private sector of these economies.[34]

Furthermore, the group's internal relations of interpersonal trust permit the formation of larger top management teams than would otherwise be possible.[35] This facilitates effective communication and delegation of authority and enables firms to overcome organizational constraints

---

[33]William J. Baumol, *Business Behavior, Value and Growth* (New York: Harcourt, Brace & World, 1959), pp. 49–50.

[34] As discussed below, the groups' activities may suffer from some forms of inefficiency. It would be easy to attribute this to nepotism and to the lack of separation of ownership from control. Many of the groups' top managers are, however, professionally trained. In addition, the keener motivation and vested interest of owner-managers may increase the pressures for superior performance. In the United States, there is some evidence of better performance in firms which are owner controlled rather than management controlled (see R. J. Monsen, J. S. Chiu, and D. E. Cooley, "The Effect of Separation of Ownership and Control on the Performance of the Large Firm," *Quarterly Journal of Economics* 82 [August 1968]: 435–51; and Harvey Leibenstein, "Organization or Frictional Equilibria, X-Efficiency, and The Rate of Innovation," *Quarterly Journal of Economics* 83 [November 1969]: 614–15).

[35] Interpersonal trust among the top owner-managers of the group is so important in these environments that Strachan (pp. 4, 22–25) considers it one of the central features of this pattern of industrial organization.

Economic Development and Cultural Change

on size and efficiency.[36] As a result, group firms can achieve economies of scale which might otherwise be foregone and can attain output levels and rates of growth within individual activities which would be beyond the scope of family-owned firms.[37]

The group pattern of industrial organization also affects rates of return to capital and the rate of capital formation in the less developed countries. The groups' capacity to marshall the managerial and technical resources necessary for entry into new activities mitigates downward pressures on rates of return to capital which would otherwise occur if firms were restricted to their existing activities. The groups' power in product markets probably also leads to a higher rate of return.[38] In addition, the diversification in the groups' activities reduces portfolio risk. Both individually and a fortiori, in interaction, these risk and rate-of-return conditions caused by the group pattern of industrial organization probably lead to a higher rate of investment than would otherwise prevail.

Further, investments made along lines of vertical integration permit the group to internalize economies which would otherwise be external to the firm and its individual activity. Thus, in addition to increasing the volume of capital formation, the group pattern also leads in this respect to a (socially) more optimal allocation of investment.[39] With their inter-activity investment allocations, the groups provide a previously unsuspected mechanism for capital mobility between activities. In fact, to some extent the groups approximate the functioning of a capital market in the less developed countries.[40] The pattern of investment and production

[36] See Penrose, pp. 28–29. On the special aspects of this managerial problem in developing countries, see Peter Kilby, *Entrepreneurship and Economic Development* (New York: Free Press, 1971), pp. 26–29.

[37] This has also been noted by White (p. 33). His data for Pakistan (pp. 150–51) indicate that group firms there experienced faster growth than nongroup firms. This result obtained even when the size of original equity investment, which was also larger for group firms, is held constant.

[38] Studies with U.S. data, for example, have indicated a strong positive relation between a firm's rate of return and its market power, as measured by its market share within an industry (see, e.g., W. G. Shephard, "The Elements of Market Structure," *Review of Economics and Statistics* 54 [February 1972]: 25–37. This relation holds even when barriers to entry are low [p. 31]). For a less developed country, Pakistan, White (pp. 145–46) has presented evidence showing a positive relation between industry concentration ratios and industry rates of return. William J. House reports similar results for Kenya (see his paper, "Market Structure and Industry Performance: The Case of Kenya," *Oxford Economic Papers* 25 [November 1973]: 405–19).

[39] In discussing their investment decisions, group firms usually express themselves in terms of the need to provide input and output quantities for complementary group activities rather than in terms of prices and rates of return. This need not be as irrational as might first appear. In effect, such decisions involve using the primal rather than the dual solution of an implicit linear programming optimizing model.

[40] White (p. 33) has also noted aspects of the groups' capital market activities. An extended analysis is presented in my "Capital Markets in the Less-developed Countries: The Group Principle," in *Money and Finance in Economic*

Nathaniel H. Leff

decisions taken in cognizance of backward and forward linkage effects helps explain the speed of the adjustment process with which interrelated investment opportunities have been taken up in less developed countries.[41] Finally, the coordination of investment and production decisions by the groups has both reduced the need for, and lessened the burden on, government planning of the modern sector in developing countries.

The preceding discussion has noted some of the ways in which the group pattern of industrial organization improves the efficiency of the less developed economies. However, the groups also create some serious distortions. These involve inefficiency within the group, interfirm and intersectoral distortions, and finally, political-economic effects on overall development patterns. In effect, the groups have taken factor-market imperfections in the less developed countries and transmuted them into product-market imperfections. In the process, rapid industrial growth has often occurred, but the groups have also created a special form of monopoly capitalism in the less developed countries. The associated distortions raise important problems for public policy in the less developed countries. However, that subject is so large that it requires another paper.[42]

VII. Conclusions

This paper has drawn attention to and analyzed a neglected feature of industrial organization which has far-reaching effects on the economies of many less developed countries, the group. As noted, the groups have their origin in well-known market imperfections of the less developed countries. Mobilizing imperfectly marketed inputs, and reducing uncertainty and risk with their diversified and vertically integrated activities, the groups in fact constitute the "intermarket operators" on which Leibenstein's theory of entrepreneurship has focused. Further, in addition to its effects on entrepreneurship, the group pattern of industrial organization also permits less developed economies to relax institutional constraints in the allocation of capital and of managerial resources. Consequently, domestic, privately owned firms can enter and can attain efficient scale in activities which might be beyond the scope of a private, locally owned firm. And because of the groups, the modern sector in many less developed countries is far less "fragmented"—both in a static and a dynamic sense—than might be expected from accounts which have not been

Growth and Development, ed. Ronald I. McKinnon (New York: Marcel Dekker, Inc., 1976).

[41] This has also been noted, in different terms, by Albert Hirschman, "The Political Economy of Import-substituting Industrialization in Latin America," *Quarterly Journal of Economics* 82 (February 1968): 1–32.

[42] See my "Monopoly Capitalism and Public Policy in the Less-developed Countries."

Economic Development and Cultural Change

aware of this pattern of industrial organization.[43] Having described the costs of factor-market imperfections in the less developed countries, economists should hardly be surprised that an institution like the group emerged to appropriate the gains to overcoming these distortions.

This paper has also provided an example of the now well-documented point that economic theory can be relevant beyond the more advanced countries where it was first developed. Thus, standard microeconomic concepts help explain the emergence of the group institutional pattern, a phenomenon which might easily be attributed exclusively to sociocultural or political conditions. Understanding the economic basis of the group is not equivalent to justifying the institution, however, and indeed is a necessary step for reforming it. Our focus in this paper on the groups' effects in mitigating factor-market imperfections should not divert attention from the product-market distortions and serious problems for public policy which this pattern of industrial organization also creates.

The group institutional form clearly resembles some features of industrial and corporate organization in the more developed countries. The similarities to the conglomerate and to the large-scale multidivisional company are evident. Moreover, some of the causes of the group pattern also overlap with those which Oliver Williamson has discussed in his work on the theory of the firm in the more advanced economies.[44] Further, as we have seen, some aspects of the microeconomic and managerial reality in the advanced sector of the less developed economies are fairly similar to those of the more developed economies. Consequently, if adapted to recognize differences such as the absence of a formal capital market, the economics of the modern firm may be more applicable to the advanced sector of the developing countries than might have been assumed. And because of the similarity in patterns of industrial organization, oligopoly theory can clearly be helpful in modeling some features of price, output, and capacity decisions in the modern sector of the developing economies.

Finally, although we have discussed some aspects of the groups in the developing countries, many important questions obviously remain unanswered. One wonders, for example, why groups or a similar pattern of industrial organization has not emerged with equal frequency in all development contexts, both contemporary and historical. Similarly, it

[43] See, for example, Ronald McKinnon's description of "the fragmented economy," in chap. 2 of his *Money and Capital in Economic Development* (Washington, D.C.: Brookings Institution, 1972).

[44] See Oliver E. Williamson, *Markets and Hierarchies: Analysis and Antitrust Implications* (New York: Free Press, 1975), and particularly his emphasis on the importance of small numbers, bounded rationality (uncertainty), informational asymmetry, and opportunism (and hence the need for trust).

Nathaniel H. Leff

would be useful to have much more quantitative information on the scale and diversification of group activities and on the size distribution of groups in individual countries and its change over time. These may clearly be related to particular phases of development and government development strategies. Provision of answers to these questions and filling in our picture of the groups must await the collection of detailed statistical data. As noted earlier, however, collection of data requires that attention be drawn to a phenomenon and that a conceptual framework be elaborated to analyze it. Hopefully, the present paper will help serve this prior need.

[22]

The Entrepreneur, the Family and Capitalism

Some Examples from the Early Phase of Industrialisation in Germany

Jürgen Kocka

The spirit and practice of capitalism emerged from non-capitalist structures and processes and were nourished by them for a long time. Max Weber illustrated this i. a. in his discussion of the relation between the Protestant ethic and the spirit of capitalism; Joseph Schumpeter generalised it and stressed the importance of pre-capitalist élites for the emergence and maintenance of the bourgeois capitalist economic and social systems. Many others have taken up the same idea, developed it further, differentiated and supplemented it. It would seem appropriate to examine it in terms of the relation between the family and (industrial) capitalism.[1]

There can be no doubt that the basic principles of family life were in crass contrast to those of the capitalist market economy and the competitive society which became fully established in the course of the process of industrialisation in the nineteenth century. The relations between members of a family were not or hardly regulated according to criteria of supply and demand, exchange and competition. On the contrary, the family was held together by ties which differed greatly from the principles of a market economy: personal dominance of one personality and loyalty, partly due to natural differences or inequalities and ties, partly to tradition and partly to emotional relations of the most complex kind. The claim of the bourgeois capitalist system to offer its members equal rights and opportunities, to secure individual freedom and distribute opportunities according to individual performance was not parallelled by any similar claim on the part of the family. Market processes were based on contracts much more than family life, which tended to be informal, generally very personal and transparent, while the market economy was highly formalised, quite impersonal and not very transparent. The family also differed from the market in the multi-dimensional and comprehensive nature of its functions and the greater diffusion of its internal structure. The market was characterised by the primacy of economic considerations and greater specification. Considered in terms of their basic features and typical examples the family and the market, the family and the capitalist economic order can be seen to have been and to be very different.

Although these characteristics appear most clearly in the middle class family which began to emerge in the eighteenth century and became fully established in the

---

1 M. Weber: Die protestantische Ethik und der Geist des Kapitalismus. Here quoted from ibid.: Die protestantische Ethik, ed. J. Winckelmann. Siebenstern Taschenbuch 53, Munich, Hamburg, 1965, pp. 29-114; J. A. Schumpeter: Kapitalismus, Sozialismus und Demokratie. Munich, 1972³; E. J. Hobsbawm: Die Blütezeit des Kapitals. Eine Kulturgeschichte der Jahre 1848-1875. Munich, 1977, pp. 284-299. – The basic idea is developed in: J. Kocka: Family and Bureaucracy in German Industrial Management, 1850-1914: Siemens in Comparative Perspective, in: Business History Review, Vol. 45 (1971), pp. 133-156.

nineteenth, some of them are also observable, occasionally in a weaker form, in families of an earlier age or other social groups, for instance the nobility and the crafts in the early modern age. But I do not wish to go into that, or the genesis of this family structure, in more detail here.[2] We can take it that the middle class family preceded industrial capitalism, which with its main characteristics – private ownership of the means of production, private enterprise, de-central investment decisions oriented to market conditions, competition and profit considerations, wage-work and the concentration of production in factories, in mechanical processes – did not become fully established in Germany until the second third of the nineteenth century.

The main argument of this article is that family structures, processes and resources furthered the break-through of industrial capitalism and helped to solve problems of (capitalist) industrialisation which could hardly have been solved otherwise.[3] This can be seen particularly clearly with problems during the first half or perhaps the first two thirds of the nineteenth century. How the family helped to solve many of these problems will be discussed in sections 1 to 5; section 6 considers what qualities made the family capable of fulfilling economic functions of this kind. Section 7 discusses some of the tensions which arose as the families became involved in the development of industrial capitalism. It also, conversely, dicusses some of the frictions which arose in enterprises through their family ties. The conclusion outlines some of the results and sketches some of the changes which can be traced in the relation between the family and industrial capitalism after the first phase of industrialisation from the 1830s to the 1870s (the "Industrial Revolution"), which, with its precursors, is the main focus of attention here.

I. Motivation and Legitimation

It is not a matter of course but for a successful process of industrialisation it is necessary that a considerable number of persons who are capable of doing so should want to become entrepreneurs. There are certain objective conditions which will greatly facilitate this: the availability of economic opportunities, a shortage of alternative ways of achieving social and economic success, the weakness of legal barriers, acknow-

---

2 For an introduction see M. Mitterauer and R. Sieder: Vom Patriarchat zur Partnerschaft. Zum Strukturwandel der Familie. Munich, 1977. D. Schwab: Art "Familie", in: O. Brunner et al. (ed.): Geschichtliche Grundbegriffe. Historisches Lexikon zur politisch-sozialen Sprache in Deutschland, Vol. 2, Stuttgart, 1975, pp. 253–301. On the family in the nobility: H.-G. Reif: Westfälischer Adel 1770–1860. Vom Herrschaftsstand zur regionalen Elite. Göttingen, 1979. On the older craft families especially: H. Möller: Die kleinbürgerliche Familie im 18. Jahrhundert. Verhalten und Gruppenkultur. Berlin 1969. See also material in: H. Rosenbaum (ed.): Familie und Gesellschaftsstruktur (seminar). Frankfurt 1978.

3 The opposite argument predominates in some of the literature on the history of enterprises and modernisation, e. g. Th. C. Cochran: The Entrepreneur in Economic Change, in: Explorations in Entrepreneurial History, Vol. 3, 1965/66, pp. 25–38, esp. pp. 26 f., 28, 36 (on the dis-functional role of the family in economic growth); D. S. Landes: French Business and the Businessman (1951), in: H. G. Aitkens (ed.): Exploration in Enterprise, Cambridge/Mass., 1965, pp. 184–200. Generally on the negative assessment of ascriptive and traditional elements in economic growth: B. F. Hoselitz: Wirtschaftliches Wachstum und sozialer Wandel. Berlin, 1969, esp. pp. 16 ff., 114 ff.

ledgement or at least tolerance of independent, profitoriented commercial activity in the dominant scale of values. There was no lack of these conditions in Germany. A wide range of subjective motives can be established for the decision to found an enterprise or take one over in the early phase of industrialisation: the desire for growing or regular profits to ward off current or threatening need or improve one's living, the desire to work independently, be one's own master, to be able to create something or exercise power, and the intention to lead a righteous and proper life, one which would be pleasing in the eyes of God.

Here I want to stress another motive which occurs frequently in the sources, although it is often interwoven with others: the desire to succeed as an entrepreneur, despite many obstacles, in order to help the family or needy relations. When – as frequently happened – a bourgeois or petty bourgeois family was threatened with poverty or decline after the early death of the head of the household or both parents, the elder son often justified his decision to go into business by the need to care for his younger brothers and sisters who were not yet old enough to work, indeed altogether by the desire to establish the family name. Alfred Krupp and Werner Siemens in the 1820s and 1840s are the most prominent examples of this. In other constellations a sense of identity with the family had a similar motivating effect.[4]

It is even more significant that after the firm was successfully established and material prosperity assured, the need for personal security well covered and social recognition achieved most entrepreneurs still continued to work; they strove for expansion, struggled, fought, made sacrifices, generally until their heirs took over or until their death, in other words they did what a quickly growing, industrial capitalist economy needed them to do. Of course there were objective conditions which favoured this but – from the point of view of the individual entrepreneur – there was no compulsion. A very pleasant "rentier" existence was one of many alternatives available during those decades to a man who had some property or state securities. Why did most of the entrepreneurs go on working, struggling, investing to expand? One motive occurs again and again in the sources: it was not primarily for themselves but for the family that the enterprise was to continue and expand. The family gave an added dimension and significance to the work. It was for the good of their children and grandchildren or – more fundamental and more abstract – for the family name, a collective identity which stretched through several generations and on into the future. This not only justified the efforts the entrepreneur himself put into the business, it also justified his demanding that others – members of the family or employees – should subordinate their individual interests to those of the firm, at least to a certain extent. Orientation to the family and its future development also enabled the entrepreneur to take a long-term view of things and made it easier for him to renounce short-term speculative advantages. He could organise his business in such a way that it probably would survive his death (making it more "objective" through the appropriate business regulations, changes in the legal form and the appropriate provisions in the will). The family united past, present and future. It provided an important ideological base for the gradual emancipation of the business from the current needs of the founder and head of the firm, a process frequently observed in the literature on later manage-

---

4 See J. Kocka: Entrepreneurs and Managers in German Industrialization, in: CEHE, Vol. VII/I, Cambridge 1978, pp. 527–536.

56   Jürgen Kocka

rial enterprises. As we see it also occurred, even though for different reasons, in large family businesses in the first phase of industrialisation. There can be no doubt of the economic efficiency of such a family orientation. Among other things, it served as an incentive and a legitimation for the reinvestment of a large part of the profit instead of distributing it for the sustenance of various members of the family.[5]

II. Motivation and Qualification

Even if family advantage was not an explicit aim of the entrepreneur, and the desire for profit, ambition or love of power and independence were the main driving forces, this motivation was itself a product of the family background. Insofar, the upbringing and education provided by the family must be seen as a contribution to the emergence of the business. For a closer analysis of this we should concentrate on the types of family from which the early entrepreneurs – nearly all male – came: first on craftsmen's and artisans' families, second on those of merchants and putters-out, and thirdly, slowly increasing, on the families of factory entrepreneurs themselves.[6] The lower middle class families (of master artisans and small retailers) were still often characterised, during the period under review (the first half of the nineteenth century), by the integration of household and business. The children were brought up in the context of production and selling. Experience of real or threatening need, in his own family or among relations, was a formative experience for many a later entrepreneur who grew up under these circumstances, as was the experience of uncertainty, dependence on market conditions and changing circumstances. These were the decades when the guilds were being dissolved or loosened, when pauperism was on the increase and capitalist principles gained influence on production as well. In these families with their potential poverty or modest prosperity – good examples are the knife-maker, Henckel, in Solingen and the miller, Bienert, in Eschdorf in Saxony – the children were brought up in the intimate family circle, by their father (if he did not die early), by their mother, who was a strong influence and often took independent family decisions alongside the father, and, very important, by elder brothers and sisters. Grandparents living in the house are rarely mentioned. School, which a boy often left early to help in the business, played a smaller part. The influence of the family was intensive and it lasted for a long time, at any rate in the artisans' families which still followed the old tradition. Even the apprenticeship, which a boy might begin at the age of 12 or 14, was sometimes in his father's workshop, though more generally he was sent to another master. Even so, his education and training until he qualified as a journeyman would be in a family: that of the new master simply replaced that of his parents.

---

5 On principle issues: Schumpeter: Kapitalismus, loc. cit., p. 258 ff.; see also: H. Schelsky: Wandlungen der Familie in der Gegenwart. 2nd edition, 1954, p. 154; F. Oeter: Familie und Gesellschaft unter dem Einfluß des Industriekapitalismus, in: Schmollers Jahrbuch, Vol. 77, 1957, pp. 513–546, esp. p. 519. For Siemens cf. below p. 75. On Krupp: H. Witt: Die Triebkräfte des industriellen Unternehmertums vor hundert Jahren und heute. Hamburg, 1929, p. 97.

6 For a summary of the origin of the first generation of industrial entrepreneurs see Kocka: Entrepreneurs and Managers, loc. cit. pp. 510–11, 516–527.

Still, it is clear that only a small percentage of these families produced entrepreneurs (although conversely nearly half of the first generation of industrial entrepreneurs came from the families of master-artisans). And we may take it that the chance to rise to the position of entrepreneur and move beyond the traditional patterns of living and working of the artisan milieu, still oriented largely to pre-industrial principles such as the honour of the "Stand" and "sustenance" ("Nahrung"), came for those sons whose up-bringing had not exactly followed the traditional mode but had been driven somewhat off course by factors such as want, reversals of fortune, unfavourable market influences, sickness or the death of one or both parents or simply through unusual contacts. There is much to suggest that in times of change or want craftsmen's families may have produced many who slid down the social scale but they produced many entrepreneurs as well.[7]

The situation was different in the wealthy merchant and trading families like the Schramms in Hamburg or already established entrepreneurs' families like the Schoellers or Carstanjens in the Rhineland. Here parents and brothers and sisters handed on much of the up-bringing of the children to the nurse, the governess and later the tutor. But again the family influence was strong and intense in the early years, especially since, as it appears, uncles, aunts and grandparents also played a part. School did not begin to compete with family influence until the later stages and it was only after this that apprenticeship took the boy to a business associate's firm, that is further away from the parental sphere. Education for independence, for the search for new paths, the expansive achievement and vision was something which could be expected in the sons of more wealthy merchants and in the early entrepreneurs' families – together with an equally strong obligation to the traditional sense of honour, middle class solidarity and the proven forms of work. So the sons of these rising bourgeois families hardly needed to loosen family ties or break away from what they had been taught in order to achieve later success as an entrepreneur, as was sometimes the case in the artisan's world. In the biographies of the better-off bourgeois families we also find attention focussed on the education of the girls, most of whom later married into commercial families. They were given a thorough training in household skills, often a certain literary education and accustomed to their role of supporting their brothers and menfolk while taking a subsidiary position. They also helped in the office or with the accounts – before they married or if they remained single.[8]

So the field from which the first generation of industrial entrepreneurs were re-

---

7 Particularly Möller: Kleinbürgerliche Familie, loc. cit., R. Stadelmann and W. Fischer: Die Bildungswelt des deutschen Handwerkers um 1800, Berlin, 1955. H. Kelleter: Geschichte der Familie J. A. Henckels in Verbindung mit einer Geschichte der Solinger Industrie. Solingen, 1924, p. 125 ff.; on G. T. Bienert (1813–1894) see E. Dittrich (ed.): Lebensbilder Sächsischer Wirtschaftsführer. Leipzig, 1941, pp. 58–73. On education also: H. Beau: Das Leistungswissen des frühindustriellen Unternehmertums in Rheinland und Westfalen, Cologne, 1959, pp. 25 ff.; see also G. Tietz, Hermann Tietz: Geschichte einer Familie und ihrer Warenhäuser. Stuttgart, 1965, p. 20 f., on the great importance of the family of a small Jewish carter for the education and training of the son, the later founder of a department store, Oscar Tietz.

8 Cf. P. E. Schramm: Neun Generationen 1648–1948. Dreihundert Jahre deutscher Kulturgeschichte im Lichte der Schicksale einer Hamburger Bürgerfamilie (1648–1948). Vol. I, Göttingen, 1963. Esp. p. 206 ff., p. 238 ff.; R. v. Carstanjen: Geschichte der Duisburger Familie Carstanjen, Cologne, 1934; B. Nadolny: Felix Heinrich Schoeller und die Papiermacherkunst in Düren. Ein

cruited – the petty bourgeois or bourgeois families, most of them Protestant and engaged in small and medium-sized businesses, was actually highly differentiated. But in every case the family was the strongest influence in childhood and early youth; this was the major factor in the later choice of occupation. There was always a strong integration of education and work; these children were indoctrinated at a very early age with a respect for independent work which was quite un-feudal and often had a religious dimension, independent work either as a means of earning an honourable living or as a satisfactory means of individual achievement in competition with others and in the battle against circumstances. The stress on the fulfilment of duty, on order and punctuality was common to all these families; the dominant position of the father was hardly questioned and the children were expected to be obedient, if necessary this was strictly enforced. At least in the commercial families of the middle and upper bourgeoisie this was combined, though often not without contradictions, with education to a sense of responsibility and independence. Permissive or indifferent, hedonistic or playful, culturally refined or intellectual, impinged with doubt or uncertainty, pessimistic or sceptical – family education for the first generation of industrial entrepreneurs was none of these. It was oriented right from the start and quite wholeheartedly to the sons' later economic activity. This was taken as a matter of course and generally desired. Certainly, in the merchant and entrepreneurial families it was assumed that one of the sons, generally the oldest, would take over the business. But it was not only the oldest who was seen as a future entrepreneur and appropriately motivated, the younger sons as well, though perhaps to a lesser extent and certainly in the early bourgeois families, were expected to go into business. They may have become partners in the family firm or – using their share of the inheritance and other help from the family – joined another firm or opened their own business.

On the one hand these early craft, commercial and entrepreneurial families did not see themselves as a transitional phase which the children would soon leave to move into a non-commercial sphere. It was a rising class, optimistic, increasingly self-confident. On the other hand, there was still a considerable objective and subjective gap separating them from the leading groups in agriculture, the bureaucracy, the army and cultural life. Unfortunately we do not have good quantitative studies of what occupations the offspring of these groups took up. Stahl established that 67% of the sons of a selection of successful founders of enterprises worked as entrepreneurs themselves, about three quarters of these had inherited their father's business or a share in it and the others worked elsewhere.[9]

This inheritance rate can certainly be regarded as high and it was the result not only of the successful motivation of the male progeny but also other factors which were due to the family background and up-bringing: specific skills and qualifications, for

Lebensbild aus der Gründerzeit. Baden-Baden, 1957. F. Zunkel: Der rheinisch-westfälische Unternehmer 1834–1879. Ein Beitrag zur Geschichte des deutschen Bürgertums im 19. Jahrhundert. Cologne-Opladen, 1962, esp. pp. 69ff., 111 ff.; and F. Decker: Die betriebliche Sozialordnung der Dürener Industrie im 19. Jahrhundert. Cologne, 1964, esp. pp. 115ff.; L. Beutin: Die märkische Unternehmerschaft in der frühindustriellen Zeit, in: Westfälische Forschungen. Vol. 10, 1957, pp. 64–74, esp. p. 69; W. Köllmann: Sozialgeschichte der Stadt Barmen im 19. Jahrhundert. Tübingen, 1960, p. 111 ff.

9 W. Stahl: Der Elitekreislauf in der Unternehmerschaft. Eine empirische Untersuchung für den deutschsprachigen Raum. Frankfurt/Zurich, 1973, p. 287 f.

example. It is difficult here to separate the role of motivation from the role of qualification. Neither before nor after this period did the family ever make such a decisive contribution to the professional qualification of entrepreneurs as in the first decades of the nineteenth century. For the traditional means of acquiring qualifications outside the family – on the basis of the guilds and corporations – had been weakened by the liberal economic reforms of the turn of the century. State provision of commercial education and training in schools was developing only slowly and markets for special skills and knowledge had hardly developed. It was still hardly possible to generalise qualifications and even less to build up theories about them – in the extreme case they were still closely guarded secrets – and hence they had to be handed on personally, through demonstration and imitation. All this goes far to explain the dominant role of the family in handing on qualification and training and hence in qualifying the first generation of industrial entrepreneurs.

The role of the family was particularly important in the provision of *technical* skills; this was especially the case for the sons of craftsmen who, when they became entrepreneurs, generally worked in industries which were the same or closely related to that in which their fathers (had) worked.[10] But the sons of great merchants also derived from their background the commercial qualifications which they needed most: they absolved their apprenticeship in the offices of one of their relations, were sent on trips abroad and enabled to build up contacts; their first job was in the enterprise of a business associate or friend, or they went into their father's firm, at first as a privileged employee and later as co-owners. The influence of the family was even stronger in the case of the sons of manufacturers or factory owners, especially where they were regarded as future heirs. Their education was often specifically designed with the later function in mind, carefully planned and varied to provide experience in many different departments of their father's business or in that of a relative or associate.[11]

So what the early entrepreneurs learned from their fathers' generation – mainly from their fathers themselves – in other words, what they acquired through family channels and not market mechanisms gave them a tremendous advantage over other members of their generation when they had to compete – now generally according to market criteria – for access to enterprises or resources to found a business.

III. Capital Formation

If the laws of inheritance or provisions in a will did not introduce modifications the same applied as to money and property: what the fathers' generation had achieved through work, performance and favourable circumstances – often in market pro-

10 See Beau: Leistungswissen, loc. cit., pp. 13–15.
11 In addition to the works by Beau already mentioned (esp. pp. 13–27), Beutin (p. 70f.), Decker (p. 114f.), Köllmann (p. 112), Schramm (p. 177, 238f.) and Zunkel (p. 72ff.) see also F. Hellwig: Unternehmer und Unternehmungsform im saarländischen Industriegebiet, in: Jahrbücher für Nationalökonomie und Statistik, Vol. 158, 1943, pp. 402–430, esp. p. 408; A. Eyberg: Umwelt und Verhalten der Unternehmer des Oberbergischen Kreises im 19. Jahrhundert. Thesis, Cologne, 1955, p. 125f.; Witt: Triebkräfte, loc. cit., p. 103ff.; F. Redlich: Der Unternehmer. Göttingen, 1964, p. 328.

cesses – was handed on to the children through non-market mechanisms, i.e. within the family, and became an *ascribed* advantage for the new generations, to be used in market and competition processes of very varying kinds.[12]

The most obvious cases of inherited advantages are those of the heirs to enterprises. As however industrial enterprises during the Industrial Revolution rarely developed in a continuous process from pre-industrial craft shops or manufactories, these heirs constituted a very small minority, albeit a rapidly growing one, among the entrepreneurs of the Industrial Revolution. Kaelble has counted them in Berlin: among persons who had founded an enterprise in Berlin or taken one over up to 1835 they accounted for 14%; of those who joined this category between 1836 and 1850 28%; but 57% of those who joined the ranks of the entrepreneurs in Berlin from 1851 to 1873 had inherited. Altogether in Berlin as in Thuringia from 1830/40 to 1870/80 every third entrepreneur had inherited his business.[13]

But inheritance also played a large part in the establishment of new businesses, most of which were founded by the sons of master craftsmen or merchants. These persons could generally draw at least on a small inheritance – or they received a payment from their fathers out of the future patrimony to help them acquire the initial capital they needed.[14] This is one of the main reasons why if not the heirs to enterprises, certainly the sons of independent craftsmen and merchants so clearly predominated in the early generation of industrial entrepreneurs. It is also one of the reasons why individual "dynasties" in the commercial middle class proved so prosperous, lasting from the pre-industrial age through the first decades of industrialisation and in some cases on into the twentieth century, even if they sometimes had to change enterprises, location and occasionally even industry.[15]

Which was the most important, the inheritance of money and property or the inheritance of qualifications and motivation can hardly be answered in general terms. The situation was different in the case of a smelting works, which cost between 200,000 and 300,000 Thalers around 1850, or a combined blast furnace and puddling works which cost 1 million, than for the 60,000 Thalers which a medium-sized mechanical engineering factory cost or the 15,000 to 50,000 needed to start a mechanised spinning works or weaving shed or a paper mill.[16] However, we know from a sample

---

12 Generally J. Kocka: Stand – Klasse – Organisation. Strukturen sozialer Ungleichheit in Deutschland vom späten 18. bis zum frühen 20. Jahrhundert im Aufriss, in: H.-U. Wehler (ed.): Klassen in der europäischen Sozialgeschichte. Göttingen, 1979, p. 140 f.

13 See H. Kaelble: Berliner Unternehmer während der frühen Industrialisierung. Herkunft, sozialer Status und politischer Einfluß. Berlin, New York, 1972. p. 55, 123 (the figures on Thuringia are from W. Huschke).

14 Examples in P. Coym: Unternehmensfinanzierung im frühen 19. Jahrhundert. – dargestellt am Beispiel der Rheinprovinz und Westfalen. Thesis, Hamburg, 1971, p. 37 f.; L. Baar: Die Berliner Industrie in der industriellen Revolution, Berlin, 1966, p. 144 f. and in most entrepreneurial histories.

15 See e. g. H. Mönnich: Aufbruch ins Revier. Aufbruch nach Europa. Hoesch 1875–1971. Munich, 1971, p. 61 ff., 91 ff.; H. Kelleter and E. Poensgen: Die Geschichte der Familie Poensgen. Düsseldorf, 1908, p. 119 (the move by old entrepreneurial families from the Eifel or Düren to Dortmund and Düsseldorf in the middle of the nineteenth century).

16 Figures from W. Herrmann: Entwicklungslinien montanindustrieller Unternehmungen im rheinisch-westfälischen Industriegebiet. Dortmund, 1954, p. 15; A. Schröter and W. Becker: Die deutsche Maschinenbauindustrie in der industriellen Revolution. Berlin, 1962, p. 72; E. Klein: Zur Frage der Industriefinanzierung im frühen 19. Jahrhundert, in: H. Kellenbenz (ed.): Öffent-

of nineteenth and twentieth century entrepreneurs that over the longer term the sons and sons-in-law of owner-entrepreneurs very much more frequently (in 89% of the cases) became entrepreneurs than did the sons and sons-in-law of manager-entrepreneurs (only 21%). The majority of the sons of owner-entrepreneurs were heading the business which their fathers had owned or headed, while only the minority of the managers' sons were doing so.[17] Both of these categories of entrepreneurs' families must have passed on very similar kinds of qualification or the access to qualifications and "connections", style of living and so on but only the sons of owners will have inherited larger amounts of funds or property, the sons of managers will hardly have done this. We do not know for certain what occupations those young men who did not follow in their fathers' footsteps and go into industrial management took up, the results are only provisional as yet and not limited to the period of the Industrial Revolution. However this example suggests that the inheritance of property and fixed assets was of relatively greater importance in the assumption of an entrepreneurial position than the mere inheritance of qualifications and motivations.

Capital to found an enterprise, to operate one or expand it was often acquired through marriage with the daughter of a wealthy family who brought a dowry and access to further credit facilities or – less frequent – through marriage of one's daughter to a man who had capital at his disposal and would perhaps come into the business as a partner. The social endogamy rate was high among the sons and daughters of entrepreneurs and there were many and intricate marriage ties between the great entrepreneurial families. Indeed marriage ties can be seen as family mechanisms of capital retention in wealthy families before joint stock companies became generally established and modern company law developed. They counteracted the tendency to divide the accumulated wealth inherent in the inheritance laws and practice.[18]

Even where there was no inheritance or dowry, or where these were inadequate or already used up, members of the family would often make payments to make up the capital needed to start a business or finance the investment which became needed as it developed or to bridge the occasional bottleneck. That applied in the first instance of course to the families of the owners or shareholders of firms who used their other income, their reserves and savings and if necessary were prepared to make sacrifices in their personal lives to enable the business to go on. It also applied to loans and deposits by brothers and sisters, parents and grandparents, brothers-in-law, uncles and aunts and cousins of all kinds. The literature and sources contain plenty of evidence of this. An American study has quantified: in Poughkeepsie in New York, a medium-sized trading town, of 249 enterprises between 1850 and 1880 (to the value of at least 1000 dollars) 153 (61%) had acquired their capital entirely or partly from relations of

---

liche Finanzen und privates Kapital im späten Mittelalter und in der ersten Hälfte des 19. Jahrhunderts. Stuttgart, 1971, p. 118–128, esp. 119f.

17 From figures and calculations by Stahl: Elitenkreislauf, loc. cit., p. 309f.

18 On the marriage ties between great entrepreneurial families see below. On the accumulation of capital through marriage generally see the study of Boston merchants in the 18th century: P. D. Hall: Family Structure and Economic Organization. Massachusetts Merchants, 1700–1850, in: T. K. Hareven (ed.): Family and Kin in Urban Communities 1700–1930. New York/London, 1977, p. 38–61, here p. 41 ff. More detailed studies on the marriage and investment policy of the great commercial families and the practices and effects of inheritance which go beyond studies of indiviual cases are urgently needed for Germany as well.

the owner(s), not including inheritances. It can be taken that members of families in comparable German cases were no less involved.[19]

The forms of financial involvement varied, ranging from fixed-interest credits to deposits with a share of the profits. Sometimes a guarantee was enough. Generally the credit was granted without a claim to co-direction or a share in the management being requested. Financial help from the family generally came without recourse to market criteria, or this did not play a primary role: the main motive was non-economic, family solidarity. Indeed, help from the family came even or because normal cover was not available, it was given on the basis of personal trust. Nor was the money withdrawn as soon as the business outlook worsened; close relations were prepared to help even when things seemed virtually hopeless. Many an enterprise only survived the initial turbulent period because it could rely on help like this, finance provided independent, indeed often in direct contravention, of capitalist rationality. As a whole, however, and over the longer term credits from relatives were not given contrary to market rationale. They were rarely given without financial considerations, certainly not by distant relatives. If the recipient was persistently unsuccessful there were requests for the money to be returned, sometimes justified by family considerations, too.[20] Nevertheless, loans and deposits from relatives were of inestimable value as there were hardly any alternative sources of funds – there was no developed capital market, for example, nor were there a powerful banking system or joint stock companies, and often the risk did appear to be too great for money to be lent according to purely economic considerations. Trust and loyalty were a necessary basis, from a non-capitalist source.[21] If he were not a member of a large family the early industrial entrepreneur had a hard time of it.

IV. Management

In the same way family resources were used to solve problems of industrial management which could not have been satisfactorily solved in any other way. The recruitment, motivation and control of senior staff was a real problem for German entrepreneurs around 1850, especially in large companies with several plants which may well have been far apart. The career and occupation of senior employees in industry were not yet clearly profiled. There was no developed market for managerial staff. The

19 S. and C. Griffen: Family and Business in a Small City: Poughkeepsie, New York, 1850–1880, in: Hareven (ed.): Family and Kin, p. 144–163, here p. 150. A few German cases in Coym: Unternehmensfinanzierung, loc. cit., p. 38 ff.

20 See the examples in W. Berdrow: Die Familie Krupp in Essen 1587–1887. Essen, 1932, p. 247 f. (Retraction of a contract handing over property to Friedrich Krupp by his mother and grandmother); pp. 296, 313. When Friedrich Krupp, aged 61, quite unexpectedly married a 21-year old girl considerable sums which had been lent by his in-laws were demanded back, completely ruining him. On this problem generally and on lawsuits between members of families see Griffen: Family and Business, loc. cit., p. 153 f.

21 Whether state credits could have helped here is doubtful. In practice they played a very minor role. See Coym: Unternehmensfinanzierung, loc. cit. p. 113 ff.; H. Winkel: Kapitalquellen und Kapitalverwendung am Vorabend des industriellen Aufschwungs in Deutschland, in: Schmollers Jahrbuch, Vol. 90/I (1970), p. 275–301, here p. 286 ff. (with a rather more favourable verdict).

work which the senior "official" in an enterprise had to do was complex, subject to rapid change, hard to standardise and hence difficult to control with bureaucratic methods. It could only be mastered with a certain independence. Particularly during the years when an enterprise was being built up the owner was often away on long business trips. If there was no other shareholder in the business the senior official had control. The employees who were in charge of a section which may have been a long way away from the centre, perhaps even abroad, were particularly hard to supervise: the post took a long time, there was no telephone and travelling was difficult.[22] All this goes to explain why the entrepreneurs of the Industrial Revolution esteemed the loyalty and honesty of their staff as highly as their technical qualification.

As far as possible posts which entailed decisionmaking functions were given to relatives. Often the first person to be appointed and paid a salary in an enterprise was a brother or nephew of the founder and the first manager his brother-in-law or cousin. When the diversification of the production programme created new management problems the entrepreneur may have reacted by building up a legally independent enterprise to produce the new article and putting a trustworthy (and not exactly inefficient) nephew or son at the head of it. Special work such as difficult business or discovery trips were, as far as possible, entrusted to the son. In all these cases business cohesion was intensified by family loyalty.[23] This helped to make constant control and regulation at least partly superfluous and achieve the necessary de-centralisation of responsibility and authority. In addition to contractual ties, financial interest and the authority of the head of the factory this form of extra-economic solidarity helped to ensure a measure of cohesion and cooperation in the management of the enterprise and largely contributed to the success which would otherwise have been hard to achieve in the initial period.

This applied to a particular degree to the management of the early "multinationals". The coordination of the three branches of the electrical concern Siemens & Halske in Germany, Russia and England was largely achieved through private correspondence and the trust between the three Siemens brothers, Werner (in Berlin), Carl

---

22 Around 1820 the Solingen knife-manufacturer Henckels needed between two and three weeks for his trip to Berlin, where he had set up a sales branch which was soon taken over by his son (Kelleter: Henckels, p. 127). In 1854 a letter from Berlin to St. Petersburg took a fortnight. The head office of Siemens & Halske was in Berlin and the company had set up a branch in St. Petersburg, which was soon taken over by the brother of the founder. See the letter from Werner Siemens, 16.6.1854, in: F. Heintzenberg (ed.): Aus einem reichen Leben. Werner von Siemens in Briefen an seine Familie und an Freunde. Stuttgart, 1953, p. 90.

23 See J. Kocka: Unternehmensverwaltung und Angestelltenschaft am Beispiel Siemens 1847–1914. Stuttgart 1969, p. 82 f.; Decker: Betriebliche Sozialordnung, loc. cit. p. 19 (on cases in Düren); an impressive account of the establishment of a department store "concern" on a family basis is in Tietz: Hermann Tietz, loc. cit., p. 19–33; Kaelble: Berliner Unternehmer, loc. cit., p. 57 f.; G. Goldbeck: Kraft für die Welt, 1864–1964. Klöckner-Humboldt-Deutz AG. Düsseldorf/Vienna, 1964 (cases of relatives travelling for the firm); for similar material: H. Kelleter and E. Poensgen: Geschichte, loc. cit., p. 110. And: Mönnich: Aufbruch ins Revier, loc. cit., pp. 62 and 91 (on Hoesch); Kelleter,: Henckels, loc. cit., p. 129 ff.; Berdrow: Familie Krupp, loc. cit., pp. 296, 306 f., 310, 349 ff. – see Schramm: Neun Generationen, loc. cit., p. 272, 365 – the de-centralisation of a business into two legally independent units in 1805/6 and its re-unification soon after on a family basis. On management organisation on family lines in British industry see S. Pollard: The Genesis of Modern Management. London, 1965, p. 145 ff.; in general: W. A. Lewis: Die Theorie des wirtschaftlichen Wachstums, Tübingen 1956, p. 125 f.; A. Marshall: Industry and Trade. London, 1959, p. 326.

(in St. Petersburg) and William (in London). Each directed his branch without over-frequent reference to the others. The loyalty of the brothers to each other was the most important base which held the business together. Conflict broke out when one of the brothers left his branch or lost his influence for some other reason. These personal methods of coordination achieved only a loose connection between the individual parts of the enterprise, which remained largely autonomous. But as long as it sufficed, family loyalty was a very fine tool with which to achieve the goal – it was cheap and accessible.[24] Most of the early enterprises were partnerships. Relations were preferred for partnership required trust and cooperation which was most likely between relatives. In Poughkeepsie, New York, between 1850 and 1880 48% of partnerships were between relatives.[25] There is nothing to suggest that comparable figures for German cities would be lower if we knew them. We do know that German entrepreneurs made their sons or sons-in-law partners in their business at a very early age.[26]

Family relationships also facilitated cooperation between enterprises. They provided a basis for early cartel-type agreements. Carefully planned marriages between the sons and daughters of the great entrepreneurial families created a complex network of connections, making the businesses like great concerns, links which could have been neither created nor maintained in those days in any other way.[27]

V. Connections and the Formation of a Class

It would be wrong to interpret the many marriage ties between the great entrepreneurial families exclusively with regard to their direct economic functions, the formation of capital and concerns. They also, like the family relations of the early entrepre-

24 See Kocka: Unternehmensverwaltung, loc. cit., pp. 76, 82, 132 f., 207, 253; S. v. Weiher: Die Entwicklung der englischen Siemens-Werke und des Siemens-Überseegeschäftes in der zweiten Hälfte des 19. Jahrhunderts. Thesis, Freiburg, 1959; ibid.: Carl von Siemens 1829–1906. Ein deutscher Unternehmer in Russland und England, in: Tradition, Vol. I, 1956, pp. 13–25.

25 Griffen: Family and the Kin, loc. cit., p. 156 f. According to Beau: Leistungswissen, loc. cit., p. 69, of 400 enterprises in North Rhine-Westphalia between 1790 and 1870 266 were headed by a technician and a merchant (partnerships) together.

26 In the sample given by Stahl (Elitenkreislauf, loc. cit., p. 241), owner-entrepreneurs of the second or a later generation became shareholders in a family business on average at the age of 24. See below and Note 62.

27 See Hellwig: Unternehmer, loc. cit., p. 429 for cartel-like agreements in the Saarland. See also Decker: Betriebliche Sozialordnung der Dürener Industrie, loc. cit., p. 113 f.: "In 1754 Anna Katharina Deutgen, daughter of the iron manufacturer Eberhard Deutgen, married Hugo Ludolf Hoesch, the head of the Düren Hoesch family. The Deutgen family was also linked by marriage with the Schüll and Wergifosse families. There were also many links between the Hoesch and Schüller families. Marriages between the Düren industrialists' families had become so frequent in the course of the centuries that industry in Düren in the nineteenth century can be described as one huge family concern. Indeed family relations worked like business relations, and in many cases they gave rise to groups of companies which functioned like concerns and included plants both in the same and different industries. One of these groups was formed by the marriages of the five daughters of Hugo Ludolf Hoesch, all of whom married leading industrialists in the metal industry. In the second half of the nineteenth century further families joined the network. Often these were young technicians and merchants, like Gustav Renker, Ernst Grebel, Richard Rhodius and so on who obtained work in Düren and then married the daughters of industrialists."

neurs in general, fulfilled important social functions as well, although these were certainly of relevance for the business. It is sometimes overlooked[28] that the entrepreneur could not as a rule act as an isolated individualist or achieve his success as a lonely genius. Of course a streak of individualism was needed, a desire for independence, an ability to look beyond what the majority thought, felt and desired – in other words a little distance. But more than anything the entrepreneur needed contacts. With no highly developed school or publication system he needed relations, friends and acquaintances for an exchange of experience. Without a very well developed communications system, without a specialised press or special correspondents, without the experts who later did nothing in the business but collect information, the early entrepreneur needed personal contracts if he was ever to recognise business opportunities of various kinds at all.[29] The low degree of insitutionalisation in the commercial and trading sphere, the weight placed on the person and his known and acknowledged qualities in the granting of credit, the attraction of qualified staff and obtaining major contracts – all this meant that the entrepreneur had to be known: not necessarily to the public at large but in not too small a circle of persons who were engaged in business, and to whom he had to be known as trustworthy and reliable.

The entrepreneur of the Industrial Revolution had also to rely on other entrepreneurs in order to implement interests which could only be represented collectively, with regard to state legislation and administration and increasingly in relations with the workforce. We need only recall the customs legislation of the "Vormärz" and the early strikes, which by the 1840s at the latest had provoked collective answers from the employers. But the means for collective interest representation were not well developed: older forms of the organisation of joint interests (guilds, corporations) had weakened since the reforms of the turn of the century. New forms of organisation (industry associations, employers' associations) only slowly emerged and they took some time to grow in influence; it was not until the second half of the nineteenth century and particularly after the 1870s that they were really effective. There were of course no special schools for entrepreneurs. Up to the 1870s/1880s very few went to the universities with their student fraternities. Only the mining sector, which had been in state ownership for a long time, had its own academies. Nor did military experience count for much, in the Rhineland military service was avoided as far as possible up to the time of the foundation of the Reich.

Beside church and communal organisations – and more than these – it was the family in the widest sense, the relations or "class" who provided the social contacts necessary to fulfil these various needs. Networks of family relationships provided contacts which went beyond the individual entrepreneur and enterprise, loyalties

---

28 See A. Gerschenkron: Social Attitudes, Entrepreneurship and Economic Development, in: Explorations in Entrepreneurial History, Vol. 6, 1953/4, pp. 1–19, here p. 13: the view of the entrepreneur as particularly lacking in tradition and relations.

29 See Redlich: Der Unternehmer, loc. cit., p. 186; R. Engelsing: Bremisches Unternehmertum, in: Schriften der Wittheit zu Bremen II, Bremen, Hannover, 1958, pp. 7–112, here p. 49. This is the great economic significance of belonging to religious minorities which were socially closely linked but geographically widely distributed. Cf. on the Jewish case D. S. Landes: The Bleichröder Bank: An Interim Report, in: Publications of the Leo Baeck Institute. Year Book 5, 1960, pp. 201–220 and a major study by Werner E. Mosse on the German-Jewish bourgeoisie in the nineteenth and early twentieth centuries to be finished shortly. See also below Note 50.

66   Jürgen Kocka

and a sense of belonging together which the business could not adequately supply but which it needed.

A large number of children and a high endogamy rate were the most important prerequisites for the emergence of this family network. The great majority of entrepreneurs' sons married daughters of the middle and upper commercial classes and a large minority or even a majority of entrepreneurs' daughters married sons of the same group. Five out of seven leading entrepreneurs in Leipzig in the 1840s had mothers who came from entrepreneurs' families; five of them in turn married entrepreneurs' daughters. Of 17 leading businessmen's sons who married in Bielefeld between 1830 and 1910 (a random sample), twelve, i. e. a good 70%, married the daughters of businessmen. Four out of the 17 brides were the daughters of public servants, one, in the Wilhelmine Reich, was the daughter of a land-owner. Conversely, of the daughters of Berlin entrepreneurs in the 1850s and 1860s 65% married into commercial families, most of them the sons of merchants, factory owners and bankers. Here too public servants, ministers of the church, officers and independent scholars formed the second largest group of origin.[30]

As marriage may have loosened ties to the parental family but hardly dissolved them, networks of relationships and loyalties were built up and could be mobilised when needed (to provide information, testimonies of character, for help in presenting a petition, in the formation of busines ties, when an employee was needed or help to acquire capital), especially since the help did not entail too much in the way of input or sacrifice on the part of the "son-in-law", "cousin" or "uncle" – the terms were very generally used. In any case the looser relationships would hardly have offered an adequate base for more.[31]

The marriage patterns also show how the middle and upper commercial classes cut themselves off from the lower classes or groups – manual workers and the lower classes altogether, those engaged in agriculture and small craftsmen or traders. On the other hand they had, at least at first, little contact with the aristocracy or the major land-owners. Their marriage ties reflected and encouraged the formation of the bourgeoisie as a class. A more frequent move was into the educated middle classes. It was only in the later decades, in the Rhineland after about 1870, that more mobility developed in marriage between the major entrepreneurs and the aristocracy or major land-owners, in keeping with the process of assimilation between the bourgeoisie and the old ruling class.[32]

The marriage patterns of the commercial bourgeoisie would need a closer examination. Here I can only point out that with the geographical expansion of markets

---

30 See H. Zwahr: Zur Klassenkonstituierung der deutschen Bourgeoisie, in: Jahrbuch für Geschichte, Vol. 18, 1978, pp. 21–83, here p. 28 (figures on Leipzig); the Bielefeld figures are calculated by K. Ditt; also cf. J. Kocka et al.: Familie und soziale Plazierung, Opladen 1980, Berlin figures from Kaelble: Berliner Unternehmer, loc. cit., p. 185.

31 The history of every enterprise, which does not completely ignore family relations, contains a large number of such cases. Cf. B. Berdrow: Familie Krupp, on the 7th and 8th generation (Friedrich und Alfred Krupp), esp. pp. 240, 245 f., 276 f., 282 ff., 287 f., 290, 293 f., 296 f. (for a crisis in these relations), 299, 300 f., 305 f., 309 ff., 316 ff., 349 ff., 352.

32 See Zunkel: Der rheinisch-westfälische Unternehmer, pp. 110 ff.; Zwahr: Klassenkonstituierung, loc. cit., pp. 41 f. (on Saxony); M. Barkhausen: Der Aufstieg der rheinischen Industrie im 18. Jahrhundert und die Entstehung eines industriellen Großbürgertums, in: Rheinische Vierteljahrsblätter, Vol. 19, 1954, pp. 135–178, esp. p. 174.

and commercial activities the geographical range of the potential marriage market also expanded. The rather local limits of the seventeenth and eighteenth centuries widened, however strong regional accents remained even in the nineteenth century.[33]

The mutual preference of two or three commercial families in marrying their offspring has frequently been shown, especially in the eighteenth century. P. E. Schramm has described how three wholesale firms in Hamburg grew together in this way to a "business clan", continuing to put chances in each other's way. Between the Krefeld silk manufacturers, von der Leyen, and the Cologne bankers Herstatt there were five marriages in two generations in the late eighteenth and early nineteenth centuries and of course intensive business relations.[34] These strong inter-relations suggest a careful marriage strategy observing economic considerations as well as family interests. They seem to have become less frequent in the nineteenth century. In the same way it can be seen that, especially in the textile industry, what had been a frequent conjunction of marriage and industry[35] became rarer. Both suggest that the social and only indirectly economic ends and functions of these networks of relations moved into the foreground – contacts, loyalties, information, collective interests, the emergence of supraregional groups or class cohesion – and the direct economic aims (capital concentration, the formation of "concerns" on family bases) became less important in the course of the 19th century.

These family networks were not sharply delineated. They were relatively unstructured and flexible. In the case of the Krupps, for instance, the contact with the big families with whom there had been close ties in the eighteenth century were largely broken off by the 1820s but an important new network was being created through new marriages.[36] Business clans of this kind and prominent groups linked by many inter-marriages and relationships on the local level could take in "new blood" if it appeared economically and socially necessary. Often cooptation into a family (sometimes the way was prepared by acting as godfather) was followed by economic suc-

---

33 The expansion beyond local areas is stressed by Zunkel after the second half of the nineteenth century. Der rheinisch-westfälische Unternehmer, loc. cit., p. 19 f., P. 13–22 contain a survey of important dynasties in the West German commercial bourgeoisie after the early modern age and shows that these generally successfully survived the first phase of industrialisation. One example of a close marriage network which extended beyond one industry but was geographically limited (for Hamburg up to the 1770s) is in Schramm: Neue Generationen, esp. p. 296 and pp. 252 f., 272 and 365. A case extending beyond regional boundaries from the same period is in Barkhausen: Aufstieg, loc. cit., p. 174, Note 27. For the marriage patterns of leading Leipzig industrialists, which went beyond regional limits but were concentrated in Saxony see Zwahr: Klassenkonstituierung, loc. cit., pp. 36–42. Hellwig: Unternehmer, loc. cit., p. 408–13, esp. p. 409 concentrates on the expansion of the marriage policy of industrialists in the Saar to the whole of the south west of Germany.

34 See Schramm: Neun Generationen, loc. cit., pp. 176, 255 ff.; Zunkel: Der rheinisch-westfälische Unternehmer, p. 21; similarly for the Saarland Hellwig: Unternehmer, p. 408.

35 See G. Adelmann: Die wirtschaftlichen Führungsschichten der rheinisch-westfälischen Baumwoll- und Leinenindustrie von 1850 bis zum Ersten Weltkrieg, in: H. Helbig (ed.): Führungskräfte der Wirtschaft im neunzehnten Jahrhundert 1790–1914, Part II, Limburg/Lahn, 1977, pp. 177–99, here p. 183; E. Dittrich: Vom Wesen sächsischen Wirtschaftsführertums in: ibid. (ed.): Lebensbilder sächsischer Wirtschaftsführer. Leipzig, 1941, p. 1–56, here p. 48 f. (on the textile industry). In Bielefeld they used to say "Linen to linen".

36 See Berdrow: Familie Krupp, pp. 284, 308. Generally on this social phenomenon see also Mitterauer/Sieder: Vom Patriarchat, loc. cit., p. 27.

68   Jürgen Kocka

cess.[37] On the other hand the family dimension meant that it was not possible to be fully accepted only on the grounds of economic success and that generally economic success and social standing – in cities like Hamburg and Barmen political power as well – went hand in hand.[38]

It was more difficult to get rid of members of the clan who were not pulling their weight. In this respect, the market mechanism, if left to itself, might have been more effective. Not even major Hamburg merchants always succeeded in getting rid of a ne'er-do-well son by despatching him to Surinam. It would appear that these families were very reluctant to disinherit. It was occasionally done and then justified with reference to the grandson.[39] But generally they went no further than threats. Clearly such a step, had it been taken more often, would have caused uncertainty and rancour, jeopardising family solidarity and perhaps the basis of the whole system.

VI. The Particular Qualities of Entrepreneurs' Families

It has been argued so far that mechanisms which were inherent to capitalism were clearly not enough for the solution of early industrial entrepreneurial problems and hence the establishment of industrial capitalism. In addition to other pre-capitalist structures, processes and resources the family played a considerable part in solving the business problems of the early industrial age. In many respects family loyalty, energy and resources functioned if not as a motor then as a vehicle of early industrial capitalist development.

The next paragraphs are meant to demonstrate that the families of the early industrial entrepreneurs which fulfilled these functions in part consciously and deliberately, but in part unconsciously and unintentionally, were a *form of transition* between the traditional "household" with the business and family under one roof and the later "middle class family".[40]

On the one hand they differed from the traditional farmers' and master artisans' families or those of the cottage workers in that the household and business were largely separate, a necessary consequence of the centralisation of production which became established with the breakthrough of industrialisation. For the family this brought a certain relief: there was no pressure, for instance, to fill all the family roles: the widow or widower could afford, if they wished, not to marry again.[41] The separa-

---

37 See Schramm: Neun Generationen, loc. cit., p. 264; Köllmann, Barmen, loc. cit., p. 112.

38 See Kocka: Stand – Klasse – Organisation, loc. cit., p. 138 f.

39 See Schramm: Neun Generationen loc. cit., pp. 248, 253; see also J. V. Bredt: Haus Bredt-Rübel: Geschichte des Hauses und seiner Bewohner. Wuppertal-Elberfeld, 1937. p. 43 ff.: the exclusion of two ne'er-do-well nephews from an inheritance, a decision which was to be re-examined and if possible revoked after six years.

40 The German concepts are "ganzes Haus" and "Hausgemeinschaft", translated here by "household", resp. "bürgerliche Familie", translated by "middle class family". On the choice of concepts see Mitterauer/Sieder, pp. 18–23, esp. p. 22 f.; O. Brunner: Das "Ganze Haus" und die alteuropäische "Ökonomik" in ibid.: Neue Wege der Verfassungs- und Sozialgeschichte, 2nd edition, Göttingen, 1968, pp. 103 ff.

41 An example of a widow who carried on the business until her son could take it over in R. L. Mehmke: Entstehung der Industrie und Unternehmertum in Württemberg, in: Deutsche

tion between household and business brought new chances and created qualities which had not been so strongly marked in the old farming or petty bourgeois households. Marriage and the family created for the entrepreneurs of the Industrial Revolution a protected, private sphere, in which moral self-realisation and emotional satisfaction were possible and "homely" pleasures could be enjoyed because the family was at a distance from the struggles of the business world and the storms of public life. Generally the young couple set up home immediately after marrying, even if the parents of one of them were in the vicinity and could have housed them. And if the son who married last and his wife did not leave the parental home and the widowed mother, the rooms and floors were carefully divided: the young family needed and were given their private quarters. The home was to be a secure refuge, where the "pains of the knocks and blows could be forgotten", a nest, from which the husband was repeatedly torn by "the inexorable demands of business" but to which he regularly returned to gather new strength.[42] However idealised and romantic this concept may have been the reality for the factory owner around 1850 was less of a contradiction to it than for the master artisan family as it had traditionally been and still was. The wife of the entrepreneur usually did not take part in her husband's business life as the farmer's wife, the master artisan's wife or the cottage worker's wife often did. Nor did the children have to work in the business, they grew up in the home and not in the workshop, even if in the first decades the factory owner's home was near the workshop, often on its site and only later, when the villa became attainable, in another quarter of the town and a better position. The people the husband worked with did not belong to the household nor to the family. When housekeeping books were kept they were clearly separate from the firm's accounts.

On the other hand, as we have seen, these families fulfilled many economic functions, their separation from the production and business sphere was not so marked as that of the public servant's family and certainly not that of the modern, twentieth century family which serves primarily reproductive, socialisation, consumption and leisure functions. A family could however only fulfil these economic functions if it had certain qualities inherited from the past. These have hardly been systematically researched and I can give here only some impressions and assumptions:

a) Only larger families could make the contributions to the management of enterprises and the formation of a social network as outlined here. In capital formation larger families were more likely to be able to help than smaller – and the families of most entrepreneurs were large. Four to eight children was the norm among seven leading entrepreneurs in Leipzig in 1840s.[43] Johann Gottfried Henckel, knife-maker and merchant in Solingen (1735–1811), was one of nine children of a father who himself had five brothers and sisters. Johann Gottfried founded his business, a supra-regional trade in metal goods and, although he married again a year after the death of

---

Zeitschrift für Wirtschaftskunde, Vol. 4, 1939, p. 113. See also E. Schmieder: Die wirtschaftliche Führungsschicht in Berlin 1790–1850, in: Helbig (ed.): Führungskräfte, pp. 1–58, here p. 57.
42 Quotations from letters by Werner Siemens to his fiancée and later wife in the 1850s, in: Heintzenberg (ed.): Aus einem reichen Leben, pp. 50, 77. On the way the "middle class family" of the nineteenth century saw itself see Schwab: Art "Familie", loc. cit., p. 293 ff. See Bredt: Haus Bredt-Rübel, p. 77 for a case in which the family of the younger son shared the same house but not the same household as the mother.
43 From Zwahr: Klassenkonstituierung, p. 28.

his first wife, had "only" four children. Of the two sons who carried on the business, one remained unmarried and childless – a rarity among entrepreneurs to the present day,[44] while the other, Johann Abraham Henckel (1771–1850), had eight children, among them three sons, one of whom died as a boy. The main heir, Johann Abraham (1813–1870) had fifteen children. Ten of them, some still living in the twentieth century, produced off-spring, altogether 31.[45] In a study of the "Deutsches Geschlechterbuch" (genealogy records) for Lower Saxony A. von Nell has shown that between 1750 and 1849 the families[46] of major entrepreneurs and merchants had on average 5.9 children and hence clearly surpassed the average family in the educated classes and the commercial petty bourgeoisie. It was not until c. 1850 that this figure declined, slowly at first and then rapidly after 1900.

b) Loosely tied and unstable families could hardly have fulfilled the functions we have outlined. The early industrial entrepreneurs' families in the narrower sense, the family which lived together under one roof, held together firmly. We can recognise four major reasons, four characteristics of these families, three of which are traditional and only one modern. First, one should stress the dominance of the father. These families had a clear centre of will and this was also the centre of direction of the firm. It was a dual role, the two aspects mutually supporting. As his family ties helped the entrepreneur in directing his firm, so his business influence helped the father in governing the family. He decided on the appointment of staff, the allocation of shares, he gave recommendations and made careers. Above all he also decided – within the broad legal limits – on the distribution of the patrimony. Tradition and custom supported his authority, as did ideology. And as long as political power in the public sphere was largely limited to the heads of household this also furthered the patriarchal, autocratic structure of the family. The head of the household and director of the firm was hence powerful enough to determine the use of family resources – within the limits set by law, tradition and custom. Certainly he decided on the education of the children, on whether relatives should live in the house and what servants should be appointed. He influenced the choice of occupation and marriage partner in the younger generation within limits which admittedly were shifting. He kept the family together; he brought up his children in this attitude of mind; he was generally powerful enough to enforce conformity to these ideals even against opposition. He did this from firm conviction and probably because he knew how well a properly functioning family served his dual role as head of the household and of the firm. The family was far too important an element in this complicated structure of personal, business and social relations to be left to itself. If necessary it was held together with pressure. The scope for individual members was very limited, and there was little room for nonconformism. The family as a unit ranked before its individual members, who of

---

44 Of 148 entrepreneurs in employment examined by Stahl (Elitenkreislauf, loc. cit., p. 302) in the 19th and 20th centuries only 7 were unmarried. On the present over-representation of married persons among entrepreneurs see B. Biermann: Die Sozialstruktur der Unternehmerschaft. Demographischer Aufbau, soziale Herkunft und Ausbildung der Unternehmer in NRW. Stuttgart, 1971, pp. 69–71.

45 From the family tree in Kelleter: Henckels, loc. cit.

46 More precisely "full marriages", those where the couples remain together until the end of the presumed fertility period of the wife (45 years of age). See A. von Nell: Die Entwicklung der generativen Strukturen bürgerlicher und bäuerlicher Familien von 1750 bis zur Gegenwart. Thesis, Bochum, 1973, p. 29.

course took very unequal parts in the definition of its aims. Generally the husband could rely on full support from his wife, he rarely encountered competition or criticism from her, for her position, self-awareness and satisfaction depended on family relationships to an even greater extent than his did. It would appear that during these decades women became more dependent and less influential the more the old links between the business and the family were broken. The housewife moved away from the world of business and work, without yet having full sovereignty in the house and the family.[47]

Second, the multiplicity of functions must be mentioned in order to explain what held these families together. It gave the family a central place in the thoughts and feelings of its members and supported a collective identity which went on from one generation to another. We have already considered many of these functions, the economic and educational particularly. There were many others. Religious observances were often largely in the family circle. Social life and games, music and other leisure pursuits were preferred at home. Family occasions such as marriages and christenings were great celebrations in the old middle and upper bourgeois families. On a wedding day the father might try his hand at writing a poem or the children would put on a play.[48] There were very few alternative means of entertainment – the father had access to some but generally these were much less highly developed than later and this lack of outside attractions strengthened the family.

There was also a shortage of alternatives in another respect. The belief must have gone very deep that in cases of individual misfortune or failure one could only expect help – to a better or worse degree – from the family. Only they would rescue a member from ultimate failure. In cases of bankruptcy and sickness, after accidents or the misfortunes of war the family came to the victim's aid as best they could.[49] Particularly during the first half of the nineteenth century there were hardly any other forms of protection or insurance, apart from the church and communal poor relief, and this must have seemed to most "respectable citizens" a nightmare and not a support.

---

47 For contrast see the extremely active, almost independent role played in the enterprise by the wife of Henckels in Solingen around 1815: Kelleter: Henckels, loc. cit., p. 129; the same applied to the wives of Hamburg merchants in the late 18th century: Schramm: Neun Generationen, p. 206; on the active roles played by the mother and grandmother of Alfred Krupp around 1800 see Berdrow: Familie Krupp, loc. cit., p. 247 f., 276. On the patriarchal role played by the father of the family in entrepreneurial households in the second third of the 19th century: Zunkel: Der rheinisch-westfälische Unternehmer, loc. cit., p. 73 f.; Köllmann: Barmen, loc. cit., p. 118; on the tradition of the patriarchal and autocratic head of the household: Möller: Kleinbürgerliche Familie, p. 10 ff. On the change in the role of women during the transition from the 18th to the 19th century see esp. K. Hausen: Die Polarisierung der "Geschlechtscharaktere" – eine Spiegelung der Dissoziation von Erwerbs- und Familienleben, in: W. Conze (ed.): Sozialgeschichte der Familie in der Neuzeit Europas. Stuttgart, 1976, pp. 367–93.

48 See the examples in Zunkel: Der rheinisch-westfälische Unternehmer, loc. cit., p. 71, 73; Berdrow: Familie Krupp, p. 284 (on the christening of Alfred Krupp in 1812); Schramm: Neun Generationen, p. 206 ff.

49 See G. Hahn: Untersuchungen über die Ursachen von Unternehmensmißerfolgen. Thesis, Cologne, 1956, p. 37 f.; Zunkel: Der rheinisch-westfälische Unternehmer, loc. cit., p. 73. On the objective limitations on the role of the family as support during the Napoleonic wars from 1806–15 see Schramm: Neun Generationen, p. 365. When Friedrich Krupp lost his house and his position in 1809 the young family moved into the mother's house, where other married brothers and sisters were living (Berdrow: Familie Krupp, p. 249). Paul Bredt moved back into his parents' house with his five children in 1879 when his wife died suddenly. See Bredt: Das Haus Bredt-Rübel, p. 85.

Since the reforms of the turn of the century guild and corporative institutions had been weakened and in some cases destroyed; new institutions of self-help were emerging only slowly; public insurance systems were not set up until the late nineteenth century and even then they did not include the bourgeoisie. One has to consider, however, whether during the first half of the century closely tied minorities, especially religious communities and sects did not develop a solidarity which functioned similarly to that of a family – perhaps even better – in providing a degree of protection and insurance, that they too formed social networks and helped to solve economic problems like those discussed above.[50]

Patriarchal authority and multi-functionality had strengthened and stabilised the middle class, farming and noble families for many generations. A third element now developed: it was in strong contrast to the two others and if not entirely new, did gain in importance with the increasing separation of the household and the enterprise and the still very limited liberation of family life which this brought. It was the romantic, idealised and emotional attitude which began to characterise the concept of the family, at first in the educated classes of the "Vormärz", then invading the entrepreneurs' households as well. The sources are scarce and seldom clear: how much is the expression of genuine love and affection in these families and how much is rhetoric, unthinking adoption of current modes of thought? What were the survival chances for delicate emotions in these multi-functional family groups, still with so many objective obligations and ties, in the early bourgeosie? There are a few instances to suggest that the chances were not lacking and that they were rather increasing than decreasing. Love and affection between affianced and then married couples, between parents and children, above all between brothers and sisters, formed ties which often bound members of a family more closely than the authority of the father or the force of contingency, but at the same time they brought greater individualisation and might stand in the way of the rationale or family sense which transcended the individual and his needs.[51]

For the families could only exercise the functions outlined above if their identity consisted of more than the sum of their individual members, if there was a family

50 For an example of one of the rare unmarried entrepreneurs: Gottfried Henckels, 1804–58, for whom obviously his relations with the Gichtelianer sect sufficed, fulfilling the role the family would otherwise have taken, even aiding the recruitment of senior staff (Kelleter: Henckels, pp. 138 ff., 153). Werner E. Mosse assumes that there was less long-term cohesion in Jewish families, although there are spectacular cases of the contrary, than in comparable non-Jewish families. C. Wilson points out that the solidarity of non-conformist religious sects in England furthered economic growth. He goes on: "The Meeting House or Chapel extended the ties of the family, and you lent or borrowed within your known community with a confidence hardly yet to be extended beyond such limits." (The Entrepreneur in the Industrial Revolution in Britain, in: Explorations in Entrepreneurial History, Vol. 7, 1954/5, pp. 129, 45, here 131).

51 There are many instances from Hamburg in the later 18th and early 19th century in Schramm: Neun Generationen, e.g. pp. 202, 206 ff., 381. On the relation between Werner Siemens and his fiancée and later wife Mathilde, daughter of a professor, in the 1850s see the correspondence between them in Heintzenberg: Aus einem reichen Leben, pp. 48–98, esp. pp. 50, 51, 52, 62, 63, 70, 72, 82 f., 85, 87; on the close relation between Werner Siemens and his brothers and its importance for the business pp. 13, 14 f., 19, 33, 64, 68, 320. Werner Siemens, the elder, had promised his mother shortly before her death to provide for his younger brothers and sisters, (pp. 60, 95). A similar promise was given by three brothers on the death-bed of their widowed mother in 1855: Schramm: Neun Generationen, p. 217. For the issues under discussion here the relations between brothers and sisters were more important than those between married couples.

sense which went beyond the happiness of individuals and was to a certain extent held to be superior to it. Only in this way could the family fulfil the legitimation function described above; only in this way did it serve as motive and reason for a decision not to consume but to accumulate. In fact we find the traces of such a supra-individual family sense in our sources. Werner Siemens, by then a successful entrepreneur, wrote in a private letter to his brother of an intention which he had had for a long time "to build up an enterprise which will last, which may perhaps one day under the leadership of our boys become an enterprise of world renown like that of the Rothschilds etc. and make our name known and respected in many lands!" and he concludes: "For this great plan the individual, if he regards the plan as good, should be prepared to make sacrifices".[52]

Particularly in the older, very self-confident commercial families, which have sometimes been compared with "dynasties", we might well find the beginnings of an emphatic, supra-individual family sense, transcending generations. And in fact they did plenty to encourage this. It is the fourth factor which favoured strong family cohesion. Again we can take the Siemens family, although they are rather an ideal and hardly representative example. When the firm of Siemens & Halske was founded in 1847 the family already had a "carefully and faithfully recorded family tree" going back through eight generations to the time of the Thirty Years' War. The record was first drawn up in 1829 and it was revised and supplemented several times in the following decades. The family had a coat-of-arms and a motto. After 1873 family reunions were held regularly, at least every five years; generally there were more than fifty and sometimes more than a hundred persons present. In the same year a family foundation was set up, its purpose "to give every member of the family of Siemens the possibility of proper education, both physical and intellectual".[53] Later family bulletins were issued (after 1905) and a family archive was set up in the old family home in Goslar (in 1931), where a Siemens library was also assembled with no lack of biographies of the more distinguished members.

Of course one cannot generalise from this. Nevertheless coats-of-arms and seals were frequent among the larger commercial bourgeois families. The older members of the wealthier Hamburg merchant families regularly had their portraits painted so as to leave a better record for posterity; later they were sometimes content with photographs. The family Bible was handed on from generation to generation and major events – births, marriages and deaths recorded in it with a respectful commentary for the benefit of future generations. The use of the same Christian names through many generations also symbolised and strengthened the family tradition, as did the early tendency to keep written records. Sometimes there were even rather legendary accounts of the family's origin.[54]

---

52 Werner to Carl Siemens 4.11.1863 in: C. Matschoss (ed.): Werner Siemens. Ein kurzgefaßtes Lebensbild nebst einer Auswahl seiner Briefe. Vol. 1, Berlin, 1916, p. 218; similarly on 25.12.1887, ibid., Vol. 2, p. 911, and to his son Wilhelm, his successor in the business, on 22.12.1883, in: Heintzenberg (ed.): Aus einem reichen Leben, loc. cit., p. 320.

53 See H. Siemens: Stammbaum der Familie Siemens. Munich, 1935, p. 26 (quotation), p. 18. Eligible acc. to §2 of the statutes were those persons numbered in the family tree and their legitimate offspring, but not adopted children.

54 See Schramm: Neun Generationen, loc. cit., p. 429 (portraits), 238 (the tradition of handing on names, which after the early 19th century gradually gave way to the desire for greater individual-

c) Where such a sense of family tradition and identity was at work, transcending individuals and generations and reminiscent of the behaviour patterns of the nobility, it certainly also furthered the cohesion of the immediate family circle, the single household, but at the same time pointed beyond it. Many of these families could only fulfil their economic functions because they were not totally absorbed in their own small household but found part of their identity in more distant kinship relations.[55] These were of course much looser than that of their immediate circle; they may have remained latent for years but could be actualised in case of need – within clearly recognisable limits – for the solution of problems. It was only in exceptional cases that the family in the wider sense, the kinship group or "clan", had a clear focal point and centre, and even so this could never develop the power and authority which the father exercised in the individual household. There were no clear external limits to these wider circles of relatives, indeed they changed according to the standpoint of the individual household concerned. That is also the reason why it is difficult to reconstruct them. Strong love and affection between their members were probably rather rare – with a few important exceptions such as closer relations which may have existed between brothers and sisters who had then founded their own families. What kept these "clans" together in such a way that they could function as described?

It is tempting to argue somewhat in a circle: the multiplicity of functions in view of the lack of feasible alternatives. How else could networks of familiarity have developed? How could the family help an individual in need if it was not itself part of a greater circle which offered protection and a distribution of risk? Also, there were few means of reducing unfamiliarity outside the direct circle in those times. Maintaining kinship ties would then seem to be a most natural strategy. Anyway, since the education process was so closely bound up with the family, since marriage partners were so consciously chosen, stressing the trend to social endogamy, kinship relations meant much more than they mean today: usually the same religion, similar values, a similar style of living and similar origins.

The tendency of families to cling together even in their outer circles was also strengthened by the tendency of the old entrepreneurial families to stay in one place. In the old industrial areas there was little geographical mobility among the entrepreneurs.[56] Relations living in the same place, if not in the same house, met frequently, even if this did not apply to all of them. "Many entrepreneurs' families had evolved a custom of meeting once a week. The Möllmanns' family day was Sunday, the Baums' Thursday. Friedrich von Eynern and his young wife Emilie Rittershaus had to devote virtually every other day, and very certainly every Sunday, to the family".[57] On journeys relations were visited, indeed these people travelled, as they said, "down the

---

isation); Moennich: Aufbruch ins Revier. loc. cit., p.61 (family legends). The family Bible with its entries was used as a source by Bredt: Haus Bredt-Rübel.

55 See R. Braun: Sozialer und kultureller Wandel in einem ländlichen Industriegebiet (Zürcher Oberland) unter Einwirkung des Maschinen- und Fabrikwesens im 19. u. 20. Jahrhundert. Erlenbach/Zurich/Stuttgart, 1965, pp. 106f. This shows how small families which were differently structured and had particularist inclinations rather hindered the development of larger enterprises and groups of enterprises.

56 See e. g. Adelmann: Führungsschichten, p. 181.

57 Zunkel: Der rheinisch-westfälische Unternehmer, p. 73; Schramm, loc. cit., also mentions family days, p. 253.

Family Business

cousins' road"[58] through Germany. For the rest many a household, many a sister, cousin or uncle may well have withdrawn from the net, refused closer contact and ignored the family bulletins. The system was flexible enough to go on functioning.

VII. Tensions

These particular qualities will show how the narrower and wider family circles of the commercial bourgeoisie could exercise the economic functions outlined above as frequently as they did. The families had maintained sufficient *traditional features* to be able to perform economic functions as the old "ganze Haus" with the enterprise and the family, servants and apprentices under one roof could do. Among these traditional features were: a large number of children, the patriarchal authority of the father and head of the household in the closer family circle, the tendency to inherit an occupation and enterprise and to social endogamy, the widespread network of kinship relations with which the smaller units were surrounded, the creation of a family identity which went beyond individuals and generations, and the importance of the multi-functionality of the family in view of the lack of alternative resources or institutions provided by the market or the state.

On the other hand these families constituted a *new element* in their environment. They were not supporting a craft shop as in the pre-industrial age or a farm which was largely selfsufficient, this was an industrial enterprise, functioning (or not functioning at all, as the case might be) according to capitalist laws, expanding, centralised. As middle class families they tended to be self-determinant, following their own rules and at some distance from the new economic rationale.

This basic tension caused repeated friction: either the needs of the enterprise infringed the principles and rules of the family, or the claims of family life threatened to disrupt the rationale of the economic sphere.

In the craft families in the eighteenth century a marriage for the son or daughter which was economically and socially "desirable" and as such planned and determined by the parents, may not have conflicted very much with the ideals and desires of the couple themselves.[59] The ideal of marriage as a self-determinant partnership only possible on a love basis, which became established mainly in the middle classes by the "Vormärz" at the latest was not in keeping with this type of "marriage of convenience". But was not the instrumentalised marriage of convenience an essential part of the family network we have just described and its economic and social functions? There can be no doubt that there were increasing conflicts between the "rational" marriage policy and the desire on the part of the young people for wedded bliss in the new style. No doubt there were marriages which were a sad contrast to what they claimed to be, full of inner conflict and compromise, tension and hypocrisy, a continuance of the old split between love and marriage which the younger generation was fighting against. What did this mean for the inner credibility of the family, which the

---

58 Berdrow: Familie Krupp, p. 258.
59 See Möller: Kleinbürgerliche Familie, p. 305 f.

popular encyclopedia of Brockhaus in 1834 described as "sacred" and was so frequently praised and celebrated as a private sphere free of conflict and instrumental-
isation?[60] Did the economic and social function it served not in turn affect the family
in such a way as to weaken its substance and hence erode the base on which it could
serve those functions? The sources are very discreet in their treatment of this inner
core of modern family life.

However, the marriage policy of the great entrepreneurial families was at least
slightly adjusted to the new ideas. We have already pointed out that although the
tendency to social endogamy did not decline there was a slackening of the tendency,
so frequent in the eighteenth century, consistently to form dynasties by frequent in-
ter-marriage between two or three families and of the tendency to marry into the same
industry or branch. The economic aspects of marriage would appear to have given
way more to the social functions, which suggests that the choice of marriage partner
was less frequently the result of a deliberate family strategy and more frequently the
result of existing social contacts, friendships and arrangements. Within these limits
the couples will have been able to choose freely, guided not first and foremost by the
business policy of their families' enterprises even if they did regard a "suitable" marriage as important, welcomed a dowry and generally regarded parental approval as
essential. Of course the marriage partner had to be suitable – not only socially and
economically but in religion as well, and this is in itself a restriction on purely economic considerations. However, it is hardly surprising in view of the great weight
placed on religion in everyday life and the attitude of the early entrepreneurs. We do
not often find an entrepreneur's son marrying hastily for love; the flower girl, the
hireling's daughter, the young girl in the factory would not have been considered. In
any case the son of an established merchant or entrepreneur did not marry in the first
full flush of passion. He generally married late, later than the sons of petty bourgeois
families or the educated classes and certainly later than the members of the lower
classes: at 33 on average between 1750 and 1849 according to A. von Nell's survey in
Lower Saxony. However, these young men generally married very much younger
girls, on average aged 22. The sons of the Bielefeld bourgeoisie in the nineteenth century also tended to wait until their thirtieth year before marrying a girl aged on average 22.[61] That was roughly the age in which according to another more comprehensive study entrepreneurs had finished their education and training at school, in apprenticeship and dependent employment and could for the first time take independent control of a business.[62] So the sons of the bourgeoisie concentrated on their business training for a relatively long time. They did not marry until they were economically and occupationally established.[63]

---

60 On these claims and this idealisation of the bourgeois family of the time: Schwab: Art "Familie",
    loc. cit., p. 291–97; Mitterauer/Sieder: Vom Patriarchat, p. 160.
61 Von Nell: Entwicklung loc. cit., p. 74, 75; for comparative figures see pp. 72, 107, 108. The Biele-
    feld data is from a random sample of 14 marriages from 1830 to 1910, by K. Ditt (Note 30).
62 See Stahl: Elitenkreislauf, loc. cit., p. 242. Heirs generally began to take over their father's business
    on average a year earlier (at 29).
63 With the effect of putting off his marriage from Werner Siemens in a letter of 13.3.1852, in: Heint-
    zenberg: (ed.): Aus einem reichen Leben, p. 60. Several authors have noted that the tendency of
    the bourgeoisie not to marry until a certain degree of commercial success had been achieved was
    apparent at the end of the 18th century as well. See Möller: Kleinbürgerliche Familie, loc. cit.,
    p. 171, esp. Note 6.

Family Business

There still remained an element of calculation in the choice of a partner. No doubt there were marriages purely for money and cases where the father dictated the choice to his heir. And families will certainly have tried to prevent economically less desirable marriages and – as in one example – kept possible suitors away from the wealthy aunt or the niece who would inherit and who was thought to be not of the soundest of intellects but very anxious to marry, even going to the point of appointing a trustee.[64] Generally, however, marriage was not calculated like a business investment or transaction. The sources rather give the impression that the sons increasingly – though the daughters less so! – had room for independent initiative and made good use of it. However, they too kept within clearly defined limits, marrying only after careful consideration of all the aspects involved and in consultation with their parents or an uncle.[65] The reality was somewhere between a love match and a marriage of convenience and no doubt there were strong variations.

But the world of business penetrated the family sphere in other respects as well, causing changes, tension and "costs". The father influenced the sons' choice of occupation and often maintained his will over theirs.[66] The eldest son or at least one of the sons generally had to submit to the requirements of the family business[66a] and prepare himself systematically – like the crown prince – for his succession. This may well have been a heavy burden if it proved too great a strain or forced the young man contrary to his inclinations and ability. If there were several sons to a marriage this lessened the likelihood of conflict. The most suitable son could then be chosen.[67] These bourgeois families were certainly flexible enough to do that; unlike the nobility or the

---

64 See Zunkel: Der rheinisch-westfälische Unternehmer, loc. cit., p. 73, esp. Note 46; see also Schramm: Neun Generationen, loc. cit., p. 248 and on Charlotte Wilhelmine Honsberg in Wuppertal around 1800, "weak in the head but very anxious to marry" Bredt: Haus Bredt-Rübel, loc. cit., p. 45 f.

65 See examples ibid., pp. 381 f. (1813/14); Kelleter: Henckels loc. cit., p. 154 f. on the marriage of one of the heirs in 1840; Mönnich: Aufbruch, loc. cit., p. 95; the letters from Werner Siemens to his fiancée, later wife (Note 51 above). One often has the impression that there were economically more rational alternatives for the entrepreneur in some cases. This also applies to Alfred Krupp's late marriage to Bertha Eichhoff, daughter of a public servant, and certainly to that of his son Friedrich Alfred to Margaretha von Ende in 1882 which the father had prevented for years (Berdrow: Familie Krupp, pp. 316, 369 f.).

66 See also H. Münch: Adolph von Hansemann. Munich, Berlin, 1932: Bredt: Haus Bredt-Rübel, p. 73.

66a For an example see W. Kurschat: Das Haus Friedrich & Heinrich von der Leyen in Krefeld. Thesis, Bonn, 1933, p. 32.

67 Werner Siemens seems to have taken it for granted that his eldest son Arnold, born in 1853, would take on the business. His second son, Wilhelm, born in 1855, was apparently first intended to go into parliament or act as the "scientific spirit of the business". The third, Carl Friedrich, was not born until 1872, in the father's second marriage and was too young to be considered for the succession, which was decided in the early 1880s. However, the eldest son proved little suited to the task. The succession then came to the second son, whose diary entries during his youth show considerable torments of self-doubt. Nevertheless, he went into the business in 1879 (without finishing his studies), where he took over various functions (with interruptions due to illness) and took over the direction of the firm in 1890. The founder, born in 1816, had therefore to carry on as head of the firm, which was growing rapidly and increasingly over-straining him, for a few years longer than he intended. See A. Roth: Wilhelm von Siemens. Berlin, Leipzig, 1922; and the diary of Wilhelm von Siemens in the Werner von Siemens Institut (Archiv) 4/Lf775. – For an example of a hard education as heir to a business which went ruthlessly over the boy's preferences, see that of Friedrich Krupp, son of Alfred Krupp: N. Mühlen: Die Krupps. Frankfurt, 1965, p. 59 f.

landowners they did not have fixed rules of inheritance and this made them economically very much more viable. A son-in-law or nephew could come into the business if there were no son or the sons were eminently unsuitable. Adoption as in Japan was apparently rare. But we do not know what conflict or heart-ache the question of the inheritance may have caused within the family.

Only closer analyses of the inheritance and dowry practice and of marriage policy altogether would show whether the choice of an heir who seemed most suitable to take over the business and the priority accorded to business interests and the general interests of the family in deciding the inheritance was purchased at the expense of other sons and daughters as can be shown, with the appropriate variations, in the case of noble families.[68] Certainly, handing on to the next generation proved a vulnerable point. Generally it would have been more in the interests of the business to maintain the accumulated capital (and not to distribute it), nor to set too many successors at its head, even if they were equally entitled to be there but to make the best qualified the head of the firm and the overall successor. But this often conflicted with the principles of justice and loyalty within the family. There is Berdrow's rather restrained account of the delay in handing over the steel works to Alfred Krupp in 1848, which must have put family feelings to a hard test and left at least one permanently damaged victim: brother Friedrich, out-bidden, who left Essen, virtually to go into banishment, becoming more and more of a strangeling, even if financially secure. There are other cases of dispute over the inheritance between the mother and children after the death of the father who had headed the business.[69] Generally an enterprise does appear to have been left to more than one person.[70]

The entrepreneurs of the Industrial Revolution, whether they founded their businesses or inherited them, would appear to have been familiar with the dilemma of having to choose between the interests of the firm and the loyalty or fairness to the closest members of their family. They resorted to various means to cope with this, sometimes handing the business on during their lifetime, reserving to themselves a regular income and a certain right of participation on matters of principle. Sometimes they founded or bought additional works in order to be able to leave one to each son,[71] though this was hardly possible in very capital-intensive industries. Sometimes they distributed shares to their children, imposing the condition that these could not be taken out of the business for some time, and not granting full codirection rights to prevent the number of managers growing to the detriment of efficiency, but leaving the direction of the enterprise to the person most suited. It is the beginning of a separation between shareholding and control in a family business. Some of the wills and contracts were very complicated.[72] But over the longer term it was not always possible

68 On the other hand it must be borne in mind that industrial enterprises and capital are on principle easier to divide than the land owned by the nobility and the rights this brings. See the excellent discussion of these problems by H. Reif, in: J. Kocka et al.: Familie und soziale Plazierung, Opladen 1980, p. 34–44. He also discusses the case of the nobility ibid., pp. 67–126, and in his book (see Note 2).

69 See W. Berdrow: Alfred Krupp, Vol. I, Berlin, 1927, pp. 221–7; on brother Friedrich ibid.: Familie Krupp loc. cit., p. 361 f. See also Note 78 below.

70 See the figures in Stahl: Elitenkreislauf, p. 284.

71 For instance in the Düren paper industry: Decker: Betriebliche Sozialordnung, p. 31, 104, 105 (esp. Note 43).

72 For examples see H. A. William: Carl Zeiss 1816–1888. Munich, 1967, p. 91–102; on obligations

to prevent heirs from claiming their full shares in the form of cash or too many or unsuitable heirs from demanding participation in the direction of the business.[73]

The only safe possibility was to change the firm into a joint stock company, a solution which became increasingly popular even during the "Vormärz". The form chosen was that of an "Aktiengesellschaft" or "Kommanditgesellschaft auf Aktien"; in 1892, the legal form of the "Gesellschaft mit beschränkter Haftung" (GmbH) was created, providing a solution to the particulary needs of the family firm.[74] Even if the old family business often continued for a long time under the new guise, these changes did constitute an important step on the way to the gradual withdrawal of the business from the family context which was becoming increasingly necessary through the growing irreconcilability of family and business interests.

Testamentary or contractual arrangements regarding inheritance and succession or changes in legal form and the arrangements which frequently had to be made between brothers and relations concerning capital participation and profit-sharing and business rights and obligations of various kinds meant that formalized contractual aspects penetrated deep into family relationships where they perhaps constituted a certain alien element. They changed one dimension of family life, institutionalising it and making it more "fixed" in order to meet the requirements of the business better.[75]

The conflict between the claims of the rapidly growing business and the family which was responsible for it could of course also negatively affect the course of business, hindering efficiency. If the owner of a factory had many sons and daughters and wanted to give them all fair shares the inheritance could prove a considerable burden on the enterprise,[76] with shares in the capital to be handed out or current earnings distributed, unless it proved possible to establish a family or business interest which was accepted as superior to the claims of individual heirs or to find other ways of avoiding distribution.[77] For this reason crises over inheritance were frequent in family firms.[78] Such crises could also arise over the problem of selection of the management. The

---

laid on sons and grandsons see Kurschaft: Haus von der Leyen, loc. cit., p. 17 for the will made by Heinrich von der Leyen (Krefeld) in 1782.

73 See S. Haubold: Entwicklung und Organisation einer Chemnitzer Maschinenfabrik. Thesis. Bonn, 1939, pp. 32 ff.; H. Rachel & P. Wallich: Berliner Großkaufleute und Kapitalisten. Vol. 2, Berlin, 1967, pp. 222, 223; Witt: Triebkräfte, p. 97.

74 See Herrmann: Entwicklungslinien loc. cit., p. 15, for an early example in 1834; see also Mönnich: Aufbruch loc. cit., p. 91 ff. on Hoesch 1871; Kelleter: Henckels, loc. cit., p. 181 on the change to a partnership limited by shares (1882); on the possibility of changing the legal form to that of a "GmbH" and Stumm's influence on the 1892 legislation: Hellwig: Unternehmer, loc. cit., p. 423 f.; on the frequency of the change even in the second generation Stahl: Elitekreislauf, loc. cit., p. 258.

75 For an example see the "Siemens'sche Vermögensgemeinschaft" of 1897 (or earlier) which collected the family capital, had statutes, and was administered by two employees. Clearly this was the only way to handle the family's claim to disposition and management, which was anchored in shareholdings, in view of the size of the enterprises, their spread and the capital involved. So a semi-public sphere developed between the level of the enterprise and the really private sphere of the individual members or branches of this huge family. See Kocka: Unternehmensverwaltung, loc. cit., p. 453.

76 I. e., if the enterprise was not sold to satisfy the claims of the heirs.

77 See A. Paulsen: Das 'Gesetz der dritten Generation'. Erhaltung und Untergang von Familienunternehmungen, in: Der praktische Betriebswirt. Jg. 21, 1941, pp. 271–280, here 278 f., and above.

78 From 1870 to 1879 in Henckels: Kelleter, loc. cit., p. 175 ff. After the death of the father there were law-suits over the inheritance. For a time the widow thought of selling to meet the various claims.

recruitment of the successor (or successors) in the direction of the business was primarily according to family criteria. But although an entrepreneur's son may have had all the advantages we described earlier in terms of up-bringing and experience this did not always guarantee that he would prove efficient at the job. If he were not, the business, which was still very dependent on the personality and ability of the head of the firm, could easily weaken or even disintegrate.[79] So dependence on the family could negatively affect the efficiency of a firm. Nor was it apparently always easy to prevent heirs who wished to do so from participating in the direction. On the other hand the factories of the Industrial Revolution could rarely be divided without seriously impairing business efficiency. This caused considerable coordination problems, as when seven members of the family wanted to take an active part in the direction of a small Düren textile firm, all claiming to represent the enterprise.[80]

The recruitment of members of the family to work below management level could also prove problematic. Of what use was the most loyal of men if his technical qualifications and general efficiency were not up to the job?[81] Moreover even in the early period it could happen that quiet, restrained growth was preferred for family considerations and many a chance to expand was not utilised because it would have made capital and staff from "outside" necessary, which might have jeopardised the family influence.[82]

VIII. Conclusion and Outlook

But these were exceptions. Generally we can say that in the first decades of industrialisation in Germany the family was one of those non- and pre-capitalist institutions which were a prerequisite, stimulus and vehicle of the process of capitalist industrialisation. It is hard to say how this process could have gone on without these families and their resources. Family structures and processes furthered capitalist industrialisation very much more than they hindered it. Family sense proved a strong motive to entrepreneurial behaviour. The desire to serve family interests, which were perceived as going beyond the individual and one generation, provided an ideological legitimation and in some cases motivation for growth-oriented entrepreneurial policy. The family helped to qualify the early entrepreneurs more than any other institution through "inheritance" of knowledge and skills and social benefits of many different kinds. The family made many a contribution to capital formation and its financial re-

---

79 In the 1880s at Siemens. See J. Kocka: Siemens und der aufhaltsame Aufstieg der AEG, in: Tradition, Jg. 17, 1972, pp. 125–42.
80 Leopold Schoeller & Söhne in 1862 in Düren. See Decker: Betriebliche Sozialordnung, loc. cit., p. 31.
81 Examples from Krupp and Siemens in Berdrow: Familie Krupp, p. 349 ff. Kocka: Unternehmensverwaltung, loc. cit., p. 352 ff.
82 See R. Braun: Sozialer und kultureller Wandel, p. 106 f.; H. J. Habakkuk: Industrial Organisation since the Industrial Revolution. Southampton, 1968, p. 12; D. S. Landes: The Structure of Enterprise in the Nineteenth Century, in: XIe Congrès International de Science Historique. Stockholm, 21.–28th August, 1960). Rapports V. Upsala, 1960, p. 115. See also the scepticism of the Stinnes brothers and sisters with regard to the joint stock company: they were only prepared to accept this in 1848 as an emergency and transitional arrangement until the family business could be re-established: Hermann: Entwicklungslinien, loc. cit., p. 14 f.

sources were of major importance. Family relations helped to solve early management problems; they served to provide information, to create trust, furthered cohesion and created a sense of class in the emergent bourgeoisie. They provided contacts
which could be used for many purposes, created a sense of belonging together which
helped entrepreneurial success. There were other functions which these families performed and which we have not been able to discuss here, for instance their role as
models and ideology for industrial staff policy and administration; much has been
written on this under the heading of "patriarchalism". Some of these functions were
more dependent on the household family, some rather performed by the more distant
circles of kinship relations.

We have put special emphasis on two of the prerequisites for this major positive
contribution which family structures and resources made to the development of early
industrial capitalism. Firstly the low state of development of viable alternatives: neither the market nor state institutions were developed enough in the first two thirds of
the nineteenth century to be able to solve the central problems of early enterprises.
Recourse to the family proved a viable and sometimes the only solution. Secondly the
economic functions of the family can be explained through its structure and position
in the strategically important sections of the commercial bourgeoisie. No doubt there
were family structures which were less favourable to the process of capitalist industrialisation.[83] This article has made only a preliminary contribution to research on the –
generally traditional – characteristics of entrepreneurs' families which enabled them
to take on these economic functions. The entrepreneur's family has been described as
a transitional phenomenon between the "ganze Haus", with the business and the
family under one roof, and the middle class family of the modern type. This duality
led to tension between some of its tasks and functions on the one hand and its claims
and aims on the other, – tensions which were ultimately due to the principal structural
difference between the family and the market as outlined at the beginning of this
article.

We have discussed some aspects of the relation between the family and capitalism in the early phase of industrialisation. During the following decades[84] this relation changed; it became looser and its dis-functional elements became more pronounced. Roughly speaking we can identify three complex processes of change as responsible for this:

Firstly: on an advanced stage of development the industrial economy needed
help from the family very much less than in its initial phases. Public institutions were
increasingly taking over the function of educating and training the entrepreneur. The
capital market was becoming developed; with the help of the banks and modern
company law new non-family means of financing were being opened up. With more
efficient methods of industrial management recourse to family relations was less and
less needed. Cartels and groupings with a formalised, tendentially bureaucratic structure were making the family rather superfluous and hopelessly old-fashioned as a
basis for the formation of concerns. The means of communication were being improved. The family and more distant relations remained important for the establishment of social cohesion in the group of leading entrepreneurs. But there were now

---

83 See Braun: Sozialer und kultureller Wandel, loc. cit., p. 106.
84 Exact dating is not possible of course here. But roughly the reference is to the last decades of the
    19th century and the 20th.

other factors as well: common experience at university, in the student corporations, in spas; cross-membership of supervisory boards and the resultant network of relationships; the centralisation of administration in Berlin; joint work in associations. The changing capitalist industrial system created its own institutions and these ensured its maintenance and further development. To a certain extent what Max Weber said with regard to the religiously motivated spiritual ascetic also applied to the family: "The victorious capitalism . . . no longer needed this support once it had become established on a mechanical base."[85]

Secondly: if in later decades entrepreneurs held to family strategies for the solution of their problems, although more efficient alternatives were by then available, this often had a negative effect on their business, especially in the large enterprises, where the requirements were in any case rather dis-proportionate to the resources of the family. Most of the examples of the inhibiting effect of family ties come from the later period. It is only after the late nineteenth century and in big business especially that the limits of the family business and the dis-functional elements in the relation between the family and industry emerged clearly although, as we have seen, they were at least latent in the initial phase.

Finally the family itself changed in a way which made it less and less of a suitable vehicle for these economic functions. The average number of children dropped; the ability to take on the entrepreneurial role declined, particularly in the third generation,[86] partly as a result of economic success which opened up new worlds to the children. Internal processes of individualisation went on in the family. The transfer of functions to alternative structures outside the family and the loosening of family ties reinforced each other.

However, these are only tendential changes. At the end of the 1930's Otto Suhr reckoned that of about 4,200 firms in mechanical engineering 120 were more than hundred years old and nearly half of these were still in the hands of the founder family.[87] Even today there are still many successful family businesses. Especially small and medium-sized companies still very strongly depend on the family background. So even in the age of advanced manager capitalism family ties have not only had a negative effect, on the contrary.[88] As far as Schumpeter's grim prognosis that capitalism will dry out if there is no motivation left at all from the family sphere[89] is concerned, the last word has not yet been spoken.

---

85 Weber: Protestantische Ethik, loc. cit., p. 188.
86 Stahl's quantitative examination (Elitenkreislauf loc. cit., p. 255 f.) of management through successive generations would appear to confirm this "law of the third generation", which certainly did not apply in the pre-industrial age: in or immediately after the third generation direction of the enterprise often passed out of the family's hands (esp. p. 264). Examples of the collapse of entrepreneurial families, which had been successful for generations or their retirement from business life around the middle of the 19th century can be found in Zunkel: Der rheinisch-westfälische Unternehmer, p. 112 ff.; see also Kurschat: Hans von der Leyen, p. 90 ff., 135 f. Hypotheses in Paulsen: Das 'Gesetz der dritten Generation', esp. 274 f. (the dangers of success) and p. 278 f. (inheritance problems).
87 Familientradition im Maschinenbau. Untersuchungen über die Lebensdauer von Unternehmungen, in: Wirtschaftskurve. Jg. 1939, Heft 1, pp. 29–50, here pp. 32, 34.
88 Examples from the Wilh. Reich in Kocka: Entrepreneurs and Managers, loc. cit., p. 583 f. H. Böhme, Emil Kirdorf: Überlegungen zu einer Unternehmerbiographie in: Tradition, Vol. 13, 1968, p. 294.
89 See Schumpeter: Kapitalismus, loc. cit., p. 258 ff.

[23]

Michael Lisle-Williams

Beyond the market: the survival of family capitalism in the English merchant banks

ABSTRACT

The disappearance of family capitalism in English society is taken for granted in most economic and sociological theory. Yet in one extremely important part of the financial system, the merchant banking sector, family-based possession and direct control continued unchallenged until the 1960s. Moreover, until that time, the survival rate of independent merchant banks was extremely high. Almost all remained in business, though some flourished and others appeared to stagnate. There was little indication that 'market forces' eliminated the inefficient. In fact, the merchant banks were embedded in a social context which limited competition, discouraged inter-bank ruthlessness and fostered co-operation. This article explores two theses, one general and one specific, that together explain the emergence of the peculiar social context and account for the continuity of family capitalism in English merchant banking.

1 THE SOCIAL AND ECONOMIC SIGNIFICANCE OF MERCHANT BANKING [1]

English merchant bankers were the acknowledged king-makers of the early nineteenth-century world. The financial empires of the Barings and Rothschilds were discussed with awe and some fear, for in wealth and power they rivalled the middle-order states of Europe.[2] Monarchs offended merchant bankers at their own peril; no state authority could rest secure without an ally among the merchant bankers who monopolized London's money pumps. In the course of the nineteenth century, the numbers of merchant bankers increased, their interests multiplied and intersected, and the map of the world was redrawn to celebrate the advance of European imperialism, funded in part through the exertions of the city of London. The apogee of the merchant banking dynasties arguably occurred in the two decades

The British Journal of Sociology   *Volume XXXV*   *Number 2*   *June 1984*

before the First World War. Their later fortunes reflected the collapse of British financial hegemony: not until the end of the second decade after the Second World War did the new functions of London's merchant banks restore prosperity and public attention. By this time, their assets were dwarfed by those of the five clearing banks while their family capitalist organization appeared anachronistic and quaint. The revival of the City as an international financial centre set in motion forces for change which may yet culminate in the disappearance of the distinctively dynastic approach to merchant banking: that point, however, appears to be more distant than financial commentators predicted in the 1960s and 1970s.[3] Several families still exhibit great reluctance to be separated from the direct control of their enterprises.

This article advances a general thesis to account for the survival of family capitalism in the English merchant banking sector. In doing so, it begins to fill a significant and surprising vacuum in the sociology of economic institutions. The absence of a sustained, historically informed sociological analysis of finance in capitalist society must bewilder anyone familiar with the writings of Marx, Weber, Sombart, Simmel and Hilferding.[4] Encouragingly, some studies reported in the last decade have pointed in the right direction. Among these are studies of elites and interlocks inspired by the analysis that Lupton and Wilson carried out, in 1958, on association among witnesses before the Bank Rate Leak enquiry.[5] Recent works by Longstreth[6] and Moran[7] are a theoretical advance in that they treat the City or financial capital as a political entity and present some stimulating hypotheses. In another vein, Thompson's more abstract Marxist analysis of the financial system is a worthwhile attempt to challenge economic orthodoxy;[8] however, the Leninist interpretation offered by Overbeek[9] suggests a serious misreading of key episodes in British financial and social history. While these studies indicate a variety of perspectives that might be accommodated within a sociology of finance, they also reveal the need for systematic, theoretically guided empirical research into the relationships between financial organization, economic power, class and status group structure, and the state. Towards that end, this article seeks to clarify the social and economic significance of the merchant banks and to explain how the characteristics of the founding families, the business of the banks, and the expanding British state interacted to protect dynastic possession from the full impact of market competition. A story emerges of dynastic ambition, the creation of a financial community, and effective control of the Bank of England by merchant bankers, set against the backdrop of the rise and decline of Britain's second empire.

Two excellent reasons can be given for concentrating on England's merchant banks: the banks themselves have been powerful organizations in shaping capitalist Britain; and the founding families have comprised a community of astounding wealth since the middle of the nineteenth century, comparable only with the brewing, shipowning and private banking clans.[10] The role of merchant bankers in the making of the English capitalist class deserves comprehensive investigation and will be discussed in detail elsewhere.[11] Here, attention will be focused on the relationships between the merchant banking dynasties, their banks and other interests, and the institutions of the City of London, including the Bank of England. Several interesting topics, among them the influence of merchant bankers on government policy and the breakdown of some aspects of financial regulation, are mentioned only in passing but merit fuller treatment in later work.

London's merchant banks in review The economic power of London's leading merchant banks is not immediately apparent from a cursory review of their balance sheets. The largest accepting house,[12] Kleinwort Benson Ltd, had assets of just over £3 billion in 1981–2, less than 10 per cent of those of Barclays Bank or the National Westminster. Unlike the much ramified clearers, the merchant banks do not have branches which deal with public deposits and loans. Rather, the modern merchant banks are essentially the powerful servants of corporations and governments, although a small part of their business consists of asset management and other services for wealthy persons. London's merchant banks borrow and lend money in the wholesale, international markets;[13] transactions involving less than a million pounds are seldom attractive. Large-scale banking is augmented by another traditional activity, bill accepting, which entails guaranteeing short-term credits in return for a commission; these functions together provide merchant banking's bread and butter. Another function with a long and colourful history is the issue of shares and bonds for companies, national governments and local authorities: in essence, it requires the successful mobilization of capital under terms that favour both the client and the issuing bank. Merchant bankers have made some of their largest profits from skilfully orchestrated issues; occasionally, there have also been serious losses. London's merchant banks were quick to exploit the investment trust concept in the late nineteenth century. Since then, management of other people's money has embraced insurance company funds, pension funds and unit trusts, and is a major factor in the post-1950s rejuvenation of merchant banking.[14] Another function which developed slowly but became a major source of income since 1960 is the provision of financial advice and organization of finance for large companies. The take-over booms of the mid 1950s and late 1960s hastened the adoption of aggressive tactics by merchant banks in corporate finance and undermined the consensual order on which City regulation depended. Leading merchant banks have acquired other significant income sources: insurance broking, bullion dealing, life assurance, international project finance, property, leasing, foreign government advice, and what can only be described as international tax minimization consultancy.

The impact of the merchant banks differs between activities, but the overall pattern is striking. Within the UK, the 10 largest merchant banks monopolize the capital markets (issues), corporate advice and finance, bullion dealing, investment management, acceptances, and leasing. In issues, corporate finance and investment management enduring relationships exist between the major merchant banks and their clients. Severing a connection with an old accepting house remains socially objectionable in the City, an act of bad faith. Nevertheless, evidence of unprecedented ruthlessness in inter-bank conduct[15] suggests that the old order, a legacy of dynastic domination, is beyond restoration.

Merchant bank power is also related to the extent of personal and formal ties between the accepting houses, the largest U.K. industrial, commercial and banking companies, and various governmental and community bodies.[16] It is necessary to recognize the variety of these ties, in terms of origins, intended functions, and wider consequences, for the web is so complex that it is a distortion simply to portray the merchant banking fraternity as the spider in command. While it is not possible to explore the pattern of connections here, previous research indicates that it generates a structure of credibility and legitimacy for merchant bank conduct. The upshot is that merchant bankers' power derives from the extensiveness of their information nets and from their position between the sources and potential users of capital.[17]

Merchant bank chairmen and directors tend more than boards of industrial and commercial enterprises or clearing banks to have upper stratum origins.[18] Although dilution of ascriptive criteria in the selection of senior management and board members has occurred in the merchant banks, most markedly since the withdrawal of some founding families from active direction, it has lagged half a century behind the clearing banks and insurance companies in this respect. Changes have been slow, but unmistakable, too, in the form of corporate organization adopted by the merchant banks. Not until 1970 did N. M. Rothschild and Sons abandon the partnership form and become a limited liability, private company. However, in the 1960s, most had developed publicly quoted holding companies within which the merchant bank proper was embedded as a subsidiary. None the less, dynastic control and the conventions of Victorian society weighed heavily upon the merchant banks, well into the second half of the twentieth century.

2 QUESTIONS AND THESES

The main question considered here is why family-based control has
persisted for so long in the English merchant banks. Family possession,
in the full sense, was the absolute rule in the merchant banks until
the early 1960s, although since then it has diminished significantly.
The nature of this diminution will be considered later. The merchant
banks were exceptional in respect of the continuity of family-based
possession. In no other branch of industry, finance or commerce had
family ownership and control endured so completely without serious
challenge from competitors. Nyman and Silberston,[19] and Francis,[20]
in arguing that the extent of individual and family capitalist control
has been underestimated in the U.K., also suggest that most companies
pass out of founding family possession at some stage. Only since the
early 1970s have a majority of merchant banks ceased to be directed
by their founding families: by contrast, all but one of the companies
in Francis's random sample of 21 of the largest 250 had ceased to be
family controlled by the 1920s.

The more general of the two theses advanced here is that the social
characteristics of merchant banking dynasties facilitated the personalized and confidential mode of capital raising and financial diplomacy
that was for so long typical of the English markets: this nexus only
came under great strain when new approaches to financial business
undermined traditional methods in the City of London in the later
1950s. The new approaches gained ground not only because of dras-
tically changed economic circumstances, but also because problems
of succession and motivation in the control of the merchant banks
became conspicuous at this time. The former were chiefly the result
of deaths in the two world wars, while the latter stemmed from the
lure of society and gentry life. The 'gentlemanly' organization of
merchant banking reduced the need for great competence or effort
on the part of family directors while ensuring that no stigma of trade
attached to the unfortunates who spent a few hours each day in the
partner's room. However, in terms of the continuity of dynastic
possession, the crucial outcome of gentlemanly organization was
widespread agreement about the limits to competition and the desirability of mutual aid as a strategy for collective survival.

The more specific thesis claims that had it not been for covert
action by the Bank of England, particularly in 1931 and 1932, several
great merchant banks would have collapsed, taking with them several
others and the fortunes of the founding families. The covert action
included a series of loans which breached the hole left by the cessation
of payments from European debtors. There were precedents for such
secret assistance, dating back to commercial crises in 1837, 1857,
1890 and 1914.[21] Nevertheless, the Bank of England had always
been selective in its aid: the prospect of failure by a major bank or

financial enterprise did not guarantee rescue. Judgments of a distinctly social sort were made by the Governor and Court of the Bank of England, within the unexamined bounds of a carefully perpetuated ideology. An important element of the situation was the prominence, and occasional predominance, of merchant banks in the Court; clearing banks were not represented until the 1950s. The long-term 'view' of the Bank was shaped by its intimate connection with and direction by partners in the most prestigious merchant banks. Within this view, the Bank's duty was to supervise, caution, protect and, if all else failed, rescue the accepting houses.

The specific thesis raises the question of the Bank of England's function and responsibility. Its spokesmen have claimed for more than a century that its responsibility is to the nation as a whole, and that the appropriate way to discharge this responsibility is by maintaining order, efficiency and integrity in the financial system. Associated with this conception of responsibility — thoroughly conservative in its assumptions — is an ideology of sound finance. The Bank's spokesmen, as advisers to governments and as public figures, have espoused fervent belief in the necessity of exposure to market forces, implying opposition to collective bargaining, economic planning, and government deficits.[22] Yet the evidence suggests that the Bank of England has protected the merchant banks and many lesser enterprises from the final judgment of the market, both directly and indirectly. In the case of the Bank Governors' actions in 1931-2, the irony is that the outstanding advocate of market individualism chose not to practise what it was preaching to wage-earners and the unemployed. The Bank's function, it is proposed, has included the maintenance of an exclusive and compliant social order in the City, one based upon informal social controls and mutual protection developed by the merchant banking dynasties. It was this order that was being rescued in the 1930s. Failure to carry the merchant banks would have meant serious disruption to financial activity in the short term, and a loss of moral authority — due to the collapse of its social base — in the longer term.

Alternative theoretical explanations of the survival of family owned and directed merchant banks are rarely made explicit. Economists seem to regard the merchant banks as curiosities, protected from the full force of competition, and only now starting to behave as proper firms should.[23] However, economists have shown little interest in accounting theoretically for this phenomenon, implicitly dismissing it as a hiccup which will pass out of the market system sooner or later. In so doing, faith is sustained in the ultimate operation of selection by efficiency, a process that has been staved off in the merchant banking sector for the better part of 70 years.

Theorists of managerial control build on the scenario provided by orthodox economics. Pockets of private capitalism are theoretically uninteresting; they are dinosaurs in the mammalian age. Managerialists assume the inevitability of concentration of corporate capital, fragmentation of individual shareholdings, and strategic control by senior employees. Merchant banks, small in terms of capitalization and manpower, are best ignored.

By contrast, the theses advanced here identify three factors that were instrumental in sustaining family capitalism in the English merchant banks:

1. dynastic ambition, ideology and resistance to loss of control;
2. compatibility between gentlemanly status and merchant banking tasks;
3. limits to competition, both informal and institutional.

The way these factors arose and affected the merchant banks is outlined in the next section. Upper stratum integration and capitalist class solidarity are major features of this context.

3 MERCHANT BANKS: DYNASTIC FOUNDATIONS

The histories of the merchant banking families reveal a struggle to convert material success into respectability and dynastic continuity. The background to this struggle, a conscious and deliberate one, was the changing relationship between class and status in nineteenth-century English society. The complacent rigidity of the old hierarchical order was challenged by competitive individualism, its political meaning expressed in bourgeois liberalism, and class conflict, rooted in labour solidarity and made coherent in various socialist ideologies. Collectively, the merchant bankers, like other capitalist contemporaries, contributed significantly to the very economic and social changes which undermined the old order, while individually they aspired to consolidate a position for their families within an exclusive, unchanging upper stratum. As early as the mid-nineteenth century, commentators expressed fears that the juggling act could not last: capitalism would erode the moral legitimacy of the old status order. Slowly, perhaps, if leading capitalists were initiated into the upper stratum and prised away from their participation in business. But eventually, they concluded, the old order would collapse as its signs and distinctions, its symbols of status, became marketable and its rural anchors gave way. Their fears were not without grounds, but the breakdown of the old order has been a long time in process. Tattered remnants of the landed status order today are embedded within the class structure, purchased by self-made men, used by politicians to buy off or placate rivals, drawn upon by the political right to present images of national harmony, and used subtly to exclude others from control of major capitalist enterprises.

Seen from the distance of the late twentieth century, the irony of unintended consequences is unmistakable. Closer to the lives of the early generations of merchant bankers, however, the ultimate contradiction between dynastic upper stratum aspirations and the actions of the capitalist class is less perceptible. At the level of most historical narrative, biography and autobiography, individual motives and conduct loom large, and situational logic reigns supreme. The solidifying structures of the emergent society appear only as shadowy premonitions of plausible futures. Merchant bankers were no more endowed with sociological imagination than the railway magnates, aristocratic colliery owners, shipping tycoons and textile manufacturers with whom they rubbed shoulders.[24]

One reason for this absence of long-sight is that the merchant bankers themselves began as a motley crowd. Certainly, their passage through nineteenth century society had a homogenizing effect, narrowing the range of variation quite spectacularly, yet religious and ethnic differences often remained in evidence, sometimes as perverse sources of pride. A further factor was the length of time that separated the first prominence of the Barings and Rothschilds from the successes of the Hambros, Grenfells, Montagus, Sassoons, Kleinworts and Gibbs. Although at least 15 major merchant banks were founded before 1850,[25] it was only in the next quarter century that their owners came to comprise a distinctive social group, identifiable in terms of economic power, wealth and political influence. And it was in the subsequent 40 years, to the First World War, that the several dozen families increasingly resembled a community within the capitalist class. By this stage, the dynastic principle was taken for granted: the unexamined conditions on which it rested, of course, were shortly to be exposed by the war and the political upheavals that followed.

The diverse origins of the main merchant banking families are well documented, if romanticized, in anecdotal and biographical accounts.[26] Contrary to some accounts, however, the preponderance of foreigners and the disproportionate representation of Jews are not due to the innate qualities of members of those categories. Rather, successful extension of credit and raising capital depended upon: an entrepreneurial orientation, without regard for injunctions against usury; a kin network which could mobilize resources, pass on information, provide trustworthy and competent partners, and act with unity when required; location in the City of London or in major commercial centres; correspondents (often kin) abroad, who could convey information and judgments and procure business; astuteness in assessing risks and minimizing bad debts and low returns; a system of complex reciprocities, encompassing contacts and informants in business and politics; and patronage or preferential treatment by a

monarch or statesman. The latter typically required subtle, complicated moves, and considerable patience: Barings, Rothschilds and
Hambros in particular adroitly built up relationships with the power-
wielders of Europe by salvaging their finances at critical times.

Recourse to anything more specific than this set of structural and
sentimental attributes as an explanation of early merchant banking
success is probably misleading. The claim that social marginality, for
instance, was a precondition of success is incorrect: by the time the
Baring, Brown, Gibbs, Gladstone, Grenfell and Hambro families
moved into merchant banking as such, they were already affluent
and prominent members of the mercantile bourgeoisie. Furthermore,
to suggest that the early merchant bankers were shrewd and ruthless
because they were driven by resentment born of deprivation, as some
accounts do, is quite wrong. Rubinstein, in his study of the very
wealthy, supports this observation:

> Almost none of the immigrant merchant bankers were literally
> penniless when they moved to London, but were mainly the sons
> of established bankers abroad, or in the case of the Barings, of
> established cloth merchants in England. . . . Indeed, it is not poss-
> ible to speak of a single wealth-holding banker who was, strictly
> speaking, a 'self made man'. At best, some came from just above
> this level, from the lower end of the middle class.[27]

Cosmopolitanism was not incompatible with an ambition to be
counted among the best in the hierarchical society of the day. To
some, the 'aristocratic embrace'[28] was given warmly and rapidly; in
other cases, an arm's length relationship developed. The pervasive
anti-semitism of the early Victorian period[29] accounts for some
barriers that Society put in the way of the Rothschilds and their
lesser brethren. By the last decades of the nineteenth century, of
course, the more visible barriers had tumbled, in large part as a result
of the Prince of Wales's gratitude for discreet rescues from financial
misadventure.[30] From 1880 onwards, the narrowing of variation in
social types within merchant banking had become evident. Several
dynasties had begun to flourish; many more were being established.
Some indication of their characteristics is warranted at this point.

Between 1880 and 1914, no less than 36 families[31] with major
merchant banking interests had, for all practical purposes, been
assimilated into the tiny upper stratum of English society. Social
histories stress that this stratum expanded while its criteria for
inclusion grew more ambiguous.[32] Often it is implied that a flood of
brash philistines, the new plutocracy, swamped the old aristocrats
and imposed their extravagant, shameless consumption on Society.[33]
However, close examination of the careers of the main merchant
banking families reveals that this is a considerable over-simplification,

indeed a significant distortion. To a very great extent, the institutions, mores and ritual occasions of the upper stratum were adapted slowly to changing circumstances by the leaders of Society.[34] The social calendar continued to reflect the importance of land-owning: appropriately, since as late as 1883, the 200 persons who owned more than 25,000 acres held 25 per cent of the private land in Great Britain.[35] Merchant banking families, like others of the wealthiest bourgeoisie, bought great houses in the West End of London and estates which encompassed several villages and prime agricultural land. Their lives were shaped by the long-established conventions that surrounded social prominence in the counties. They dispensed local justice and patronage, represented the county in the House of Commons, organized the rural militia, supported parishes and entertained their social equals with hunts, shoots, balls and house parties. May to August each year saw a return to London and the enactment of the Society Season. Old landed families and their new neighbours engaged in elaborate summertime rites, celebrating the timelessness of the status order and paying homage to the watchful, judgmental gate-keepers of Society, the grand ladies of the great class. Certainly, the upper stratum expanded to include people like merchant bankers, but it was a controlled expansion conditional upon their adoption of approved social qualities.

Several aspects of the creation of upper stratum identities are relevant here. Members of the merchant banking families subjected themselves to various forms of institutional processing once they had acquired the necessary resources. Hierarchy and exclusion in society were reinforced in the household: the small army of servants clung to their rigid pecking order, supervised by the mistress of the household and her daughters, who were excluded from and appendages to the masculine public world. The paterfamilias tended to be remote from his heirs, who were nursed through infancy by servants, sent to often austere, all male public schools for upwards of 10 years, and then routed through an exclusive Oxbridge college before being released into the male domains of public life. Elements of these relationships were refracted into the organization of the banks and other enterprises which the families controlled. Generational conflict was suppressed by a strong dynastic ideology that applauded duty, dignity and respect, reinforced by the years of accommodation to hierarchical relations imposed on each rising generation.[36] To take one example, by 1914 all the main merchant banking families had sent their sons to Eton, Harrow or Winchester, predominantly to the former.[37] By this time, too, family traditions of military service, parliamentary representation,[38] club membership, participation in blood sports, racing and yachting, and cultural patronage had been firmly established. With a few exceptions, too, the generation who governed the merchant banks and associated financial enterprises

were not founders but heirs to fortunes: despite their names, the
Goschens, Sassoons, Kleinworts and Rallis convincingly presented
the persona of English gentlemen.

Although the ethos of upper stratum Victorian family life strongly
favoured dynastic control of resources, including merchant banks,
the largeness of many families created practical difficulties. In principle, the preferred solution to this problem was primogeniture, such
that the eldest son inherited the business or the estate intact and
governed it personally, while the other sons received lifetime incomes
but were expected to contribute to society through the church, military, civil service or higher learning. Daughters remained dependent
upon the household until they married. Where there were numerous
siblings, then, an estate would be inherited with large, fixed expenditures attached. In practice, though, variations were common.[39] As
early as the eighteenth century, private banking families had developed solutions which departed considerably from primogeniture.
Family lands usually were inherited by the eldest son, who participated as a partner with his younger brothers in the family bank.
Sometimes, control of the bank was consolidated when one partner
bought his brothers out. Occasionally, kin outside the senior branch
of the family bought back in. In the absence of heirs, control of a
family bank passed to the female line.[40] Merchant banking solutions
resembled these. The merchant bank remained in the family, governed
by a small group of kin, but supporting a much larger group who
occupied themselves with the land and the service of monarchs,
temporal and spiritual. The Baring family is the archetype for this
arrangement, in part because of the great fecundity of Henry Baring
and his two spouses who produced 13 children in 40 years. Branches
of the family established their own rural fiefdoms, while retaining
control of the great merchant bank and providing it with occasional
new blood.[41] Like other merchant banks, Barings had to achieve a
balance between accommodating kin who wished to occupy themselves in the bank and maintaining a modicum of efficiency and competence. It was not uncommon for family members to have brief
merchant banking careers, or to be given positions where they could
go through the motions without damaging the business.

While there were often obvious material reasons for striving to
keep a merchant bank within the founding family, resistance to loss
of control cannot be attributed simply to expected returns. Family
histories and memoirs repeatedly stress the symbolic and sentimental
value of dynastic continuity to the founders and subsequent generations. No less than the family estates, the merchant bank testified
to the social worth of the clan. The much-remarked peculiarities of
pre-1960 merchant banks express dynastic success — solidity, traditionalism, quiet order and hierarchy.[42] It is not surprising, therefore,
that a sense of duty towards the family was realized in service within

the bank: scrupulous attention was given to preparation of the younger generation to govern the enterprise. Duty, however, was not always felt to be enough, especially when the elders came to recognize the profligacy of some of their heirs. Some family members spent more than they received, although the bank's capital could be protected while it remained a partnership. But when commercial strategy favoured adoption of limited liability corporate form, with publicly disposable shares, several families set up trusts to safeguard their banks from individuals' whims. In 1929, for example, 'The Hambro Trust Limited was established to ensure that the divergent family interests should remain cohesive, and so keep the power vested within the family'.[43] Barings had done the same thing when they bought back the family bank from its rescuers four years after the crash of 1890; Rothschilds set up Rothschild Continuations in 1939; and the Schroder family kept their interests in harmony through the Veritas Trust.

Subsequent sections outline the impact of external factors, including war and economic depression, on the merchant banks' business. Here, it might be noted that these environmental changes coincided with some strains internal to the controlling families, chiefly problems of succession and motivation. In the numerically small families, such as the Rothschilds, Flemings, Waggs, Samuels and Bensons, unexpected deaths jeopardized continuity of direction. These circumstances prompted the survivors to offer special friends and loyal employees a greater role in directing the banks. However, these conscripts acted in trust on behalf of the family, indeed as regents until a new generation could exercise dynastic authority for themselves. In some cases, appeals to duty could not induce family members to take a banking career seriously; regency was required in these circumstances, too, and became more common through the 1930s and 1940s.

From the First World War onwards, the weaknesses of dynastic control grew more obvious. Several once great merchant banks, including Frederick Huth and Co., Goschen and Cunliffes, Ogilvy Gillanders (the Gladstone family bank), and the two Sassoon enterprises, had begun to languish and were in danger of failure by the early 1920s. In a more competitive and open economic environment, such firms would almost certainly have been taken over by rivals or pushed towards extinction. A change of management and a re-orientation of business probably would have restored profits.[44] However, these things could not occur while the legitimacy of dynastic control was defended by the City fraternity. A hostile takeover, as occurred in industry and commerce in the 1950s, was unthinkable. The culture of the City prohibited overt confrontation. Instead, a family's allies were expected to assist discreetly, typically with the knowledge and approval of the Governor of the Bank of England:

Beyond the market   253

new capital might be injected into the bank and loyal friends might
be invited to replace old family members in directing the enterprise.[45]
A premium was placed on co-operation, discretion and at least a façade
of order; open antagonism had ceased when the Rothschilds on the
one side and Hambros, Barings and Morgan Grenfell on the other
buried their differences in the 1890 crisis.[46]

4 SURVIVAL

Intense belief in the value of dynastic control was not enough in
itself to ensure that the merchant banks would prosper in an era of
global change. Economic forces beyond the ken and command of the
City shifted the centre of international financial activity across the
Atlantic. Within the U.K., too, the decade before 1920 had been
marked by major changes in capitalist organization: industrial concentration had occurred and executive power increasingly was in the
hands of a new managerial elite;[47] while in the City itself, a multitude
of private and joint-stock banks had been merged to form five great
clearing banks.[48] Even the very conservative insurance companies,
many closely aligned with merchant banks, had joined together in
great composites and had begun to push meritocracy of sorts into
the boardroom.[49] Yet this reorganization had proceeded with great
deference towards the claims of owning families, whose disappoint-
ments were cooled out and obscured by public displays of unity on
the newly constituted boards. A model was at hand, then, for the
development of the merchant banking sector: weaker firms could be
absorbed into a small number of large, more bureaucratic banks in
which shareholding families played a diminished role. That this did
not occur despite the economic pressures requires some explanation.

An adequate explanation must go beyond the desire of individual
families to retain control of their banks, for it needs to show how
these families were able to keep control in spite of poor performance
and impending financial failure. A vital part of this picture, of course,
is the Bank of England, which by the 1920s had legitimated its dual
function as central bank and voice of the City. It was an unwritten
law that bank insolvencies were to be averted; where firms were in
danger of failure, therefore, one would find the attention of the
Governor of the Bank and his functionaries. One explanation, then,
is that the Bank of England allowed and enabled founding families
to keep charge of their merchant banks. But, of course, this raises
two crucial questions immediately: how did the Bank do this? and
in whose interests did the Bank act? Neither has a simple answer.

Taking the second question first, one might observe that the
organization of the Bank of England favoured the representation of
certain financial interests above others. Until well into the inter-war

period, these interests were those of the merchant banks, the overseas banks, the fraternity of great merchant houses and the remnants of the private banks: their representatives comprised the Court of the Bank of England, the 26 men who supervised British financial policy.[50] Domestic joint-stock banks were excluded from representation. Of course, the clearing banks' interests could not be ignored any more — far less, in fact — than those of the discount houses or the stockbroking firms. But the Bank of England's Court operated with a world view that above all was sympathetic to the needs and risks of merchant banking. Two merchant banks had been represented for a century or more;[51] others provided directors who, like many of their colleagues, served for three or more decades.[52] It was inconceivable that the Bank would act to the detriment of the established names in the City. By the turn of the century, in some part because of the galvanizing effect of the Barings crisis, the Bank was cast in the role of guarantor and supervisor of a social order as well as a system of markets. On occasion, the Bank of England might challenge the activities of a particular merchant bank, but this was done to maintain procedures and principles which offered collective security. On similar grounds, the Bank strove to exclude 'undesirables', either those whose reputations preceded them or those whom the Bank feared would elude the restraint of the financial community. One basis of this conservative world view was an acute, institutionalized mistrust of non-gentlemen. Although occasionally pragmatism triumphed over principle when it became clear that an undesirable was going to succeed financially, subtle forms of dishonour were inflicted on the parvenu within the City. It was accepted that the Bank's Court, dominated by the grandees of merchant banking, functioned as the City's moral enforcer.[53]

Under these circumstances, the myth of identity between City interests and those of the nation legitimated the Bank's predominant attention to the former. The conflicts inherent in this claim were fully exposed in the restoration and abandonment of the gold standard, in 1925 and 1931 respectively. The prerequisite for restoration of the gold standard at the pre-First World War parity between the pound sterling and the dollar was a rise in the sterling exchange rate. The strategy used to achieve this was an increase in interest rates, which brought a flow of foreign funds into London. But the cost of this was domestic deflation: investment levels dropped, exports became less competitive, and the working class paid the price in increased unemployment. Further difficulties arose because British industry was in poor condition after the war, weakening the export base on which the City had relied in better days. As a result, the Bank was preoccupied with maintaining the exchange rate throughout the brief resurrection of the gold standard.[54] The myth that what was good for finance was good for society as a whole was challenged in some quarters, but it was not discredited. Indeed, the events surrounding the fall of the second Labour Government in 1931 and the election of a Nationalist replacement suggest that public belief in the Bank's guiding myth was extraordinarily tenacious.

It may not have been entirely coincidental that during the gold standard regime of 1925–31, London's merchant banks enjoyed an Indian summer, a new boom in sterling loans to foreign governments. Defaults on some of these, particularly by Central European states, in 1931 created the circumstances that led to direct Bank of England aid to several leading merchant banks. This aid was the most dramatic form of encouragement given to the maintenance of family ownership and control, but it comprises only a single episode in a much broader, enduring context of support. This context is described briefly, by way of an answer to the first question, before considering the salience of Bank-led rescues of merchant banks.

Since its foundation in 1694, the Bank had been — physically as well as figuratively — at the centre of the social organization of the City. Over the two centuries to the zenith of the merchant banks, there had been crucial changes in this social organization, produced by the increased size, complexity and diversity that accompanied the global ascendancy of British trade and finance. From the middle of the nineteenth century, merchant bankers had become increasingly prominent in the Bank's oligarchy. By this time, the Bank's role in the financial system had become less competitive and more authoritative as its masters sought to construct a rational order. As Checkland[55] cogently demonstrates, that order was limited, but none the less it reflected the gradual transformation of *laissez faire* into a system of instrumental reason. The Bank gradually distanced itself from sectional interests. Great care was taken to establish its discretionary authority and trustworthiness. Minimization of the conflict between the Bank's dual roles of city mouthpiece and city policeman depended upon the solid foundation of a community-like social system in the City as well as astute impression management to stave off public criticism and investigation. Trenchant criticisms of the Bank's secrecy[56] failed to puncture the myth of congruence between City and national interests; the Bank exercised the widest discretion — and arbitrariness — behind this shield, almost always without dissent from the City. But essential to this harmonious façade was the exclusiveness of the banking fraternity, which in turn was facilitated by dynastic control.

By the later 1920s, diffuse and dense social ties integrated most of the owners of the City's 20 or so major merchant banks in a community of interest. Kinship and intermarriage brought the Barings, Smiths, Hambros, Morgans and Grenfells together in a clan system which encompassed the wealthiest and most powerful aristocrats in the country. Further links were developing rapidly during this period:

the extended kinship organization absorbed many other banking families in subsequent decades. Ties of friendship and business partnership reinforced those links, and extended to other families, notably the Jewish and Germanic ones, which for various reasons were marginal to the aristocratic-banking kinship structure. To these could be added common membership of clubs, committees, political parties (and parliament), and, of course, the Bank of England. Additional structuring emerged from repeated association and interaction in routine business activity.[57]

Cultural flesh can be put on these bare bones. In the later 1920s, the period of threat and decline, the merchant banks were directed by men whose formative years had been spent in country house comfort, Etonian rigour and privilege, and, in many cases, in the uniform of exclusive military regiments in the Boer War or the First World War. They were natural rulers, patriarchs in a paternalistic enclave around which a more bureaucratic form of capitalism was developing. Hierarchy and ascribed status were taken for granted, but the barbarians could be heard at the gates. Society was the natural habitat of the post-First World War plutocracy: its locale shifted according to the season, from London to the estates, and to snow or sun in winter. Merchant bank owners, with some important exceptions, participated fully in Society's round of activities, sometimes to the detriment of their firms.[58] At all times, in the City and out, merchant bankers presented themselves as gentlemen, although gentlemen proved to be capable of an astounding range of conduct. Perhaps the most that can be inferred from their gentlemanly status is that merchant bank owners acted towards each other with integrity and honour within the City. Limited as this normative order might have been, it extended to mutual assistance and protection under certain conditions, and solidarity in the face of external stress. In particular, the normative order ruled out ruthless competition among the established merchant banks and made hostile take-over attempts unthinkable. Men brought up to control and command with natural ease abstained from following the logic of capitalist accumulation to its conclusion. They co-operated with their competitors, who were also their cousins and friends, in a self-perpetuating community of mutual regard.

Mutal support and tacit agreements to restrain competition had been firmly established by the later years of the nineteenth century. A cluster of merchant banks co-operated most closely with each other: Barings, Brown Shipley, Hambros, Morgan Grenfell and Lazards in particular.[59] Kinship and association underpinned these commercial relations, which had developed over several decades, partly in opposition to the power of the Rothschilds. Co-operation ranged from syndication of issues, non-poaching agreements with regard to customers, maintenance of individual territorial interests, provision of guarantees to each other, sharing information, and joint control of investment trusts and other ventures. Co-operation was not restricted to this group of merchant banks, however; others, including Rothschilds, shared in loan issues and investments.[60] A tradition of mutual support had begun to evolve in the middle of the nineteenth century through joint involvements in diverse ventures, from foreign banks, mines and railways to pastoral companies and plantations: it had been formalized in joint-stock companies and in protective associations like the Corporation of Foreign Bondholders. The Barings crisis of 1890 strengthened this tradition and gave it a moral character. When the First World War had differential effects on the merchant banks — the central and western European specialists' business disappeared — the stronger ones assisted the weaker ones to survive liquidity crises. The Bank of England formalized and gave official endorsement to merchant bank mutuality at this time by sponsoring the Accepting Houses Committee, and extending certain rights and privileges to its members. Although the A.H.C. now seems to have little future,[61] for half a century it functioned as an exclusive club, protected by the power and 'moral suasion' of the Bank of England.

The responsibility that the Bank of England accepted on behalf of merchant banks can be gauged by reviewing its assistance to two old but declining houses which were eventually wound up, and to three major merchant banks which were threatened with extinction because of unforeseen events in 1931.

Frederick Huth and Co. was founded in the early nineteenth century and prospered as a central European specialist under the direction of the Huth and Meinertzhagen families. Its senior partner, Frederick Huth Jackson, was a director of the Bank of England from 1892 until his death in 1921. His brother-in-law, George Macaulay Booth, a member of the Liverpool shipping dynasty, also served as a Bank director. However, the firm ran into difficulties during the First World War, and was in danger of failure by 1921. The Bank had given Huth's special rediscounting facilities — essentially unlimited credit — while assuring the financial world that all was well. For 14 years after Huth Jackson's death, the Bank of England provided the firm with covert loans and assisted in its reorganization. However, this was of no avail, as Huth's continued to lose money, so the firm was finally liquidated. The Bank justified its continuing and expensive aid to Huth's by quoting the convention that

> Huth Jackson's . . . place in the Bank's Court carried with it a traditional obligation on the part of the Bank to support. Since 1841, it had been the Bank's practice to answer any enquiry about a Director's firm by 'undoubted and unqualified' reports and to discount their acceptances without limit.[62]

Montagu Norman's insistence that Huth's not be allowed to fail enabled the owning families to retreat in honour and comfort to their country estates.

The once-great merchant bank of Fruhling and Goschen merged with the firm of the First World War Governor of the Bank of England (Walter Cunliffe) to become Goschens and Cunliffe. The loss of European business weakened their position significantly, aggravated by succession problems within the Goschen dynasty.[63] Goschens and Cunliffe, like Huths, was not to fail suddenly but was to be helped into dignified sale and liquidation over a long period. It eventually ceased business in 1939, when some of its interests as well as one partner (Kenneth Goschen, a Director of the Bank of England) were absorbed amicably into Antony Gibbs and Co.

Less conspicuous than these prolonged withdrawals, but more vital to the survival of family control in the merchant banking sector was the secret assistance given to three major accepting houses in the 1930s.[64] The Bank was never compelled to justify these covert loans, since their existence was revealed only after nationalization. Professor Sayers, however, suggests that the Bank would not allow any of the great names to go under without struggle, because to do so would have jeopardized the reputation of the City and might have led to a run on other banks with disastrous effects for the financial system. It is certainly unlikely that Montagu Norman, the Governor from 1920–44, would have acted primarily on sentimental grounds. The global financial situation was gloomy from a banker's viewpoint, particularly because gold was being siphoned out of London and the pound sterling was so patently over-priced. Bank failures in Europe and the U.S.A. terrified British bankers. Whether failure of the three accepting houses would have brought a chain of crashes in other financial institutions is incapable of resolution with finality. The probability of collapse must have been high: in view of the structural connections, possible economic consequences and tradition of Bank regulation and supportiveness, it was a foregone conclusion that assistance would be given. Irrespective of other results, it is almost certain that failure of the three accepting houses would have brought down at least four others with European interests, spelling the end of family dominance in the merchant banking sector.

Lazard Brothers and Co. was on the verge of ceasing business in July 1931.[65] The Wall Street crash had occurred in October 1929, beginning the great depression that undermined Rothschild's Credit Anstalt in Vienna, in May 1931. The Austrian bank failure was compounded by a moratorium on short-term central European debts in June 1931, which seriously affected the liquidity of the accepting houses. Lazards at this time was one of the great six merchant banks, and with its ally, Morgan Grenfell, a leader in the reorganization of British industry. Three families controlled Lazards. The chief shareholder was Viscount Cowdray, who through his industrial-financial company S. Pearson and Son, possessed a majority of the equity. Sir Robert Kindersley, later awarded a peerage, was chairman and Robert (later Lord) Brand was senior managing director. Kindersley was a Director of the Bank of England. When Montagu Norman, the Governor, returned from a meeting in Basle on 14 July, 1931, Kindersley requested a secret interview immediately. In the interview, Kindersley disclosed that Lazards needed £3 million from the Bank to prevent failure, because of a £6 million loss due to 'maladministration' in the Brussels office. Norman took the proposal to rescue Lazards to the Committee of Treasury, the governing body within the Court, where it was endorsed on the grounds that it was necessary to avoid panic in the City. The Bank loan averted the crisis, but Lazards returned for another £2 million a year later. The accepting house repaid the Bank over several years: foreign bankers were none the wiser.

Surreptitious aid was given to two other accepting houses. Both loans were much smaller than Lazards', but equally essential to their survival. The Bank also operated extensively in the discount market to enable the financing of bills to continue. Hambros, Barings, and Rothschilds, together with the three firms above, were forced to withhold a large part of their acceptances from the market after the moratorium on German, Austrian and Hungarian short-term debts. The Bank bought otherwise unsaleable bills from the accepting houses, ensuring their liquidity and solvency.

It is not suggested here that the Bank conspired to save family control in the merchant banks whatever the cost to the rest of the financial system or the British economy. Rather, the Bank — the Governor and Court, guided by precedent and pragmatism — resolved to prevent failure or embarrassment in the City. The world-view of banking leaders implicitly assumed that the liquidation of prestigious merchant banks was against the national interest. Young, no friend of the left, none the less observed that

> The family-like atmosphere of the whole British ascendancy (in the City) up to 1930 misled its members too often into thinking that the public good was at stake when they were organising their own comfort.[66]

If attention is confined to the specific difficulties of the accepting houses, alternative courses of action do not appear politically or economically feasible. The logic of the sitation suggests that covert loans and market intervention were appropriate actions, given the Bank's objectives. However, this conclusion begs much larger questions about the Bank's long-term relationship with the government, its responsibility for Britain's over-priced pound and subjection to

the gold standard, and its direction by merchant bankers. It is difficult to avoid the conclusion that the Bank's priorities were established
with special attention to the interests of the financial institutions and
with myopic disregard for their impact on the rest of British society.

5 STAGNATION AND BEYOND

Stagnation set in to the merchant banking sector for two decades
after the close escapes of 1931–2. Kellett[67] found that

> Allowing for a threefold depreciation in the value of the pound
> the merchant banks' deposits in the period 1955–57 were only just
> level with their equivalent thirty years earlier. The average of
> deposits in 1955–57 of £156 million, or £52 million at 1936 prices,
> compared with £54 million in the year 1927. Acceptance credit
> business was equally flat. The credits outstanding in 1955–57 of
> £104 million, equivalent to £34 million at pre-war prices, compared
> with an actual level of around £34 million in 1927–30.

But these figures, and the continuity of control during this period,
obscure some important nascent changes.

One was a modification of merchant banking business, away from
acceptances and foreign loans towards industrial finance and investment management. Inevitably, much of the traditional craft of
merchant banking became redundant, as did the practical contributions of some senior employees and partners. The corollary, of
course, was an influx in the 1950s of new men, many with specialized
training, who were poorly suited to a regime of paternalism.[68]

Second, several new merchant banks grew to rival the great names
in size and skill. Most important among these was S. G. Warburg and
Co., founded in the City in the early 1930s by the scion of a long-
established Jewish-German banking family. No respecter of conventions, Warburg's hallmark was aggressive dealing. Warburg's success in
the 1957 takeover struggle for British Aluminium[69] rewrote the rules
of corporate finance. Another innovator was Philip Hill, whose investment trust-cum-merchant bank became a leader in industrial issues
and corporate advice; its speculative activities also came under
scrutiny from the City. Hill's successors merged their merchant bank
with three older, dynastic enterprises: Higginson & Co., Erlangers (in
1959), and M. Samuel and Co. in 1965. The result was Hill Samuel.

Third, the average age of merchant bank boards increased considerably during the decades of stagnation. Death provided the only exit
from merchant banking for hereditary directors (if one excludes gross
incompetence). For example, Lords Kindersley and Brand were still
governing Lazards in 1951, 20 years after the Bank rescue, aged 82

and 73 respectively. Other merchant banks also exhibited remarkable continuity of direction, remaining under the control of men whose minds and characters were shaped by the experiences of Victorian upper stratum life.[70] It appears that wartime deaths of heirs — particularly in the Great War — destabilized the merchant banks no less than the landed aristocracy and gentry, by depriving the older generation of choice of successors.[71]

The willingness of some old families to dispose of their merchant banks during the 1950s indicated an awareness of significant changes in the financial world. The time of the small, family run bank staffed by loyal retainers had passed; but the thick walls of the City had long kept out the challengers. In the 1950s and early 1960s, sales occurred to other families or to entrepreneurs, and created merchant banks on a par with the great names. It was only in the later 1960s, with the sale of a majority holding in William Brandt's Sons to the National and Grindlays Bank that the trend towards large-scale bureaucratic control began. By then, the City had been transformed by the development of 'parallel' money markets, notably the Eurocurrency market, and an influx of foreign banks and aspiring entrepreneurs. Moreover, diversification of clearing bank functions had begun to challenge areas of business that the merchant banks had believed to be secure. Merchant banks required reorientation and reorganization to exploit the new opportunities presented by the rejuvenated City.[72] Some dynasties, such as the Hambros, set about doing this systematically and with clear intent of retaining control.[73] Others, like the Gibbs in 1980 and the Arbuthnots in 1982, cashed in their chips without fuss and left the scene that both had inhabited for 150 years.

Change has characterized the period since the late 1960s. A substantial transition has occurred from a merchant banking system overwhelmingly controlled by dynasts and their appointees to one in which bureaucratic-entrepreneurial control is becoming typical. Bureaucratic-entrepreneurial control refers not only to the separation of legal ownership from strategic control and to the coordination and regulation of the enterprise by bureaucratic means, but also to the construction of entrepreneurial roles occupied by salaried employees within an explicitly rule-bound bureaucratic structure. The latter feature obviously generates organizational divisions and tensions, but it is an inevitable compromise between the type of personalized flexibility essential to certain merchant banking tasks and the large-scale organization resulting from recent growth. Although consequent tensions and divisions may be more acute in contemporary merchant banks than in insurance companies and clearing banks, for example, the problem of reconciling enterpreneurship with large-scale administration is by no means absent in the latter.

This is not the place to explore how the diminution of family possession has affected organizational relations within the merchant

262 *Michael Lisle-Williams*

banks, since this article's focus is on the factors which led to the extraordinary tenure of family capitalism in the merchant banking sector. However, it should be emphasized that the process of transition has occurred chiefly in the 1970s and 1980s during a period of growth and prosperity for the merchant banks, and not, as might have been predicted, during the troubled years of 1931–2. Moreover, the transition to non-hereditary, non-owner control has begun to occur in the merchant banks several decades after a similar shift in the clearing banks.

6 IMPLICATIONS OF THE ARGUMENTS

This article has explored two theses which explain the prolonged survival of family capitalism in the English merchant banking sector. Throughout the preceding sections, emphasis has been given to the significance of the mediation of economic forces by social organization. The counterfactual employed here was that in the absence of a cohesive system of social relationships in the merchant banking sector — extending to the Bank of England itself — global changes in the organization of capitalism would have undermined family-based control more dramatically and rapidly than has been the case.

It is implied in this argument that the much-remarked trend from status to contract was reversed in the English financial world. In the last decades of the nineteenth century, *laissez faire* and no-holds-barred competition in the merchant banking sector were replaced by a mode of allocation that depended on duties and reciprocal obligations derived from a stable status order. Competition became less direct by the turn of the century; income and profits were determined as much by agreement within the merchant banking community as by market forces. This situation increased the likelihood of individual bank survival, particularly when traditional sources of revenue were destroyed by the First World War. Co-operation was a rational strategy through the long years of stagnation.

However, by the later 1950s, when the old club of merchant bankers could not prevent changes that were profiting new rivals, both domestic and foreign, the relationships, norms and beliefs inherited from the Victorian era were increasingly recognized as redundant and even dangerous. Far-reaching changes in the international financial system resulted in the displacement of the old status order in favour of less personalized organization. Dynastic representatives bowed to the imperatives of capitalist progress. They relinquished active control to join their old cronies and kin in the genteel ceremonial order maintained by the rentier segment of the capitalist class.

In this final section, implications of the arguments advanced here are considered for three topics of outstanding sociological concern.

Beyond the market 263

These are ownership and control of corporate resources, class action, and power in British society. The narrowness of the substantive area explored here and the numbers of questions as yet only tentatively answered suggest that a broad brush is needed in the following discussion.

(i) *Ownership and control* The arguments presented here contain implications for research into the distribution of corporate ownership and control. Obviously, it is implied that the shift from family-directed to manager-directed enterprise is significant, but not in the sense that managerialist theorists might suppose. For one thing, the transition from family to managerial direction is less clearcut than it might seem. There are several degrees of family involvement between complete strategic control and operational management and complete disposal of shareholdings: joint direction, rights of veto, and privileges of influence based on long association. Variations of this sort exist in the present-day merchant banks. Second, the social role of salaried employees differs between sectors and over historical time. In the merchant banking sector, it was noted, there were precedents for managerial control on behalf of owners, based on a relationship infused with status considerations and legitimated by a wider context of reciprocal rights and duties. In other sectors, where ownership was less visible and continuous, the shareholder-manager relationship was more openly contractual and, on occasions, conflictual. A third factor which complicates the issue is that what appear from share registers to be instances of managerial control may actually be entrepreneurial control: insurance companies, pension funds and merchant banks sponsor and support entrepreneurs by buying large blocks of shares in particular companies.

Managerialists generally contend that the fragmentation of private shareholdings and the decline of dynastic direction have freed managers from accountability to owners and thereby, from preoccupation with profits and growth. However, trends in the merchant banking sector lend weight to the opposite conclusion: managerial control means less variation in both the ends pursued and the means employed. Reliance on the capital market rather than retained profits and family fortunes entails constant attention to the visible symbols of competitive success: balance sheet size, profits, 'innovation', and share price. The result appears to be more formally rational, relative to the end of competitive success, than family capitalist organization within the pre-1960 City order.

Assumptions of corporate independence are unrealistic. An adequate theory of corporate ownership and control needs to recognize and incorporate the constraints of oligopoly in many sectors, large shareholdings of financial institutions, networks of board-level association, and patterns of merchant banking advice. Combined with these structural constraints, of course, is the culture of big business, which further limits the scope of autonomous corporate action.

Over the past century, the organization of authority and benefit in the capitalist economy has become more formally structured; more impersonal; more differentiated; and less directly connected with the private ownership of capital. The growth of large-scale bureaucratic transnational enterprises, specialized financial institutions and state economic agencies is symptomatic of the systematization of capitalism.[74] So too is the construction of an edifice of statutory regulation. Within this framework, the role of the merchant banks increasingly has been to mediate between the major beneficiaries and the executive controllers of systematized capitalism. In other words, merchant banks mobilize, reconcile and integrate interests associated with the accumulation of private capital. They help to impose the interests of particular entrepreneurs on complex corporate organization, while collectively acting to extend the scope of profit-oriented formal rationality within the company sector. In performing this dual function, the merchant banks link class to corporate structure.

(ii) *Theories of class action* The study of merchant bank owners revealed how a diverse, largely alien group of traders and money lenders was transformed over a few generations into a morally integrated community within the capitalist class. Individuals within the merchant banking dynasties came to resemble each other in their cultural attributes, recreations, ways of life, and even demeanour and appearance. Association and kinship ties reinforced this unifying cultural moulding. The signs of status and class manifested themselves in the persons, residences and enterprises of merchant bankers.

Identification of class action involves some ambiguity. Of course, in many cases, merchant bankers and their kin acted deliberately as members of the capitalist class or the governing class. In the later nineteenth century, such action was legitimated by an ideology of duty and responsibility. Parliamentary representation, county administration, advice to Cabinet, and even the maintenance of standards of display and entertainment were justified in these terms. In practice, there was almost always disagreement about the best strategy and the correct policy — issues such as electoral reform, Irish home rule, the South African war, and free trade were highly divisive. However, the class action of merchant bankers may have been most significant where it was depicted as protecting the national interest, revered British tradition or the like. Broadly, class action would have included continuing support for cultural institutions which legitimated inequality; for state institutions which were instruments of capitalist imperialism; and for the Bank of England

and its ideology. The distinctive feature of class action was that it dismissed, discredited or opposed the attempts of organized labour to challenge the authority of private capital. As such, class action must be inferred; it cannot be confined simply to those behaviours which capitalists intended to be class-effective. This topic will be pursued elsewhere in respect of financial capitalists, but the point is that an historically adequate analysis of class action requires investigation of the relationship between institutional dynamics and the conscious strategies of groups and individuals.

(iii) *Theories of power in British society*   Sociologists scarcely need reminding that the study of power remains one of the discipline's great headaches. Certainly Lukes' formulation of the problem highlighted the inadequacies of issue-based or decision-making conceptualizations of power and shifted the focus back onto the institutional structures of society.[75] To assess the relative power of different social groupings — classes, status groups, communities, organizations or loose associations — one must investigate their access to material and symbolic resources. The main implication of this study is that financial institutions are major determinants of access to material resources and deserve prominence in sociological theories of power in British society.

The transition from dynastic control to bureaucratic control in financial institutions is significant for theorizing social power. In considering the access of particular groups to material resources, one needs to recognize the gatekeeping function performed by lenders and creditors. If the gatekeepers cease to be aristocratized private owners, extending credit on the basis of particularistic criteria and moralistic assumptions, and are replaced by financial technocrats with professional ideologies and universalistic market-rational criteria, the sort of people and organizations being funded may be much less 'socially acceptable' and much more ruthless and egoistically rational than was formerly the case. Under these circumstances, the composition of the British capitalist class may alter dramatically to include more 'self-made' men, while the power of the remnants of the old aristocratic-bourgeois status group may decline greatly. British society may become more thoroughly capitalist, especially if moral distinctions between 'responsible' and 'irresponsible' business fall away further, and arms dealers, drug traffickers, and organizers of prostitution find willing creditors in the legitimate banking system. This is not a sentimental epitaph for the passing of dynastic control, but a hypothesis, following Hirsch,[76] that the end of family capitalism may mean the extension of capitalist rationality to once morally objectionable undertakings and a major shift in the balance of power within the capitalist class. Such a change may further limit the legitimacy and effectiveness of state regulation of economic life,

266   *Michael Lisle-Williams*

and challenge the compatibility of liberal democracy and amoral capitalism.

Michael Lisle-Williams
School of Humanities
Griffith University, Australia

NOTES

1. This article is based on a larger study whose findings are set out more fully in the author's doctoral thesis: 'A Sociological Analysis of Changing Social Organisation and Market Conduct in the English Merchant Banking Sector', unpublished D.Phil. thesis, Oxford University, 1982.

2. See L. H. Jenks, *The Migration of British Capital to 1875*, Alfred A. Knopf, 1927.

3. Cf. B. Lardner, 'Merchant Banks Rebuild their Image', *The Banker*, May 1978; D. F. Channon, *British Banking Strategy and the International Challenge*, Macmillan, 1977.

4. Especially K. Marx, *Capital*, vol. 3, Foreign Languages Publishing House, Moscow 1962; M. Weber, *Economy and Society*, G. Roth and C. Wittich (eds), University of California Press, 1978, vol. 1, ch. 2; W. Sombart, *The Jews and Modern Capitalism*, Free Press, 1951; G. Simmel, *The Philosophy of Money*, Routledge & Kegan Paul, 1978 (trans. by T. Bottomore and D. Frisby); and R. Hilferding, *Finance Capital*, Routledge & Kegan Paul, 1981 (ed. and intro. by T. Bottomore).

5. The Parker Tribunal Report (*Report of the Tribunal Appointed to Inquire into Allegations of Improper Disclosure of Information Relating to the Raising of the Bank Rate*, Cmnd. 350, HMSO Jan. 1958) examined the actions of directors of Lazards and Morgan Grenfell, two prestigious merchant banks. T. Lupton and C. S. Wilson revealed a pattern of social ties — particularly kinship — amongst these persons and other 'establishment' figures in their study, 'The Social Backgrounds and Connections of Top Decision Makers', *Manchester School*, 1959, 27, pp. 30-51. Subsequent enquiries which have explored the social characteristics of bank directors include: S. Aaronovitch, *The Ruling Class*, Lawrence & Wishart, 1961; M. Barratt Brown, 'The Controllers of British Industry', in K. Coates (ed.), *Can the Workers Run Industry?*, Sphere, 1968; P. Stanworth and A. Giddens, 'An Economic Elite', in *Elites and Power in British Society*, Cambridge University Press, 1974; and R. Whitley, 'Commonalities and Connections Among Directors of Large Financial Institutions', *Sociological Review*, 1973, 21, pp. 613-32.

6. F. Longstreth, 'The City, Industry and the State', in C. Crouch (ed.), *State and Economy in Contemporary Capitalism*, Croom Helm, 1979.

7. M. Moran, 'Finance Capital and Pressure — Group Politics in Britain', *British Journal of Political Science*, Oct. 1981, 11(4), pp. 381-404.

8. G. Thompson, 'The Relationship Between the Financial and Industrial Sector in the United Kingdom Economy', *Economy and Society*, 1977, 6, pp. 235-83.

9. H. Overbeek, 'Finance Capital and the Crisis in Britain', *Capital and Class*, 1980, p. 11.

10. See W. D. Rubinstein, *Men of Property: The Very Wealthy in Britain Since the Industrial Revolution*, Croom Helm, 1981, esp. pp. 91-7.

11. Merchant Banking Dynasties in the English Class Structure (forthcoming, *British Journal of Sociology*).

12. There are now 16 accepting houses, members of the Accepting Houses Committee. They include most but not all the larger merchant banks. Excluded are the subsidiaries of three

Beyond the market

clearing banks, and two foreign owned banks, as well as small merchant banks without substantial acceptance business. Table 1 compares the accepting houses on various dimensions. Numbers of corporate clients and the scale of investment management business are not perfectly correlated with asset totals.

industrial and commercial companies have regular merchant bank advisers. Merchant bankers are on the board of 36 of the top 150 companies, while directors of another 20 of the top 150 are also on merchant bank boards. Less formal links, such as common club or committee membership, are extensive. However, the meaning of

TABLE 1: *London's accepting houses, business indicators, 1979.*

Accepting house	Balance sheet totals (£m)	Capital plus disclosed reserves (£m)	Pension funds managed (£m)	Investment trusts (£m)	No. of 'top 1000' corporate clients
Arbuthnot Latham*	185	13.4	1.5	—	1
Baring Bros.	475	25.0	675	69	27
Brown Shipley	253	19.0	17	—	5
Charterhouse Japhet	211	15.4	207	81	13
Robert Fleming	215	34.0	1,034	651	16
Guinness Mahon	304	22.7	3	—	6
Hambros	1,524	81.9	274	93	27
Hill Samuel	1,411	81.9	1,450	254	73
Kleinwort Benson	2,388	110.4	405	205	54
Lazards	729	41.9	941	83	32
Mercury Securities†	1,156	79.1	1,591	—	68
Morgan Grenfell	1,265	45.3	1,293	—	67
Rea Bros.	111	4.9	4	—	4
N. M. Rothschild	528	25.0	377	22	47
Samuel Montagu	1,368	57.1	96	302	31
Schroders	1,817	57.9	1,384	150	74
Singer & Friedlander	317	n/a	8	15	14

Sources: Annual reports; Directory of City Connections 1980–81; Pension Funds Yearbook, 1981; Investment Trust Yearbook, 1981.

* Resigned after take-over, 1982.
† S. G. Warburg & Co.

13. See the publications *Euromoney* and *The Banker* for up-to-date summaries and surveys.

14. Richard Minns's book, *Pension Funds and British Capitalism*, Heinemann, 1980, emphasizes the power of merchant banks in the allocation of capital.

15. Informed accounts include R. Heller and N. Willatt, *Can You Trust Your Bank?* Weidenfeld & Nicolson, 1977, and Anthony Sampson, *The Moneylenders*, Viking Press, 1982. Revealing evidence of changes in inter-bank conduct is found in Sir A. Johnston's, *The City Take-Over Code*, Oxford University Press, 1980.

16. 550 of the largest 1,000 U.K.

these dense, variegated connections is less obvious than Aaronovitch or Barratt Brown have suggested. Constraint and communication are two dimensions of the resultant pattern (see Lisle-Williams, *Note 1* above).

17. Similar to the finding of J. Scott and M. Hughes in 'Capital and Communication in Scottish Business', *Sociology*, 1980, 14(1), pp. 29–48.

18. See P. Stanworth and A. Giddens, above; and for an analysis of directors of financial institutions, M. Lisle-Williams, 'Continuities in the English Financial Elite, 1850–1980', unpub. B.S.A./P.S.A. paper, Sheffield University, Jan. 1981.

19. S. Nyman and A. Silberston, "The

268 *Michael Lisle-Williams*

Ownership and Control of Industry', *Oxford Economic Papers*, 1978, 30 (1).

20. A. Francis, 'Families, Firms and Finance Capital', *Sociology*, Feb. 1980, 14 (1).

21. For a detailed description of the rescue of Baring Brothers from financial illiquidity in 1890, see M. de Cecco, *Money and Empire*, Blackwell, 1974.

22. See Susan Strange's *Sterling and British Policy: A Political Study of an International Currency in Decline*, Oxford University Press, 1971; Sir Henry Clay's biography of *Lord Norman*, Macmillan, 1957; and D. Moggridge's *British Monetary Policy 1924-1931: The Norman Conquest of $4.86*, Cambridge University Press, 1972.

23. Cf. H. Carter and I. Partington, *Applied Economics in Banking and Finance*, Oxford University Press, 1979.

24. S. G. Checkland's *The Rise of Industrial Society in England, 1815-1885*, Longmans, 1964 places the 'suppliers and manipulators of capital' in this context.

25. Almost all early merchant banks continued to deal in goods as well as finance. The distinction between merchant houses and merchant banks became clearer in the final quarter of the nineteenth century. With this qualification, the following merchant banks were founded before 1850: Baring Bros.; Brown Shipley; Frederick Huth & Co.; Fruhling & Goschens; N. M. Rothschild & Sons; Samuel Dobree & Sons; J. S. Morgan & Co.; Kleinworts; Seligmans; J. Henry Schroder; Morton Rose & Co.; Ralli & Co.; P. P. Rodocanachi & Co.; Arbuthnot Latham; Antony Gibbs & Sons; Morrison & Co.; C. J. Hambro & Co.

26. Biographies, family histories and memoirs used in the study of merchant bankers include: R. Bramsen and K. Wain, *The Hambros, 1779-1979*, Michael Joseph, 1979; P. Magnus, *Gladstone*, Dutton Books, 1954; S. G. Checkland, *The Gladstones 1764-1851*, Cambridge University Press,
1971; E. Corti, *The Rise of the House of Rothschild*, Gollancz, 1928; V. Cowles, *The Rothschilds*, Weidenfeld & Nicolson, 1973; C. Douglas-Home, *Evelyn Baring*, Collins, 1978; T. Spinner, *George Joachim Goschen: The Transformation of a Victorian Liberal*, Cambridge University Press, 1973; D. Farrer, *The Warburgs*, Michael Joseph, 1974; D. Hart-Davis, *Peter Fleming*, Jonathan Cape, 1974; R. W. Hidy, *The House of Baring in American Trade and Finance*, Harvard University Press, 1949; N. Mosley, *Julian Grenfell*, Weidenfeld & Nicolson, 1976; G. Wechsberg, *The Merchant Bankers*, Weidenfeld & Nicolson, 1966; P. Ferris, *The City*, Random House, 1961; R. Palin, *Rothschild Relish*, Cassell, 1970; S. Jackson, *The Sassoons*, Heinemann, 1968; R. Henriques, *Marcus Samuel*, Barrie & Rockcliffe, 1961; C. Bermant, *The Cousinhood*, Macmillan, 1971; W. L. Fraser, *All to the Good*, Heinemann, 1963.

27. W. Rubinstein, *Men of Property*, above, p. 96.

28. F. M. L. Thompson, 'Britain', in D. Spring (ed.), *European Landed Elites in the Nineteenth Century*, Johns Hopkins University Press, 1977, p. 29.

29. See e.g. S. Aris, *The Jews in Business*, Jonathan Cape, 1970. F. Donaldson's *The Marconi Scandal*, Hart-Davis, 1962 also highlights the strength of anti-semitism in the years before the First World War. C. Holmes, *Anti-Semitism in British Society, 1879-1939*, Edward Arnold, 1979 refers at some length to the social obstacles encountered by Jewish bankers.

30. See B. Tuchman, *The Proud Tower*, Macmillan, 1966, p. 18.

31. This figure refers to those families which had (a) acquired substantial wealth through merchant banking or related business; (b) purchased a major London residence, a country estate, or both; (c) been mentioned in Society news, particularly in The Tatler, between 1900 and 1914; (d) participated regularly in the Society calendar; (e) sent sons to Eton, Harrow, Rugby, or Winchester; (f) joined one or more

of the 10 most exclusive London clubs; and (g) married members of Peers' families or the landed gentry. Most families had also obtained at least one hereditary title, although in a few cases knighthoods only had been offered (or accepted). Family names are:

Arbuthnot
Baring
Benson
Brand
Brandt
Brown
D'Erlanger
Fleming
Gibbs
Gladstone
Glyn
Goschen
Grenfell
Guinness
Hambro
Huth
Keyser
Kindersley
Kleinwort
Mills
Montagu
Morrison
Norman
Pearson
Ralli
Rodocanachi
Rose
Rothschild
Samuel
Sassoon
Schroder
Schuster
Smith
Stern
Tiarks
Wagg

32. See F. M. L. Thompson, *English Landed Society in the Nineteenth Century*, Routledge & Kegan Paul, 1963: ch. XI, 'Indian Summer, 1880-1914'.

33. Cf. J. Camplin, *The Rise of the Plutocrats*, Constable, 1978.

34. The role of Society leaders is sensitively portrayed by L. Davidoff in *The Best Circles*, Croom Helm, 1973.

35. J. Bateman, *Great Landowners of Great Britain and Ireland*, 4th ed., 1883.

36. These generalizations are based on the accounts of family life included in *Note 26* above, as well as in other records of Victorian upper stratum life, including K. Rose, *Superior Person: A Portrait of Curzon and his Circle in Late Victorian England*, Weidenfeld & Nicolson, 1969; and *The Later Cecils*, Weidenfeld & Nicolson, 1974. P. Magnus, *King Edward VII*, 1975; Consuelo Vanderbilt Balsan, *The Glitter and The Gold*, 1953; and R.R. James, *Lord Rosebery*, Weidenfeld & Nicolson, 1963.

37. An analysis of school lists (see *Note 1*) revealed that 29 of the 36 banking families investigated had sent one or more sons to Eton.

38. Members of at least 24 families had been Members of the Parliament by the First World War. As in so many other pursuits, the Barings were most prolific; not less than 17 Barings had sat in the House of Commons.

39. Some are indicated by W. D. Rubinstein, in 'Men of Property: Occupation, Inheritance and Power', in Stanworth and Giddens, above, pp. 144-69.

40. Coutts and Co., the aristocratic private bank, is one such case (R. M. Robinson, *Coutts': The History of a Banking House*, John Murray, 1929).

41. Brothers-in-law and close business associates (Labouchere, Hodgson) were brought in as junior but active partners (see Hidy, *Note 26* above).

42. Graphic accounts are given by Ferris, Fraser and Palin, among others (*Note 26* above).

43. Bramsen and Wain, above (*Note 26*), p. 380.

44. The success of several new merchant banking firms during the early inter-war period suggested that some re-orientation of traditional business was feasible. Among these firms were Rea Brothers, closely linked to North of England shipping interests; Gray Dawes, part of the Earl of Inchcape's empire; S. Japhet and Co., capitalised by Sir Ernest Cassel, King Edward VII's adviser; and Singer and Friedlander.

45. This occurred in M. Samuel, Helbert Wagg, Arbuthnot Latham and Erlangers during the inter-war period.

46. See Bramsen and Wain, above.

47. L. Hannah, *The Rise of the Corporate Economy*, Methuen, 1976, ch. 5.

48. J. Sykes, *The Amalgamation Movement in English Banking, 1825-1914*, P. S. King, 1926, provides a detailed history.

49. See Barry Supple, *The Royal Exchange Assurance: A History of British Insurance, 1720-1970*, Cambridge University Press, 1970, esp. ch. 12.

50. R. S. Sayers, *The Bank of England, 1891-1944*, Cambridge University Press, 1976, vol. 2, ch. 22 outlines the relationship between the City, the Court of the Bank, and its salaried officials.

51. Barings, for 123 years, and Morgan Grenfell, through the Grenfell and Smith families, for 138 years.

52. Both of Montagu Norman's grandfathers were Directors for several decades: George Warde Norman for 50 years (1822-72), and Mark Collet for 39 years (1866-1905). Montagu Norman was the Bank's longest serving Governor (1920-44).

53. S. G. Checkland emphasizes the narrow conservatism of financial morality, in 'The Mind of the City', *Oxford Economic Papers*, 1957, 9, pp. 261-78.

54. D. E. Moggridge, *British Monetary Policy, 1924-1931: The Norman Conquest of $4.86*, Cambridge University Press, 1972.

55. S. G. Checkland, *The Rise of Industrial Society in England, 1815-1885*, Longmans, 1964, ch. 6.

56. Criticism of the 'money power' was widespread in Victorian times; its sources and targets were many and contradictory. Gladstonian liberals, radicals, and landed conservatives were dissatisfied with various aspects of City conduct (see Checkland, above, pp. 210-12).

57. See *Note 1* above.

58. Suggested by Cowles, Douglas-Home, and Palin, among others (*Note 26* above).

59. Detailed by J. Crosby Brown, *A History of Brown Shipley*, 1909, and Bramsen and Wain, above.

60. Outlined in L. H. Jenks, (*Note 2* above), and in H. Feis, *Europe, The World's Banker, 1870-1914*, Yale University Press, 1930.

61. See recent discussions in *The Banker* and *Euromoney*.

62. R. S. Sayers, *Note 50* above, p. 268.

63. George J. Goschen was Chancellor of the Exchequer from 1887-92; he had been a Liberal minister (First Lord of the Admiralty, 1871-74), but joined the Conservatives after the Irish home rule split in 1886. Three of his brothers were active in the City — one was a Director of the Bank of England.

64. Sayers disclosed the existence of these loans in 1976. A senior director of one rescued bank confirmed that Bank of England loans were not repaid in full until the 1950s (interview 18.8.1981).

65. The details which follow are attributable to Sayers, above.

66. G. K. Young, *Merchant Banking: Practice and Prospects*, Weidenfeld & Nicholson, 1971.

67. R. Kellett, *The Merchant Banking Arena*, Macmillan, 1967, p. 29.

68. See Young, above, and also G. Wechsberg, *The Merchant Bankers*, Weidenfeld & Nicholson, 1966.

69. This episode dramatized the conflict between the dynastic establishment and the innovative new banks. It was widely understood as a major challenge to the authority of the old City oligarchy. Accounts of the 'Aluminium war' can be found in Bramsen and Wain, above; Young, above; and R. Spiegelberg, *The City: Power without Accountability*, Blond & Briggs, 1973. The development of the conflict can be reconstructed from contemporary newspaper reports: see e.g. the *Financial Times*, November, 1958 to January, 1959.

70. Upon the death of Lord Aldenham, the *eminence grise* of Antony Gibbs and Sons, *The Times* stressed the formative effect of a Victorian upbringing on his character: 'Lord Aldenham was an old fashioned man. He might almost have been described as a Victorian. He had all the virtues of

that age. Born into a great merchant banking tradition, he had to the full the high qualities for which is family had always been renowned . . . he had not only the trust but the respect of all members of his staff . . . When he was in the chair, the annual general meetings of the Westminster Bank were conducted with the informality of a family affair'. (*The Times*, 2.6. 1969, p. 10.).

71. For example, four of the five sons of Francis Henry Baring (1848–1914) died in the Great War; so did two of William Grenfell's three sons; four of Pascoe du Pre Grenfell's nine sons died in war.

72. The pressure of new opportunities is emphasized by D. Channon, *British Banking Strategy and the International Challenge*, Macmillan, 1977, ch. 4.

73. See *Euromoney*, April 1978.

74. There is concurrence on this point with John Scott, *Corporations, Classes and Capitalism*, Hutchinson, 1979; and with Graham Salaman's conclusions (pp. 245–7) in *Class and the Corporation*, Fontana, 1981.

75. Steven Lukes, *Power: A Radical View*, Macmillan, 1974.

76. F. Hirsch, *Social Limits to Growth*, Routledge & Kegan Paul, 1977.

[24]

Volume XVII, No. 1   Journal of Southeast Asian Studies   March 1986

The Khaw Group: Chinese Business in Early Twentieth-century Penang

J. W. CUSHMAN

Khaw Sim Bee's 許沁美 premature death in 1913 at the hands of an assasin, allegedly torn by jealousy over Sim Bee's advances towards his wife, marked the end of an era in the family politics of peninsular Siam. Sim Bee was the youngest son of Khaw Soo Cheang 許泗漳 (1797–1882), a Hokkien immigrant who rose to the governorship of Ranong and founded the Khaw dynasty in Siam. Through his position as High Commissioner of Monthon Phuket, Sim Bee came to dominate the political and commercial life of the region. The man who King Vajiravudh ranked "as a personal friend who will be sincerely mourned by me as a personal loss"[1] headed a family that was equalled by few others in the kingdom.[2]

But the Khaw family was not just another of the many Chinese families that made good in Siam's accommodating cultural milieu in this period. Through political patronage and commercial acumen, they had become one of the wealthiest and most powerful of Siam's bureaucratic families. While their political influence derived from the bureaucratic appointments they were granted in Siam itself, their commercial influence extended across Siam's southern borders into Malaya and the Netherlands East Indies. Penang, with its framework of British laws and commercial facilities, was the nerve centre of the Khaw business empire.

What marked Khaw Sim Bee and his relatives from other Chinese families in Siam was the duality inherent in their positions as political representatives of the Court in Bangkok,

---

This article is a revised version of a paper presented at the Colloquium on Malaysian Social and Economic History held at the Australian National University, June 8–10, 1985. The research was funded in part by a grant from the Social Science Research Council, New York and by assistance from the Department of Far Eastern History, the Research School of Pacific Studies, Australian National University. I am grateful for their support. I also wish to thank Craig Reynolds, Hong Lysa, Tony Kevin, Howard Dick, Ben Batson, Sharon Carstens and John Butcher for reading and commenting on earlier drafts of this paper. The following abbreviations are used in the footnotes: *PG* (*Pinang Gazette and Straits Chronicle*), F.O. (Foreign Office), C.P. (Confidential Print), N.A., R. 5 (Bangkok: National Archives, Reign 5), B. (Misc Documents in the National Archives), T. (Ministry of Foreign Affairs), K. Kh. (Office of the Financial Adviser), M. (Ministry of the interior).

[1]Quoted in *PG*, 22 April 1913.

[2]For a history of the family, see Prince Damrong Rajanabhab, "Tamnan mu'ang Ranong" [History of Ranong] in *Prachum phongsawadan*, pt. 50 and *Xu shi xongpu* [A genealogy of the Hsu (Khaw) clan] (Singapore, 1963); pp. B161–B165. For a biography of Khaw Sim Bee, see Senanuwongphakdi, *Prawat lae ngan khǫng phraya Ratsadanupradit (Khǫ Simbi na Ranǫng)* [The life and work of phraya Ratsadanupradit] (Bangkok, 1970); Darunee Kaewmauang, "Phraya Ratsadanupraditmahitsornphakdi (Khǫ Simbi na Ranǫng): Phunamkanpokkhrong huamu'ang Thai fang tawantok phǫ sǫ 2444–2456" [Phraya Ratsadanupraditmahitsornphakdi (Khǫ Simbi na Ranǫng): leading governor general of the west coast provinces of Thailand, 1901–1913] (M.E. diss. Srinakharinwirot University, 1983).

and commercial representatives of their own family's interests. Many of the tributes paid to Khaw Sim Bee on his death hinted at the importance of the interplay between political patronage and commercial success as the crucial underpinning for the family's autonomy of action in peninsular Siam.[3] A particularly perceptive tribute came from the British Chargé d'Affaires in Bangkok, W.R.D. Beckett, a less than total admirer of Khaw Sim Bee but a long-time observer of the family's activities. Because, he argued, "... they gauged to a nicety...the limits to which autocracy could be stretched, [and] in Bangkok ... played the role of courtier to perfection", the Khaw family was able to monopolise all the commerce in their realm. Their monopoly was, he continued, "... a direct outcome and corollary of the paternal administration of the Siamese representative, whose policy for twenty-three years was but a faithful index of the wishes of the Court and Cabinet at Bangkok".[4]

The duality of their political and economic roles was mirrored at another level by the duality of the family's locus of power between Siam and Penang. The security they derived from their preeminence as the leading political figures along the west coast of the Thai peninsula on the one hand, and from their access to the Chinese networks, British legal guarantees and sophisticated commercial infrastructure of Penang on the other, provided them with a greater range of opportunities than if they had been based in only one area.

While the interplay between the family's economic and political position and between its Siam and Penang bases was a significant overall factor in their successful rise from immigrants to "courtiers", this interplay was particularly fruitful in the expansion of their business ventures around the turn of the century. The business organisation of what I shall call the Khaw "group" in the following pages owes much to these complementary assets at the family's disposal.

Chinese Business Formations: The Group

One by-product of the present focus of social science interest on how development strategies in Southeast Asian countries are affected by questions of ownership and control within their economies has been the emergence of a clearer picture of Chinese business formations. Large-scale, publicly subscribed Chinese firms, staffed and managed by personnel recruited without regard to particularistic ties or connections to ownership, are becoming common within the modern industrial sectors of these economies.[5] Businesses organised on corporate lines, with interests in diverse economic activities are not, however, a feature of the present-day industrial landscape alone.

---

[3]*PG*, 11 April 1913; 14 April 1913; 22 April 1913; 17 May 1913. *Bangkok Times*, 18 April 1913; 22 April 1913; 30 April 1913; 23 May 1913.

[4]F.O. 422/68/21, Beckett to Grey, 30 April 1913 (C. P. 10656). Great Britain, Foreign Office, Confidential Prints. Confidential Prints are bound individually by print number and have also been collected together under the heading: *Correspondence Respecting the Affairs of Siam and the Malay Peninsula*, i.e., F.O. 422. The citations below are to this file but the C.P. number will be included in parentheses.

[5]See, for example, Kevin Hewison, "The Financial Bourgeoise in Thailand", *Journal of Contemporary Asia* 11.4 (1981): 395–412; Sieh Lee Mei Ling, *Ownership and Control of Malaysian Manufacturing Corporations* (Kuala Lumpur, 1982); Tan Tat Wai, *Income Distribution and Determination in West Malaysia* (Kuala Lumpur, 1982); Lim Mah Hui, *Ownership and Control of the One Hundred Largest Corporations in Malaysia* (Kuala Lumpur, 1981); Krirkkiat Phipatseritham and Kunio Yoshihara, *Business Groups in Thailand* (Singapore, 1983); Robert H. Silin, *Leadership and Values: The Organization of Large-scale Taiwanese Enterprise* (Cambridge, Mass., 1976).

60   *J. W. Cushman*

The Kian Gwan conglomerate of Oei Tjie Sien and his son, Oei Tiong Ham,[6] Yap Ah Loy's mining concerns,[7] the shipping and trading companies of Thio Thiau Siat (Chang Pi-shih), Loke Yew and Wee Bin[8] and the vertically integrated companies of the Khaw group are but a few examples of what appear to have been precursors of the Lee Loy Seng or Liem Sioe Liong multinational empires of today.

By setting the industrial enterprises organised by the Khaw family in the early 1900s in the analytical category of the group, the features which distinguished these formations from what are often depicted in the literature on the Chinese in Southeast Asia as the more common pattern — the "traditional", small-scale, family-run firm — may be drawn more sharply.

Following the analysis of group formation as developed by Leff and Strachan, the "group" is defined here as a "multicompany firm ... under common entrepreneurial and financial control ... [with] capital and high-level managers [drawn] from sources which transcend a single family". Its activities are often vertically integrated and its capital is supplemented by its own financial institutions.[9] In the absence of banking facilities, the group itself acts as a "financial intermediary" in the distribution of credit and provides such services as the preferential allocation of credit to group members.[10] The "essence" of group organisation, according to Strachan, lies in the "network of relationships" between the men who control the firms within the group. A high degree of "loyalty and trust similar to ... that ... normally associated with family or kinship groups",[11] is the hallmark of such networks which are forged by years of cooperation and experience of honest dealings among their members.

While perhaps not a completely satisfactory category for analysing the organisational features of the Khaw enterprises in the early twentieth century, the "group" is, nonetheless, a useful label. It helps us to identify its financial component, which, although not as central to its activities as the financial intermediary services provided by Strachan's sample of Latin American groups,[12] is a major feature distinguishing it from the classic vertically integrated firm. More importantly, the relationships among the firms and individuals in the Khaw group conform almost perfectly with Strachan's requirement that the group's "design incorporates a business strategy which is, in large part, a response to particular environmental conditions".[13] In this case, forays by British firms into the Khaw family's traditional mining and shipping preserves in the west coast states of the Thai peninsula were the most pressing "environmental conditions". To counter these moves, all aspects of the mining industry were integrated under the umbrella of interlocking

---

[6]J. Panglaykim and I. Palmer, *Entrepreneurship and Commercial Risks: The Case of a Schumpeterian Business in Indonesia* (Singapore, 1970); J. Panglaykim and I. Palmer, "Study of Entrepreneurialship [*sic.*] in Developing Countries: The Development of One Chinese Concern in Indonesia", *Journal of Southeast Asian Studies* 1.1 (March, 1970): 85–95.

[7]Research for a new history of Yap Ah Loy's economic and political position in Selangor is being carried out by Sharon Carstens, Department of Anthropology, Beloit College, Beloit, Wisconsin.

[8]Michael Godley, *The Mandarin-capitalists from Nanyang: Overseas Chinese Enterprise in the Modernization of China, 1893–1911* (Cambridge, Mass., 1981); Song Ong Siang, *One Hundred Years' History of the Chinese in Singapore* (Singapore, reprint: 1967).

[9]Nathaniel H. Leff, "Industrial Organization and Entrepreneurship in the Developing Countries: The Economic Groups", *Economic Development and Cultural Change* 26.4 (1978): 663–64.

[10]Harry W. Strachan, "The Role of the Business Groups in Economic Development: The Case of Nicaragua" (DBA diss., Harvard University, Cambridge, Mass., 1973), p. 113.

[11]Strachan, pp. 4, 29.

[12]Strachan, pp. 53–60, 89, 101.

[13]Strachan, p. 52.

companies, managed by associates of the family, drawn from various sectors of the Penang business community (see Table 2), and who were bound to one another by relations of loyalty and trust. The Khaw group was the product of this "coordinated business strategy".

Britain and Siam

Nineteenth-century British commercial sentiment generally held that Britain's rightful sphere of influence in the peninsula should extend from Singapore to Burma. Under the altruistic guise of introducing "progress and civilization with all their humanizing influences ... amongst their fellowmen of the East"[14] British merchants vigorously sought to promote their own commercial and industrial ventures. Certain factions within both the Colonial Office and Foreign Office were of like mind. The belief that British strategic and commercial interests would be ill-served if a European power other than Great Britain were to "obtain any footing in the Malay Peninsula at any point on either side, from the boundary of the Province of Tenasserim to Singapore ..." surfaced in official documents at regular intervals.[15]

As Siam's sovereignty appeared to falter under the onslaught of France and Britain in the 1890s, those advocating British paramountcy in the peninsula became more vocal. Their demands reached a crescendo after the Anglo-Siamese Convention was signed on 6 April 1897. Siam promised "not to cede or alienate to any other Power" territory to the south of Bang Tapan (Isthmus of Kra — see map). Furthermore, "... any special privilege or advantage, whether as regards land or trade..."[16] granted by Siam to another country required the written consent of the British government. Because the British government saw a potential danger to British influence in the commercial and mining concessions applied for by nationals of other countries, the peninsula came to assume as important a part in Britain's commercial, as in her political, sphere of influence.

Rather than settling the issue of British rights in the peninsula, the Convention of 1897 merely created a basis for new tensions between Siam and Great Britain. Fears that Siam was about to cede various of her islands — most notably Langkawi and Phuket — to foreigners raised afresh the spectre of foreign encroachment into British preserves.[17] While Britain was able to bring the full weight of her diplomatic clout to bear on Prince Devawongse, Siam's Minister of Foreign Affairs, to prevent outsiders from gaining a foothold, diplomatic efforts to speed British commercial ambitions in peninsular Siam were not as successful.

---

[14]N.A., R. 5, B. 1. 1/6: Quoted from *The Straits Independent*, 14 May 1890.

[15]F.O. 422/36/340, C.O. to F.O., 29 August 1893 (C.P. 6479). These views were expressed as early as the 1780s. See the "Extract from Captain Kyd's Memoir on Pinang", 1 September 1787, in John Anderson, *Political and Commercial Considerations relative to the Malayan Peninsula, and the British Settlements in the Straits of Malacca* (Singapore, 1965), appendix, p. lxvi. For a more recent analysis of the British position, see C.D. Cowan, *Nineteenth-Century Malaya: The Origins of British Political Control* (London, 1961); Jeshurun Chandran, "The British Foreign Office and the Siamese Malay States, 1890–97", *Modern Asian Studies* 5.2 (1971): 143–59; Chandran, *The Contest for Siam 1889–1902: A Study in Diplomatic Rivalry* (Kuala Lumpur, 1977); V.G. Kiernan, "Britain, Siam and Malaya: 1875–1885", *The Journal of Modern History* 28.1 (1956): 1–20; Ira Klein, "British Expansion in Malaya, 1897–1902", *Journal of Southeast Asian History* 9.1 (1968): 53–68; Eunice Thio, "Britain's Search for Security in North Malaya, 1886–97", *Journal of Southeast Asian History* 10.2 (1969): 279–303; Thio, *British Policy in the Malay Peninsula*, vol. I (Singapore, 1969).

[16]Likhit Dhiravegin, *Siam and Colonialism [1855–1909]: An Analysis of Diplomatic Relations* (Bangkok, 1975), pp. 102–103; F.O. 422/47, passim (C.P. 6950).

[17]See, for example, the discussion in F.O. 422/53/18, 20, 21, 24 (C.P. 7525); F.O. 422/54/4, 14 (C.P. 7800).

PENINSULAR SIAM C. 1900

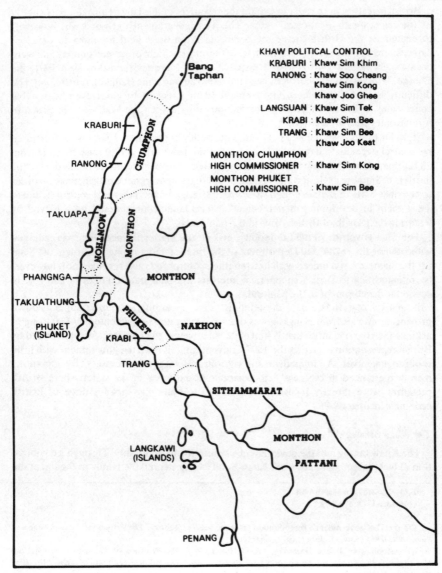

KHAW POLITICAL CONTROL
KRABURI : Khaw Sim Khim
RANONG : Khaw Soo Cheang
Khaw Sim Kong
Khaw Joo Ghee
LANGSUAN : Khaw Sim Tek
KRABI : Khaw Sim Bee
TRANG : Khaw Sim Bee
Khaw Joo Keat

MONTHON CHUMPHON
HIGH COMMISSIONER : Khaw Sim Kong
MONTHON PHUKET
HIGH COMMISSIONER : Khaw Sim Bee

Bang
Taphan

KRABURI

RANONG

CHUMPHON

TAKUAPA

MONTHON

MONTHON

MONTHON

PHANGNGA

TAKUATHUNG

PHUKET
(ISLAND)

PHUKET

KRABI

NAKHON

TRANG

SITHAMMARAT

LANGKAWI
(ISLANDS)

MONTHON

PATTANI

PENANG

Source: Damrong; Bunnag.

British investors were eager to exploit the resources of the Thai peninsula, particularly of the mineral-rich west-coast states. The Thai government did not wish, however, to encourage the British to see the peninsula as an open field for them to develop. Concessions applied for by the British were therefore seldom processed quickly and were occasionally refused outright. In a dispatch to the Marquess Lansdowne in 1901, the Chargé, William Archer, correctly read the mood among some Bangkok reformers: "The difficulty is that the Siamese Government seem reluctant to grant even reasonable concessions to British subjects, preferring possibly to keep the Malay States closed to foreign enterprise altogether."[18]

If, as Sir Frank Swettenham believed, "the policy of the King of Siam is to strengthen his control over the Malay States in his part of the peninsula, and to raise revenue from all his dominions"[19] then Britain's course was clear. She needed but to break down "the barriers of Siamese exclusion and obstruction", suggested Archer a trifle naively, in order to convince Siam of Britain's "honest desire to strengthen their [Siam's] control ... and to assist them in developing their revenue".[20] The latter course would be achieved by fostering the growth of British firms in the peninsula.

The Thai government held different views on the matter. Prince Damrong, charged with running the revitalised Department of the Interior and a strong proponent of "Siam for the Siamese", did indeed wish to strengthen control and raise revenue; not, however, by relinquishing to British commercial interests the Thai state's authority and role in economic development in the peninsula.

A general consolidation of the administrative apparatus and closer supervision of provincial officials from Bangkok was one long-term step implemented by Damrong to achieve the goal of a more tightly knit state.[21] However, the constant demands raised by British representatives, citing the 1897 Convention, left the Thai government with little room to maneuver. An immediate and vigorous response was necessary. By appointing men "experienced in business"[22] to positions of authority in the states where British pressures were directly focused, Siam hoped to blunt the forward drive of British economic incursions.[23]

The Khaw Strategy[24]

The Khaw family met the government's requirements admirably. Through a combination of luck, talent and hard work Khaw Soo Cheang steered the family to the top of the

---

[18]F.O. 422/54/27, 26 March 1901.

[19]Quoted in F.O. 422/54/27.

[20]Ibid.

[21]On the Thai government's centralisation reforms, see Tej Bunnag, *The Provincial Administration of Siam, 1892–1915* (Kuala Lumpur, 1977), chapter 3.

[22]Translation from Prince Damrong, "An Explanation of the Province of Takua-pa", in Chatthip Nartsupha, Suthy Prasartset and Montri Chenvidyakarn, eds., *The Political Economy of Siam, 1910–1932* (Bangkok, 1978), p. 105.

[23]Tej Bunnag has argued (pp. 138–39) that the Thai government could not push centralisation in the southern provinces too forcefully for fear of alienating both the British, who were "'to protect [Siam] against France'" and the "provincial nobility" who might "'run to the foreigners'". This is plausible to the extent that the interests of the provincial nobility and state did not coincide. The members of the Khaw family appointed to positions on the west coast recognised, however, that their own interests could be promoted more advantageously under a Thai administration than under the British.

[24]Britain's and Siam's conflicting political and economic claims to the Thai peninsula and the role of the Khaw family in strengthening Thai control in the region are dealt with more fully in chapters 3–4 of my forthcoming book, *Family and State: A Sino-Thai Tin Mining Dynasty, 1810–1932*.

peninsular bureaucratic hierarchy during the nineteenth century. As the first "rajah" of Ranong, which, when he arrived in the 1830s, was said to be "more like a forest than a town",[25] he became well known for developing the province's mining and smelting industries. After building up a trade with Penang in the region's tin, he bid successfully for Ranong's tin monopoly in 1842. He carried out his duties for the central government so conscientiously — "not delaying the payment of tin royalties" — that he was appointed governor in 1854 with the title of Phra Rattanasethi when the former incumbent died. Soo Cheang's stewardship was further rewarded in 1862, when, in a royal proclamation raising his title to *phraya*, the second highest bureaucratic rank, he was commended by the King for turning the "forest" into a prosperous, well-populated commercial centre, and thereby adding to the government's revenues. His new title was appropriate, the King argued, because of the high regard in which he was held by "foreign dignitaries and business individuals" with whom he came into contact in his official capacity.[26]

Khaw Soo Cheang's sons were appointed to similar positions elsewhere in the peninsula. His eldest surviving son, Khaw Sim Kong 許心廣 (d. 1912), succeeded him as governor of Ranong after a period as assistant governor. Khaw Sim Khim 許心欽 (d. 1903) became assistant, then later honorary, governor of Kraburi. Khaw Sim Tek 許心德 (d. 1920s), later known for his "real or professed ignorance of everything in his province",[27] was appointed governor of Langsuan. Soo Cheang's youngest son, Khaw Sim Bee, was first appointed governor of Kraburi, was later appointed to Trang in 1890 and in 1900 was put in charge of the west coast states from Ranong to Trang as High Commissioner of Monthon Phuket.[28] Judicious marriage alliances with other important families and astute connections with members of the Thai aristocracy, further cemented their political supremacy.

From their various bases in the peninsula, members of the Khaw family were able to control and direct much of the economic life of the region. They operated many of the large commercial tin concessions, as well as the local smelters which handled the tin from Ranong and the neighbouring provinces. Their Penang-based steamship company, Koe Guan 高源, which served the coastal ports dotting the peninsula, was a major carrier of Chinese workers for their mines. Their steamers also had a virtual monopoly in the import-export trade along the coast, transporting locally mined tin to Penang and in return supplying provisions for the mining communities. By the time Sim Bee was appointed to head Monthon Phuket, the Khaw family was politically and commercially well placed to block British investors' attempts to turn the peninsula into an outpost of British commerce. Several years later, in 1906, Consul-General Sir John Anderson expressed the British attitude that had evolved from contact between British investors and the Khaw family when he wrote from Singapore that "... no enterprise [in Phuket] will ever get a fair chance so long as it is run by the present High Commissioner [Khaw Sim Bee], who has his finger in every pie, and by himself or his family levies toll on everything". [29]

Just a few years earlier, however, there had been no guarantees that the Khaw strategy would succeed. Indeed, as Britain strengthened her position in Siam's Malay dependencies and as British companies renewed their efforts to secure a share in the economic life

[25]Damrong, *Tamnan mu'ang Ranong*, p. 16.
[26]Ibid.
[27]H. Warington Smyth, *Five Years in Siam*, 2 vols. (New York, 1898), vol. 2, p. 62.
[28]Damrong, *Tamnan*, p. 21.
[29]F.O. 422/61/6, incl. 2, Anderson to Beckett, 13 September 1906 (C.P. 9308).

of the peninsula north of Penang, no one could have foreseen in 1896 that local Chinese might impede "... the preponderant interest which Her Majesty's Government cannot but take in those regions...."[30]

That "preponderant interest" had manifested itself in a growing involvement of British companies in the Malayan tin industry. The Straits Trading Company, Ltd., set up in 1887 to smelt the ore from Selangor, Sungei Ujong and Perak, expanded rapidly under exclusive contracts from the Selangor and Sungei Ujong governments.[31] The company erected a modern smelter on Pulau Brani, off Singapore, in 1890 and opened branch offices throughout the Malay States to purchase ore for its smelters. With "the tin ore piling up on Pulau Brani",[32] it erected another smelter across from Penang at Butterworth in 1901 by which time the company was processing over half the tin exported from the Straits Settlements.[33]

Smelting and finance were not the only Chinese preserves that were being supplanted by Western-dominated firms. The Straits Steamship Company, Ltd. was formed in 1890 by "Singapore businessmen and Straits Chinese" and offered serious competition to local Chinese firms in both passenger and cargo traffic. Its close association with the Straits Trading Company for whom it carried "the whole of the tin"[34] helped to ensure its success.

By the turn of the century, the two companies were intent upon expanding into the rich tin market in the Thai states north of Penang. With equal determination, the Khaw family moved to strengthen its own position in the region. The commercial war that followed was the inevitable result of the mutually exclusive economic interests on both sides.

In January 1902 the Straits Trading Company applied to the Thai government for permission to open an agency for buying ore in Phuket on the understanding "that in serving our own interests by extending our business operations to Siamese Territory we should at the same time contribute to the welfare of the Country by extending the present and opening up new fields of enterprise".[35] The concession was granted later in the year with the proviso that its business was "not to ... be prejudicial to Siamese Subjects engaged in similar or kindred forms of trade".[36]

The initial reception in Phuket to the new office was not, however, a welcoming one. Frank Adam, who acted as manager for the Agency, lived according to one of the longtime coastal shipping captains, in "a veritable fortress with six-foot Sikhs manning the palisades".[37] The company began buying ore in 1904 but, on its own admission, "... our business has not made the progress we had hoped for and lately it has suffered a serious setback".[38] Property leases were refused, the Phuket Treasury was uncooperative about currency transactions, and the rules for conducting business were constantly amended to suit the whims of local administrators. After four years of this treatment the company's manager in Singapore, C. McArthur, was driven to observe that "The present game at

---

[30]F.O. 422/47/1, de Bunsen to Salisbury, 30 November 1896 (C.P. 6950).

[31]Wong Lin Ken, *The Malayan Tin Industry to 1914* (Tucson, 1965), pp. 163–64.

[32]K.G. Tregonning, "Straits Tin: A Brief Account of the First Seventy-five Years of the Straits Trading Company, Limited", *Journal of the Malayan Branch of the Royal Asiatic Society* 36.1 (1963): 100.

[33]N.A., R. 5, T. 2.12/23: McArthur to Damrong, 23 January 1902.

[34]K.G. Tregonning, *Home Port Singapore: A History of the Straits Steamship Company Limited, 1890–1965* (Singapore, 1967), pp. 17, 19.

[35]N.A., R. 5, T. 2.12/23: McArthur to Damrong, 23 January 1902.

[36]N.A., R.5, T. 2.12/23: Sri Sahadheb to Straits Trading Company, 6 June 1902.

[37]William Blain, *Home is the Sailor: The Sea Life of William Brown Master Mariner and Penang Pilot* (New York, 1940), p. 95.

[38]N.A., R. 5, K.Kh. 0301.1.23/6: McArthur to Williamson, 17 August 1906.

Tongkah [Phuket] seems to be one in which we and our particular customers figure as the ball, while a select circle of well-informed and powerful Chinese are in the position of the players."[39]

Despite such unpropitious beginnings, the Straits Trading Company was prospering by 1907. Its Penang smelter, in operation by 1902, was an attractive alternative to the local smelters run by the Khaw, Tan and other families on Phuket and the mainland. The Chinese had formerly smelted most of Phuket's tin but, by 1907, most of the 3,228 tons of ore exported from the region was being shipped to the Straits Trading Company's smelter in Penang.[40] When the Straits Steamship Company began a service to Phuket in 1906 using the S.S. *Ban What Hin* and S.S. *Sri Helena* to transport the tin ore, the Khaw family was already fully alive to the danger these companies posed for their monopoly in the region. The Khaw group of enterprises was launched to meet this challenge.

The Khaw Group

The Khaw family, with part of its commercial base firmly located within Penang's more advanced commercial environment, had actually begun to marshall its forces well before 1907. With Khaw Sim Bee's appointment to Monthon Phuket in 1900, members of the family became more conspicuous in Penang social and commercial circles. Their activities were reported regularly by the English-language *Pinang Gazette* which seldom failed to remark on Sim Bee's visits to Penang and neighbouring states. The weddings they attended, the donations they made to the Penang Free School, and the parties and receptions they held in the Italian Renaissance style "home beautiful" Khaw Sim Bee built off the exclusive Northan Road, were faithfully recounted in its pages.[41]

The close identification of the Khaw family with the Penang settlement (even when the Khaws were serving in their official capacities in Siam, Westerners often referred to them as "Penang Chinese"),[42] led some observers to speculate that they might help to introduce British trade into the peninsular states where they ruled. After a visit to the peninsula C.W.S. Kynnersley even went so far as to suggest that the interests of British subjects in Trang "... may safely be entrusted to Mr Khaw Sim Bee who is himself a British subject".[43] This early optimism proved groundless, with the more common view emerging that "... things will never be right until the present High Commissioner is removed".[44] The expansion of the Khaw shipping company, Koe Guan, from 1902, however, signalled the family's intention to strengthen its own position rather than that of British companies in the economies of the Malay and Thai peninsula.

The Eastern Shipping Company, Ltd.

A full-page advertisement at the front of the 1904 edition of the *Singapore and Straits Directory* announced that Koe Guan Co., Shipowners of 63 Beach Street, Penang, ran a regular service of sixteen steamers from Penang to Burma, Siam, Sumatra, Singapore and

---

[39]Ibid.

[40]Great Britain, Foreign Office, Diplomatic and Consular Reports, Annual Series, *Siam: Report for the Year 1907 on the Trade and Commerce of the Monthons of Saiburi and Phuket* (London, 1908), p. 7.

[41]See, for example, *PG*, 29 October 1900; 1 November 1900; 19 February 1901; 13 January 1904.

[42]See, for instance, the remarks in F.O. 422/56/40, incl. 5: Memorandum by Sir F. Swettenham, 1 February 1902 (C.P. 7968); F.O. 422/59/3, incl. 1: Anderson to Lyttelton, 6 December 1904 (C.P. 8714).

[43]C.W.S. Kynnersley, "Notes on a Tour through the Siamese States on the West Coast of the Malay Peninsula, 1900", *Journal of the Straits Branch of the Royal Asiatic Society* 36 (1901): 53.

[44]F.O. 422/61/6, incl. 3: McArthur to Anderson, 12 September 1906.

China.[45] Up to this date the Khaw shipping enterprise had been a modest affair. A few small steamers, purchased in the 1890s by Khaw Joo Ghee 許如義, who succeeded his father, Sim Kong, as governor of Ranong, were engaged mostly in the coastal trade from Penang to Moulmein or Rangoon.[46] They had, according to one of their captains, William Brown, "… a monopoly [on] this foredeck traffic … [and] lucrative carrying trade".[47] In June 1902, they bought eight vessels belonging to the Kong Hock fleet (Chuan Yu Kay)[48] and seven months later purchased four steamships from New Zealand. With the acquisition of these vessels, Koe Guan became the largest shipping firm in Penang. The *Hong Kong Free Press* reported that Koe Guan "decided to have their own fleet" after failing to obtain a share in the Straits Steamship Company.[49] Equally, Koe Guan may well have decided to expand once the Straits Trading Company made it clear that it wanted a slice of the Khaw "pie" on the Siamese peninsula.

The *Rotorua, Omapere, Janet Nicoll* and *Waihora*, the four steamers acquired from the Union Steamship Company of New Zealand, were brought to the attention of the Khaw family by an Australian, Captain Edward T. Miles (1849–1944).[50] "Teddy" Miles, who later became "something magnificent in Malaya",[51] was a Tasmanian who arrived in Penang late in 1902 after an eventful career as a ship's master, a shipping broker, charterer and salvager and, most latterly, as a politician in Tasmania where he was Minister for Lands, Mines, Works and Railways in 1899. After resigning from this office, he turned his past experience to effect by joining the Union Steamship Co. of New Zealand as a broker and as a trade representative for Henry Jones & Co. of Hobart, who were best known at the time for their jams and preserves under the trademark, IXL. It was in his capacity as broker that he met with the principal members of the Khaw family in Penang when he sold Koe Guan the four vessels owned by Union Steamship.[52]

Armed with its new steamers, the Koe Guan Company — which was also the agent for Singapore's largest Chinese shipping firm, Wee Bin — moved beyond the coastal trade into the south China traffic. It became a major carrier of coolie labour from China to Penang. Much of this labour found its way to the plantations and the mines operated by the Khaw family in Siam. The Khaws also began working more closely with another expanding Penang shipping company, Guan Lee Hin, owned by Quah Beng Kee and his brothers.[53] Listed as Beng Brothers, "Ship Agents, Owners & Charterers" in the 1904

---

[45]*The Singapore and Straits Directory for 1904* (Singapore, 1904), p. 24.

[46]W.A. Laxon and R.K. Tyers, *The Straits Steamship Fleet, 1890–1975* (Singapore, 1976), pp. 42–43 lists the early vessels in the Khaw fleet. I am grateful to Howard Dick for bringing this material to my attention.

[47]Blain, p. 81.

[48]*PG*, 12 June 1902.

[49]Quoted in Song, pp. 349–50.

[50]Biographical Information on Captain Miles can be found in Thomas A. Miles, *The Life Story of Captain Edward Thomas Miles, Master-Mariner.* Typescript, Australian National Library (Canberra, 1969). The letters of Captain E.T. Miles and his sons, especially those of T.A. Miles, are held privately by E.T. Miles' grandson, Richard Miles, in Sydney. I am most grateful to Richard and his wife, Sue, for kindly allowing me complete access to these files. Captain Miles' role in the formation of Tongkah Harbour is also treated in Francis David Birch, "Tropical Milestones: Australian Gold and Tin Mining Investment in Malaya and Thailand 1880–1930" (M.A. diss., University of Melbourne, 1976), a seminal work on Australian investment in Southeast Asia.

[51]*PG*, 28 January 1908, quoting the *Sydney Bulletin.*

[52]See the *PG*, 10 January 1903 for further particulars about the date and sale of these vessels. Cf. Miles, *Life Story*, p. 148.

[53]Arnold Wright (ed.), *Twentieth Century Impressions of British Malaya* (London, 1908), p. 177.

Singapore and Straits Directory, this company owned nine steamships and shipped to Burma, Singapore and Sumatra with weekly departures for south China.[54]

Early in 1907, a freight war between Beng Brothers (also called Beng Kee and Co.) and the Straits Steamship Company, during which Beng Brothers had "the active sympathy, if not the business co-operation of the wealthy and influential shippers, the Koe Guan Company...",[55] appears to have brought the two Chinese firms into closer commercial association. They were certainly portrayed as offering realistic alternatives in both cargo and passenger traffic to the service provided by Straits and other steamship companies.[56] When they joined together with several other Penang shipping companies, most notably Ban Joo Hin, owned by Thio Thiau Siat,[57] to form the Eastern Shipping Company in late 1907, the new company emerged as a formidable challenge to their western-run competitors.

Eastern Shipping Company, Ltd. was one of nine joint stock companies registered in Penang in 1907. With an initial capital of $1,400,000 and a fleet of sixteen vessels (Table 1), Eastern Shipping was now in a better position to meet the threat posed by the

TABLE 1
VESSELS OF THE EASTERN SHIPPING COMPANY LTD., 1907

FROM KOE GUAN*	FROM BENG BROTHERS*
Deli	*Jin Ho*
Langkat	*Pin Seng*
Mary Austin	*Ben Whatt Soon*
Cornelia	
Taw Tong	
Avagyee	
Petrel	
*Resident Halewyn***	
Vidar	
Rotorua	
Omapere	
Janet Nicoll	
Perak†	

Notes: *Khaw Joo Tok and Quah Beng Kee were also managing agents under the name Taik Lee Guan & Co. for the *Glenogle* which was engaged in the coolie trade and was said to carry 2,000 deck passengers (Wright, p. 177).
**Resold in 1907.
†Known as the "Black" *Perak* to distinguish it from the vessel of the same name owned by the Straits Steamship Company.
Source: *Pinang Gazette* 1906–1907; Laxon and Tyers, pp. 12–14, 42–46.

[54]*Singapore and Straits Directory* (1904), pp. 25, 208. The nine vessels were the *Pin Seng*, *Jin Ho*, *Thye Seng*, *Tung Seng*, *Say Seng*, *Lum Seng*, *Pak Seng*, *Jit Seng* and the *Guat Seng*.
[55]*PG*, 7 May 1907, quoting the *Straits Free Press*.
[56]Ibid. See also the notice in the *PG*, 1 August 1903, about competition between the Khaws and the British India Steam Navigation Company.
[57]Godley, pp. 11–12.

Straits Steamship Co., particularly on its runs to the ports in the Siamese Malay states, and by the Dutch-owned *Koninklijk Paketvaart Maatschappij* (K.P.M.) line in the trade with north Sumatra.[58] The Board of Directors was composed of the men who headed the individual firms that made up the company as well as some of the larger Chinese mine owners in the Malay States (see Table 2). These included members of the Khaw family and Quah Beng Kee (b. 1872),[59] who were directors of the two principal firms, as well as the mining magnates, Foo Choo Choon, said to be "the richest Chairman in the world"[60] and Cheah Choo Yew. Just as the Straits Steamship and Trading companies were linked through the carriage and smelting of tin, Eastern Shipping was connected in a similar fashion to two other companies formed in these years — the Tongkah Harbour Tin Dredging Company, N.L. and the Eastern Smelting Company, Ltd.

Tongkah Harbour Tin Dredging Co., N. L.

The rising price of tin on world markets from the late 1890s[61] and the acknowledged backwardness of Siam's mining industry in comparison with the industry in the Federated Malay States were important considerations in the Thai government's decision to upgrade support for the industry at the turn of the century. To strengthen Bangkok's control over mining, the Mines Department, formed in December 1891, was placed under the Ministry of the Interior in 1896 and a branch office was set up in Phuket to supervise concession licenses.[62] Steps were also taken to improve communication facilities in mining areas and to transform Phuket, the centre of the mining industry on the west coast, from a "rotten and unhealthy ... collection of Chinese huts and hovels" to a place holding out "attractions for capital and enterprise".[63]

Khaw Sim Bee was a central figure in the modernization of the tin regions. His many innovations as governor of Trang (1890–1900), during which time it became the "banner province of Siam", were appreciated by Westerners and Thai alike.[64] His reputation as an able administrator must have weighed heavily in the Court's decision to appoint him as High Commissioner of Monthon Phuket, especially as Britain was pressing home the point that "... unless the Siamese Government takes action and adopts a progressive policy in regard to Puket ... The British Government will insist that the country shall be opened up either by Siam, or, if she is unwilling, then by Great Britain herself".[65]

With Siam's tin output lagging far behind that of the F.M.S. in 1900 (Siam produced only 3,900 tons; the F.M.S., 42,444 tons in that year),[66] positive steps were needed in addition to the administrative changes just mentioned. One of the first was to provide

---

[58]*PG*, 17 March 1908; Tregonning, *Home Port*, p. 56. The company's fleet grew rapidly through the further purchase and construction of vessels after 1908. Based on the shipping arrivals and departures listed in the *Pinang Gazette*, the company appears to have acquired almost forty vessels by 1912. See also Anthony Reid, *The Conquest for North Sumatra: Acheh, the Netherlands and Britain, 1858–1898* (Kuala Lumpur, 1969), pp. 259–70.

[59]For a short biography of Quah Beng Kee, see Wright, p. 755; W. Feldwick (ed.), *Present Day Impressions of the Far East and Progressive Chinese at Home and Abroad* (London, 1917), pp. 858–61.

[60]*PG*, 7 September 1907.

[61]Wong, p. 243.

[62]Bunnag, pp. 96–97; Thailand, Ministry of Commerce and Communications, *Siam: Nature and Industry* (Bangkok, 1930), p. 108.

[63]*PG*, 27 January 1903.

[64]*PG*, 22 April 1913; Kynnersley, pp. 52–53.

[65]N.A., R.5, M. 2.14/50: Report on a Journey through the Malay Peninsula, 24 December 1906, p. 16.

[66]Wong, pp. 247–49.

TABLE 2

INTERLOCKING DIRECTORATES IN THE KHAW GROUP

	Penang Khean Guan Insurance Co., Ltd.	Opium Farms Penang–Kedah–Perak–Bangkok–Singapore	Eastern Trading Co., Ltd.*	Tongkah Harbour Tin Dredging Co., N.L.**	Eastern Shipping Co., Ltd.	Eastern Smelting Co., Ltd.
KHAW Joo Tok	X	X	X	X	X	X
KHAW Sim Bee	X	X		X	X	
KHAW Joo Choe	X	X				X
KHAW Bian Kee	X	X			X	
KHAW Joo Ghee	X				X	
QUAH Beng Kee					X	
FOO Choo Choon		X	X		X	
CHEAH Choo Yew	X	X				
CHUNG Thye Phin	X	X				X
CHUAH Yu Kay	X					
GOH Boon Keng	X	X	X		X	
JESSEN, H.						
LOKE Chow Thye			X		X	X
LEE Chin Ho		X				X
LIM Kek Chuan		X	X			X
NG Boo Bee	X	X				X
YEOH Wee Gark				X		
ONG Hun Chong				X	X	X
MILES, E.T.						
MILES, E. Leslie						

Notes: *Proposed directors.

**Of the 30,000 shares sold to Chinese investors in Penang, Khaw Joo Tok took 21,250. Not all of these were held by him but were to be distributed to other Penang investors at a later date (M les Papers: Share Distribution Certificate, May 1907; 2 January 1907 letter to Khaw Joo Tok).

Source: Straits Settlements and F.M.S., Opium Commission, *Proceedings* (Singapore, 1908); *Penang Gazette* 1900–1911; *Singapore and Straits Directory* 1896, 1899, 1901, 1904, 1910, 1912.

additional labourers for the mines in Phuket. Mine owners had complained that coolies brought from China never reached Phuket because when they landed in Singapore, "they were enticed away from the ship and were lost".[67] As we have seen above, Koe Guan's expansion into the coolie trade enabled the Khaw family to supply the necessary workers to the west-coast mines. But even with an adequate supply of labour, it was unlikely that production could be increased significantly unless more modern extraction methods were used. The Tongkah Harbour Tin Dredging Co., N.L. was to offer the solution. And just as the Khaw's Penang base was important in the extension of their shipping facilities to Phuket, it was also useful in the formation of the dredging company.

Khaw Sim Bee approached Captain Miles when he returned to Penang to sell Koe Guan timber for jetties they were building. He mentioned that he had a "good tin property in Southern Siam which he was anxious to have worked by modern European methods". "Would Captain Miles be interested in inspecting the property?"[68]

Miles agreed to go, but several months were to elapse before he was able to meet this commitment. Finally, having been warned by Sim Bee that he could not indefinitely "keep [the offer] open for others are enquiring about it", he arrived in Phuket in September 1905 to see what the place offered.[69] As a result of Miles' decision to bid for the concession, bucket dredging — one of the major technological innovations in the Thai mining industry — was introduced to Phuket.[70]

According to Miles' account, after considering the property Sim Bee had in mind, Miles suggested instead a harbour site that could be mined using a bucket dredge. When he began test boring, he found that tin deposits ran at least a mile into the harbour. He then approached Sim Bee with a request for the exclusive dredging rights to the entire harbour, approximately six square miles, for a period of twenty-five years. In return, he undertook to excavate a channel and dock in the heavily silted harbour. This would enable ships to enter the inner harbour, reduce the lighter charges on the exported tin ore and raise revenue in the form of dockage.

Sim Bee suggested that Miles put the matter before Prince Damrong, who, as Minister of the Interior, had jurisdiction over mining, when he next visited the province. Prince Damrong was also favourably impressed and asked Miles to draw up a draft of the concession he wished to acquire. This was reviewed and approved in Bangkok by a Royal Commission, one of whose members was Khaw Sim Bee himself, and was signed on 11 September 1906. Under the terms of the concession agreement,[71] Miles was given dredging rights to the harbour and a rebate on the duty usually attached to imported plant and machinery. For his part, Miles was to complete the excavation of the dock and channel within six years and was to pay the government royalties on the tin. The latter ranged

[67]N.A., R.5, M. 2.14/50: Report on a Journey, p. 18.

[68]Miles, *Life Story*, p. 148.

[69]Ibid., p. 151; E.T. Miles, "Notes on Tongkah Tin Dredging, A Challenge", *The Industrial Australian and Mining Standard*, 2 July 1909.

[70]The impact of the bucket dredge on the Thai tin industry is explored in greater depth in chapter 5 of my forthcoming book, *Family and State*. Briefly, however, the bucket dredge enabled a larger volume of tin to be recovered from both prime and marginal sites. By boosting production, the state's revenues from the tin royalty grew in the post-1906 period. These were reinvested to improve the peninsula's infrastructure and silence the complaints from British businessmen.

[71]For the original concession agreement, see N.A., R. 5, K.Kh. 0301.1.11/2: Memorandum of Agreement between Captain Edward T. Miles and the Government of Siam, 11 September 1906; Rachan Kanchanawanich, "Some Notes on the Dredging History by Tongkah Harbour Tin Dredging Berhad", *The Milestone, Commemoration of the First Tin Dredge in Thailand* (n. p., 1969), pp. 52–55.

from 10 to 25 per cent of the market price[72] and was said by one of the early Australian investors in Siam to amount to £1,500 per month.[73]

The Tongkah Harbour Tin Dredging Co., N.L., was registered in Hobart, Tasmania on 23 November 1906. With an authorised capital of £150,000 divided into 150,000 shares, 115,000 were reserved for the former directors of the prospecting syndicate, the IXL Prospecting Company, N.L. and 35,000 were offered to the public at 10 shillings per share. While Miles and his Australian associates, including Henry Jones, W.A. Palfreyman, E.A. Peacock and A.H. Ashbolt, were major shareholders in the company, at least 30,000 shares were reserved for "Eastern shareholders" — represented on the Board of Directors by Sim Bee's nephew, Khaw Joo Tok (許如琢 1871–1951).[74] The 35,000 publicly subscribed shares netted the company £17,500 in working capital from which the costs of the first dredge were partly met.[75]

With its finances on a more secure footing, and once the teething pains of the new dredging technology developed by Miles had been overcome, the company began recovering ore on a regular basis from early in 1908. By 1911 the firm had five dredges operating in the harbour and it had already paid out over £30,000 in dividends.[76] In 1910 Tongkah Harbour was the only company using dredges in Siam and it accounted for 25 per cent of Siam's tin output. By 1918, almost half of Siam's output was attributed to dredging (Table 3), and dredging overtook other more traditional methods of extraction in the next two years.[77]

The Eastern Smelting Company, Ltd.

Having acquired a reliable supply of ore and an expanded shipping service to carry it, all that was lacking was an up-to-date smelting plant. Tin from Thai mines had traditionally been smelted in small Chinese blast furnaces made of clay known as *relau Tongka* (lit. a Tongkah furnace).[78] The principal advantage of these smelters over the more sophisticated western smelters was cost: the Chinese-style smelters required little capital outlay whereas the technologically advanced western smelting plant required large capital inputs. The principal disadvantage of Chinese smelting methods was that the

---

[72]W.A. Graham, *Siam*, 2 vols. (London, 1924), vol. 2, p. 75; James C. Ingram, *Economic Change in Thailand, 1850–1970* (Stanford, 1971), p. 99 and note 9. The royalty was put on a sliding scale in the twentieth century and was reduced when tin prices declined below the level where the mine owners could make a profit: Bangkok, N.A., R.6, K.Kh. 0301.1.11/3: Scale of Royalty on tin from 1904, 20 February 1915.

[73]Herbert Pratten, *Through Orient to Occident* (Sydney, 1908), p. 14.

[74]Khaw Joo Tok's obituary can be found in the *Straits Echo and Times of Malaya*, 26 July 1951. Details of shareholdings can be found in the Miles Papers: Letter to Khaw Joo Tok, 2 January 1907, Share Distribution Certificate, May 1907; Tongkah Harbour Tin Dredging Co., N.L., *Prospectus*, 23 November 1906; The IXL Dredging Company Ltd., *Prospectus* n.d. (c. Sept. 1906).

[75]Birch, p. 120.

[76]*The Industrial Australian and Mining Standard*, 3 August 1911, 14 December 1911.

[77]Birch, pp. 169–70; Royal Department of Mines, *Notes on Mining in Siam with Statistics to March 31, 1921* (Bangkok, 1922?), p. 3.

		tons
1919:	Dredging	= 4998.2
	Other	= 4566.3
1920:	Dredging	= 3933.2
	Other	= 3010.5

[78]Wong, pp. 157–58.

TABLE 3
TIN EXTRACTION BY DREDGING
OVER OTHER METHODS, SIAM 1910–18

	Dredging Tons	Other Tons	%
1910	1,250	4,900	25.5
1911	1,260	4,900	26
1912	2,140	5,900	36
1913	2,320	6,750	34
1914	2,430	6,590	37
1915	2,890	9,000	32
1916	3,440	8,700	40
1917	4,140	9,150	45
1918	4,110	8,830	46.5

Source: Modified from·Birch, p. 170; these figures are of the same order of comparison as those in Royal
Department of Mines, *Notes on Mining in Siam*, Bangkok, 1922 (?), p. 3.

smelted product contained a high impurity content which required further treatment to
achieve the "almost theoretical purity ... demanded for ... the [European] tin plate
trade".[79] Nor were Chinese smelters able to effect the economies of scale possible to the
bigger smelting enterprises.

In addition to the "vast numbers of small Chinese smelting works scattered all over the
various centres of tinstone production",[80] some Chinese were experimenting with more
modern smelting methods. The most important of these was the plant begun in Penang
by a close associate of the Khaws, Lee Chin Ho (b. 1863).[81] He opened the Seng Kee
smelting works in 1898 on an acre of land off Dato Kramat Road. With four reverberatory
furnaces, electrically driven equipment and a laboratory for testing ore samples,[82] the
Seng Kee smelter provided an alternative to the Butterworth smelter of the Straits
Trading Company, and a solid base from which the Chinese-run smelting industry could
expand.

Lee Chin Ho's works were purchased towards the end of 1907 by the Eastern Smelting
Company, Ltd., a new company formed in that year with a capital of $1,500,000. The
company's object as expressed by its secretary, James Donald, was "to encourage the
miner in the development of his property, and to stimulate the tin industry so far as we
possibly can".[83] Its first Board of Directors read like a Who's Who of the F.M.S. and Thai
mining industries: Eu Tong Sen, Chung Thye Phin, Ng Boo Bee, Ong Hun Chong, Khaw
Joo Tok and his nephew, Khaw Bian Kee.[84] Its Managing Director, Herrmann Jessen,
had, moreover, gained extensive experience in the smelting business during his years
with Behn, Meyer and Co. Besides smelting the ore from their own mines, the new

[79]Arnold Wright and Thomas Reid, eds., *The Malay Peninsula: A Record of British Progress in the Middle
East* (London, 1912), p. 276.
[80]C.G.W. Lock, *Mining in Malaya for Gold and Tin* (London, 1907), pp. 161–62.
[81]On Lee Chin Ho, see *"Pinang Gazette" Centenary Number* (1933); Feldwick, pp. 856–57.
[82]Wright, p. 817.
[83]*PG*, 18 January 1908.
[84]*PG*, 17 March 1908.

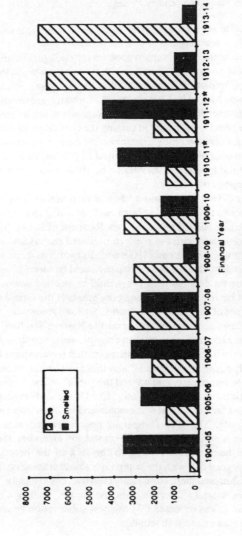

TABLE 4

TIN EXPORTS, MONTHON PHUKET, 1904–1914 (TONS)

Note: *The increase in smelted tin over ore exports for these years may reflect seller uncertainty during the transition from Chinese to European ownership of the Eastern Smelting Company.

Source: Great Britain, Foreign Office, Diplomatic and Consular Reports, Annual Series, *Siam*, 1907–1915.

company also hoped to attract ore from the many small mines that were continuing to use traditional methods of smelting.

One of the first steps the new company took was to open ore-buying agencies throughout the F.M.S. These proved to be popular with the miners who, in the past, had felt that the Straits Trading Company did not always offer the fairest prices for their tin.[85] Because Eastern Smelting was backed by Chinese, most of whom were themselves mine owners, it had an advantage over the Straits Trading Company when it came to doing business with other Chinese miners. Its success in gaining the confidence of the mining community can be judged by Eastern Smelting's dramatic increase in production figures over the three years it was in operation. In 1908 it smelted 11,400 tons of ore and unrefined tin, or 18 per cent of the tin shipped from the Straits; by 1910, it was smelting 16,000 tons or 29 per cent of total shipments.[86]

Eastern Smelting did not remain under Chinese direction for long however. In 1911 the company, "an established and thriving business" according to the *Pinang Gazette*,[87] was sold to British interests headed by the former Resident of Perak, Sir Ernest Woodford Birch. Birch's involvement with the concern predated the takeover in 1911. Birch had visited the Seng Kee works in the early 1900s and afterwards suggested to Lee Chin Ho that "it would be an excellent idea if a large company could be formed" involving the "leading mine owners as shareholders" so their ore "could be smelted down at one place, and at cheaper rates...."[88] He had also been among the guests at the formal opening of the company by the Governor of the Straits Settlements, Sir John Anderson, on 17 January 1908.

Birch may well have acquired an option on the Eastern Smelting Company after the one held by George Meudell, an Australian entrepreneur, had lapsed when tin prices fell in 1908–1909.[89] Meudell remarked in his memoirs that the company he had "bonded for sale in London only needed more capital" and that after he had let his option go, "somebody else floated the tin smeltery and bagged the profit".[90] The "somebody else" appears to have been Ernest Birch and his associates, Cecil Budd and David Currie.

The original firm's lack of capital was emphasised in all the contemporary discussions of the company's sale. The 1911 *Prospectus* noted, for instance, that "the principal object of this issue is to provide working capital for extending the said business...." Business had even been refused "owing to the lack of the necessary capital".[91] The Chinese directors argued that with the company's shares trading on the London market, "they could get fresh capital there more easily than they could locally".[92] Fresh capital was also needed if they were to compete with the Straits Trading Company which was planning to expand. It was expected that the new subscription would provide sufficient funds to overcome past financial shortfalls.

Finance

The sale of Eastern Smelting in 1911 highlights a fundamental weakness of the Khaw group: its limited access to financial resources. The financial arm of the group — the

---

[85]*PG*, 17 July 1901.
[86]Eastern Smelting Company, Ltd., *Prospectus*, July 1911 (Lim Keong Lay Collection, Rare Book Room, Penang Public Library).
[87]*PG*, 31 August 1911.
[88]*PG Centenary Number* on Lee Chin Ho.
[89]Wong, p. 243; Birch, pp. 156–57.
[90]George Meudell, *The Pleasant Career of a Spendthrift* (London, 1933), p. 136.
[91]*Prospectus*, 1911.
[92]*PG Centenary Number* on Lee Chin Ho.

Penang Khean Guan Insurance Company founded in 1885, the opium farm syndicates composed of Khaw family members and their associates. and the proposed Eastern Trading Company, a lending institution floated in April 1907[93] — did not generate enough free capital to allow the group to grow to its full potential.

The Penang Khean Guan Insurance Company and the revenue farms gave good returns over the years on the money invested in them. The insurance company paid regular dividends to its shareholders, even in years when the company "had suffered a heavy loss".[94] The opium farms, which one colleague has called "virtual money trees",[95] were so lucrative that they provided approximately one-half of the revenue of the Straits Settlements in 1904–1905.[96] Opium was a main prop of the Khaw fortune and members of the family had been actively involved in various syndicates in the Straits Settlements. the F.M.S. and Siam. While the insurance company and revenue farms were not financial institutions as such, each could generate substantial income that was not then required for reinvestment in capital equipment. They would have acted as channels for investment funds among the participating members and as financial intermediaries generally. providing credit information and information about new investment opportunities.

Another possible source of funds open to the Khaw family was the Koe Guan Trust (Koe Guan Kong Lun 高源公輸) which, according to the will of Khaw Soo Cheang, was to be set up with sixteen of the sixty shares from his estate. These sixteen shares were worth on the order of $320,000 in 1905 when Khaw Sim Kong, Sim Tek and Sim Bee — Soo Cheang's surviving sons — organised the trust.[97] The trust was to cover the usual expenses incurred during the *cheng-beng* festival (sweeping the tombs), as well as marriage gifts and funeral costs for impoverished family members. It was also, however, to provide "a yearly investment income for male descendants" — and quite possibly the trustees took advantage of their position to borrow money to invest in such activities as Eastern Shipping and Eastern Smelting.[98]

Proceeds from the insurance company, revenue farms and trust would not, however, have been adequate to meet the demands, immediate or anticipated, on the group's resources. Access to dependable investment funds must have been a paramount consideration behind the floating of the proposed Eastern Trading Company, Ltd., in 1907. The company's *Prospectus* announced that it was to be in the business of "carrying on ... every description of banking and mercantile exchange, discount and loan business...."[99] There seems to have been general agreement that the time was ripe for such a venture because funds from European financial institutions were not adequate to finance local planters and miners.

Because of the tight credit market and unreasonable rates of interest, the *Pinang Gazette* suggested that "both European and native planters and business men will seek accommodation" from the new venture. The promoters argued, moreover, that as a local

[93]*PG*, 8 April 1907, 27 April 1907.

[94]*PG*, 3 January 1900.

[95]Letter from Howard Dick, 3 July 1985. The revenue farmers could lose money as well: see, for example. John G. Butcher, "The Demise of the Revenue Farm System in the Federated Malay States", *Modern Asian Studies* 17.3 (1983): 398–400.

[96]Wright, p. 152.

[97]*PG*, 30 June 1903. In the report of the suit brought by Khaw Soo Cheang's granddaughter to inherit part of the estate. the shares were said to be worth $20,000 each.

[98]This was suggested in an interview with one of the Koe Guan trustees, Mr Khaw Cheng Joey, Penang, March 1984.

[99]27 April 1907.

enterprise, the money it generated would remain in the F.M.S. to the benefit of the Malayan eonomy. Finally, the promoters hinted at the connection they expected would materialise between Eastern Trading and the Khaw business group: "by uniting what may be termed legitimate banking business *with enterprise in the wider spheres of activity available to such companies*, the highest measure of success should be achieved" (italics added).[100]

Unfortunately for the Khaw group, Eastern Trading was not fully subscribed and the plan had to be abandoned. An editorial in the *Pinang Gazette* of 18 July 1907, while admitting it was a timely exercise, argued that because "the Board was to have been exclusively Asiatic", potential investors, European and Chinese alike, had been frightened off. This mistake was not to be repeated. When the Eastern Smelting Company was floated some months later, "the composition of the Board of Directors" was said to "inspire confidence" with well-known Europeans (e.g., the Secretary, James Donald and the Managing Director, Herrmann Jessen) figuring prominently in the company's management structure.[101]

The Decline of the Khaw Group

Access to finance was recognised as an essential prerequisite to the success of large-scale business by the more go-ahead Chinese entrepreneurs of the early twentieth century. Oei Tiong Ham, for instance, had realised early on that unless he 'had ready access to a reliable supply of funds, he would not be able to diversify. The N.V. Bankvereniging Oei Tiong Ham was the result.[102] Other Chinese arrived at similar conclusions. Lim Peng Siang, the founder of the Ho Hong Company (successor to Wee Bin) for instance, organised the Ho Hong Bank, Ltd., to finance his oil, rice and cement companies.[103] All of these companies were making their debut in the early twentieth century in the face of growing competition from European firms supported by substantial European backing.

The Khaw family and its business partners also recognised the central role of finance to the implementation of their plans. Had Eastern Trading been successfully launched, there was every chance that the Khaw group would have continued to prosper. As we have seen, lack of finance for expansion was the apparent reason behind the sale of The Eastern Smelting Company, one of the core businesses within the group. An institution like Eastern Trading might well have enabled the original promoters of the smelting firm to carry their ideas for modernising the Malayan tin industry further. As it turned out, the directors, while losing majority control, did rather well financially from the sale of the company; the ordinary shares they received in lieu of a cash payment were valued at £133,000.[104]

The other core firm in the Khaw group, Eastern Shipping, suffered a similar, though less clear-cut fate. It maintained its association with Eastern Smelting even after the latter was sold because it had contracted with the company to ship all the ore smelted at the

---

[100]Ibid.

[101]*PG*, 14 November 1907.

[102]Panglaykim and Palmer, *Entrepreneurship*, p. 16.

[103]Tregonning, *Home Port*, pp. 65–66.

[104]Eastern Smelting Company, Ltd., *Prospectus*, July 1911. As part of the sale agreement, the old company was allowed to nominate two Directors in the new company. Lee Chin Ho appears to have been the only former Chinese Director to sit on the restructured Board (Wong, p. 267).

Penang refinery.[105] The fleet was gradually allowed to deteriorate over the years as the managing director, Quah Beng Kee, became embroiled in a series of legal wrangles over accidents blamed on the firm. He and Khaw Joo Tok were also at loggerheads over company policy.[106] When the fleet was requisitioned by the British government during World War One[107] the company appears to have lost impetus altogether. With its contracts going to other firms and its vessels becoming increasingly unseaworthy, the company looked to be even more lack-lustre after the war ended. But the firm still controlled certain routes and monopolised parts of the coastal trade, especially with the tin provinces of peninsular Siam. Accordingly, when the Khaw family, after much soul-searching, decided to sell in 1922, the Straits Steamship Company bought it to prevent other British firms or the K.P.M. from taking it over.[108] Its sale in 1922 for 2 million dollars marked the end of the Khaw group.

On the face of it, the Khaw group should have been a model business venture. The group's management practices, combining as they did western expertise and technology with the local contacts and networks open to its Chinese directors, were sound. The industry around which the group's activities were centred — tin — continued to be one of the major revenue earners for the F.M.S. and Straits Settlements.[109] And, while the financial institutions associated with the group were becoming somewhat uncertain by the end of the first decade of the twentieth century, the group still had access to funds through a number of channels. Why, then, did the group not become self-sustaining?

The absence of a single guiding hand in the group's direction must certainly rank as one of its great eventual weaknesses. Unlike the far-flung Oei empire in which Oei Tiong Ham was the key policy figure, the Khaw group developed as a looser confederation of equals with Khaw Sim Bee the *primus inter pares* (even if behind the scenes) until his death in 1913. E.T. Miles was to remark years later that Sim Bee did not stand out in Penang's commercial circles because "he was then a very high placed, and much esteemed Siamese official ...",[110] implying that his official position precluded him from appearing to run major commercial enterprises from British territory.

The duality of the Khaw family's locus of power was cited at the beginning of this paper as an explanation for their extraordinary success in peninsular Siam. This duality also helps to account for the Khaw group's initial strength, as well as to explain its subsequent decline. Although the group lacked a degree of unity because of its various management coalitions, its competitive position was strong against Western firms as long as the Khaws, and especially Sim Bee, were able to secure the necessary concessions from Bangkok to allow the Khaw companies a major share in the peninsular trade. The death of a man noted for "his remarkable activity of mind and body, and capacity for sustained and continuous work, and untiring energy"[111] must have profoundly affected the diverse economic empire he headed. Khaw Joo Tok, who had represented the family's interests

[105]The retiring directors may well have insisted that the connection between the shipping firm and the smelting company be maintained in order to ensure the continued viability of Eastern Shipping.

[106]Interview with Khaw Cheng Joey, Penang, March 1984.

[107]*Report of the Trial in the Supreme Court of the Straits Settlements of the Action Brought by the Eastern Shipping Co., Ltd., of Penang against His Majesty's Attorney General for the Straits Settlements concerning the Requisition of Ships* (Penang, 1921).

[108]I am grateful to Howard Dick for providing this information.

[109]In 1914, for instance, of Perak's revenue of $19,338,374, over one-fifth, or $4,181,077, came from the collection of the tin duty: Wong, pp. 251, 261.

[110]Miles Papers, E.T. Miles, *Memoirs.*

[111]F.O. 422/68/21, Beckett to Grey, 30 April 1913.

Family Business

in Penang's commercial circles with Sim Bee, was now the family's senior commercial figure. Although described as "a big man with an imposing personality"[112] he may have lacked the strength and drive to hold together the disparate interests within the Khaw group.[113]

There were political consequences as well. Khaw Sim Bee's death in 1913 and that of his brother, Sim Kong, the year before signalled the beginning of the erosion of the family's political influence in the Thai administration of the peninsula. Although the family continued to enjoy certain advantages, especially in the mining industry, appointees from Bangkok came in to take over the political positions they had once monopolised. The interaction between the Penang commercial base and the Thai political base became less effective just as it was perhaps most needed: at a time when Western companies were gaining the upper hand, with the backing of home governments and financial institutions.

As the political and economic circumstances that had initially given impetus to the group began to change, the ties that had bound together this alliance "of diverse firms controlled by a number of different men and families"[114] were not adequate to carry the group into the new economic climate of post-World War I Southeast Asia. The Khaw family and its business partners had boldly experimented with a business formation, but the successful implementation of this model still lay in the future.

---

[112]A. Pratt, *Magical Malaya* (Melbourne, 1913), p. 34.

[113]Interview with Dato Khaw Bian Cheng and Khaw Cheng Joey, Penang, March 1984: Khaw Joo Tok came to rely increasingly on his associate, Tan Swee Tin, in the management of Koe Guan's affairs. By all accounts, Joo Tok was not as forceful a figure as Khaw Sim Bee.

[114]Strachan, p. 29.

[25]

By *Johannes Hirschmeier*

PROFESSOR OF ECONOMICS
NANZAN UNIVERSITY

The Japanese Spirit of Enterprise, 1867-1970

❡ *Tradtional Japanese disdain for business was overcome by making in-dustrialization synonymous with the esteemed value of public service in the face of foreign economic competition. The alien corporate form of organization was made palatable by characterizing it as a family group which attracted traditional loyalties. Professor Hirschmeier attributes Japan's rapid industrialization at the turn of the century and her remark-able recovery after World War II to such pragmatic social compromises and uses them to identify and explain a uniquely Japanese "spirit of enterprise."*

The search for a specific Japanese spirit of enterprise may seem at this stage of technological development to have little prac-tical value. Indeed, Marx was to a large extent right in saying that the substructure of economic organization resulting from techno-logical progress would shape the superstructure, and with it our value system. Do we not today move with almost frightening speed toward something like a uniform world culture with almost identical business practices, wherein the sole differences seem to lie mainly in language and color of skin?

While not denying the tendency toward some convergence of the spirit of enterprise in various countries, there do remain, and shall continue to be for quite some time, marginal differences in practice that have their root in basic mentalities. Westerners doing business in Japan *do* discover such differences, at times to their puzzlement or even displeasure. Yet those differences are not necessarily oddi-ties or signs of underdevelopment; they have their roots in both his-torical precedence and something we could call national character. It is this common denominator, the Japanese spirit of enterprise, that I wish to analyze as it manifests itself under various historical conditions and in business practices and institutions which differ from western patterns.

Business History Review, Vol. XLIV, No. 1 (Spring, 1970). Copyright © The President and Fellows of Harvard College.

The western spirit of capitalism has undergone constant modification, from the stress on fulfilling one's calling by God in a secular asceticism of hard work and accumulation, through the optimistic belief that an "invisible hand" would establish a beneficial harmony out of individual egotisms, toward an ever growing realization of the need for conscious control by the state as well as self-control by business. Today, the West aspires to almost the opposite of the Darwinian market jungle — the age of the "soulful corporation" and the "organization man." Are there any remaining constants which could be called central to the western spirit of enterprise? I think we can, notably if compared with Japan, discover two such basic constants. First, no matter what role his firm or social group may play, the westerner still evaluates everything with respect to the individual person. This seems so self-understood that westerners become aware of their basic individualist or rather personal value system only when it is compared with the Marxian or, in this case, the Japanese way of thinking and acting. Second, somehow westerners judge economic behavior as well as other activities against norms that are independently established, things called "truth" or "right," and which can be asserted against mere practicability and utility or against group and state. It is obvious that we touch here upon the basis of western normative thinking, with wars over religious or ideological belief as tragic testimony.

One of the strongest concerns of the Japanese, however, is harmony (*wa*), to which both rigid principles and the individual person as such must usually take a back seat. As far as principles are concerned, the Japanese are not known to be keen philosophers. In the realm of ideas that have no direct practical application, they are amazingly tolerant: they marry in the Shintō rite, are buried according to the Buddhist faith, and may, in addition, belong to some "modern" religion that has made a very nice, happy-go-lucky stew of Buddhist, Christian, and Shintō tenets. The stress on harmony further manifests itself in their attitude toward the group and toward nature. The Shintō myths make man appear as part of nature: the individual must not subdue or coerce nature but must subordinate himself to it. The elegance and softness of Japanese arts have one of their sources here. The same basic attitude as to nature is maintained vis-à-vis the group: belonging, being part of it, is valued above self-assertion of the individual person. To sum up briefly this one trait: non-dogmatic pragmatism in the service of harmony within the group and for the group, not primarily for the individual.

There exists yet another basic element, at times totally contradictory to the first: the Japanese can be hard and unbending in their determination, and fierce fighters. During World War II the world wondered whether there was any connection between the polite behavior of the Japanese and the harmony in their arts, and the self-sacrificing and often cruel way they fought. It seems that whenever the Japanese feel challenged, notably as country or as group, they completely lose their sereneness and the hard, unbending fighting spirit of the *samurai* comes to the surface again. In terms of the spirit of enterprise, we can see that in periods of outside challenge economic nationalism takes precedence over the interests of the individual group. This asserted itself strongest in the Meiji period, but is notably felt throughout the modern period because the Japanese feel challenged by the very fact of being still behind, of still not having attained the first place somehow due to them.

Throughout this article I shall try to point out that, and how and why these two basic elements have influenced business behavior. I shall place particular emphasis on historical continuity on the one hand and the changing emphasis between these two elements according to the degree of challenge on the other.

BUSINESS FOR THE SAKE OF THE NATION

The Tokugawa Merchants

Tokugawa society was not, until the very last decades, confronted with any major outside challenge. It was dominated by group interests: the commoners lived and worked within the extended family and occupational groupings, according to their house rules and customs handed down by tradition and influenced by Buddhist as well as Confucian teachings. The idea of Japan as a nation state lay dormant for, in spite of the unification of the country, primary loyalties belonged to the *han*. The country, *tenka*, was more or less synonymous with society as a whole, the concept used as basis for the Confucian social ethics.

According to Sokō Yamaga the *tenka* was conceived of as a human body of different members with different functions which all cooperate to the welfare of the whole. The diversity of social functions was laid down in the particular "way" (*michi*) of the social groups. Robert Bellah puts it like this: "The word *shokubun* . . . implies that the occupation is not merely an end in itself but part of society. One's occupation is the fulfillment of what one owes to society, it is the part one plays which justifies one's receiving the

benefits of society." [1] The *samurai* were the mind and willpower
giving guidance to and bearing responsibility for the harmony of
the rest of society. In the rigid framework of agrarian feudalism,
where the *samurai* lived on rice stipends and suffered impoverishment apparently through the hands of the merchants, the official
verdict on business pursuit could not but be quite similar to that
reached by the medieval Scholastics in Europe — that merchants performed a parasitic albeit necessary function in society. Sayings like,
"warrior means willpower, peasant means taxpaying, artisan means
work, merchant means smiling," [2] reveal how hard the Tokugawa
merchant class was pressed to justify their pursuit of profits in terms
of the official Confucian social ethics though, in fact, their daily
routine was hardly touched by it; they did business by their handed-
down house and guild rules.

In their *shingaku* philosophy the Tokugawa merchants made an
attempt to justify their profits in terms of their service to the *tenka*
(whole society), proving that their activity, their way, was as necessary for the well being of society as that of the samurai. While
their stress on honesty, thrift, and accumulation reminds us of the
Puritan mentality, we find nowhere an attempt to emphasize the
individual, his rights as a person, and his business pursuit as following the calling of God. Practically, the merchant's way was a subordination of the individual to the house and the group; only,
vis-à-vis the criticism of the feudal class, the service function toward the whole society was extolled. Public recognition was sought,
then, in terms of the ruling class and its ideology, both in theory
and, to some extent, also in practice. By way of the adoption system
and by acquiring, through diverse services, at least part of the
paraphernalia of the *samurai* class, the right of the family name
and the sword, the merchants tried to emulate the feudal class itself. Incidentally, they followed here the example of the early
English industrialists who also sought social recognition in terms of
the established value system by infiltrating into the ranks of the
aristocracy, and by vying for seats in Parliament. [3]

While the service function of business for the welfare of society,
the *tenka*, was all there in theory, two changes were needed in order
to transform this philosophical speculation into a dynamic force that
would push aside the predominance of groupism: the agrarian-
oriented economic theory had to give way to a new and realistic

[1] Robert Bellah, *Tokugawa Religion* (Glencoe, 1957), 115.
[2] Mataji Miyamoto, *Osaka* (Osaka, 1957), 119.
[3] Reinhard Bendix, *Work and Authority in Industry* (New York, 1963), 22–34.

evaluation of the usefulness of business; and the *tenka* had to become a nation under challenge.

The first change came about when the *bakufu* leaders themselves fully realized, in the course of time, how useful business was, be it only in terms of the taxes which they began to levy upon the merchants. Yet they did not dare upset the already unbalanced apple-cart of society by calling the merchants outright a productive class. But scholars who studied conditions of western countries began to sing a different tune. Thus, Kohei Kanda pointed out: "When a country depends on commerce, it always enjoys economic prosperity; whereas, when a country relies upon agriculture, it always suffers poverty. Hence, Oriental countries are persistently poor because they depend on agriculture, while Occidental countries are at all times wealthy because they rely on commerce." [4] Yet it was only after the Meiji Restoration that business could fully be proclaimed to be not only useful but of paramount importance for the very survival of Japan as nation.

The second change began when the shock of being suddenly confronted with the superior western powers began to awaken in the Japanese a new national self-consciousness. Above all status and *han* differences, people began to take on an overriding sameness. Loyalties to the *han*, which had been also called *kokka* (nation), were transferred to the new *kokka*, the nation state. The bifocality of authority — ideal authority of the Emperor in Kyoto and real political power of the Tokugawa *bakufu* in Edo — merged into one strong central power located in Tokyo. The Emperor personified traditional values (Shintō) and national unity. He became the source of real power that rested in his government, composed of young radicals, and the symbol of progress which soon meant mainly economic development.

Meiji Economic Nationalism

Economic centralism is certainly one of the most conspicuous features of Meiji nationalism which has left its permanent imprint on the Japanese economy. This centralism, in fact, has a dual direction: from the center toward the periphery in terms of guidance, help, and investments; and a movement from the periphery toward the center creating, as by-product, a backwash-effect on the rest of Japan.

Meiji national awakening could only reach its high emotional

[4] Yasuzo Horie, "Confucian Concept of State in Tokugawa Japan," *Kyoto University Economic Review*, XXXII (October 1962), 29.

JAPANESE SPIRIT OF ENTERPRISE   17

watermark because of energetic and systematic guidance from the center. Institutionally, this meant the government with cooperation from the circle of the avant-garde of intellectuals and entrepreneurs. Geographically, this meant Tokyo as distinct from the rest of Japan. The government provided some initial guidance by directly establishing pioneering enterprises based on modern, western technology. It took the brunt of initial losses that resulted from technical inexperience, and then sold cheaply to businessmen willing and capable to turn the losses into profits. It experimented with new laws and policies designed to favor modernization on a broad front and create the needed atmosphere for modern business. From the very outset the Meiji officials never thought in terms of permanent state enterprises as mainstay of the economy, but rather their primary concern was to help private business to its feet.

The wealthy merchant houses were first relied upon and prodded to join "the battle of enterprise," under conditions laid down from above — modern technology, large scale, joint-stock form, and competitive against the foreigners. The almost pathetic failure of this attempt is well known; it did not jibe with merchant attitudes and old traditions. Hence, the government was forced to look for its own favorite agents of enterprise, the so-called "political merchants." Actually, the officials were not so much playing a game of favoritism as they were looking almost desperately for able and willing agents to carry out what they themselves deemed necessary without having the fiscal means nor the time and experience to carry out. They acted like quarterbacks in a football game, looking for receivers to catch the ball and run with it. The best runners eventually became *zaibatsu* (financial oligarchs), out of a unique combination of government subsidies, monopolistic practices, and personal capabilities and ambitions. The *zaibatsu* entrepreneurs shared with government officials a strong sense of national purpose which they discharged with vigor, albeit not to their own disadvantage. A capitalism for the "national interest," with the government willing to grant special privileges or design policies toward this end, and the business elite docilely following the official line, has remained a lasting heritage of that Meiji economic centralism.

The other direction of economic centralism created a lasting backwash-effect upon initiative from the periphery, and upon local independence. The Tokugawa *bakufu* had established a strong centrist administration, with the *daimyō* making their *sankin-kōtai* (alternate residence) pilgrimages to the center; but the *han* economies had remained independent economic units. After the Meiji

Restoration, Tokyo became simply *the* center, politically, ideologically, and economically. Since guidance and help came from there, the progressive elements gathered in Tokyo, cooperating with both the officials and among each other, and coming into living contact with the new era. Soon the former economic capital of Osaka was pushed into the backwaters of relative stagnation. Thus, something happened which is today often pointed out in the literature of economic development: modernization spreads from a center, attracting new business into that center via the advantages of cooperation and external economies of various kinds while the rest of the country may for some time be pushed into more pronounced stagnation as capital and entrepreneurship are syphoned away into the modern sector.

This backwash-effect was enforced by the typical mental make-up of the Japanese "vertical society." [5] People refer from their directly involved group, not toward the next group horizontally, but toward the center where all converge. The idea of nation too easily coincides with government itself, resulting in a marked lack of local initiative and care for local needs. As a result of all this Tokyo has retained its absolute position as center of initiative, the major firms establishing their headquarters there, imposing on the rest of Japan the necessity of continuing *"sankin-kōtai* travels," since major decisions must be made in Tokyo.

After the Meiji Restoration a revaluation of business activity became both possible and urgently necessary. As late as 1900 a leading entrepreneur, Takashi Masuda of Mitsui Bussan, complained of low public estimation of business: "The men of commerce and industry . . . are not the equal of other classes in social prestige. . . . Power in this society is monopolized by politicians, and men of commerce and industry have hardly any share in it. Although you would think that even a half-grown child would laugh at anyone who said that artisans and merchants should be placed beneath the samurai and the peasants, in fact even educated men have not yet completely cast off these feudal ideas." [6] The entrepreneurs themselves, fully aware of their own contribution to the nation, chafed under this lingering contempt for business. Among them were former *samurai* and some who had deliberately "stepped down" from higher government positions in order to engage re-

[5] Chiye Nakane, *Tate shakai no ningenkankei* (human relations in the vertical society), (Tokyo, 1967). Nakane points out the various practices and attitudes that result from the lack of horizontal orientation with almost exclusive stress on the vertical line of group-center, and within the group vertically with heavy stress on hierarchy.

[6] Byron K. Marshall, *Capitalism and Nationalism in Prewar Japan* (Stanford, 1967), 45.

JAPANESE SPIRIT OF ENTERPRISE   19

sponsibly in entrepreneurial activity, like Eiichi Shibusawa and Tomoatsu Godai. Furthermore, these men were fully aware that, unless the public image of modern businessmen would reach a similar esteem to that of government officials, it would be difficult to attract ambitious and talented men into often-enough lower paid and more risky business pursuits.

Eiichi Shibusawa [7] and the other leading entrepreneurs, who often cooperated closely, worked toward a new public image of the businessmen in stressing the differences vis-à-vis the Tokugawa merchants as well as the idea of continuity of values. Just as the era of the *bummei kaika* (civilization and enlightenment) was propagated as a rejection of backward practices and an embrace of all that was progressive, gathering new knowledge from the whole world, so the "businessmen of the *bummei kaika*" had to appear as the very opposite of the old merchants and their ways. If the old merchants had acted for private profits, the "entrepreneurs" (a new name was coined) would act like government officials for the sake of the nation. If the former had adhered to old house rules and traditions, the entrepreneurs would apply the new western knowledge and engage in new types of enterprises that needed school records and theoretical knowledge gained mainly from books. If the old merchants had been unreliable (this had been their public image), the entrepreneurs had to follow the path of absolute honesty. All the glory went to the modern, large scale enterprises thus eventually strengthening the double structure of small, backward versus large scale, modern enterprises. And the stress of school records contributed to a dichotomy between employees' and workers' positions based solely and formalistically on a college degree, a problem we shall touch upon later.

In terms of continuity of values, the entrepreneur was painted as the legal heir of the *samurai*. The *samurai* had been the learned class par excellence, and the entrepreneur acted upon and thus represented the ideals of the *bushidō* (the "way of the *samurai*"). Magnanimity and courage, loyalty, public service, and honesty were to characterize, according to Shibusawa, the modern businessman. Indeed, by stressing along with the *bushidō* the differences from the western capitalist who was supposed to seek only his own profits, Shibusawa not only tried to prevent a break and a vacuum in the value system but also to successfully compensate the tech-

---

[7] Johannes Hirschmeier, "Eiichi Shibusawa: Industrial Pioneer," in William W. Lockwood (ed.), *The State and Economic Enterprise in Japan* (Princeton University Press, 1965). The importance of a new public image as well as the approach to achieve it are elaborated in greater detail, as is the leadership role of Eiichi Shibusawa.

nical inferiority complex with an ethical superiority-stress. Since the "barbarians" from the West had proven to be superior in knowledge, they at least had to remain inferior, "barbaric," ethically in order to strengthen the sense of national identity which was necessary for the drive of modernization.

Investment decisions of entrepreneurs were affected by nationalist attitudes in various ways. The leading men of business displayed a veritable "Sturm und Drang" mentality toward innovations. Under a pervading sense of a mission they seldom confined themselves to one single line of enterprise but fanned out in various unconnected directions. Hence, the entrepreneurial avant-garde rushed forward leaving the details to lesser men. Their courage was bolstered by the assurance that the government would not let them down, as well as by some kind of half-knowledge which made them overlook real difficulties until they stumbled over them. Their eventual success was then mostly assured by both government assistance, and the working of external economies and various linkage effects which developed all along.

While the glamor of achievement was bestowed on the large scale, new-type ventures, Japanese private consumption remained largely traditional and was catered to by the old style, small scale establishments. The new industries worked mainly for the public sector and competed directly with foreign firms. Furthermore, the entrepreneurs purposely shunned the merchants' smiling salesmanship; they were interested in production first. This linkage of modern industry with the public sector (transportation, shipping, arms production, cement for public buildings, western-type paper for newspapers and government consumption), leaving Japanese consumer habits traditional (house, furniture, eating habits), strengthened the dual structure of the Japanese economy. The progressive sector of the economy adopted a "consumer-be-damned" neglect of sales effort, disdainfully leaving to the small establishments the menial job of catering for the small man.

Economic Nationalism after World War II

Defeat in World War II caused not only sincere soul searching in Japan with respect to prewar nationalism but also, in a typical pragmatic about-face, a veritable enthusiasm for anything American. The democratization of Japanese industry — the dissolution of the *zaibatsu*, diffusion of shareholdings and the establishment of a strong labor movement — was thus carried out with much goodwill. Management eagerly absorbed new American techniques and methods, from modern accounting to public relations and marketing. Sooner than anyone had expected, the Japanese economy gained strength, and Japanese firms began to flex their muscles in the international market.

The first stirrings of a new kind of economic nationalism appeared in the mid-1950's. The national managers' association, *keizai dōyūkai*, passed at its general meeting in 1956 a resolution calling on managers to "realize and act upon a sense of public responsibility." This new stress on public responsibility soon became a "new doctrine of management," sparking research efforts and expositions of typical "Japanese managerial attitudes." To the western way of thinking this emphasis of public responsibility could only be welcomed, yet some Japanese intellectuals were quick in sensing here a disguised resurgence of nationalism.[8] To westerners, public responsibility of business means things like fair pricing, a cooperative attitude, and care for the workers, as well as cooperation and contribution toward local needs, avoiding public damage in terms of water pollution, and the like. To put it differently, the West thinks in horizontal terms, "the public" meaning the people directly involved within the enterprise or locally outside of the firm. The Japanese, too, readily think vertically of the state and the government when they say "public." Japanese industry has been too long neglectful of the horizontally conceived public to change this quickly. With company headquarters usually located in Tokyo, civic responsibility is underdeveloped and local needs, outside the company members themselves, are conspicuous by their neglect. "Japan is a poor country" and "industrial production must come first" are the standard refrains to excuse the constant neglect of public needs by big industry.

Along with the thus interpreted "public responsibility," Japanese managers began to rediscover their historic national heritage. Company histories were compiled which stressed the great achievement of the Meiji beginnings. Japanese business ethos on the line of Shibusawa's early argument was reasserted, and business strategy was studied in terms of the military genius of Ieyasu Tokugawa. The aforementioned *keizai dōyūkai* began, in 1962, a research program on the "managerial philosophy contained in the Japanese business climate." Such attempts resemble Shibusawa's stress on

---

[8] Jūichi Nakase, "gendai keiei shisō to nationalism" (today's managerial mentality and nationalism), *gendai no me* (March 1965), and "sengo nihon no keieisha no shisō; shakaietki sekininron to rijun dai ichi-shugi" (Japanese managerial mentality after the War; the theory of social responsibility and the principle of profits-first), *keizai hyōron* (February 1966).

bushidō at the time of Japan's first competitive confrontation with the more advanced West.

The Japanese government as well as the industrial leaders presently think very much in terms of confrontation and challenge coming in the shape of imminent capital and trade liberalization. The "danger to the national economy" resulting from the "invasion" of foreign capital is painted vividly to the public, in an effort to convince the people that they should condone and even welcome measures that aim at strengthening the position of the big firms. On the one hand, the international achievements of Japanese industry are extolled, showing statistically its truly remarkable growth and the rise of Japan to the position of number two in the free world in terms of gross national product. On the other hand, American capital is characterized as a giant against whom the still inferior and capital-scarce Japanese industries need protection and subsidies. The government thus encourages mergers of large companies, including the two giants, Yawata and Fuji Steel, probably at the expense of the consuming public, but definitely "for the sake of Japan." At times, a veritable xenophobia, or rather a revived *jōi*-mentality (*sonnō-jōi*, "revere the emperor, expel the barbarians," the battle cry of the anti-*bakufu* forces that eventually established the Meiji Restoration) comes to the fore, as in the case of the Toyota Motor Company which changed its articles of incorporation so that no foreigner could become a company officer. The board chairman explained this measure by saying, "defense of our own castle is the first prerequisite for service to the state." [9]

Economic nationalism today differs, of course, from that of the Meiji period. It is less open and reflects the large degree of internationalism that became a positive force after World War II. But it is there, and it does at times tip the scales in favor of decisions both on the part of the government and of private business, which can only be fully understood against the background of the Japanese vertical society to which, in the last analysis, each group interest must be subordinated, notably in times of outside challenge.

The Role of Economic Familism

Service to the House (Iye)

The "house" was the smallest unit in which the individual fulfilled his service to Tokugawa society. The term *iye* also meant, of

---

[9] Herbert Glazer, *The International Businessman in Japan* (Tokyo, 1968), 72. Glazer gives interesting details gained by practical dealings with Japanese executives which provide ample illustration for the return of Japanese economic nationalism.

course, the building, but mainly it meant the family enterprise of which the living family was only a trustee. Employees as well as family members were equally obliged to loyally observe the many detailed house rules and traditions handed down from the ancestors like a spiritual blood stream superior to the physical blood. For the sake of the house's prosperity a son could be subordinated to the commands of an employed manager (*bantō*) or even disinherited in favor of an outsider who would take up the house name as his own.

The merchants' business ethics were strongly dominated by the service idea toward the house's perpetual prosperity, and thus virtue meant parsimony, accumulation, hard work, and clever calculation for the increase of profits. To accumulate was the way of the merchant, and he "revered gold and silver like Buddha and the Gods until death."

But subservience to the house and its traditions meant also subordination of the individual and his initiative. The rules of the house stifled progress and prevented innovations. On the other hand, the larger merchant families could for the same reason establish a division between ownership and control, and impose limits on the amount of consumption which family members were allowed. The *bantō* (manager) was given practical power but he would never forget his position as retainer of the house and the family, maintaining meticulously the proscribed attitude of deference, which somehow resembled the relationship between the emperor and the *bakufu* leaders who wielded real power over the emperor while bowing to him. Some merchant families, like the Mitsuis, would even adopt some prototype of joint-stock system where all branch families became co-owners of an undivided family enterprise.

This division between ownership and management, as well as the joint ownership of branch families of an undivided house enterprise, enabled some leading merchant families to modernize effectively and eventually to become top financial and industrial empires in the new era. Both the Mitsui and Sumitomo merchant houses succeeded in their modernization on account of the almost absolute power wielded by their progressive *bantō* who could impose their views on the family. Both not only made strategic business decisions but effectively reeducated the owner families for the new era. The top *bantō* of Mitsui, Rizaemon Minomura, sent five of the younger Mitsui sons to the United States in 1872 to study modern banking, as preparation for the establishment of the Mitsui Bank. Both Minomura of Mitsui and Saihei Hirose of Sumitomo had the old family laws revised to fit the new era of progress. The revised Mitsui House Law of 1889 contains as paragraph two this sentence: "It is our duty to study the fast changes of the time, and start or liquidate our enterprises so that we shall not lag behind the progress of the world." [10]

Most of the emerging *zaibatsu* (financial empires), however, were not old merchant houses but upstarts beginning almost or totally from scratch after the Meiji Restoration. Yet some of these, too, modeled their enterprises according to the house idea, making use of the important service ethics and the long time horizon which is implied in the individual's subordination to the house, as an economic unit. Most typical of these new *zaibatsu* with strong emphasis on its family or house aspect is probably Yatarō Iwasaki's Mitsubishi *zaibatsu*. Although Iwasaki received most of his top men from the liberal Keiō College, there was no yielding to any democratic principle. Although some, like Heigorō Shōda, were given far-reaching decision power, they were never permitted to forget that they were nothing but retainers of the House of Iwasaki.

The familism which was carried over from the Tokugawa merchant house into modern type enterprises, notably of the *zaibatsu*, had a special appeal for the Japanese. Professor Yasuzō Horie mentions that many university graduates, chiefly sons of samurai, preferred lower paid employment with the large *zaibatsu* enterprises to higher paid government jobs, precisely because the lifelong employment in the service of one family appealed to their traditional values of loyalty.[11] Although the general evidence points rather in the opposite direction of *samurai* sons crowding into government employment because of the higher public esteem of anything connected with government service and a lingering contempt for business, the point is well taken. As far as the traditional value system was concerned, familism and groupism had deep roots irrespective of merchant or samurai background, and the idea of service and loyalty — the subordination of the individual to the group rather than his self-assertion — were carried over into the modern era.

The question is, then, whether familism became a handicap or a force for progress. In itself, familism is ambivalent. In the Tokugawa period it encouraged thrift and hard work, but on balance became, in the critical time of change, a handicap due to the backward-looking servility to tradition, house rules, and stifling of in-

[10] Fujiyoshi Sakamoto, *Nihon keiei Kyōikushi josetsu* (introduction to the history of Japanese management education), (Tokyo, 1964), 16.

[11] Yasuzo Horie, "Nihon keieishi ni okeru iye no mondai" (the problem of the House in Japanese business history), *Keieishigaku* (Business History Review), II (1967), 128.

dividual initiative. Yet under some conditions, where a progressive leader could assert himself, familism could become an enormous power, as in the case of the *zaibatsu*. The sense of perpetuity of the house, to which the living family owed service, had probably something to do with the tremendously long time horizon that was displayed by the outstanding Meiji entrepreneurs. I have shown elsewhere [12] that the low returns in modern large scale investments can hardly be explained by rational calculations alone if compared with the going interest rates. Rather, they indicate attitudes whereby some absolute future goal rather than the living individual's time preference scale must have been taken as basis for discounting. Such interpretation does, of course, not deny that the amounts of government subsidies made the waiting for returns easier and left little choice but to invest in modern large scale ventures, or that the very dynamics of development with new economies of scale and external economies could at times turn *ex ante* irrational decisions into *ex post* profitable ones. All I want to say here is that the service idea toward the house, given dynamic leadership, probably was a positive force at times where individualist and rational thinking alone would not have carried the day.

Perhaps the Japanese idea of house could be contrasted with the well known French family business attitudes where management was not willingly delegated to outsiders and where opportunities for enlargement were often passed up because too large an enterprise was considered bothersome for the living members and threatening to direct family control. [13]

Since World War II the idea of the house has almost vanished within the large modern enterprises, including the *zaibatsu*. This is not only due to the official dissolution of the *zaibatsu* for, clearly, in the large modern corporation family ownership, quite apart from control of management, fast reaches its limits, as even the Krupp family of Germany had to realize. But the mentality of service to the house is still very much alive in the small, traditional businesses. There, in the spirit of handed-down customs, the family members and employees keep up that total dedication to the house, patiently working long hours with no clear demarcation between work and leisure, not claiming rights but fulfilling their duties. It has been asserted that this type of small family enterprise in the best tradition

[12] Johannes Hirschmeier, *The Origins of Entrepreneurship in Meiji Japan* (Cambridge, Mass., 1964), 196–210.

[13] David S. Landes, "French Business and the Businessman: A Social and Cultural Analysis" in Hugh G. J. Aitken (ed.), *Explorations in Enterprise* (Cambridge, Mass., 1967). See also Peter N. Stearns, "Individualism and Association in French Industry, 1820–1848," *Business History Review*, XL (Autumn 1966).

of the Osaka merchants, with thrift and hard work as expression of filial piety toward the House, has really been the basis of Japan's post-war recovery even though all government support and public acclaim went to the large modern enterprises.[14]

Groupism in the Joint-Stock Companies

The company form of enterprise found little understanding and cooperation on the part of the merchant class after the Meiji Restoration. The merchants had no quarrels with the features of separation of ownership and control but objected to the emphasis on joining up with other, wholly unrelated people in a common enterprise. Without the house traditions at the center, a company must have appeared to them as a soulless entity to which they could not subordinate the interests of their ancestral house. The early joint-stock companies that were established by the merchants, as result of heavy government pressure and even outright threats, ended accordingly in total failure.[15]

In contrast to the merchants, the *samurai* found an easier access to the company system for various reasons: they lacked the house business tradition, they had no other choice but join together on account of their meager resources, and, finally, they were responsive to the idea of being on the modern, progressive side championed by the government. Indeed, it is one of the lasting achievements of Shibusawa to have made the company system a success against the familism of the merchant traditions.

Lifelong employment was one of the decisive features that was carried over from the house idea and that could give the company a quasi-family semblance. Initially, only administrative employees and not laborers were employed for life by the companies. Workers were usually hired in smaller, subcontracting units and worked directly under their own labor boss (*oyakata*), to whom they owed loyalty and by whom they were paid. In this fashion, even very large establishments could work with a minimum of direct company supervision. Mitsubishi's Nagasaki shipyard employed almost 1,000 workers, and the Ashio mine 8,000–9,000. In 1896, Ichibei Furukawa's mining empire is said to have had not more than fourteen employees

[14] Takao Tsuchiya, *Nihon no keieisha seishin* (the Spirit of Japanese managers) (Tokyo, 1959), 63–67. Tsuchiya is very emphatic on the great contribution of the small and medium enterprises where work is done in the spirit of the old merchant houses, quoting as illustration the famous novel by Yamasaki Tomio, *Noren*, an epic of an Osaka merchant house continuing the business through to present day, in the best of the house traditions.

[15] Detailed accounts on the problem of introducing the joint stock enterprise system are furnished in the large volume by Kanno Wataro, *Nihon kaisha kigyō hasseishi no kenkyū* (Studies in the emergence of the Japanese company form of enterprise), (Tokyo, reprinted 1966).

under direct company jurisdiction while all others — the whole blue
collar working force — was subcontracted through the system of
labor bosses.[16]

By the mid-Meiji period lifelong employment was increasingly extended to include workers. This became necessary partly because
machine-paced operations required a steady labor force which the
oyakata could not provide, but partly also because loyalty relationships could be made use of to prevent the establishment of labor
unions. Managers could pay lower wages and demand longer working hours than otherwise would have been possible. Management
tried to counter the drive for establishment of unions with a variety
of arguments. Since all company members, including workers, were
like a family, management would and should discharge paternal
responsibilities rather than introduce the principle of disputed rights.
The stress of rights rather than duties, as done in western capitalism,
would go counter to the best of Japanese ethical traditions and
would destroy the spirit of harmony. And finally, Japanese industry
could not yet pay wages according to western standards because
this would hurt its competitiveness and thus damage the national
economy. At this early stage, even labor leaders would go along
with such argumentation. Bunji Suzuki, the leader of the first
workers' movement, himself stressed the difference in attitudes
between western and Japanese workers and the need of the latter
for family-type relations within the enterprises.[17]

The sense of belonging was strengthened by the fostering of
specific company atmospheres (*shafū*). The employee or worker
with lifelong employment identified himself with *his* company, sharing burdens and accepting low wages in times of distress, but being
remunerated with extra gratifications if things went well. In peak
times he worked long hours without overtime pay but could take it
easier in times of slack. Not only the employee but also his children
were taken care of in company schools and recreational facilities,
and later through arrangement of marriages. The employee's social
life centered around his company, without separating working and
leisure time the way Westerners are prone to do. For the husband
the private home was often more or less only a place to sleep.

Entrepreneurs and managers were well aware of the positive value
of group consciousness and identification for harmony and efforts
within the company. When in 1906 the national railroads had to

---

[16] Hiroshi Hazama, *Nihonteki keiei no keifu* (the genealogy of Japanese management),
(Tokyo, 1963), 82–85.
[17] Marshall, *Capitalism and Nationalism in Prewar Japan*, 79.

absorb seventeen private lines, Shinpei Gotō, the chief of national organization, was quick to see a danger in the loss of identity sentiments and started his famous "the railways are one family" (*tetsudō-ikka*) campaign.[18] Gotō proclaimed that employees and workers of the national railways should foster three basic attitudes as distinctive family characteristics: first, work should be considered as expression of gratitude for being permitted to serve the passengers; second, in mutual respect all should foster the spirit of harmony and avoid disruptive strife; and third, each should be content to discharge his duty in the position to which he was assigned knowing that he fulfills an important function. We find here, in a nutshell, three elements that characterize much of the earlier familism which have not disappeared to this day as typical group mentality: service, harmony, *mibun* (minding one's position).

The groupism after World War II did incorporate a good deal of democratic elements. The labor unions claimed the rights of the workers and brought, by and large, an end to paternalism. But unions did not organize according to skills but rather according to companies, thus becoming themselves a positive factor to foster the feeling of belonging to the same enterprise. In Solomon B. Levine's words: "The main interest of the industrial workers now was seen as focused upon unionism imbedded in the web of traditional Japanese culture." [19] And as before the war, the companies kept stressing identity with the enterprise by a host of means, such as common recreations and excursions, club activities, fringe benefits, and company housing projects. Recently, the larger companies have become even more emphatic in fostering their own company identity image; entering college graduates are in many cases put through a tough "boot camp" (*kenshūkai*), lasting anywhere from one week to two months or longer, where they not only learn about the company's history and discipline but are melted into a closly knit group through menial work, *zazen* (Zen-squatting), and the like. One of my students graduating this year told me he will have to spend a whole month with his fellow company freshmen in a Zen temple, with such routines as getting up at four, squatting, scrubbing floors, and even being beaten if needed. New employees are "broken in" first, and then on-the-job training is offered, also under strict discipline.

One side effect of this company groupism is that most of the employee's social life centers around the company and not the private

---

[18] Hazama, *Nihonteki keiei no keifu*, 136–138.
[19] Solomon B. Levine, *Industrial Relations in Postwar Japan* (Champaign, 1958), 102.

individual family. The Japanese family house is not a place of parties as in the West; it is almost "off limits" to anyone but the closest friends and relatives. When questioned about this peculiarity, most Japanese answer that their homes are too poor and too small and that they are hence ashamed to receive visitors. This may be another reason so that better private houses, and improving transportation along with the spread of a more individualist attitude toward the company may eventually put the private family into the center of social life, but, as yet, this trend is slow in emerging.

While the large companies keep fostering the group mentality and have no plans to abolish lifelong employment, the small enterprises are characterized by a high turnover without lifelong employment. This phenomenon certainly needs an explanation which can only be given in terms of hard economic necessity. With low wages and an exaggerated susceptibility to business cycles small firms simply cannot keep a permanent staff of employees and workers. Since they depend on subcontracting, small enterprises are the first to suffer in recessions and many bankruptcies result. They can get only those workers and employees who can find no other place of work and those leave whenever there is a chance; a man who has worked a couple of years as a laborer in a small enterprise tends to take the first opportunity to establish his own workshop.

Again, as in the case of the house idea, we must ask, what is the significance of groupism in terms of economic efficiency and progress? Here, too, we discover a certain ambivalence. The group can be used as cover for the most naked egotism, notably by those who are on the top, but it also can cover incompetence by individuals, and thus may hamper progress to some extent. But on the whole, as far as the Japanese are concerned, group belonging tends to act as stimulus toward effort. As members of a permanent group the Japanese tend to work harder and achieve better results than under purely temporary contract. Professor Chiye Nakane has mentioned that the Japanese have an underdeveloped sense of contract; they prefer to work out of some kind of loyalty with permanent ties. In the feeling of many a Japanese to change the group for pecuniary reasons would probably come close to changing his family for higher pay.

Japanese tend to appraise this group mentality as expressed in lifelong employment, and even more in seniority promotion, as a remnant of feudalism and hence a sign of economic underdevelopment. Thus, they follow the Marxian model of thinking, postulating that Japan has to follow the exact western pattern of development. I doubt whether this is true, and my own thinking is that we find here a different view of man and his position in society, rather than a sign of "underdevelopment." Indeed, the individualist West seems to be past the peak of individualism, as witnessed by the quests for cooperation, group belonging, and management's efforts to strengthen a sense of identification among company members. Hence, there should really be no need for Japanese management to steer in the direction of classic capitalist mentality when they can, in effect, take a shortcut by carrying their non-capitalist group attitudes straight over into the post-capitalist era.

SOME CONSEQUENCES OF ECONOMIC FAMILISM

Social Mobility and Oversupply of Potential Managers

The process of economic modernization in the Meiji period necessitated a radical break with the merchant way of rising to the top gradually through experience and long, loyal service to the house. Theoretical knowledge and a good school record were deemed absolute prerequisites for managerial positions. Like government officials, top managers were often young men who had been given high positions on account of personal ability and academic achievement. Out of that early Meiji necessity evolved a permanent pattern — an unbridgeable dichotomy between those with and those without proper school records, the former alone being eligible for leading positions in the large companies. Since college graduates were at a premium, the large enterprises developed special demand-supply relations with particular colleges, the top grade colleges serving the *zaibatsu*. It was not only a matter of securing the best graduates, for economic familism also influenced this special *gakubatzu-zaibatsu* (school clique-financial clique) relationship. The new employee would find in his new place of work a good number of his former co-students, perhaps some from his college club, who would readily introduce him to the details of work in the fashion of quasi-*oyabun* (parent) and give the new quasi-*kobun* (child) a feeling of continuity and belonging which helped to establish firm loyalty relations.

The introduction of the American educational system after World War II resulted in a sudden proliferation of colleges and an oversupply of graduates. With open as well as disguised unemployment (in the many small sweatshops) parents would do their utmost to secure their sons' college education and thus lifelong security, hopefully in a large company. A veritable Darwinian struggle for the survival of the fittest was the result with each prospective student aiming at the "highest" college he dared in terms of his own knowledge, but being forced to take examinations, just in case, in four or five others. This selective process of the "examination hell" is reinforced by two considerations: first, the state universities are incomparably cheaper, and hence anyone who has a slight chance will try to enter, and second, in Japan something *kokuritsu* (national) is deemed automatically better than anything private, on account of the vertical society mentality mentioned before. Of course, both reasons work together in the fashion of a self-fulfilling prophecy. If all try to get in and only the best are admitted, then it is clear that graduates of state universities are the best and hence are offered the best employment opportunities.

Thus, Japanese companies enjoy a buyers' market facing a neatly graded supply of graduates. Independent of what type of instruction is offered in the colleges and what kind of political activity the student might have engaged in during his four years in college, he has proven himself to be a capable man in the fiercest of competitive struggles, and is thus worth the initial salary differential which the large firms pay over the smaller ones. Graduates from Tokyo University receive 30 per cent higher initial salaries than the average of college graduates, and this difference rises after ten years of service to 50 per cent.[20] On the other hand, graduates from third-rate colleges are not at all assured of finding commensurate employment, and some wind up as taxi drivers, surprising a casual foreign visitor with their few remembered phrases in English or German.

The fierce competitiveness of the college entrance examinations is, of course, a direct result of economic familism. Japanese society works like an escalator. The problem is to board the right one, and there at the entrance to it is the place, the only place, to compete directly and ruthlessly. Once on it, nobody should pass the other but must wait to be pushed upward in his turn. It would hurt group harmony to compete on the escalator by running up the stairs in front of a member of the group. This is the spirit of seniority promotion; after all, the grading had been done before entering.

The Japanese school system operates to give Japanese society something close to perfect mobility, and hence to offer business the broadest possible base for selection. Even the poorest boy from northern Japan or a small village in Kyushu has, at least theoretically (in practice local schools will recommend only extraordinary talents)

[20] Hazama, *Nihonteki keiei no keifu*, 155.

the same chance of entering Tokyo University, and hence to attain the highest positions in society, as any son of a top executive. Though personal connections and money do play a role, each Japanese nevertheless has some chance to rise high. For, once inside the company, talent does play a considerable role for promotion to top positions in spite of the seniority system.

Finally, due to the lure of lifelong employment, Japanese firms are able to shift the cost of investment for education almost totally back to the consumers. About two-thirds of all colleges are private, paid for by the household sector with business making almost no contribution at all. Education is part of the "dowry" which the son is supposed to bring along when he "marries" into his company so that the college acts as marriage go-between. Those who wish may use this as a supplementary version of the now thread-bare, cheap-labor argument of Japanese industry.

As one side effect of the heavy emphasis on college achievement, and hence on passing examinations, I should mention a marked lack of creative thinking. Individual thinking is not rewarded and not trained. Ready formulas are accepted, often only half understood. Indeed, this, too, has its roots in the need, during the Meiji period, to copy and get quick results. Western things were taken over as far as they were useful while the mind itself was supposed to remain Japanese. This tendency to copy readily without grasping the underlying principles lingers on, making the Japanese admire western technical know-how and strengthening their determination to catch up, in typical follower mentality. It is only now that determined efforts in the direction of creativity are being made, with rising criticism of the examination system that puts a premium on mechanical memorizing at the expense of thinking and of the formation of individual convictions.

Competition among Groups

The idea of competition itself was new in the Meiji period. The merchants were quite shocked when they realized that the neatly ordered market with government guaranteed monopoly rights had turned into a disorderly free for all, notably on account of the opening of the ports and the rushing in of a new breed of venturesome men without house rules and traditions.

The necessity of competition was, of course, preached by the government and the new business leaders. But to avoid chaos, an urgent need was felt to establish rules and standards of performance, and to exchange experiences and work together for favorable policies. A new kind of business community had to emerge to replace the old guilds, competitive and democratically open, working on the principle of division of labor and mutual help and trust. Together with the urgent need to meet common problems, Eiichi Shibusawa felt that trade associations could become training grounds for democratic thinking and fair business practices, and he founded first an association of bankers, because banking was new and most in need of common policies and reliability, and a few years later the Chamber of Commerce followed and the Spinners Association.

Such an approach, however, did not become typical. Instead, the *zaibatsu* came to dominate the economy so much that they could establish their own empires with direct and indirect control. Competition was then carried out between whole groups or sets of enterprises. This approach has persisted even after the dissolution of the *zaibatsu* until present time. After World War II the former member firms of the *zaibatsu* groups again formed associations for close cooperation. Thus, the presidents of the Mitsubishi line of firms have their Friday meetings and those of the Mitsui group their Monday meetings where common policies are established. Moreover, the large banks which were not touched by the scattering of the *zaibatsu* now form the very core of the new groupings due to a huge backlog of investment needs and rapid economic growth. Firms not allied to one of those powerful groups that have a large bank at the center may find themselves shy of capital and not able to compete with a rival firm which is a member of such a group.

The outcome of these *zaibatsu*-type groupings is a one-set approach. If, for example, the Mitsubishi group introduces a new product or establishes a new firm to produce it, the other groups will follow suit although each knows that the market can hardly absorb such a sudden production increase. Hence, fierce competition follows which is all the more cut-throat like because behind each such firm stands a whole group which is vitally interested in increasing its total share of the market and its economic power. This obvious waste in recent years which results from overinvestment and a desperate scramble for a larger market share, has become possible because the Japanese have not yet accepted wholeheartedly the principle of division of labor. They think in terms of groups, and if one comes out with a new product, the competing group feels challenged to produce the same, with some minor alterations, of course.

Needless to say, this one-set type of group competition is only one and perhaps not even the most important feature of market competition in Japan. More severe is the problem of imbalance between large and small enterprises that compete in the same market. The large companies with the latest equipment can often sell at considerably higher prices and yet increase their market share, on account of their superior quality and sales organization.[21]

INTRA-GROUP HARMONY AND EFFICIENCY

The *nenkō joretsu* (promotion according to seniority) is one of the well known Japanese devices to avoid outright competition within the group. This seniority principle had no place in the Meiji period as long as able businessmen and managers were at a premium. But when the pace of dramatic change slowed down, the emphasis was back on loyal service proven in long years as basis for promotion. Both lifelong employment and the seniority principle are, of course, mutually connected and arise from the attitudes of economic familism. Without going into details of application I shall make a few comments as to how the seniority principle influences efficiency.

The selection and, hence, basic grading of capability of each individual employee is done before entering the group; the large company not only chooses according to college but also gives its own tests which include attitude testing. Whatever practical knowledge is further desired, together with background on the firm and its special "spirit," is taught after entry into the firm. There remains, then, the problem of individual efficiency. Here the group itself functions as an excellent agent to elicit efforts, probably in many cases producing more than open competition would be able to do. George A. De Vos [22] and others have shown that the Japanese have strong guilt feelings if they fail to do their duty in terms of work with respect to the family and the economic group. Work and cooperation toward the group are felt as strong ethical imperatives quite independent of pay; to work only for money appears somehow morally base, something to be ashamed of. Laziness as well as luxurious living and conspicuous consumption have always been branded as depraved behavior, at least to the extent that they hurt group or family interests. Samurai were not at all ashamed to be poor, and rich landlords kept on working with their hands in Tokugawa Japan.

[21] Professor Nakamura has followed up this problem in the field of ceramics: Tsutomu Nakamura, "Nagoya chihō tōjiki kōgyō soshiki ron" (a treatise on the organization of ceramic industry in the Nagoya area), part 2, *Academia, Journal of the Nanzan Academic Society,* Economics Series No. 17 (July 1967), 75–76.

[22] George A. DeVos, "Achievement Orientation, Social Self-Identity, and Japanese Economic Growth," *Asian Survey,* V (December 1965).

The seniority principle obviously results in later promotion of capable men into high executive positions than is objectively desirable. Ten years ago the average age of Japanese top executives in large firms was 57.2 years with only about 10 per cent being under 50 years of age.[23] But again we have to take this fact and evaluate it in the context of Japanese behavior: Japanese managers, notably in the lower ranks, are much less ready to hand down orders than their counterparts in the West and are not even supposed to be "too clever" because they might make others feel inferior. The most valued men are those who can cooperate well, understand their subordinate's problems, and listen to them. The decision mechanism is much more cumbersome than Westerners would like to have it. Prolonged talks with all concerned are held (*sōdan*) with much tea sipping and many tentative statements that are purposely left open-ended, finishing sentences with, ". . . according to my personal opinion this may be so, however." Thus, dissent is possible without direct confrontation, since Japanese take direct opposition or criticism very personally. Hence, to preserve harmony and to give each person ample chance to gradually adjust his view to that of all others, the rigamarole of many words and much tea sipping is needed. In the end each has the feeling that it was his own opinion, after all, and all are ready to back up the decision. It is said that Japanese are poor in reaching decisions but excellent in carrying them out. We can also add that the Japanese are pragmatists, they do not become bogged down in hard principles but can move along the path of least resistance which, in economic terms, often is quite rewarding. Lofty principles are nevertheless needed as window dressing *ex post*, or at the starting line *ex ante*; the real thing, however, must remain fluid and is a function of group interest, and, hence, of joint group opinion. The best leaders, then, are those who can wield group opinion, and these are usually those with the longest experience in the company.

Conclusion

In confining myself to the influences of the state and the group, I am quite aware of the incompleteness of my treatment of the spirit of Japanese enterprise. Probably, important things could be said on such aspects as authority (the verticality within the enterprise), work ethos, and the way technology is absorbed and diffused. Furthermore, even in what I have touched upon, more penetrating

[23] Kazuo Noda, *Nihon no jūyaku* (Japanese executives), (Tokyo, 1960), 320.

things could probably be said by competent sociologists, anthropologists, and perhaps even by men with more firsthand experience in dealing with Japanese businessmen than I have.

I have presented something of an ideal-type; yet real life seldom closely follows a model, but is shot through with a blend of various factors that are difficult to define and may even seem contradictory. Thus, in spite of all that has been said about "doing business for the sake of society" and "acting within a group," the Japanese are, in many respects, also rugged individualists who can either disregard group interests or use them as camouflage to cover their blatant egotisms. Similarly, notwithstanding the seniority promotion principle, there are ways for strong personalities to assert themselves and grasp leadership, as evidenced by the leading entrepreneurs and successful innovators of whom, of course, Kōnosuke Matsushita is a prime example.

A final word on the future effectiveness of these two influences of national interest and groupism. I tried to point out that the relative importance of the group receded in favor of national interest during the time of national challenge and fast economic change. Today, a similar trend can be discerned. With the "black ship" of capital and trade liberalization fanning economic nationalism, the pressure is on to rapidly close the technical and efficiency gap vis-à-vis the West, and hence the group-centered seniority principle is going to be one of the first casualties. James C. Abegglen has suggested that at the time of his investigation in 1957 Japanese productivity per worker was only 60–70 per cent of that of the American counterpart under identical conditions. He puts the blame chiefly on the effects of groupism.[24] While this view may be disputed as far as the will to work is concerned, new problems of technology and organization will bring growing pressure for the abolition of the seniority promotion principle.

Recent surveys clearly indicate an accelerating trend both among younger employees and managers toward opposition of this system. Management is pressed from two sides: by the need to assign positions of responsibility and thus higher pay to younger staff members who can cope with the ever more complex problems of organization and technology, and by the other demand to move the age of retirement up which, with the seniority principle in action, would push costs too high. But opposing the seniority system in favor of efficiency pay does not mean opposing life-long employment. On the

[24] James C. Abegglen, *The Japanese Factory: Aspects of its Social Organization* (Glencoe, 1958), 111.

JAPANESE SPIRIT OF ENTERPRISE   37

contrary, most employees emphatically favor the retention of this system, for the sake of security and stability. As for the younger employees, they move ever more toward a western-like, less respectful attitude toward work, and dislike of familism and "feudal" atmosphere. With more responsible work to do, they demand higher pay which allows them to become independent of their parents' support when they marry. The tendency in the "age of the three C's" (*c*ar, room *c*ooler, *c*olor television) is toward moving the social aspects of life into the small family unit, away from the company, thus in the direction of American suburbia.

While such is the present mood, nobody can predict what will happen should a real labor scarcity develop after the large enterprises have absorbed the sweat shops and subcontracting units. But with the trend in the West, in the age of the Organization Man, toward higher valuation of security and belonging, Japan is not likely to move too far in the opposite direction toward cold individualist rationalism. If, as I have tried to show, the Japanese tendency toward groupism has deeper roots than mere economic opportunism, both a relative stronger national sentiment and group-orientation may be there to stay for quite a long time.

[26]

Siu-lun Wong

The Chinese family firm: a model*

ABSTRACT

Three aspects of Chinese economic familism are distinguished —
nepotism, paternalism, and family ownership. This essay is mainly
concerned with the last aspect and the resultant phenomenon of the
prevalence of family firms among privately-owned Chinese commercial and industrial enterprises. It is argued that such firms are
not necessarily small, impermanent and conservative because they
tend to behave differently at various stages of their developmental
cycle. Four phases of development — emergent, centralized,
segmented, and disintegrative — are identified and discussed. This
Chinese pattern is then compared with its Filipino and Japanese
counterparts.

The essence of Chinese economic organization is familism. Let us
start with this proposition and see how far it can take us in
understanding Chinese business conduct. It would not be long before
we realize that this generalization might only apply to circumstances
where private property is respected and individual pursuit of profit is
regarded as legitimate. Even with this qualification, the validity of the
statement still depends on the exact meaning of the term 'familism'. It
can mean at least one of three things. When Milton L. Barnett
characterizes the behavioural pattern of Cantonese entrepreneurs in
the USA as familial, he is talking about nepotism or the preferential
recruitment and promotion of kinsmen within a firm. 'Priority is given
to relatives and fellow villagers when a proprietor engages a staff of
employees,' he writes.[1] But in a second usage, the substance of kinship
obligations gives way to an ideal image of how superiors and
subordinates should interact in a company. 'The principles of family
organization were applied in the business unit,' asserts a Hong Kong
Chinese businessman. He elaborates as follows:

> There were those who governed and there were those who were
> governed, each according to his ability but all having an equal
> interest in the success of the operation. Acceptance of the

established order, as advocated by the Confucian school, made it possible for persons of diverse origin to fit into a family pattern.[2]

It is clear that what he has in mind is paternalism. In the third sense, the emphasis is on the ownership and control of business assets by the family. Oksenberg is explicitly concerned with this aspect when he observes that 'all the spinning and weaving companies [in Hong Kong] might loosely be labelled "family firms".'[3]

It is important to distinguish among these three possible connotations of familism because, in my view, they are not inherently tied to one another although very often they do coexist. In other words, a paternalistic enterprise may not be nepotistic in its appointments policy, and it is possible for a family-owned firm to be impersonal and universalistic in its internal administration. It is now apparent that we have to break down 'familism' into its various components to see which one of them, if any, forms the core of Chinese economic life. The overblown importance of nepotism has already been punctured by Freedman. 'It is important to remember', he reminded us,

> that outside the family, a kinsman has few specific economic claims, . . . and that in general we must not look to see preference being shown to a kinsman in economic matters on the grounds simply that he is a kinsman.[4]

What is relevant is not the dichotomy between kin and non-kin, 'but between personal and impersonal'.[5] We are less certain of the role of paternalism because of the scarcity of systematic studies. Since its linkage with the Chinese family is basically a metaphorical one, I shall not go into it here except to note that its occurrence probably has more to do with the nature of the labour market and the manpower requirement of a particular industry than with cultural factors. It is the issue of family firms that I shall explore in the rest of this essay as I feel that much of our knowledge about the Chinese family (or *jia*) has not yet been applied to illuminate the nature of this particular mode of business ownership and control.

There is little doubt that family firms have been prevalent in Chinese commerce and industry operating on capitalistic principles. In his study of a Chinese county town in the late 1940s, Morton Fried found three distinct types of financial organization which he called nuclear family enterprises, extended family stores, and partnerships respectively. 'The two most popular forms, regardless of size', he said, 'are family ownership, which in operational actuality might be called the individually owned store, since the head of the family generally operates the store as if it were his alone, and the partnership'.[6] Another anthropological study of a Chinese community carried out in the early 1960s, this time in the overseas context of the Philippines, revealed that

> most Chinese firms started as a family concern. As the family of the founder increased, the firm often grew into a large corporation which remained in the family. Examples of such firms are: Yutivo Sons Hardware Company, Cham Samco and Sons, Inc. (hardware), La Perla Cigar and Cigarette Factory, Inc., and practically all of the cigar and cigarette manufacturing establishments in Manila.[7]

This identity between family and business among the Philippine Chinese was reaffirmed a decade later by Omohundro who noted that

> [in] conversation among themselves, Chinese merchants habitually equate the business name, the name of the firm's founder or present head, and the business family as a group.[8]

In the area of finance, a Chinese banker based in Hong Kong said in a recent interview that 'all overseas Chinese banks [are] run by banking families'.[9] I have been able to make a quantitative estimate of the extent of family ownership in the cotton spinning industry in Hong Kong where there were about 1.2 million households, some 98 per cent of which were Chinese by origin, and approximately 38,000 manufacturing enterprises by the end of the last decade.[10] Over 90 per cent of these enterprises were small concerns employing less than fifty workers. Thus the cotton spinning factories, with an average of about 500 employees and 25,000 spindles per mill, constituted the modern, large-scale sector of the economy. Half of the thirty-two spinning mills existing in 1978 had the majority of their stock held by single families, as revealed in their company records filed with the Hong Kong government. This is almost certainly an under-estimation of the number of family firms as eleven of the mills were public companies whose share-holders could remain anonymous. My informants maintained that many of these public companies were actually possessed by families, given the lax company regulation that they were only required to offer a quarter of their shares to the public.[11] On the basis of the above evidence, we may say that the family firm as a major form of Chinese business organization is not restricted to a particular locale or a special line of economic endeavour.

When industrial capital is held by the family as a unit, what effects will this have on the enterprise? While the family may facilitate the establishment of the firm by furnishing the initial capital, it is generally believed that the growth of the enterprise will be hindered.[12]

The Chinese family firm: a model   61

The family firm, it is often said, is limited both in scale and life span. Amyot asserts that as far as the Manila Chinese are concerned, 'the structure of the family corporation is admirably suited to small, limited enterprises' and 'there seems to be a principle of limitation to the growth of family businesses beyond a certain point'.[13] Two arguments have been advanced to support this assertion. The first rests on the self-evident fact that there is only a finite number of members in a family. Thus expansion would quickly exhaust the supply of managerial competency, and the firm cannot grow any further.[14] Other than this personnel problem, the family enterprise is also alleged to be intrinsically conservative in its financial policy because it is particularly wary of external interferences or takeover. Landes has expressed this view clearly in the case of French family business:

> In such a system, the compulsive urge toward growth inherent in business for the sake of business is either diluted or absent . . . the main objective is to avoid use of credit and to make the highest rate of profit possible on a given turnover; to amortize expenses rapidly and build up huge reserves; and to finance expansion out of such reserves, or by what the French called *autofinancement*.[15]

Despite this purported concern with 'conservation and consolidation', family enterprises in their Chinese guise are apparently short-lived. As common wisdom has it, they seldom last beyond three generations. The practice of equal inheritance among male heirs and the nearly inevitable emergence of the proverbial prodigal son are usually held to be reponsible. In this view, the family is regarded as a poor vehicle for sustaining capital accumulation and the entrepreneurial drive.[16]

It is not hard to find exceptions to the generalization that family firms are limited in scale and tend to be impermanent. We know of the Rong family which controlled nine spinning mills in China in the 1930s with over one-fifth of the entire spindleage of Chinese-owned mills,[17] the Guo (Kwok) family in Hong Kong which holds the Wing On group of companies with the department store business valued at over 300 million Hong Kong dollars in 1979 as its main pillar,[18] and the Huang (Ooi) family which operated the Oei Tiong Ham Concern with offices in nine Indonesian cities and fifteen overseas commercial centres. Before it was nationalized by the Indonesian government in 1961, the Oei Tiong Ham Concern owned at least ten factories, a bank, an insurance company and a construction firm.[19] There are also indications that, when the market situation is favourable, Chinese family firms do not hesitate to make use of external capital supplies such as bank loans to finance expansion. A prominent Hong Kong banker has pointed out that the Colony's firms have a higher proportion of their capital in the form of bank loans than companies in most other industrial countries except Japan. The average borrowings from banks in Hong Kong's spinning and weaving companies, most of which were family-owned as I have already shown, amounted to 75 per cent of proprietor's funds in the 1960s.[20] The significance of these facts is not so much in falsifying the generalization, but in suggesting that the issues involved have most probably been over-simplified because a static view of the *jia* has been adopted. Family enterprises may appear to us to be large or small, vigorous or enervated, depending on the point in their developmental cycle at which we make our observation.

Let me try to build a model of the evolution of a Chinese family firm, beginning with its formation. It is not surprising that, as Fried found in the town he studied, 'the primary source of capital is either the individual himself or his relatives.'[21] But we should not too hastily deduce from this that 'most Chinese firms [start] as a family concern'[22] because it is unlikely that the funds mustered by an individual and his *jia* alone are sufficient to set up an enterprise other than a very modest one. The common format for a new business to assume, it seems to me, is that of partnership in which financial resources are pooled by persons largely unrelated by ties of descent or marriage.[23] Thus when Fried discovered that partnerships and family enterprises were the most popular modes of commercial organization in his Chinese town,[24] he might actually be looking at firms with varying degrees of maturity. Partnerships are notably unstable. Half of the thirty-two cotton spinning mills in Hong Kong for which I obtained information were actually incorporated by partners, but only four remained as partnerships at the time of my investigation.[25] Most individuals apparently enter this form of business alliance as an expedient, fully aware that one must fend for oneself. As a consequence, this type of economic organization is generally under-capitalized. Partners typically defer paying up on their shares and demand maximum returns for their investments. The Dai Sheng Cotton Mill initiated by Zhang Jian, for instance, had to pay eight per cent 'guaranteed dividend' annually to all partners before actual production started.[26] In the absence of mutual trust, factions and cliques tend to be rife with each partner attempting to place his own men inside the firm. If the business manages to take off despite these obstacles, then we see an asymmetrical growth in the distribution of shares. Some partners are in a more advantageous position to increase their portion of ownership relative to others. The usual method is to capture the key managerial positions as these carry an entitlement to extra 'red' shares as an incentive to effort.[27] Those who have close relatives among the partners will have an obvious edge over others as they can act jointly. This can explain why teams of brothers are so frequently found at this precarious stage.[28] In this initial phase, the family firm is just emergent. It becomes fully-fledged when a share-holder and his *jia* ultimately attain majority ownership in the company.

In discussions on the foundation of the family firm, the second phase in my model, the term 'extended' family recurs. We can leave aside the loose usage of this concept where it is sometimes stretched to mean a group of kinsmen, and concentrate instead on the connection between this particular form of domestic organization and business activities. It is often assumed in the literature that the extended family precedes the creation of the economic enterprise.[29] The reverse, I think, is more likely to be the case as far as the Chinese are concerned. Given the general patterns in which 'wealth and social standing are associated with family complexity',[30] and landed property used to be a more secure and prestigious form of ownership than commercial or industrial capital, the extended family is hardly the best breeding ground for self-made entrepreneurs. I shall argue that those who pool resources with partners and later found their own their enterprises generally come from the simpler form of elementary families. As they become successful, they are in a position to delay the division of the *jia* estate they have created, thus turning the original elementary families into extended ones. This brings us to the authority of the father-entrepreneur. As a father, the head of the family firm has maximum flexibility in his action. In theory, he can run the business as he sees fit without consultation with other *jia* members, as long as he does not 'rob a son of his inheritance, curtail one son's share of the legacy in order to benefit another son, or reduce his sons' shares unjustly in order to make a bequest or confer a gift on some other person.'[31] Decision-making power is thus highly centralized in the hands of the entrepreneur. Such power is sometimes institutionalized, as shown in the article of association of one of the Hong Kong spinning mills I have studied. There were two kinds of stocks in this mill — the founder's shares and ordinary shares. Only the father-entrepreneur held the 100 founder's shares, and this qualified him to be the 'governing' director as well as the 'permanent' director of the company. The 100 founder's shares were equal in voting power to all of the 99,900 ordinary shares put together. This made the founder an incontestable leader as he could block any decisions of the Board of Directors, which consisted mainly of his family members, or the General Meeting of the Company.[32] Centralization in decision-making entails a low degree of delegation of responsibility to subordinates. As Zhang Jian had complained, the father-entrepreneur is a busy man carrying the entire business on his shoulders. 'Every letter is drafted by me, and every matter depends on my deliberation. For sleep, I can have no more than three hours a night; for meals, I cannot find time even for two bowls of rice.'[33] This highly personalized style of leadership has two major implications for capital formation. The possibility for profits to be retained and re-invested is much enhanced. When an economist described some family businesses in Hong Kong as 'progressive' and that they 'used *all* their profits to finance expansion',[34] it is almost certain he was referring to those which were in this second phase of their development. Besides reinvestment, the father-entrepreneur is also able to transfer funds from one line of business to another for lateral expansion and mutual sustenance. Capital is mobile within the family group of enterprises because it belongs to a common, unified *jia* budget.[35] But these are just options open to the father-entrepreneur. Whether he will take advantage of them or not rests on the level of his motivation to enlarge the *jia* estate.[36] Although he has nearly absolute authority in utilizing the capital of the family firm, it is not his personal property. He is just a trustee of the *jia* estate which ultimately belongs to his children. But here, the cultural emphasis on the continuation of the family line acts as a powerful spur to effort. A good trustee must create an endowment to the family estate to ensure that there are valuable assets to transmit to future generations. The more successful he is in enriching that endowment, the greater the social recognition and esteem that will accrue to him. But while this encourages exertion, it simultaneously discourages the abdication of managerial power. Retirement from the family firm will remove the very basis on which the entrepreneur's social status and prestige in the wider community are built. A superannuated father is also powerless to contain the centripetal tendency among his sons as inheritors to the business. Yet, even if health permits, he cannot hold on to the reins of the enterprise for too long after his sons have become fathers themselves, lest this be interpreted as a sign of his sons' incompetence and hurt the reputation of the family business.[37] This tug of war between the father-entrepreneur and sons-inheritors usually drags on until fate intervenes by removing the former.

After the father-entrepreneur has relinquished control, the centralized family firm enters the third phase of its evolution and gradually becomes segmented. Traditionally, the legitimate heirs who were normally the sons had equal rights of inheritance. This principle had been modified in Republican China by enlarging the circle of heirs to include the wife/wives and daughters of the head of the family. It is often held that this system of equal division would splinter *jia* properties and dissipate family fortunes. But this depends on what is being divided — whether it is the *jia* estate itself, the profits that it yields, or the responsibility for managing it. Some assets are more amenable to division than others. As Freedman has suggested, 'business property [is] a more effective centripetal force than agricultural property'.[38] In West Town which was primarily an agricultural community, estates were evenly divided among heirs when *fen jia* happened. But Hsu found two exceptions in which *jia* properties were kept intact to be jointly managed by the inheritors.

One family was engaged in horse-trading, and the other was in retailing. Both had little land.[39] Several factors act against the fragmentation of business capital. Industrial and commercial assets are usually in the form of integrated entities that would cease to function once split. Even where subdivision is feasible, efficiency and productivity will suffer as a result because an economy of scale is often involved. Moreover, the worth of a family firm is more than the sum of its physical possessions. There are intangible assets such as its business reputation which cannot be apportioned to individual heirs. The legal framework, at least in Hong Kong, also provides some means for private companies to retain their capital. Most family-owned spinning mills, for instance, have company regulations stipulating that shares cannot be freely sold to outsiders. Boards of Directors are empowered to refuse to register any transfer of shares. If family members want to give up company ownership, they must first offer their portions for sale to existing share-holders 'at fair value'. Since mortgages and outstanding debts are essential components of business capital, the 'fair value' of company shares when converted into cash is substantially lower than their nominal value.[40] It is therefore more advantageous for inheritors to keep their shares with a promise of steady future income. In sum, the likelihood of splintering the estate of the family firm at this stage is not very great.

The same cannot be said of the profit derived from that estate. A common family budget is relatively easy to administer while the heirs are still single. There is no conflict between what Cohen calls the principal of jural equality which states that heirs have 'rights to arithmetically identical fractions of the estate' and the practice of consumer equality that caters for the needs of family members on a *per capita* basis. But once the brothers acquire wives and children, friction arises. It is because '[brothers] marry in sequence; by the time of the wedding of the youngest, some children of the oldest may be students. In addition, the brothers' wives bear or raise to maturity differing numbers of offspring'.[41] Some brothers may then feel that their domestic units or *fang* are getting less than the fair share of the family 'cake'. Pressure to create separate budgets is thus built up. Profit derived from the *jia* estate is the first thing to be divided among the inheritors, often while the father-entrepreneur is still at the helm of the enterprise. Such a division is shown in the allotment of an identical number of company shares to sons in the Hong Kong cotton mills so that they can have independent sources of income in the form of dividends. Daughters generally get smaller allotments than sons, though parity in shares distribution is still maintained among the female heirs themselves. This may indicate a discrepancy between the actual practice of inheritance among contemporary Chinese family firms and the legal prescription of strict equality among both male and female inheritors since Republican times. But it is possible that the balance between a son's and a daughter's allotment is actually given to the latter in the form of dowry when she marries. We cannot decide which is the case until we have more information on the system of dowries in these business families.

But when it comes to the management of *jia* property, it is unambiguous that the traditional bias against women in the family still prevails. Succession to managerial positions in the family firm is largely the prerogative of male heirs. How are business responsibilities distributed among brothers? Theoretically, they can take turns to play the role of chief executive. But for reasons yet unclear to me, this is rarely done.[42] In actual cases, the eldest son is better able to assume the mantle of chief executive when succession occurs because he has the earliest opportunity to work in the firm and establish himself there. But the younger brothers are unlikely to defer to his authority because of what Margery Wolf describes as 'the inconsistent preparation of the brothers for their adult roles'.[43] As she says,

> Younger brothers learn very early and very concretely that older brothers yield to younger brothers, and yet as adults the expectation is exactly the reverse — the younger is expected to yield to his older brother's decisions and guidance, a situation for which he has been poorly prepared.[44]

To fend for their own interests, the younger heirs normally adopt either one of two strategies. They may anticipate the situation by acquiring skills which are different from their elder brothers. Thus when the eldest brother becomes the chief, they can act as powerful deputies as plant managers, accounting managers, and personnel managers etc. Alternatively, they may press for the creation of new ventures of which they will be the heads. In either case, the result is the emergence of distinct 'spheres of influence' and a proliferation of departments, factory plants, or subsidiary companies within the family concern. This trend of segmentation inevitably leads to decentralization of decision-making. A vivid illustration can be found in the following case of the Kian Gwan Company in Indonesia

> The Concern experienced a great loss with the death of Oei Tjong Hauw in January 1951. According to Chinese tradition the eldest son should have taken over but in this case the candidate chose to reside in Amsterdam and the youngest was elected in his place. Now the highest authority in the entire former Concern was the Board of Managing Directors, consisting of eight shareholders, linked by two co-ordinators, the youngest brother in Singapore and Djakarta and the eldest in Amsterdam. Each office was autonomous except in the matter of personnel where the Djakarta office took all decisions to avoid embarrassments and loss of good faith in family members.[45]

It is clear that consensus among brothers cannot be taken for granted, and the power of the new chief executive is greatly curtailed. He no longer enjoys his predecessor's flexibility in re-investment and transferring funds laterally. His hands are commonly tied by a formal agreement drawn up among heirs as to the manner in which company profits should be distributed.[46] He is closely checked in his entrepreneurial decisions. As noted by Cohen,

> the management of family funds takes on a public character if the eldest son shares with his younger brothers a desire to maintain the family intact. A brother in charge of finances is at pains to justify his activities thoroughly, and he is under far closer scrutiny than was his father. In each of at least two Yen-liao joint families the oldest brother keeps detailed account books, which are frequently inspected by other family members.[47]

We may expect the chief executive to resign himself gradually to the role of care-taker instead of innovator. Thus the characteristic features of this phase are the outward expansion of the enterprise owing to segmentation, and a reduction in the flexibility for re-investment and risk-taking.

The mutual watchfulness among brothers in a segmented family firm is very similar to the relationship among partners during the emergent phase. The same opportunity for the asymmetrical growth in share-holding is present because of the continual existence of the practice of conferring red shares to top executives who succeed in leading the enterprise to prosperity. In some cases, therefore, a brother in a segmented family firm may manage to build up a majority stake and the enterprise is taken over by his *fang*. The firm will then re-enter the centralized phase. If this does not happen and the brothers remain in partnership until it is their turn to yield to their own offspring, then the family enterprise will pass into the final phase of disintegration.

As individual brothers usually produce more than one son, there will be more inheritors in the second succession. The sheer increase in the number of share-holders will by itself heighten the possibility of internal bickering. But the rule of equal inheritance among heirs will ensure that first cousins (brothers' sons) will have divergent interests. Brothers may still co-operate because they begin on an equal footing as owners. But cousins are much less likely to see eye to eye because of the disparity in share-holding created by the differential fertility among various *fang*. This tendency is analogous to the situation in the transmission of ownership rights in ancestral trusts in lineages as described by Freedman

> Once established, this 'trust' was the joint property of all the heirs and its management and fruits fell to be enjoyed by them in turn

(usually on an annual basis) or collectively . . . if instead of being rotated the estate was managed in such a way that its annual profits were distributed among the owners, then the sharing of the profits was made on the basis of *per stripes* shares. It follows that if at the foundation of the 'trust' there were three or more sons, and after the lapse of several generations the male agnatic descendants of these sons differed greatly in numbers, then the members of the most prolific line enjoyed the smallest shares of the total benefit of the 'trust' and those of the least prolific the greatest.[48]

For this reason, I would argue that although relationships among Chinese brothers are doubtlessly brittle, the most fragile family bonds are to be found among first cousins if they remain in the same *jia*. This may account for the conspicuous absence of groups of first cousins working in the cotton mills of Hong Kong.[49] After cousins have become co-owners, the danger of fission is ever present in the family firm. The economic considerations against the sale of family shares are less inhibitive at this stage. The value of individual portions has become much smaller due to sub-division, and this reduces the attraction of the regular income derived from the shares. Those in a weaker bargaining position may decide to break off the economic ties to the family enterprise, especially when they are brought up with little emotional attachment to it. Family members as share-holders will then be more concerned with immediate, tangible benefits than long term business prospects.

To summarize the key features of the four phases of the Chinese family firm, I shall use the schematic presentation seen in Table I with a plus sign indicating unity and a minus sign representing division.

TABLE I

| Phases | Aspects of family firm | | |
	Estate	Management	Profit
I Emergent	+	+	+
II Centralized	+	+	−
III Segmented	+	−	−
IV Disintegrative	−	−	−

How effective is the Chinese family firm as an organization for economic competition? Davis has argued that it is superior to its Filipino counterpart because of a difference in the way descent is traced. In his words,

Kinship among most Philippine groups is reckoned bilaterally; that is, the kin of both of one's parents are equally important, and true

descent groups are generally lacking . . . Because kinship is reckoned
bilaterally from the individual's perspective, and not from a fixed
point of remote ancestral origin, membership in kin groups
overlaps considerably, so a given individual is a member of the kin
groups of many other persons and ideally, at least, owes support
(and gets support) from all with whom he reckons a kinship
bond . . . individuals may easily be caught by conflicting claims for
support in such a system, and except for the nuclear family, kinship
alone does not provide the basis for corporate economic activities.[50]

Even the nuclear family will be easily broken up at the time of
succession because of the potentially large number of claimants on the
family estate, each of whom owes loyalty to several other kin groups.
In the Chinese case, because of the principle of patrilineal descent,
more discrete and enduring corporate kinship units can be formed for
the management of resources and investment.[51] The durability of the
Chinese family firm is of course a relative matter. Compared with its
Japanese equivalent, it would appear to be transitory. Since the
Japanese practise primogeniture in the sense that only one male heir
is chosen for succession, it is easier for the ownership and management of
the family estate to remain intact. This facilitates the persistence of an
enterprise held by the Japanese family or the *ie*.[52] The different
degrees of durability of Filipino, Chinese, and Japanese family firm
can be tentatively stated in the following ideal types of their life cycles
(see Table II).

TABLE II

Family firms	Phases of development*		
Filipino	I→IV	I→IV	I→IV............
Chinese	I→II→III→II→III→II→III		......
	IV ↘	IV ↘	IV ↘
Japanese	I→II→II→II→II......................		

* I   Emergent phase
 II   Centralized phase
III   Segmented phase
IV   Disintegrative phase

There are bound to be many external factors that would alter these
cycles. In real life, the family firms can hardly be dissociated from
their outside environment. To acknowledge this is to court questions
such as the following: Under what conditions will family firms
flourish? How would they affect the patterns of social mobility and
industrialization? What impacts will they have on the tendencies

70   *Siu-lun Wong*

towards the separation of ownership and control and the emergence of professionalism in modern business communities? These are all interesting and important lines of enquiry, but they will lead me away from the primary aim here which is 'to escape from reality long enough to be able to grasp [the] underlying principles' of the development of the Chinese family firm.

Siu-lun Wong
Department of Sociology
University of Hong Kong

NOTES

* This essay is dedicated to the memory of my teacher, Professor Maurice Freedman (1920–75). I am indebted to Professor Murray Groves and the late Miss Barbara Ward for commenting on an earlier draft.

1. M. L. Barnett, 'Kinship as a Factor Affecting Cantonese Economic Adaptation in the United States', *Human Organization*, vol. 19, no. 1, Spring 1960, p. 45.

2. S. N. Chau, 'Family Management in Hong Kong', *Hong Kong Manager*, vol. 6, no. 2, March/April 1970, pp. 20–1.

3. M. Oksenberg, 'Management Practices in the Hong Kong Cotton Spinning and Weaving Industry', unpublished paper read at Seminar on Modern East Asia, Columbia University, November 1972, p. 7.

4. M. Freedman, 'The Family in China, Past and Present' in Skinner, *The Study of Chinese Society: Essays by Maurice Freedman*, Stanford, Stanford University Press, 1979, p. 243.

5. M. Freedman, *Chinese Family and Marriage in Singapore*, London, Her Majesty's Stationery Office, 1957, p. 88.

6. M. H. Fried, *Fabric of Chinese Society: A Study of the Social Life of a Chinese County Seat*, New York, Praeger, 1953, p. 138.

7. J. Amyot, *The Manila Chinese: Familism in the Philippine Environment*, Quezon City, Ateneo De Manila University, second edition, 1973, p. 118.

8. J. T. Omohundro, 'The Chinese Merchant Community of Oloilo City, Philippines', unpublished Ph.D. thesis,

University of Michigan, 1974, p. 231.

9. 'A Retail Boom in Hong Kong', *Asiaweek*, 11 July, 1980, p. 50.

10. See Census and Statistics Department, Hong Kong, *Hong Kong 1981 Census Main Report, Volume 2: Tables*, Hong Kong, Government Printers, 1982, p. 107; C. K. Rao, *Hong Kong 1981*, Hong Kong, Government Printers, 1981, p. 224; V. F. S. Sit, S. L. Wong, and T. S. Kiang, *Small Scale Industry in a Laissez-Faire Economy: A Hong Kong Case Study*, Hong Kong, Centre of Asian Studies, University of Hong Kong, 1979, p. 25.

11. See S. L. Wong, 'Industrial Entrepreneurship and Ethnicity: A Study of the Shanghainese Cotton Spinners in Hong Kong', unpublished D. Phil. thesis, University of Oxford, 1979, p. 75–6; 286–7.

12. For two representative views, see C. Kerr *et al.*, *Industrialism and Industrial Man: The Problems of Labour Management in Economic Growth*, Harmondsworth, Penguin, 1973, p. 94; E. W. Nafziger, 'The Effect of the Nigerian Extended Family on Entrepreneurial Activity', *Economic Development and Cultural Change*, vol. 18, no. 1, October 1969, p. 33.

13. Amyot, op. cit., p. 119.

14. Ibid, pp. 119–20.

15. D. S. Landes, 'French Business and Businessman: A Social and Cultural Analysis' in Aitken, *Explorations in Enterprise*, Cambridge, Harvard University Press, 1967, pp. 186–7.

16. On the Chinese case, see H. D.

Fong, 'Industrial Capital in China', In-
dustrial Series, Bulletin No. 9, Nankai
Institute of Economics, 1936, p. 48; and
D. E. Willmott, *The Chinese of Semarang: A
Changing Minority Community in Indonesia*,
Ithaca, Cornell University Press, 1960,
p. 52. As a general argument, see Kerr *et
al.*, op. cit., pp. 94, 151; and W. A. Lewis,
The Theory of Economic Growth, London,
George Allen and Unwin, 1955, p. 120.

17. Wong, op. cit., p. 291.

18. The Wing On Co. Ltd, *Annual Report
and Accounts 1978-1979*, Hong Kong, The
Company, 1979, p. 9.

19. Willmott, op. cit., pp. 49-50; and J.
Panglaykim and I. Palmer, 'Study of
Entrepreneurship in Developing Countries: The Development of One Chinese
Concern in Indonesia', *Journal of Southeast Asian Studies*, vol. 1, no. 1, March
1970, pp. 85-95.

20. P. A. Graham, 'Financing Hong
Kong Business', *Far Eastern Economic
Review*, 17 April, 1969, p. 152.

21. Fried, op. cit., p. 144.

22. Amyot, op. cit., p. 118.

23. My usage of the term partnership is
broader than the British legal definition
that a partnership is distinct from a
private limited company and does not
have limited liability or a separate legal
personality. See P. Smith, *The Family
Business — Company or Partnership*, London,
Sweet and Maxwell, 1979, p. 7.

24. Fried, op. cit., p. 138. On the high
frequency of partnership as a form of
business association, see also Willmott,
op. cit., p. 54; and Amyot, op. cit., p. 65.

25. Wong, op. cit., p. 288. For other
examples, see Y. H. Lin, *The Golden Wing:
A Sociological Study of Chinese Familism*,
London, Kegan Paul, Trench, Trubner
and Co., 1947, pp. 133-41; B. E. Ward,
'A Small Factory in Hong Kong: Some
Aspects of its Internal Organization' in
Willmott, *Economic Organization in Chinese
Society*, Stanford, Stanford University Press,
1972, pp. 353-85.

26. S. C. Chu, *Reformer in Modern China:
Chang Chien, 1853-1926*, New York and
London, Columbia University Press, 1965,
p. 29.

27. For an illustration of the distribution
of these 'red' shares, see Lin, op. cit., p.
99.

28. Examples include the Nanyang
Brothers Tobacco Company, the Shaw
Brothers in film-making, the Rong Brothers who started the Shen Xin Textile
and flour mills, and the Guo Brothers
who founded the Wing On Group.

29. See for example Nafziger, op. cit.,
pp. 25-33 and Lewis, op. cit., pp. 113-15.

30. M. Freedman, 'Introduction' in
Freedman, *Family and Kinship in Chinese
Society*, Stanford, Stanford University
Press, 1970, p. 3.

31. S. Shiga, 'Family Property and the
Law of Inheritance in Traditional China'
in Buxbaum, *Chinese Family Law and
Social Change in Historical and Comparative
Perspective*, Seattle and London, University
of Washington Press, 1978, p. 149.

32. Wong, op. cit., p. 293.

33. Zhang Jian, *Zhang Sean Xiansheng
Shiye Wenchao* (Mr Zhang Jian's Essays
on Industry), Nantong, Hanmolin Publishers, 1947(?), pp. 14-15. The trans-
lation is mine.

34. D. W. Stammer, 'Money and Finance in Hong Kong', unpublished Ph.D.
thesis, Australian National University,
1968, p. 262, original emphasis.

35. Zhang Jian, for example, 'used a
part of Dah Sun's excess profits to
support his numerous other Na-t'ung
projects, without keeping the accounts
absolutely clear'. See Chu, op. cit., p. 35.
The same phenomenon is observed by
Stammer, op. cit., p. 262.

36. For a definition of the *jia* estate, see
M. L. Cohen, 'Developmental Process in
the Chinese Domestic Group' in Freedman, *Family and Kinship*, p. 27.

37. For a good illustration of this dilemma, see the case of Mr. Lo, owner of
Friendship Store, in Omohundro, op.
cit., pp. 309-11.

38. M. Freedman, *Lineage Organization
in Southeastern China*, London, The Athlone
Press, p. 30.

39. F. L. K. Hsu, *Under the Ancestor's
Shadow: Kinship, Personality and Social Mobility in China*, Stanford, Stanford University Press, 1971, pp. 115-21. Cohen
also finds different propensities for family
division between tobacco cultivators and
rice farmers in Taiwan in M. L. Cohen,
*House United, House Divided: The Chinese
Family in Taiwan*, New York and London,

Columbia University Press, 1976, pp. 218–25.

40. For an illustration, see The Economic Research Institute of the Shanghai Academy of Social Sciences, *Heng Feng Shachang Di Fasheng Fazhan He Gaizao* (The Establishment, Development and Transformation of the Heng Feng Cotton Spinning Mill), Shanghai, Shanghai People's Press, 1958, p. 35.

41. Cohen, op. cit., p. 197.

42. There was a reported case of brothers taking turns to utilize the machinery in paper-making mills in Yunnan, but in effect the management was separate. See Fei and Chang, *Earth-bound China*, Chicago, University of Chicago Press, 1945, pp. 178–81.

43. M. Wolf, 'Child Training and the Chinese Family' in Freedman, *Family and Kinship*, p. 61.

44. Ibid., p. 53.

45. Panglaykim and Palmer, op. cit., p. 94.

46. For samples of these contracts, see Economic Research Institute of the Shanghai Academy of Social Sciences, op. cit., p. 35; and The Shanghai Economic Research Institute of the Chinese Academy of Sciences and the Economic Research Institute of the Shanghai Academy of Social Sciences, *Nanyang Xiongdi Yancao Gongsi Shiliao* (Historical Materials on the Nanyang Brothers Tobacco Company), Shanghai, Shanghai People's Press, 1958, pp. 11–12.

47. Cohen, op. cit., p. 217.

48. M. Freedman, *Chinese Lineage and Society*, London, The Athlone Press, 1971, p. 51.

49. I found brothers, brothers-in-law, uncles and nephews working in the same companies, but not first cousins. See Wong, op. cit., p. 277.

50. W. G. Davis, *Social Relations in a Philippine Market*, Berkeley, University of California Press, 1973, p. 198.

51. Ibid., p. 199.

52. See e.g. J. C. Pelzel, 'Japanese Kinship: A Comparison' in Freedman, *Family and Kinship*, pp. 277–8.

53. The quotation is from M. Freedman, 'The Chinese Domestic Family: Models' in Skinner, op. cit., p. 239.

[27]

Ownership and Management of Indian Zaibatsu

Shoji Ito
Institute of Developing Economies

Introduction

It is already more than a century since the most progressive among the adventurous merchants of India established modern cotton textile mills in Bombay in the 1850s. Until roughly the close of the nineteenth century, Indian modern enterprises in various fields, including cotton textiles, were more advanced than contemporary Japanese counterparts. Jamsetji Nusserwanji Tata (1839–1904) adopted one of the newly invented devices of ring spinning for the first time in the world. Even at the beginning of the present century, the history of Indian entrepreneurship got another feather in its cap: establishment of an integrated iron and steel mill (TISCO) solely with indigenous funds (but with the help of foreign technical experts).

The development of entrepreneurship in India, however, had been slow and lopsided, particularly because the colonial government was hostile to balanced industrial development in India, especially by the Indians. The circumstances in which the Indian entrepreneurs developed were in sharp contrast to the Japanese ones which were created by strong nationalist government.

On the other hand, India shared two common features with Japan. Firstly, both countries were latecomers, in terms of industrialization, compared with the Western countries, and the industrialists of both countries had to face stiff competition from the developed industrialists of the world. Secondly, both countries observed traditional customs of cohesion among family members or groups of families, though different in nature.

147

The first factor caused, at least partially, the early emergence of large-size enterprises and corporate groups, which after the Indian Independence were often called "finance capital," "empire" or "monopoly capital." The second factor partially explains the continuing hold by particular families over the undivided, expanding corporate groups.

This paper attempts to highlight the salient features of ownership and management of Indian "zaibatsu" today. The reason why the present paper limits its concern to the zaibatsu of India, even though the framework (i.e., 'family firms') of this conference is a much wider one, is mainly that, while family firms are the dominant form of enterprise in the Indian private sector, the zaibatsu assume a dominant position among them. In a way, it is representative of all the Indian family firms.

In Section I, general features of the Indian zaibatsu are described. Section II is devoted to a study of how a family's hold over a large group of companies is maintained in an unchallenged manner regardless of their relatively small amounts of capital ownership. In Section III and IV, a few characteristics of the moves toward professionalization of management in India will be highlighted. Firstly, the ultimate decision making power of the group of companies rests in the hands of the zaibatsu family's members. Secondly, as managerial work has expanded and become complicated, more and more responsible tasks have tended to be gradually entrusted to the salaried managers who were brought up through in-service training, but the families appear to have preferred men of their own caste/community. Thirdly, a rational system of recruiting bright young men to be promoted to the top managerial rank is being tried by a few zaibatsu groups.

In the concluding section, the validity of the theorem[1] put forward by Professor Yasuoka, relating to the interrelationship between the nature of ownership and that of management, is tested in the light of the above analyses.

I. A Bird's-Eye View of Indian Zaibatsu

The public sector assumes a leading role in India's economic

development. Its share in the whole of gross domestic capital formation and gross fixed capital formation are 41 and 53%, respectively
(1977/78). Moreover its share in the total paid-up capital of the
limited companies is as much as 76% (1978).

However its productivity is so low that it has no inherent capacity
of its own for expansion, and it requires extra-economic forces for
extended reproduction. The private sector is much more dynamic.
Take for instance the ratio of gross profit to total capital employed
in Indian factories: the ratio for the public sector is 0.06 while that
for the private sector is 0.30.[2]

The Indian factory sector is characterized by its high concentration in large-size enterprises. Factories that employ 1,000 or more
workers are 1.2%, but they employ no less than 43.8% of all factory
workers (1974). The corresponding figures for Japan are 4.5 and
36.8%, respectively. The high concentration of large-size factories
in India was caused by the establishment of huge factories by the
public and private sectors, which in turn reflects the availability of
scale-merit technologies in the world.

As of 1977/78, 67 companies out of the top 200 limited companies
of India belong to the public sector. Of the remaining 133 companies, 31 companies are considered to be substantially controlled
by foreign capital. Some of them are under the control of MNCs
such as the Lever Group of Netherlands-Britain (one company),
Imperial Chemical (three companies), and the Inchicapes (two
companies). Many of the remaining 102 Indian companies are under
the control of the dominant business groups of India. The Tatas,
one of the two largest groups, control 10 companies including the
TISCO, which is the largest company in the Indian private sector,
and the Tata Engineering & Locomotives Co., Ltd. (TELCO),
which is the second largest. The Birlas, another of the largest groups,
control 16 companies including Gwalior Rayon Co., Ltd., their
largest company. And among the remaining companies are 4
companies under the Mafatlals, 2 companies under the Walchands,
2 companies under the Singhanias, 1 company under the Shri Rams,
3 companies under the Thapars and 2 companies each under the
Modis and the Mahindras.[3]

According to a census of public limited companies in the private

150   *S. Ito*

TABLE 1 List of the Larger Zaibatsu of India (1966).

Name (1)	Community (2)	No. of Cos. (3)	Total Net Assets (4)	Main Business Interests (5)
1. Tata	Parsi	74	585	Various
2. Birla	Marwari Maheshwari	265	576	Various
3. Mafatlal	Gujerati Kunbi	21	136	Textiles, Chemicals, Petro-chemicals, Sugar
4. Bangur	Marwari	85	125	Finance, Textiles, Cement, Paper, Cable
5. Bajoria-Jalan	Marwari Agarwal	105	107	Eng., Textiles, Sugar, Railway
6. Shri Ram	Agarwal	36	107	Textiles, Chemicals, Electricals, Eng., Ceramics
7. Thapar	Punjabi Khatri	53	103	Electrical, Paper, Coal, Sugar, Textiles, Eng., Vanaspathi
8. Walchand	Gujerati Jaina	27	80	Car, Industrial Machinery, Sugar, Construction
9. Sahu-Jain	Marwari Jaina	27	80	Cement, Textiles, Paper, Sugar, Plywood, Printing & Publishing, Eng.
10. J. K. Shinghania	Marwari Agarwal	47	79	Textiles, Paper, Sugar, Metals, Chemicals
11. Goenka	Marwari Agarwal	54	65	Textiles, Tea, Generation

Source: Government of India, *Report of the Monopoly Inquiry Commission, 1965*, 1965, pp. 373–414 for Column (5) and Govt. of India, *Report of the Industrial Licensing Policies Inquiry Committee*, Appendices Volume II, pp. 1–45 for Columns (3) and (4).

Note: Column (4); in Rs. 10 million (US$1 ≒ Rs. 9).

sector,[4] the larger the companies are, the higher the net profit ratios are: the companies whose net assets were below Rupees 2.5 million showed a negative profit rate, and those with assets between Rs. 2.5 million and 5 million had a net profit rate of 1.3%. These rates increased steadily to 26.5% for the largest companies with net assets over Rs. 200 million (1971/72).

It is estimated that, while the "foreign capital controlled companies" accounted for 30% of the total turnover of the private companies in 1971/72, the 20 largest Indian groups accounted for 35% in 1975.[5]

All of these facts taken together indicate that the large national and foreign groups of companies have fostered giant and profitable concerns.

Professor Shigeaki Yasuoka defines the term 'zaibatsu' as a group of companies that is owned by a family (or a group of families) and is controlled through a holding company as an appex with some of its larger members enjoying oligopolistic positions. When this definition is applied to the Indian model, some 10 or 20 of India's largest groups can be called zaibatsu as well.

Except for the Associated Cement Company groups (A.C.C.), they have been controlled by particular families. The groups' nomenclature is often suggestive of this: they usually adopt the family names.

Having passed through the initial stage, almost all the private enterprises have been essentially family business. Groups like the Birlas or the Tatas are two cases in point; they employ no less than 300 thousand people and account for more than one tenth of the assets of the companies in the private sector.

Table 1 shows some salient features of the 11 largest zaibatsu.

II. Family Ownership of Group Companies

The zaibatsu in India are the outcome of expansion of the once small family business. The expansion was both through creation of new enterprises and takeover of ongoing or bankrupt concerns. Therefore, there are normally no two public opinions as to who owns an enterprise. In the rare case where the takeover bid is being disputed, the noisy 'proxy war' occurs at the time of the general meeting of the company concerned.

But more often than not, the family's shareholding is much less than a majority, particularly in the case of large manufacturing companies. Take for instance Hindustan Motors Ltd., the then largest company of the Birla Group; the members of the Birla families owned less than 2% of the paid-up ordinary shares as of December 1971.[6]

According to Dr. Hazari's thoroughgoing study, assisted by Professor A. N. Oza, the zaibatsu family members owned less than 12%, in face value, of the total ordinary share capital of the 888 companies belonging to the 20 "corporate groups" as of 1958.[7] Even if the shareholdings of the charitable trusts (endowments) established by the families are also taken into account, the picture does not change much (15%).

The main reason why family ownership is not challenged by outsiders, in spite of such minority shareholding is due to, according to Dr. Hazari, the extensive networks of intercorporate investments among group companies: the group companies held 33% of the total ordinary shares issued by the group companies as of 1958.

Further, he found in the Tatas case:

1) the family and their trusts owned, rather exclusively, an appex company (Tata Sons Private Ltd.),

2) the family, the trusts and the appex company owned an investment company, and then

3) all the above four institutions jointly owned many of the large industrial companies of the group, which in turn jointly or singly owned other minor companies.

This pyramidal structure reminds us of the structure of the old Japanese zaibatsu.

However, he found many a circular chain of investments in the cases of the Birlas and the Bangurs, in which company A held some shares in company B, company B in company C, C in D, D in E and E, in turn, in A. Chains of this sort were especially observed among investment companies. He concluded that it was not clear just where the chain started.

While this appears to be a labyrinth, the puzzle is not a difficult one to solve in light of the pyramidal order observed in the Tatas or Japanese zaibatsu of large size. According to a study by the present author, a few of these investment companies are very closely held by the zaibatsu family members. These companies can, therefore, be regarded as the starting points of the chain. All the so-called invest-ment companies are not investment companies in the usual sense of the term. They are in practice joint holding companies, from any point of view. Thus, the zaibatsu of India, with numerous compa-nies under a common authority, have holding companies in disguise which play the role of keeping the family's claim of ownership over group companies intact.[8]

III. Family System and Control over Management

1. Family System

Unlike the traditional system in Japan, all the sons (not daughters in traditional India) had equal rights over the father's property. Adoption was not common practice. And rigid conditions restricting the manner of adoption have been established and observed.

However, many of the richer families have maintained the custom of an extended family—the Hindu joint family. The ancestral prop-erties tended to be kept undivided in joint ownership (coparcenary) among the members (coparceners). According to Hindu Law, joint ownership was to be presupposed unless expressed otherwise. And management of the property used to be entrusted to the family head, called *karta*, usually the most senior and able male member of the family. It was the duty of *karta* to properly maintain the property for the sake of all the members, and it was a virtue for the juniors to obey whatever the *karta* did: The latter was not accountable to the former for his conduct, though he had to be *bona fide* and show, through account books, the net results of his conduct when so demanded by any member. In the case of traditional trading castes/communities, they used to keep the ancestral family business as a "joint family firm."

These traditions of coherence among the extended family members must have contributed to the tendency of maintaining an undivided family business even after the death of its head.

TABLE 2   Common Directorship with Tata Sons Pvt., Ltd. (1972).

Name of Company	Name of Common Director
TISCO	J.R.D. Tata (Ch), S. Moolgaokar (Vice-ch), M.A. Wadud Khan.
TELCO	J.R.D. Tata (Ch), S. Moolgaokar (Vice-ch), N.H. Tata
Indian Tube	None
Tata Power	N.H. Tata (Ch), J.D. Choksi
Tata Hydro	N.H. Tata (Ch), N.A. Palkhivala
Andhra V. Power	N.H. Tata (Ch)
Tata Chemicals	J.R.D. Tata (Ch), N.A. Palkhivala
TOMCO (Tata Oil Mills)	J.R.D. Tata (Ch), N.H. Tata (Vice-ch), M.A. Wadud Khan (Mg. Dr)
Voltas	J.D. Choksi, A.B. Bilimoria

Source: Data available at the office of the Registrar of Companies, Bombay.
Note: Ch stands for chairman of the board of directors, Vice-ch for vice-chairman, and Mg. Dr for Managing Director. The nine largest companies of the Tatas are included.

However, individualism among family members has been rapidly developing because of British influence. It should be noted that the traditional Hindu law had inherent elements for "individualism" such as equitable rights over property among brothers, right of co-parcener to ask at liberty for separation of his own share of property from joint ownership, etc. The Hindu family laws enacted during the 1950s gave a further impetus to division and recently, increasing feuds among brothers in quite a few zaibatsu families are reportedly leading to division of the group companies after the head's death.

The family system in the zaibatsu of India appears to be at a crossroad. However, in view of the scale-merits of larger groups consisting of multiple activities, as well as the traditional cordial relationship between brothers in India, the process for division is slow.

The Birlas' case is suggestive of it. In terms of management, they have divided responsibility, but they maintain cordiality as well as networks of intercorporate investments, both leading to a federation of group companies.

TABLE 3   Community Distribution of Directorships for the Birlas' 14 Largest Companies (1972).

Community	No. of Directors	No. of Directorships Held by the Directors
The Birlas	9	15
Other Marwaris	44 (2)	55 (2)
Parsis	1	1
Gujaratis	8 (6)	9 (7)
Bengalees	7	8
Tamilians	4	4
U.P.-Kayastha	1	1
Muslim	1	1
Punjabi	1	1
Foreigners & Unidentifiable	9	10
Total	85 (8)	105 (9)

Notes: 1. The names of directors were compiled with the help of Kothari & Sons ed., *Kothari's Economic & Industrial Guide of India, 1973-74* (n.d.) and the data available at the offices of the Registrars of Companies in Bombay and Calcutta. Then they were classified by community, often with the names themselves.

2. The figures in brackets show the number of directors that belong to other zaibatsu including the Sahu-Jains, Kanorias, Mafatlals, Kasturbhai-Lalbhais and Thackerseys, and that of the directorships held by them.

2. Indian Ways of Maintaining Family Control over Group Companies

In the case of typical pre-war Japanese zaibatsu, the zaibatsu families tended to entrust loyal and brilliant salaried managers with management of enterprises *en bloc.*

In the case of India, the zaibatsu family members have been active leaders of management. All the important decisions have been made by themselves with the help and advice of loyal salaried managers.

Their hold over the management of the group companies has been maintained by various arrangements. The managing agency system had been the most important one until its abolition in 1970.[9] Multiple directorship is another one, with members of the zaibatsu family occupying the key management positions in the various companies. Table 2 illustrates the case of the Tatas.

Special attention should be paid to the nature of Indian society and to its bearings on the continuing managerial control by a par-

TABLE 4   Community Distribution of Directorships for the Tatas' 10 Largest
Companies (1972).

Community	No. of Directors	No. of Directorships Held by the Directors
The Tatas	3	12
Other Parsis	14	25
Marwari	1 (1)	1 (1)
Gujaratis	11 (4)	14 (4)
Bengalees	6	7
Marathis	3	5
Punjabis	3 (1)	4 (2)
Muslim	3	6
Tamilians	2	2
Mysorian	1	3
Malayalees	2	2
Foreigners & Unidentifiable	24	27
Total	73 (6)	108 (7)

Notes: Cf. the preceding table. The figures in brackets relate to the Mafatlals,
Mahindras, Kilachands, Thackerseys, Bajajs, and Khataus.

ticular family. Indian society is divided into a large number of communities which are either minor religious communities, such as the Parsis, or sub-castes of the Hindus. Each community has exclusivity, particularly in the matter of marriage and adoption, as well as cohesion. It is only natural, under these circumstances, that a man in business could trust, and has trusted, the members of his own community.

Resort, in various manners, to the traditional community ties in business management has been one of the conspicuous characteristics of Indian business. It was in fact the most important factor behind the successful emergence of the Marwari community as India's dominant trading firm during the last century.[10]

An analysis of community distribution of the company directors belonging to India's two representative zaibatsu would indicate the extent to which community ties are utilized by the zaibatsu families. Tables 3 and 4 show the community-wise distribution of the directors of the companies, belonging to the Birlas and the Tatas, respectively, whose net assets were over Rs. 100 million, around 1972. The Birlas' companies are considered by the general

TABLE 5   The Birlas, Marwaris and Non-Marwari Directors in 76 Companies Belonging to the Birla Group, and Percentage of Directorships Held by Them in the Birlas' Companies (1972).

			Number of Directorships			
		Number of Directors (1)	Total (2)	Of which, Directorships in the Birlas' Companies (3)	Directorships in the Second Tier (4)	$\frac{3+4(\%)}{2}$ (5)
The Birlas	A	0	0	0	0	—
	B	18	106	104	0	98
Other Marwaris	A	28	272	73	9	30
	B	83	382	286	20	80
Of which, Other	A	(5)	(61)	(8)	(0)	(13)
Groups	B	(0)	(0)	(0)	(0)	(—)
Others (including	A	16	133	41	2	32
Unidentifiable)	B	17	79	63	0	80
Total	A	44	405	114	11	31
	B	118	567	453	20	83

Note: Those directors whose communities were not identifiable constitute about half of the "Others." The identifiable ones include the Bengalees, Gujaratis, U.P. Banias, etc.

public to be managed exclusively by the family members or their "henchmen." On the contrary, the Tatas are considered to be the most modern and open minded of the Indian zaibatsu, relying on salaried professional managers to a great extent.

As Table 3 shows, two-thirds of the directorships (at least 70 out of 105, i.e., 67%) were held by the Marwaris, the Birlas' own community. In the Tatas' case, it is surprising to see, Table 4, that the Parsi directors occupied an unduly large percentage of directorships (37 out of 108, i.e., 34%) in lieu of the community's rather small size; its population was hardly 100,000. Particularly in the case of the appex company, Tata Sons Pvt. Ltd., the Parsis accounted for 6 of the 7 directors in 1968 and 8 of the 10 in 1972.

As regards the Birlas, Birla Brothers Pvt. Ltd. had been the most important managing agent. The directors of this company mainly consisted of members of the Birla family.

As mentioned before, the Birlas hold a number of investment

companies. Table 5 shows those directors who held directorships in any of the Birlas' investment, trading or financial companies. These directors were singled out because they can be regarded as those persons most trusted by the Birlas in view of the nature of the business.

The figures in lines B of Table 5 show that out of 118 such directors, no less than 101 persons (86%) were the Marwaris.

The directors of some 20 companies belonging to the Birlas but working in other activities were also studied, the results are shown in lines A of the Table. Those having no directorships in any company in the fields of investment, finance and trade numbered 44. They held as many as 405 directorships. However, only 125 directorships (31%) were held in the companies belonging to the Birlas. The corresponding percentage figure for the 118 directors was no less than 83%.[11]

Last, but not least, apart from the resort to community ties, Indian zaibatsu have established a variety of family charitable trusts. As Isamu Hirota points out, these trusts have a function of maintaining the family's controlling interests (i.e., vote-carrying shares) undivided among the individual members.[12]

The members of the zaibatsu family do not always hold the most powerful legal status in the management of the companies: a young member may be merely a general manager or president who is not legally responsible to the general meeting of the companies. Still, it is because of the above mentioned arrangements that they have unchallenged managerial power in the group companies.

IV. Subtle Changes toward Professionalization of Management

Almost all of the zaibatsu families belong to some trading community. Even when examining exceptions, the founders of such groups have usually accumulated their initial capital by trading and speculation, as was the case with the Tatas. The family members have not lost their traders' acumen and traits, even today. The profitability of industrial enterprises depends to a good extent on factors other than productivity and quality of products. For instance,

TABLE 6   Increasing Importance of Salary Earners among Total Employees (1951–70).

(in 1,000 persons)

	Both Wage & Salary Earners (1)	Of which, Salary Earners (2)	$\frac{(2)}{(1)}$ % (3)
1951	1,633	154	9.4
1955	1,784	195	11
1960	2,904	323	11
1965	3,986	641	16
1970*	4,311	797	18

Sources: For 1951 and 1955, *Tenth Census of Indian Manufactures, 1955,* Govt. of India; for the later years, various issues of *Annual Survey of Industries,* Govt. of India.

Note: * The figures for 1970 are in million man-hours.

the availability of raw materials, and hence their prices, fluctuate volatilely in India. Thus, shrewdness in speculative activities can be numbered as one of the more important qualifications of a successful entrepreneur.

However, given the favorable conditions created by the independent government's policies toward heavy industrialization in the 1950s, business groups started to increasingly diversify their manufacturing activities into more sophisticated fields. This necessitated employment of an increasing number of qualified engineers and other technicians. Table 6 suggests this tendency.

A series of fiscal incentives, many governmental financial institutions and licensing systems such as Industrial Licensing and Capital Goods Import Licensing, have been created in order to guide private business activities into priority fields, as defined by the government from time to time. Both incentive and prohibitive measures accompanied increasing administrative and accounting burdens in all the large companies, which in turn required the zaibatsu to employ legal specialists, accountants (including Chartered Accountants), and other experts, including those who had undergone rigorous training in post-graduate courses at MIT or Harvard Business School.

The qualitative and quantitative expansion of managerial responsibility has led to employment of unrelated personnel for not only middle management but also upper management, though at a much slower pace in the latter case. The Tatas were in the forefront in this matter even before the Independence. In the case of the British groups which emerged in colonial India, the partners used to be selected from among the British who served the group well, but toward the end of British rule, they started recruiting some Indian staff as junior or even senior partners. Dr. R.N. Mukherji, a Bengalee engineer in Indian Iron & Steel (Burn Group) was perhaps the first such case. Mahindra, in the Burn Group, and Ananthramakrishnan, in the Simpson Group, are other conspicuous examples.

On the contrary, most of the Indian zaibatsu groups, particularly those belonging to the Marwaris, were much slower to introduce unrelated persons into top management personnel. When the ownership of British firms was taken over, senior officers were sometimes dismissed and replaced by the new Indian owner's "henchmen," who were often connected with the owner through blood ties, community ties or at least village ties.

However, the members and relatives of the family, even if its size was large, could not continue to handle the expanding tasks of top management. Hence, there emerged various measures to employ unrelated persons in top managerial positions. In the following subsections, new measures are described, including references to in-service training which retained a somewhat traditional nature.

1. In-service Training and Promotion to Upper Echelons

It is more than one hundred years since modern university education was introduced in India. But merchants of India, even the richest of them, rarely sent their children to formal educational institutions for middle and higher education. They used to train the young boys in their own firms until they became competent enough to join as partners in the family business or start new firms of their own. This type of in-service training was the predominant form of education up until the 1950s.

Most of the elderly bosses of the present-day zaibatsu received primary education only. This does not necessarily mean that they are dull, rough and uncivilized; to the contrary, they are highly intelligent, paying attention to worldwide news relating to politics, economy, commerce and technology. G. D. Birla, the founder of the Birla group, was a typical example.

As business interests widened, the family started depending on unrelated, but in-service-trained, persons for daily matters and, in course of time, even for more responsible matters.

The case of the Birla zaibatsu is illustrative of fostering and promoting unrelated, in-service-trained persons to upper echelon position.

D. P. Mandelia, T. C. Saboo, G. D. Thirani, M. D. Dalmia, S. N. Hada, M. L. Bagrodia and R. K. Birla are important topmost salaried managers in the Birla zaibatsu.

According to a lawyer, "M. L. Bagrodia started his life as a clerk in a Birla concern drawing less than Rs. 100 per month. He proved himself very useful to Birlas as he brought fortune to Birlas and to himself by his magic wand."[13]

As regards S. N. Hada (born in 1924), he "started his life in Birla concern as a lowest paid mill-hand and had no technical or university qualification or experience. It is a mystery as to how he paved his way to the top-most position in a Birla concern and how he amassed more than Rs. 5 lakhs (100,000) to buy shares in Hada Textiles after honouring heavy Income Tax Liabilities."[14] He has come to assume very important positions in the Birla zaibatsu in the course of time; as of 1972, he acted as the Managing Director of New Swadeshi Mills of Ahmedabad, and Director in Indore Exporting & Importing Co., Ltd., which is an important holding company, Bharat General & Textile Industries Ltd. and six other important companies, including two Birlas' companies which were working in Ethiopia and Nigeria.[15]

The most important of them all is perhaps D. P. Mandelia (born in 1907). He started his life as a warehouse keeper of a Birla concern. By 1950 he had directorships in 14 Birla companies including the Birla Brothers (Gwalior) Private Ltd. which was an important managing agent of the Birlas, Gwalior Rayon Co., Ltd. and Textile Machineries Corporation (Gwalior) Ltd. Today he is advisor to the head of the Birlas, G. D. Birla. As of 1971, he had directorships in 10 companies; these included Pilani Investment Co., Ltd., the most important holding company of the Birlas, and Zuari Agro-Chemicals

Ltd. which was then the latest and huge chemical fertilizer manufacturer.[16] He drew remunerations from various Birla companies
amounting to Rs. 30,000 per month, and resided in "a palatial
house" at Gwalior City, paying as rent Rs. 2,100 per annum (which
the Income Tax department estimated at Rs. 6,000 per annum).[17]

When the present author of this paper interviewed such an important manager in 1973, he said categorically that "family background, capability and loyalty" were the very conditions requisite
to promotion to higher positions. This is reminiscent of the old
Japanese custom.

Though further details have yet to be explored, it may not be out
of context to refer to a college professor who has been on good terms
with the Birlas and is being well looked after by them as well. He
told me that the Birlas have continued to be quite sympathetic and
generous to those who had contributed to them whole-heartedly.

There is, however, a conspicuous difference between the positions
of Indian and Japanese employed managers: the Indian ones are
often allowed to start and run their own business enterprises separately while serving the masters.

The in-service training mentioned above is not sufficient for
bringing up engineers and other specialists in particular fields who
become immediately necessary when any zaibatsu ventures into
any new activities in big way. In such cases, the necessary specialists
are taken on from any firms within the country (and even from
abroad). Thus the turnover of specialists is fairly high in India.

According to the present author's impression, the in-service
trained persons are weak in technological aspects, but they are much
more "loyal" to the particular firm or group to which they belong.

2. "Tata Administrative Service"

In order to assure both the merits of in-service training and those
of obtaining brilliant persons with high qualifications, the Tatas
have introduced a modern system called "Tata Administrative
Service" (TAS).

The TAS was started in 1956.[18] Dr. Fredy Mehta (1928–), a
London-educated economist who has been a director in Tata Sons
Pvt. Ltd. since 1972, is the first person to be recruited by TAS. While

only a few persons were recruited at the initial stages, 12 persons were recruited last year (1981–82), and the total strength of the TAS has reached over one hundred. It is of interest that they are recruited through a central body called the TAS Committee for all of the Tata companies. Its influence is such that quite a few of those persons who passed the most prestigious examinations for the Indian Administrative Service or Indian Foreign Service joined TAS instead.

It should be added that the TAS is not likely to undermine the authority of the Tata family in the near future. One should not be astonished by the news that a young member of the family, 45-year old Ratan Tata, was appointed Chairman of Tata Industries Ltd. in spite of the availability of more senior and "competent" persons within the company. This is taken as a gesture signifying his likely appointment as the leader of the Tatas in the future.[19]

3. Professionalization of Family Members Themselves

Zaibatsu families' excessive power has been severely criticized by various kinds of people, not only by the leftist or egalitarian intellectuals but also by wide varieties of officials and liberal professionals.

In the 1950s, the zaibatsu families started sending their young children to formal higher educational institutions in India, and sometimes abroad, for scientific as well as managerial study. Today, those members in their 30s or below are mostly college graduates. They often go abroad (especially to the U.S.A.) for short-term training courses.

This is a response to the above mentioned criticism as well as their own need to become capable of executing scientific management and exercising leadership over their highly qualified experts who are often much older and abler. A young, college-educated member of one of largest zaibatsu families reportedly said that, without first becoming highly professionalized himself, he could not direct his specialists properly or with authority.

V. Concluding Remarks

Though the zaibatsu families' holds over both ownership and

management have been diluted quantitatively in the process of growth among the groups, control over their companies has been maintained by resorting to various means which are either of universal nature or those very peculiar to Indian nature.

Though professionalization of management has started and is a welcome development, it is still within the overall framework of maintaining the families' firm control. One of the TAS's functions is to integrate the group, as we have seen. In the case of the Birlas, in which many companies are managed by employed managers, the performances of these companies are closely monitored by the family.

However, relationships among the family members are elastic and opportunistic. While many a zaibatsu extended family enjoy amicable internal relationships, quite a few, such as the Mafatlals, Singhanias and Jaipurias, are suffering from family feuds. This is perhaps because the norms of family members have not been rigidly defined. Further, the basic reason behind this is perhaps that all the individual members, at least male members, of the family have traditionally had equal ownership rights over ancestoral property.

This is in sharp contrast to Japanese traditional merchant families which were based on primogeniture and collective ownership of property.

Professor Yasuoka presumes that, as against the case of collective ownership, families based on individual ownership tend to actively manage their businesses themselves while making efforts to exclude undesirable members.[20] Such tendencies have also been observed in the Indian cases where all the members have been expected to be active leaders of the family business. Moreover, there have been a few cases of ousting undesirable members, such as the late G. Birla.

However, the individualistic attitude is a fairly new phenomenon in India, and efforts to consolidate the ownerships dispersed through equal succession have been continuously made by way of establishing, from time to time, a series of "charitable" family trusts, holding companies and chains of intercorporate investments. It may be that careful studies are necessary in order to see whether these efforts are due to traditional ideas favoring extended family or the scale merits of business. The present author of this paper presumes that the latter is the major, albeit not the sole, factor.

Acknowledgements
    Professor P. N. Agarwala, New Delhi, and particularly Professor
A. N. Oza, Bombay University, kindly made many comments on a
rough draft of this article, many of which have been incorporated in
the present edition. But whatever bias or mistakes that remain are
wholly the author's.

NOTES

1. Shigeaki Yasuoka, "Ownership and Management of Family Busi-
    ness: An International Comparison," (HSDRJE-63/UNUP-414),
    The U.N. Univ., Tokyo, 1982, 29p.

2. Government of India, *Annual Survey of Industries; 1977–78, Summary
    Results for Factory Sector*, New Delhi, 1980, pp. 26, 30.

3. According to the present author's own classification of the 200
    largest companies listed in *The Times of India Directory & Year-book
    1980/81*, Bombay, 1981.

4. "Census of public limited companies, 1971–72," *Reserve Bank of India
    Bulletin* (June 1978), p. 447.

5. Nirmal K. Chandra, "Role of foreign capital in India," *Social
    Scientist* (April 1977), pp. 3–20; S. K. Goyal, *Monopoly Capital and Pub-
    lic Policy*, Allied Publishers Pvt. Ltd., New Delhi, 1979, pp. 52–53.

6. Shoji Ito, "Indo no aru dai-kigyō no kabunushi-kōsei" [An analysis
    of the share-holders' list of a large public limited company in India],
    Ajia Keizai (Oct., 1974), pp. 84–90.

7. R. K. Hazari, *The Structure of the Corporate Private Sector, A Study of
    Concentration, Ownership and Control*, Bombay, 1966, 400p.

8. For further details, cf. Shoji Ito, "On the basic nature of the invest-
    ment company in India," in *The Developing Economies*, XVI-3 (Sept.
    1978), pp. 223–238; Ito, "Studies in Indian zaibatsu; roles of inter-
    corporate investment," in *The Journal of Intercultural Studies*, No. 2
    (1975), pp. 51–56.

9. P. S. Lokanathan's Study (*Industrial Organization in India*, London,
    1935, 413p.) is the classical work on the Managing Agency System.
    Many studies have been made since. Kenji Koike's study (*Keiei
    Dairi Seido Ron* [*On the Managing Agency System*], Tokyo, 1979) puts
    forward a novel idea that the system's aim was to basically preempt
    industrial profit by corrupt entrepreneurs, while Shin'ichi Yone-

kawa in one of his articles ("Indo boseki kabushiki kaisha ni okeru keici dairi seido no teichaku katei" [The settlement process of the managing agency system in Indian textile companies], *Hitotsubashi Roso*, Vol. 85, No. 1, 1980) proved that the mercantile approach of the ealier entrepreneurs was its origin.

10. Tomas A. Thimberg, *The Marwaris; From Traders to Industrialists*, New Delhi, 1978, 268p. The community ties were important also for the Nattukottai Chettiars, Parsis, Gujerati Banias at the time when they started expansion of their networks of transaction in remote places.; Shoji Ito, "A note on the 'business combine' in India—with special reference to the Nattukottai Chettiars," in *The Developing Economies*, IV-3 (Sep. 1966), pp. 370–372; Ito, "Indo ni okeru zaibatsu no shutsuji ni tsuite; 19-seiki–dai-ichiji-taisen" [On the origins of Indian zaibatsu; from the 19th century to World War I] in *Shakai Keizai Shi-gaku*, Vol. 45, No. 5 (1980), pp. 29–54. These remind us of a similarity shared by the Ōmi merchants of Japan who used village ties for building up wide networks; Eiichiro Ogura, *Ōmi Shōnin no Keifu* [*Genera of Merchants from Ōmi Region*] Tokyo, 1980.

11. For more details, cf. Shoji Ito, "Indo ni okeru dai-zaibatsu no dōzoku-teki seikaku no sai-kentō" [A reexamination of family characteristics of large Indian zaibatsu], in *Keizai to Keizaigaku* (Mar. 1978), pp. 35–46.

12. Isamu Hirota, "Indo ni okeru kazoku-teki keiei no seiritsu jijō" [Circumstances pertaining to the establishment of family management], in *Shōgaku Ronshū*, No. 14 (1979), pp. 1–27.

13. N. C. Roy, *Mystery of Bajoria-Jalan House*, Calcutta, 1972, p. 208.

14. Ibid., p. 208.

15. From the "List of Directorships" available in "D" files at the office of Registrar of Companies, Calcutta.

16. Ibid.

17. Roy, op. cit., pp. 204–205.

18. The following information was collected from the Tatas' office in Bombay, Sept. 1982.

19. "The Tatas: changing of the guard," *India Today*, Dec. 31, 1981, p. 96ff.

20. Shigeaki Yasuoka, *op. cit.*, pp. 23–24.

[28]

Pakistan's Big Businessmen: Muslim Separatism, Entrepreneurship, and Partial Modernization*

Hanna Papanek
University of Chicago

In Pakistan, as in other developing countries, the role of indigenous capitalists has been an extremely complex economic, social, and political question. In the past few years, the very large business-industrial combines —the "Big Houses" or the "Twenty-two Families"—have been the focus of a great deal of political controversy. At this particular juncture, therefore, it should be useful to examine some of the aspects of the growth and development of the new capitalists of Pakistan in the context of the development of Pakistan as a separate state since 1947. By going back to the pre-Partition years, it may be possible to see some of the connections between the Pakistan movement and some of the big businessmen; similarly, a brief look at the first post-Partition decade should indicate some of the roots of the elite of the business-industrial class.

Three major themes characterize the development of this class and, in turn, provide some linkages to other aspects of Pakistan's society and economy. Muslim separatism, its probable economic and social antecedents, and its political expression is the first of these themes; its culmination in the creation of a separate state and an increasingly separate economy provided the initial impetus for the creation of a new Pakistani capitalist class. Another crucial aspect of the growth of Pakistan's economy and of the major firms which emerged—is entrepreneurship of a vigorous, aggressive, and manipulative sort which is often characteristic of the initial phases of a

* This paper was written in January 1971 and presented at the annual meeting of the Association for Asian Studies, Washington, D.C., on March 30, 1971, before East Pakistan became the independent state of Bangladesh. Because the paper deals with events of the period before 1969, it has not been rewritten to take specific account of the events of 1971–72. The designation "East Pakistan" has been retained in this paper to describe a political unit during its period of existence and which has now become the independent state of Bangladesh. The research on which the article is based was supported by the Center for International Affairs, Harvard University, and carried out with the cooperation of the Pakistan Institute of Development Economics. The assistance of Pakistani colleagues is gratefully acknowledged. I am also indebted to Shahid Javed Burki and Gustav F. Papanek for their comments and criticism of this paper, but the responsibility for errors is, of course, mine.

1

Economic Development and Cultural Change

private-enterprise economy. Third, the rapid development of indigenous industrial enterprises, especially in cities which had been characterized by largely nonindustrial economic activities in pre-Partition days, had important consequences in terms of the social, economic—and, eventually, political—modernization of the country. At the same time, the entrepreneurs themselves underwent a process of modernization of values and life-styles. But, in both the broader sense of the modernization of the society and of the entrepreneurial class, the modernization was at best partial. In the present paper, the role of Muslim separatism and partial modernization will be stressed, especially since earlier discussions of the new class have tended to concentrate on questions of entrepreneurship and regional disparities in economic power between East and West Pakistan.[1]

Separatism and Modernization

Since it became obvious, in retrospect, that the opportunities created by the establishment of a separate economy and by the large-scale emigration of Hindus, especially from West Pakistan, were the major factors in the initial establishment of the new Muslim capitalist class, it is tempting to speculate that this was the major root of the separatist effort of the Muslim League. Levin has indeed argued that "the process of capitalist competition pushed the big Muslim bourgeoisie on the path of religio-communal separatism, through the benefits promised to them by the formation of Pakistan."[2] But, although big businessmen certainly profited from the establishment of the new state eventually, other factors seem to have been more significant in the establishment and success of the Pakistan movement. The economic arguments for separatism were more broadly based, although a careful historical analysis is needed to establish this aspect of Pakistan's development. Some hypotheses are offered here which are relevant to the development of this approach.

While the creation of Pakistan represented the success of a political movement aimed at setting up a separate state for India's Muslims on the grounds of religious differences and incompatibilities between them and Hindus, it is well known that some of the major supporting arguments used in making the case were based on the economic position of Muslims. In

---

[1] G. F. Papanek, *Pakistan's Development: Social Goals and Private Incentives* (Cambridge, Mass.: Harvard University Press, 1967; and Karachi: Oxford University Press, 1968). Hanna Papanek, "Entrepreneurs in East Pakistan," in *Bengal: Change and Continuity*, ed. R. and M. J. Beech (East Lansing: Michigan State University, Asian Studies Center, 1971), and idem, "Pakistan's New Industrialists and Businessmen: Focus on the Memons," in *Entrepreneurship and the Modernization of Occupational Cultures in South Asia*, ed. Milton Singer (forthcoming).

[2] S. F. Levin, "About the Evolution of Muslim Trading Castes and the Development of Capitalism," in *Kasty v. Indii* [Castes of India], ed. G. G. Kotovskii (Moscow: Izdaletsvo Nauka Glavnaya Redaktziya Vostochnoi Literatury, 1965); passage translated by Thomas Timberg.

Hanna Papanek

examining this argument, in retrospect, it is essential to distinguish specific groups in the Muslim population in economic terms and to relate their economic status and prospects to the extent of their participation in the separatist movement.

In such an analysis, it is indispensable to examine the nature of the division of labor within the Indian social structure and its relationship to factors of religious differences, on the one hand, and the distinctions between castes (or their non-Hindu equivalents), on the other. Obviously, the lines dividing Hindus and Muslims in socioeconomic terms in undivided India were extremely complex, and it was not possible to distinguish—in overall terms—between Hindus and Muslims along the lines of socio-economic class differences. While in some regions, such as the Punjab, Muslims were generally cultivators, and many of the landlords and money-lenders were Hindus—a fact which had been recognized by the passage of the Punjab Alienation of Land Act of 1900[3]—such religious distinctions often did not exist in other areas. Members of both religions were represented in all classes and most occupations in undivided India.

Instead, the economic distinctions between Hindus and Muslims were shaped in more indirect ways through the operation of the caste system. Within the context of this system, the division of labor between castes generally meant that a given occupation was the specialty of a given caste and that the entrance of outsiders into the occupation tended to be prevented by practices favoring fellow caste members in employment. This type of occupational specialization was common in both Hindu castes and Muslim "quasi-castes" or "communities," at all social levels. Similar occupations have typically been held by Hindu groups in one locality; Muslims, in another; sometimes Muslim and Hindu occupational groups coexist in the same village or larger region. It is probably accurate to say that, for the mass of Hindu and Muslim cultivators, artisans, and urban workers, there was not much difference in undivided India in economic terms in a given occupation between the two religions.

However, in the more modern occupations, particularly those for which a measure of formal education was required, caste and religious factors played a somewhat different role. Traditional claims to such occupations by particular castes were often weaker, and access to them might be open to members of several different groups in the population, depending on opportunities, political factors, the foreclosing of alternatives, and so on. Formal education, provided by the British, proved to be a critical factor in the degree of access to the newer occupations, and it is here that the consequences of the Muslim failure to enter new educational institutions for a generation or more after Hindus did so in the nineteenth century were very marked. The effects were likely to be felt most acutely in

[3] See Norman G. Barrier, *The Punjab Alienation of Land Bill of 1900*, in *Duke University Commonwealth Studies Center Monograph*, no. 2 (Durham, N.C.: Duke University Press, 1966).

Economic Development and Cultural Change

the professions, government service, and in the more modern sectors of commerce and industry, all of which required varying degrees of modern education. It was undoubtedly also in these occupations that upward social mobility was likely to be most rapid. In terms of this analysis, then, one would expect that the individuals most highly motivated to join a separatist movement would be Muslims whose access to modern, middle-class occupations was felt to be foreclosed, or advancement made difficult, by the overwhelming dominance of Hindus in these same occupations. The continuing operation of factors which favored the entry of fellow caste members into a given enterprise or occupation probably exacerbated a situation in which Hindus were not only numerically more prevalent but also had the advantage of much earlier entry.

While these hypotheses remain to be more fully substantiated by detailed studies, an approach stressing the social structural characteristics of Indian society and their economic consequences would represent an important new method for analyzing the separatist appeal of the Pakistan movement. As will be shown, such an approach is particularly relevant to the role of private enterprise before and after Partition.

A closely related argument deals with a more general aspect of the dynamics of separatist movements. Such a movement, be it religious, racial, or linguistic, must aim for the mobilization of the entire group which it claims to represent. In the case of the Muslim League, its claim to represent all of India's Muslims tended to foreclose its ability to make more specific class-based appeals and perhaps also to minimize the importance of specific economic and social plans for the new state. The striking absence of well-developed economic plans by the Muslim League leadership—especially in comparison with Indian National Congress efforts in this respect—was probably one of the factors which later produced such a pronounced bias in favor of private enterprise by the early government of Pakistan (see next section).

Finally, it is also important to remember that no specific statements were made by advocates of separatism about the possible exchange of populations between the two new contemplated states until the very eve of Partition. It is difficult to imagine exactly what kind of vision of the new state of Pakistan was held by the leadership of the separatist movement if one remembers the extent of Hindu control over existing economic institutions in the areas which were to become Pakistan.[4] What patterns of economic and political relationships were expected to develop without significant demographic and institutional changes? Apparently, Jinnah was alone in even broaching the possibility of a planned exchange of populations between India and Pakistan. In January 1947, in an interview with an English journalist, he "expressed his conviction that only a wholesale

[4] C. N. Vakil, *Economic Consequences of Divided India* (Bombay: Vora & Co., 1950), pp. 130–33.

4

Hanna Papanek

exchange of minority populations between the future states of India and Pakistan could offer a solution to the ever-growing conflict between the communities."[5] The idea was categorically opposed by Gandhi as "unthinkable and wrong"; Nehru admitted that such a solution might be possible for the Punjab but would be disastrous to the survival of India if it were to be extended to other areas.[6] After Partition had occurred, Liaqat Ali Khan stated (in Lahore on October 10, 1947) that, "although Pakistan would not refuse shelter to any Muslim settler," he strongly opposed supporting the evacuation of Muslims from Indian areas outside the Punjab.[7] Thus, while a systematic plan for the exchange of populations seems not to have been part of separatist thinking, the events which did occur make it necessary to question whether the dynamics of separatism, when once set in motion, do not inevitably lead to large-scale population movements. As broadly based studies of refugee movements will perhaps show, such population displacements may occur for reasons of underlying economic and political power, regardless of the intentions of the separatist movement. In any event, the development of Pakistan's society and economy would have been very different if major population shifts had not occurred. The enormous opportunities facing businessmen and industrialists—especially after the Karachi riots of January 1948—were very closely related to the existence of an economic "vacuum," particularly in West Pakistan, as will become clear in the later discussion.

With respect to the role of the new capitalists in the process of "modernization," several distinctions must first be made. In general, the definitions of modernity or modernization which have been developed stress the importance of cities and of factories in various ways. Lerner sees modernity as a "consistent whole," a complex in which are associated such phenomena as "urbanization, industrialization, secularization, democratization, education [and] media participation."[8] Inkeles, in his cross-cultural studies of villagers and factory workers, has focused on an empirical complex of attitudes and values which could be defined as "modern." These attitudes are often strikingly associated with numbers of years of formal schooling but sometimes even more so with numbers of years spent as a worker in a factory.[9] Huntington, discussing political development, defines political modernization as "rationalization of authority, differentiation of structure,

[5] Joseph B. Schechtman, *Population Transfers in Asia* (New York: Hallsby Press, 1949), p. 21.

[6] Ibid., pp. 21–23.

[7] M. Rafique Afzal, *Speeches and Statements of Quaid-i-Millat Liaquat Ali Khan (1941–51)* (Lahore: Research Society of Pakistan, 1967), pp. 124–26.

[8] Daniel Lerner (with Lucille Pevsner), *The Passing of Traditional Society* (Glencoe, Ill.: Free Press, 1958), p. 438.

[9] See, e.g., Alex Inkeles, "Making Men Modern: On the Causes and Consequences of Individual Change in Six Developing Countries," *American Journal of Sociology* 75, no. 2 (September 1969): 208–25; and idem, "Participant Citizenship in Six Developing Countries," *American Political Science Review* 63, no. 4 (December 1969): 1120–41.

5

Economic Development and Cultural Change

and expansion of political participation" but stresses the fact that this is only the theoretical rather than the actual direction in which social, economic, and cultural modernization affect the movement away from a traditional polity.[10] Bellah, in a discussion of the role of religion and modernization in Asia, notes that "increased effectiveness in goal attainment" must be accompanied by an "increase in the rationalization of the goal-setting process [otherwise] very serious pathologies can result." Such pathologies are the product of "partial or disturbed modernization, not the inevitable result of modernization itself."[11]

Some of the common elements which can be taken from these definitions and discussions of various aspects of modernization—and which have been variously elaborated in the larger literature in this field—apply to the role of the new capitalists in several different ways. First of all, it is clear that the development of new economic institutions by a relatively small group of owners and managers has social and political implications going far beyond the economic consequences. In Pakistan, the growth of manufacturing industries in large urban centers resulted in the creation of a new class of urban industrial workers, generally drawn from rural landless laborers, urban casual workers, and others. Despite the fact that industrial wage rates rose only very little in the decades following Partition,[12] while industrial profits rose tremendously, especially at the beginning,[13] the creation of this new urban class differentiated them from rural and urban casual laborers in economic terms, with probable long-range political consequences. The creation of an urban proletariat was clearly one of the early effects of economic "modernization"; the failure of the government to assure more equitable income distribution indicated one of the failures of the modernization process, resulting from increased political power by the industrial owners. Furthermore, new consumer goods began to be locally manufactured and to be more widely visible than ever before, while at the same time large masses of the population continued to be unable to buy such goods. Finally, the development of the new economic institutions provided many opportunities for great profit and very rapid social mobility by relatively few families and resulted in the development of a new group of businessmen and industrialists with higher status than most of them had ever had before. In terms of class formation, there is no doubt that the new state rapidly developed newly demarcated social groups in its structure, which included a group of *nouveaux riches* as part of the upper class, and a segment of the middle class engaged in business and manufacturing occupations in various capacities ranging from self-employed entrepreneurs to

[10] Samuel P. Huntington, *Political Order in Changing Societies* (New Haven, Conn.: Yale University Press, 1968), p. 35.

[11] Robert N. Bellah, "Epilogue," in *Religion and Progress in Modern Asia*, ed. R. N. Bellah (New York: Free Press, 1965), pp. 195–96.

[12] Azizur Rahman Khan, "What Has Been Happening to Real Wages in Pakistan?" *Pakistan Development Review* 7 (Autumn 1967): 317–48.

[13] G. F. Papanek, p. 39.

6

Hanna Papanek

managers and clerks. In addition, the industrial labor force, which occupied a position above that of the urban unemployed and casual workers and well above that of rural landless laborers, began to develop increasingly, especially in the larger cities where industries were concentrated.

The term "partial modernization" is also peculiarly applicable to the new rich themselves as well as to their efforts to adjust and assimilate to "the existing order [and to gain] political power and social status commensurate with their new economic position."[14] This group of entrepreneurs constitutes, in Pakistan, a clear example of persons undergoing value changes in the direction of modernization, with many of these changes apparently following their movement into new occupations rather than preceding this process. Among the most striking findings of studies of Pakistani industrialists,[15] and of the survey of businessmen and industrialists on which this paper is based, are aspects of the "traditional" values and actions of those who became businessmen and industrialists in Pakistan. A large proportion of the new industrial-business class, particularly among the elite of this group, were persons who had been in some kind of business (more rarely, industry) before Partition, and very many of them belonged to Muslim "business communities" (see section 5 below). Their "traditional" values, going back two or three generations, at least, included a strong orientation toward profit, high importance attached to savings, willingness to take considerable risks, a pattern of migration in search of business opportunities by men who left their families behind, and acceptance of a view of Islam which sees trade as a valued occupation and the injunctions against "usury" as inapplicable to ordinary interest. With respect to values and attitudes not directly connected with their occupation, on the other hand, many of these men traditionally showed a distinct social conservatism, favoring arranged marriage within the quasi-caste community, *purdah* (segregation of women), and a rather simple middle-class life-style which emphasized conspicuous consumption only in highly visible public occasions associated with family status, such as weddings. With respect to education, the prevalent attitudes of members of "business communities" tended to be highly instrumental, that is, a minimum level of formal education was customary before an intensive period of business apprenticeship. Some of the changes which this group underwent following their economic success will be indicated in the more detailed discussion of twelve Big Houses later in this paper, in an attempt to give some support to the notion of "partial modernization" in one respect.

The view of "partial modernization" as "pathology" needs, however, to be discussed further. It may be more useful to see the pattern of development of Pakistan's new capitalist class as being a logical outcome of the contradictions inherent in a private enterprise economy in which the consolidation

[14] Huntington, p. 50 (based on Mancur Olson, Jr., "Rapid Growth as a Destabilizing Force," *Journal of Economic History* 23 [December 1963]: 532).
[15] G. F. Papanek, chap. 2.

7

Economic Development and Cultural Change

of economic power by a small elite becomes transformed into considerable political power. Both the initial inclinations of the Muslim League in favor of private enterprise, and that of later governments favoring rapid economic growth, made it almost inevitable that such a consolidation of power was not resisted either by strongly established bureaucratic forces or through the exercise of controls by political parties responsive to a wide popular constituency. While it is therefore true that the "partial modernization" in the economic sphere was carried out very rapidly by the new business-industrial class of Pakistan, it would be wrong to assume that economic modernization, like political modernization, can be expected to proceed smoothly. The contradictions of power inherent in this process can certainly not be overcome by the frequently voiced hopes that, "if only" entrepreneurs were more educated or had a greater sense of "social responsibility" or "patriotism," there would be smooth economic modernization. The contradictions are inherent in the process not in the personnel, especially since, in their own terms, the entrepreneurs of Pakistan have shown both patriotism and social responsibility by having established enterprises at all, particularly in the early high-risk years from 1947 to 1952.

Private Enterprise and the Pakistan Movement
Writing in 1967, Chaudhri Muhammad Ali stated that "the movement for Pakistan was inspired by the urge to develop the human and material resources of Muslim homelands so as to promote the moral and material welfare of the people."[16] Yet, in the days preceding Partition, the thrust of the Pakistan movement seems to have been primarily political, and there is little evidence that the separatist leadership was making specific efforts to address itself to economic problems beyond the general proposition that more opportunities would open up for Muslims in a predominantly Muslim state. With some exceptions—for instance, at their thirty-first session in 1943 at Karachi[17]—the Muslim League apparently did not put high priorities on problems of planning for economic development or income distribution as central issues in themselves. The Indian National Congress, on the other hand, was more specifically concerned with these issues and more productive in terms of policy discussions and resolutions.[18] One of the obvious reasons for this difference was the more deliberately ideological orientation of the Congress leadership, including both Gandhian and explicitly socialist approaches to economic problems. On the other

[16] Chaudhri Muhammad Ali, *The Emergence of Pakistan* (New York: Columbia University Press, 1967), p. 340.
[17] Syed Sharifuddin Pirzada, ed., *Foundations of Pakistan: All-India Muslim League Documents, 1906–1947*, vol. 2, *1924–1947* (Karachi: National Publishing House, 1970), pp. 468–70.
[18] K. N. Chaudhuri, "Economic Problems and Indian Independence," in *The Partition of India: Policies and Perspectives, 1935–1947*, ed. C. H. Phillips and Mary Doreen Wainwright (Cambridge, Mass.: M.I.T. Press, 1970), pp. 299–304.

Hanna Papanek

hand, the Muslim League, which was trying to develop a position of exclusively representing all Muslims, may have found it difficult to make specific pronouncements which might have emphasized class differences among Muslims. Sayeed notes that "after 1945, there seems to be an attempt on the part of Jinnah to be all things to all people. It was true that he wanted Muslim capitalists to establish Muslim enterprises, but at the same time he was expressing grave concern about the gross inequalities that existed."[19]

At the same time, it is difficult to imagine that a political movement in whose Council the two largest groups were landlords (163 out of 503) and lawyers (145)[20] would take a particularly radical stance on economic issues. Efforts in provincial Leagues to introduce resolutions calling for the nationalization of public utilities, public control of private industry, and a tax policy directed to a sharp equalization of incomes were not made part of the general policies of the Muslim League at the national level.[21]

In the immediate circle around Jinnah, several big businessmen and industrialists played important roles, not only in helping to finance the Pakistan movement, but also in helping to organize businessmen, and in more specifically political roles. These men were also active in setting up private firms which were to fulfill important economic roles in the new state, as will be discussed in some detail.

Muslims in commercial occupations also clearly felt that it was high time for Muslims to occupy more—and more important—positions in the economy, and these feelings were obviously shared by at least some of the political leaders. When Pakistani businessmen spoke of the early post-Partition years, they almost unanimously stressed their eagerness at that time to prove that Muslims like themselves could be successful businessmen and industrialists. In terms strikingly reminiscent of resentment against colonial rulers, many of them described how Hindu contempt of Muslim business skills had rankled, and how they had been angered by statements that Muslims "obviously" were not capable in business and finance or industrial management. This feeling was probably part of the general Muslim wish for greater access to jobs and for greater prestige in modern occupations in all sectors of the economy, which would be easier if Muslims were employers.

In any event, Jinnah made his government's position explicit soon after Partition, with regard to the role of private enterprise, in the first "Statement on the Industrial Policy of Pakistan (1948)." In describing this policy to businessmen, he told the Eighty-eighth Annual Meeting of the Karachi Chamber of Commerce in April 1948 that:

---

[19] K. B. Sayeed, personal communication.
[20] Khalid Bin Sayeed, *Pakistan: The Formative Phase 1857–1948*, 2d ed. (London: Oxford University Press, 1968), p. 224.
[21] Ibid., p. 225.

Economic Development and Cultural Change

> Government will seek to create conditions in which industry and trade
> may develop and prosper . . . . I would like to call to your particular
> attention the keen desire of the Government of Pakistan to associate
> individual initiative and private enterprise at every stage of industrializa-
> tion . . . . Commerce and Trade are the very lifeblood of the nation.
> I can no more visualize a Pakistan without traders than I can one without
> cultivators and civil servants. I have no doubt that in Pakistan, traders
> and merchants will always be welcome and that they, in building up their
> own fortunes, will not forget their social responsibility for a fair and
> square deal to one and all, big and small.[22]

It is not surprising, then, when businessmen recall that there was "not the
slightest doubt in my mind that Jinnah and the Muslim League were in
favor of private enterprise; there was no question at the time of any other
system."[23]

These facts should dispel any tendencies to see the early post-Partition
period, when Jinnah was still alive, as one in which private enterprise was
being kept at bay. In 1970, Wahidul Haque wrote that "the leader of the
revolution, Quaid-e-Azam, himself coming from a merchant family, unified all segments of the Muslim society in order to create a homeland for
them free from feudal-capitalist-ecclesiastical oppression . . . . After the
death of the Quaid-e-Azam on September 11, 1948, the process of capitalistic development of the new state was launched under the hegemony of the
bourgeois elite."[24] Whatever else might be said about the achievements of
Jinnah and the Pakistan movement, it does seem to be evident that the
actual alignment between at least some big businessmen and the Muslim
League leadership had begun long before Independence.

When Partition came with its attendant horrors and violent population displacements, events further reinforced an initial government inclination toward private enterprise because the economy was in chaos, and
the very small number of available government officials were needed for
tasks other than the management of state enterprises. The result of the ambivalent position of the Muslim League leadership on the question of
economic organization and power was that there existed no ideological
commitment to any economic policies which might have counteracted, however faintly, the general disposition to continue the system as it stood.

The most clear-cut evidence of Jinnah's relationship with businessmen
before Partition is provided by the role which he personally played in the
mobilization of Muslim businessmen through the organization of Muslim
chambers of commerce and through the establishment of "nation-building"

---

[22] "Address by His Excellency the Quaid-i-Azam Mohammed Ali Jinnah, First
Governor General of Pakistan," Minutes of 88th Annual General Meeting, Karachi,
April 27, 1948, *Annual Report for the Year 1947* (Karachi: Karachi Chamber of
Commerce, n.d.), pp. xxxix, xl, xlvii.

[23] Personal communication.

[24] Wahidul Haque, "Development Policies and Regional Justice in Pakistan"
(paper presented to the Conference on Pakistan, Rochester, N.Y., July 29–31, 1970).

10

Hanna Papanek

companies which were to function in the new state. In both these efforts, leading roles were played by men most of whom later came to Pakistan, where
they rose to positions of importance in the economy. This group included
Sir Adamjee Haji Dawood (the father of the present head of the Adamjee
firm), the two Ispahani brothers (M. A. and M. A. H.), Mahomedali Habib
(of the Habib Bank), Habib Ibrahim Rahimtoola, as well as several others
who included men active in provincial League activities, such as G. Allana
in Karachi. The families of most of these men already owned considerable
wealth, and it is certainly not surprising that their firms became large and
important in Pakistan. What is perhaps more interesting is that these
firms remain politically highly visible and their names remain powerful
symbols, even though, by the late 1960s, some of them were far out-
distanced in economic terms by other big enterprise groups. While association with the Pakistan movement was an important factor in the initial
rise of these firms, it is probable that wealth, business experience, and aggressive entrepreneurship were far more crucial. In the initial establishment of Pakistan's industrial giants, politics of the visible sort were not
the key factor, as may become clearer in the discussion of the twelve
largest Big Houses in a later section of this paper.

Chambers of Commerce

Trade associations and chambers of commerce have existed in the subcontinent for some time. Most of the associations were of the guild or caste
type, usually organized by men of a single trade, often belonging to the same
caste. A typical contemporary example of such associations are the
numerous "Kirana Merchants Groups" which represent the interests of
dealers in food grains and spices and are intended also to preserve harmony
among members, most of whom happen also to be Memons. Other types
of associations have also existed at least since the mid-nineteenth century:
the Karachi Chamber of Commerce (which is now for foreign firms only)
was founded in 1860 to advance and represent the interests of the merchants
of the city, both indigenous and foreign.[25]

At the time of Partition, there were fewer than 100 associations of
Muslim businessmen; the *Muslim Year Book*[26] of this period lists eighty-
eight organizations for undivided India, most being of the single-trade
type. Very few were listed for areas which were to become Pakistan, reflecting the relative scarcity of Muslim businessmen in these areas. A few
organizations had larger constituencies and some actual or potential
significance as pressure groups. In 1932, some of the men connected with

[25] Cf. Herbert Feldman, *Karachi through a Hundred Years: The Centenary
History of the Karachi Chamber of Commerce and Industry 1860–1960* (Karachi:
Oxford University Press, 1960).

[26] S. M. Jamil, comp. *Muslim Year Book of India and Who Is Who Complete,
1948–1949* (Bombay: Bombay Newspaper Co., under the auspices of the All-India
Muslim Chamber of Commerce and Industry, n.d.).

11

Economic Development and Cultural Change

the "New Muslim Majlis" in Calcutta founded the Muslim Chamber of Commerce in that city,[27] and this chamber continued to be active. At the time of Partition, M. A. H. Ispahani was its president. In 1939, an All-India Muslim Chamber of Commerce was organized in Bombay, by S. M. Jamil, and was headed for several years by Sir Sultan Chinoy, who was prominent in Bombay civic and political affairs.[28] One of the objectives of the Bombay-based chamber was "to secure organized action on all subjects relating to the interests of the Muslim business community" in addition to encouraging unanimity among Muslim merchants, and spreading commercial and economic knowledge among them.[29]

In 1943, efforts for a Pakistan-oriented national organization of Muslim businessmen were begun by some in the group around Jinnah, which included M. A. H. Ispahani and Chinoy's son-in-law Habib Ibrahim Rahimtoola, with Nurur Rehman, secretary of the Calcutta-based chamber, as organizing secretary.[30] There were evidently some problems connected with the setting up of this new organization, which was, in fact, competing with the Bombay-based group but had to be careful to avoid an open conflict with it, either on personal or ideological issues. Jinnah seems to have pressed hard for the formation of the new group, which finally held its first annual meeting in Delhi in 1945. The new Federation of Muslim Chambers of Commerce and Industry had as its stated objectives: "to focus commercial opinion and to represent the corporate and collective view of the Muslim commercial community; to play a vigorous and an ever watchful part in the political and economic life of the country."[31] The first President was Sir Adamjee, apparently after negotiations to have this post held by Chinoy broke down. The statement of objectives stops just short of claiming an openly representative role for Muslim businessmen, and, although the federation was officially neutral politically, it was clearly in sympathy with the Pakistan movement. Both in the national and provincial chambers, leading figures were men who were also associated with the Muslim League and who had been active in business as well as civic affairs. The groups in Karachi and Lahore involved men like Yusuf Haroon, G. Allana, Nasir A. Shaikh, and Maratib Ali Shah (of the Wazirali family) in leading positions.

Whether the new federation had any direct political effect is not clear, but it does represent one of several instances in which the Pakistan movement

[27] M. A. H. Ispahani, *Qaid-e-Azam Jinnah: As I Knew Him* (Karachi: Forward Publication Trust, 1966), pp. 4–6.

[28] Sultan Chinoy, *Pioneering in Indian Business* (Bombay: Asia Publishing House, 1962).

[29] Jamil, p. 6.

[30] Z. H. Zaidi, "Aspects of the Development of Muslim League Policy, 1937–47," in *The Partition of India: Policies and Perspectives, 1935–1947*, ed. C. H. Phillips and Mary Doreen Wainwright (Cambridge, Mass.: M.I.T. Press, 1970), p. 270; Ispahani, pp. 130–42.

[31] Jamil, p. 9.

12

Hanna Papanek

mobilized Muslim sentiment through the creation of groups or institutions which were not particularly new in type, except that they were specifically by and for Muslims.

The "Nation-building" Companies

Another type of mobilization of Muslim sentiment and resources in the immediate pre-Partition period was the formation of new companies by a few Muslim big businessmen, mainly at Jinnah's urging. The fact that these companies were organized before Partition to meet some of the economic needs of the new state must have indicated to Muslim businessmen that the government of Pakistan might be expected to be favorable to private enterprise. Also, it is possible that they, in turn, influenced the leadership of the Pakistan movement in the course of the organization of the companies, at least in the sense of raising some issues of interest to them.

Four companies were organized in the period immediately before Partition; all were privately financed, owned, and managed by largely Muslim capitalists. Most of the investors in the four firms were either personally close to Jinnah or had gradually moved into positions of support for the establishment of a Muslim state, whether or not they themselves intended to migrate there. They came from families which were among the wealthiest Muslims in commerce and industry in undivided India: Adamjee, Ispahani, Rahimtoola, Dada (and other Bantva Memons), Habib (of the Habib Bank) and several others. Eventually, all these families did migrate to Pakistan, and most of them are among the leading business-industrial families today —but it is important to remember that many of them had not initially intended to do so.[32] Until riots in their hometowns forced them to migrate (as was the case for the Bantva Memons), many of these families had planned to carry out their business activities in both of the new independent states, while remaining in their original places of residence. Their decision to invest in the new companies was based both on the expectation of good profits and the political significance of the move. The actual investments, however, represented only very small fractions of these families' total assets. It is also important to note, finally, that only one of the major investors in the four companies was a resident of the area which was to become Pakistan—Rustom Cowasjee, a Karachi Parsi shipping magnate.

A very important forerunner of the four companies was the Habib Bank, which, in its turn, played a crucial role in the establishment of the later firms. The Habib Bank had been set up as a public limited company in Bombay in 1941 by the Habib family, who had previously been in internal trade and private banking. M. A. H. Ispahani recalls that it was after the revitalization of Muslim politics and the Muslim League by Jinnah in 1936, "in this politically charged atmosphere, that the Habibs decided to break the Hindu-British monopoly in the banking field. They were encouraged

[32] Based on personal interviews with leading businessmen; it is important to note that, in retrospect, this was an embarrassing admission to make.

13

Economic Development and Cultural Change

by Qaid-e-Azam and the Muslim League, and in their turn, to their eternal credit, were able to help and in some measure strengthen the Muslim League cause."[33] The Habib Bank was subsequently appointed banker to the Muslim League Fund, the Pakistan Fund, and the Qaid-e-Azam Bihar Relief Fund.[34] In early 1947, Jinnah reportedly "told Mr. Habib to pack up from Bombay and proceed to Karachi to establish the Habib Bank";[35] in any event, the bank's headquarters were shifted to Karachi on August 7, 1947. In the immediate post-Partition period, it played an extremely significant role in transferring Muslim assets into Pakistan, both for small depositors and large accounts, although there are no exact figures available concerning the total transfers. The relations between Jinnah and Mahomedali Habib were apparently quite close. It may prove to be a significant personal detail that it was in 1937 that the Habibs became Isnasheri Shias, largely at Mahomedali Habib's urging. They had previously been Khoja Ismaili followers of the Aga Khan but later became key figures in the Khoja Isnasheri community. Jinnah himself was of course both a Khoja (by birth) and an Isnasheri Shia by faith. Because of Jinnah's apparently very high regard for Mahomedali Habib and Habib's important role in other business enterprises supported by Jinnah, it would be important to explore further the role of the Habib family and of the bank in the Pakistan movement.

The four "nation-building" companies included three new ones: an airline, a shipping line, and a bank, plus a reorganized existing insurance company. The airline, Orient Airways, was founded in 1946, at the specific request of Jinnah, by members of the Adamjee and Ispahani families. Its board of directors specifically did not include any Hindus, and ownership of shares was reported to be widespread among Indian Muslims, including Jinnah himself.[36] After a difficult beginning, the airline came to play a role in the transport of refugees during Partition, but became really crucial to internal transportation and communication after the boundaries and hostilities between India and Pakistan became consolidated. In 1956, the Government of Pakistan organized Pakistan International Airlines Corporation as a government-owned corporation which took over Orient Airways and greatly expanded operations.

Muhammadi Steamship Company was the largest and, in many ways, the most interesting of the four companies since it was a joint venture of several important commercial families. It is indicative of the strength of the single-family pattern of corporate organization that no joint venture among indigenous business families on a comparable scale has been

[33] M. A. H. Ispahani, "Good Luck to Habib Bank," *Finance and Industry* (Karachi) 5, no. 11 (November 1966): 41.

[34] S. A. Meenai, *Money and Banking in Pakistan* (Karachi: Allies Book Corp., 1966), p. 45.

[35] Hatim A. Alavi, "House of Habibs," *Finance and Industry* (Karachi) 5, no. 11 (November 1966): 43.

[36] Ispahani, *Qaid-e-Azam Jinnah*, pp. 143–44.

Hanna Papanek

organized in Pakistan since. It was clearly the pressures exerted by Jinnah
and the leadership of Mahomedali Habib which made the company possible
in the first place, but, even so, it survived as a joint venture only until 1963,
when it passed into the control of a single family (Valika). Mahomedali
Habib was one of the two largest investors in the company, but it was the
position of respect and power which he held among Muslim businessmen
and his commitment to active leadership in the company which persuaded
most of the other large investors—who were commercial rivals—to join
it. These others included one non-Muslim (Cowasjee), and six families of
Bantva Memons, of whom three (Dada, Arag, and Adam) were among the
largest food-grain shippers of the subcontinent. Habib Bank, Cowasjee,
Dada, Arag, and Adam all ranked among the top thirty family business-
industrial groups in terms of net assets in the late 1960s in Pakistan. The
other, somewhat smaller investors in Muhammadi Steamship also play
important commercial and industrial roles but have remained less prominent. The board of directors of the company, at its inception, included
several prominent Muslim businessmen who were not major investors
(Adamjee, Ispahani, Haroon, Valika) as well as another Parsi and a
Hindu public accountant in addition to representatives of major investors.[37]

The insurance company was Eastern Federal Insurance, an existing
firm which had been founded in 1932 for a specifically Muslim clientele by
men associated with the "New Muslim Majlis" in the Calcutta corporation
elections. This was the same group also involved in setting up the Muslim
Chamber of Commerce in Calcutta. Abdur Rahman Siddiqui, editor of
Morning News (Calcutta) developed the idea for the company, with the
support of prominent Muslims including the Nawab of Bhopal, Ghulam
Mohammed (later Governor General of Pakistan), and others. At an early
period of this company, M. A. Ispahani agreed to place his business with
it to provide further financial support.[38] During the immediate pre-Partition period, the firm received additional financing and management from
Sir Adamjee and H. I. Rahimtoola. By 1965, the management control of
this company was in the hands of the Arag group together with the Ispahani
family; much of its importance in the life insurance market (where there
was by then a great deal of competition) was due to contract coverage of
army personnel.

Muslim Commercial Bank was established in July 1947, a month before Partition, with Jinnah's strong encouragement, by Sir Adamjee and
M. A. Ispahani. The founder-directors of the new bank included men from
the large commercial or industrial Muslim families (Ispahani, Adamjee,
Dada, Arag, Amin Jute) as well as Khwaja Shahabuddin, who had been a
prominent member of the first Muslim ministry in Bengal (1937–40) as well
as, much later, a member of the Ayub government (most recently, 1965–69,

[37] Interviews and personal communications.
[38] Typewritten statement provided by Eastern Federal Union Insurance Co.,
Karachi (no author, n.d.).

15

Economic Development and Cultural Change

Minister for Information and Broadcasting). Muslim Commercial Bank became a part of the Adamjee group of companies; in 1964, M. M. Ispahani was on its board of directors, along with members of the Arag and Valika families and two Adamjees, of whom one was chairman.[39]

Those business and industrial families which supported the Pakistan movement generally considered Pakistan a desirable goal, both from an ideological and commercial point of view, even though, as has been noted, some big business familes did not intend to move there. The extent of their influence in the circle around Jinnah, of course, needs to be explored much more thoroughly than has been done so far—and the appearance of personal memoirs by these men, such as M. A. H. Ispahani's volume, should prove extremely interesting. There is certainly no question that these businessmen understood the potential which might be offered by an independent Pakistan in terms of economic opportunities, but it would be a gross oversimplification to see this as the major causative factor in the separatist movement. Other forces of social and economic discontent were probably much more significant than simply a drive for capitalist expansion of markets—which of course played a role—and these forces need to be studied by social and economic historians.

In most of these efforts, only a small group of families was involved, most of whom were of western Indian origin. The Ispahani brothers, whose family came to Bombay from Iran in 1820, later shifting to Calcutta, were perhaps an exception. But, in this group, wealthy Punjabi business families were very few, the major exceptions being Nasir A. Sheikh of Colony, and the Muhammad Amin family (Amin Jute). The relations between Punjabi businessmen and the various competing Punjab-based Muslim political movements in the pre-Partition period need to be explored further in order to explain some aspects of the role of private enterprise in Muslim politics.

From a narrower point of view, it is important to follow the post-Independence business histories of the commercial and industrial families which were prominent in supporting the Muslim League. In retrospect, it is striking that, although most of these families have remained very wealthy and some have grown substantially in economic power, they constitute only a small segment of the most powerful Big Houses. Many of the most aggressively entrepreneurial and fastest-growing big firms had no connection whatever with the Pakistan movement, and none—with the exception of Gandhara, under Gauhar Ayub, son of President Ayub—was the result of political power directly transformed into economic terms. The usual transformation, of course, was the other way around and much less explicit. Some of the most politically active members of the Jinnah circle, among the businessmen, never came to hold leading positions among the Big Houses, such as Rahimtoola or Ispahani, despite their

[39] Muslim Commercial Bank, Ltd., "Prospectus and Memorandum of Association," mimeographed (Karachi: Muslim Commercial Bank, 1947); and idem, *Annual Report and Accounts 1964* (Karachi: Muslim Commercial Bank, n.d.).

16

Hanna Papanek

public reputations and their obvious considerable wealth. At the same time, however, these few men held powerful political offices in the government of Pakistan during various regimes, as was true for a few other leading business families, but very different from the generally prevailing pattern. In Pakistan, unlike some other developing countries, the first generation (post-Partition) of big businessmen were a group apart, rather than members of existing social or political elites who were expanding their spheres of influence into the economy. Although political influence obviously played an important role in the development of the Big Houses, it was not in itself sufficient for large-scale growth of the enterprises. The political power which relative newcomers, such as Dawood, Valika, Fancy, or Saigol, came to enjoy was the result of spectacular economic success and careful cultivation of informal contacts. It was the combination of such contacts, in the very early years, with aggressive and daring financial maneuvers, often of a sort which the more established enterprises found unacceptable, coupled with great skill in the use of existing regulations and incentives, which accounts for the spectacular rise of many of the newer firms. Considering the modest antecedents of some of the big businessmen and industrialists in Pakistan today—particularly those who were not closely involved with the Pakistan movement—it is important to examine some of the large family firms in somewhat more detail.

The growth of the new capitalist class in Pakistan after Independence was determined in broad outline by the generally pro-private-enterprise position of the early governments, while the specific composition of the top of this class was influenced only in part by patterns of political involvement before 1947. The factors which became far more crucial in both the composition and the consolidation of power of the new class were the economic and political events following Partition and resettlement of immigrants, most particularly the pattern of occupational specialization in various regions.

The New Class

The development of a new class of largely Muslim industrialists and businessmen in the new state of Pakistan was the result of several related factors. The most important of these was the separation of India and Pakistan into quite independent economies, forcing a complete reorganization of trade patterns in both East and West Pakistan. In this connection, a close look must be taken at the specific economic policies of the immediate post-Partition period in order to determine the pattern of breakdown of trade relations between the two new states. It may be possible that people on both sides of the border were interested in seeing a definite economic separation and that the economic "vacuum" which resulted in Pakistan, for example, was more closely related to these policies than has generally been assumed.[40] In addition, the almost complete emigration of

---

[40] I am indebted for this suggestion to Shahid Javed Burki.

Economic Development and Cultural Change

Hindus from West Pakistan and a much smaller outflow from East Pakistan resulted in a severe "vacuum" in some of the occupations and institutions providing goods and services, particularly in the nonagricultural sector, which had been manned largely by Hindus in urban areas.

Third, as has already been noted, the policies of the new government strongly fostered private enterprise and encouraged both commercial and, later, industrial investment by immigrant and resident entrepreneurs. Fourth, the heavy influx of Muslim immigrants and the economic and political needs of the new state provided strong pressures toward policies of rapid economic development. Economists have analyzed this process in some detail[41] and have stressed particularly that government policies strongly supported industrial growth at the expense of other sectors, such as agriculture, and favored industrial locations in West Pakistan over those in East Pakistan, especially in the first decade or more.

All of these factors placed a premium on entry into business, first in commodity imports and later in the manufacture of basic consumer goods, particularly textiles. Because of the virtual interruption of trade ties with India, commodity importing was crucial in the immediate post-Partition years. In the early 1950s, the boom produced by the Korean War increased both the availability of foreign exchange and the demand for imports, rendering the import business extremely profitable. When this boom ended, the government's action in restricting further imports, particularly in textiles, caused many businessmen to shift rapidly into textile manufacturing. For economic reasons, and because it was possible to import foreign technology along with technicians, the manufacturing plants which were established in this early period were almost all quite large in size and extremely profitable. The pattern of opportunities, in which both accident and improvisation played an important role, was such that considerable assets could be accumulated in the immediate post-Partition period in commercial activities. Consequently, both established business families with large assets from pre-Independence times and comparative newcomers to big business were subsequently able to make the initial investments in large-scale industrial enterprises which generally formed the basis for the Big Houses.

The composition of the new class was deeply influenced by the exact nature of the economic disruption which occurred after Partition. The initial economic policies of the new government created first a group of Muslim businessmen who reaped very high profits from commodity-import trade, but who were then barred from this profitable line by the imposition of controls on textile and other imports during the foreign-exchange crisis following the end of the Korean War boom of the early 1950s. These circumstances made entry into business most likely for those

[41] Cf. G. F. Papanek; and Stephen R. Lewis, *Pakistan: Industrialization and Trade Policies* (London: Oxford University Press, 1970).

18

Hanna Papanek

who had experience in commerce, access to an existing network of commercial intelligence and credit, as well as fairly substantial assets; all of these plus even more substantial assets were required to make the subsequent entry into manufacturing industry.

An additional set of factors derived from the South Asian social structure accounts for the particularly important role played in Pakistan's economic growth by members of "business communities."[42] Obviously, the existing economic opportunities placed a premium on the availability of large amounts of capital, business skills, and knowledge of suppliers, markets, and so on. While some of these factors might have been available to educated persons from other occupational backgrounds, such people lacked the incentives in the early years to enter business occupations, since they were often well established in existing positions. Refugees displaced from other middle-class occupations did try to enter business, but these enterprises were generally at a lower level, requiring little capital. But over and above the possession of individual skills and assets, members of business communities were affected by a set of additional factors which proved to be crucial.

Within the South Asian social structure, the occupational specialization of entire ascriptive groups, such as castes or their non-Hindu counterparts ("communities"), has meant, in the case of commercial communities, that a range of socioeconomic classes exist within the community and that a wide variety of commercial jobs, ranging from street hawker to company president, is held by members of the group. There may well be some specialization by a given community in a single group of products, such as grains or textiles, but there is a considerable amount of social mobility within the confines of the community. Group loyalties play an extremely important role in hiring and employment in commercial enterprises (though not in the case of factory labor). Potential entrepreneurs can come from various class levels within the community, which retains its strong emphasis on self-employment in business as the most desirable occupation, thus assuring a continuing supply of both manpower and entrepreneurial replacements. Within the business communities, there is also a well-functioning information network, producing not only intense rivalries among competitors, but also diffusion of information and a system for assessing credit worthiness, and much better access to credit facilities than would be available to unaffiliated individuals. Rivalry, information, and access to capital produced a tendency toward more innovative entrepreneurial behavior, especially in a situation with as many opportunities for business profit as existed in the early years of the new state.

At the same time, people in business occupations as a group held relatively low status with respect to the educated elites, even though wealth itself plays an important role in the status evaluation of individuals and

[42] For a more detailed discussion of the structure and role of business communities in Pakistan, see H. Papanek, "Pakistan's New Industrialists and Businessmen."

19

Economic Development and Cultural Change

families. Persons from other middle-class occupations, or wealthy landlords with available capital, were not highly motivated to shift to business in the early period. The relative lack of formal education of the first generation of entrepreneurs contributed further to this evaluation of the status of businessmen, and this was particularly true of the newcomers, especially the most enterprising ones.

These were some of the reasons why the entrants into modern industry in the first decade of Pakistan's existence were primarily men from business backgrounds who belonged to business communities. This pattern has been well documented by studies of Pakistan's industrial sector, such as G. F. Papanek's 1959–60 survey of industry and the survey of businessmen and industrialists on which this paper is based. The regional distribution of occupationally specialized Muslim business communities—whose historical origins are still not well understood—accounted also for the fact that entrants into industry were largely persons who had worked outside Pakistan areas before Partition, including many of western Indian origin. In this respect, one of the factors accounting for the domination of East Pakistan's commerce and industry by non-Bengali Muslims has been the relative absence of occupationally specialized Muslim Bengali business communities. Other significant factors for this disparity were, of course, political—such as the location of the capital at Karachi and the nature of economic policies.

The Twelve Biggest "Big Houses"

These factors in the development of the new class are shown particularly clearly in the business histories of the largest company groups. Among the largest of the Big Houses, it is obvious that early entry—in the first five years—into industry after Partition was a crucial factor in their rise to the top. By the same token, the largest company groups cannot be taken as typical of the development of an industrial class in Pakistan; in later years, other entrepreneurs moved into industrial activities from backgrounds in occupations other than those of the pioneering entrepreneurs. But, because of the great importance of the large companies in the economy—and in social and political matters as well—it is instructive to look at some of them more closely. The leading families which make up this top group have considerable political significance, both as symbols and as actors, but fully accurate facts are not available in detail, despite frequent public references to them. Systematic data, presumably available to government sources, will be needed to present a complete picture of the economic role of these families; the public records, such as annual company reports of public companies, show only a part.

In very general terms, the pattern of business organization in Pakistan (1971) closely resembles that of the private sector in India.[43] Each of the

[43] Cf. R. K. Hazari, *The Structure of the Corporate Private Sector: A Study of Concentration, Ownership and Control* (New York: Asia Publishing House, 1966).

Hanna Papanek

Big Houses is controlled by a single family, usually through a central private firm which may also function as a trading firm or which is an outgrowth of the original trading firm of the family. The central firm may also function as a managing agency for public limited corporations controlled by the family, or there may be separate managing agencies. Each family group among the Big Houses typically controls several industrial enterprises, diversified in terms of products. Families continue to exert effective control even though many of their enterprises have in recent years become public firms, if they were not public earlier, and the government has placed limits on the holdings permitted individual shareholders in order to dilute control. Many groups also include a commercial bank, an insurance company, and a private sales organization. Some also have a construction firm, an investment firm, a trading company which may even include a retail operation, and perhaps a shipping line. More recently, there have been investments in large agricultural estates as well as firms for the exploitation of natural resources, but these are relatively less important than the industrial ventures. Several of the industrial enterprises may be joint ventures with foreign firms. Many of the Big Houses have also established foundations as part of their group or have various kinds of trust funds handling charitable and educational activities. In addition to all of these, there is a complex pattern of directorships in public limited firms, in which members of the Big Houses play important roles in big ventures of other families. These may or may not indicate financial interests held in additional firms by members of a Big House.

There is widespread agreement among businessmen and some others as to the membership of the top group of Big Houses, but, beyond about ten or fifteen names, agreement becomes more difficult and the bases for choice vary. But the fact that a small group of families control a very substantial share of the country's industrial assets has, of course, been clear for some time. Figures for 1959–60, for example, indicated that seven families controlled about one-fourth of all private industrial assets, and sixteen families about 40 percent of private industrial assets.[44] Other estimates and calculations have continued to stress the role of the top families.

Here, a comparison has been made of two lists; one, a privately compiled ranking made by highly knowledgeable businessmen, based on estimated net worth of Houses, as of late 1968. This list includes families whose assets are mainly commercial, or in shipping or urban real estate, rather than mainly industrial; it does not include large landowners. The second list is based on totals of paid-up capital in public corporations controlled by Big Houses and listed on the Karachi Stock Exchange as published in late 1969 in the *Pakistan Times*,[45] Because of the exclusive emphasis of the

[44] G. F. Papanek, p. 68.
[45] Economist, "Monopolies in Pakistan—II: Some Significant Facts," *Pakistan Times*, October 7, 1969.

21

Economic Development and Cultural Change

second list on industrial enterprises and public limited companies, the first gives a somewhat more accurate picture of the largest business-industrial houses. The two lists show a very high degree of agreement: the first five names are identical, although differing somewhat in rank, indicating that the top positions are held by families primarily in large industry. Out of the first fifteen names on both lists, twelve are the same, again differing slightly in rank. These twelve names are as follows, in order of net worth as estimated by business informants: (1) Dawood, (2) Habib Bank, (3) Adamjee, (4) Crescent (Mohd Amin Mohd Bashir, Ltd.), (5) Saigol, (6) Valika, (7) Hyesons, (8) Bawany, (9) Amin Jute, (10) Wazirali, (11) Fancy, (12) Colony (Nasir A. Shaikh, Farooq Shaikh: undivided company. On the business-informant list, the undivided company appears; but, on the paid-up capital list, the two companies resulting from a split appear in slightly different ranks).

In terms of net worth, the first eight Houses were estimated in late 1968 to be above ten crores rupees ($20 million at the official rate); of these, the two or three leading Houses were thought to be worth almost twenty crores. Of course, in comparison with large U.S. companies, these amounts are quite small, but in the Pakistani context and in view of the estimated starting assets of some of these companies, they are quite startling.

If the list is expanded to twenty or twenty-five, it includes, in terms of net worth, many of the very large commercial Houses which were also active in undivided India, particularly Dada, Adam, and Arag (all Bantva Memons), as well as some of the newer Punjabi Houses based on cotton exports and industry, and a number of Parsis in industry, trade, and real estate. The Ispahani family (so prominent in pre-Partition Muslim League politics) is included toward the bottom of the list of twenty-five and fairly well down the list ranked in terms of paid-up capital of public companies.

Most of the twelve industrial-commercial combines on the above list are relative newcomers to large-scale *industrial* activity, even though the scope of *commercial* activity in which some of them engaged—as did some not on the present list of twelve—was very large in the Indian context. It is quite clear that in undivided India there were few Muslim industrialists who had large enterprises; in the group of twelve considered here, only Adamjee in Calcutta was a large-scale industrialist. In addition, Bawany held several industrial enterprises in Rangoon. Some of the others (Saigol, Colony) had begun relatively small industrial enterprises. At the same time, several families in this group of twelve were very wealthy, mainly as a result of successful commercial ventures, including government contracting and especially army-supply contracting.

In the case of all twelve families, business activity was not a new occupation but generally went back several generations. None of the present heads of firms are new-entrants to business, although all of them have undergone considerable shifts within their basic occupation in the sense of

Hanna Papanek

moving from commercial to manufacturing operations and in vastly increasing the size of their enterprises. At the same time, only very few in this group belong to families who had so consolidated their commercial success in a preceding generation that they had been able to establish themselves in a fairly high status position. In very broad terms, high status in the generation preceding the major entrepreneurs of these twelve families had been achieved only by Adamjee and Wazirali, and to a lesser extent by Amin, Colony, Bawany, and Habib. Among the others, the most dramatic status change—from newcomer to magnate—was probably achieved by Dawood, Valika, and Fancy. The rest constitute a kind of middle group, where changes in wealth, economic power, and status were only slightly less dramatic than in the case of the most pronounced newcomers.

An interesting indication of these status changes is provided by the educational achievements of entrepreneurs. Among businessmen-industrialists as a whole, there has been a dramatic change in educational achievement between generations: the sons of the major entrepreneurs in large firms generally have achieved between five and ten years more formal education than their fathers. In a group of eighty-six business firms of various sizes, all holding import licenses, surveyed in the present study, 37 percent of heads of firms claimed they had at least ten years of formal schooling, while only 6 percent of their fathers had achieved this level. In a group of twenty-five very large firms surveyed, slightly over half of the current heads of firms said they had between zero and ten years of schooling while nearly 90 percent of their fathers were in this category. Not enough sons of heads of firms were old enough to make statistical comparison possible, but the data support a very large further shift upward.

Within the group of twelve Big Houses discussed here, a similar development has resulted in sharp differences within the group itself. Generally, in those families where wealth and high status had been achieved in an earlier generation, the major entrepreneurs of the twelve firms were educated at least to the level of matriculates or better (ten years of school or more), while the more newly mobile families had stressed formal education less than immediate entrance into business at the time when the major entrepreneurs of the present firms were growing up. Only five of the major entrepreneurs (i.e., men primarily responsible for the establishment and growth of the firm after Partition) in this group of twelve were educated to matriculation or better, including one B.A. and two B.Sc.'s. The remaining seven entrepreneurs were educated to levels below matriculation, including instances where formal education was very rudimentary indeed. Among some of these seven—and this includes major entrepreneurs who have since died or been replaced by a younger generation—knowledge of English was very scant at the time of Partition, although it was improved as the enterprises grew, sometimes by formal lessons.

Economic Development and Cultural Change

In addition to their significance in terms of status, educational achievements are also important in another sense. The Pakistan experience makes it quite clear that entrepreneurial success, in the circumstances which existed, was much less dependent upon formal education than on other skills and assets. If formal education in the institutions provided by the British colonial administration could be said to have played a role in changing the values as well as skills of South Asian students, then it is likely that these particular values were not very important in the business context or in entrepreneurial activities. In fact, the biographies of businessmen collected in this study as a whole indicate that a basic level of educational achievement was important—that is, literacy, some arithmetic, and perhaps enough English to send and receive telegrams—but that very high levels of education—that is, beyond matriculation—were in some sense dysfunctional for business success.[46] This was also indicated in G. F. Papanek's survey of industrialists: men with low educational achievements were about as likely as men with high educational achievements to be successful entrepreneurs, if not somewhat more so.[47]

Another dimension, religion and community, is also illustrated in this group of twelve Big Houses. All of these families are Muslims. While the top ranks of big business include several Parsi families (three out of the top twenty in terms of estimated net assets), only one of these three is primarily involved in large industry (Hirjina), while the others are in shipping, trade, urban real estate, and some industry (Cowasjee, E. M. Dinshaw). Parsis living in Pakistan areas did not enter large industry in the immediate post-Partition period, even though one might have expected them to do so because of their relative wealth, high levels of education and modernization, business skills, and established residence. In fact, however, the established Parsi business families did not make major industrial investments until much later, even though they did invest in large immovable enterprises such as hotels and urban real estate. The largest of the Parsi industrial firms (Hirjina) is controlled by a family which came to Pakistan after Partition from Bombay, in a highly unusual move, since there was almost no immigration or emigration by Parsis at the time of Partition.[48] Large Hindu firms have also not played an important role in the Pakistan economy since the early 1960s, although G. F. Papanek's industrial survey indicated that in 1959–60 Hindu-owned firms controlled 12 percent of private industrial assets, mainly in East Pakistan.[49]

[46] H. Papanek, "Pakistan's New Industrialists and Businessmen."

[47] G. F. Papanek, "The Industrial Entrepreneurs—Education, Occupational Background and Finance," in *Development Policy II: The Pakistan Experience*, ed. W. P. Falcon and G. F. Papanek (Cambridge, Mass.: Harvard University Press, 1971), pp. 237–59.

[48] Elizabeth B. Gustafson, "A Demographic Dilemma: The Parsis of Karachi," *Social Biology* 16, no. 2 (June 1969): 120.

[49] G. F. Papanek, *Pakistan's Development*, p. 42.

Hanna Papanek

An additional dimension of religious differences is closely related to occupational specialization of quasi-caste groups and to minority status. With only two exceptions (Hyesons, Wazirali), all the families in the top group of twelve belong to quasi-caste groups with a traditional occupational specialization in commerce, known as business communities. The Punjabis in this group often refer to themselves as "Chiniotis," or at least as related to the Sheikhs specialized in business who are particularly concentrated in the West Punjabi town of Chiniot. In both group structure and historical development, the Sheikhs of the western Punjab are quite different from the business communities of western India, particularly those centered in Kathiawar, Gujarat, and Bombay City.

The most important Muslim business community of Kathiawar origin is the Memons; from the Bombay area come the Khoja Ismailis, the Khoja Isnasheris, and the Dawoodi Bohras. These four communities are— at least in Pakistan—cohesive, fairly structured groups, with some degree of internal organization, including some *panchayat*-like councils and some voluntary organizations. Each group is endogamous. In addition, there are some religious factors: the three groups from the Bombay area all belong to different sects of Shias, for whom religious observances and internal religious organizations are significant bonds of solidarity and marks of distinctiveness from other groups.

Overall, the distribution among the business families of various religious allegiances within Islam is as follows: Memons and Punjabi Sheikhs are Sunnis, while Khoja Ismailis, Khoja Isnasheris, and Dawoodi Bohras are Shias. Syed families are also Shia. Since the majority of Pakistanis are Sunnis, and since the most significant business communities—in terms of numbers and economic activities—are also Sunni, it is difficult to see the role of business communities as illustrative of a minority-group hypothesis in the usual sense. However, there is no doubt that the strong commitment to a business occupation, which is very prevalent among Memons, and to slightly lesser degrees in the other groups, does constitute a self-defining characteristic for members of these communities which differentiates them from others.

It is only in this very special sense of self-definition that the business communities might be considered "minorities" within the population. Although a wider discussion is beyond the scope of this paper, the role of Pakistani business communities does raise some questions about the generally accepted role of "minority groups" as entrepreneurs. In this view, a causal connection is sometimes assumed between a group's minority status within the population, as defined in some generally accepted religious or racial terms (Jews, Chinese, Lebanese, etc., in various settings), and their entrepreneurial activities and successes. In the case of India and Pakistan, at least, the existence of occupationally specialized castes and communities raises the possibility of many other causal factors which may be more important.

25

Economic Development and Cultural Change

Some reference has already been made to the fact that many Muslim businessmen and industrialists, whether originally from Pakistan areas or not, typically worked in non-Pakistan areas before Partition. The differences between resident Muslims and refugee Muslims, which are crucial in the political sense,[50] need to be modified in the case of the business families to include also the category of "returnees." The special significance of this category lies in the fact that, even if these families were engaged in business or manufacturing in places distant from their hometowns, the men often left their wives and children behind in the hometowns and also maintained a network of personal and commercial connections in their province of origin. This network often proved to be immensely important, either as part of the commercial enterprise carried on in distant places or as part of a new enterprise begun after Partition. For example, the large Punjabi firms which engaged in the export of cotton from the Punjab (such as Crescent and Nishat) built up their buying networks after Independence on the basis of existing personal and commercial connections within their home province. Similarly, those commercial firms in undivided India who had established branches in areas which became Pakistan were at an advantage in setting up their new distribution networks after Partition; this group included some of the very large Memon firms of food-grain dealers as well as others and is not restricted to returnees. Finally, the fact that so many Muslim businessmen and industrialists who became prominent in Pakistan had previously worked in non-Pakistan areas serves to indicate two important points. First, businessmen who were already established in Pakistan areas at the time of Partition apparently were less highly motivated to make early investments in new industrial ventures. Presumably, they had less liquid capital than newcomers, and their existing enterprises preoccupied them. Second, it reinforces the observations made in connection with Partition population movements that, in areas which became Pakistan, effective control of commercial and industrial enterprises was in the hands of non-Muslims.

Details concerning these various aspects of social and business background of the twelve Big Houses are presented in table 1.

In terms of numbers of Houses, this top group divides almost exactly into families of western Indian origin and families from the Punjab. After their migration to West Pakistan, of course, there has been a tendency to see all of them as undifferentiated "West Pakistanis," and, although this is not true in terms of even recent origin, it is very largely true in terms of criteria of economic action. The absence of indigenous Bengalis from the ranks of the large entrepreneurs is very marked, but the absence of Muslims from the United Provinces and other areas with strong Muslim elite

[50] Shahid Javed Burki, "Group Politics in a Praetorian Society—a Case Study of Ayub's Pakistan," mimeographed (Cambridge, Mass.: Center for International Affairs, Harvard University, 1970), pp. 33–42.

26

Hanna Papanek

TABLE 1
SUMMARY OF SOCIAL AND BUSINESS BACKGROUND OF THE
TWELVE BIG HOUSES

Name	Community	Family Origin	Business Headquarters Location, Pre-1947
1. Dawood	Memon	Kathiawar (Bantva)	Bombay
2. Habib ..	Khoja Isnasheri	Bombay	Bombay
3. Adamjee	Memon	Kathiawar (Jetpur)	Calcutta
4. Crescent	Punjabi Sheikh	Western Punjab (Chiniot)	Delhi
5. Saigol...	Punjabi Sheikh	Western Punjab (Chakwal)	Calcutta
6. Valika ..	Dawoodi Bohra	Bombay	Bombay
7. Hyesons.	(None)	Madras	Madras
8. Bawany .	Memon	Kathiawar (Jetpur)	Rangoon
9. Amin ...	Punjabi Sheikh	Western Punjab	Calcutta
10. Wazirali.	(None, Syed)	Western Punjab (Lahore)	Lahore
11. Fancy...	Khoja Ismaili	Kathiawar	East Africa
12. Colony..	Punjabi Sheikh	Western Punjab (Chiniot)	Lahore

groups is only somewhat less remarkable. In terms of the present head-quarters of firms, at least in the late 1960s, all of the above firms (with the possible exception of Adamjee) were located in West Pakistan, although many had substantial enterprises in East Pakistan.

In terms of starting resources available at the time of Partition, there are substantial differences between the twelve firms, even given the very unsatisfactory nature of information on this point. Some of the firms which can be described as newcomers to big business are generally considered to have begun their enterprises with available assets considerably below one crore rupees ($2 million), and some estimates indicate that they have multiplied their net worth in twenty years by factors ranging from twenty- to sixty-fold. Outstanding in these terms, that is, modest beginnings and large growth, are Dawood, Crescent, Fancy, Valika, and Colony. Such dramatic rates of increase in economic assets do not apply to the same extent to many other business families who entered Pakistan with substantial assets and who have remained among the Big Houses without comparable increases in their holdings. This latter group includes many of the families who were most closely connected with the Pakistan movement, while the owners of some of the most rapidly growing firms were not.

In making the point that the top group of entrepreneurs (either the top twelve or top twenty or thirty) were not part of an already-existing elite but represented a newly risen group, three of the characteristics which have been mentioned are particularly relevant: prior wealth, prior political prominence, and educational attainments. On a combination of these three criteria, only very few families in this group could be considered to qualify or to have been even marginally accepted into existing elite groups. In terms of their life-styles, and despite the considerable wealth

27

Economic Development and Cultural Change

of many families, most of these business families were essentially middle-class. It was not until the 1960s that conspicuous luxury spending by this group became obvious and widespread, even in terms of urban middle-class standards.

In the business histories of the larger sample of Pakistani businessmen as well as in the case of the group examined here, it also becomes quite clear that political or civic activity becomes important to a business family only when some manpower can be spared from the business. This is typically a task of the second generation or occurs quite late in the life of an entrepreneur after the firm has been well established. Civic activity within the "community" is likely to begin somewhat earlier and is considered to be a definite obligation to be met by prominent or wealthy persons. It is expected that their wealth and prestige should be used on behalf of the community to at least some extent. The most dramatic illustration of such a combination of activities and the use of leadership prestige to advance economic goals is provided by the Khoja Ismailis. One of the major functions of the well-known Jubilee "weighings" of the Aga Khan has been the collection of funds from his followers as a religious obligation. In the last such weighing, conducted in Pakistan in the early 1950s, these funds were collected in terms of shares in a finance corporation (Platinum Jubilee Finance Corporation), and capital was subsequently lent out to members of the community through credit cooperatives and other community institutions.[51] A more common pattern is for prominent businessmen to be elected presidents of various community institutions in order to represent the community in the outside world, give personal donations, lend prestige to arbitration between contending parties, and provide business acumen and personal connections for the solution of financial problems. Such positions in the community may lead to wider recognition in business organizations or civic activities, but business leaders have generally been conspicuously absent from the world of politics as representative figures, except in a few rare instances. Of course, they have been reported to have played important roles in the financing of various political parties of both the Right and the Left, but these activities have generally not been well publicized. Nevertheless, prominent businessmen have been very significant symbolic figures in Pakistan's political development, especially in the last few years.

Summary: Growth and Development of an Elite
The few Big Houses which have been discussed here are obviously not the whole story of Pakistan's industrial and commercial development. But they have played an extremely significant role in economic as well as political terms, because of the extent of concentration of economic control in the

---

[51] H. Papanek, "Leadership and Social Change in the Khoja Ismaili Community" (Ph.D. diss., Harvard University, 1962).

Hanna Papanek

hands of a few, the speed of industrial growth, and the high political visibility of the industrial-commercial family combines. Within the general context of separatism, modernization, and entrepreneurship, the detailed data on individual large family firms begin to form something of a pattern.

To begin with, there is a definite overlap between the pre- and post-Partition periods in terms of the participation of big businessmen in economic activities connected with Pakistan. It is clear that the mobilization of Muslim businessmen in support of the Pakistan movement came rather late in the game—starting only after about 1943 in any serious way—and only very few big businessmen participated actively in the movement's leadership. Those who had been active, however, as well as those who had participated in setting up the "nation-building" companies eventually came to Pakistan. They brought large amounts of private capital into the country, and, as they felt assured of the pro-private-enterprise position of the new government, began to establish commercial and industrial enterprises.

At the same time, Muslim businessmen with almost no prior contact with the Muslim League leadership came to Pakistan and soon gained a realization of the opportunities which might be offered by the new state. These men were mainly newcomers to the ranks of big business, but they included a few extremely skillful and aggressive entrepreneurs who established themselves very rapidly in the front ranks of the new elite. With a few exceptions, these newcomers established new industrial enterprises more rapidly than the commercial Houses who had earlier been among the leading Muslim business groups. Among these relative newcomers, there are large numbers of Punjabi entrepreneurs—many of whom had been in business outside Pakistan before returning—who entered large-scale industry and became extremely powerful in the economy. In the list of twelve Big Houses, which emphasizes industrial interests more than commercial ones, the large majority consists of families with no prior connection with the Pakistan movement; a somewhat smaller proportion consists of families with relatively little prior wealth, although all had been in business before.

Obviously, the large commercial Houses are also still at the top of the business-industrial class, just below these top twelve, as an expansion of the list of Big Houses would show, although this has not been done in the present paper. This indicates the importance of large assets, business skills, and business connections in the establishment of large enterprises but also shows that the earlier political connections of the immigrant Muslim business families were less important than some other factors in the achievement of large-scale industrial control. At the same time, it is important to recall that many newcomers lacked all of these advantages and yet established enterprises which were the foundation of later Big Houses or somewhat smaller but still significant firms.

Another major feature of the business-industrial elite is the predominance of members of occupationally specialized business communities

29

among the leading families. This is as true for the list of twelve analyzed here, as it is for a longer list of twenty-five or-thirty; it is further supported by broader studies of all industrialists (as of 1960) and of segments of the business-industrial group (as of 1967–68). The significance of this business-community background extends over several areas of social and economic activity. On the one hand, members of business communities have had extensive training in business skills and established connections with a network of information and credit facilities within the community itself. In addition, membership in a business community serves to identify a person in terms of a significant network when his credit worthiness is evaluated by outside agencies or when he seeks employment. Rivalry between members of the same business community is also an important feature of the entrepreneurship shown by these people, as is the tendency for businessmen to imitate the business decisions of others whom they know, envy, and respect. Preference in hiring members of one's own community further strengthens community bonds and also serves to insure a continuing commitment to business occupations by younger, lower-status members of the community who may later move up into entre-preneurial positions not pre-empted by the sons of wealthier families. These factors of a continuing supply of manpower for business occupations and their relationship to the business community's typical tendency to include a range of socioeconomic classes are extremely significant aspects of the operation of these traditional social groupings in a modern economy. Additional features of the business communities include the prevailing traditional custom of arranged marriages within the group, which often affects the ownership and inheritance of assets, and a frequently highly conservative tendency with regard to the status of women and the role of formal education.

With respect to formal education, the business-industrial elite occu-pies an interesting position when compared with other Pakistani elite groups. In the case of earlier generations of businessmen, it was clear that the British system of formal education was of very limited use in com-mercial activities. Unlike those seeking admission into administrative, clerical, professional, or educational occupations, businessmen could generally carry out their occupations with very limited knowledge of English, limited vernacular literacy, and basic mathematics. This was even true, although to a lesser extent, with more modern business occupations such as manufacturing and foreign trade. Although Muslim businessmen did feel, in the years before Partition, that their opportunities were restric-ted through the competition of Hindu businessmen, this was based less on the Muslim lag in participating in English education than was probably true for others who joined the separatist movement.

The relation between formal educational achievements and status is indicated by several shifts between generations and among families. Among the twelve Big Houses discussed here, entrepreneurs from well-

Hanna Papanek

established wealthy families were fairly well educated, while the new-comers to elite status are generally much less educated. In addition, there are very considerable intergenerational changes in educational attainment, both for the larger group of Big Houses (not listed here) and for other samples of businessmen and industrialists. This is particularly marked in the case of sons of very large industrialists and businessmen and will have some bearing on the future role of trained managers from outside the family in executive positions.

The relative lack of formal education by businessmen as a whole and big businessmen in particular has also been a serious problem in the achievement of status. Educated elite groups in Pakistan have tended to look down on businessmen and to assume a high level of corruption, inefficiency, and greed. Although this expectation was frequently confirmed, it also affected the particular pattern of relationships which developed among big businessmen, government officials, and politicians. A general feeling of working together to make Pakistan a reality, which often characterized government officials in the early years, existed between government and business to a much smaller extent. Educational achievement was one of the symbols used in maintaining some degree of social distance between businessmen, as a group, and members of the existing establishment.

Status, education, wealth, and political connections affect the role of big businessmen in the modernization process, particularly with respect to establishing connections with newer political forces emerging in the country. The small group of leading businessmen-industrialists who have developed Pakistan's industrial establishments in the private sector have, of course, played an important role in the modernization of the country simply by developing industry. At the same time, there is no doubt that the concentration of economic control in the hands of a very small number of families has had very serious effects on the distributive aspects of growth. Both the overt and hidden participation of businessmen in various aspects of the administrative and decision-making process and in the activities of political parties has been in the interests of maintaining their pattern of control relatively unimpaired. Future relationships with new political elites will clearly be affected, not only by the existing power relationships between business and government, but also by a pattern of attitudes regarding the role of businessmen and their presumed status attributes which are held by other elite groups. Of particular importance in this respect is the role of entrepreneurship and educated management, since it is clear that the establishment of the large family combines was based on a particularly aggressive entrepreneurial style, which is now associated with business activities in general. One major question which will deserve careful consideration from several angles will be the future role of educated managers in executive positions in business firms and the relationship of these managers to interest groups and political parties.

31

Economic Development and Cultural Change

A particularly salient feature of the role of the Big Houses is the absence of indigenous Bengali entrepreneurs, not only from among the top twelve, but essentially from the first thirty. This has been partly based on the historical development of Muslim society in Bengal and the absence of occupationally specialized business communities corresponding in structure and function to those from western India. However, the greater political power held by groups based in West Pakistan has played a crucial role in this process, particularly in the allocation of resources. The location of the capital in West Pakistan has also been of considerable importance in determining the location of businesses and industrial plants. The effect of the economic dominance exercised by big firms based in West Pakistan has been severely felt in East Pakistan, not only in terms of investment decisions, but also in retarding the development of an East Pakistani business and industrial middle class. In many respects, the feelings of Bengali Muslims vis-à-vis West Pakistani Muslims parallel those which were held earlier by Indian Muslims vis-à-vis Hindus—that their entry into the economy and into positions of political and administrative participation was retarded by other groups who had the benefit of earlier entry, greater starting assets, and more effective political support. In this context, it is very relevant to note that East Pakistani industrialists are reported to be among the important supporters of the Awami League leadership.

Despite the earlier lack of close relationships between the business-industrial elite and decision makers in government, except on an individual level, there is now a much closer tie between these groups, based on shared interests. To a very limited extent, this is indicated by an increase in intermarriage between important business and civil-service families and an increase in the number of young men from other elite backgrounds entering business occupations as trained executives. Although few big businessmen are running for political office in Pakistan, their role in the changing political situation is likely to become increasingly critical. The relationship between the leading families discussed here and the other entrepreneurial groups who have made later and small-scale entry into both manufacturing and commerce is also likely to change. In any event, the complex pattern of social, economic, and political antecedents and consequences in the growth of Pakistan's existing business-industrial elite needs to be understood to evaluate the role of this type of group in a developing, postcolonial society, in whose history separatism has played a crucial role.

Name Index